In Nature's Name

Linley Sambourne, cartoon, *Mistress of Creation, Punch*, 3 January 1874

In Nature's Name

An Anthology of Women's Writing and Illustration, 1780–1930

EDITED BY

Barbara T. Gates

THE UNIVERSITY OF CHICAGO PRESS
Chicago and London

Barbara T. Gates is Alumni Distinguished Professor of English and Women's Studies at the University of Delaware. She is the author of *Victorian Suicide: Mad Crimes and Sad Histories* and *Kindred Nature: Victorian and Edwardian Women Embrace the Living World,* the latter published by the University of Chicago Press. Her edited works include *Critical Essays on Charlotte Brontë,* the *Journal of Emily Shore,* and, with Ann B. Shteir, *Natural Eloquence: Women Reinscribe Science.* In the year 2000, she was awarded the Founders' Distinguished Senior Scholar Award by the American Association of University Women.

The University of Chicago Press, Chicago 60637
The University of Chicago Press, Ltd., London

Printed in the United States of America
11 10 09 08 07 06 05 04 03 02   1 2 3 4 5
ISBN: 0-226-28444-1 (cloth)
ISBN: 0-226-28446-8 (paper)

Library of Congress Cataloging-in-Publication Data

Gates, Barbara T., 1936–
In nature's name : an anthology of women's writing and illustration, 1780–1930 / edited by Barbara T. Gates.
p. cm.
Includes bibliographical references (p.).
ISBN 0-226-28444-1 (hardcover : alk. paper)—
ISBN 0-226-28446-8 (pbk. : alk. paper)
1. Nature—Literary collections. 2. English literature—Women authors. 3. American literature—Women authors. 4. Nature—Pictorial works. I. Gates, Barbara T., 1936– .
PR1111.N3 I5 2002
820.8′09287—dc21

2001005012

∞ The paper used in this publication meets the minimum requirements of the American National Standard for Information Sciences—Permanence of Paper for Printed Library Materials, ANSI Z39.48-1992.

This book is dedicated to the incomparable women who haunt its pages and to their understanding of nature.

Life calls to us . . .
Above us, or below us, and around:
Perhaps we name it Nature's voice.

Elizabeth Barrett Browning,
Aurora Leigh I: 673–76

Contents

SECTION TWO: PROTECTING

Illustrations

Acknowledgments

Acknowledging scholarly debts is always both a pleasure and a concern: pleasurable because it lends a chance to thank, and a concern because one might forget—or even misspell the name of—an important colleague. So let me begin with an apology to Sara Triller, my research assistant both for *Kindred Nature* and the early stages of this book. Sara's surname appears as Trillet in the acknowledgments for the earlier book. Sara and Kathryn Miele have been my right-hand women. Both have transcribed documents and helped with the editing of *In Nature's Name.* Kathryn is also largely responsible for generating the chronology and for choosing many of the fine selections for the section "Protecting." Help with garnering pictures for the book came from Megan Riggs, another assistant on the project. Dates and hard-to-find biographical materials were often tracked by Linda Stein of the Morris Library, University of Delaware. Page numbers for some of the poems were traced by Angela Leighton and Jonathan Grossman. And absolutely essential aid came from Suzanne Potts, loyal, as always, in the final preparation of the manuscript.

My main debt is to my editor extraordinaire, Susan Abrams, who encouraged me with this project from start to finish. Susan and the editorial staff at the University of Chicago Press, especially David Aftandilian, always believed that this anthology should come into being and have consistently worked toward that end. To you and your associates, my sincerest thanks.

Marilyn Ward at the library of the Royal Botanical Gardens at Kew and Christopher Mills and Julie Harvey of the British Museum of Natural History, who were equally helpful with *Kindred Nature,* again lent their expertise to this project. And Kate Newell patiently helped read proofs.

Preface

This book grew as a scion from *Kindred Nature* (University of Chicago Press, 1998), a cultural study of Victorian and Edwardian women and nature. In the parent book I tried as much as possible to tell my story through the words of the earlier women, quoting liberally and, when I could, remaining in their grip. Readers of *Kindred Nature* have, however, requested longer selections from the women who were my primary sources, and I have added still other authors who might reveal other facets of nature interpretation in their day. Certainly, I have had a great deal of pleasure in compiling this material—pleasure not just of reacquaintance but of discovery. If feminist scholarship has been diligent in rediscovering Victorian and Edwardian texts by novelists and poets, it has largely ignored writers about nature, science, and species preservation. There are still many to recuperate. To me this seems especially ironic, since most of these writers hoped above all else to aid in the diffusion of knowledge about nature that took place during their lifetimes. They wanted their work to be known because they felt their subjects to be so important.

In Nature's Name began, then, as a supplement, a companion text. Like all offspring, however, it has demanded the right to grow in its own way. Throughout the many months it has taken first place on my desk, the book has kept extending not just its range, but its categories and level of inclusiveness. It still centers in natural history but could easily have been expanded to include more of the physical sciences and astronomy—the latter being a field in which women were very active. Space simply did not allow. As it stands, *In Nature's Name* includes not just multiple aspects of natural history study but multiple genres as well. Poetry, fiction, artwork, and nonfiction prose are all accommodated here. A thematic anthology like this one permits multiple genres to be gathered together in complementary arrangements that can offer new insights into women's role in redefining nature, nature study, and nature writing.

On the question of genre and generic approaches to the literature of nature, I would like to add a word or two about the nature of nature writing, in part by referencing Patrick Murphy's recent book, *Farther Afield in the Study of Nature-Oriented Literature* (Virginia, 2000). Murphy offers the most comprehensive representation of the modes of nature and environmental writing produced to date. He subdivides writing about nature into four groups: nature writing, nature literature, environmental writing, and environmental literature. The "modes and genres" portion of his schema (page 11) is reproduced below:

Nature Writing

Natural history essay
Rambles and meditations
Wilderness living
Travel and adventure
Agrarian and ranch life
Philosophizing

Nature Literature

Poetry

Observations
Pastoral odes
Agrarian and rural elegies
Domestic and garden life
Interaction with animals

Fiction

Sport stories
Animal stories and fables
Regionalism
Wilderness living
Travel and adventure

Agrarian and ranch life
Science fiction and fantasy

Environmental Writing

Environmental degradation
Community activism
Wilderness defense
Recreational responsibility
Sustainable agriculture and grazing
Environmental ethics
Inhabitation

Environmental Literature

Poetry

Observation of crisis
Agrarian values
Alternative lifestyles
Encountering the other

Fiction

Environmental crisis and resolution
Wilderness defense
Destruction of agrarian life
Cultural conservation
Dystopias, utopias, fabulations

Murphy's lists are useful for the study of British women's nature writing. With the exception of concern for wilderness as such—something most of their European lives had little contact with except when they became colonial lives—the women in this book wrote in all of the categories and subgenres listed by Murphy. In their case, however, one can also discern areas where gender determined genre. Even in their diversity, as a group they are notable both for their interest in domestication of plants and animals and for their focus on education, especially in their desire to educate the young. *In Nature's Name* therefore includes large sections of writing about nature study and science education—areas not specifically outlined by Murphy. Careful consideration of its importance in British nature writing by women moves me to add science popularization to Murphy's categories and to expand popularization's subgenres. These would necessarily include early modes like conversations, dialogues, journeys, and the nature rambles that included conversations; midcentury modes like parables; and later-century modes like the science–fairy tale comparisons developed by Arabella Buckley. All of these are discussed in the introduction to my section "Popularizing Science." In this book I have also chosen not to separate nature writing from nature literature nor environmental writing from environmental literature, since essays and expository writing are, to my mind, quite as literary as poems and fiction.

Beginning in the late eighteenth century, nature and environmental writing grew in popularity in Britain and appealed to a number of women who were prolific over extended periods of time. The individual sections of this book therefore follow the contours of what is now called "the long nineteenth century," a period that extends from the late eighteenth to the early twentieth centuries. Strict chronological order has, however, taken second place to thematics in this anthology. Consequently, I have also prefaced the book with a chronology that places the works represented alongside the social, political, and scientific events of their day. This stems from a realization that some readers are more comfortable with a chronological approach and that students new to the subjects of this anthology might like to see just where the women included in *In Nature's Name* fit into a larger historical picture.

Despite the importance of genre and of time, I have nevertheless deliberately chosen to arrange this anthology by theme and subject rather than by type or chronological order. Throughout the period covered here (from just before 1790 to 1930), women took special interest in a number of issues surrounding nature study and natural history: the protection of species, the introduction of plants and animals into the home, the evolution of the animal story, the adventure story about women, the popularization and dissemination of science, and the development of the art of gardening, to name just a few. To bring such issues, movements, and interests into prominence, I have endeavored to find documents and pictures that would group together subjects like these and have developed the book's divisions accordingly.

In terms of its specific organization, the anthology opens with a section "Speaking Out," one that points out some of the difficulties women encountered when they tried to speak in nature's name. They needed to pave their own ways as spokeswomen for nature and at the same time counter a trend, pervasive in their culture, toward essentializing them as more natural and less intellectual than men. Could women, they wondered, be considered authoritative on the subject of nature at the same time that they shed unwanted stereotypes about their own nature? The women included in this section show just how they went about answering this question and assuming this difficult task. The second section shows how crucial to women was the protection of nonhuman species. "Protecting" is concerned mainly with environmental literature—writing that deals with perceived threats to the natural world. As their writing clearly shows, in the nineteenth century, women were in the forefront of movements intended to save animals and plants from destruction. In sections three and four, the anthology continues by exploring nature writing in its many guises: animal stories, narratives about farming and gardening, and travel and adventure narratives, for example. In the fifth section, I pause to offer selections illustrative of some of the important aesthetic movements of the Victorian and Edwardian timeframe, their bearing on women's nature writing and vice versa. The book concludes with two sections devoted to the significance of women as science writers: section six explores the wide variety of popular science writing, a field on which women left a strong mark, while section seven probes the vexed question of just who in science study was considered a professional and who an amateur.

Throughout, I have created subsections that I hope will be useful to students using this book—one on women and Darwin, and others on seaweed study, various types of conservation, and on the appreciation of color, to name just a few. Overall my hope is to encourage a dialogue of texts that might have pleased the inhabitants of this book, many of whom felt quite alone in their endeavors and few of whom would have considered themselves working within what we now call "traditions" of women's writing. What most of these writers did have in common of course was an overarching desire to study, protect, and represent aspects of nonhuman nature, whether wild or domestic.

In terms of the editing of individual texts I have corrected little—only a few glaring typographical errors—and have left spellings and usage entirely intact. In general the footnotes to the selections are those of the women themselves, some of whom, in their desire to be authoritative, were avid footnoters. Occasionally, however, I have created a new note to explain a reference or term that might be unfamiliar to today's reader. These are inserted and numbered consecutively with original footnotes, but in every case I have labeled new notes as the work of this editor. So as not to confuse my own contemporary readers by causing them to hunt for something they are not going to find, I have also now and then deleted references to figures or tables that I have not been able to reproduce.

The book includes a chronology and a set of brief biographical sketches of the writers and artists included here. These are designed to give the reader a basic familiarity with their subject, but not to be comprehensive. Believing that the primary selections are the heart of this book, it has been my deliberate choice to give essentials and summaries rather than to repeat gossipy speculation about the women's lives or to offer a thicket of information that might be only tangentially relevant to the selections that follow. For one or two women, I have unfortunately, despite many months of searching, been able to find no biographical or more extensive bibliographical information. Their work must stand self-contained.

Each of the seven sectional divisions of this book is preceded by a short essay-introduction to its texts and writings. A fuller context for the work represented in this book is always available through reference to my *Kindred Nature: Victorian and Edwardian Women Embrace the Living World*, in which many of the women whose work is here represented made earlier appearances. *In Nature's Name* concludes with a bibliography of primary and secondary works of possible interest to the reader. These are arranged to complement the seven sections. The bibliography for the section "Speaking Out" has been further expanded to include an extensive list of relevant titles in gender studies; the bibliography for "Amateurs or Professionals?" is similarly extended to include titles in science studies.

I have opened *In Nature's Name* with two short poems intended to emphasize the passion for nature felt by most of the women in this book. Cecil Frances Alexander's "All Things Bright and Beauteous," a famous hymn still sung today, suggests a religious view of nature held by many women throughout the first half of the nineteenth century. Mary Webb's poem "The Secret Joy," written at the far end of this book's timeframe, brings the reader "face to face" with nature with no intervening presence. More sensual than Alexander's poem, it nevertheless represents what Webb calls "a gospel of earth," a connection so profound that "we think that there is some deep meaning in it all, if we could only find it" (*The Spring of Joy* 130). These poems serve as a prelude to writings and pictures of many sorts, all intended to draw human beings closer to nature, one way or another.

PRELUDE

CECIL FRANCES ALEXANDER

"All things bright and beauteous"

1848.

All things bright and beauteous,
All creatures great and small,
All things wise and wondrous,
The LORD GOD made them all.

Each little flower that opens,
Each little bird that sings,
He made their glowing colours,
He made their tiny wings.

The rich man in his castle,
The poor man at his gate,
GOD made them, high or lowly,
And ordered their estate.

The purple-headed mountain,
The river running by,
The sunset, and the morning,
That brightens up the sky,

The cold wind in the winter,
The pleasant summer sun,
The ripe fruits in the garden,
He made them every one.

The tall trees in the greenwood,
The meadows where we play,
The rushes by the water,
We gather every day;—

He gave us eyes to see them,
And lips that we might tell,
How great is GOD Almighty,
Who has made all things well.

MARY WEBB

"Face to face with the sunflower"

The Secret Joy. 1917. New York: Charles Scribner's Sons, 1937.

Face to face with the sunflower,
    Cheek to cheek with the rose,
We follow a secret highway
    Hardly a traveller knows.

The gold that lies in the folded bloom
    Is all our wealth.
We eat of the heart of the forest
    With innocent stealth.
We know the ancient roads
    In the leaf of a nettle,
And bathe in the blue profound
    Of a speedwell petal.

FIGURE 1 Mary Webb

SECTION ONE

Speaking Out

As the nineteenth century unfolded, human sexual and gender differences were explored and then keenly debated by scientists like Charles Darwin (1809–82) in *The Descent of Man* (1871) and philosophers like Herbert Spencer (1820–1903), who followed Darwin's ideas but extended his arguments to encompass society. Simultaneously, women were themselves requesting new roles in society—more education, the vote, work outside the home, a place in the professions—and their requests prompted further rethinking about the nature of womanhood. Women came to represent a "question," the "Woman Question," a catchall phrase that referred to the parameters of women's nature and to women's consequent place in culture. Most Victorians were little likely to distinguish between sex and gender, between reproductive functioning and culturally assigned value, and their own culture began to elide womanhood and biological nature. Women were essentialized—looked at primarily in terms of their reproductive functions, childbearing in particular. But this raised another question: if women *were* nature, could they then better speak for nature, or should they not speak at all? This in turn raised still more questions, the relationship between women's bodies and minds being central among them. Were women designed only to bear and foster children, or could they withstand mental or physical strain other than childbirth? Women's skulls were measured, their temperatures gauged, their nerves assessed. Could women work and be wives and mothers? Should women engage in sports? in higher education? Notice figure 2, cartoonist Linley Sambourne's 1885 illustration for Charles Kingsley's *Water Babies* (1863), where Sambourne depicts a full-bosomed woman in cap and gown as the "Great Fairy Science." This sketch, meant to be playful and ironic, also visually presents the anomaly of woman as body and mind. In his book, Kingsley had transformed all the figures representing nature and evolution into women. Later his niece, Mary Kingsley, would sport with such representations of nature and science when, tongue in cheek,

FIGURE 2 Linley Sambourne, *The Great Fairy Science,* illustration for Charles Kingsley's *Water Babies* (London: Macmillan, 1885), p. 98 (originally published 1863)

she set out to find fish and fetish in West Africa under the aegis of a personified "Science" (preface, *Travels in West Africa,* 1897). She knew full well that she was traveling at the behest of male ichthyologists and anthropologists, as we shall see in section five.

Debates raged around the female mind/body controversy and other subjects involving women's nature, and most relied on an appeal to an august, personified "Nature" as the final determiner. A male-driven culture largely determined this determiner, and throughout the historical periods covered in this anthology, this culture represented itself as the proper assessor of personified Nature's intents. In the name of Nature, prominent male intellectuals often decided that women were indeed limited by their reproductive roles and that the "advancement" of women seemed unlikely. Take Herbert Spencer for another example. Spencer posited that women had evolved so as to be slowed down mentally in order to conserve their physical energy for reproduction. In his *Education: Intellectual, Moral, and Physical* (1861), he observed that "nature is a strict accountant; if you demand of her in one direction more than she is prepared to lay out, she balances the account by making a deduction elsewhere" (179). On the Spencerian ledger, women's intellects were what paid the price.

This book sets out to show how significantly women too spoke in Nature's name, and its opening section paints the backdrop for the entire book by emphasizing the work of intelligent Victorian and Edwardian women who contested ideas like those of Spencer. Such women needed to clarify just who they were and what nature was—to claim the right to speak on Nature's behalf without themselves being essentialized. In claiming this right they had important forerunners like Mary Wollstonecraft (1759–97). Concerned that her own period's preoccupation with "natural law" might constrain women, Wollstonecraft had suggested in her *Vindication of the Rights of Women* (1792) that women were first determined by "natural law" to be inferior and then made inferior by their culture. She called upon women to resist such an idea and assert their own "natural right" to intellectual development.

In "Speaking Out" we enter the debates over women's nature later in the story, in the wake of Darwinism and after laymen and -women alike had become interested in the study of gender. This section is intended to show that even throughout the later part of the nineteenth century, women had to prepare the ground for their own endeavors, particularly their endeavors in natural history, the subject of this entire volume. Observe, for example, the satirical cartoon from *Vote,* where women strike back at antisuffragism by classifying its proponents as dinosaurs (figure 3). If we turn from looking to listening and turn first to Lydia Becker, we hear just one of the many voices suggesting that nature study was not just the province of men. Becker was a feminist, suffragist, and strong advocate of maximizing women's educational opportunities as well as an amateur botanist. She believed that men had no right to appropriate Nature's voice on behalf of the whole of the human species. Significantly, Becker's essays were written in the late 1860s, shortly after the 1865 census, which was the first to separate professions by gender and thereby call attention to the large gulf between male and female professionals. In the essay "Is There Any Specific Distinction Between Male and Female Intellect?" (1868) Becker answers her own question with a resounding "no." Nor, she argues, can any sort of "natural law" prove that this is so. Such distinctions are arbitrary and man-made, not "natural" at all. Education will, she believes, make the difference that in time will prove her point. In the meantime, her essay finds no connection between gender and intelligence, only between intellectual opportunity and the lack thereof.

FIGURE 3 *The Antysuffragyst, Vote,* 26 September 1913

Becker's essay is interesting from many points of view, not the least of which is that it predates John Stuart Mill's more famous work, *The Subjection of Women* (1869).

Becker's first essay paved the way for her second, "On the Study of Science by Women," and suggests that women often needed to prepare the ground for their own subsequent writing. Throughout the 1830s and 1840s people of both genders had taken part in the "crazes" of the science of natural history—collecting and cataloging fossils, rocks, and plants and animals in order to build collections or simply immerse themselves in the natural world. But most women so interested were limited in just how far they might extend these pursuits. By the 1860s science was becoming professionalized, which meant that they were excluded not just from its professional ranks, but even from understanding its discoveries and theories. Becker suggested that this was because of their lack of formal training in the sciences, and again not because of any innate inability. She deplored this entire state of events and argued for the many advantages science study by women might confer upon her society. Like others who advocated for women's intellectual rights, in the latter portion of her essay she cited example after example of women who have excelled in the sciences.

Emma Wallington, the next person represented in this section, is one of the few women for whom I was unable to find any other reference. Wallington was sufficiently respected to have won a voice in and to have presented a paper at the Anthropological Society in 1874, no mean feat for a woman of her day, when many professional societies were entirely closed to female participation. What is especially interesting about Wallington in "The Physical and Intellectual Capacities of Woman Equal to Those of Man" is her direct rhetorical appropriation of Nature's intentions—an appropriation far more common in the work of her male contemporaries.

Like Becker, to whom she refers, Wallington argues from illustrious examples, although she includes examples of women's physical as well as mental strength. But unlike Becker's arguments, Wallington's are immediately challenged in the sections of discussion following her paper. Here we see, as close as we can get to first hand, the kind of rebuttal offered when women argued from outstanding examples: yes, said the women's critics, but your exemplars are exceptions, not the rule.

Mona Caird (figure 4) entered debates over women's nature during the 1890s, when the wild woman controversy raged in the pages of *Nineteenth Century,* an influential Victorian periodical. This controversy included a number of prominent female voices. It began in 1890 when Lady Jersey (née Margaret Elizabeth Leigh [1849–1945]) wrote that women need not be bound by motherhood from accepting mental or physical activity of other sorts. The next year, conservative novelist Eliza Lynn Linton (1822–98) (figure 5) responded with an essay entitled "Wild Women and Social Insurgents," which derided women aspiring to social equality with men. Caird, a New Woman radical who wanted total equality in all spheres, countered with the essay reprinted here. Constructed Nature she calls a "fetish"; women's "nature" she calls the result of "the system of things"; and Linton's arguments she calls "strange reasoning." Throughout, she tries to answer Linton with a sweep and humor that make her essay both readable and enjoyable but fail to mask her earnest hope for a better civilization.

Lady Florence Dixie too looked forward to such a civilization. In her *Gloriana; or The Revolution of 1900* she offers a feminist utopia in which the future is envisioned as a brighter place for women. Like others in this section, Dixie takes it upon herself to appropriate Nature's voice in order to correct male pronouncements that have been made through that vehicle. She begins this process in her preface, reprinted here in full, and continues it in the selection from Gloriana's speech to parliament. Here her heroine pleads with her peers to reappraise their views of women's roles and strengths. Dixie's utopia is visionary but tame in comparison with the work of the visionary who concludes "Speaking Out." Turning male supremacy entirely on its head, Frances Swiney was an out-and-out radical in her day. For her, women were the most highly evolved, the finest developments of humankind. This is her ceaseless cry, one might say her creed, and Swiney cites a train of authorities to prove it true. "Man has not gone about dropping the end of a tail here, or a superfluous rib there. The mother's womb alone has been the crucible and workshop wherein Nature has formed her evolving handiwork," she tells us. Hence, women are the be-all and end-all of life. In

"Man's Necessity," reprinted in this volume, Swiney answers those who would elevate motherhood to women's sacred mission. She answers with a nod of agreement, suggesting that since this is so, women should not be utilized as vessels for male sexuality. Men should practice abstinence except when children are desired and should continue this practice when women are pregnant. "Nature," she reminds them with utter seriousness, "never wastes"; nor should men then waste nature's sperm. In turning male logic back on itself in this way, Swiney moved from being a radical to being an extremist. Her writing reveals just how far one woman was willing to go, even so late as the early twentieth century, in order to speak in Nature's name.

LYDIA E. BECKER

"Is There Any Specific Distinction Between Male and Female Intellect?"

Englishwoman's Review 8 (1868): 483–91 (paper read at a meeting of the Manchester Ladies' Literary Society).

The superiority in muscular strength of the male to the female sex in the human species is a fact beyond all dispute. Many persons, reasoning from analogy, maintain that there is a difference in the minds of men and women corresponding to the difference in their bodily organisation—that because women are weaker in body than men they must be weaker in mind; and in order to soften this rude assertion of superiority, men have endeavoured to make out that to compensate women for the intellectual powers denied to their sex, they are gifted with a certain fineness of perception, an intuitive apprehension of truths, to be reached by the slower minds of the other sex only by a cumbrous process of reasoning. The persons who believe that the distinction of sex extends to mind are accustomed to maintain that the intellects of men and women should be cultivated in a different fashion and directed in different ways, and that there is a "sphere" or "province" assigned to each, within which it is the bounden duty of one sex, at least, to confine erratic genius. There would seem more reason for this division of intellectual labour if the terms imposed affected both sexes alike. But while men have been permitted to wander at will over the whole range of human thoughts and capacities without danger of being warned off any region, as "beyond the province of their sex," women have been pent in a small corner, and though they have lately succeeded in considerably enlarging the boundary of what is considered their legitimate sphere of exertion, they have not yet been able to obtain the recognition of the principle that the boundary itself, in so far as it is a restriction on natural tastes and capacities, ought not to be imposed on one sex more than on the other. Men have been left free to think and act according to their natural bent, while women have been and are subjected to artificial restraint; and this circumstance has produced the same inevitable result as would have arisen from a corresponding difference in the training of two classes of men. Suppose all dark-haired boys were encouraged to join in athletic sports and exhilarating games, and trained to strive for all the honours and rewards of active life, and all light-haired ones were kept chiefly indoors, allowed exercise only in the shape of walking, set to quiet occupations, and instructed that their vocation in life consisted mainly in being useful to the others, there would arise a difference between the mental and moral complexion of the two sets, quite as striking as that which subsists between girls and boys, or men and women.

The propositions to which I invite your assent this afternoon are—

1. That the attribute of sex does not extend to mind, and that there is no distinction between the intellects of men and women corresponding to and dependent on the organisation of their bodies.
2. That any broad marks of distinction that may exist at the present time between the minds of men and women collectively, are fairly traceable to the influence of the different circumstances under which they pass their lives, and cannot be proved to inhere in each class in virtue of sex.
3. That in spite of the external circumstances which tend to cause divergence in tone of mind, habits of thought, and opinions, between men and women, it is a matter of fact that these do not differ more among persons of opposite sexes than they do among persons of the same; that comparing any one man and any one women, the difference between them in these points will not be greater than what may be found between two men or two women.

In illustration of the first of my propositions, I would observe that sex is an attribute common to all organised beings who rise above the very lowest forms of animal or vegetable life. The higher vegetables, though possessing the attribute of sex, have never manifested any signs of consciousness or intelligence. They do possess a certain amount of sensitiveness to external impressions not strictly mechanical, and a capacity for spontaneous movement till they find the support or nourishment they need. Yet these appearances, curious and interesting as they are, do not warrant us in ascribing any degree of intellect to plants. These cannot therefore afford us any assistance in the inquiry as to the effect of sex upon mind, but they may help to disabuse us of the notion that superiority in strength is necessarily masculine—every botanist being aware that female plants are quite as strong and big as male ones of the same species.

When we turn to the animal kingdom, we do not proceed far up the scale from the lowest organisms before detecting the existence of mind in the creatures whose habits we observe. Mind of a very low order, it may be, still we observe signs of consciousness, of pleasure and pain, of voluntary action, and of ingenious adaptation of means to ends, long before we quit the kingdoms of the invertebrata. And I am not aware that any naturalist has reported that there is a greater development of intellect in one sex than in the other, as a general rule. Exceptions there are, certainly. In the hive bee, the ingenuity to work and the power to govern are vested in actual or potential females, while the males, kept within their "sphere," are ignominiously hustled out of existence, whenever they are tempted to step beyond it, or unreasonable enough to ask for a share of the good things of the hive. But it seems fair to conclude that this subordination is not due to any inherent inferiority in masculinity, as such, but simply to the fact that their bodily organisation leaves them defenceless against the terrible weapons of the superior sex. Had nature gifted the males with stings, they would assuredly assert their right to live on equal terms with other members of the community.

In another class of invertebrata we are presented with the view of numerous species of animals having the sexes united in the same individual; a puzzling anomaly for those who maintain that difference of sex extends to mind. They may try to escape by denying that snails and oysters have any intellect, and certainly their mental powers seem greatly below those of ants and bees—still, we are not justified in saying they have none at all.

Passing to the kingdom of which man is a member, we do not find universal among vertebrate animals the rule as to feminine subordination deduced from the relative strength of the sexes in the human species. Where there is inequality in this respect among brutes, the difference is not always in favour of the male. Whichever sex is stronger will have the mastery, but there is no ground for the assertion that the male is necessarily the superior. In the birds of prey, from the eagle to the sparrow-hawk, the female exceeds her mate in size, strength, and courage; the male bird is an inferior creature, who was always rejected by the falconers on account of his comparative deficiency in these qualities. The lordly eagle, the monarch of the peak, is the female bird, and should not be spoken of by names denoting the masculine gender.

If the birds of prey were to reason, from experience in their own species, that there was any inherent superiority of one sex over the other they would unquestionably assign the palm of dominion to the female. But the eagles would undoubtedly be mistaken if they affirmed that the dominant sex reigned among them by any more recondite title than that of an accidental superiority of physical strength. The male is bodily weaker among eagles, the female among men, therefore there is no ground for the assumption that one sex is naturally and inherently superior, even in strength, to the other.

But in animals, and in the lower stages of civilization among human beings, superiority in physical strength counts for, and brings in its train, superiority in everything else; the weakest go to the wall—the strong oppress and enslave the less powerful. In the long dark night of ignorance and superstition which represents the past history of our race, brute force has been the one thing worshipped. Men have bowed down in adulation before the conquerors who came with sword in hand to oppress them, and put to death those who came with intellect to enlighten and free them. Now the dawn of a brighter day is breaking, and we rejoice in the promise of the light to come. It is true, we have not ceased to idolize military despotism, but we have at least learned not to put to death the philosophers. We still seem, however, a long way off the time when he will not be considered the greatest man who boasts the "greatest faculty for coercing mankind."

The second proposition to which I ask your assent is, that any broad marks of distinction existing at the present time between the minds of men and women collectively are fairly traceable to the influence of the different circumstances under which they pass their lives, and cannot be proved to inhere in each class in virtue of sex.

In illustration of this assertion, I point to the fact, that when minds are classified into groups, the male and the female mind are not the only species recognised. Whenever a class of persons are united by similarity of profession or pursuits, there is generated among them a peculiar tone of thought, distinguishing them from men engaged in other occupations.

We have the legal mind, the military mind, the clerical mind, the commercial mind, the scientific mind, the scholastic mind, and others. Suppose a company of soldiers, another of lawyers, another of priests, another of artists were gathered together, the conversation of each assemblage would have a marked tone peculiar to the members of the profession of which it was composed; and suppose the separate parties then gathered into one, and a conversation to take place on general subjects—the lawyer, the doctor, the artist and the soldier would each bring into the discussion, not only his own individual peculiarities of thought and feeling, but something of the influence exerted on these by the exigencies of his calling in life.

We do not attribute this result to any inherent natural distinction in the minds of those who pursue each profession, but entirely to education, and circumstances. Men are not born soldiers, lawyers, or doctors, and though some are undoubtedly predisposed by natural bent to one vocation, in which only they can excel, the great majority would make indifferently good members of any trade or profession which circumstances caused them to embrace.

Now I believe that a similar reason accounts for all the differences that may be observed to exist between men and women. The difference in their vocation in life, in their daily habits, in the things each has got to do, would tend to make a divergence between men and women, even if their education and training had been in common.

But how far is this from being the case! Boys are encouraged to develop their bodily powers, to mix with the world, to regard personal distinction in their calling in life as an object of honourable ambition. Girls are usually discouraged from hard play, or exercise calculated to develop bodily strength; their natural aspirations for a career or pursuit in life by which they may win their way in the world are repressed as unbecoming, and they are told that the highest reward of any excellence they may attain consists in living unrecognized and unknown.

The one thing to be sedulously and religiously shunned is publicity. When boys or men do a thing worthy of approbation their friends think it something to be proud of, and give honour where honour is due, their names are given that others may be encouraged to persevere in the good work.

But if a girl or a woman renders a public service, or distinguishes herself in any way, it seems to be regarded as something to be ashamed of; it is considered wrong to give honourable public distinctions to women, and that they ought to deprecate rather than desire them. This principle is acted on by the University of Cambridge, which admits boys and girls on exactly equal terms to its local examinations. But the boys who pass honourably have their names published, while the girls who pass honourably have their names suppressed. It is just as natural for a girl as for a boy to be pleased to see her names in a list of those who have done well. This desire is thought praiseworthy in a boy and worthy of encouragement—it is thought blameworthy in a girl and to be sternly reproved. An artificial distinction is made where nature has made none.

No one would wish to see either girls or boys ostentatiously putting themselves forward. But there may be just as much egotism and self-consciousness in ostentatiously hiding their heads. Arrogance is a very unpleasant quality. But a man who is "'umble" may be more trying to deal with. At least we give the first credit for honesty.

With this and other marked differences in the mental training and moral code imposed on the two sexes, it is only wonderful that the distinction between men and women is not greater than we find it; and this brings me to my third proposition, namely—That in spite of the circumstances which tend to cause divergence in the tone of mind, the habits of thought, and the opinions of men and women, it is a matter of fact that these do not differ more among persons of opposite sexes than they do among persons of the same—that comparing any one man with any one woman, the difference between them will not be greater than may be found between two men or two women.

One of the most natural and obvious divisions of labour between the two sexes, is that which assigns to men the occupations of soldiers and sailors. Women would seem to be unfitted physically to engage in them. But do we find a corresponding mental or moral disability? On the contrary, instances are by no means uncommon of the natural taste of a woman leading her so decidedly to one or other of these professions that she has overcome all obstacles and actually engaged in them. Disguised as men, women have more than once been detected as soldiers and sailors, some having performed their duties creditably, and maintained the secret of their sex for years. We may assume that all have not been detected, and that a careful scrutiny might possibly reveal others scattered among the ships and armies of the world. These instances are not adduced with a view of proving that it is desirable to open such professions to women, but merely in support of my proposition that sex does not extend to mind. As these military and naval heroines were feminine in body they would have bad minds to correspond if it were truly a law of nature that there was such a thing as sex in taste and intellect.

Needlework is a trade seemingly peculiarly adapted to the powers and tastes of women. Yet surely it is not hard necessity which leads so many men to embrace it. Men can do it, and do it well, and as there is no legal nor social restraint on them, they set to work to make clothes, I presume with satisfaction to themselves, as well as to those who employ them.

Many professions are common to both sexes; and the votaries of art and literature are taken from the ranks of men and women indiscriminately, though the opportunities of study and the prospect of reward are greatly in favour of the dominant sex.

If we take an assemblage of persons of opposite sexes and test the difference of thought and opinion existing among them by putting before them any proposition on which opposite views can be held, I believe it would be impossible to find one which would range all the men on one side, and all the women on the other. If it were true that there is a specific difference, however slight, between the minds of men and women, it would be possible to find such a proposition, if we took one which corresponded to this distinction. When a naturalist seeks to group a number of individuals into a distinct class, he fixes on some character, or set of characters, common to them all, and distinguishing them from other individuals. When he finds such a group distinctly defined he calls it a species. But when he finds two individuals differing very widely from each other, yet so connected by numerous intermediate forms that he can pass from one extreme to the other without a violent break anywhere in the series, he considers them to be of one and the same kind. Taking the conventional masculine type of mind as one end of the scale, and the conventional feminine type as the other, I maintain that they are connected by numerous intermediate varieties distributed indiscriminately in male and female bodies; that what is called a masculine mind is frequently found united to a feminine body, and sometimes the reverse; and that there is no necessary, nor even presumptive connexion between the sex of a human being, and the type of intellect and character he possesses.

LYDIA ERNESTINE BECKER

From "On the Study of Science by Women"

Contemporary Review 10 (1869): 388–404.

. . . Most of the inducements for pursuing scientific studies are common to men and women. But there are some considerations which render such pursuits of greater value to women than to men. Prevalent opinions and customs impose on women so much more monotonous and colourless lives, and deprive them of so much of the natural and healthy excitement enjoyed by the other sex in its freer intercourse with the world, that the necessity for some pursuit which shall afford scope for the activity of their minds is even more pressing in their case than in that of men. In default of mental food and exercise, the minds of women get starved out. Numbers end by falling a prey to morbid religious excitement; while others, after vain struggles against their destiny, sink at last into a weary kind of resigned apathy, and men say they are content. But no one can measure the pain that has been endured ere the yearnings for a wider and freer existence subside into deadened calm. Many women might be saved from the evil of the life of intellectual vacuity, to which their present position renders them so peculiarly liable, if they had a thorough training in some branch of science, and the opportunity of carrying it on as a serious pursuit, in concert with others having similar tastes. Many a passing moment would then be made bright with a flash of thought which would otherwise have stolen away unmarked into the irrevocable past.

Men, who have been in the habit of enjoying the advantages attending systematic study and of the liberty of thought and speech not yet attained by women, do not need to be reminded of the benefits they derive from them. But women, who have never had the opportunity of finding out by experience the value of these conditions of mental life, do not always appreciate the magnitude of the loss they endure. If they did, I think they would not be content with their enforced exclusion from the pale of scientific society.

One of the greatest benefits which intellectual pursuits bring in their train is that of affording a peaceful neutral ground in which the mind can take refuge from the petty cares and annoyances of life, or even find diversion from more serious troubles. Like prudent investors, who keep a part of their capital in the funds, those who place the sources of a portion of their income of enjoyment in some pursuit wholly unconnected with their personal affairs, will find they have an interest which is perfectly safe amid the chances and changes of life. I do not for a moment maintain that intellectual pursuits can afford consolation in sorrow—for that we must look elsewhere; but they are undoubtedly capable of giving solace and diversion to the mind which might otherwise dwell too long on the gloomy side of things, and of beguiling the tedium of enforced solitude, or of confinement to a sick room. For an instance of this I may refer to the example of one of the most illustrious naturalists of the age. Mr. Charles Darwin has informed us that some of his most curious and interesting observations respecting the habits of climbing plants were made when he was a prisoner, night and day, to one room; and we cannot doubt that the occupation they afforded him not only served to lighten the weary hours, but occasioned him an amount of positive enjoyment which one less gifted might have failed to secure, though at liberty to participate in the ordinary pleasure of social life.

Such an example should encourage others to do likewise. Many particulars respecting the commonest of our wild plants, animals, and insects, are as yet imperfectly understood; and any woman who might select one of these creatures, and begin a series of patient observations on its habits, manner of feeding, of taking care of its young, of communicating with its kind, of guarding against danger, on its disposition and temper, and the difference in character between two individuals of the same species, would find such occupation not only exceedingly entertaining, but, if the observations were carefully noted, the result would be something of real, if not of great, scientific value. Gold is gold, whether our amount be an ingot or a spangle; and we need but to open our eyes, and carefully observe what is passing around us, to add perpetually to our store of the pure gold of knowledge.

No one should be deterred from either making or reporting original observations by the feeling that they are trifling or unimportant. Nothing that is real is considered insignificant by the naturalist, and observations apparently the most trifling have led to results which have turned the whole current of scientific thought. What could be a more trifling circumstance than the fall of an apple from a tree? Yet the appearances presented contained the clue that unravelled the mystery of the planetary movements. The law of gravitation maintains stability of the universe, yet the fall of a pin to the ground is as truly a manifestation of this force as the movement of the earth in its orbit. With the sentiment of the poet in our hearts,—

"That very law that moulds a tear,
  And bids it trickle from its source,
That law preserves the earth a sphere,
  And holds the planets in their course."—[1]

we shall never regard any appearance as trifling which the tremendous forces of nature concur to produce.

How seemingly unimportant are the movements of insects, creeping in and out of flowers in search of the nectar on which they feed! If we saw a

1. Samuel Rogers (1763–1855), "On a Tear," lines 21–24. *Ed.*

man spending his time in watching them, and in noting their flitting with curious eyes, we might be excused for imagining that he was amusing himself by idling an hour luxuriously in observing things which, though curious, were trifling. But how mistaken might we be in such an assumption! For these little winged messengers bear to the mind of the philosophical naturalist tidings of mysteries hitherto unrevealed; and as Newton saw the law of gravitation in the fall of the apple, Darwin found, in the connection between flies and flowers, some of the most important facts which support the theory he has promulgated respecting the modification of specific forms in animated beings.

It is true we are not Darwins nor Newtons, and cannot expect to make surprising discoveries; but we may be sure that these, and all other philosophers, have found an exquisite pleasure in tracing the workings of nature, and this enjoyment may be had by all who follow, however humbly, in their footsteps. And if we wish to understand their theories, it is refreshing to find our attention directed at the outset to pleasant and familiar natural objects—to varieties of pigeons, to humble-bees sucking clover flowers, to beetles swimming with their wings, to primroses and crimson flax, and grotesque orchids with their wild, weird beauty, setting traps for unwitting insects, and making them pay for their feast of honey by being the bearers of love-tokens from one flower to another—to be sent, in fact, to the Book of Nature, and bidden to read its wondrous stories with our own eyes.

Besides the addition to our store of positive knowledge, there is another important advantage to be derived from scientific study; namely, the cultivation of those habits of accuracy in speech and thought which are so absolutely necessary to its successful prosecution. One of the first lessons which a scientific student learns is, that he must not take a mere impression on his own mind as representing a positive fact, until he has carefully verified its accuracy by comparing it with the results of observation, and is prepared to state exactly on what grounds he entertains it. And when he hears an assertion made, he will pause before accepting it as true, for the mental inquiry whether the asserter is likely to be personally acquainted with the fact he alleges; and if not, what are his probable sources of information. On the answer to these expressed or unexpressed queries will depend the measure of credence to be given to the assertion in question. A reverence for accuracy of this kind would arrest many a baseless and painful rumour; and if it is the tendency of scientific investigation to conduce to such a tone of mind, the most inveterate sceptic as to the benefits of intellectual culture for women might be induced to confess that it is better that maids, old and young, should graduate in the School for Science, rather than in the School for Scandal.

If we turn from the consideration of the advantages women would gain from taking an active part in scientific pursuits, to the means accessible to them for prosecuting these studies, we perceive a very deplorable state of affairs.

The necessity for some common ground on which all interested in intellectual pursuits may meet, has been so strongly felt, that there exist all over the country institutions and societies, devoted either to literature and philosophy in general, or to the cultivation of special departments of knowledge. But most of these institutions, especially such as are devoted to the higher branches of scientific investigation, have one strange and injurious deficiency. They do not throw open such opportunities as they afford for acquiring knowledge freely to all who desire it; they draw an arbitrary line among scientific students, and say to one half of the human race, "You shall not enter into the advantages we have to offer; you shall not enjoy the facilities we possess of cultivating the tastes and faculties with which you may be endowed; and should any of you, in spite of this drawback, reach such a measure of attainments as would entitle one of us to the honour of membership or fellowship in any learned society, we will not, by conferring such distinctions on any of you, recognise your right to occupy your minds with such studies at all." It is no light mortification to a woman, who is desirous of prosecuting a study, to find that those best qualified to help her on her way are sedulous in affording her all the discouragement in their power, and that the doors of the high places of science are rigorously closed against her.

In order to have definite information on this head, I applied to the secretaries of one or two of the scientific societies of the metropolis, with the following result. Mr. White, Assistant-Secretary of the Royal Society, writes:—

"In answer to your inquiry as to what is the position of women with regard to the Royal Society, I beg leave to say that the Society is not open to women; that ladies are not admitted to the meetings, and have never been elected Fellows.

"Mrs. Somerville[2] many years ago was elected honorary member of the Astronomical Society, but I am not aware that she has ever written F.R.A.S. after her name."

2. Mary Somerville, author of *On the Connexion of the Physical Sciences* (1834), excerpted in this book. *Ed.*

Mr. Henry Walter Bates, Secretary to the Royal Geographical Society, kindly furnished me with the following statement:—

"1. Women are not entitled to become members or Fellows of the Royal Geographical Society. But they are allowed to attend the meetings as visitors introduced by Fellows, and, if they are teachers of geography, they can obtain a Council card of admission for the season.

"2. There is no instance on record of the Society bestowing medals or other rewards on women. Lady Franklin received a medal on behalf of her deceased husband. Women have distinguished themselves as explorers, both singly—Madame Pfeiffer—and with their husbands—Lady Baker, Madame Helfer, Madame Semper—but I do not think it has been proposed in our Council to bestow a reward for geographical merit on a woman.[3]

"3. Women are admitted as visitors to the Ethnological Society; but I am not aware that this is allowed or practised in any other scientific society.

"Ladies are Fellows of the Royal Horticultural Society; but this is not for scientific purposes, but to obtain admission to the gardens. Ladies are not generally invited even to the *soirées* of learned societies such as the Royal, the Linnæan, etc. Ours is an exception, a small number being invited as friends of the President. They are, however, invited freely to the *soirées* of the microscopical clubs and societies, and seem to avail themselves very largely of the privelege, and to look through microscopes quite as eagerly as the men. They are also invited freely to the *soirées* of the Society of Arts. I think if a lady was to offer a really good paper on a scientific subject to any of these societies, it would be accepted and published like a man's paper in their transactions. I have seen papers by ladies (I think) in the transactions of the Linnæan Society."

Mr. Bates speaks of a lady offering a really good paper on a scientific subject. But so long as ladies are shut out from the association of those who are engaged in such pursuits, it is hardly to be expected that they would have either the stimulus or the opportunity of producing much that was valuable; and he seems not quite certain that if they did, their papers would be accepted and published.

To the list of ladies enumerated by Mr. Bates, as having distinguished

3. Mr. Bates writes with regard to the ladies last-named in his statement:—"Madame Helfer accompanied her husband, Dr. Helfer, to Burmah and the Andaman Islands, and assisted him in his scientific investigations. Madame Semper travelled with her husband, Dr. Semper, in the Philippines. Their narrative is not yet published, but it will, I have no doubt, show how much Dr. Semper owed to the enterprise, endurance, courage, and scientific enthusiasm of his partner. They travelled in a small boat round the islands, dredging the sea bottom for marine animals, and had sometimes to run in ashore to escape from pirates. The result was a most magnificent collection of the animal productions of the Philippine archipelago."

themselves in geographical exploration, I may add the name of Mademoiselle Alexandrine Tinné,[4] who, a few years ago, fitted out a steamer at her own expense, to explore the Bahr el Ghazal, one of the tributaries of the White Nile, and accompanied the expedition, along with her mother and aunt. I remember that, at one of the meetings of the British Association, some one asked Sir Roderick Murchison,[5] whether the Royal Geographical Society would mark its sense of her munificence and courage in geographical enterprise by electing her a Fellow of the Society. The learned president received the proposition with something very like disdain, making an observation to the effect that they never had conferred such a distinction upon a lady. The gentleman who asked the question read a letter from Mademoiselle Tinné, giving intelligence of the progress of the expedition, which, at that time, was tolerably prosperous, but subsequently became entangled among the dreary swamps of the equatorial Nile regions, and fever and disaster arrested its progress. But the enterprising lady is still bent on making further explorations, and when last heard of, in December, 1868, she was on the point of setting off from Tripoli to Lake Tschad and the kingdom of Borran. The expeditions of these ladies in Central Africa have been often referred to in the proceedings of the Royal Geographical Society.

We cannot claim the honour of numbering any of these distinguished ladies among our countrywomen. Madame Helfer and Madame Semper are probably foreigners, and the ladies Tinné and Baker certainly so. I call them distinguished because, though they have not attained the honours or distinctions bestowed on other explorers, they have done the deeds which merited such reward.

I have been informed that on one occasion the authorities of the Royal Astronomical Society had a discussion as to whether they should award their gold medal to Miss Caroline Herschel[6] for her discovery of five comets. It was understood that it would undoubtedly have been given had the discoverer been a man. But they came to a determination akin to that of the Royal Geographical Society—not to recognise or reward services to science when rendered by a woman, and the medal was withheld.

When the Meteorological Society was formed it was decided to admit women, and four ladies were elected on the original foundation; among them the Countess of Lovelace—Byron's daughter "Ada." In a little while

4. Alexander Tinné (1835–69), a Dutch explorer who mapped the River Nile. *Ed.*

5. Sir Roderick Murchison (1792–1871) was the first geologist to establish the sequence of Paleozoic strata. He was president of the Geological Society of London. *Ed.*

6. Caroline Herschel (1750–1848) was a German-born British astronomer who actually discovered eight comets (contra the text) and three nebulae. *Ed.*

one of these ladies, the wife of an eminent meteorologist, wrote to say that she had been told it would be injurious to the Society to have women as members; she, therefore, thought it her duty to resign, and she hoped the other ladies would follow her example. One of them did so; but another, who could not be made to comprehend the necessity for maintaining the scientific disabilities of women, refused to withdraw, and no one even suggested the propriety of resignation to Lady Lovelace. But the two ladies who remained members are since dead, and no others have been elected; for it appears that the Royal Charter which was subsequently obtained would not have been granted to any Society which admitted women to participate in its advantages.

The story of the connection of women with the scientific societies of the metropolis being chiefly of a negative character, is thus soon told. That a different complexion would be given to the tale, were the advantages and the honours they possess open freely to all lovers of intellectual pursuits without invidious distinction, may be reasonably inferred from the results obtained where this principle has been acted on.

. . . So long as intellectual pursuits were confined to a select few, and the masses of people, men and women alike, cared nothing for these things, the disadvantages of the exclusion of women from participation in these pursuits were but slightly felt. There was nothing in this exclusion to cut them off from the sympathy of those with whom they lived, or to cause divergence or estrangement between their minds, and those of persons with whom they habitually associated. If they were on a low level intellectually, the men around them were on the same, and so the balance was preserved. But now we see symptoms of a change. Everywhere educational institutions of more or less pretensions and efficiency are springing into being. Scarcely a town but has its mechanics' institute, debating society, literary society, or some kindred mechanism for promoting intellectual activity. But almost invariably the efforts of those who promote these institutions are directed to producing a divorce between the thoughts and sympathies of those who should be mates and helps to each other in all the concerns of life. They see man and woman, ignorant and undeveloped, grinding at the mill of life's daily toil. They desire to lighten this toil, by affording a glimpse of something beyond the narrow horizon of each day's mechanical duties. They go to the man, and they open to him the vista of intellectual enjoyment, leaving his companion uncheered in her solitude, unthought of, uncared for. Should she cast a wistful glance at the prospect, and ask why she may not share in the good things they set forth, she is encountered by the assurance that the pathways that lead to the higher regions of thought were never meant for her to tread, and with a contemptuous reproof for her presumption in wishing to stir a step beyond her appointed "sphere." So, bereft of the companionship of her partner in ignorance, the last condition of that woman is worse than the first. After profiting by the advantages denied to her, he returns elated with the consciousness of superior wisdom, and complacently propounds theories as to the "radical inequality of the sexes—the radical inferiority, physical, moral, and intellectual, of woman."

The danger of producing disunion in families by teaching all the men, and leaving all the women out in the cold, is no fanciful one. It is already beginning to be felt, and will increase with the success of every attempt to promote popular education that is not based on comprehensive principles. A very intelligent working man in one of the manufacturing towns of Lancashire, with whom I was conversing on the subject of a public movement in which he was greatly interested, informed me that it was a source of serious trouble to him that his wife had not kept up with the advance of his mind, and for want of knowledge and cultivation, was unable to understand the importance of the work on which he was engaged, and unwilling to see him devoting his attention to it, or to sympathise with his efforts for its advancement. He spoke in sorrow, as feeling it a real misfortune, and as if his were but a representative case as regards the effect on domestic happiness of the present one-sided system.

Some of the educational institutions so far recognise the existence of the other sex as to make a feeble effort to supplement their main provisions by the establishment of supernumerary "women's classes." I have not heard whether these well-meant but ill-advised efforts to combat the evil have done much good. The little I have heard leads me to the belief that the result has been what one might from the first have anticipated, and that the interest displayed in these classes has been languid. There are not a sufficient number of women as yet roused to the interest of such subjects to afford material for the promotion and continuance of such isolated classes, and the fact of their exclusion from the companionship of the other sex acts as a damper on their spirits. They would not care much for social pleasures if they were only admitted to women's balls, women's dinner parties, women's croquet parties, and women's concerts; and if they are only allowed to participate in intellectual pleasures on these exclusive terms, they will certainly not derive from them either the advantages or the healthful stimulus which these are capable of affording.

It seems to me a matter for sincere regret that any effort made to promote the intellectual activity of women should be based on this system of separation and exclusion. Whatever difficulties may be thought to stand in the way of studies conducted in concert, none can exist, even in imagination, when the proposal is simply that of simultaneous and identical examinations; the placing of all the papers together for judgment, and making out the class list in order of merit, with absolute impartiality and indifference as to whether the papers were the production of male or female students. The success of the local examinations in connection with the University of Cambridge, where no difference of any kind is made in the examination of girls and boys, should point out the principle to be acted on in further efforts in the same direction. The only matter for regret in respect of these examinations is the treatment of the successful students, in the invidious distinction implied in the exclusion of girls from the class lists. The boys who pass honourably have their names published; the girls who pass honourably have their names suppressed. It is just as natural for a girl as for a boy to be pleased to see her name in a list of those who have done well. The University encourages the boys by marking the proficiency they have attained as something to be proud of; it discourages the girls by implying that the acquirements they have gained are something to conceal, or be ashamed of.

A still further departure from the principle of equality has been made by the University of London. They have instituted a special examination for women, to which no male student is admitted, and the recognition attached to success is a mere certificate of having passed, without the honours of a University degree.

Perhaps I ought to consider the step that has been taken by the London University not so much a departure from the principle of intellectual equality as an advance towards it. It is the pleasanter, and possibly the truer way. Certainly, before this concession was made, women were not allowed by the authorities to have any rights at all in the matter. Now that their eyes have become partly open to the needs of women in this respect, we may hope that the process will not stop till complete justice has been done.

From all that I can gather respecting the proposed examination, it is in no way inferior in what examinees call "stiffness" to that provided for the other sex. A woman who passes in any subject will do quite as much as a man who passes the men's examination corresponding in grade. But though she will have worked as hard and done as much as the men, she will not have equal honour. The men will say to her: "You are not on our level; you have only passed the women's examination;" and she will not be admitted as a graduate whatever the amount of intellectual power or attainments she displays. The whole arrangement proceeds on the principle that it is very womanly to work, but "unfeminine" to receive pay or reward for work.

Women may be admitted to the course of study, but not to the honours or advantages to which that course of study leads men.

It will not be very wonderful if an experiment based on what seems a radically false principle should prove a failure, and if high-spirited and accomplished women who are conscious of no moral nor intellectual inferiority to the other sex, should refuse to enter an examination which does not place them on a level with others. It is only to be hoped that the possible failure of an experiment of this nature will not be used as an argument against better devised future attempts to extend the educational privileges of women.

The efforts made by the London University to help women up the ladder of learning remind me of the history told by Mr. Frank Buckland[7] of his endeavours to facilitate the ascent of salmon up rivers, the natural course of which had been obstructed by weirs and dams placed there by man. After exhausting his ingenuity in providing a way for the salmon up these artificial barriers, by means of a contrivance "nicely adapted to their special tastes and capacities," he found, to his dismay, that his pains had been entirely thrown away, for "the ungrateful beasts wouldn't go in!" But Mr. Frank Buckland is a man of resources, and failure is no word in his vocabulary. He informed us that the only plan then available was to catch a salmon, and ask it what it wanted. Of course the creature very soon told him, and the moment arrangements were made in accordance with its real needs, of it went, like an arrow, up the stream, on its way to the mountains. Now, if those who are sincerely, but perhaps somewhat blindly, trying to open the way to a higher life for women, will be as wise as Mr. Frank Buckland in seeking to adapt their means to the real feelings and wishes of those whom they are striving to benefit, instead of to what they imagine women ought to feel and desire, they will be as successful as he was in setting the struggling creatures, free, and in peopling the stream of life with fish worth catching, instead of leaving nothing for the angler but the minnows and sticklebacks "of the period."

Besides the special benefits to women themselves, results of a yet more important nature with respect to the happiness and welfare of mankind, would follow from making them acquainted with the results of scientific inquiry, and imbuing their minds with the principles on which such researches are based. The importance of scientific knowledge is not yet appreciated by the general public. A knowledge of science is frequently treated as if it were merely a branch of learning, like Latin or Greek, and the question of making it a part of general education is regarded as if it were simply a

7. Frank Buckland (1826–80) was an English zoologist and expert on fish and fishing. He was the son of William Buckland, famous English divine and geologist. *Ed.*

question of what course of study was best fitted to train the faculties or suit the taste of the student.

But surely there is a more important aspect of the study of science than that which regards it as merely a mass of curious and interesting information. Men and women constitute an integral portion of a universe governed by uniform and undeviating laws. It is the object of scientific explorers to discover these laws, a pursuit in which they may be said as yet to have hardly made a beginning. Every step gained in advance reveals something which can be turned to account in ameliorating the hardships and discomforts of life, and promoting the happiness of mankind. With complete knowledge of the conditions under which we live, and complete conformity to these conditions, we might hope to see most of the evils that afflict our race entirely disappear. This knowledge is presumably attainable by human faculties, if the search be conducted with sufficient perseverance, and based on right principles. The greater the number of minds that are impressed with this belief, the greater the encouragement that will be given to the inquiry, and the greater the probability and the proximity of success. When the conviction of the preventability of misery shall have become the prevailing one, men and women will cease to meet its existence chiefly with endeavours to palliate its effects, but will set resolutely to work to remove its causes. They will then no longer accuse either chance or Providence of sending the ills that afflict mankind, but perceive that they are traceable to the action of inexorable and undeviating law, and that most, if not all of them, may be averted or avoided by human foresight acting on human knowledge.

When the science, the practice, and the principles which lead to this habit of thought shall cease to be considered the exclusive privilege of the dominant sex, and become the heritage of humanity at large, the progress of the race will receive an impetus which shall carry it on at a pace hitherto undreamed of. The rate of advancement will be far more than doubled, because the untrained and stationary half of mankind necessarily acts as a drag on the other. We seek to unloose the locked wheels of the car, and to set free the imprisoned energies now pining for scope.

There is a strong tendency greatly to undervalue the extent the intensity of the feeling that exists among women of dissatisfaction with their present condition, and with their exclusion from participation in the pursuits that interest and occupy men. It is assumed that the majority are contented, and that the desire for an amelioration of their lot is felt only by a few exceptional natures. But let not those in whose hands the power lies, pass over the cry so lightly. Many are the signs of the times which tell a different story. Among many voices, one has been raised that had no strength in itself, but in the truth of the note that it rang. That note has found an answering chord in thousands of women's hearts, and has come back from near and far, over the length and breadth of the land. Not in loud and turbulent cries, but in tones unmistakably clear to an ear attuned to catch the delicate harmonics that breathe from sorrowful and suffering souls. And not from our land alone, for women's hearts are everywhere the same. Voices have resounded from the Alps; signs have reached over the Pyrenees; echoes have bridged the Atlantic. No false note could awaken so deep and so wide a response; no harsh tone could evoke such loving sympathy.

The cry for equal rights for all human beings proceeds from the irrepressible consciousness of equal needs, and the possession of common feelings. The movement now hourly gaining strength for the social, educational, and political enfranchisement of women, arises from no spirit of opposition or rivalry with men, but from deep and intense sympathy in their noblest aims and aspirations.

~ EMMA WALLINGTON

"The physical and intellectual capacities of woman equal to those of men"

Anthtropologia 1 (1874): 552–65.

ORDINARY MEETING

Held at 37, Arundel Street, Strand, London, on Tuesday, 2nd June, 1874, at 8 p.m.

PROFESSOR LEITNER, PH.D., IN THE CHAIR.

The Minutes of the preceding Meeting were read and confirmed. Elections announced:—

Fellows: E. RICHMOND HODGES, Esq., CHARLES HAMILTON, Esq.

The following paper was read:—

THE PHYSICAL AND INTELLECTUAL CAPACITIES OF WOMAN EQUAL TO THOSE OF MAN.

By EMMA WALLINGTON.

Believing that the progress of the human race is greatly facilitated by patient investigation of facts and fair discussion, I venture to bring under your notice the oft-debated question of woman's physical and mental capacities.

The doctrine of averages respecting the innate superiority of man's bodily and intellectual powers only affords us an approximation to the truth. For the sake of argument, it may be admitted the majority of men are stronger and more intellectual than the majority of women. But is it true that superiority is exclusively a *male* attribute? We are willing to accept the answer which Nature gives; her voice tells us this superiority is shared by women, and it is the object of this paper to offer evidence of the opinion advanced, in the hope that your kind consideration may cast new light on a vexed question.

The oft-repeated assertion that women are inferior to men, physically and intellectually, has tempted me to investigate the matter, in order to discover whether the said assertion is based on the solid foundation of truth and accurate knowledge, or the superficial one of imperfect observation and loose inference.

First, as to the physical part. Many of the arguments brought forward in support of woman's natural deficiency of muscular strength are clearly founded on data in which feeling and prejudice bear much larger proportions than correct reasoning and strict attention. Facts are proverbially stubborn things, and the chief difficulty in affairs of warm controversy is our reluctance to consider impartially the facts we most dislike; every attempt to ignore or pervert them only serves to prolong and embitter the controversy and delay the advancement of truth. In calling your attention to the physical capabilities of women, I wish it to be understood that the examples I adduce are not always such as I am pleased with, neither am I now discussing what employments I desire to see a woman's physical energy expended in; your attention is drawn to the following illustrations for the purpose of showing that—whether we like it or not—hundreds of thousands of women have always performed, and do to this day perform some of the hardest work of the world. In this country, less than a quarter of a century ago, large numbers of women worked in mines; it was not until an Act of Parliament was passed prohibiting female labour in this direction that the employment of women in mines ceased. Nature had evidently given women the requisite strength to undergo the needful toil, otherwise employers would not have found it worth their while to engage them. Of out-door women agricultural labourers we have between forty and fifty thousand; numbers of these may be seen with their infants on their backs while at their labour, and when the day's field work is finished they can seldom rest until their male partner's evening meal is prepared and the children seen to. To come nearer home, we have only to observe the amount of hard work daily gone through by large numbers of domestic servants; the physical powers they continuously display would put to shame the muscular efforts of many men. Many women are also excellent pedestrians, runners, and rowers; but as matches are seldom or never started on their account, we hear next to nothing of their powers and skill. Elihu Burritt, in his "Walks in the Black Country and Green Border Land," gives a vivid description of the labour of women in brickfields. He was informed that seventy-five per cent of the persons employed were females. He describes the different operations the women were engaged in, and saw many of the girls carrying loads of clay averaging 50 lbs. each—some of the girls carrying, it was computed, as much as 30,000 lbs. in a day. This was in 1869, and it was stated that as many as 1,200 females were employed in the district. In April, 1872, appeared in the *Daily Telegraph* an account of the women blacksmiths. In the districts of Netherton, Rowley, Lye Waste, and Bromsgrove, in Staffordshire, the writer found thousands of women employed in this laborious occupation; he gives a full description of their work, and observes that their arms were of prodigious size and strength. If we go abroad we find similar examples. The Indian women led lives as laborious as their lords. Mrs. Jameson[1] has shown what powers of physical endurance are required for the life and the heavy toils the women undergo. Rassam, in his "British Mission to Abyssinia," says, "Few, if any, Abyssinian women can sew; and even if they could it would be deemed highly unbecoming in them to ply the needle in public. Sewing and laundry work are left to the males; spinning and carrying wood and water are tasks apportioned to what we are pleased to term the weaker sex." In the "Recollections of Massimo D'Azeglio," by Count Maffei, we read:—

"Here, on the Lago Maggiore, where I live, suppose a load of chopped wood of half a hundredweight and a few chickens have to be brought from a village halfway up the mountain to the market on the shore, the work of the family is thus distributed:—The wife takes up the heavy load of wood and the husband the poultry. It is curious to hear the peasants, when they try to lift a heavy weight and find it too heavy, drop it, saying, 'It is a woman's work.' In mountainous countries this is the general custom."

A traveller, who had recently returned from Africa, spoke at the first annual meeting of the Female Medical Society as follows:—

"I am a medical man. I have spent several years in Africa, and have seen human nature among tribes whose habits are utterly unlike those of Europe. I had been accustomed to believe that the *muscular* system of

1. Anna Jameson (1794–1860), a social and cultural critic who wrote about women and work. Wallington probably refers to Jameson's reaction to an 1842 report on factories and mines. *Ed.*

women is necessarily feebler than that of men, and perhaps I might have dogmatized to that effect, but, to my astonishment, I found the African women to be as strong as our men. Not only did I see the proof of this in their work, and in the weights which they lifted, but on examining their arms I found them large and hard beyond all my previous experience. The men, on the contrary, were weak, and their muscles small and flabby. Both facts are accounted for by the habits of the people; the men there are lazy in the extreme; all the hard work is done by the women."

On a recent occasion, Sir Garnet Wolseley, in his speech at the Mansion House banquet given in his honour, alluded to the superiority of the Ashantee women over men as soldiers. With such instances as these before us, it is idle to assert that woman's physical strength is less than man's. The fact of a person's being born a male is no guarantee of his strength; else we should find all men stronger than any women, which we never do. Natural muscular physique, combined with training, produces differences in physical strength equally in both sexes.

Let us now turn to the intellectual side. In a society having kindred objects to your own, a paper was recently read to the effect that the mental function and physical constitution of the brain in woman differed essentially from that of men. I have not had the advantage of hearing or seeing the paper, and cannot therefore examine its arguments. It is no doubt true there *are* differences, but whether such differences are sufficiently appreciable to warrant the inference of there being a marked and distinguishing dissimilarity in the mental capacity of the sexes appears to me extremely problematical.

It is frequently urged that relatively and absolutely men have larger brains than women, and from this it is concluded women cannot possess an equal amount of intellectual power. For my own part, I think the size of the brain is not always a criterion of mental ability. When we observe what Nature has to declare on the subject, we perceive quality and temperament have more to do with intellectual excellence than quantity. I do not of course dispute that—other things being equal—a large brain has the advantage in power over a smaller one, and man having in proportion to his body the largest brain, gives him the pre-eminence over other animals. But it must be borne in mind that woman, comparatively, has not been surrounded by the same intellectual influences and circumstances as man; the chances of her mental development have been more accidental. Whatever the size of the female brain may be, it cannot be denied many women have, in proportion to their bodies, much larger brains than men, and that some women have larger brains than some men; in such cases, what becomes of the argument of the mental superiority of the male? It is worthy of note, that where men and women, either in physical or intellectual labour, are placed under equal conditions, there you will have an equality of power; *all* the women may not labour with equal success, neither will *all* the men. This is an affair of every day occurrence, which anyone may verify for himself.

As an ounce of fact is of more worth than any quantity of theory, I now proceed to cite a few examples of woman's mental capacity. Curiously enough the mechanical and mathematical sciences are those in which women have particularly distinguished themselves.

Maria Cunitz, born at Scheweidnitz in the beginning of the seventeenth century, was educated in ancient and modern languages, medicine and mathematics, and ultimately devoted herself chiefly to astronomy and astrology. In 1651, her book of astronomical tables, entitled "Urania Propitia," was published at Frankfort, having appeared previously at Oels, in Silesia. Her object in these astronomical tables was to dispense with the use of logarithms in employing the tables published by Kepler; the preparation of this work must of necessity have required superior intelligence and an immense amount of labour. The Marquise du Châtellet, in the eighteenth century, was the French translator of Newton's "Principia." Voltaire, who was acquainted with her, and taught her the English language, says that mathematics and metaphysics were her favourite studies. She first attached herself to Leibnitz, and gave an explanation of a part of his system, in a work written with great ability entitled "Institutions de Physique." Clearness, precision, and elegance, were the leading characteristics of her style. Her translation of Newton's great work stood so high that Delambre always used it whenever he had to make a quotation from Newton in his "History of Astronomy."

Madame Lepaute, wife of the eminent Parisian clockmaker, had from her childhood evinced a decided love for the sciences. She became an invaluable assistant to her husband, and in his celebrated work "Traité d'Horlogerie," published in 1755, a table of the lengths of pendulums was contributed by his wife.

"Her most important and memorable achievement is the part she had in the performance of the toilsome calculations for Clairaut's investigation of the perturbations of Halley's comet, the expected return of which had already begun to occupy the astronomical world in 1757. When Lalande first proposed the investigation to Clairaut, the latter declined undertaking it alone; whereupon Lalande offered to take upon himself the astronomical calculations, and for this purpose he obtained the co-operation of Madame Lepaute. . . . 'During six months,' he says, 'we calculated from morning till night, the consequence of which was that I contracted an illness which changed my constitution for the remainder of my life. Without her assistance Clairaut and I could never have dared to undertake this enormous labour.'" [Single quotes added. *Ed.*]

Maria Agnesi, of whom it has been said "she would be a prodigy, even without her sex being taken into account," was a native of Milan, and a contemporary of the two last-mentioned ladies. In 1738, when only "twenty years of age, she published at Milan a collection in Latin of nearly two hundred philosophical propositions, embracing every branch of natural and moral science, which, the title page declared, she had been in the habit of explaining extemporaneously, and defending from objections in frequent disputations held at her house in presence of learned men of the highest eminence; and it appears from the preface that a number of these theses had been in circulation for some time." In 1748 was published, at Bologna, her "Instituzioni Analitiche ad uso della Gioventu Italiana," in two vols., quarto. The late Professor de Morgan described this work as a "well-matured treatise on algebra, and the differential and integral calculus inferior to none in its day in knowledge and arrangement, and showing marks of great learning and some originality." A translation of a portion of this work was inserted by the French mathematician, Bossut, in a course of mathematics which he had published in 1775, as the best treatise he could present to his readers on the elements of the differential and integral calculus. An English translation of the whole, which had been made long before by the Rev. John Colson, Lucasian Professor of Mathematics at Cambridge, and commentator of Newton's "Fluxions," was published in 1801.

Maria Bassi, a native of Bologna, in 1732, at the age of twenty-one, had the degree of Doctor of Philosophy conferred upon her by the University of Bologna. "The same year the Senate appointed her to a chair with a respectable salary, and with liberty to lecture on any subject in the faculty of philosophy she preferred. She selected natural philosophy, to which, and to the connected studies of algebra and geometry her genius most inclined."

Caroline Herschel's stupendous astronomical labours are, perhaps, too well known to need enlarging upon. The splendid renown attached to Sir W. Herschel's name was largely due to his sister's superior intelligence, unremitting zeal, and systematic method of arrangement.

The career of the late Mrs. Somerville affords a striking illustration of noble devotion to the most abstruse science, and of successful effort through all the vexatious delays and formidable obstacles which obstruct the intellectual path of many women who are born with a strong impulse for achieving higher things, but who are denied that leisure and freedom of action which the majority of learned men generally secure. Her intellectual capacity was extraordinary, and what is more remarkable, it shone in undiminished vigour to the last. Writing of herself, in her ninety-second year, she says, "I am still able to read books in the higher algebra four or five hours in the morning, and even to solve the problems."

The late Mrs. Janet Taylor was for many years a teacher of navigation. For her improvements in nautical instruments she received medals from the Board of Admiralty and the Trinity Brethren, and several from foreign powers. She was an acknowledged mathematician of the first class, and her logarithmic tables are said to be correct and complete in no ordinary degree.

Miss Maria Mitchell, an American lady, has distinguished herself as an astronomer. In 1865, she was appointed Professor of Astronomy in the Vassar College, Poughkeepsie, New York; she has an excellent observatory under her charge, and teaches astronomy with great success.

Before leaving the mathematical examples, it may not be out of place to offer the testimony of one or two competent teachers as to the abilities displayed by many girls in this branch of study. Miss Jex Blake,[2] in her "Record of Experiences of American Schools and Colleges," says, "In mathematics especially I have heard the proficiency of female students commended." In the report of the third session of the Working Women's College, Mr. R. B. Litchfield observed that "he had never seen better papers than those of the successful candidates." In reference to the Cambridge examination for girls, the *Athenæum* for January, 1868, remarks:—

"Not only do the girls acquit themselves in their favourite studies, as well as the boys, but they shine equally in such studies as mathematics. The examiner in Euclid last year informed us that it was quite a treat to read the girls' Euclid papers, they were so neat and precise; and he also stated a very notable fact, that whereas boys, as a rule, never seem to distinguish between the *essential* steps of a proof and the mere *formal ones,* but as often omit the one as the other, the girls, without an exception, never omit a vital step in their proof, but always exhibit a thorough appreciation of Euclid's method. To estimate rightly the value of this testimony, the reader must bear in mind that this gentleman examined all the Euclid papers, both of boys and girls,

2. Sophia Jex-Blake (1840–1912), physician famous for "storming" the University of Edinburgh to promote medical education for women. *Ed.*

throughout England, and could, therefore, accurately compare the relative value of the answering."

In geographical explorations, women have taken an active part. Among them may be mentioned Madame Pfeiffer, Madame Helfer, Madame Semper, Lady Baker, Miss Emma Roberts, Mademoiselle Alexandrine Tinné, and Mrs. Jackson Gwilt.

The study of geology possesses attractions to women. Mrs. Somerville followed it with ardour. In her "Recollections," she speaks of Lady Murchison's superior knowledge of this subject, and her familiar acquaintance with it long before the late Sir Roderick Murchison had given his attention to it. If I have been rightly informed, Miss Lydia Becker[3] is another good geologist.

Botany and natural history have also found their adherents. In the former science Mrs. Somerville again meets us. We have come across the names of Elizabeth Blackwell,[4] who published a "Curious Herbary," in 1739; and Elizabeth Christina Von Linné, one of the daughters of the illustrious Swedish naturalist, who discovered the luminous property of the flower of the Tropæolum (nasturtium or cress), of which she sent an account to the Royal Academy of Sciences at Stockholm.

Among the lady naturalists we find the name of Maria S. Merian, Lady Bunbury, a friend of Mrs. Somerville's, possessed a great knowledge of conchology. Mary Anning, who died in 1847, is described as of "European fame as a discoverer of fossils—more particularly those of the Ichthyosaurus, Plesiosaurus, Pterodactyle, and many fish in the blue seas of Lyme Regis." It is said the great Ichthyosaurus, now in the British Museum, was purchased by Mr. Hawkins from Miss Anning.

In the Royal College of Science for Ireland, where both sexes study together with the most beneficial results, several ladies have taken prizes and good positions in geology, botany, zoology, chemistry, and physical science. In the session of 1867–8, Matilda Coneys—who had previously highly distinguished herself in chemistry, the laboratory examination, and physical science—gained the first prize for pure mathematics, all her male competitors being exhibitioners. It may be seen, on application for them, that the examination papers of the School of Science bear comparison with those of any college or university in the kingdom. A Madame Emma Chenu, spoken of by Mrs. Somerville, received the degree of M.A. from the Academy of

3. Lydia Becker is represented by two selections in this book. *Ed.*

4. Elizabeth Blackwell (1821–1910), a British-born American physician who worked both in the United States and in Britain to further women's medical education. *Ed.*

Sciences in Paris; and afterwards obtained the diploma of Licentiate in Mathematical Sciences from the same illustrious society, after passing a successful examination in algebra, trigonometry, analytical geometry, the differential and integral calculi, and astronomy. A Russian lady also took a degree, and a friend of Mrs. Somerville's received a gold medal. It is stated in the "Recollections" that "Mrs. Marcet's[5] conversations on chemistry" first opened out to Faraday's mind that field of science in which he became so illustrious.

Women have also made names for themselves as doctors of medicine, and law, as theological and philosophical writers, as translators, as sculptors, painters, poets, modellers and designers; as enlightened rulers and administrators, and as orators. I could give you examples, past and present, in all these professions and callings, but I refrain, from fear of exhausting your patience. The illustrations I have offered are, I think, of sufficient importance to support my position; and I have confined myself chiefly to those relating to the highest branches of knowledge, because they are generally the most strongly debated, and the examples in the less scientific departments are more frequently brought under our notice.

Looking at what women have achieved, and are achieving, based as the results are on practical experience—the test of all others the most conclusive—the weight of the evidence goes to show that the intellectual capacity of woman does not differ from man's more than that of men differs among themselves; in other words, the differences are not so much of *sex* as *individuals.* As far as I know, it has not yet been proved that the mental functions of all men are precisely the same. Given a number of men in any subject of scientific discovery, collectively, they may arrive at similar results; individually, the intellectual process of investigation has varied according to each one's personal constitution, temperament, and previous knowledge.

In a barbarous state, men do not commonly exhibit high mental powers; it is only when civilization has advanced considerably, thereby leaving men free to cultivate their minds, that the intellectual faculties begin to bear fruit—the nervous energy, not being wholly required for the satisfaction of Nature's most pressing wants, seeks with an irresistible impulse to develop itself in other directions. If it be conceded that surrounding circumstances have much to do in determining the mental pursuits of men, the same may be conceded in respect to woman, with this difference: in her case opinions

5. Jane Marcet (1769–1858) is represented in this book. *Ed.*

and usages have repressed to a much greater extent the natural growth of her faculties. A refined woman dreads nothing so much as being stigmatized as unwomanly; the more intellectual men are, the more thy find themselves objects of respect and admiration; but, till within a recent period, the contrary opinion has generally prevailed in regard to the other sex. In reading the biographies of many celebrated women of former times, one fact is continually forced upon us, namely, the fear those women had of losing the esteem and admiration of their male relatives and acquaintances; the higher their intellectual attainments, the greater their fear of their attainments being known. Bearing in mind the strong influence which circumstances often exert, remembering that the term "learned," as applied to females, has generally conveyed the sting of reproach instead of the sweet balm of commendation, our wonder is—not that women have accomplished so much entitling them to enter the highest intellectual ranks—but that they should have done anything at all. Many of them must have been endowed with decided genius and uncommon talent, and also great moral courage, thus to have distinguished themselves in spite of the difficulties thrown in their way of acquiring knowledge, and in the face of the depressing influence of opinion.

Many persons are disposed to decry the recent efforts for improving the education of girls; but, as Miss Becker has truthfully pointed out, previous to the agitation for educational improvement, the general mass of men were as ignorant as the women. Now all this is changed; we have encouraged the mental advancement of boys, leaving the girls far behind, thus making the intellectual gulf between the sexes wider.

If, as I trust will be admitted, I have shown that physical and mental superiority are not essentially *male* attributes—if the manifestations of trained human intelligence are of any value—let us no longer strive, by dogmatizing on woman's supposed natural inferiority, to lessen the sum total of intellectual excellence. If we believe men and women are intended to live in the world as co-partners and not as aliens, as helpers in all things and not as hindrances in some, as joint partakers in all that calls forth the higher faculties of thought and feeling, let us cast off the mischievous dogma that encourages a faith in *man's* power to elevate himself, while it denies the possession of this power to *woman,* and meets her attempts at emancipation from intellectual thraldom with covert sneers and chilling depreciation. Preconceived notions cannot for ever withstand the assaults of truth and right reason; believing this we may, while using every legitimate aid to amelioration, hopefully trust to time to gradually remove the obstructive artificial barriers to woman's mental progress. Turning from the tempting, but oft bewildering masses of speculation, resolutely confining ourselves to the hard and fast, but safer grounds of indisputable fact, we needs must conclude the nearer the sexes are on an intellectual equality, the greater the sum of improvement and happiness occurring to each.

DISCUSSION

The thanks of the Meeting were voted to the Authoress, and, after some remarks by Dr. CARTER BLAKE,

Mr. GRAZEBROOK said: It is with some reluctance I rise to criticise a most able paper written by a lady, claiming for her sex a mental and physical equality with our sex. But, in the very paper itself, I find an argument essentially feminine, both in its line of reasoning and deductions, although it is written with great ability. Thus you find the feminine tendency to argue from exceptions, and to draw rules from a few remarkable instances. The lady has cited a great number of remarkable women, each equal to, or greater than most men; but I will engage, if you will take any one of these most remarkable women, that you will find fifty remarkable men at least equal to her in every respect. The lady argues, that because women were employed at severe labour in the coal mines and in agriculture, hence that they were capable of entering into competition with man successfully. But everyone practically engaged in such trades knows, that women were employed at such labour simply owing to the smaller wages paid them, that they cost much less than men, and that you could hire three women for the wages of one man. Now, if they were generally equal, they could demand and would obtain the same pay for the same time! As regards the mental comparison, the lady inadvertently defined the difference when she claimed that the girls' exercises in Euclid were more *neatly* written and *exactly* reasoned. Women can compete successfully with man in following out a beaten path; they can transcend man in attention to minute details, and they can follow where bolder spirits have led. But they have not the grasp of intellect and the vigour and the boldness which make the great discoverer of the unknown. Then, in confirmation of my view that in the divine scheme of creation woman are born inferior to man, both in body and mind, I look around to the varying conditions of all parts of the world, and in no race, nor country, nor tribe, nor remote island, excepting one of doubtful authenticity, do I find an instance of woman having the upper hand, and reducing all the males to subjection. Now, if man and women were born equal, out of every hundred of these remote races and peoples in islands and localities apart from each other you would find fifty races where the women had subjected the men, and fifty where the men had subjected the women. Hence, gentlemen, in conclusion, I find that there is no evidence nor proof in this lady's paper that woman is the equal of man in physical power, nor in the larger attributes of the mind which denote mental power, and all the evidences of the outer world seem to prove the direct negative to the proposition.

Mr. J. T. DEXTER wished he had been able to point to examples of genius in women; but they were so rare as almost to justify the doubt of their possibility. But, on the other hand, there were few men who stood in the first rank of great intellects, and, hitherto, the competition had been unfavourable in its conditions to the development of extraordinary powers in women. Yet, conceding the point that woman had been wanting in the creative faculty which gave to the world invention, explanation, and discovery, the acquisition of knowledge already discovered was made with readier facility and far less strain and exhaustion of nervous energy with woman than with man. This point was conclusively established by the experience of university examiners in arts and medicine, as well as by the rapid strides with which every logical induction and every means of persuasion was mastered by woman applying herself to the pursuit of professional matters. Miss Wallington's historical examples of great excellence in attainments could be paralleled to-day by women making no special pretensions; and it was significant of something more than equality in the mental power of woman that a Master of Arts and a lady, some years his junior, ran so evenly for the highest prize the University of London had to bestow, that it almost needed the consideration of sex to turn the scale in favour of the male competitor; the lady having shown equal capacity in other fields, and all the while discharging the duties (not light ones) of an honorary secretary to a political movement.

Mr. CHURCHILL thought that the fact of the women on the Gold Coast doing all the hard word was evidence of their inferiority. If they could oblige the men to do it and walk beside them, they would, as no one does hard work who can avoid it. Women had shown great power in acquiring knowledge, and in analyzing and arranging. They had followed in mathematics as far as men had led, but not even Mrs. Somerville had advanced a step beyond. They had written good poetry, but not the best; and clever plays, but none that retained their places on the stage. The best play written by a woman is, perhaps, Joanna Baillies'[6] "De Montfort;" but, though acted by Mrs. Siddons and John Kemble, it was coldly received, and soon withdrawn. Angelica Kauffman[7] had painted beautiful pictures; but neither she nor any other woman had painted the best picture in any exhibition.

Mr. PYCROFT, F.S.A., said Sir Isaac Newton and other great men had acknowledged their obligations to their mothers. Rosa Bonheur[8] was equal as a painter to Landseer, and he thought the authoress had proved her case as regarded mathematics.

After some remarks from the Rev. T. R. LLOYD, Dr. KAINES, Mr. WYLLIE, and Mr. JEREMIAH,

Mr. LEWIS said that women, to do physical work equal to that of men, must almost necessarily abjure the maternal functions. The sexes were not so much unequal as different, and to employ a woman to do a man's work was like using a chisel instead of a screwdriver, a practice, by the way, to which ladies were rather addicted.

Professor LEITNER said it seemed to him that those who in this country opposed the complete equality of woman with man based their objections on a supposed physical inferiority. When on a tour in the hills of Thibet, which required a great deal of endurance, he found the female coolies equal, if not superior, in that respect to the men. A friend of his, when in Abbeokuta, had been called on to resist an attack by the female soldiers of Dahomey, and bore testimony to their ferocity and prowess. The great facility with which women of savage races deliver children, even while working in the fields, and go on afterwards with their work, was well known. He believed education had had much to do with the alleged inequality of the sexes in Europe. He though that "difference" was a better term than either superiority or inferiority. There was much secondary literary work done by women now, such as magazine articles and reviews, which, perhaps, accounted for the fluency and want of thoroughness which characterized those productions as a rule. With respect to mathematics, the natives of India, who were not supposed to be superior in intellect, excelled in mathematics, so far as the text-books went, but were deficient in the critical faculty or in discovering the truth of any matter. It was true clever men owed much to clever mothers; but, on the other hand, clever fathers seldom had time to attend to their children, who were left almost entirely with their mothers. The proper sphere for woman was to excel as a daughter, a sister,

6. Joanna Baillie (1762–1851), a Scottish dramatist and poet. *Ed.*

7. Angelica Kauffman (1741–1807), artist and member of the Royal Academy of Arts. *Ed.*

8. Rosa Bonheur (1842–99), animal painter of great skill. *Ed.*

a wife, and a mother. The proudest position any human being could occupy was that of guiding and preparing the young for important stages of life.

The PRESIDENT said: There is no doubt that women have excelled in a great deal of intellectual work. The names of De Stæl, Dacier, De Genlis, Corinna, and Sappho might be added to Miss Wallington's list. There is no doubt, also, that women are, to a great extent, kept back by their social status, especially by their inexperience of the realities of life; but treble the cases that can be produced on their behalf, they would, at most, amount to exceptions to the general rule, viz., that intellectually women are inferior to men. Women have never attained the summit of any art or science. Among the female sex we do not find either great composers or great metaphysicians. As artists they are only third rate. We might naturally have expected them to have excelled in cookery; but the noble art of gastronomy is represented by the male sex only. Neither do women possess the faculty of invention. Homer speaks of a Mæonian or Carian woman staining with purple the ivory cheeks of horse bits; and a woman is said to have invented the art of painting. The latter assertion would seem to be founded on a statement in Pliny. The story runs thus: "Butades, of Corinth, invented the art of modelling portraits in the earth, which he used in his trade. His daughter (called by Athenagoras Core, from her birthplace, Corinth), being deeply in love with a young man, who was about to depart on a long journey, traced the profile of his face, as thrown upon the wall by a lamp. Thereupon her father filled in the outlines by compressing clay upon the surface, and so made a face in relief, which he then hardened by means of fire." Assuming that Core did what she is reported to have done, it does not amount to very much after all. There is no doubt also that in some countries the women work harder than the men, and, in fact, do the work of the men; but the laziness of the men does not add to the strength of the women. Allowing for the circumstances in which woman is placed, the physical and mental difference between the sexes may be accounted for by the difference of organization, &c. The female skull is smaller than that of man, not only in horizontal circumference, but also in internal capacity. Its base is more extended, and there is a greater tendency to prognathism. The type of the female skull resembles, to a certain extent, that of the infant, and, in a still great degree, that of the lower races. Craniologists, indeed, assure us that the female skull preserves very nearly the earlier stage from which the race or tribe has been developed. The weight of the brain is also less than in man. It is likewise laid down that the difference between the sexes as regards the cranial cavity increases with the development of the race, so that the male European excels more the female than does the negro the negress;

and hence, with the progress of civilization, the men are in advance of the women, so that the inequality of the sexes increases with civilization.

Miss WALLINGTON replied as follows:—Mr. Grazebrook has declared I have adduced rules from exceptions. My main proposition is that physical and mental superiority are not exclusively male attributes. If facts count for anything, I have shown that this proposition is true; to tell me the illustrations I have given in support of this truth are exceptions does not destroy it. When we speak of man's capacity for high mental acquirements, no one for one moment supposes we mean the whole male race: compared with the mass of mankind we find a small number of men pre-eminently distinguish themselves, and on the strength of the superior attainments of these few we say man possesses the power of climbing the loftiest intellectual heights. To say the examples I brought under your notice, in regard to intellectual women, are exceptions, applies equally to celebrated intellectual men; they are also exceptions; yet we do not allow this fact to destroy the data of our reasoning, neither should we be justified in maintaining that males, as a race, are devoid of mental power because only a few may make that power manifest. Speaking generally, men intellectually inclined have always felt sure of obtaining honour and renown for superior attainments, to say nothing of pecuniary rewards. Women, generally, have had no such inducements held out to them; the contrary has too often attended the intellectual efforts of women, and this prevailing tone of discouragement must at all times have exercised an influence over the sex very prejudicial to feminine mental progress. Mr. Grazebrook also expresses it as his opinion that men evince greater aptitude than women. Those who have had experience in teaching both sexes, whether in the elementary or the higher branches, science included, are generally agreed that the female sex are quite equal, and sometimes much superior to the male in quickness and mental grasp of the subjects studied. With regard to the same speaker's objection respecting woman's non-entrance into the unknown, I must be allowed to say that my paper only concerned itself with the known; at the outset, I stated my intention to confine the argument to established facts. As far as my experience allows me to judge, I do not perceive that the mind of woman is deficient in the power of conducting a mental inquiry into new fields; it is acknowledged that the mothers of many celebrated men have directed the minds of their sons into channels they might never have entered had not a farseeing judgment and superior mental endowments, combined with striking original power, been near at hand to give them the requisite impulse. Mr. H. B. Churchill has told us that in the great number of instances I have given of women undergoing the heaviest labours, they—the women—do it because they are compelled. I do not for one instant dispute this, but the fact that women *do* perform it still remains, and it proves they have the natural requisite power, whether they like it or not. I also apprehend that the question of liking the work is outside my paper, and that it is one which applies to both sexes equally; many men dislike hard work, when compelled to perform it, and it is very questionable whether the majority of men would systematically endure it if left to follow their own inclinations. With respect to a want of originative power in women, I do not think this has by any means been proved. Some people declare no one *can* be original after Shakespeare. With all due admiration for the bard of Avon, I am disposed to say no one can hope to claim an indisputable originality in arts and politics after the Greeks—a people counting several noted women among its brightest spirits.

MONA CAIRD

From "A Defence of the So-Called 'Wild Women'"

Nineteenth Century 31 (1892): 817–29.

. . . To the time-honoured argument that nature intended man to be anything and everything that his strength of muscle and of mind permitted, while she meant woman to be a mother, and nothing else, the rebels reply, that if a woman has been made by nature to be a mother, so has a cow or a sheep; and if this maternal capacity be really an infallible indication of function, there is nothing to prevent this reasoning from running down-hill to its conclusion, namely, that the nearer a woman can become to a cow or a sheep the better.

If popular feeling objects to this conclusion, and yet still desires all women to make maternity their chief duty, it must find another reason for its faith, leaving nature's sign-posts out of the question. On these sign-posts man himself is privileged to write and rewrite the legends, though of this power he seems at present to be unconscious, persistently denying it even while his restless fingers are busy at their work.

This dear and cherished appeal to nature, however, will never be

FIGURE 4 Mona Caird

abandoned by the advocates of the old order while breath remains to them. But if they use the argument they ought not to shrink from its consequences, nor, indeed, *would* they, but that it happens that women, as a matter of fact, have risen above the stage of simple motherhood, accustoming their critics to attributes distinctively human; and these having by this time become familiar, no longer seem alarming or 'unnatural.' In our present stage of development we demand of a woman that she shall be first of all a mother, and then that she develop those human qualities which best harmonise with her position as such. 'Be it pleasant or unpleasant,' Mrs. Lynn Linton says, 'it is none the less an absolute truth—the *raison d'être* of a woman is maternity. . . . The cradle lies across the door of the polling-booth and bars the way to the Senate.'[1]

We are brought, then, to this conclusion: that if there be any force in what is commonly urged respecting nature's 'intentions' with regard to woman, her development as a thinking and emotional being beyond the point where human qualities are superficially useful to her children is

1. In this essay, Caird is responding to Eliza Lynn Linton's essay "The Wild Women. No. 1: As Politicians," which appeared in *Nineteenth Century* in July of 1891. I have chosen not to reprint Linton's essay because Caird here replays most of Linton's arguments in order to refute them. *Ed.*

FIGURE 5 Eliza Lynn Linton

'unnatural' and false, a conclusion which leads us straight away to Oriental customs and to Oriental ethics. Moreover, another consideration confronts us: nature, besides designing women to be mothers, designed men to be fathers; why, then, should not the man give up his life to his family in the same wholesale way? 'The cases are so different,' it will be said. Yes, and the difference lies in the great suffering and risk which fall solely to the share of the mother. Is this a good reason for holding her for her whole life to this painful task, for demanding that she shall allow her tastes and talents to lie idle and to die a slow and painful death, while the father, to whom parenthood is also indicated by 'nature,' is allowed the privilege of choosing his own avocations without interference? Further, if woman's functions are to be determined solely by a reference to what is called nature, how, from this point of view, are we to deal with the fact that she possesses a thousand emotional and intellectual attributes that are wholly superfluous to her merely maternal activities? What does Mrs. Lynn Linton consider that 'nature intends' by all this? In the present order of society, speaking roughly, a woman, to whom maternity seems unsatisfying or distasteful, has either to bring herself to undertake the task for which she is unfitted, or to deny her affections altogether. To man, the gods give both sides of the apple of life; a woman is offered the choice of the halves—either, but not both.

Yet every new development of society, every overthrow of ancient landmarks, tends to prove more and more conclusively that this fetish 'nature,' who is always claimed as the patroness of the old order, just when she is busy planning and preparing the new, has *not* separated the human race into two distinct sections, with qualities entirely and eternally different. If this were so—if women were, in fact, the only beings under heaven not modifiable by education and surroundings, then we should be forced to reconstruct from the foundation our notions of natural law, and to rescind the comparatively modern theory that it is unwise to expect effects without causes, and causes without effects, even in the mysterious domain of human nature. We should live once more in a world of haphazard and of miracle, in which only one fact could be counted upon from age to age, viz., the immutable and stereotyped 'nature' of women.

Unless we are prepared for this antique and variegated creed, we cannot consistently pronounce, as Mrs. Lynn Linton cheerily pronounces, what the sphere and *raison d'être* of either sex are, and must be, for evermore. It seems, indeed, safe to predict that women will continue to bear children, but it is far from safe to prophesy to what extent that function will in the future absorb their energies and determine the horizon of their life. We know that although men have been fathers from the beginning of human history, they have not made fatherhood the keynote of their existence; on the contrary, it has been an entirely secondary consideration. They have been busy in influencing and fashioning a world which their children are to inherit—a world that would be sorrier than it is if men had made the fact of parenthood the central point of their career. Women have been forced, partly by their physical constitution, but more by the tyranny of society, to expend their whole energies in maternal cares, and this has been the origin of a thousand evils: it has destroyed the healthy balance of their nature, thrown work on to unfit shoulders, formed a sort of press-gang of the most terrible kind, inasmuch as unwilling motherhood is worse than unwilling military service; and it has deprived the very children in whose behalf this insane cruelty has been wrought of the benefit of possessing mothers and teachers whose character is developed all round, whose faculties are sound and healthy, whose minds are fresh, buoyant, and elastic, and stored with such knowledge of nature and life as would make them efficient guides and guardians to those helpless ones who are at the outset of their career. It may seem paradoxical, but is none the less true, that we shall never have really good mothers until women cease to make their motherhood the central idea of their existence. The woman who has no interest larger than the affairs of her children is not a fit person to train them.

For the sake of men, women, and children, it is to be hoped that women will come to regard motherhood with new eyes; that the force of their artificially fostered impulses will become less violent; and that there may be an increase in them of the distinctly *human* qualities and emotions in relation to those merely instinctive or maternal. It is this *change of proportion* in the force of human qualities that virtually creates a new being, and makes progress possible. In the light of this truth, how false are all the inferences of phrases such as 'Nature intends,' 'Nature desires'; she intends and desires nothing—she is an abject slave. *Man* intends, *Man* desires, and 'Nature,' in the course of centuries, learns to obey.

This worship of 'nature' is a strange survival in a scientific age of the old image-worship of our ancestors. She is our Vishnu or Siva, our Odin and Thor, a personal will who designs and plans. This is a subtle form of superstition which has cunningly nestled among the folds of the garment of Science, and there it will lurk safe and undetected for many years, to discourage all change, to cast discredit on all new thought, to hold man to his errors, and to blind him to his own enormous power of development.

It is this insidious superstition that prevents even intelligent people from recognising the effect upon women of their circumstances. Professions are known to leave their mark on men, although the influence of a man's profession is not so incessant and overwhelming as are the conditions of women's lives, from which there is no escape from the cradle to the grave; yet it is always grudgingly and doubtfully admitted, if at all, that this fact offers an explanation for any bad quality in the feminine character, any weakness or excess of which women may be guilty. No one seems to realise how age after age they have been, one and all, engaged in the same occupations, subjected to the same kind of stimulus and training; how each individual of infinitely varying multitudes has been condemned to one function for the best years of life, and that function an extremely painful and exhausting one. No one seems to understand that these causes must produce effects, and that they have produced the effect of creating in women certain tyrannous and overwrought instincts which we say, reverentially and obstinately, 'Nature has implanted in woman.' We might more accurately say 'Suffering, moral and mental starvation, physical pain, diseases induced by the over-excitement of one set of functions, one-sided development—these have implanted impulses which we have the assurance to call sacred.'

At the present time, some very interesting researches are being carried on, which tend to show, so far as they have gone, that the physical nature of women has been literally destroyed by the over-excitement and ill-usage, often unwitting, which public sentiment has forced them to submit to, while their absolute dependence on men has induced them often to endure it as if it were the will of Heaven.

These researches show that through these centuries of overstrain, one set of faculties being in perpetual activity while the others lay dormant, women have fallen the victims of chronic disease, and this condition of disease has become also a condition of a woman's existence. Have we not gone far enough along this path of destruction, or must we still make motherhood our chief duty, accept the old sentiment about our subservience to man, and drive yet farther into the system the cruel diseases that have punished the insanities of the past, taking vengeance upon the victims of ill-usage for their submission, and pursuing their children from generation to generation with relentless footsteps? Such is the counsel of Mrs. Lynn Linton and her school. Upon the effects of all this past ill-treatment is founded the pretext for women's disabilities in the present. They are physically weak, nervous, easily unstrung, and for this reason, it is urged, they must continue to pursue the mode of life which has induced these evils. This is strange reasoning.

The suffering of women to-day is built upon their suffering of yesterday and its consequences. It is surely a rather serious matter to cut off a human being from whatever the world has to offer him in this one short life! From this point of view what force or meaning have Mrs. Lynn Linton's taunts and accusations against her sex, even though they were all perfectly just? It is possible that women, in virtue of their susceptible physical constitution and nervous system (a quality, by the, way, which distinguishes the man of genius from the ordinary being), are more responsive than men are to their surroundings, and all that Mrs. Lynn Linton says, if true, about the wildness of ignorant women in times of excitement—she cites for an example the *tricoteuses* of the French Revolution[2]—might perhaps be explained on this ground. A quick response to stimulus is *not* the mark of a being low in the scale of existence, though it may lead to extravagant deeds when untutored. But Mrs. Lynn Linton will not look at this question philosophically; she hurls accusations at her sex as if it pleased her to add another insult to those which the literature of centuries—with that exquisite chivalry which we are so often warned our freedom would destroy—has never tired

2. Those women, like Madame Defarge in Dickens's *Tale of Two Cities,* who knit relentlessly as aristocrats were guillotined. *Ed.*

of flinging at the defenseless sex. It does not strike Mrs. Lynn Linton to inquire into the real causes that underlie all these problems of a growing human nature; she prefers the simple finger of scorn, the taunt, the inexpensive sneer.

Why does she so harshly condemn the results of the system of things which she so ardently approves? To make her position more difficult to understand, Mrs. Lynn Linton dwells with some insistence on the effects upon her sex of their training. She speaks of 'ideal qualities which women have gained by a certain amount of sequestration from the madding crowd's ignoble strife. . . . Are the women at the gin-shop bar,' she demands, 'better than the men at the gin-shop door; the field hands in sun-bonnets more satisfactory than those in brimless hats?' This is to prove that women have no real moral superiority. Elsewhere is asked: 'Can anyone point out anywhere a race of women who are superior to their conditions?' All this is strange reasoning from one who takes her stand in the fiats of 'nature' as distinguished from the influences of surroundings.

One might ask: 'Can anyone, point out anywhere a race of men who are superior to their conditions?' But this possible question never seems to strike Mrs. Lynn Linton, for she exposes herself all through the article to the same form of demand, and she nowhere attempts to meet it. Her mode of warfare is indeed bewildering, for she attacks from both sides, makes double and antagonistic use of the same facts, and she does not at all object to assertions clearly contradictory, provided they are separated in time and space by the interval of a paragraph or two.

Her arguments, when formidable, mutually and relentlessly devour each other, like so many plus and minus quantities which, added together, become cancelled and leave a clean zero between them.

Unconscious, however, of this cannibalism among her legions, the authoress finds herself at the close of her article with a gigantic and robust opinion which nothing—not even her own arguments—can disturb.

As an instance of this strange suicidal tendency of her reasoning we may compare the already quoted paragraphs setting forth the effects of environment upon the woman's temperament with the even more determined assertion of its eternal, unalterable, and God-ordained nature. Confront these two statements, and what remains? Mrs. Lynn Linton seems to half surrender her position when she says that '. . . there are few women of anything like energy or brain-power who have not felt in their own souls the ardent longing for a freer hand in life'; but the following sentence seems to play still more into the hands of the enemy: 'Had Louis the Sixteenth had Marie Antoinette's energy and Marie Antoinette Louis's supineness, the whole story of the Reign of Terror, Marat, Charlotte Cordé, and Napoleon might never have been written.' What doctrine of Mrs. Lynn Linton's does it even seem to support?

In unblushing contradiction of this sentiment Mrs. Lynn Linton asserts that political women have always been 'disastrous,' and that even Mme. Roland 'did more harm than good when she undertook the manipulation of forces that were too strong for her control, too vast for her comprehension.'

Were the forces of the French Revolution within the grasp of any one person?

'Women are both more extreme and more impressionable than men,' Mrs. Lynn Linton says; 'and the spirit which made weak girls into heroines and martyrs, honest women into the yelling *tricoteuses* of the blood-stained saturnalia of '92, still exists in the sex, and among ourselves as elsewhere.'

In short, when a 'weak' girl espouses martyrdom she is prompted thereto by a sort of hysteria, male heroism alone being heroic.

While admitting, nay, emphasizing, on the one hand the fact of the remodelling force of circumstances, Mrs. Lynn Linton denies that feminine character and intelligence can ever be altered by one hair's breadth, except—and here comes the third and crowning contradiction—except for the worse.

Among the many other minor points which Mrs. Lynn Linton has touched upon are several which call for special comment from the point of view opposed to hers. For example, we are asked to believe that the peace of the home practically depends on the political disabilities of woman; or, in other words, that a man is unable to endure in his wife opinions differing from his own. I do not believe that men are quite so childish and petty as this; but if they are, it is indeed high time that they should learn the lesson of common courtesy and tolerance.

The device of keeping peace between two persons by the disarmament of one of them is ingenious and simple, but there is a temptation to think that such peace as that, if peace it can be called, would be well exchanged for strife. Does peace, indeed, mean the stagnation that arises from the relationship between the free and the fettered, or does it mean the generous mutual recognition of the right of private judgment? Identity of opinion between two people, even when not produced artificially, is not always inspiriting to either of them. The denial of political power to women, if it ever does prevent dissension, achieves at best, on the part of the wife, unreasoning acquiescence and not rational agreement.

Mrs. Lynn Linton says that 'amongst our most renowned women are some who say with their whole heart, "I would rather have been the wife of a great man, or the mother of a hero, than what I am—famous in my own person."' That is a matter of taste, but it seems strange that those famous women should not have acted upon their predilections. Against the following sentence I cannot refrain from expressing a sense of revolt; but the revolt is on behalf of men rather than of women. 'But the miserable little mannikin who creeps to obscurity, overshadowed by his wife's glory, is as pitiful in history as contemptible in fact. The husband of the wife is no title to honour; and the best and dearest of our famous women take care that this shall not be said of them and theirs.'

Are men, then, to be treated as if they were a set of jealous schoolboys, or superannuated invalids whom the discreet person allows to win at chess, because they have a childish dislike to being beaten?

It is consoling to remember that the ideas on which such feelings rest are giving way slowly but surely in all directions. It is only when the rebellion is extended over evidently new ground that Mrs. Lynn Linton and her followers begin to sound the tocsin, assuring the rebellious woman that she shows 'a curious inversion of sex, disdaining the duties and limitations imposed on her by nature.' As a final taunt, Mrs. Lynn Linton says: 'All women are not always lovely, and the wild women never are.' This reminds one of the exasperated retort of an angry child who has come to the end of his invention—a galling if somewhat inconsequent attack upon the personal appearance, which is the last resort of outraged juvenile nature.

Nothing perhaps can better show the real attitude of this lady and her followers on this question than her irritation against those who are trying to bring a ray of sunlight into the harems and zenanas[3] of the East:—

Ignorant and unreasonable (she says), they would carry into the sun-laden East the social conditions born of the icy winds of the North. . . . In a country where jealousy is as strong as death, and stronger than love, they would incite women to revolt against the rule of seclusion, which has been the law of the land for centuries before we were a nation at all. That rule has worked well for the country, inasmuch as the chastity of Hindu women and the purity of the family life are notoriously intact.

If Mrs. Lynn Linton approves of the relation of the sexes in the East, and looks upon it with an eye of fondness because it dates back into ages whose savagery clings to us, and breaks out in the blood of civilised men to this day, then she may well set herself in opposition to the rebellion among

3. Parts of the house in which women are or were sequestered. *Ed.*

modern women against the infinitely less intolerable injustice which they suffer in the West. Did we happen to be living in harems in South Kensington or Mayfair, with the sentiment of the country in favour of that modest and womanly state of seclusion, it is easy to imagine with what eloquence Mrs. Lynn Linton would declaim against the first hint of insurrection—although in that case, by the way, the strictly unfeminine occupation of writing articles would be denied her.

The really grave question raised in these essays is that of the effect of the political and social freedom of women upon the physical well-being of the race; for while past conditions have been evil, future ones may conceivably be equally so, though they could with difficulty be worse. This is indeed a serious problem which will require all the intelligence of this generation to solve. But first I would suggest what appears to be a new idea (strange as this may seem), namely, that the rights of the existing race are at least as great as those of the coming one. There is something, pathetically absurd in the sacrifice to their children of generation after generation of grown people. Who were the gainers by the incessant sacrifice? Of what avail was all that renunciation on behalf of those potential men and women, if on their attainment of that degree they, too, have to abandon the fruits of so much pain and so many lost possibilities, and begin all over again to weave *ad infinitum* this singular Penelope's web? The affairs of the present are carried on by the adult population, not by the children; and if the generations of adults are going to renounce, age after age, their own chances of development—resigning, as so many mothers do, opportunities of intellectual progress and spiritual enlightenment for the sake of their children—how in the name of common sense will they benefit humanity? For those children also, when their minds are ripe for progress, must, in accordance with this noble sentiment, immediately begin in *their* turn to renounce, and resign, and deny themselves, in order to start another luckless generation upon the same ridiculous circle of futility! I fear that it is not unnecessary to add that I do not here inculcate neglect of children, but merely claim some regard for the parent whom it cost previous parents so much to bear, and rear, and train. I protest against this insane waste of human energy, this perpetual renunciation for a race that never comes. When and where will be born that last happy generation who are to reap all the fruit of these ages of sacrifice? Will they wallow in the lost joys of sad women who have resigned ambitions, and allowed talents to dull and die in this thankless service? Will they taste all the experience that their mothers consented to forego? Are all these things stored up for them, like treasure that a miser will not spend, though he perish in his garret for lack of warmth and nourishment? Not so, but rather for every loss suffered by the fathers the children will be held debtors.

As regards the fears that are entertained on all sides at the prospect of women taking part in political life, or in any occupation which custom has not hitherto recognised as feminine, the advocates of freedom might ask why nobody has hitherto felt the least alarm about the awful nervous strain which the ideal submissive woman has had to undergo from time immemorial in the bearing and rearing of vast families, and the incessant cares of a household, under conditions, perhaps, of straitened means. Is there anything in the world that causes more nervous exhaustion than such a combination of duties? Doctors are, for once, agreed that worry is the most resistless of all taxes upon the constitution. Monotony of life has the same tendency, and a lack of variety in interests and thought undeniably conduces to the lowering of the vitality. Yet nobody has taken fright at the fatal combination of all these nerve-destroying conditions which belongs essentially to the lot of woman under the old *régime.*[4]

The one sort of strain which seems to be feared for the feminine constitution is the strain of brain-work, although, as a matter of fact, mental effort, if not prolonged and severe, enhances and does not exhaust the vitality.

It is true it cannot be carried on simultaneously with severe physical exertion of any kind. To go on having children year after year, superintending them and the home while doing other work outside, would indeed have disastrous consequences for women and for the race, but who would wish to see them do anything so insane? Such a domestic treadmill is stupid and brutal enough without the addition of the mental toil. It is the treadmill that must be modified.

If the new movement had no other effect than to rouse women to rebellion against the madness of large families, it would confer a priceless benefit on humanity. Let any reasonable woman expend the force that under the old order would have been given to the production of, say, the third, fourth, or fifth child upon work of another kind, and let her also take the rest and enjoyment, whatever her work, that every human being needs. It is certain that the one or two children which such a woman might elect to bear would have cause to be thankful that their mother threw over 'the holiest

4. 'The idea of the pilgrimage [to the hill-top] was to get away from the endless and nameless circumstances of everyday existence, which by degrees build a wall about the mind, so that it travels in a constantly narrowing circle. . . . *This is all—there is nothing more;* this is the reiterated preaching of house-life . . . the constant routine of house-life, the same work, the same thought in the work, the little circumstances daily recurring will dull the keenest edge of work.'—*The Story of my Heart,* by Jefferies.

traditions of her sex,' and left insane ideas of woman's duties and functions to her grandmothers.

But there are many modern women who in their own way are quite as foolish as those grandmothers, for they are guilty of the madness of trying to live the old domestic life, without modification, while entering upon a larger field of interests, working simultaneously body and brain under conditions of excitement and worry. This insanity, which one might indeed call by a harsher name, will be punished as all overstrain is punished. But the cure for these things is not to immerse women more completely in the cares of domestic life, but to simplify its methods by the aid of a little intelligence and by means which there is no space to discuss here. The present waste of energy in our homes is simply appalling.

Surely the imprisonment and distortion of the faculties of one sex would be a ruinous price to pay for the physical safety of the race, even if it secured it, which it does not, but, on the contrary, places it in peril. If it were really necessary to sacrifice women for this end, then progress would be impossible, for society would nourish within itself the germ of its own destruction. Woman, whose soul had been (by supposition) sacrificed for the sake of her body, must constitute an element of reaction and decay which no unaided efforts of man could counteract. The influence, hereditary and personal, which women possess secures to them this terrible revenge.

But there is another consideration in connection with this which Mrs. Lynn Linton overlooks. If the woman is to be asked to surrender so much because she has to produce the succeeding generation, why is the father left altogether out of count? Does *his* life leave no mark upon his offspring? Or does Mrs. Lynn Linton, perhaps, think that if the mother takes precautions for their welfare to the extent of surrendering her whole existence, the father may be safely left to take no precautions at all?

'The clamour for political rights,' this lady says, 'is woman's confession of sexual enmity. Gloss it over as we may it comes to this in the end. No woman who loves her husband would usurp his province.' Might one not retort: No man who loves his wife would seek to hamper her freedom or oppose her desires? But in fact nothing could be more false than the assertion that the new ideals imply sexual enmity. On the contrary, they contemplate a relationship between the sexes which is more close and sympathetic than the world has ever seen.

Friendship between husband and wife on the old terms was almost impossible. Where there is power on the one hand and subordination on the other, whatever the relationship that may arise, it is not likely to be that of friendship. Separate interests and ambitions, minds moving on different planes—all this tended to make strangers of those who had to pass their lives together, hampered eternally by the false sentiment which made it the right of one to command and the duty of the other to obey. But now, for the first time in history, we have come within measurable distance of a union between man and woman as distinguished from a common bondage. Among the latest words that have been said by science on this subject are the following from the *Evolution of Sex,* by Professors Geddes and Thompson:—

Admitting the theory of evolution, we are not only compelled to hope, but logically compelled to assume, that those rare fruits of an apparently more than earthly paradise of love, which only the forerunners of the race have been privileged to gather, or, it may be, to see from distant heights, are yet the realities of a daily life to which we and ours may journey.

As for Mrs. Lynn Linton's accusations against the 'wild women' as regards their lack of principle and even of common honesty, they are surely themselves a little 'wild.'

The rest of her charges are equally severe, and they induce one to wonder through what unhappy experiences the lady has gone, since she appears never to have encountered a good and generous woman outside the ranks of her own followers—unless it was a born idiot here and there! Even the men who disagree with her are either knaves or fools!

I would exhort the 'wild women' to be more tolerant, and to admit the truth that they number many wise opponents, as well as many wise and generous supporters, among men. The matter is too serious to be wrangled about. The adversaries of the 'wild woman' have hit upon not a few truths in their time, and have done much service in forcing the opposite party to think their position out in all its bearings. From the 'wild' point of view, of course, their conclusions seem false, because they deal with facts, when they find them, without sufficiently comparing and balancing them with other facts, perhaps rather less obvious, and, above all, without taking into account the one very significant fact that human nature is as sensitive as a weather-glass to its conditions and susceptible of infinite modification.

Mrs. Lynn Linton expresses herself with indignation against the mothers who allow their daughters to have a certain amount of freedom; 'they know,' she says, 'the dangers of life, and from what girls ought to be protected.' If they disregard the wisdom of experience, on whose soul lies the sin? Is the wolf to blame who passes through the open fence into the fold? Yes, certainly he is; the negligence of the shepherd does not turn the wolf into a lamb. But, as a matter of fact, the illustration is not a true one. The social 'wolf' attacks the lambs only if the lambs exceed the limits of what society expects from them as regards liberty. A girl walking alone in London meets with no trouble, whereas in Paris or Vienna she might run the risk of annoyance. It is clearly in the interests of every one that those limits should be as much as possible extended. The greater number of girls who are allowed this independence the less the risk, and the less the hindrances and difficulties for all concerned. The burden on mothers of an army of daughters who cannot stir from their home without a bodyguard is very severe. Mrs. Lynn Linton does her best to check this tendency, to give more self-reliance to girls, and would throw society back upon its path towards its abandoned errors.

The quarrel, in fact, between Mrs. Lynn Linton and her opponents is simply the time-honoured quarrel between yesterday and to-day, between reaction and progress, between decaying institutions and the stirrings of a new social faith.

There was a time when Mrs. Lynn Linton had sympathies with the struggle of a soul towards a new faith, but that is all over; and she has no sympathy left for any belief which is not 'hallowed by time,' for any attitude of mind (at least in her own sex) that is not unquestioning and submissive.

The world will occupy itself in fighting out the question for a long time to come; and the question will entangle itself inevitably with the great economic problems that this age has to solve, the whole matter of the relation of the sexes being involved in these.

The emancipation of woman and the emancipation of the manual worker will go hand in hand. If this generation is wise and sane, it will conduct these two movements in a fashion new to history. Taking warning by the experience of the past, it will avoid the weak old argument of violence (even in language) as a strong and intelligent teacher avoids the cowardly and senseless device of corporal punishment. It will conduct its revolution by means of the only weapon that has ever given a victory worth winning: Intelligence.

Mankind has tried blood and thunder long enough; they have not answered. The counter-stroke is as strong as the original impetus, and we expiate our error in the wearisome decades of a reaction. No revolution can be achieved to any purpose that is not organic; it must rest upon a real change in the sentiment and constitution of humanity. We are not governed by armies and police, we are governed by ideas; and this power that lies in human opinion is becoming strengthened with every advance that we make in civilisation, and in the rapidity with which ideas are communicated from man to man, and from nation to nation. The whole course of civilisation tends towards the dethronement of brute force in favour of the force of thought and of sentiment. It behoves women, above all, to conduct their movement in a quiet, steady, philosophic, and genial spirit; regarding the opposition that they receive, as much as possible, from the point of view of the student rather than of the partisan; realising that in this greatest of all social revolutions they must expect the fiercest resistance; that men in opposing them are neither better nor worse than all human beings of either sex have shown themselves to be as soon as they became possessors of power over their fellows. The noblest cannot stand the test, and of average men and women it makes bullies and tyrants. If this general fact be borne in mind throughout the struggle, it will be easier to avoid the feelings of bitterness and rancour which the sense of injustice creates; it will remind those engaged in the encounter to regard it with calmer eyes, as one would regard the history of past events; it will teach them to be prepared for defeat while hoping for success, and not to be too much dismayed if the change for which they have striven so hard must be delayed until long after they are dead, and all those who would have rejoiced in it are no longer there to see the sun rise over the promised land. It will teach them, too, to realise more strongly than most of us are inclined to do, that men and women are brothers and sisters, bound to stand or fall together; that in trying to raise the position and condition of women, they are serving at least as much the men who are to be their husbands or sons; that, in short—to quote the saying of Hegel—'The master does not become really free till he has liberated his slave.'

~ FLORENCE DIXIE

From *Gloriana; or The Revolution of 1900*

London: Henry & Co., 1890, vii–ix; 128–34.

[pp. vii–ix]

I make no apology for this preface. It may be unusual but then the book it deals with is unusual. There is but one object in "Gloriana." It is to speak of evils which DO exist, to study facts which it is a crime to neglect, to sketch an artificial position—the creation of laws false to Nature—unparalleled for injustice and hardship.

Many critics, like the rest of humanity, are apt to be unfair. They take up a book, and when they find that it does not accord with their sentiments, they attempt to wreck it by ridicule and petty, spiteful criticism. They forget to ask themselves, "Why is this book written?" They altogether omit to go to the root of the Author's purpose; and the result is, that false testimony is often borne against principles which, though drastic, are pure, which, though sharp as the surgeon's knife, are yet humane; for it is genuine sympathy with humanity that arouses them.

There is no romance worth reading, which has not the solid foundation of truth to support it; there is no excuse for the existence of romance, unless it fixes thought on that truth which underlies it. "Gloriana" may be a romance, a dream; but in the first instance, it is inextricably interwoven with truth, in the second instance, dreams the work of the brain are species of thought, and thought is an attribute of God. Therefore it is God's creation.

There may be some, who reading "Gloriana," will feel shocked, and be apt to misjudge the author. There are others who will understand, appreciate, and sympathise. There are yet others, who hating truth, will receive it with gibes and sneers; there are many, who delighting in the evil which it fain would banish, will resent it as an unpardonable attempt against their liberties. An onslaught on public opinion is very like leading a Forlorn Hope. The leader knows full well that death lies in the breach, yet that leader knows also, that great results may spring from the death which is therefore readily sought and faced. "Gloriana" pleads woman's cause, pleads for her freedom, for the just acknowledgment of her rights. It pleads that her equal humanity with man shall be recognised, and therefore that her claim to share what he has arrogated to himself, shall be considered. "Gloriana," pleads that in woman's degradation man shall no longer be debased, that in her elevation he shall be upraised and ennobled. The reader of its pages will observe the Author's conviction, everywhere expressed, that Nature ordains the close companionship not division of the sexes, and that it is opposition to Nature which produces jealousy, intrigue, and unhealthy rivalry.

"Gloriana" is written with no antagonism to man. Just the contrary. The Author's best and truest friends, with few exceptions, have been and are men. But the Author will never recognise man's glory and welfare in woman's degradation.

[pp. 128–34]

"The bestowal of the suffrage on woman is a practical acknowledgment by man that woman has a right to be considered as a being who can reason, and who can study humanity in its various phases, and act on her own responsibility. It is not for me here to seek for the causes which have hitherto led man to believe to the contrary. His belief, in a great measure, has been due to woman's weak acceptance of his arbitrary laws; for I do not suppose it will be pretended by any one that the laws laid down for the sacrifice of woman's freedom were the creation of a woman's brain. But this weak acceptance of these arbitrary laws cannot fairly be ascribed entirely to the fault of woman. 'Slavery in no form is natural'; it is an artificial creation of man's; and woman's slavery cannot be taken as an exception to this maxim. She has, in point of fact, been subjected to bondage, a bondage which has, in a manner, become second nature to her, and which custom has taught her to regard as a part of the inevitable.

"But if honourable gentlemen will believe me, Nature is stronger than custom, and more powerful than law. Nature is a force that cannot be repressed finally and absolutely. It is like an overwhelming torrent against which you may erect monster dykes, which you may dam up for a time, but all the while the waters are rising, and will find their level in the end. Through countless years woman has been repressed. Every human force and ingenuity of man have been employed to establish her subjection. From religion downwards it has been the cry, 'Women, submit to men!' a cry which I may safely say was never originated by herself.

"Now Nature has established a law which is inviolable. It has laid down the distinction between the sexes, but here Nature stops. Nature gives strength and beauty to man, and Nature gives strength and beauty to woman. In this latter instance man flies in the face of Nature, and declares that she must be artificially restrained. Woman must not be allowed to grow up strong like man, because if she did, the fact would establish her equality with him, and this cannot be tolerated. So the boy and man are allowed freedom of body, and are trained up to become muscular and strong, while the woman, by artificial, not natural laws, is bidden to remain inactive and passive, and in consequence weak and undeveloped. Mentally it is the same. Nature has unmistakably given to woman a greater amount of brain power. This is at once perceivable in childhood. For instance, on the stage, girls are always employed in preference to boys, for they are considered brighter and sharper in intellect and brain power. Yet man deliberately sets himself to stunt that early evidence of mental capacity, by laying down the law that woman's education shall be on a lower level than that of man's; that natural truths, which all women should early learn, should be hidden from her; and that while men may be taught everything, women must only acquire a narrow and imperfect knowledge both of life and of Nature's laws.

"I maintain to honourable gentlemen that this procedure is arbitrary and cruel, and false to Nature. I characterise it by the strong word of Infamous. It has been the means of sending to their graves unknown, unknelled, and unnamed, thousands of women whose high intellects have been wasted, and whose powers for good have been paralysed and undeveloped. To the subjection and degradation of woman I ascribe the sufferings and crimes of humanity, nor will Society be ever truly raised, or ennobled, or perfected until woman's freedom has been granted, and she takes her rightful place as the equal of man. Viewing this great social problem in this light, we have deemed it our duty to present to Parliament a bill, establishing as law, firstly, the mixed education of the sexes, that is to say, bringing into force the principle of mixed schools and colleges, in which girls and boys, young men and young women, can be educated together; secondly, the extension of the rights of primogeniture to the female sex, so that while primogeniture remains associated with the law of entail, the eldest born, not the eldest son, shall succeed the owner of property and titles; also that all the professions and positions in life, official or otherwise, shall be thrown open as equally to women as to men; and thirdly, that women shall become eligible as Members of Parliament, and peeresses in their own right eligible to sit in the Upper House as well as to undertake State duties. Such is the drastic, the sweeping measure by which we desire to wipe off for ever and repair, though tardily, a great wrong. Honourable gentlemen will perceive that we take no half-way course. We are not inclined to accept the doctrine of 'by degrees,' believing that this would only prolong the evil and injustice which daily arise from the delay in emancipating the female sex; and I will now as briefly as possible set forth to honourable gentlemen the arguments in favour of the three clauses contained in this bill.

"With regard to the first one, namely, the advisability of educating girls and boys, young women and young men, together, it is necessary to point out that the system of separating the sexes throughout their educational career has arisen chiefly from the totally different forms of education meted out to each. We hold that these different forms are pernicious and morally unhealthy, calculated to evilly influence the sensual instincts of the male sex, and to instil into the other sex a totally wrong and mischievous idea of the right and wrong side of Nature. We are convinced that this system has been productive of an immense amount of immorality and consequent suffering and degradation in the past, and that the system of elevating Nature into a mystery is the greatest conceivable incitement to sensuality and immorality. We hold that there should be no mystery or secrecy anent the laws of God. We hold that in creating mystery we condemn God's law—namely, Nature, to be what it is not—indecent; and we hold that the system of separating the sexes, of telling all to the one and enshrouding everything in silence and mystery to the other, has had the evil effect of producing immorality, so wide and far-spreading as to be frightful in its hideousness and magnitude; while it has been productive of millions of miserable marriages, of disease, and of evil immeasurable and appalling.

"Nature tells us truths which we cannot condemn as falsehoods, however much we may avert our eyes from their light. Nature tells us that it is natural for the male and female sex to be together. If we bring up the young to face this truth, if we bring up the young to accept as natural and rational the laws of pure and unaffected Nature, they will accept it as it is. But if we clothe it in boys' and men's eyes in fanciful garments, and leave girls and women in ignorance of its truths, we must expect the terrible and horrible results which have followed such unnatural teaching through centuries of time.

"We therefore emphatically in this clause record out protest against the system of teaching the young to regard Nature in a false light, in other words, to judge of God's laws as impure. We believe such a system of education to be, as we have said, an incentive to the male sex to do wrong, while totally unfitting the female sex to do right. The beginning of all immorality on woman's side has sprung from ignorance, and from the system of mystery and the tendency to declare indecent that which cannot be so, being God's law. In regard to the physical condition of the sexes, we hold that where equal opportunities are afforded to both of strengthening, developing, and improving the body, little material difference will be found in the two. There are many strong men in this world, and there are many strong women, as there are weakly men and weakly women. I have never heard it yet argued, that because a man is not strong in body he is therefore unfitted to take part in the affairs of State. Yet woman's weakness is one of the reasons adduced for excluding her therefrom. We believe that in a big public school, say, for instance, at Eton, if girls and boys were admitted together, that girls would very soon prove that neither physically nor mentally were they inferior to boys, nor should such a pernicious doctrine be ever inculcated into the boy's brain. He should not be brought up as he is now, to look down on his sisters as inferior to him, nor should those sisters be told that he is their superior in strength and mental capacity. It is a doctrine the perniciousness of which is far-reaching, and a distinct infringement of the natural."

~ FRANCES SWINEY

From *Woman and Natural Law*

2d ed. London: C. W. Daniel, 1912. 5–27.

PART I: THE BIOLOGICAL LAW

> The female contains all qualities and tempers them,
> She is in her place and moves with perfect balance,
> She is all things duly veil'd, she is both passive and active,
> She is to conceive daughters as well as sons, and sons as well as
> daughters.
>
> Walt Whitman

The thinker of the present day is confronted by a great problem. He has, if a sincere seeker after the truth of things, visible and invisible, to ask himself this crucial question: "How can I reconcile the philosophies, religions, creeds, and social codes of the past and of the present with the recognised facts that science is daily revealing of immutable natural laws?"

For the human mind has become intensely analytical and severely skeptical of assumptions that cannot be proved by practical demonstration, or through the logical reasoning of critical analysis. The old faiths, the time-honoured dogmas, customs, and traditions, are all in turn put through the mill of merciless investigation, and only the grains of gold come out unscathed. The worn-out husks fall away, pulverised to atoms, that ignorance, prejudice, falsehood, and injustice have for long regarded as divinely revealed or wisdom-inspired truths; and lo! the truth that survives is utterly different from the popular belief and accepted dicta of the past, sunk deep in error and misconception.

In no field of scientific research has there been a greater revolution in specious assumptions than in the relative position the feminine factor holds in the natural law of evolution. The change of aspect that the latest discoveries in biology, psychology and sociology have brought about is so stupendous and important in its bearing on the woman movement, that I purpose briefly to bring a few of the leading facts to the notice of those women who, through various circumstances, are unable to procure or read the scientific books dealing with this subject.

Woman, to play her true part in the cosmic scheme, must know the basic facts of her existence; she must realise that there is only one divinely-inspired law, the law regulating, controlling, and dirigating all the manifold activities of the universe; nowhere contradictory, uncertain, or variable, but ever insistent, immutable, and inexorable. She must bring all her reasoning powers to bear on the discrepancies between human theories and indubitable facts that no sophistry can controvert. They are written large on the face of nature; they reveal the mysteries of the truths of life, and no soul pressing on to individual development can afford to disregard them. I say more; no soul can advance on the road of true progress unless this knowledge becomes the invincible weapon, the Sword of Truth, by which old fallacies, pernicious customs, and worn-out creeds can be overthrown and demolished.

> As a star feels the sun and falters,
> Touched to death by diviner eyes—
> As on the old gods' untended altars
> The old fire of withered worship dies.[1]

The old is passing away. All things are becoming new. "I overturn, overturn, overturn, saith the Lord."

I will first take the truths that biology teaches us, which we shall find on many important points are subversive of previously held opinions.

In Professor Lester F. Ward's illuminative work, *Pure Sociology,* occurs the following suggestive sentence:—

"We are probably in about the same position and stage with reference to the question of sex as were the men of the eighteenth century with reference to the question of evolution. . . . The advancement of truth has always been in the direction of supplanting the superficial and apparent by the fundamental and real."[2]

Now, what is the fundamental and real at the base of all phenomena?

1. Algernon Charles Swinburne, "At a Month's End," lines 45–48. *Ed.*
2. Page 302.

Is it not Life itself? Life has at last been tardily discovered as the one thing needful to individual existence, as the one positive, personal possession without which nothing is possible.

This re-discovery in the last decade by philosophers, biologists, and scientists generally, of the sovereignty of Life, has led to another of equal importance, viz. the re-discovery of motherhood.

"Life," states Bergson,[3] and re-echo Burke[4], Saleeby,[5] and a score of other thinkers, "is the great Reality."

"Woman," declares Wells,[6] "is the greatest discovery of the twentieth century."

"Woman is Nature's supreme instrument of the future," writes Dr Saleeby.[7] "Fatherhood," he continues, "is historically of mushroom growth compared with motherhood."

We are thus being brought back and back to the archaic conception of universal Monism: to Life, the one Reality, and to Eve, the embodiment of Life—the Mother of all Living. Now what does this imply by logical deduction? It implies a marvellous sequence of irrefutable fact or truths.

Life—the one Reality—and the woman, or the female organism, the transmitter of life, lead to the recognition of the one Force of Life, the one Law of Life, the one Substance of Life, the one Standard Form of Life, and the one Purpose of Life. All proceeding from the One.

In man-made religious philosophies and theoretical dissertations the masculine principle and the male organism are primary in the cosmic scheme, the feminine principle and female organism are secondary.

The natural law, however, at all points, substantiates the fact "that originally and normally all things centre, as it were, about the female. In a word, life begins as female."[8]

Life is feminine. On the physical plane the first living organism was a mother-organism, the first organic substance was mother-substance, the first standard of form was the mother-form, and the one purpose throughout creation is to bring, relatively, all units approximately to the full development of the potentialities of creative life processes; to evolve the highest

3. Henri (Louis) Bergson (1859–1941), French philosopher and author, winner of the Nobel Prize for Literature in 1927. *Ed.*

4. Edmund Burke (1729–97), Dublin-born statesman and author of *Philosophical Inquiry into the Origin of Our Ideas of the Sublime and the Beautiful* (1756). *Ed.*

5. C. W. Saleeby (1878–1940) fought for feminism in the name of eugenics. *Ed.*

6. H(erbert) G(eorge) Wells (1866–1946), journalist and author of science fiction. *Ed.*

7. *Parenthood and Race Culture*, p. xiv.

8. *Pure Sociology*, p. 313.

expression of the forces of Life through the creative powers and the transmissive functions of the female.

Priority of existence, then, belongs to the female. The Feminine is the primary and fundamental basis of existence from which all proceeds in organic evolution.

"The female is not only the primary and original sex, but continues throughout as the main trunk . . . the male is therefore, as it were, a mere afterthought of Nature. Moreover, the male sex was at first and for a long period, and still throughout many of the lower orders of beings, devoted exclusively to the functions for which it was created, viz. that of fertilisation. Among millions of humble creatures the male is simply and solely a fertiliser."[9]

The female represents the centre of gravity of the whole biological system, what Herbert Spencer[10] terms "the moving equilibrium," which regulates, dirigates, and controls the process of evolution. "The female sex being the organism proper," states Lester F. Ward, "the female not only typifies the race, but, metaphor aside, she is the race," for she is the creative focus from whom proceed the daughter and the son.

Here we come face to face with a long-forgotten truth. The first male, the first son of the mother, was ever virgin-born. The deep significance of this biological fact of life cannot be over-estimated. From the mother's own chemico-physics was formed what physiology terms the male-element—and wrongly. For parthenogenesis, or virgin-birth, alone proves the oneness of the substance out of which all living things are made, and the differentiation is simply owing to the proportions and the conditions in which the substance is utilised.

The male, then, is secondary to the female. Therefore from Nature's point of view, the male is of little importance in comparison with the female; hence, among many species, there is a great superabundance of males, and only comparatively few individuals among them are able to fulfil the function for which they were brought forth, as is seen among the drones of the bees and the useless males of the ants.

Moreover, biology proves that fertilisation is not a necessary adjunct of reproduction, but is, on the contrary, in reality a method of the female organism proper to further variations of type and diversity of chemico-physics. The male, besides, brings back to the mother-organism the hereditary traits of the species and the disintegrating waste-products of proto-

9. *Pure Sociology,* Prof. Lester F. Ward, p. 313.

10. Herbert Spencer (1820–1903), British evolutionary philosopher and journalist. *Ed.*

plasm (the Life-stuff), so that nothing may be lost of the Life-substance in the transmutation of old forms of life into new.

"The Masculine," writes a profound thinker, "is but a means or mode put forward by the Feminine, to be recalled after being used, as a tool is laid aside by the worker."[11]

And this is just what is done by the females of many species. When environmental conditions are approximately in harmony with the maternal organism, it then reproduces parthenogenetically, without the aid of male fertilisation, and, after producing numerous generations of females, only brings forth male-offspring when the conditions become less favourable both as to nutrition and temperature.

Thus the old and popular fallacy, that with the male is the gift of Life, dies a natural death. As Professor Winterton C. Curtis affirms, "the old conception of sexual and asexual reproduction must be given up entirely."

Life, growth, development, and reproduction are solely feminine properties; the male element is simply the vehicle by which new variations are added to the maternal organism, so as to bring about the greater variations of species through the choice of females among numerous males of the most attractive and best developed individuals, and, as Letourneau points out in his *Evolution of Marriage,* whether the so-called *sexes* "are represented by distinct or united individuals, whether the accessory organic apparatus is more or less complicated, are matters of no consequence; the essential fact re-appears always and everywhere of the conjugation of two cellules, with absorption, in the case of superior animals, of the male cellule by the female cellule."[12]

Professor Weismann also recognises the basic oneness of sex in many passages in his celebrated work, *The Germ Plasm,* by the implied deduction that the male element, reabsorbed by the female, is but a disintegrated portion of the creative, feminine element of which the male is an integral part.

Thus we find that there is sex differentiation, but only *one* sex or organism proper, the female. This basic truth is brought prominently forward by recent researches in embryology.

According to natural law, like produces like. According to natural law, all is by number, weight, and measure.

First, then, the mother, and under the best conditions for herself and her offspring, produces a daughter. The first male cell, and the first male

11. Henry R. S. Dalton, B.A., *Short Essays on the Woman Movement.*

12. Page 4.

organism, as an entity separated from the mother, was an initial failure on the part of the maternal organism to reproduce its like, and was due to a chemical deficiency in the metabolism or physique of the mother.

In the standard work, *The Evolution of Sex,*[13] and in the treatise on *The Determination of Sex,*[14] this fact is insisted upon with constant reiteration and demonstration. The leading biologists agree that a "very favourable condition in both ovum and sperm will probably lead to the formation of a female"; that "there is for the ovum a certain minimum mass, which must be surpassed if it is to develop at all; and a second minimum which the ovum must attain if the female is to be produced."

Thus better nourishment assists the production of females, as "male reproduction is associated with preponderating katabolism, or waste of substance, and the female with relative anabolism," or conservation or growth of substance.

Therefore such well-known authorities as Düsing, Pflüger, Ploss, Heape, Maupas, Loeb, Geddes, and Thomson conclusively prove that the female, whether in plant or animal, so far from being the result of an arrest in development, as was erroneously supposed by Darwin and Spencer, is the direct outcome of the most favourable nutritive and environmental conditions. Male plants and male flowers predominate in bad seasons. "A male flower . . . is an intermediate stage between a perfect leaf and a perfect, or, we may say, a female, flower."[15]

A cold, inclement spring fills the farmyard with cockerels, as the farmer knows to his cost; and, in the human race, male births are in the ascendant during times of war, famine, and pestilence. Nature puts forth her best efforts to produce a female, as the female is the natural standard of each species. Therefore, given relatively sympathetic conditions for both mother and offspring, first births are invariably female, the result of anabolic constructive processes, when the maternal organism is in the full height of its strength and vitality. The natural law of primogeniture is entailed on the female. As Schenk observes, "these sex-determining impulses originate, like all other development-determinating influences, from the mother, since it is she that supplies to the embryo, as agencies of impulse, the juices derived from the food she has received. In addition to these, the embryo receives also from the mother such products as are required for the growth that follows the impulse."

13. Geddes and Thomson.
14. By Dr Lenhossek, Professor of Anatomy, Budapest.
15. Professor Meehan, U.S.A.

"It is obvious," states Dr Marshall, "that the sperm contributes comparatively little material to the fertilised ovum, being provided with only sufficient protoplasmic substance to form a locomotive apparatus by means of which it gains access to the ovum. The predominantly destructive metabolism of the spermatozoön, as contrasted with the ovum, has been strongly emphasised by Geddes and Thomson." [16]

Moreover, biology, through microscopic research, has revealed the law of number, weight, and measure governing sex differentiation. We now know that the somatic or body-cells of the females of each species contain more chromosomes than those of the males, *i.e.* the nuclear lines of protoplasm which carry the hereditary and individualistic traits of the unit are more numerous in the complex organism of the female than in that of the male. For instance, in some species the male-cell has ten chromosomes, while the female has twelve; in another, the female-cell has thirty-eight chromosomes while the male has only thirty-five. Hence the conclusion of the Mendel school of biologists, as expressed by Professors Hurst and Castle, is as follows:—

"Femaleness is due to the presence of a chromosome absent in the male. . . . We may, therefore, regard the female as of more complex organisation than the male. And, in that sense, the female may be said to be physiologically the superior sex. We may thus further conceive that either the female is an extra-developed male, and has arisen by the addition of a new factor to maleness, or, perhaps more probably, that the male has arisen as a defective variation from the female." [17] The male-cell, therefore, is a variant daughter-cell not developed to the full potentiality of the female. It is an intermediary between the parent-cell and its like, the daughter cell.

Now, as I have pointed out, the first male organism was unlike the mother; it was deficient in all vital organs and functions. It was "exceedingly small, frail, and ephemeral"; but the mother was not content with the abnormal deficiency in her offspring; and, as "cells feel stimuli," and this feeling is a mental activity, and when it is caused to be systematically repeated a structure will arise which is the embodiment of that kind of mental action," [18] the female organism began to create the male in its own image, and from a shapeless sac it gradually assumed a definite form, agreeing in general characteristics with that of the original organism, the mother. Moreover, as the female, by natural law, is the selector of mates, the male, while

16. *The Physiology of Reproduction*, p. 175.

17. "Mendelism and Sex," *The Mendel Journal*, October 1909.

18. Professor Elmer Gates on *Cell Formation.*

approaching the form and stature of the female, becomes endowed with numerous secondary sexual characteristics, in many cases highly ornamental, due to the strongly developed esthetic faculties of the female in choosing the most attractive and brightly-coloured mate. But it must be noted that these distinctive characteristics are entirely superficial and exterior; they never even modify vital organs, though they become in many instances exaggerated developments in feathers, horns, and hair; and, irrespective of any extraneous traits of abnormal male differentiation or male efflorescence, the irresistible law of organic evolution ever tends to render the male more like the female, and to become independent of her, as a perfected, complete being, as the species rise in complexity of organ and function.

Many anthropologists assert that primitive man was smaller, weaker, and less capable than the woman. Travellers among primitive peoples always express astonishment at the strength and vigour of the women, who often surpass the men in height, can carry heavier burdens, and are superior in endurance and longevity. It is presumed that it was during the long ages of the Matriarchate, when woman was the selector and controlled all sexual relations, that man advanced towards humanity, becoming more and more like the woman.

For a little observation will disclose the fact that instead of the dual differentiation of the *one* sex (the female) being more accentuated in the human species than in the subhuman, the very reverse is found to be the case. For, consider to what genus the human race belongs—to the mammalia, the greatest division of vertebrated animals, and so designated from the distinctive organs and functions of the female. Does not logical deduction teach us that superiority of standard rests with the organism in which the typical organs and functions are perfected, are fully developed, are, in a word, active, instead of with the organism in which these same organs are rudimentary and ineffective?

Physiologists are at last grasping this basic anatomical truth; and Professor Albrecht, writing on the obscure diseases of men, plainly avers that "males are rudimentary females." While Mr T. H. Montgomery concludes, from a general review of the leading facts of development, physiology, and anatomy, that the male is less developed and more embryonic than the female. He points out the fact that when one sex is rudimentary in comparison with the other, it is almost always the male; though, as I have before remarked, in no species does the female more lead evolution than in the human; and no male has more approximated to the organic development of the female than has man.

For instance, there are many well-authenticated cases known in which men have suckled children; among animals only one species of rabbit found in Central America has evolved a male capable of this active functional power. Again, "the *prostate* in man is simply a womb 'out of employment.'"[19]

The distinctive sex organs of the male are the organs of the female placed outside the body for expulsive action instead of for constructive.[20] In other vital physiological modifications, that I will not enter upon, but well known in the medical profession, men are developing more and more the organism of the woman. Even the most casual observer can mark how in height, bearing, vigour of muscle, equality of brain-power, decrease of hairiness and facial traits, the boy and the girl of the higher civilisation are becoming closely assimilated, and how the boy, especially, is losing the distinctive features of masculinity.

For "woman," writes Dr Havelock Ellis, "represents more nearly than man the human type to which man is approximating."[21] "It would not be difficult," he further remarks, "to multiply examples of the ways in which women are leading evolution." He notes how in the shape of the head women are in advance. The dolichocephalic skull is more primitive than the brachycephalic, and women are "much more brachycephalic than men.... In the shape and size of the face woman is in advance of man, while man is also higher than the apes.... In the number of teeth women are leading evolution; the wisdom teeth are more frequently absent, and the second dentition more frequently late in appearance. This is in conformity with the tendency of evolution to decrease the size and number of the teeth, and the size of the mouth.

"Not only by his large brain, but by his large pelvis, the modern man is following a path first marked out by women.... Women remain nearer than men to the infantile state which approximates nearer to the type of the race; while men approach nearer to the ape-like and senile state which is the ancestral past of the race."[22]

Thus the first development of progressive, constructive and eliminating change is, as a rule, found in the female; as the larger pelvis, which accentuates the difference between man and the lower animals, and gives the organic structure necessary for sustaining an erect position. Women walk

19. *The Alternate Sex,* Leland, p. 33.
20. See *What a Young Husband Ought to Know,* p. 50.
21. *Man and Woman,* p. 392.
22. *Man and Woman,* p. 392.

with greater balance and equipoise than men. The *grace* of women is simply the physical expression of more perfect harmony between anatomical structure and consequent rhythmic motion than man has yet attained. The lesser jaw, the larger brain, the less teeth and the less hair on the body point to women as higher in the line of evolution than man. Whereas, when there is retrogression towards ancestral types, the male alone carries the visible signs, as in the appearance of the caudal appendage, the eighth rib, hare-lip, ape-like ears, splay feet, supernumerary digits and nipples, and other malformations of like character, due to atavism or a falling back on sub-human traits.

Common-sense observation shows us that it is the female alone that can initiate or instigate a change of construction; first, by eliminating some useless factor, and then supplementing it by some organic modification of structure tending towards a higher stage of development. These changes could only take place in the forming embryo. Nothing can be evolved except through and by the female of each species. That is the basic law of evolution and the Law of Life. It is so simple that we are in danger of forgetting it. "Man is not a fallen god but a promoted reptile,"[23] is the verdict of science, learning slowly the natural law.

Man has not gone about dropping the end of a tail here, or a superfluous rib there. The mother's womb alone has been the crucible and workshop wherein Nature has formed her evolving handiwork. Obviously, also, it would be the female embryo that would be the first to benefit from the change, as being the one taking the longer to develop, and the one requiring the most vital energy and the best condition on the part of the mother to produce, it would be the organism best adapted for transformation from a normal to an abnormal phase of being, *i.e.* abnormal, until by hereditary transmission the changed condition or structure has become a racial characteristic.

For, let us reflect for a moment what woman has done already for humanity-in-the-making. Place a native Australian beside a Greek statue, when Greece was at her apotheosis of physical and intellectual achievement, and realise by a practical illustration what the mothers of the race have accomplished in anatomical structure alone. Compare a Madonna of the Italian school at its zenith with a negress of the African coast, and it will be gauged somewhat how stupendous has been the task of the mothers of mankind.

No wonder that Henry Drummond[24] came to the following conclusion:—

23. *The Universal Kinship,* J. Howard Moore, p. 107.

24. 1786–1860, founder of the Catholic Apostolic Church. *Ed.*

"Life is exalted in proportion to its organic and functional complexity. Woman's organism is more complex, and her totality of function larger than those of any other thing inhabiting our earth. Therefore, her position in the scale of life is the most exalted; the sovereign one."

Unfolded out of the folds of the woman, man
Comes unfolded, and is always to come unfolded;
Unfolded only out of the superbest woman of the
Earth is to come the superbest man of the earth:
. . . .
Unfolded only out of the perfect body of a woman
Can a man be form'd of perfect body.

Walt Whitman[25]

ROSA FRANCES SWINEY [MRS. FRANCES SWINEY]

From "Man's Necessity"

The League of Isis (National Union of Woman's Suffrage Societies, London), no. 2 (1907), 1–3.

Woman's redemption from sexual slavery can only be achieved through man's redemption from sex-obsession. There is no living organism so completely under the tyranny of sex as the human male. The majority of men are utterly incapable of freeing themselves from the limitations of masculinity. They cannot view humanity whole. Religion, legislation, habits, customs, conventions, prejudices, and superstitions are tarred with the same brush of sex-differentiation. Consequently, being absorbed in the contemplation of his own sex-limitations, man has had little time to give attention to the consequences to the other half of humanity—women—of this sex-concentration, until these said consequences, by the law of reflex action, return with disastrous force upon himself.

No sex-sophistry has been more upheld by man than the double standard of morality, the illogical device by which man has cloaked masculine licentiousness under the specious plea of sexual necessity. Humanity, as a

25. "Unfolded Out of the Folds," from *Leaves of Grass* (1872). *Ed.*

whole, is now confronted by the results of this perversion of physiological truth; and, diseased in mind and body, mankind despairingly cries out for some remedy to heal its open sores. For the history of pathology plainly reveals that through male incontinence the whole human race suffers all the ills to which corrupt flesh is heir. Yet if man had given attention to the study of Nature's laws instead of devoting his energies to self-gratification through sex-obsession, he would have discovered how essential to the furtherance of male development was the restriction on male sex-functions. In the sub-human species the male, except for the purpose of reproduction of the species, never sexually approaches the female, who only permits of one act of fertilization at the proper time and season. The conditions of polygamy and monogamy are governed by the requirements of the female and the offspring, not by the necessity of the male. Throughout the sexual life of the animal world the male is the servitor to the creative demand of the female to produce offspring after her kind. For long periods of latent sexuality the male has no call on the exercise of sex-functions, and lives a life free of sex-obligations. With what result? Naturalists assert that practically disease is unknown among the sub-human species unless introduced through man's agency and unnatural conditions; that, chances being equal, animals live the full extent of their natural life limit. They die of old age, and among the higher mammalians retain all their senses intact to an extreme old age. Their limbs also keep their elasticity of muscle and tissue. The males in many species are larger, stronger, and adorned with more outward secondary sexual characteristics—such as horns, feathers, manes, etc.—than the females. These appendages grow during the period of latent sexuality, and are at their full development at the breeding season, so as to be the means of attracting the sexual selection of the females. Now, it is computed that the generative organs of all living creatures contain thousands upon thousands, in some cases millions upon millions, of germ-cells in excess of any possible requirements for the reproduction of species. Yet Nature never wastes. She is of all mistresses the most parsimonious with her substance and her means. Therefore the law of life regulates and controls the expenditure of the germ-cells in outward manifestation to the extent requisite for the normal continuance of the species, but the vast reservoir of vital forces concentrated in the sex-organs is utilized in building up, renewing, and keeping in health, strength, vigour, and vitality, the whole complex system of brain, nerve, tissue, muscle, and bone. With this retained life-force the horns and manes of the stag and the lion are developed; the feathers and the vocal chords of the cock-birds are brought to perfection; and all male animals replenish their strength and vitality through the diffusion and absorption of the vital germ-cells. No law of Nature is more strictly enforced upon the male organism than the necessity for its own individual development of keeping within the limits of normal exercise for a definite use any expenditure of human vitality *outside* of the body. Many polygamous males at the end of the breeding seasons are physical wrecks depleted of all vitality—for instance, the bull seal and the male salmon. They have to recuperate during a long period of continence. Man is not exempt from the same law of control, and must for his own advancement be obedient to the same restriction. Among the sub-human species the male has no sex-dominance over the female; he fights for sex-supremacy among the males, and it is obvious that as there are, as a rule, many more males than females, many males never, or very late in life, exercise their sex-functions. With them reproduction of species is incidental to the life-history. In no case is use made an excuse for abuse, or any waste permitted of means to obtain ends.

Immature males do not mate under Nature's supervision. The young of the higher mammalians are carefully segregated by the old leaders or members of the flock or herd until they are fully grown. No careless breeding, as with the human race, between unformed girls and undeveloped boys. No exercise of the vital powers until the organism is fully prepared by Nature for the exercise and task of the reproduction of species under the best conditions, and the functions and faculties are at their best. The sex-energy in the boy and the man is capable of the same transmutation into sources of individual development as among the lower but wiser animals. It is with the human male the fount of the higher activities, of the greatest mental achievements, of the supreme spiritual gifts, as in the chemico-physical laboratory of the body life transforms, assimilates, and changes one form of energy into another, and of the physical substance, feeds, nourishes, and sustains brain, nerve, muscle, and tissue, and keeps in working order all the different organs. Until man learns the great lesson taught and enforced by Nature he will remain under the stigma symbolized in the allegory of the Hindu cosmology, where it is represented that Ananta, the male element, is the means by which creation was accomplished. "Ananta, the serpent, is said," writes Forlong[1] in "Rivers of Life," "to do the necessary though menial work of creation, from over-zealous performance of which he caused or created wickedness, incurring Vishnoo's anger. Some poems even represent him as an enemy of Vishnoo or true religion." True religion is the knowl-

1. *Rivers of Life; or Sources and Streams of the Faiths of Man in All Lands Showing the Evolution of Faiths from the Rudest Symbolisms to the Latest Spiritual Developments* by James George Roche, d. 1904, a popular anthropologist of religions. *Ed.*

edge of truth practised in life observance. No natural truth has been more flagrantly disobeyed and ignored by man than the law of male continence, with the result that no species but the human is diseased by sexual vice, over-populated with degenerates, imbeciles, and malformed individuals. No species but the human suffers from hereditary diseases, or is decimated by infant mortality due to inborn defects.

Yet in all times, in all places, there have been the philosophers, the seers, who, above the current customs and the pernicious religious dogmas, taught and foresaw that the human male's individual advancement, development, and redemption lay in the continence, in the non-fulfilment of sex-male subserviency to the generation of species. For the male this sex-subserviency to the needs of the female was a term of probation, a time of trial of the soul's evolution, when not able to create out of its own substance on the physical plane, it had to retain in purity and discretion the vital forces for its own individual development during its sojourn in the elementary male form. As it used the life-energy in that crucial test of experience, so it entered the woman-plane of fuller creative powers, either burdened with the Karma of sex-excesses in the masculine plane, or equipped with the pure and supreme qualities of motherhood. For the soul learns the truth of motherhood only through the path it has carved out for itself as the servant, the tool, the helper of the mothers of the race. It enters the woman-phase either as the revered mother or as the harlot thrust out into the mire of the streets.

SECTION TWO

Protecting

Many Victorian and Edwardian women worked hard to preserve nonhuman species. As advocates for vulnerable animals and landscapes, they might have been engaged in activities such as speaking, writing, and picketing, any of which could have brought them into the public eye and subsequently led to their censure. Because much of animal and plant life had been humbled—even razed—in the name of progress, there was much work to be done in their day. Horses were abused daily in the streets and in pursuit of sport; other large and powerful animals were caged in inhumane confinement, displayed for public viewing; foxes were hunted for the sake of tradition; rabbits and dogs were vivisected in the name of scientific advancement; birds were killed to provide feathers for uniforms and women's hats; ancient trees were felled to clear the way for an ever-expanding urban system of residential, commercial, and industrial buildings.

If they were prepared to undergo a bit of taunting or satirizing—as, for example, was Octavia Hill for her work on behalf of land preservation (see figure 6) or Frances Power Cobbe on behalf of animal rights—women were especially well positioned to take a stand against such abuses. Their culture had already authorized them to protect other species. From the late eighteenth century, women had been informed that one of their roles was to teach the young how to be kind and respectful toward nonhuman creatures. Connection and gentle affinity toward nature, not harming or teasing, was what was wanted. Books like Erasmus Darwin's *Plan for the Conduct of Female Education in Boarding Schools* (1797) had recommended such behavior and had showed how women could themselves inculcate it. Even earlier, Mary Wollstonecraft's *Original Stories from Real Life* (1783) had argued that the rights of animals were to be placed alongside the rights of women. By the 1820s, the decade that saw the establishment of the Royal Society for the Prevention of Cruelty to Animals (1822–24), there was a larger cultural awareness of the need for sensitivity toward other species. And as late as

FIGURE 6 Linley Sambourne, cartoon of Octavia Hill, *Punch,* June 1883

1851, Maria Grey and Emily Shirreff's *Thoughts on Self-Culture, Addressed to Women* echoed Erasmus Darwin in reminding women that a part of the special self-culture that was gendered female involved teaching gentleness toward animals (see figure 7). Still, throughout the nineteenth century abuses toward animals and the environment proliferated, and the chorus of women's voices raised in protest swelled as the century progressed. By the 1890s, women were founders of or active in dozens of animal-rights organizations—for example, the Victoria Street Society to halt vivisection, which

FIGURE 7 A. C. H. Luxmoore, *Sympathy, Illustrated London News,* cover for 8 March 1873

was begun by Frances Power Cobbe in 1870, and the Royal Society of the Protection of Birds, a part of whose history will come into focus in the selections that follow.

Treating a large and complex topic, "Protecting" is divided into two subsections that shade into one another. The first includes various expressions of sensitivity toward other species and encompasses protests against blood sports and vivisection. The second offers various points of view with regard to conservation and is grouped according to some of the animals and plants in need of protection. Both sections include women who linked human rights to issues of preservation.

"Protecting" opens with an excerpt from Sarah Trimmer's *Fabulous Histories* (1786), an early example of the teaching of morality to youngsters through discussion of kindness toward animals. Here Trimmer's narrator carefully details for the fictional Benson children just how to treat both wild birds like a robin family and domesticated birds like a canary and thereby distinguishes a domestic/wild discrimination often made in this type of writing. Written at the end of the eighteenth century, when Europeans were beginning to keep pets in earnest and when there was a general interest in childhood education, Trimmer's popular book went through edition after edition and paved the way for other work anthologized in this section—Mary Sherwood's, for example. Like Trimmer, the prolific Sherwood was beloved in her day. Her *Soffrona and Her Cat Muff* (1828) carefully instructs children just how closely beneficence toward human life is connected to kindness toward animals. Young Soffrona needs to learn that a concentration on pets to the exclusion of needy human beings can be self-defeating. Despite her rescue of tiny Muff from rowdy boys, only by helping the elderly Martha does Soffrona find a way ultimately to help the little kitten.

If the stories by Trimmer and Sherwood focus on instruction of the young, Anne Brontë's novel *Agnes Grey* (1847) centers instead on the life of a governess who already knows the lessons learned by the Bensons and Saffrona. What decent but naïve Agnes still has to learn is a harder lesson involving human callousness and indifference. The parents of the unruly children Agnes is meant to govern have little respect for otherness of any sort, and that includes respect for Agnes herself. As a matter of fact, they and the children's uncle are actually opposed to the lesson in bird protection that Agnes takes for granted and tries to impart to their children. In contrast to this fictional family, Anne Brontë was herself tender-hearted and religious and especially sensitive to the needs of animals. A native of the moors, she watched her older sister Emily rescue and restore injured moorland creatures, some of which—like Emily Brontë's hawk, Hero—could never be returned to the wild. In "A Captive Dove," she reveals a personal disdain for captivity of any sort. In Brontë's day, captured birds like this dove were often snared, then sold by professional bird catchers such as the one reviled in Eliza Cook's short poem, "On Seeing a Bird-Catcher" (1869).

By the late 1870s interest in animal life had grown in England, and large audiences eagerly awaited stories about animals. Within months of its publication, Anna Sewell's famous novel, *Black Beauty* (1877), had, for example, sold over 91,000 copies. Excerpted in this section is the well-known episode involving Poor Ginger. It takes place late in the story, after the beautiful thoroughbred Black Beauty has been made a cab horse—an animal used to draw passenger vehicles in the cities. Here Black Beauty rediscovers his old acquaintance, Ginger, now an abused cab horse with little time left

FIGURE 8 *Black Beauty and Ginger Meet Again,* from *Black Beauty* (London: Jarrolds, 1922), p. 209

and less desire to live (see figure 8). Sewell permits Black Beauty—whose story is written as though it were his autobiography—to tell us the moral of this vignette straight from the horse's mouth: "Oh! if men were more merciful, they would shoot us before we came to such misery" (366).

The remaining selections in the section on sensitivity poetically deplore indifference or cruel disregard toward smaller, even more helpless creatures than the cart horses. Christina Rossetti's beautiful lyrics from *Sing-Song* (1872) all advise stewardship rather than abuse of the small and delicate in nature. In "On a Forsaken Lark's Nest" (1889), Mathilde Blind imagines her way into the eggs of a bird whose nest is destroyed by reaping. And Mary Howitt's "Cry of the Suffering Creatures" (1872) exhibits a deep religious commitment to otherness of all sorts. Howitt's animals, like the slaves whose freedom she also championed, are made to serve, and for this they too suffer more than they pose a threat through rebellion. If only people would try to understand animals rather than fear them, they might love rather than abuse them, suggests Howitt; such behavior on the part of human beings might even create a heaven on earth. Trimmer, Sherwood, Brontë,

Howitt—all these writers again remind us that for over a century women remained the appropriate teachers of both morality and religion, the two being intimately linked.

It took everything Brontë's Agnes Grey had to crush her charges' young birds with a stone so that they would not starve to death. But whereas middle-class women like the fictional Agnes might be shocked or appalled by animal abuse, many landed women hunted side by side with men in what have been classified as blood sports, those that resulted in the death of an animal like a fox. Since it conferred status, fox hunting in particular was a means to upward social mobility and a very popular pastime for Victorians and Edwardians. In this anthology riding to hounds is described by three separate writers from three distinct points of view. In the second passage from *Black Beauty,* we again see through the eyes of Beauty, this time when he is still a colt and witnesses the death of a rider and subsequent shooting of a horse—all because of someone's seemingly needless desire to give chase to a hare. Sewell's novel often turns on ironies and role reversals, imparting a wisdom and sensitivity found wanting in humans toward animals. Adopting a role normally attributed to people, Sewell's humane horse, for example, views hunting as a tragic waste of life, both human and animal.

So does Florence Dixie's "Horrors of Sport" (1892), which is autobiographical like *Black Beauty,* though certainly not fictional. Here Dixie offers her readers a true-life human conversion story. As a self-styled "Female Nimrod," well-to-do Dixie spent years riding to hounds and hunting on several continents. Full of reproach for her earlier life, she recants by confessing. For those unlike herself who cannot relinquish hunting, she recommends dragging an animal to provide a scent and enable a chase but not using a living animal like a fox. For her own part, Dixie vows she will never again "raise a gun or rifle to destroy the glorious Animal Life of Creation." Nor certainly would Mary Webb's animal-loving heroine, Hazel, in Webb's 1917 novel *Gone to Earth.* Hazel is deeply attached to a wild fox named Foxy. In the first passage reprinted here, Foxy awakens and reflects about the "death pack," the hounds that hunt and haunt her species. Webb's exquisite sensitivity toward Foxy is reflected both in passages like this and through the sensibility of Hazel, who in the end dies to save Foxy from the hunt. The final passage in this section describes the dual deaths of mistress and fox, when, in a futile effort to escape the pack, Hazel dashes toward a fatal fall with the frightened Foxy clutched to her breast.

In addition to teaching children to be humane and advocating the abandonment of cruel traditions like the hunt, women took a strong stand against vivisection—the dissection of living animals—which many Victorian and Edwardian women thought the ultimate form of cruelty to non-human creatures. Some even feared that what was practiced on animals might translate to what could be practiced on human beings. Physician Elizabeth Blackwell (1821–1910) and novelist Ouida (1831–1908), for example, both suggested that if vivisection were condoned, poor, sick, or disabled people might become the next victims of vivisection. Nevertheless, despite various kinds of protests against their work throughout the late nineteenth and early twentieth centuries, scientists continued arguing in favor of animal experimentation, understood to include vivisection. Then as now, vital breakthroughs were envisaged as the probable result of experimentation on the living, and vivisection continued more or less unabated up until the end of our time period. Outspoken opponents like feminist journalist Frances Power Cobbe were nevertheless shocked by the practice, which Cobbe believed created "an *agony* such as simple Nature never knew."[1] Criticized for her strong stand and jeered by medical students who also poked fun at the women in her audiences who cried over such agonies, the undaunted Cobbe continued objecting to vivisection. She had begun this work early, even before the 1870s, and throughout her long career developed many allies. Some of those allies, the mystic Anna Kingsford and the Roman Catholic cardinal Henry Manning, for example, made strange bedfellows for a rational journalist like Cobbe, but protectionists like Cobbe knew the importance of political coalitions.

The section on antivivisection presents a diversity of voices and points of view. Vernon Lee, for example, normally known for her aesthetics and not her political concerns, approaches vivisection as an evolutionist. Lee argues that far from advancing human society, the practice of vivisection retards the growth of the moral qualities by which humanity defines itself. Lee sees justice as the natural moral goal toward which humanity reaches. As an unjust means of acquiring scientific knowledge, vivisection works against moral progress of human society and as such impedes the evolution of humanity. Like Lee, Anna Kingsford also refers to the evolution of the human race as more than just a physical phenomenon. Kingsford's argument in the section from *Spiritual Therapeutics* (1883) excerpted here is more unabashedly religious and spiritual than is Lee's, but Kingsford, like the women whose work appears in "Sensitivity," opens a space for the discussion of the spiritual alongside the scientific. A physician herself, and one who was appalled by the vivisections she had witnessed in medical school,

1. "The Future of the Lower Animals," *The Modern Rack: Papers on Vivisection* (London: Swann Sonnenschein and Co., 1889), 91.

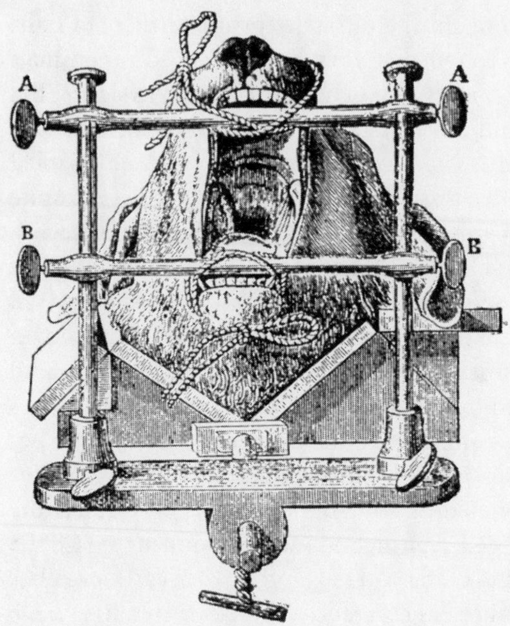

FIGURE 9 Illustration from Bernard's *Physiologie Opératoire,* from Frances Power Cobbe, *Light in Dark Places* (London: Victoria Street Society, 1896), p. 15

Kingsford closely examines the most common justification given by scientists for the practice of vivisection. She explains that although scientists try to argue within the realm of the materialistic and atheistic, they encounter a problem when they try to rationalize animal vivisection by emphasizing its contribution to the welfare of humanity as a higher species. Such a justification is logically flawed, for its reasoning defeats their purely materialist argument, which views the human race as just another species of animal. If there is in fact no materialist argument for the superiority of humankind, then there can be no need for humanity to utilize other animals in such a way. Like Frances Power Cobbe, Kingsford argues that science alone cannot justify an act of cruelty, for human society cannot be advanced by something that depletes its very humanity.

For her part, Cobbe did not much like Kingsford, who in her religious righteousness became a far more radical antivivisectionist than did Cobbe. In the end Kingsford vowed to will the deaths of eminent vivisectors like Claude Bernard and M. Paul Bert through her religious powers. In "Light in Dark Places," Cobbe included illustrations from Bernard's manuals (see figure 9) in order to provide readers with a look at what so distressed the antivivisectionists. Also reprinted here is a wicked spoof of vivisections,

"Science in Excelsis" (1889), wherein Cobbe resurrects a race of beings that are higher on the evolutionary scale than humans—the angels. Angels, of course, could be expected to act in ways morally superior to humanity, just as humans might suppose themselves morally superior to other animals. In this essay, Cobbe's angels therefore assume the same rights over humans that humans do over other animals. Inspired to pursue the study of human physiology for the sake of knowledge, they vivisect human vivisectors—performing experiments dictated by the humans' own laboratory manuals. What, the ironic Cobbe wonders, could be more just than that?

Vernon Lee mentions that it is easier to deny one's own natural sympathy when those who are supposed to act as role models—and as model citizens—are practicing cruel acts of vivisection without remorse. Louise Lind-af-Hageby and Liese Schartau's *The Shambles of Science* (1903) also calls for a reevaluation of a revered role model—the medical professor. In "Fun," Lind-af-Hageby and Schartau describe in graphic detail a vivisection they witnessed in medical school. In this case, students were deterred from sympathy for a dog that was obviously wide awake, terrified, and suffering tremendously. As described by the two women, the laboratory theater was devoid of any consideration for the dog's pain. Instead, the room was pervaded by a perverse spirit of jocularity, fueled by the personality of the charming and entertaining professor. It was a similar spirit—not uncommon in medical schools—that had shocked Kingsford when she sat in lecture halls and that had tested Cobbe when she lectured against vivisection.

In the first decade of the twentieth century, however, the vivisected dog of "Fun" became the subject of a controversy that actually led to rioting in London's Battersea area. Lind-af-Hageby and Schartau's mention of wounds on the dog from a prior vivisection and their suggestion that the dog was not properly anesthetized both indicated that the vivisection described in "Fun" was not performed in accordance with the Vivisection Act, which allowed an animal to be vivisected only once. The women were convinced to testify to this effect, and the professors were accused of breaking the law. Unfortunately for the two women, their statements could not be proven, and the chapter called "Fun" had to be removed from later editions of *The Shambles.* Public sympathy remained with the dog, however, until a statue was erected in its honor in Battersea Park engraved with an inscription condemning the professors and affirming the statements of Lind-af-Hageby and Schartau. A suit to have the inscription removed followed. Then, a group of medical students, led by Joseph Lister (1827–

1912)—discoverer of antiseptic surgery—destroyed the statue in the night, and rioting ensued.[2]

Turning from this brand of active protesting and more toward persuasion, the remainder of "Protecting" is devoted to women actively engaged in the conservation of animals and natural resources. The section on conservation opens with the protection of birds. Because birds were widely used in the decoration of women's hats at the end of the nineteenth century, a number of women made bird protection a women's issue. The section on birds begins with a tribute by Eliza Cook, who wrote large numbers of bird poems that attempted to characterize birds from the inside out in order to gain greater sympathy for them. It then briefly crosses the Atlantic in order to suggest something of the international scope of the movement for bird preservation. In America, efforts toward bird protection paralleled those in England, where the Royal Society for the Protection of Birds supported the cause of the American egret both through its pamphlets and through efforts like the sandwich board protest of 1911 (see figure 10). The American Audubon Society was established in 1905 and also worked toward the protection of egrets and the end of feathered millinery. To my mind, one of the most haunting of American writings on this subject came not from the polemicists, however, but from novelist Sara Orne Jewett. Jewett's short story, "A White Heron," tells of a young woman's coming of age and her crucial decision to protect a white heron from a bird collector. In order to save the bird, Sylvia must relinquish the favors of the young male hunter who seeks the bird. For this isolated, impoverished girl, this is a painful choice.

Returning to England, "Protecting" turns to two of the many women who attended the International Congress of Women in 1899. Both Winifred, Duchess of Portland, and Margaretta Lemon devoted much of their lives to the protection of birds, a campaign that, by the time of the international congress, had been under way for more than three decades and would continue for years to come. Birds, especially seabirds, had been used in the decoration of hats worn by the British military as well as those donned by fashionable women (see figure 11). Once seabirds were protected by the Sea Birds Protection Act of 1869, milliners turned to other species, primarily imported birds. By the time that the Society for the Protection of Birds (SPB) was established in 1889 (it received a royal charter in 1904 and was renamed the Royal Society for the Protection of Birds), an entire industry—known as the bird trade—had come to depend on the continuation of this

2. For further discussion of this moment in history, see Coral Lansbury's *The Old Brown Dog: Women, Workers, and Vivisection in Edwardian England* (Madison: University of Wisconsin Press, 1985).

FIGURE 10 Sandwich board protest on behalf of egret, 1911

fashion. In the 1880s, in only one year's time, over 400,000 West Indian and South American and 350,000 East Indian birds were sold on the London market (see figure 12). This state of affairs prompted the founding of the society, whose first members included both Lemon and the Duchess of Portland.

The International Congress of Women had designated an entire session to protecting bird and animal life; the Duchess of Portland (figure 14) opened the session in the speech excerpted here. The duchess was the first president of the SPB, an office she loyally held for over sixty-five years. Like Frances Power Cobbe, Portland here urges women to hold to their tenderheartedness as a strength, not a weakness, and to continue their necessary work on behalf of the liberty of animals. Her cofounder and coworker at the SPB, Margaretta Lemon, followed upon the Duchess of Portland's introduction, eloquently elaborating on the duchess's statements and focusing upon what she considered the most important issue: the loss of ornamental birds through the bird trade. In her speech, Lemon is careful to credit the men who helped the women of the SPB to accomplish their goals. Throughout the history of this organization—and Lemon was the SPB's historian—this attitude was a given. Although the organization was always managed by women, it had many male allies and always gave these allies full credit either for being experts or for being supporters.

FIGURE 11 Linley Sambourne, cartoon of a protest against the slaughter of egrets for women's hats, *Punch,* September 1899

The section on birds concludes as it began, with fiction, this time with Mary Webb's short story, "The Cuckoo Clock," a clever piece that turns the tables on its protagonist, a young male hunter of birds' eggs. He too is a collector, a conspicuous consumer of eggs for his new egg cabinet. Tried for his crimes by a tribunal of birds, he stands condemned and in a surprise ending is confined in a manner befitting one who so avidly hunted birds' eggs simply in order to encase them.

Turning from the birds of the sky to the life of the land, the next selections reveal that from the beginning, women were in the forefront of the movement for land conservation. Mary Russell Mitford's narrator in *Our Village* (1826) finds a walk in the wood an occasion to comment, journal-style, on human beings and their pets, wild animals and their protection, wildflowers, and the tragedy of the felling of trees. Mitford's selection is followed by an essay from the pen of Octavia Hill, one of the founders of the

Society for the Protection of Birds.—No. 20. *16th to 20th thousand.*

[Illustration from the "Royal Natural History," by kind permission of Messrs. Fredk. Warne & Co.]

THE BIRD OF PARADISE.

THE month of May, 1895, was the culminating point of a deplorable fashion in London. Few bonnets and hats were to be seen without the adornment of a graceful spray of soft, fine plumes, with drooping or curly tips. These beautiful "Bird of Paradise" feathers could be purchased in quantities at every milliner's shop, and the assurance that they were real, which there is little reason to doubt, could usually be elicited. Mixed in the same spray, and forming a contrast to these soft plumes, might be seen the delicate Osprey tips, which, to the shame of womanhood, have so long been in fashion, and, in spite of the indisputable cruelty involved in obtaining them, are still largely used. It can be stated on reliable authority that, during the season, one warehouse alone of the many that are engaged in the traffic so detrimental to bird life, disposed of no less than 60,000 dozens of these mixed sprays. What can be more significant of the wholesale destruction which this fashion involves, than the impression which is prevalent throughout the trade that it must soon disappear, as the supply of birds is almost exhausted?

FIGURE 12 First page, pamphlet 20, Royal Society for the Protection of Birds (c. 1895)

National Trust for Historic Sites and Natural Scenery. The famous writer Beatrix Potter, by the way, followed in Hill's footsteps, in the end using some of the royalties from her books to preserve property in the English Lake District and offer it to the National Trust. Hill's essay, "Our Common Land," was a political document, a plea for the passage of a bill to promote open spaces for the public. Hill here realizes the pitfalls of such a bill—the landed have little incentive to provide space for others—but argues brilliantly for its passage by reminding her readers-listeners of the human need for holidays away from cities and smoke and fatigue. Edith Nesbit (figure 15) too finds charity toward others' needs as the "one thing needful." Civilization, she argues, takes a huge toll on human resources, especially spiritual resources. It is a restoration of the spirit that human beings most need. Her essay therefore calls for a different kind of education. Nesbit believed that the inclusion of moral education along with scientific learning must become a primary aim of Edwardian educators—much as it was of those earlier women included at the beginning of "Protecting."

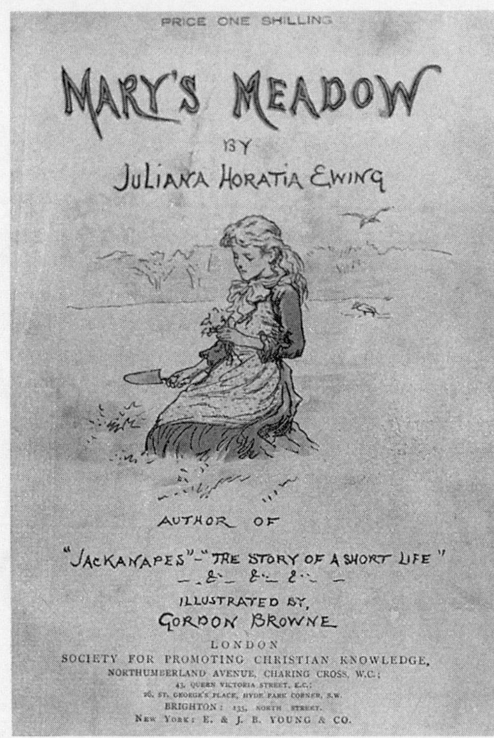

FIGURE 13 Cover, Juliana Ewing, *Mary's Meadow*

Juliana Horatia Ewing (figure 16), like her famous mother, Margaret Gatty, the science popularizer, aimed to provide such education through her short stories. In her famous *Mary's Meadow* (see figure 13), she showed how children might save a meadow by providing it with rare flowers and thereby forcing its protection. The story became so well known that people began "Mary meadowing," or beautifying and planting what seemed to be waste spaces (rather like the roadside seeding and planting one sees today). It also led to the establishment of the Parkinson Society for Lovers of Hardy Flowers, an association that "meadowed" and worked to preserve vanishing species of plants. In "Our Field" (1911), the short story by Ewing reprinted here, a group of children saves an abandoned dog by assembling plant collections from a field and then winning monetary prizes for the collections. In so doing, they create a small ecosystem and microeconomy of children, animals, and plants—all stemming from a neglected field whose owner is unknown. They also echo Ewing's own belief that land is not owned but held in trust and that all must behave as stewards toward it, something similar to Octavia

Hill's belief that "buttercups are more abidingly beautiful and blessed than sovereigns."[3]

Such ideas were not new in Ewing's day; they had only become more pressing by then, and they would continue to be. As in the case of our first selection on land and plants, trees garner a final word of sympathy in Charlotte Mew's "The Trees Are Down" (1929), written a hundred years after Mitford's *Our Village.* The free verse of the talented Mew echoes the deep concern of her latter-day narrator, who, on a beautiful May day, would not even wish a rat dead. Acts like felling plane trees "unmake" spring with the magnitude of their destruction. This last plea for protecting other species asks the reader's heart to beat in time with the sympathetic narrator's as with those of the angels who cry all day over the loss of one of nature's grandest forms.

3. *The Life of Octavia Hill as Told in Her Letters,* ed. C. Edmund Maurice (London: Macmillan, 1913), 333.

Sensitivity to Other Species

SARAH TRIMMER

From *Fabulous Histories, Designed for the Instruction of Children, Respecting Their Treatment of Animals*

London: T. Longman, G. G. J. and J. Robinson, 1786. 28–35.

Robin was a very strong robust bird, not remarkable for his beauty, but there was a great briskness in his manner, which covered many defects, and he was very likely to attract notice. His father judged, from the tone of his chirpings, that he would be a very good songster.

Dicky had a remarkably fine plumage, his breast was of a beautiful red, his body and wings of an elegant mottled brown, and his eyes sparkled like diamonds.

Flapsy was also very pretty, but more distinguished for the elegance of her shape, than for the variety and lustre of her feathers.

Pecksy had no outward charms to recommend her to notice; but these defects were amply supplied by the sweetness of her disposition, which was amiable to the greatest degree. Her temper was constantly serene, she was ever attentive to the happiness of her parents, and would not have grieved them for the world, and her affection for her brothers and sister was so great, that she constantly preferred their interest to her own, of which we lately gave an instance.

The kind parents attended to them with unremitting affection, and made their daily visit to Master and Miss Benson, who very punctually discharged the benevolent office of feeding them. The Robin Redbreasts, familiarized by repeated favours, approached nearer and nearer to their little friends by degrees, and at length ventured to enter the room and feed upon the breakfast-table. Miss Harriet was delighted at this circumstance, and

Frederick was quite transported; he longed to catch the birds, but his mamma told him, that it would be very mean and to drive them away. Miss Harriet entreated him not to frighten them on any account, and he was prevailed on to forbear; but could not help expressing a wish that he had them in a cage, that he might feed them all day long.

And do you really think, Frederick, said Mrs. Benson, that these little delicate creatures are such gluttons, as to desire to be fed all day long? Could you tempt them to do it, they would soon die; but they know better, and as soon as their appetites are satisfied, always leave off eating. Many a little boy may learn a lesson from them. Do not you recollect one of your acquaintance, who, if an apple-pie, or any thing else that he calls nice, is set before him, will eat till he makes himself sick? Frederick looked ashamed, being conscious that he was too much inclined to indulge his love of delicacies. Well, said his mamma, I see you understand who I mean, Frederick, so we will say no more on that subject; only, when you meet with that little Gentleman, give my love to him, and tell him, I beg he will be as moderate as his Redbreasts.

The cock bird having finished his breakfast, flew out at the window, followed by his mate; and as soon as they were out of sight, Mrs. Benson continued her discourse. And would you really confine these sweet creatures in a cage, Frederick, merely to have the pleasure of looking at them? Should you like to be always shut in a little room, and think it sufficient if you were supplied with victuals and drink? Is there no enjoyment in running about, jumping, and going from place to place? Do you not like to associate with little boys and girls? And is there no pleasure in breathing the fresh air? Though these little animals are inferior to you, there is no doubt but they are capable of enjoyments similar to these; and it must be a dreadful life for a poor bird to be shut up in a cage, where he cannot so much as make use of his wings—where he is excluded from his natural companions—and where he cannot possibly receive that refreshment, which the air must afford to him when at liberty to soar to such a height. But this is not all, for many a poor bird is caught, and separated from its family, after it has been at the trouble of building a nest—has perhaps laid its eggs—or even hatched its young ones, which are by this means exposed to inevitable destruction. It is likely that these very Redbreasts may have young ones, for this is the season of the year for their hatching; and I rather think they have, from the circumstance of their always coming together. If that is the case, said Miss Harriet, it would be pity indeed to confine them.—But why, mamma, if it is wrong to catch birds, did you at one time keep Canaries? The case is very different in respect to Canaries, my dear, said Mrs. Benson. By keeping them in a cage, I do them a kindness. I consider them as little foreigners who claim my hospitality. This kind of bird came originally from a warm climate, they are in their nature very susceptible of cold, and would perish in the open air in our winters: neither does the food which they feed on grow plentifully in this country; and as they are always here bred in cages, they do not know how to procure the materials for their nests abroad. And there is another particular which would greatly distress them were they to be turned loose, which is, the ridicule and contempt they would be exposed to from other birds. I remember once to have seen a poor Canary, which had been turned loose because it could not sing; and surely no creature could be more miserable. It was starving for want of victuals, famishing with thirst, shivering with cold, and looked terrified to the greatest degree; whilst a parcel of Sparrows and Chaffinches pursued it from place to place, twittering and chirping with every mark of insolence and derision. I could not help fancying the little creature to be like a foreigner just landed from some distant country, followed by a rude rabble of boys, who were ridiculing him, because his dress and language were strange to them.

And what became of the poor little creature, mamma? said Miss Harriet. I was going to tell you, my dear, replied Mrs. Benson. I ordered the servant to bring me a cage, with feed and water in their usual places; this I caused to be hung on a tree, next to that in which the little sufferer in vain endeavoured to hide himself amongst the leaves from his cruel pursuers. No sooner did the servant retire, than the poor little wretch flew to it. I immediately had the cage brought into the parlour, where I experienced great pleasure in observing what happiness the poor creature enjoyed in her deliverance. I kept it some years, but not chusing to confine her in a *little* cage, had a *large* one bought, and procured a companion for her of her own species. I supplied them with materials for building, and from them proceeded a little colony, which grew so numerous, that you know I gave them to Mr. F. to put in his aviary, where you have seen them enjoying themselves. So now I hope I have fully accounted for having kept Canary birds in a cage. You have indeed, mamma, said Harriet. I have also, said Mrs. Benson, occasionally kept Larks. In severe winters vast numbers of them come to this country from a colder climate, and many perish. Quantities of them are killed and sold for the spit, and the bird catchers usually have a great many to fell, and many an idle boy has some to dispose of. I frequently buy them, as you know, Harriet, but as soon as the fine weather returns, I constantly set them at liberty. But come, my dears, prepare for your morning walk, and afterwards let me see you in my dressing-room.

I wonder, said Frederick, whether our Redbreasts have got a nest? I will watch to-morrow which way they fly, for I should like to see the little ones. And what will you do should you find them out? said his mamma. Not take the nest, I hope? Why, replied Frederick, I should like to bring it home, mamma, and put it in a tree near the house, and then I would scatter crumbs for the old ones to feed them with. Your design is a kind one, said Mrs. Benson, but would greatly distress your little favourites. Many birds, through fear, forsake their nests, when they are removed, therefore I desire you to let them alone if you should chance to find them. Miss Harriet then remarked, that she thought it very cruel to take birds' nests. Ah! my dear, said Mrs. Benson, those who commit such barbarous actions, are quite insensible to the distresses they occasion. It is very true, that we ought not to indulge so great a degree of pity and tenderness for such animals, as for those who are more properly our fellow-creatures; I mean men, women, and children; but as every living creature can feel, we should have a constant regard to those feelings, and strive to give happiness, rather than inflict misery. But go, my dear, and take your walk. Mrs. Benson then left them, to attend her usual morning employments; and the young Lady and Gentleman, attended by their maid, passed an agreeable half hour in the garden.

MARY MARTHA SHERWOOD

From *Soffrona and Her Cat Muff*

London: Houlston and Son, 1828. 6–31.

. . . Soffrona and Sophia lived in a very lovely house, surrounded with woods. Wherever you looked from the windows of that house, you might see trees growing thickly together, forming beautiful arbours, and pleasant shades, with little paths winding about among those trees; and here and there, near the trees, were fountains of water springing from the hills, and running down into the valleys: for there were hills there, and the tops of some of them were covered all through the winter with snow, though in summer they appeared green or blue, according to the time of year, and wore a very pleasant aspect.

Soffrona and Sophia were allowed to play in these woods, and they had learned to run and skip upon the hills like young fawns. It was very pleasing to see them, and they found many treasures in those wild places which children who have never been in woods have no idea of. They found snail-shells, and painting-stones, and wild strawberries, and bilberries, and walnuts, and hazel nuts, and beautiful moss, and many kinds of flowers; and there they heard birds sing—cuckoos, and linnets, and blackbirds, and thrushes; and saw beautiful butterflies with gold and purple plumes, and dragon-flies, whose wings look like fine silk net.

One morning in the month of May, Soffrona and Sophia had leave given to them to play in the woods, after they had finished their lessons, and they took a basket with them, to bring home any treasures which they might find. And they went a long way through the woods,—I dare say as much as half a mile,—till they came to a place where an old tree had been blown down by the side of a brook; and there they sat down, and each of them took a little penny book to read out of their basket: and while they were reading, they heard a noise of boys shouting and laughing, and they jumped up and hid themselves behind some bushes.

So the boys came nearer, and went down close to the water's side; and the little girls heard them say one to another, "Let us put it in the deepest place, where it cannot scramble out." And they saw the boys stoop over the water and put something into it, and at the same time they heard a very young kitten cry; and the two little girls could not stop themselves from screaming out, quite loud, from the midst of the bushes, saying, "Wicked, cruel boys! what are you doing?"

Now the boys heard the cries of the little girls; and, as the Bible says, *The wicked flee when no man pursueth;* (Prov. xxviii. 1.) so they all took to their heels, and ran away as fast as they could, leaving the poor little kitten in the water.

Soffrona and Sophia did not lose one moment after the boys were gone, but ran to the brook, and found the little kitten almost dead. However, they got it out, though they wet themselves up to the knees in so doing, and they returned to the tree, and Soffrona sat down, and laid it upon her lap, while Sophia wiped it dry; and as she rubbed it, she found warmth returning to its little body, and presently it opened its eyes and began to mew. "O my dear little Puss!" said Soffrona, "how very glad I am that you are not dead! You shall be my Puss, and I will call you Muff. Will you let her be mine, Sophia? Will you give me your share of her?"

. . . So it was agreed that the kitten should belong to Soffrona, and be called Muff; and when the little girls had dried it as well as they could, they put it into the basket upon some soft moss, and ran home with it.

The lady was not angry with them for having wetted themselves in the brook to save a poor little animal's life, but she hastened to change their clothes; and then they took the kitten out of the basket, and procured some milk to feed it with.

When the fur of the little cat was quite dry, it was seen that she was very beautifully marked. Her legs, and face, and breast, were quite white, and her back was streaked with yellow and black; so that she appeared like a fine polished tortoise-shell. But she was only nine or ten days old, and was not able to lap milk; and this was a great grief to Soffrona and Sophia, for they feared that although she had been saved from the water, she would surely die of hunger. The little girls tried to force milk down her throat with a spoon; but the milk ran down the outside of her mouth, instead of the inside of her throat, and the little creature's sides became quite hollow for want of nourishment.

Soffrona was thinking of nothing but Muff all the evening, and she kept her on her lap while she was reading and while she was eating her supper. She was, indeed, so much occupied by her little kitten, that, when the lady asked her to help to make a flannel petticoat for a poor old woman who lived in a cottage among the hills, not very far off, she took the needle in her hand, it is true, but I do not think that she took twenty stitches; for she was looking down every minute upon the kitten on her lap: and the petticoat would not have been done that night, if Sophia had not been doubly diligent.

Now it was much to be wished that the petticoat should be done that night; for it was intended for a good old woman who lived in the woods, a very poor woman indeed, and the March winds had given her great pain in her limbs, and she was in much need of a warm petticoat; and, more than that, the lady had promised the little girls the pleasure of taking the petticoat, with some tea and sugar, the next morning, after they had repeated their lessons, to the cottage. But, as I before said, Soffrona's heart was with her kitten, and she could think of nothing else, and of no other creature. She had no pity left for the old woman, so much was she thinking of little Muff. We ought to be kind to animals; but our first affections should be given to our Maker, our second to our fellow-creatures, and our third to any poor animals which may be in our power.

The last thing Soffrona did in the evening, was to try to put some milk down Muff's throat, and this was the first thing she did in the morning: and so far she did right, for the poor little thing depended on her. But when she had done all she could for Muff, she should have given her mind to her other duties; but she could not command herself to attend to any thing else all that morning, and learned her lessons so ill, that, if the lady had not been very indulgent, she would have deprived her of the pleasure of walking with Sophia to see the old woman, and to carry the petticoat.

There was a neat little maid-servant, called Jane, who used to walk out with Sophia and Soffrona when they had a long way to go; and Jane was ready waiting for the little girls by the time the lessons were done.

Sophia had asked leave to carry the basket with the petticoat and the tea and sugar; and Soffrona took another basket, and put a bit of flannel at the bottom of it, and laid Muff in it, and tied the cover over it; and when Sophia took up her basket to carry, Soffrona also put her arm under the handle of Muff's basket, and went down stairs with it.

When they were got out of the house, Jane said, "What, have you two baskets, young ladies, full of good things, to carry to old Martha? Well, I am very glad; for she is a good and pious old woman."

Soffrona coloured, but did not answer; and Sophia smiled, and said, "She has not got any thing for the old woman in her basket: she has only got Muff, wrapped in flannel, in it."

"O, Miss!" said Jane, "how can you think of doing such a thing? What a trouble it will be to you to carry the kitten all the way! and we have two miles to walk, and most of it up hill. Please to let me carry the kitten back to the house."

"No, no, Jane," said Soffrona, "no, you shall not."

"*Shall* not, Miss!" said Jane: "is that a pretty word?"

Soffrona looked very cross, and Jane was turning back to complain to the lady: but Sophia entreated her not to do it; and Soffrona submitted to ask her pardon for being rude, and promised to behave better, if she would permit her to carry the kitten where she was going. So that matter was settled, and Jane and the little girls proceeded.

I could tell you much about the pretty places through which they passed in going to poor Martha's cottage, which were quite new to the little girls. They first went through some dark woods, where the trees met over their heads like the arches in a church; and then they came to a dingle, where water was running at the bottom, and they crossed the water by a wooden bridge; then they had to climb up such a steep, such a very steep hill, covered with bushes; then they came to a high field surrounded with trees, and in a corner of that field was old Martha's thatched cottage. It was a poor place: the walls were black-and-white, and there were two windows, one of which was in the thatch, and one below, and a door, half of which was open; for it was such a door as you see in cottages, the lower part of which can be shut while the other is open. There was a little smoke coming out of the chimney, for Martha was cooking her potatoes for her dinner.

"Do you think Martha has any milk in her house?" said Soffrona; "for poor Muff must be very hungry by this time."

"I fear not," replied Jane: "but come, young ladies, we have been a long time getting up this hill, and we must be at home by three o'clock."

So they went on, and came close to the door, and stood there a little while, looking in. They saw within the cottage a very small kitchen; but it was neat, and there was nothing out of its place. There was a wide chimney in the kitchen; and in the chimney a fire of sticks, over which hung a little kettle. Old Martha was sitting on a stool within the chimney. She was dressed in a blue petticoat and jacket, and had a high crowned, old-fashioned felt hat on her head, and a coarse clean check handkerchief on her neck. Before her was a spinning-wheel, which she was turning very diligently, for she could not see to do any work besides spinning; and by the fire, on the hob, sad a fine tortoise-shell cat, which was the old woman's only companion.

"O!" cried little Soffrona, "there is a cat! I see a cat!"

"Dear, Miss," said Jane, "you can think of nothing but cats."

"Well, Jane," answered Sophia, "and if she is fond of cats, is there any harm in it?"

Jane could make no answer, for by this time old Martha had seen them, and came halting on her crutch to meet them, and to offer them all the seats in her house; and these were only a three-legged stool and two old chairs.

Sophia then presented the old woman with what she had brought from her mamma, and Jane gave her a bottle of medicine from her pocket: and the old woman spoke of the goodness of Almighty God, who had put it into the lady's heart to provide her with what she needed most in this world.

Now, while Sophia and Jane and Martha were looking over the things which the lady had sent, the old cat had left the hob, and had come to Soffrona, and was staring wildly, and mewing in a strange way round the basket; and at the same time the kitten within began to mew. "Puss! Puss! pretty Puss!" said Soffrona, for she was half afraid of this large cat, and yet at the same time very well inclined to form a friendship with her.

At length, those that were with her in the cottage saw what was passing; and Martha said, "Don't be afraid, Miss; Tibby won't hurt you. Poor thing! she is in great trouble, and has been so ever since yesterday."

"What trouble?" said Soffrona.

"Some rude boys came in yesterday, and stole her kitten," replied

Martha. "I was in the wood, picking a few sticks, and left the door open; and the boys came in, and ran away with the kitten; and the poor cat has been moaning and grieving like a human being,—poor dumb thing,—ever since. The cruel lads! I saw them go down the hill!"

"O!" said Soffrona, "and I do believe"

"And I am sure," said Sophia.

"And I am so glad!" said Soffrona.

"And how happy she will be!" said Sophia.

And Soffrona immediately set down her basket and opened it, and put the little kitten on the floor, for the kitten was indeed poor Tibby's kitten.

It was a pretty sight, an agreeable and pleasant sight, to behold the joy of the old cat when she saw her kitten. The poor creature seemed as if she would have talked. Martha took up the kitten, and laid it on a little bit of mat in the corner of the chimney, where it used to be; and the old cat ran to it, and lay down by it, and gave it milk, and licked it, and talked to it in her way, (that is, in the way that cats use to their kittens,) and purred so loud, that you might have heard her to the very end of the cottage. It was a pleasant sight, as I said before, for it is a pleasure to see any thing happy; and Soffrona jumped and capered about the house, and knew not how sufficiently to express her joy: and as for little Sophia, her eyes were filled with tears; and poor old Martha was not the least happy of the party.

And now, when it was time to go, Soffrona took up her empty basket, and giving the kitten a kiss, "Little Puss," she said, "I will rejoice in your happiness, though it will be a loss to me, for I must part with my little darling. But I will not be selfish: mamma says that I can never make myself happy by making other things miserable. Good-bye, little Puss: if God will help me, I will try never to be selfish." And she walked out of the cottage, wiping away her tears.

"But you will let her have Muff, won't you, Martha," said Sophia, "when her mother has brought her up, and can part with her?"

"To be sure I will, dear Miss," replied Martha; "for I was delighted to hear her say that she knew she never could make herself happy by making others miserable."

When Muff was a quarter old, she was brought to Soffrona, and became her cat, and lived in her service till her yellow and black hairs were mingled with grey.

ANNE BRONTË

"The Uncle"

Agnes Grey. 1847. Ed. Ian Jack. Oxford: Clarendon Press, 1988. 42–46.

Besides the old lady, there was another relative of the family, whose visits were a great annoyance to me—this was "uncle Robson," Mrs. Bloomfield's brother, a tall, self-sufficient fellow, with dark hair and sallow complexion like his sister, a nose that seemed to disdain the earth, and little grey eyes, frequently half closed, with a mixture of real stupidity and affected contempt of all surrounding objects. He was a thick-set, strongly built man, but he had found some means of compressing his waist into a remarkably small compass, and that, together with the unnatural stiffness of his form, showed that the lofty-minded, manly Mr. Robson, the scorner of the female sex, was not above the foppery of stays.

He seldom deigned to notice me; and, when he did, it was with a certain supercilious insolence of tone and manner that convinced me he was no gentleman, though it was intended to have a contrary effect. But it was not for that I disliked his coming, so much as for the harm he did the children—encouraging all their evil propensities, and undoing, in a few minutes, the little good it had taken me months of labour to achieve.

Fanny and little Harriet, he seldom condescended to notice; but Mary Ann was something of a favourite. He was continually encouraging her tendency to affectation, (which I had done my utmost to crush,) talking about her pretty face, and filling her head with all manner of conceited notions concerning her personal appearance, (which I had instructed her to regard as dust in the balance compared with the cultivation of her mind and manners); and I never saw a child so susceptible of flattery as she was. Whatever was wrong, in either her or her brother, he would encourage by laughing at, if not by actually praising; and people little know the injury they do to children by laughing at their faults, and making a pleasant jest of what their true friends have endeavoured to teach them to hold in grave abhorrence.

Though not a positive drunkard, Mr. Robson habitually swallowed great quantities of wine, and took with relish an occasional glass of brandy and water. He taught his nephew to imitate him in this to the utmost of his ability, and to believe that the more wine and spirits he could take, and the better he liked them, the more he manifested his bold and manly spirit, and rose superior to his sisters. Mr. Bloomfield had not much to say against it, for *his* favourite beverage was gin and water, of which he took a considerable portion every day, by dint of constant sipping—and to that, I chiefly attributed his dingy complexion and waspish temper.

Mr. Robson likewise encouraged Tom's propensity to persecute the lower creation, both by precept and example. As he frequently came to course or shoot over his brother-in-law's grounds, he would bring his favourite dogs with him, and he treated them so brutally that, poor as I was, I would have given a sovereign any day to see one of them bite him, provided the animal could have done it with impunity. Sometimes, when in a very complacent mood, he would go a-bird-nesting with the children, a thing that irritated and annoyed me exceedingly, as, by frequent and persevering attempts, I flattered myself I had partly shown them the evil of this pastime, and hoped, in time, to bring them to some general sense of justice and humanity; but ten minutes' bird-nesting with uncle Robson, or even a laugh from him at some relation of their former barbarities, was sufficient, at once, to destroy the effect of my whole elaborate course of reasoning and persuasion. Happily, however, during that Spring, they never, but once, got anything but empty nests, or eggs—being too impatient to leave them till the birds were hatched; that once, Tom, who had been with his uncle into the neighbouring plantation, came running in high glee into the garden with a brood of little callow nestlings in his hands.

Mary Ann and Fanny, whom I was just bringing out, ran to admire his spoils, and to beg each a bird for themselves.

"No, not one!" cried Tom. "They're all mine: uncle Robson gave them to me—one, two, three, four, five—you shan't touch one of them! no, not one for your lives!" continued he, exultantly, laying the nest on the ground, and standing over it, with his legs wide apart, his hands thrust into his breeches-pockets, his body bent forward, and his face twisted into all manner of contortions in the ecstacy of his delight.

"But you shall see me fettle 'em off. My word, but I *will* wallop 'em! See if I don't now! By gum! but there's rare sport for me in that nest."

"But, Tom," said I, "I shall not allow you to torture those birds. They must either be killed at once, or carried back to the place you took them from, that the old birds may continue to feed them."

"But you don't know where that is, madam. It's only me and uncle Robson that knows that."

"But if you don't tell me, I shall kill them myself—much as I hate it."

"You daren't. You daren't touch them for your life! because you know papa and mama and uncle Robson would be angry. Ha, hah! I've caught you there, Miss!"

"I shall do what I think right in a case of this sort, without consulting any one. If your papa and mama don't happen to approve of it, I shall be sorry to offend them, but your uncle Robson's opinions, of course, are nothing to me."

So saying—urged by a sense of duty—at the risk of both making myself sick, and incurring the wrath of my employers—I got a large flat stone, that had been reared up for a mouse-trap by the gardener, then, having once more vainly endeavoured to persuade the little tyrant to let the birds be carried back, I asked what he intended to do with them. With fiendish glee he commenced a list of torments, and while he was busied in the relation, I dropped the stone upon his intended victims, and crushed them flat beneath it.

Loud were the outcries, terrible the execrations, consequent upon this daring outrage; uncle Robson had been coming up the walk with his gun, and was, just then, pausing to kick his dog. Tom flew towards him, vowing he would make him kick me instead of Juno. Mr. Robson leant upon his gun, and laughed excessively at the violence of his nephew's passion, and the bitter maledictions and opprobrious epithets he heaped upon me.

"Well, you *are* a good un!" exclaimed he, at length, taking up his weapon, and proceeding towards the house. "Damme, but the lad has some spunk in him too! Curse me, if ever I saw a nobler little scoundrel than that! He's beyond petticoat government already:—by G——, he defies mother, granny, governess, and all! Ha, ha, ha! Never mind, Tom, I'll get you another brood to-morrow."

"If you do, Mr. Robson, I shall kill them too," said I.

"Humph!" replied he, and having honoured me with a broad stare, which, contrary to his expectations, I sustained without flinching, he turned away with an air of supreme contempt, and stalked into the house.

Tom next went to tell his mama. It was not her way to say much on any subject; but, when she next saw me, her aspect and demeanour were doubly dark and chill.

After some casual remark about the weather, she observed—

"I am sorry, Miss Grey, you should think it necessary to interfere with Master Bloomfield's amusements; he was *very* much distressed about your destroying the birds."

"When Master Bloomfield's amusements consist in injuring sentient creatures," I answered, "I think it my duty to interfere."

"You seemed to have forgotten," said she, calmly, "that the creatures were all created for our convenience."

I thought that doctrine admitted some doubt, but merely replied—

"If they were, we have no right to torment them for our amusement."

"I think," said she, "a child's amusement is scarcely to be weighed against the welfare of a soulless brute."

"But, for the child's own sake, it ought not to be encouraged to have such amusements," answered I, as meekly as I could, to make up for such unusual pertinacity.

> "Blessed are the merciful, for they shall obtain mercy."

"Oh, of course! but that refers to our conduct toward each other."

> "The merciful man shews mercy to his beast,"

I ventured to add.

"I think *you* have not shewn much mercy," replied she, with a short, bitter laugh; "killing the poor birds by wholesale, in that shocking manner, and putting the dear boy to such misery, for a mere whim!"

I judged it prudent to say no more.

ANNE BRONTË

"The Captive Dove"

October 31, 1843. *The Poems of Anne Brontë: A New Text and Commentary.* Totowa, NJ: Rowman and Littlefield, 1979. 92–93.

Poor restless Dove, I pity thee,
And when I hear thy plaintive moan
I'll mourn for thy captivity
And in thy woes forget mine own.

To see thee stand prepared to fly,
And flap those useless wings of thine,
And gaze into the distant sky
Would melt a harder heart than mine.

In vain! In vain! Thou canst not rise—
Thy prison roof confines thee there;
Its slender wires delude thine eyes,
And quench thy longing with despair.

O! thou wert made to wander free
In sunny mead and shady grove,
And far beyond the rolling sea
In distant climes at will to rove.

Yet hadst thou but one gentle mate
Thy little drooping heart to cheer
And share with thee thy captive state,
Thou couldst be happy even there.

Yes, even there, if listening by
One faithful dear companion stood,
While gazing on her full bright eye
Thou mightst forget thy native wood.

But thou, poor solitary dove,
Must make unheard thy joyless moan;
The heart that nature formed to love
Must pine neglected and alone.

ELIZA COOK

"On Seeing a Bird-Catcher"

The Poetical Works. London: Frederick Warne and Co., 1869. 126.

Health in his rags, Content upon his face,
He goes th' enslaver of a feathered race:
And cunning snares, warm hearts, like warblers, take;
The one to sing for sport, the other, break.

ANNA SEWELL

"Poor Ginger"

Black Beauty. 1877. London: J. A. Allen, 1989. 362–66.

One day, whilst our cab and many others were waiting outside one of the parks, where a band was playing, a shabby old cab drove up beside ours. The horse was an old worn-out chestnut, with an ill-kept coat, and bones that showed plainly through it. The knees knuckled over, and the forelegs were very unsteady. I had been eating some hay, and the wind rolled a little lock of it that way, and the poor creature put out her long thin neck and picked it up, and then turned round and looked about for more. There was a hopeless look in the dull eye that I could not help noticing, and then, as I was thinking where I had seen that horse before, she looked full at me and said, 'Black Beauty, is that you?'

It was Ginger! but how changed! The beautifully arched and glossy neck was now straight and lank, and fallen in, the clean straight legs and delicate fetlocks were swelled; the joints were grown out of shape with hard work; the face, that was once so full of spirit and life, was now full of suffering, and I could tell by the heaving of her sides, and her frequent cough, how bad her breath was.

Our drivers were standing together a little way off, so I sidled up to her a step or two, that we might have a little quiet talk. It was a sad tale that she had to tell.

After a twelvemonth's run off at Earlshall, she was considered to be fit for work again, and was sold to a gentleman. For a little while she got on very well, but after a longer gallop than usual, the old strain returned, and after being rested and doctored she was again sold. In this way she changed hands several times, but always getting lower down.

'And so at last,' said she, 'I was bought by a man who keeps a number of cabs and horses, and lets them out. You look well off, and I am glad of it, but I could not tell you what my life has been. When they found out my weakness, they said I was not worth what they gave for me, and that I must go into one of the low cabs, and just be used up; that is what they are doing, whipping and working with never one thought of what I suffer; they paid for me, and must get it out of me, they say. The man who hires me now, pays a deal of money to the owner every day, and so he has to get it out of me too; and so it's all the week round and round, with never a Sunday rest.'

I said, 'You used to stand up for yourself if you were ill-used.'

'Ah!' she said, 'I did once, but it's no use; men are strongest, and if they are cruel and have no feeling, there is nothing that we can do, but just bear it, bear it on and on to the end. I wish the end was come, I wish I was dead. I have seen dead horses, and I am sure they do not suffer pain. I wish I may drop down dead at my work, and not be sent off to the knacker's.'[1]

I was very much troubled, and I put my nose up to hers, but I could say nothing to comfort her. I think she was pleased to see me, for she said, 'You are the only friend I ever had.'

Just then her driver came up, and with a tug at her mouth backed her out of the line and drove off, leaving me very sad indeed.

A short time after this, a cart with a dead horse in it passed our cab-stand. The head hung out of the cart tail, the lifeless tongue was slowly dropping with blood; and the sunken eyes! but I can't speak of them, the sight was too dreadful. It was a chestnut horse with a long thin neck. I saw a white streak down the forehead. I believe it was Ginger; I hoped it was, for then her troubles would be over. Oh! if men were more merciful, they would shoot us before we came to such misery.

~ MATHILDE BLIND

"On a Forsaken Lark's Nest"

The Ascent of Man. London: Chatto and Windus, 1889. 138.

Lo, where left 'mid the sheaves, cut down by the iron-fanged reaper,
Eating its way as it clangs fast through the wavering wheat,
Lies the nest of a lark, whose little brown eggs could not keep her
As she, affrighted and scared, fled from the harvester's feet.

Ah, what a heartful of song that now will never awaken,
Closely packed in the shell, awaited love's fostering,
That should have quickened to life what, now a-cold and forsaken,
Never, enamoured of light, will meet the dawn on the wing.

1. A professional horse slaughterer. *Ed.*

Ah, what pæans of joy, what raptures no mortal can measure,
Sweet as honey that's sealed in the cells of the honeycomb,
Would have ascended on high in jets of mellifluous pleasure,
Would have dropped from the clouds to nest in its gold-curtained
home.

Poor, pathetic brown eggs! Oh, pulses that never will quicken
Music mute in the shell that hath been turned to a tomb!
Many a sweet human singer, chilled and adversity-stricken,
Withers benumbed in a world his joy might have helped to illume.

CHRISTINA ROSSETTI

"Hurt no living thing"

Sing-Song: A Nursery Rhyme Book. 1872. London: Macmillan, 1893. 105.

Hurt no living thing:
Ladybird, nor butterfly,
Nor moth with dusty wing,
Nor cricket chirping cheerily,
Nor grasshopper so light of leap,
Nor dancing gnat, nor beetle fat,
Nor harmless worms that creep.

CHRISTINA ROSSETTI

"Hopping frog, hop here and be seen"

Sing-Song: A Nursery Rhyme Book. 1872. London: Macmillan, 1893. 58.

Hopping frog, hop here and be seen,
I'll not pelt you with stick or stone:
Your cap is laced and your coat is green;
Good bye, we'll let each other alone.

Plodding toad, plod here and be looked at,
You the finger of scorn is crooked at:
But though you're lumpish, you're harmless too:
You won't hurt me, and I won't hurt you.

CHRISTINA ROSSETTI

"Hear what the mournful linnets say"

Sing-Song: A Nursery Rhyme Book. 1872. London: Macmillan, 1893. 14.

Hear what the mournful linnets say:
"We built our nest compact and warm,
But cruel boys came round our way
And took our summerhouse by storm.

"They crushed the eggs so neatly laid;
So now we sit with drooping wing,
And watch the ruin they have made,
Too late to build, too sad to sing."

MARY HOWITT

"The Cry of the Suffering Creatures"

Sketches of Natural History; or Songs of Animal Life. 1834. London and New York: T. Nelson, 1872. 13–15.

Oh! that they had pity, the men we serve so truly!
Oh! that they had kindness, the men we love so well!
They call us dull and stupid, and vicious and unruly,
And think not we can suffer, but only would rebel.

They brand us, and they beat us; they spill our blood like water;
We die that they may live, ten thousand in a day!

Oh, that they had mercy! for in their dens of slaughter
They afflict us and affright us, and do far worse than slay!

We are made to be their servants—we know it, and complain not;
We bow our necks with meekness the galling yoke to bear;
Their heaviest toil we lighten, the meanest we disdain not;
In all their sweat and labour we take a willing share.

We know that God intended for us but servile stations,
To toil, to bear man's burdens, to watch beside his door;
They are of earth the masters, we are their poor relations,
Who grudge them not their greatness, but help to make it more.

We have a sense they know not, or else dulled by learning—
They call it instinct only, a thing of rule and plan;
But oft when reason fails them, our clear, direct discerning,
And the love that is written within us, have saved the life of man.

And in return we ask but that they would kindly use us
For the purposes of service, for that for which we're made;
That they would teach their children to love and not abuse us,
So each might face the other, and neither be afraid.

If they would but love us, would learn our strength and weakness,
If only with our sufferings their hearts would sympathize,
Then they would know what truth is, what patience is and meekness
And read our hearts devotion in the softness of our eyes!

If they would but teach their children to treat the subject creatures,
As humble friends, as servants who strive their love to win,
Then would they see how joyous, how kindly are our natures,
And a second day of Eden would on the earth begin.

The Horrors of Sport

ANNA SEWELL

"The Hunt"

Black Beauty. 1877. London: J. A. Allen, 1989. 8–14.

Before I was two years old, a circumstance happened which I have never forgotten. It was early in the spring; there had been a little frost in the night, and a light mist still hung over the plantations and meadows. I and the other colts were feeding at the lower part of the field when we heard, quite in the distance, what sounded like the cry of dogs. The oldest of the colts raised his head, pricked his ears, and said, 'There are the hounds!' and immediately cantered off, followed by the rest of us to the upper part of the field, where we could look over the hedge and see several fields beyond. My mother and an old riding horse of our master's were also standing near, and seemed to know all about it.

'They have found a hare,' said my mother, 'and if they come this way, we shall see the hunt.'

And soon the dogs were all tearing down the field of young wheat next to ours. I never heard such a noise as they made. They did not bark, nor howl, nor whine, but kept on a 'yo! yo, o, o! yo! yo, o, o!' at the top of their voices. After them came a number of men on horseback, some of them in green coats, all galloping as fast as they could. The old horse snorted and looked eagerly after them, and we young colts wanted to be galloping with them, but they were soon away into the fields lower down; here it seemed as if they had come to a stand; the dogs left off barking, and ran about every way with their noses to the ground.

'They have lost the scent,' said the old horse; 'perhaps the hare will get off.'

'What hare?' I said.

'Oh! I don't know *what* hare; likely enough it may be one of our own hares out of the plantation; any hare they can find will do for the dogs and men to run after'; and before long the dogs began their 'yo! yo, o, o!' again, and back they came altogether at full speed, making straight for our meadow at the part where the high bank and hedge overhang the brook.

'Now we shall see the hare,' said my mother; and just then a hare wild with fright rushed by, and made for the plantation. On came the dogs, they burst over the bank, leapt the stream, and came dashing across the field, followed by the huntsmen. Six or eight men leaped their horses clean over, close upon the dogs. The hare tried to get through the fence; it was too thick, and she turned sharp round to make for the road, but it was too late; the dogs were upon her with their wild cries; we heard one shriek, and that was the end of her. One of the huntsmen rode up and whipped off the dogs, who would soon have torn her to pieces. He held her up by the leg torn and bleeding, and all the gentlemen seemed well pleased.

As for me, I was so astonished that I did not at first see what was going on by the brook; but when I did look, there was a sad sight; two fine horses were down, one was struggling in the stream, and the other was groaning on the grass. One of the riders was getting out of the water covered with mud, the other lay quite still.

'His neck is broken,' said my mother.

'And serve him right too,' said one of the colts.

I thought the same, but my mother did not join with us.

'Well! no,' she said, 'you must not say that; but though I am an old horse, and have seen and heard a great deal, I never yet could make out why men are so fond of this sport; they often hurt themselves, often spoil good horses, and tear up the fields, and all for a hare or a fox, or a stag, that they could get more easily some other way; but we are only horses, and don't know.'

Whilst my mother was saying this, we stood and looked on. Many of the riders had gone to the young man; but my master, who had been watching what was going on, was the first to raise him. His head fell back and his arms hung down, and every one looked very serious. There was no noise now; even the dogs were quiet, and seemed to know that something was wrong. They carried him to our master's house. I heard afterwards that it was young George Gordon, the Squire's only son, a fine, tall young man, and the pride of his family.

There was now riding off in all directions to the doctor's, to the farrier's, and no doubt to Squire Gordon's, to let him know about his son.

When Mr. Bond, the farrier, came to look at the black horse that lay groaning on the grass, he felt him all over, and shook his head; one of his legs was broken. Then someone ran to our master's house and came back with a gun; presently there was a loud bang and a dreadful shriek, and then all was still; the black horse moved no more.

My mother seemed much troubled; she said she had known that horse for years, and that his name was Rob Roy; he was a good bold horse, and there was no vice in him. She never would go to that part of the field afterwards.

Not many days after, we heard the church bell tolling for a long time; and looking over the gate we saw a long strange black coach that was covered with black cloth and was drawn by black horses; after that came another and another and another, and all were black, while the bell kept tolling, tolling. They were carrying young Gordon to the churchyard to bury him. He would never ride again. What they did with Rob Roy I never knew; but 'twas all for one little hare.

~ FLORENCE DIXIE

"The Horrors of Sport"

Westminster Review 137 (1892): 49–52.

Many people have no doubt read Lord Randolph Churchill's tenth letter from Mashonaland[1] to the *Daily Graphic.* It was divided into two parts, and its reading proved distasteful to many people, who view with disapproval the wounding, maiming, and torture of wild animals under the name of SPORT. But it also proved unwelcome to numerous sporting readers, by reason of the wilful destruction of life in a cruel and unsporting manner which it gave evidence of, as well as the utter callousness displayed in the recital, to the sufferings of the hapless victims of that day of butchery and funk combined.

"Sport" is horrible. I say it advisedly. I speak with the matured experience of one, who has seen and taken part in sport of many and varied kinds, in many and varied parts of the world. I can handle gun and rifle as well and

1. A region in northeast Zimbabwe. *Ed.*

efficiently as most "sporting folk," and few women, and not many men, have indulged in a tithe of the shooting and hunting in which I have been engaged both at home and during travels and expeditions in far-away lands. It is not therefore as an novice that I take up my pen to record why I, whom some have called a "female Nimrod," have come to regard with absolute loathing and detestation, any sort or kind or form of sport, which in any way is produced by the suffering of animals. Many a keen sportsman, searching his heart, will acknowledge that at times a feeling of self-reproach has shot through him, as he has stood by the dying victim of his skill. I know that it has confronted me many and many a time. I have bent over my fallen game, the result of alas! too good a shot. I have seen the beautiful eye of deer and its different kind, glaze and grow dim as the bright life, my shot had arrested in its happy course, sped onward into the unknown; I have ended with the sharp yet merciful knife the dying sufferings of poor beasts who had never harmed me, yet whom I had laid low under the veil of sport; I have seen the terror-stricken orb of the red deer, dark, full of tears, glaring at me with mute reproach as it sobbed its life away, and that same look I have seen in the eyes of the glorious-orbed guanaco of Patagonia, the timid, gentle gazelle, the graceful and beautiful koodoo, springbok, &c., of South Africa, seemingly, as it were, reproaching me for thus lightly taking the life I could never bring back. So, too, I have witnessed the angry, defiant glare of the wild beast's fading sight, as death, fast coming, deprived him of the power to wreak his vengeance on the human aggressor before him. And I say this. The memory of those scenes brings no pleasure to my mind. On the contrary, it haunts me with a huge reproach, and I fain I never had done those deeds of skill—and cruelty.

It is a remnant of barbarism in our natures that we should take pleasure in displaying our skill on living animals. Deer-stalking is no doubt a healthy and exhilarating exercise, requiring skill, stamina, a clear sight and a steady hand. Yet the last act in a successful stalk is, if we come to think about it, disgusting and brutal. In close proximity to us we see a lordly animal, happy, peaceful, and enjoying fully the gift of life. We draw a trigger, and, if we do not miss, we wound or kill. Happy it be if it is the latter. More often than not it is the former, and then, if limbs are not broken, a fierce tracking ensues, resulting sometimes in the death of the beast, sometimes in its loss, and, as a consequence, many an hour of torture ere death closes its sufferings. Yet thousands are spent yearly on deer forests, and the pæan of animal woe that goes up therefrom throughout the stalking season expends itself year after year unheard, unfelt, unthought of amidst the throng of men.

I wonder how many sportsmen who tramp turnips after partridges and heather after grouse have studied the happy ways and manners of these quiet, unpretending grey and brown birds? Both grouse and partridges manifest the same characteristic affection for their young. It is a touching sight, when coming unexpectedly upon a young covey, to watch the frantic efforts of the cock and hen to simulate being badly wounded, so as to draw attention from their brood. It is a piteous sight to see a wounded grouse or partridge striving to escape some beater, who with uplifted stick pursues the poor, helpless, stricken animal, striking at it amidst the laughter and evident amusement of his fellow-beaters. It is a mere trivial incident, no doubt, and yet, those who know and have studied the habits of these birds, their instinctive eagerness to be together, their sharp cry and outstretched necks when separated and calling for reunion, can guess and feel what the agony of terror must be to a wounded bird situated as I have described, and which when caught is killed by having its brain bitten[2] in, or its breast pinched tightly till it dies of suffocation.

What more beastly sights does one see anywhere than at a covert shoot, when driven before beaters, into the very jaws of death, thousands of tame, hand-reared pheasants are literally mown down by the rows of guns awaiting their advent? Let us watch some "warm corner" in one of these shoots. Falling pheasants hardly risen from the ground meet our view. Some fall dead, others dying, others legged, some winged. On one side, we see dishevelled heaps of struggling feathers, pheasants with a leg and both wings broken striving to wriggle back to the woods, where hitherto they have been peaceful and happy. Now arises the piteous squeal of the wounded rabbit, or the more childlike human cry of terrified agony from the maimed and timid hare, striving alas! in vain to escape from the army of noisy beaters advancing their way, whose shouts must add to the pandemonium of horror which surrounds their last dying moments.

What more aggravated form of torture is to be found than coursing with greyhounds, the awful terror of the hare depicting itself in the laid back ears, convulsive doubles, and wild, starting eyes which seem almost to burst from their sockets in the agony of tension which that piteous struggle for life entails?

And what sadder sight is there to be found in the records of the hunted, than the one of a dead-beat fox, worn out, with lolling tongue, heaving sides, bedraggled brush, with the bay of the nearing pack growing every moment more distinct, struggling on in search of safety for his doomed life, dodging

2. The biting in of a wounded partridge's, or grouse's, or pheasant's brain is a brutal method of killing, much adopted, and is not productive of instantaneous death.

now here, now there, surrounded by a hostile field, the fiendish tally-ho sounding in his ears, the cracking of whips which warn him against any further attempt at escape? Then the hounds rush in. For one brief moment he turns at bay. *Cui bono?* The next all is worry, worry, worry, as the poor, weary but gallant Tod is torn limb from limb, disembowelled, and reduced to a shapeless mass of bloody, draggled fur. A fitting death it is, indeed, following as a sequel on the hunted torture which the poor brute has suffered from find to finish.

I have ridden to hounds over many a hard fought field, yet even in the days when I did not scruple to join in this animal torture, the death of a gallant fox always affected me unpleasantly, and reproach knocked at my heart louder and louder each time, and I have asked myself, "Cannot we have sport without cruelty?"

Assuredly we can. Well-laid drags, tracked by experts would test the mettle both of hounds and riders to hounds, but then a terrified, palpitating fleeing life would be struggling ahead, and so the idea is not pleasing to those who find pleasure in blood. Much of this barbarous taste and callous indifference to the sufferings of animals is bred with out childhood and upbringing. Youth, especially of the male sex, is taught to regard shooting and hunting as manly accomplishments, without which a man is regarded rather as a poop than otherwise. Women, myself included, are, in many instances, brought up to indulge in sporting amusements, and it follows as a natural sequence that in the large majority of cases where this is so, a callous indifference to the agony and misery caused to the victims is imperceptibly engendered. Sometimes, as in my case, and in the cases of several men, whom I have known as "mighty sportsman," reproach knocks at the heart's door and finds inside a responsive echo. None but those who have indulged largely in sport in its many and varied branches, can realise the holocaust of animal suffering that is day by day offered upon the altar of sport. I have seen and gauged it to its fullest, and I can safely say, that save in self-defence, I will never in life again raise a gun or rifle to destroy the glorious Animal Life of Creation, which alas! I have so often and so wantonly taken part in bringing to destruction. And I say this. Savagedom still dominates us in a great degree. A higher education and civilisation will teach us to despise amusements which are purchased at the expense of suffering to animals. Let those in high places consider well how meet a good example in this respect would be, and lead youth forward to find relaxation and pleasure in feats of skill, endurance and physical adroitness without the aid of blood and torture to make of us skilled sons and daughters of the chase and the field. In our national schools, both high and low, kindness, and our duty to animals, should form part of the curriculum, while every effort that science and investigation can command should be put forth to attain for such animals as are needed for food, a speedy, painless, and merciful end. As we have framed laws for the protection of domesticated and tame animals, so we should teach mercy—and where destruction is necessary—a painless mode of death. And high time it is, that the machinery of the law be put in force to do away with the torture of wild animals, which under the name of "Sport," we daily immolate upon the altar of suffering, breeding and preserving them merely for the gratification of the still lingering savage instinct in us, which delights in taking life. The idea will no doubt be unpopular and create resistance, and yet, the day must dawn when that savage instinct will become eradicated and man will cease to seek and find pleasure in destroying our glorious animal life.

~ MARY WEBB

From *Gone to Earth*

1917. New York: Dial Press, 1982. 16–17; 62; 283–87.

[pp. 16–17]

. . . In the middle of the night Foxy woke. The moon filled her kennel-mouth like a door, and the light shone in her eyes. This frightened her—so large a lantern in an unseen hand, held so purposefully before the tiny home of one defenceless little creature. She barked sharply. Hazel awoke promptly, as a mother at her child's cry. She ran straight out with her bare feet into the fierce moonlight.

'What ails you?' she whispered. 'What ails you, little un?'

The wind stalked through the Callow, and the Callow moaned. A moan came also from the plain, and black shapes moved there as the clouds drove onwards.

'Maybe they're out,' muttered Hazel. 'Maybe the black meet's set for to-night and she's scented the death pack.' She looked about nervously, 'I can see summat driving dark o'er the pastures yonder; they'm abroad, surely.'

She hurried Foxy into the cottage and bolted the door.

'There!' she said. 'Now you lie good and quiet in the corner, and the death pack shanna get you.'

It was said that the death pack, phantom hounds of a bad squire, whose gross body had been long since put to sweeter uses than any he put it to in life—changed into the clear-eyed daisy and the ardent pimpernel—scoured the country on dark stormy nights. Harm was for the house past which it streamed, death for those that heard it give tongue.

This was the legend, and Hazel believed it implicitly. When she had found Foxy half dead outside her deserted earth, she had been quite sure that it was the death pack that had made away with Foxy's mother. She connected it also with her own mother's death. Hounds symbolized everything she hated, everything that was not young, wild and happy. She identified herself with Foxy, and so with all things hunted and snared and destroyed.

Night, shadow, loud winds, winter—these were inimical; with these came the death pack, stealthy and untiring, following for ever the trail of the defenceless. Sunlight, soft airs, bright colours, kindness—these were beneficent havens to flee into. Such was the essence of her creed, the only creed she held, and it lay darkly in her heart, never expressed even to herself. But when she ran into the night to comfort the little fox, she was living up to her faith as few do; when she gathered flowers and lay in the sun, she was dwelling in the mystical atmosphere as vivid as that of the saints; when she recoiled from cruelty, she was trampling evil underfoot, perhaps more surely than those great divines who destroyed one another in their zeal for their Maker.

[p. 62]

. . . Hazel expressed things that she knew nothing of, as a blackbird does. For, though she was young and fresh, she had her origin in the old, dark heart of earth, full of innumerable agonies, and in that heart she dwelt, and ever would, singing from its gloom as a bird sings in a yew-tree. Her being was more full of echoes than the hearts of those that live further from the soil; and we are all as full of echoes as a rocky wood—echoes of the past, reflex echoes of the future, and echoes of the soil (these last reverberating through our filmiest dreams, like the sound of thunder in a blossoming orchard). The echoes are in us of great voices long gone hence, the unknown cries of huge beasts on the mountains; the sullen aims of creatures in the slime; the love-call of the bittern. We know, too, echoes of things outside our ken—the thought that shapes itself in the bee's brain and becomes a waxen box of sweets; the tyranny of youth stirring in the womb; the crazy terror of small slaughtered beasts; the upward push of folded grass, and how the leaf feels in all its veins the cold rain; the ceremonial that passes yearly in the emerald temples of bud and calyx—we have walked those temples; we are the sacrifice on those altars. And the future floats on the current of our blood like a secret argosy. We hear the ideals of our descendants, like songs in the night, long before our firstborn is begotten. We, in whom the pollen and the dust, sprouting grain and falling berry, the dark past and the dark future, cry and call—we ask, Who is this Singer that sends his voice through the dark forest, and inhabits us with ageless and immortal music, and sets the long echoes rolling for evermore?

[pp. 283–87]

. . . In spite of her bird-like quickness of ear, she was too much overwhelmed by the scene she had just left to notice an increasing, threatening, ghastly tumult that came, at first fitfully, then steadily, up through the woods. At first it was only a rumour, as if some evil thing, imprisoned for the safety of the world, whined and struggled against love in a close underground cavern. But when it came nearer—and it seemed to be emerging from its prison with sinister determination—the wind had no longer any power to disguise its ferocity, although it was still in a minor key, still vacillating and scattered. Nor had it as yet any objective; it was only vaguely clamorous for blood, not for the very marrow of the soul. Yet, as Hazel suddenly became aware of it, a cold shudder ran down her spine.

'Hound-dogs!' she said. She peered through the trees, but nothing was to be seen, for the woods were steep. With a dart of terror she remembered that she had left Foxy loose in the parlour. Would they have let her out?

She ran home.

'Be Foxy here?' she asked.

Edward looked up from the chapel accounts. James was trying to browbeat him over them.

'No. I expect she went out with you.'

Hazel fled to the back of the house, but Foxy was not there. She whistled, but no smooth, white-bibbed personality came trotting round the corner. Hazel ran back to the hill. The sound of the horn came up intermittently with tuneful devilry.

She whistled again.

Reddin, coming up the wood at some distance from the pack, caught the whistle, and seeing her dress flutter far up the hill, realized what had happened.

'Bother it!' he said. He did not care about Foxy, and he thought Hazel's affection for her very foolish; but he understood very well that if anything happened to Foxy, he would be to blame in Hazel's eyes. Between him and Hazel was a series of precipitous places. He would have to go round to reach her. He spurred his horse, risking a fall from the rabbit-holes and the great ropes of honeysuckle that swung from tree to tree.

Hazel ran to and fro, frantically calling to Foxy.

Suddenly the sound, that had been querulous, interrogative and various, changed like an organ when a new stop is pulled out.

The pack had found.

But the scent, it seemed, was not very hot. Hope revived in Hazel.

'It'll be the old scent from yesterday,' she thought. 'Maybe Foxy'll come yet!'

Seeing Reddin going in so devil-may-care a manner, a little clergyman (a 'guinea-pig' on Sundays and the last hard-riding parson in the neighbourhood on weekdays) thought that Reddin must have seen the fox, and gave a great view-hallo. He rode a tall raw-boned animal, and looked like a monkey.

Hazel did not see either him or Reddin. With fainting heart she had become aware that the hounds were no longer on an old scent. They were not only intent on one life now, but they were close to it. And whoever it was that owned the life was playing with it, coming straight on in the teeth of the wind instead of doubling with it.

With an awful constriction of the heart, Hazel knew who it was. She knew also that it was her momentary forgetfulness that had brought about this horror. Terror seized her at the dogs' approach, but she would not desert Foxy.

Then, with the fearful inconsequence of a dream, Foxy trotted out of the wood and came to her. Trouble was in her eyes. She was disturbed. She looked to Hazel to remove the unpleasantness, much as Mrs. Marston used to look at Edward.

And as Hazel, dry-throated, whispered 'Foxy!' and caught her up, the hounds came over the ridge like water. Riding after them, breaking from the wood on every side, came the Hunt. Scarlet gashed the impenetrable shadows. Coming, as they did, from the deep gloom, fiery-faced and fiery-coated, with eyes frenzied by excitement, and open, cavernous mouths, they were like devils emerging from hell on a foraging expedition. Miss Clomber, her hair loose and several of her pin-curls torn off by the branches, was one of the first, determined to be in at the death.

The uproar was so terrific that Edward and the six righteous men came out to see what the matter was. Religion and society were marshalled with due solemnity on God's Little Mountain.

Hazel saw nothing, heard nothing. She was running with every nerve at full stretch, her whole soul in her feet. But she had lost her old fleetness, for Reddin's child had even now robbed her of some of her vitality. Foxy, in gathering panic, struggled and impeded her. She was only half-way to the quarry, and the house was twice as far.

'I canna!' she gasped on a long terrible breath. She felt as if her heart was bursting.

One picture burnt itself on her brain in blood and agony. One sound was in her ears—the shrieking of the damned. What she saw was Foxy, her smooth little friend, so dignified, so secure of kindness, held in the hand of the purple-faced huntsman above the pack that raved for her convulsive body. She knew how Foxy's eyes would look, and she nearly fainted at the knowledge. She saw the knife descend—saw Foxy, who had been lovely and pleasant to her in life, cut in two and flung (a living creature, fine of nerve) to the pack, and torn to fragments. She heard her scream.

Yes; Foxy would cry to her, as she had cried to the Mighty One dwelling in darkness. And she? What would she do? She knew that she could not go on living with that cry in her ears. She clutched the warm body closer.

Though her thoughts had taken only an instant, the hounds were coming near.

Outside the chapel James said:

'Dear me! A splendid sight! We'll wait to verify the 'apenny columns till they've killed.'

They all elbowed in front of Edward. But he had seen. He snatched up his spade from the porch, and knocked James out of the way with the flat of it.

'I'm coming, dear!' he shouted.

But she did not hear. Neither did she hear Reddin, who was still at a distance, and was spurring till the blood ran, as in the tale of the death-pack, yelling: 'I'm coming! Give her to me!' Nor the little cleric, in his high-pitched nasal voice, calling: 'Drop it! They'll pull you down!' while the large gold cross bumped up and down on his stomach. The death that Foxy must die, unless she could save her, drowned all other sights and sounds.

She gave one backward glance. The awful resistless flood of liver and white and black was very near. Behind it rose shouting devils.

It was the death-pack.

There was no hope. She could never reach Edward's house. The green turf rose before her like the ascent to Calvary.

The members of the hunt, the Master and the huntsmen, were slow to understand. Also, they were at a disadvantage, the run being such an abnormal one—against the wind and up a steep hill. They could not beat off the hounds in time. Edward was the only one near enough to help. If she had seen him and made for him, he might have done something.

But she only saw the death-pack; and as Reddin shouted again near at hand, intending to drag her on to the horse, she turned sharply. She knew it was the Black Huntsman. With a scream so awful that Reddin's hands grew nerveless on the rein, she doubled for the quarry.

A few woodlarks played there, but they fled at the oncoming tumult.

For one instant the hunt and the righteous men, Reddin the destroyer, and Edward the saviour, saw her sway, small and dark, before the staring sky. Then, as the pack, with a ferocity of triumph, was flinging itself upon her, she was gone.

She was gone with Foxy into everlasting silence. She would suck no more honey from the rosy flowers, nor dance like a leaf in the wind.

ANTIVIVISECTION

VERNON LEE

From "Vivisection: An Evolutionist to Evolutionists"

Contemporary Review 41 (1882): 803–11.

. . . Honour, dishonour—very fine-sounding words, but meaning how much? Figments, useful enough in their day when only figments had power; effete expressions inherited from a time (answers my historical and sociological friend), when it appears that people committed abominations with much greater impunity than nowadays. This code of honour is scientifically merely a museum curiosity. True enough. But remember what I said when we began our moral discussion, about the standard by which we were going to judge vivisection being a sort of Janus, presenting a very old and a very new face. The old face I have spoken of; it is this god of other days, called Honour. But there is another face, or rather the same thing presents a younger one seen from the other side. And this newer face is what is called evolutional morality. For the old name and the new mean but one thing. The old code of things to be done and things to be avoided, which used to be considered as a mysterious, inexplicable something, of no particular origin, miraculously given, I suppose, is in truth a now intelligible something, whose reason and origin we understand. As the sudden word of command by which things were created, is now understood as the mere inevitable adjustment and development of physical things, so also this old principle of honour is now comprehensible as the instinct, the ingrained habit due to ages of deliberate choice, of preferring certain sets of motives to certain other ones. For as our physical nature has been evolved by the selection and survival of those physical forms which are in harmony with the greatest number of physical circumstances; so also has our moral nature been evolved by the more and more conscious choice of the motives including consideration for the greatest number of results from our actions, of the motives which, instead of merely enlarging the shapeless and functionless moral polyp-jelly of *ego,* work out, diversify and unify, lick into shape, the complicated moral organism of society, with all its innumerable and wondrously co-ordinated limbs and functions. And thus has evolved itself that which was formerly called *Honour,* and whose other name is natural morality: the preference of justice to expediency. Slowly and with difficulty, indeed; every single preference of right to desire having been as a touch which has moulded the wonderful instinct into existence; every single preference of desire to right having been the rude thumbing which obliterates the nascent form; every single just action making easier a score of just actions, every single unjust decision having begotten a score of future unjust decisions. A very arduous work has been this making of man's conscience, which seems to be at once the greatest requisite and the most crowning perfection of the evolution of society; for if mere overbalance of pleasure above pain had been the highest goal of our gradual evolution, evolution might have ended with those half-existing things whose happiness is more complete than that of the most noble mind. And the making of man's conscience has been the evolution of a spiritual organism which perceives and chooses justice within ranges ever and ever extending: justice, at first (when the moral sight was a mere titillating all-overishness on the contact of some adjacent thing, and the moral limbs were fastened like those of a limpet to one spot) limited to the mere family, then to the tribe, then to the class and the race; and nowadays, when the times of justice, limited to class and race, are separated from us by barely a century,—nay, by barely a score of years,—extending to whatever can feel, to whatever can have its poor little portion of happiness exchanged by fraud and violence for misery. Nature, many tell us, is not thus just; she uses as her instruments starvation, pestilence, continuous sacrifice of weaker to stronger; and Nature having made us, shall we be wiser or more pharisaical than she? But this Nature of which you speak, what is she, when you tear away the allegorical and mythical rags of religion with which we still mumm up our scientific conceptions? What is this Nature? contending forces, a chaos which has not made us, but out of which we have gradually emerged. If Nature—that is, the course of continually clashing and reacting events—has been unjust, why should we be unjust, who are not an abstraction formed out of abstract ideas, but living men and women, with eyes and ears to see and hear, and minds to judge and wish and hope and choose; why should we, with our reason and conscience, pretend to take lessons from a mere abstract entity, a mere expression by which we symbolize phenomena? Indeed, we do not; and had we done so, society would never have existed.

Hence, when I say that honour rejects vivisection as an unjust and cheating practice, I mean thereby also that it is contrary to the nature of the highest result of our gradual evolution. I mean that by preferring in this case the advantages which our race might gain at the expense of wholesale and profitless agony to another race, we are laying obliterating fingers upon those delicate moral features which have thus slowly and arduously been moulded into shape. For, in the first place, we are deliberately buying our good with the evil of others, and thus running counter to the great moral principle of obtaining advantage only in return for advantage, of being spared pain only by sparing it, of making the actions of men into the transactions of those who barter, lend, and repay, instead of those of men who cheat and rob. And, in the second place, this great movement of moral retrogression consists of a number of minor movements of moral retrogression. For we are making our perception of the evil of others give way to our perception of our own desire: we are letting ourselves slip instead of holding ourselves erect, and thus weakening our moral muscle. We are diminishing our most precious quality, the power of submitting to justice, of foregoing our wishes. And with this weakening of our moral will, goes inevitably the diminution also of our moral perception; for every time that we prefer desire to right, we not only increase the tyranny of covetousness, but, by jostling the one wrong choice with the many right ones which all except an utterly immoral life must contain, we let our soul lose its keenness, its moral scent: it endures foulness, gets pimply, weak, diseased, sometimes loses a limb, and always loses somewhat of its most precious power, of its elasticity, its endurance, its resistance. Moreover, every time that we prefer desire to justice, we are warping not only our moral, but also our intellectual nature. For a man, who is naturally inclined to morality and thoughtful as well, finds in his life numbers of opportunities of eschewing evil, and doing good with either no cost at all to his selfishness, or only so little as merely to enhance the natural pleasure which he takes in virtue; thus he develops for himself a moral nature in which acknowledged evil cannot dwell without constant moral discomfort from its presence; hence if the temptation of some evil choice overcome him, he will, in proportion to his honesty of habits and ideals, be anxious to persuade himself that this choice was not evil, but good; he will persuade himself that what was culpable self-indulgence was wise self-sacrifice, that the mud with which he has bespattered himself while seeking his pleasure is the trace of honourable moral labour, and thus he will, after giving way to a lower motive, listen to a false argument; and strange and lamentable are the sophisms which have ever, from Plato to Machiavelli, from the well-intentioned society-reorganizing Jesuit moralists of the seventeenth century to the honest and humane advocates of the modern vice of vivisection, followed upon a choice in which the desire or the habit of evil has conquered the perception of good.

And thus, after having given my reasons for considering that the deliberate choice of advantages to mankind, bought by unrequited and cheating infliction of agony upon creatures who cannot participate in the gain, while they sustain all the loss, is a retrogression in the path of moral evolution, inasmuch as it is the preference of desire to right; I wish to point out one or two instances of the blunting of moral judgment and stultification of intellectual argument which has already appeared as an inevitable secondary deterioration by the side of the largest principal degradation of our conscience. The temptation to recognize vivisection as a legitimate practice, is to any person imbued with modern scientific views a very great temptation; vivisection means a most valuable instrument, or rather a most valuable short cut, for the attainment of a kind of knowledge, with which are connected not only a great number of problems of body and soul, of present and future life, of moral health and disease, having an almost religious importance to us, who have forsworn our old creeds; but also a kind of knowledge at the same time bearing upon the actual well-being of mankind, upon the diminution of misery, which has become the mission of the men and women who would formerly have wasted their energies in prayers and crusades. It is a practice, therefore, which—to us who are scarcely weaned of our beloved old creeds, and but ill-accustomed as yet to the rude bracingness of a new faith which merely tells us to do right without reward, and endure pain without compensation,—still craving for the imaginative stimulant, the almost physically rapturous self-unconsciousness of complete surrender to a single object,—to us still so unable to dispense with a superstition—is in reality an ingredient in the heady elixir with which we comfort our chilly souls, in the spiritual cordial of a religion of science and humankind which has replaced the old religion of Christ and His wounds, until the world be fit for the religion of justice. Hence those, and they are among the noblest of us, who have been seeking strength and warmth in this belief, are, when the sense of this horrible ingredient of vivisection comes home to them, tempted by the strongest of all temptations, habit, to gulp down the poisonous moral absinthe of acquiescence in injustice together with the strengthening and purifying things with which it has lamentably got mingled. They have not the strength to bear the dreary soul-chilliness which they know they must suffer while carefully analyzing this creed of complete subservience of all good to human progress; they prefer to take it as it is, and they persuade themselves that all its ingredients are good. Thus to a large class of men, not merely physiologists and physicians dependent upon physiology, but a multitude of generous thinkers to whom the idea of a loss to science or to medicine is unendurable, vivisection has become as much a vicious necessity as any beastly vice to a swinish sinner;—a necessity which it has become necessary to their conscience to make from a vice into a virtue, or at least to exclude from any moral analysis. And while they have thus sophisticated or silenced their own conscience into acquiescence with evil, their example—the example of men eager in the cause of good which is agreeable to them, earnest against evil with which they do not sympathize, noble with all that nobility which is inherent in a fine nature and costs it no more than would vice to a vicious one—the apparently deliberate sanction of vivisection by these moral censors of our day, implies also the blind acquiescence of those conscientious men and women who feel that they must accept the decisions on right and wrong of their intellectual superiors. There stands before the eyes of the honest mediocrity, which in all such matters has the casting vote, an irresistible array of sanction of vivisection by men who are the highest authorities in the new philosophic morality. But this seeming strength is mere weakness, this apparently energetic decision is for the most part mere apathetic acquiescence. The knowledge that vivisection is conducive to progress of ideas and human welfare; the sense of the solidarity of science, of free thought with experimentalism; the habit of abetting anything which is modern and due to a modern movement; all this goes to make up that imposing display of approbation by which progress, freedom, generous thought are made responsible for a huge act of injustice. Nay, something lower than all this, lower and yet more irresistible and natural: the social habit, the official solidarity, of thinking men, which makes the historian, the philologist, the political man meet the physiologist on terms of familiarity, perhaps of professional comradeship; and which has for results that the clean-handed man, who has been writing of Buddha, or Christ, or the new basis of morality, who has been moralizing back slums or speaking against Nubian slave-dealers; persuading himself that there must be a frightful deal of exaggeration in the stories told about Professor A.'s or Dr. B.'s laboratory, that Professor A. or Dr. B. is the best authority about his own doings, that his own statements about the mere tickling pains he inflicts, and the gallons of anæsthetics which he employs, are surely the most reliable; and finally, that vivisection must be perfectly justifiable and praiseworthy, since it is practised by his colleague and friend, Professor A. or Dr. B., who must be an altogether exemplary man, willing to sacrifice his profession and his fame on the least suspicion of immorality, since he is the necessary colleague and friend of himself, the noble, humane, conscientious writer on ethics or reformer of abuses. This that I say may seem unjust; but let any of us ask his conscience how often he has successfully resisted the desire of believing in the moral cleanness of the hands which he is forced to shake in comradeship, or pleased to squeeze in friendship and admiration; let us ask ourselves whether one of the reasons of most acquiescence in evil has not always been, in all mankind, the reluctance to perceive the foulness and injustice and cruelty mixed up with the greatness of our heroes and our gods.

. . . Shall physiology be fettered? shall the discovery of facts and laws be retarded? shall one science be separated by a moral barrier from the full data which it covets? It seems a very frightful decision to come to; yet not so frightful, nor, when we look well at the matter, by any means unique. For in reality there are few, if any, sciences, which are permitted to obtain directly all the materials they require; barriers exist for them, sometimes almost enclose them—barriers across which only the strong muscle of analogical argument can raise itself to peer, the strong wing of imaginative reason can fly—barriers, which we are apt to forget, of place and time, hopeless barriers of chaos and vacuity and obliteration which separate the historian, the geologist, the astronomer, the physicist, the sociologist, from the facts which he covets. Moreover, this very science of physiology, in its higher levels of human biology, of mental physiology, has between it and its facts a wall as yet solid and unbroken, the wall of public opinion, of long habit, perhaps almost prejudice, which will not let the investigator experiment on the living nerves and brain, the living imagination and passions of a human victim. These walls exist for all science; their presence is borne with patience, and mankind does not fret at the long and roundabout ways by which knowledge must wearily proceed. A bit more wall or a bit less, a little more patience and a little more fortitude, a little more ingenuity in hewing out the difficult paths of thought where we cannot follow the broad highway of experiment: this is what would be meant to men of science by the prohibition of vivisection. A little more manly endurance of physical and mental pain; a little more wise recognition that with the pain mankind has equitably drawn a possible and probable lot of pleasure; a little more truthful perception that the pains which we suffer are largely due to the folly and vice of ourselves and our fathers; a little more grateful perception that the joys of mind, and eye and ear and heart, are multifold with which man can compensate himself for the sufferings of the body—a certain amount of gained moral vigour: this is what the prohibition of vivisection would mean to mankind at large. There is on either side a loss and a gain. Which shall we choose? To me it seems that to the man who not merely superficially knows and repeats, but whose thoughts and feelings are saturated with our new creed of the perpetual development of the nobler by perpetual elimination of the baser motives of our nature, it will be clear, sooner or later, that the improvement of bodily condition, the advancement of our knowledge, must be a retrogressive step if bought at the expense of the infliction of manifold and daily increasing tortures on creatures who will participate in no way thereby; on creatures who have not our innumerable consoling pleasures of thought, sentiment, hope, and æsthetic perception; who, if they suffer, lose all and everything they possess, nay rather, are basely cheated and robbed like some poor serf of their miserable birthright of painless existence by us, their lords, rich with a hundred inherited riches, rich with a hundred riches within our grasp. And similarly, it seems to me, that to every man imbued with the noble religion of choice and improvement, it should appear that the patient foregoing of knowledge thus to be bought, the manly endurance of suffering at such a price to be diminished, must be a great step in the great journey of human bettering; must be, both in the large act of preference of justice to injustice, and in the minor attendant acts of cherished forbearance from the coveted, of fortitude in pain, of thoughtful weighing of good and evil, of candid listening to our conscience, one of those choices of the higher rather than the lower which have made us what we are, which shall make us what we should be.

ANNA KINGSFORD

"Unscientific Science: Moral Aspects of Vivisection"

Spiritual Therapeutics. Ed. Wm. Colville, Jr. Edinburgh, 1883. 292–308.

Apologists of the practice appear to think that the desire of knowledge is in itself sufficient to vindicate all the cruelties and injustices imaginable. They do not seem to recognize the fact that every branch of intellectual research has its *moral limits,* and that the quest of pleasure, of wealth, of power, or of knowledge must never, in a civilized state, be permitted to outrage justice or the law of humanity.

In the ancient religious mysteries of all the nations of the globe, it is said that the fall of man ensues when he sacrifices moral obedience to the intellectual desire to *know.* Ah, it is primal and profound truth, and for this reason it finds its place in the initial chapters of the occult Book. *There are certain means of acquiring knowledge of which man can not make use without forfeiting his place in the Divine Order.*

We know well that there exist many practices which are extremely profitable in their results, but which are not legitimate, and which civilization does not tolerate,

In former times human lives were sacrificed to the interests of the fine arts. It is related that a certain painter of celebrity, wishing to seize the effects of violent death, caused a negro slave to be decapitated in his studio; and that another artist, famous for the talent he displayed in the interests of the Church, crucified an unfortunate youth in order to secure a faithful model for an altar-piece portraying the expiring of Christ.

Such acts as these are not in the category of legitimate practices, whatever may be the artistic or other value of their results; and the same may be said of many other pursuits constituting so many sciences invented by man to enrich, to amuse, or to aggrandize himself, but which are, by the *consensus* of modern opinion, discountenanced and outlawed.

It is necessary that men should understand the mere plea of "science" to be insufficient as justification of human action. There are sciences of a legitimate and civilized nature, tending toward light, wisdom and righteousness, and there are others which are neither legitimate nor civilized, and whose results can only end in the obliteration of sentiment, the negation of humanity, and the destruction of true science and true civilization. The progress made by vivisection is an advance upon the downward path.

And here we are brought face to face with the fact that the vivisecting school is pre-eminently the materialistic and atheistic school; while the school of spiritualistic thought is, by the very nature of its philosophy, opposed to vivisection.[1]

The materialist has no fundamental notion of Justice. For him everything is vague, relative, inexplicable. He is acquainted only with physical atoms, chemical elements, protoplasm and the theory of the evolution of forms without aim and without order. In his view there is only a blind force acting in the midst of darkness. Consequently, morality is not for him a

1. Of course I use the word "spiritualist" in its real and original sense, as opposed to "materialist."—*e.g.*, regarding the universe as having a spiritual and intelligent basis. I do not employ the word as a synonym for any special doctrines other than this.

determined and positive quality, having its source in the divine and inviolable Mind which directs and dominates all material manifestation; it is but a matter of human habit and convention, differing according to the particular time, place and race concerned. The man who adopts this view of morality of course accepts the civil law as the soul arbiter of action, and regards conduct as reprehensible, or the reverse, according to the light in which it is popularly viewed by his own nation and era. The sentiments, such as honor, justice, courage, pity, love, loyalty, are for him but idiosyncracies, varying according to such and such a temperament and depending for their manifestation and development on physical and accidental causes. Naturally, then, he laughs at appeals to sentiment, and boasts of being inaccessible to the "hysterical attacks" of "sensitive and weak-minded fanatics." When he says this, and other similar things, he simply means that the words "pity" and "justice" have no sense for him. There is but one only thing in the world which appears to him worthy of desire and attainment, and that is knowledge—knowledge always, and before all things, without any restriction or limitation of the means employed in its attainment.

The materialist does not understand that the Source and Substance of every series of phenomena, material and physical, the origin of which he seeks so eagerly to interpret, is equally the necessary Cause of the evolution which has produced humanity, whose distinctive appanage is the *moral nature.* To think otherwise would be to create illogical and absurd confusion between science and morality, by opposing intellect and intellectual interests to justice and the interests of the psychic being.

Thus is brought about the inevitable negation of philosophic unity.

But it is no uncommon thing to hear partisans of vivisection meet the charge of injustice and immorality made against the practice by the reply that it is a work of the highest intrinsic merit, because it has for its object the welfare of humanity.

Let us stop and consider what is meant by "the welfare of humanity." What is the signification of the word "humanity," so often used, so little understood? For the materialistic and vivisecting school we know very well that humanity imports nothing else than the special physical form of an animal belonging to the family of apes, a creature having such and such conformation of cerebral convolutions, skeleton, and organs. It is the body, the physical form, which constitutes humanity, and that is all. But for the spiritualistic school of thought, humanity means the manifestation of certain qualities and principles which find no expression among irresponsible beings—a condition raised above animality in virtue of a special moral capacity. Consequently, even were it true (which it is not) that *physical* human life could be saved, and bodily advantages obtained by means of cruel and tyrannical practices, such practices would still be, from the human point of view, completely unjustifiable. The human race can not be saved or enriched by acts which destroy and rob humanity. The physical life and health of individuals would be too dearly preserved or bought by the sacrifice of the high qualities which alone constitute man's superiority over all other creatures. The champions of vivisection demand the abasement of the moral standard of our race to the level of the primitive instinct of purely animal existence—the preservation of the body at any cost. Such a surrender would involve the destruction of that which is infinitely more precious than our physical life, of that which gives to this life all its worth and all its glory,—the dignity of human sentiment, and the privilege of responsibility.

What would be said of any person who, being sick or in pain, should cause a number of highly sensitive animals to be tortured for hours or days in his presence, on the remote chance of thereby discovering some means of alleviation for his own malady? Who among us, hearing of such an act as this, but would say that such a man was not worth the saving? And why should the motives of a whole people which act thus in accepting the practices of vivisection as the means of healing its physical ailments be held worthier our respect than those of the individual?

There can be but one reply. The human race, once beggared of all the attributes which alone enrich and elevate it, has no claim to royalty over the animals, and its salvation can in no wise profit the world.

For the unjust king is no longer a king, but a tyrant.

Vivisection has upon its hands the blood of violence and of abuse of force. No man ought to seek the relief of his suffering or the advance of his power at the price of the agonies of his lower brethren, even if such relief or advance should be really proved possible by these means. But it would seem that some physiologists of the modern school are only anxious to prove our common origin with the animals, and consequently the ties of brotherhood which link them to us, in order the more tranquilly to claim the right to torture and misuse them.

To vindicate the practices of vivisection by appeal to the "law of Nature," and to the habits of certain beasts who live by carnage, is to seek to regulate the conduct of the being highest in the series of evolution by the manners of those beings which are lowest in the scale, and to degrade the code of human morality to the plane of that of the wolf, the tiger, or any other irresponsible and noxious creature.

What is the good of being a man—of being a "king"—if this high rank, this glorious title, imply no superiority to gross natures and to the common lot? What is the meaning of all the mystery of development and of the transmutation of forms which, according to the teaching of science, have occupied so many thousand ages of painful evolution, and by which alone we men have gained our majesty of moral force and responsibility, if at the bidding of the vivisector we are to abandon our royal privilege, and sink again into the slime beside the last and most obscure of our vassals?

Ay, and lower even than they. For the "struggle for existence" among irresponsible beings, about which the vivisectors talk so much, rarely implies torture, but only death. The claim of the vivisector is for the right to inflict torture, in which but very few animals, and these the most ferocious and loathsome, appear to take pleasure. If, then, it be true that man has the right to kill certain animals, as he has that to kill certain men, this right does not involve the infliction of prolonged and horrible sufferings. At the present day, in civilized countries, condemned criminals are given over to death, but never to the flames, never to the rack or the *oubliette.* We have no right to inflict upon innocent animals torments to which pity forbids us to subject guilty men.

The force which ought to dominate the world is not physical force, nor even purely intellectual force; but it is, above and beyond all other, moral and philosophical force, which alone differentiates man from the beast and distinguishes the civilized being from the barbarian.

In fact, the distinctive glory of humanity is based on the sentiments—those divine qualities which have ever inspired all the noble and worthy actions of our race, and which are everywhere recognized as the most precious heritage of mankind.

It is probably because the beliefs of materialism stifle the sentiments in its devotees that they fail to perceive how inapposite are many of the comparisons drawn by them between the practices they defend and others recognized as useful and necessary to the State. A favorite argument is that which likens the craft of the vivisector to the profession of the soldier. Yet what is easier than to see that sentiment here enacts an enormously important part, and that there is all the difference in the world between the courage which gives itself of its own accord to danger and to death, and the cowardice which, at its ease at home, maltreats and martyrizes dumb and inoffensive creatures.

Where is the analogy between the vivisector's laboratory, with its gagged, bound, and trembling victims, carved to death in cold blood, and the field of battle, where every man in each contending army fights for home and country under the inspiration of enthusiasm, ambition or the desire for renown?

Neither is there any resemblance between the practices of vivisection and the great enterprises of civilization, such as engineering, exploration in unknown seas, and similar undertakings of a perilous nature, by appeal to which it has been sought to justify the scientific torture of animals; for these last do not voluntarily devote themselves to the knife. Men who take part in difficult works of construction, adventurers who traverse the arctic wastes or engage in other hazardous enterprises, are volunteers who follow the interest of their own satisfaction or personal profit at their own risk.

There is a complete contrast between the free sacrifice of oneself for the good of others and the enforced sacrifice of others for the good of oneself. The first is divine; the second is infernal. And vivisection represents a sacrifice of the latter kind.

Moreover, as already has been said, death is not torture. Let us remember that the right of vivisection differs from every other right assumed by men over animals by its peculiar nature, and that its defenders, if not wholly illogical or ignorant, vindicate the propriety of inflicting, not violent deaths, nor average pains merely, but horrible and prolonged agonies, such as that of the curarized dog cut to pieces by inches, and lingering hour after hour, in the silence and darkness of the night—dying in torment in the laboratory of Paul Bert,[2] the *moralist!*

It is vain to appeal to the vivisectors themselves against the cruelties daily perpetrated in their chambers of horror. Formerly, when the priests of the mediæval church burnt and tortured men for the salvation of souls, under the auspices of the Holy Office, it was not to the eminent deans and prelates of the sacred hierarchy that the world addressed itself in order to obtain the abolition of the Inquisition and of its infamous practices. The priests of the religion of the middle ages, like the priests of science to-day, found fine phrases with which to defend themselves as a body of conscientious and disinterested men. Nevertheless, the question between the Church and the world was decided by the laity against the members of the ecclesiastical corporation, and there has never yet been reason to regret the loss of stake and rack and dungeon.

A science based upon torture can no more be true science than a religion based upon torture can be true religion. It is a new Reformation that we want—but this time in the domain of science!

For the rest, the instruments used in our laboratories of vivisection are much the same as in mediæval times. The modern arsenal is fully as

2. Paul Bert (1833–86), born in Auxerre, France, was a professor of physiology at the Sorbonne. He advanced the study of blood gases and anesthetics. *Ed.*

complete as was that of the days of Torquemada, or Isabella of Spain—only now the dumb and innocent dog replaces the Jew or the heretic, and creatures which man judges his inferiors are bound to the wheel and tortured, with the hope of extorting from them the secret of life, in blind ignorance of the fact that Nature, outraged and agonized, replies like the human victim on the rack, more often by a lie than by a truth.

Attempts have again and again been made to dissuade antivivisectionists from the crusade they have undertaken, by inviting their attention and that of the public generally, to other abuses more or less grave, with the inquiry, "Why do not you kind-hearted people occupy yourselves with reforming the cruel practices of drovers, cab-drivers, sportsmen, slaughter-men, and their like? Why do you not try to solace the misery that everywhere reigns outside the vivisector's laboratory, before you think of attacking the methods of men and science?"

To all this we reply that we do most strenuously occupy ourselves with these matters, but that every such effort is paralyzed by the fact that not only is vivisection by its very nature the most cruel of all cruelties, and therefore the head and front of offending, but that it is, alone of all cruelties, protected by State legislation, although other and minor barbarisms are officially condemned. So long as the *principle* of cruelty is thus encouraged and kept alive by law, in the highest walks of science, all attempts to extirpate lesser cruelties elsewhere must prove unavailing.

How, for instance, can we teach our children the duties of humanity toward dumb animals, when, in the course of their studies at school and college, they learn what horrors are perpetrated in the work-rooms of science by the masters and professors they are expected to revere and to imitate? Or how can we profitably interfere to check the barbarities of the streets, when it is in the power of the brutal carman or drover to retort that, no matter how he may maltreat his beast, he can not approach the cruelties of the physiological laboratory which have the full sanction of the law? How can we urge him to cease working some old and worn out horse, broken down by fatigue in the service of man, when the result of our charitable interference may possibly be, not the well-earned rest of a life-long toil, nor even quick death under the blow of the knacker's axe, but a long and horrible agony in some infernal school of vivisection for the benefit of "science"? Alas, we can but stand by silent, praying only in our hearts that the poor, ill-used creature may rather be worked till he drops dead in his harness, than be delivered over to the tormentors to end his innocent life of faithful service in the pains of hell. Everything, rather than the scalpel, the saw and the hot iron of the vivisector!

We demand justice! Justice not only for innocent and defenseless animals, but for men themselves.

The present law of this country is a law manifestly unjust and cowardly. It attacks the dwarfs and respects the giants of cruelty. The poor man who, in the interests of his livelihood, accidentally over-drives his horse or his donkey, is punished by the very Legislature which protects the learned professor who flays and burns alive scores of living creatures systematically.

The law ought to be administered equally to all men, whether rich or poor, professors or laics, ignorant or learned. Either it ought to be admitted that there is no harm in illtreating animals—and in such case a law which protects them is ridiculous—our the man who cuts up a dog alive in a laboratory merits punishment as much as the man who flogs a horse in the street, and in such case the law ought not to favor the social rank or pretext of the first malfactor at the expense of the last. If vivisection is to be permitted, encouraged and endowed by the State, then societies for the protection of animals from cruelty have no *locus standi,* and ought to be abolished as anomalies at once absurd and illogical.

A good Christian once said to me, "I should never be happy in the joys of Heaven if I knew that other souls were condemned to eternal torment. Such a thought as that would render all my own felicity bitter to me." Well, this is something like the feeling of anti-vivisectionists with regard to the suffering of the victims of the physiological laboratory. The frightful thought that every day the rising sun will witness the commencement of hundreds of long drawn martyrdoms of inoffensive creatures throughout Christendom; the thought that every evening when we go to our rest the silence of night will but bring to these unhappy beings prolonged suffering, terror and agonizing death; the thought that such things take place, not by accident, or by nature, in far-off uncivilized countries, but here, in our midst, in the heart of our towns, next door, maybe, to our home, by deliberate, organized, systematic law-abiding act—this is what tears the heart, embitters life and forces us to the reflection that, after all, human civilization and human progress are but fever dreams, futile, meaningless and grotesque.

And this is why, when the vivisectors ask us angrily, "What right have you to meddle with the researches of scientific men?" that we turn upon them with greater anger and retort in our turn, "What right have you to render earth uninhabitable and life insupportable for men with hearts in their bosoms?"

It is not the fact, as the partisans of vivisection are never weary of declaring, that the public has shown itself incapable of judging scientific necessities, but rather that the scientists have shown themselves incapable of recognizing the obligations of public morality. If in matters of technical physiology it be fair to regard the public as "profane," it is equally correct to regard the experts of vivisection as "profane" in relation to the principles of moral conduct. Does the diploma of physiologists entitle them to pose as the exclusive arbiters of morality? Or is it not rather the truth that, being themselves indifferent to the interests of morality and incompetent to deal with psychic considerations, they assume the defenders of these to be ignorant of scientific exigencies and incapable of understanding them, solely because of their own moral blindness?"

Now, the fact is that the question is quite as much of moral as of physical interest.

If society be right in refusing to recognize the infallibility of a purely ecclesiastical caste in matters affecting the public conscience—as, for instance, in respect of religious persecution—it is equally right in refusing to admit the assumption of infallibility on the part of a caste exclusively scientific and materialistic in matters similarly affecting the public conscience. It was in the teeth of powerful vested interests that the world rejected compromise with the Inquisition and with the slave traffic, and the same considerations which influenced civilized men in dealing with these institutions must equally influence them to-day, face to face with the claims and interests of vivisection.

It is vain to urge that the majority of modern torturers for science's sake are educated, intelligent and eminent men, illustrious savants, venerable professors, who are themselves the best judges of what is necessary for science—who may safely be trusted to act for the best, and who are preeminently humane and sympathetic in their conduct and methods. Precisely the same was said with equal truth of the majority of torturers for religion's sake. They, too, were the learned, reverend and eminent men of their time, and like the vivisectors, were often genial and polished members of society, chiefs of distinction, dignitaries of high importance in the State. And there is no reason to doubt that the atrocities of which they were the eager authors and contrivers were instigated, not by a love of cruelty, but by zeal for the honor of religion and for the advance of the church, and by ardor for the good of humanity.

Every custom that the world has seen, whatever its barbarity, has found apologists, simply because of its being a custom.

History shows us that the abolition of human and other sacrifices in religious cults was in its time denounced as a menace for the faith, as an evidence of morbid sensibility and a symptom of degeneracy. Gladiatorial combats, cruel and barbarous amusements of all kinds, formerly popular, have in their turn been suppressed, and always in spite of the clamorous protestations of persons interested in their maintenance. No pretext based on the pretended utility of vivisection ought to exempt it from the category of practices unworthy of a civilized era.

The abuse of force is an inexcusable crime and shame in those who claim despotic authority, and to seek to justify such abuse by representing it as a means of attaining a praiseworthy end is to argue, as did a certain celebrated brigand, who attempted to excuse his acts of violence by saying, "If I have committed robbery, I have robbed only heretics with the intention of enriching the coffers of the true Church."

Cruelty is always cruel, and only Jesuits and Paul Bert will dare to rehabilitate the sophistry expressed in the ecclesiastical axiom, "The end justifies the means," even when the "end" is "scientific progress," the means "suffering the most atrocious that the imagination can conceive," and the victims, beings incapable of defending themselves or of avenging their wrongs.

Happily for humanity, the arbiters of the national conscience are neither the ecclesiastics nor the biologists, but the people.

I reflect on the history of the inquisition, of slavery and of despotism, and I have confidence in the future!

There is a better gospel than that of intellectual science, there is a higher law than that of physical utility. Do not let us fear, any of us, that by living up to the best and noblest in us we shall miss any good thing that might have been ours by baser means. The greater includes the lesser, and the science of Heaven[3] encompasses all lower knowledges. Only let us seek first the kingdom of God and God's justice, and all these things shall be added unto us. There is nothing the righteous man may not know, for the spirit in him is divine, and able to unfold all secrets in their order.

For love is the universal solvent, and love's method is in all its unfoldings consistent with its object and intent.

In conclusion, I recommend specially to my brethren of the medical faculty those brave and worthy words which Dr. Samuel Johnson addressed to the physiologists of his day:

"May all men of heart who follow the noble science of medicine, the aim of which is the relief of suffering, publicly condemn the practices of vivisection, for they are of a nature to discredit their profession, and will end by extinguishing in their votaries those sentiments which alone deserve the

3. This refers to Kingsford's own version of theosophy. See Barbara Gates, *Kindred Nature* (University of Chicago Press, 1998), 147–52. *Ed.*

confidence of the public, and the absence of which is more to be dreaded than the worst of physical evils."[4]

FRANCES POWER COBBE

"Science in Excelsis: A New Vision of Judgement"

The Modern Rack. London: Swan Sonnenschein & Co, 1889. 239–51.

SCENE I.

An outlying region of Paradise. A group of Cherubim reclining on clouds. In the midst, the Archangel St. Raphael on a crimson bank of sunset. Eloa, the sister of the Angels (the Angel of Pity), leaning on the frustrsum of a rainbow in the background.

ST. RAPHAEL. My friends and fellow Cherubim, it seems to me that we and some of our former associates, now in "another place," have dissertated long enough on Fixed Fate, Free Will, Foreknowledge Absolute. If I mistake not, it is nearly nine hundred thousand years since the subject was first mooted by my illustrious brother Saint Uriel, and since that epoch we have spent many ages in talking the matter over, without arriving at any satisfactory conclusion. In fact (as one of these poor little intelligent creatures who move on the planet Tellus ventured to surmise), we have—

"Found no end, in wandering mazes lost."[1]

It is high time, surely, for us to turn to some more practical study, lest our special glory of being the "Spirits who *know* most" be eclipsed, and no question will remain but that the Seraphim, who *love* most, have the better of us.

THE ANGEL ISRAFEL. I rise to second the motion of the most wise and noble Archangel. His observation is just. We have spent time enough on scholastic and metaphysical riddles which no Angel can be expected to understand. Science, as everyone now admits, is superior both to Learning and Philosophy. Let us turn our attention to it forthwith.

4. Johnson was a convinced opponent of vivisection. See his essay in the *Idler* 17, August 5, 1758. *Ed.*

1. John Milton. *Paradise Lost* 2:561. *Ed.*

MANY CHERUBIM AT ONCE. By all means! By all means! Let us immediately establish a "Celestial Association for the Promotion of Science."

RAPHAEL (*graciously*). I am pleased, my friends, to see that my suggestion meets with your approval. We will take up Science with angelic vigour forthwith. Let us consider a moment how we shall pursue the various branches. As to Astronomy (for which we possess, of course, very special advantages), I think our Celestial Association might very properly "endow research" by sending out an Exploring Expedition round the Universe, to bring us in the latest intelligence from all the worlds of space. A Report drawn up on such a scale would be both instructive and entertaining.

THE ANGEL SAMIASA. A splendid proposal, Saint Raphael! I am ready to volunteer for the Expedition on the spot.

MANY OTHER ANGELS. And I! And I! And I!

RAPHAEL. This is highly gratifying. Our distinguished colleagues will doubtless return, within a million years or so, laden with interesting intelligence. I would only warn the less far-sighted not to lose themselves by mischance in a Nebula, a misfortune to which scientists in general seem liable. The next science to be considered (since we need not trouble ourselves with petty details, such as Geography or Geology) is Physiology; and here, I venture to foretell, our most interesting studies will be found. What do any of us, Angels, know, for example, of that singular little Automaton, Man—a tiny creature of bone and muscle, blood and nerves, who yet sends his thoughts up to our very dwelling-place, looks through our ethereal forms with his telescope even to the remotest suns, penetrates the history of past ages, and writes poems which, like the *Divina Commedia* and *Paradise Lost*, even Angels are wont to peruse with satisfaction? How, I ask, does that little lump of pulpy matter which the creature calls his Brain help him to do these things? How does he move his little legs and arms by those bands he calls his muscles; and what is the meaning of that curious internal bag, into which he is always cramming bread and fruit and (horrible to think!) the flesh of other animals? Truly, I believe, my dear fellow-cherubim, we could scarcely find, in any of the hundred million spheres around us, a more interesting point whereat to commence our studies than this very Physiology of Man; and I for my part, as the Archangelic Healer, confidently hope to hit on some beneficent discoveries which, as in the case of Tobit, may enable me to cure these poor creatures' maladies.

[*All the Angels tumultuously applaud, and St. Raphael continues:*]

To effect our purpose, it will be desirable to adopt their own method of scientific research and make investigations into the structure of these little beings, especially into their nervous systems; and to collect and verify as many facts as possible about their various organs—how they are kept alive, and how long it takes to kill them when they are dipped in boiling water, or starved, or put in an oven, and so on.

ELOA (*starting up*). Oh, Saint Raphael! you don't mean to say you would suffocate, or starve, or bake those miserable creatures? Consider, they are evidently sensitive to pain.

RAPHAEL (*reprovingly*). Dear Eloa! do not be so excitable! Nothing will be attempted, I can assure you, beyond the legitimate demands of Science. Grave doubts may be entertained as to whether Men are anything more than Automata; but, even granting they have some dim feelings of pain and pleasure, it would surely be absurd for a moment to put their sensations in competition with the noble thirst for knowledge now stirring in the Angelic mind? Only think of placing *man's* existence or suffering in the balance against the acquirement of some great truth by Archangels like Gabriel, Michael, or myself!

ELOA (*weeping and clasping her hands*). Oh, Saint Raphael! when you speak thus, and draw up your majestic form a thousand fathoms high and shake your iridescent wings, I feel how poor and low, and all too base, to claim your consideration, are the feeble creatures of earth! But yet, O mighty and wise and generous Archangel, have pity on these miserable beings! To the greater part of them Science is but a name, a word of no meaning. To live their little day in the sun; to play and eat and sleep; to love their mates and their offspring; this is what existence is to them—harmless, even if ignoble. Say, great and glorious St. Raphael, that you will not turn that humble existence into a curse by putting them to tortures of which they can understand neither reason nor end?

[*Two or three Cherubim touch her on the shoulder.*]

Sister Eloa! It is a pity when charming Angels talk of things which they don't understand.

ST. RAPHAEL. Well, well, Eloa shall have her way thus far. We will not try any experiments on those simple mortals for whom she pleads, who know nothing about the glories of Science, and cannot be supposed to take any sympathetic interest in our investigations into their brains and stomachs. We will confine our researches entirely to those eminent Physiologists who have devoted themselves to the same pursuit, and have tried every experiment upon creatures nearly as much lower than they as they are lower than we; I mean on cats, dogs, and monkeys. They have been so ingenious in inventing and so candid in recording all their practices, that we shall have nothing to do but to order up a few of their *Handbooks* and *Reports,* and then set to work to go over the contents *seriatim* on their own persons. At the end—though it seems doubtful whether these human Physiologists have obtained anything of value by tormenting the brutes—of course we, with our keener vision and deeper knowledge, shall advance Science much more by experimenting on the higher animal.

THE ANGEL ITUHRIEL. Nothing can be more to the purpose than our great President's observation. I only wish to know how his Wisdom means to proceed.

RAPHAEL. Well, I think we must first command a new Physiological Laboratory to be built in connection with our College of Science, and let it be placed in such a position that it cannot be overlooked, and also where good south and north light may be obtained. So far as my recollection goes, there has not hitherto been any edifice of the kind in Heaven, though there are several closely resembling it in an opposite locality. Then we shall furnish it suitable with tables, Bernard's gags, experiment troughs, forceps, saws, clamps, chisels, cannulæ, knives and actual cauteries; a furnace or two, and an engine for maintaining artificial respiration when the subjects are curarised. When all is ready, Azrael will, I am sure, be so obliging as to run down and tell all the Physiologists they are "wanted" up here; and we may then immediately set to work without further delay.

ALL THE CHERUBIM. An excellent plan! So be it. Glory to Science in the highest! Amen.

[*Scene closes.*]

SCENE II.

A celestial Laboratory, or lofty hall, filled with a variety of singular troughs and tables of sundry shapes. A formidable collection of instruments is ranged along the wall. An engine works in the corner. Galvanic batteries, kymographions, hœmodromometers, and other philosophical machines, lie about the tables. Over the door is the inscription LICENSED AS THE ACT DIRECTS, FOR THE TORTURE OF VERTEBRATE ANIMALS, *beneath which a boy-cherub has written in chalk* "MANGLING DONE HERE." *Enter Raphael and the Cherubim. Eloa timidly following.*

RAPHAEL. Our architect has done his work with his usual rapidity. Our Laboratory has "risen like an exhalation." I hope, my friends, we shall soon be enabled to quench our noble thirst for knowledge at the fountains of life. Ha! here comes the ever-punctual Azrael and our "subjects."

[*Enter Azrael (the Angel of Death), leading in a score of eminent Physiologists, who stand, pale and shivering, near the door.*]

GERMAN PHYSIOLOGIST. Mein Gott! What is that for a place! It mooch remind me of a well-known spot.

FRENCH PHYSIOLOGIST. Mais qu'est-ce donc? Un laboratoire de physiologie? But where are the dogs, and the cats, and the rabbits? Mon Dieu! Serait-il possible que . . .

ENGLISH PHYSIOLOGIST. Well! what do those tremendous swells of Angels over there want with us? Can they intend to take some lessons out of our handbook of the Physiological laboratory, and do they mean to invite us to give them a course of lectures, like the students at the dear old Hospital?

RAPHAEL (*approaching with a smile*). Not so far wrong, most learned doctor. We mean to learn Physiology from you, only not perhaps quite in the way you expect. You have always loudly proclaimed that theory without experiment is of little worth, so we intend to try some of your own choice examples on yourself and your friends.

ALL THE PHYSIOLOGISTS IN CHORUS. Oh! oh! oh! No! no! no! Oh, how shocking! Oh, how cruel! Oh, how insulting to Science!

RAPHAEL (*turning to the Cherubim*). Did you ever hear anything so inconsistent? Why, these are the very men who have been repeating again and again that only by actual Vivisection could Physiological Science be advanced, and that Science is an end so noble and glorious that it was not worth while considering the pain any creature might endure to advance it! I have really no patience with them; but still I will condescend just to say a few words in explanation. [*He beckons to the Physiologists, and whistles, as if calling dogs.*] Come hither, you poor little two-legged trembling creatures! Don't growl and whine, but think yourselves very much honoured by what we Cherubim are going to do to you.

PHYSIOLOGISTS. Oh, my Lord! Oh, your Saintship! Oh, your Holiness! Don't try your experiments on us! We were not made to be experimented on—indeed we were not; and we are *quite certain* the UNKNOWN AND UNKNOWABLE would not approve of it at all!

RAPHAEL. I should like to know why you are not to be experimented on, when you have tried your own devices on nearly every creature which breathes.

PHYSIOLOGISTS. Why? Because we are men and they were brutes. We had of course a right to do as we pleased with them.

RAPHAEL. Well! we are angels and you are men; and by the same logic *we* have a right to do as we please with you, being quite as much above you as you are above the dogs and monkeys. Moreover, these same monkeys, by your own showing, are your near relations; whereas we angels disclaim any kind of connection with you miserable mortals.

PHYSIOLOGISTS. Oh, but, you see, we are intelligent beings.

RAPHAEL. If I am not greatly mistaken, dogs are intelligent too; much nearer to the level of your intelligence than you are to ours.

PHYSIOLOGISTS. We have reason.

RAPHAEL. So have they.

PHYSIOLOGISTS. We have affections.

RAPHAEL. So have they! More than you, I suspect.

ENGLISH PHYSIOLOGIST. We have immortal souls.

RAPHAEL. *A la bonne heure!* I was waiting for somebody to say that; and I suppose the French and German and Italian Physiologists felt a little diffidence in bringing out the argument. You have certainly immortal souls, as your presence here, after Azrael has delivered his death-warrant, sufficiently testifies. But will you please to explain to me why the fact that an animal has (as you imagine) only one life should justify you in making that solitary life such a curse as that it were better it had never been given?

GERMAN PHYSIOLOGIST (*loftily*). We don't want to be justified. We are Philosophers, and can allow no superstitious moral considerations derived merely from the inherited prejudices of our ancestors to interfere with our pursuit of knowledge.

RAPHAEL. Herr Professor! though you don't believe in the story of Adam and the Forbidden Tree of Knowledge, you talk uncommonly like one of his descendants. May I ask if you think it equally becoming for a Philosopher to steal and lie and cheat, as well as to be cruel, for sake of knowledge?

FRENCH PHYSIOLOGIST. Quel tracasserie àpropos de quelques malheureux chiens! Enfin—we are the strongest, and that is the long and the short of the matter.

RAPHAEL. Perfectly true, Monsieur! You have hit the nail on the head. Your argument is unanswerable, and of course you will acquiesce cheerfully in our application of it to the present case. We Cherubim are stronger than you men, and we mean to treat you precisely as you treated the dogs.

[*Physiologists are silent and stand, with chattering teeth, looking at the apparatus and at the Cherubim, who are tucking up their sleeves.*]

ELOA (*sinking on her knees*). Oh, my beloved Archangel, have mercy upon them!

RAPHAEL. Tut-tut! Eloa, you are really too weak, I cannot let these creatures escape. The slight resemblances which exist between their nature and ours make them (as they have said of dogs) "creatures which it would be a pity to withdraw from research"; and in the sacred interests of Science—

ALL THE CHERUBIM. Oh, yes! The sacred interests of Science! The sacred interests of Science!

PHYSIOLOGISTS (*unanimously*). D——n Science!

RAPHAEL. Come, come; we have no time to lose. Just hand me that curly-haired one, Sandalphon, and I'll begin by paralysing him with curare!

PHYSIOLOGISTS (*screaming*). O mercy, mercy! not curare!

RAPHAEL. What a miserable cur it is, whining and crying before he is hurt! We can have no more of this. Let the assistants secure the whole pack as fast as possible on the operating troughs. Where are their books?

ATTENDANT CHERUB. Here, your Grace. Here is the *Handbook of the Physiological Laboratory,* and the *Lezioni di Fisiologia Sperimentale,* and the *Leçon sure le Système Nerveux,* and the *Physiologie Opératoire,* and the *Pression Barométrique,* and the *Méthodik,* and the *Archives de Physiologie,* and the *Centralblatt,* and many more lectures and papers.

RAPHAEL. Enough for the present. Let us begin at once and take the Englishmen, for their experiments are not quite so ingeniously cruel as the others. When we have sawn through their backbones, and irritated the stumps of the nerves, and rubbed caustic on their eyes, and made a few other interesting demonstrations, we shall be in better mood to bake, and skin, and try many curious experiments with the rest. See, here is quite a facetious idea. [*Reads.*]

"It seems, indeed, wonderful to see animals (of course Men are included) sometimes, after a slight puncture of some part of the encephalon with a needle, turn round just like a horse in a circus, or roll over and over, for hours, and sometimes for days. . . . The animal is bent like a corkscrew as much as the bones allow, in cases of rolling."[2]

Think how instructive it will be to see a philosopher rolling over and over, twisted over like a corkscrew, for hours and days together! Then there are many other experiments to be verified. I say deliberately *verified,* because it seems that after being tried on dogs and cats and horses, even if all the Physiologists come to the same conclusion, which is very seldom, it always remains doubtful whether the same result will follow in the case of man. [*Turns over the books.*] Here is a good case for one of our English—or ought I to say Scotch?—subjects. It is recorded, I find, in the *British Medical Journal* for Oct. 23, 1875—a periodical, I think, edited by the very gentleman who so loudly proclaimed, in a newspaper called *The Times,* that no cruel-

2. Lecture by Dr. Brown-Séquard, *Lancet,* vol. ii., p. 600.

ties are ever practised by vivsectors. [*Aside.*] I hope you have not forgotten to bring him up, Azrael? Of the whole crew he will be the most entertaining subject, as we shall be able to see what sort of brain secretes these kind of statements. [*Aloud.*] Well, our Professor, like his dogs, will need to be starved for eighteen hours. Then we shall curarise him and establish artificial respiration, and when this is done we shall cut open his abdomen, squeeze out his gall-bladder, clamp his cystic-duct, dissect out his bile-duct, tie a tube in it, inject various things into his intestine, and carefully note the results. It will not take more than seven or eight hours, it appears, to do all that is needful.

Here is another very amusing experiment to be tried upon one of the authors of the *Handbook of the Laboratory.* He directs it to be tried by the student on the eye of a "frog or small mammal," but I have little doubt a large mammal will answer quite as well. We must first take off the Professor's spectacles, and then "scrape the cornea of the eye, so as to remove the epithelium completely. Hereupon, the caustic is to be rubbed two or three times lightly over the whole surface, after which the eye is washed with saline solution, and the animal (or professor) is left to itself for twenty or thirty minutes," during which interval spectators have recorded that it is apt to perform antics of a very diverting description.

But we will not be severe on these Englishmen, who, as I said, are not so cruel *yet* as their continental colleagues. Here, good Israfel, will you be so obliging as to catch that slippery little German who gives the *Lezioni di Fisiologia* to his pupils? We will just try two of his tricks mentioned in his book, pages 38 and 40. First, we will take hold of the sciatic nerve (the great nerve of the thigh, my dear fellow-cherubim, which in all these earthly creatures is exquisitely sensitive), and *tear out its roots at the pelvis,* as he did to the nerve of a dog. After a little while we shall then treat him to a curious experiment he is fond of trying on frogs. We will force open his mouth, seize the epiglottis with a hook, pull up the lungs, and snip them off with scissors.

As to the French gentlemen, we have plenty of interesting experiments to make on them. Here is one or two we will try on the author of the *Traité de Physiologie Humaine:*

"We must first strip the skin completely off the legs and lay bare the nerves, and then apply to the nervous branches some exciting substance."

Still more instructive will be this:

"In order to suppress the functions of the skin, it is advisable to lay bare, by shaving, the whole skin of the dog, sheep, or horse (it will not be necessary to shave the man), and to cover the exposed surface with a thick drying varnish. Animals thus treated rarely survive twelve hours. After death the organs are found gorged with black blood."

The state of the creature while it is thus simmered alive in its own blood must be very curious indeed to witness; indeed, it would seem there can be little use in the experiment, except to afford pastime to the spectators. Quite a new interest will be afforded by baking some of these gentlemen in ovens variously prepared at different degrees of heat. Several of them have ascertained in this way, as M. Gavarret mentions, that dogs bear being kept in an oven at 120° *centigrade* for eighteen minutes, or survive for thirty minutes if the oven be only heated to 80°.[3] It will be new to see how long Men can endure having the blood parched in their living veins like these animals.

Lastly, we shall take one peculiarly ingenious gentleman, and treat him as he tells us he treated a "middle-sized, vigorous dog.[4] We shall place some curare under his skin, which, we are told,[5] "will cause him to become perfectly paralysed; while his intelligence, his sensitiveness, and his will, will remain intact"—"a condition," we are assured by the same great authority, "accompanied by the most atrocious sufferings which the imagination of man can conceive." When our friend is in this state of redoubled sensitiveness, but utter helplessness, we shall make him breathe, by means of a machine blowing through a hole in his wind-pipe, and then we shall dissect out the nerves of his face, neck, fore-arm, interior of abdomen, and hip. We shall continue to excite them with electricity for ten hours, and then we shall leave him with the engine working on him, while we go and refresh ourselves for a second bout of the same interesting experiments.

ELOA (*whose eyes have grown large with horror during this reading, flings herself into the arms of St. Raphael*). Oh, my brother! my glorious Archangel! spare these poor wretches! It is impossible your noble nature can descend to inflict such torment even on the meanest of God's creatures.

RAPHAEL. Dear Eloa! Must I remind you that your unfortunate habit of compassionating unworthy objects has ere now led you into terrible mistakes? Do you forget how you followed Lucifer himself into Gehenna when he told you his pitiful tale, and how, when he had got you there, he clutched you fast, and said you should remain and be lost with him for ever; and how it was JUSTICE, and not PITY, which delivered you, so that you might warn your sex never to follow your foolish example?

3. See M. Gavarret's Treatise, p. 156.

4. *Archives de Physiologie*, vol. ii., p. 650.

5. *Revue des Deux Mondes*, Sept. 1, 1864, pp. 173, 182.

BAHMAN, LORD OF THE ANIMALS[6] (*here stands forward among the group of student-Cherubim*). Most noble Archangel and brother Cherubim! I think it becomes me to speak in this matter. Do you understand, beloved and gentle Eloa, that these men have already done all these hideous things to my poor, harmless, unoffending birds and brutes? Do you know that they have tortured them for hours and days, by scores and by hundreds, and taught thoughtless youths to stifle every emotion of compassion and do the like, multiplying and repeating every form and kind of agony again and yet again? Do you know that the clanking engines, which maintain breath in the curarised and doubly-suffering creatures, never cease working in their accursed laboratories by day or night; and that they lie down to sleep leaving their mangled victims on their torture-troughs, waiting for the morrow's fresh anguish? Do you know that one of these men alone has been known to have tried his infernal devices on no less than fourteen thousand dogs, beside uncounted numbers of other sensitive creatures?

[*Eloa sobs convulsively, and at last covers her face and slowly leaves the hall.*]

RAPHAEL. My brother Angels! there now remains nothing to stay our hands. PITY has fled before SCIENCE, who alone will henceforth direct our proceedings.

[*A veil falls and conceals the scene.*]

A voice from behind the veil:

With what measure ye mete, it shall be measured to you again.

An Anthem of Seraphs heard from a great Distance:

Blessed are the merciful, for they shall obtain mercy!

6. One of the seven Amshaspands. *Vide* Zend-Avesto.

LOUISE LIND-AF-HAGEBY AND LIESE SCHARTAU

"Fun"

The Shambles of Science: Extracts from the Diary of Two Students of Physiology. London: Ernest Bell, 1903. 19–26.

His weary eyes . . . were full of the measureless pity that is in the eyes of the surgeon who is about to vivisect of a dumb creature because it is necessary for the welfare of the human race.

Hall Caine[1]

There is a barking and howling, a groaning and snarling—a chorus of inarticulate voices which make the air vibrate with the music of the physiological laboratories. It is a strange music brought about by chords played upon by pain and terror.

That music never stops in this physiological laboratory, and it seems to have an exhilarating influence on all who go there to benefit from the advanced teachings of that institution.

To-day's lecture will include the repetition of a demonstration which failed last time. A large dog, stretched on its back on an operation-board, is carried into the lecture-room by the demonstrator and the laboratory attendant. Its legs are fixed to the board, its head is firmly held in the usual manner, and it is tightly muzzled.

There is a large incision in the side of the neck, exposing the gland. The animal exhibits all signs of intense suffering; in his struggles he again and again lifts up his body from the board, and makes powerful attempts to get free. The lecturer, attired in the blood-stained surplice of the priest of vivisection, has tucked up his sleeves and is now comfortably smoking his pipe, whilst with hands coloured crimson he arranges the electrical circuit for the stimulation that will follow. Now and then he makes a funny remark which is fully appreciated by those around him.

Students, young and old, enter and take their seats, there is a spirit of jocularity prevailing, a loud conversation is going on, jokes and laughter everywhere. The lecturer places a lamp with a strong light near the dog; with the utmost kindness and consideration he tells the students sitting near that he hopes the light will not hurt their eyes.

There is nothing of the serene dignity of science about the place,

1. Hall Caine (1853–1931), British novelist and secretary to Dante Gabriel Rossetti. *Ed.*

everybody looks as if he expected an hour's amusement; if he gets instruction in the bargain—well, it is all the better.

The lecturer has gone out of the room, the apparatus is ready, the dog will not run away nor will he offend our ears by any loud yelps; besides, if he did try both it would only be rather amusing. It is so ridiculous to see him trying to tear off the strings and to get loose; why, he looks as if he wanted to fly, working his shoulders as if they were cut wings. The attendant stands near the animal to see that nothing goes wrong. The general hilarity has also reached him.

When the lecturer re-enters, the dog's struggles are changed into convulsive trembling of the whole body. This is nothing unusual; the animals seem to realise the presence of their tormentors long before these touch them. Dogs whose heads are covered so that they cannot see will nevertheless show signs of the utmost terror when their vivisectors approach them.

The demonstration begins. There is a cannula[2] in the duct of the submaxillary gland, and we are going to study changes in the rate of flow of saliva. The apparatus is arranged in such a manner that we can all watch the differences in the rate of the flow, as an image of it is projected on a screen by means of a lantern. The chorda tympani is stimulated. The rate of flow ought now to be "greatly accelerated," but it does not behave nicely and refuses to be accelerated. Laughter and applause. Of course the clever demonstrator cannot take the responsibility for any breach of etiquette on the part of a particular kind of saliva in a particular dog. Let us now see the result of stimulation of the sympathetic. *In a dog* the rate of flow ought not to be influenced by this kind of stimulation. But, what is this? The rapidity of the flow increases. Do we see right? Yes, there is no doubt about it. The saliva once more clearly demonstrates its want of salivary education and appears like a gush from a waterfall. Roars of laughter and uproarious stamping of feet.

"I am afraid this experiment is not very successful," says the lecturer with a sigh, after various other forms of "stimulation." Laughter and applause. Physiological experiments so often come in contact with "the unknown," let us, therefore, have a good stock of humour to carry us through situations that otherwise might make us melancholy.

The dog is shaking the board in his efforts to escape. During the stimulation these efforts have been redoubled. The brute is the only one of the party who is lacking in true humour. But then—he is only a dog. . . .

The lecturer, in spite of his splendidly good temper, seems a little ir-

2. A tube inserted into a cavity, for drainage or for the insertion of fluids or substances. *Ed.*

ritated at the result of the experiment that was made in order to correct a former one. Besides, the animal is not quiet. He touches a bell; the laboratory servant enters and is told to take out the dog. The lecturer has not mentioned anæsthetics, nor has he told us that the animal is not under anæsthesia, we suppose because he thinks that there is no need of telling us such an evident thing. The attendant disconnects the operation-board from the electrical apparatus, lifts up the board, and walks out with the animal. The man ought to be skilled in carrying operation-boards with dogs fixed to them about, but it may be, as we have said before, that the general spirit of mirth and pleasure has so affected him that he gets careless, for he is balancing the board in such a manner that it swings from one side to another. Fancy, if he should drop it! The board and the electrical coils might be injured.

He passes through the door all right, but when he is going to shut it, he cannot manage everything, and the board is banged against the door. The man does not understand properly the value of the doors. . . . The poor fellow must have got annoyed, for we hear another bang when he puts down the board, in order not to be encumbered by it when he now shuts the door.

The banging has not in the least disturbed us. We are listening to some interesting accounts of "sham-feeding." The lecturer describes certain experiments on dogs amid the laughter of the audience. The œsophogus had been cut and a fistula established, so that the food taken fell down on the floor instead of passing into the stomach. The dogs ate and ate and ate—they were frightfully hungry—and were much surprised to see the food fall out; they tried again with the same result. They could go on like that for hours. How comical! How clever of the physiologist who tried this! Aren't animals stupid?

During the process of eating, the stomachs of the dogs secreted gastric juice. This is an instance of "psychic secretion." Awfully interesting. Marvellously clever!

When describing some other experiments, where food had been introduced directly into the stomachs by means of fistulæ[3] when the animals had been asleep, the lecturer jokingly said that this was rather difficult, for you had to be careful not to awake the dogs, but only their stomachs. Laughter and applause.

When this lecture was over we suddenly remembered Mr. Hall Caine's description of the "measureless pity" in the eyes of the surgeon who is about to vivisect a dumb creature because it is necessary for the welfare of the human race. What a lovely picture! But things are not so beautifully sentimental, and the welfare of the human race is sometimes rather far away.

3. Canals formed by imperfectly closed wounds. *Ed.*

Conservation: Birds

ELIZA COOK

From the Preface

The Poetical Works. London: Frederick Warne and Co., 1869.

It is with considerable pride, and more pleasure, that I now present to my readers in one volume the whole of my poems, at a price which, I hope, will be within the means of those who could not afford the purchase of my previous editions; and if I can still retain the sympathy and support of "the people" I shall be amply rewarded, and wish for no more richly-gilded laurel.

I have been too long before the Public to have anything new to express or explain relative to the compositions now again tendered for their reception. I can only offer my earnest thanks for the generous patronage which has always followed the numerous editions of my works; and declare that I am still, as I ever have been, inspired alone by "love and goodwill" toward those who have so kindly helped me along my chequered path, by freely responding to my simple effusions. Let me add, that I am very happy in the assurance afforded me through that response, of many genial ears and hearts being as open to the whistle of the woodland robin, as they are to the pæan of the cloud-piercing skylark.

ELIZA COOK

"Birds"

The Poetical Works. London: Frederick Warne and Co., 1869. 214.

Birds! Birds! ye are beautiful things,
With your earth-treading feet and your cloud-cleaving wings!
Where shall Man wander, and where shall he dwell,
Beautiful birds, that ye not come as well?
Ye have nests on the mountain all rugged and stark,
Ye build and ye brood 'neath the cottagers' eaves,
And ye sleep on the sod 'mid the bonnie green leaves.
Ye hide in the heather, ye lurk in the brake,
Ye dive in the sweet flags that shadow the lake;
Ye skim where the stream parts the orchard-decked land,
Ye dance where the foam sweeps the desolate strand;
Beautiful Birds, ye come thickly around,
When the bud's on the branch and the snow's on the ground;
Ye come when the richest of roses flush out,
And ye come when the yellow leaf eddies about!

SARAH ORNE JEWETT

"A White Heron"

"A White Heron" and Other Stories. Boston and New York: Houghton Mifflin Co., 1886. 1–22.

The woods were already filled with shadows one June evening, just before eight o'clock, though a bright sunset still glimmered faintly among the trunks of the trees. A little girl was driving home her cow, a plodding, dilatory, provoking creature in her behavior, but a valued companion for all that. They were going away from whatever light there was, and striking deep into the woods, but their feet were familiar with the path, and it was no matter whether their eyes could see it or not.

There was hardly a night the summer through when the old cow could be found waiting at the pasture bars; on the contrary, it was her greatest pleasure to hide herself away among the huckleberry bushes, and though she wore a loud bell she had made the discovery that if one stood perfectly still it would not ring. So Sylvia had to hunt for her until she found her, and call Co'! Co'! With never an answering Moo, until her childish patience was quite spent. If the creature had not given good milk and plenty of it, the case would have seemed very different to her owners. Besides, Sylvia had all the time there was, and very little use to make of it. Sometimes in pleasant weather it was a consolation to look upon the cow's pranks as an intelligent attempt to play hide and seek, and as the child had no playmates she lent herself to this amusement with a good deal of zest. Though this chase had been so long that the wary animal herself had given an unusual signal of her whereabouts, Sylvia had only laughed when she came upon Mistress Moolly at the swampside, and urged her affectionately homeward with a twig of birch leaves. The old cow was not inclined to wander farther, she even turned in the right direction for once as they left the pasture, and stepped along the road at a good pace. She was quite ready to be milked now, and seldom stopped to browse. Sylvia wondered what her grandmother would say because they were so late. It was a great while since she had left home at half-past five o'clock, but everybody knew the difficulty of making this errand a short one. Mrs. Tilley had chased the hornéd torment too many summer evenings herself to blame any one else for lingering, and was only thankful as she waited that she had Sylvia, nowadays, to give such valuable assistance. The good woman suspected that Sylvia loitered occasionally on her own account; there never was such a child for straying about out-of-doors since the world was made! Everybody said that it was a good change for a little maid who had tried to grow for eight years in a crowded manufacturing town, but, as for Sylvia herself, it seemed as if she never had been alive at all before she came to live at the farm. She thought often with wistful compassion of a wretched geranium that belonged to a town neighbor.

"'Afraid of folks,'" old Mrs. Tilley said to herself, with a smile, after she had made the unlikely choice of Sylvia from her daughter's houseful of children, and was returning to the farm. "'Afraid of folks,' they said! I guess she won't be troubled no great with 'em up to the old place!" When they reached the door of the lonely house and stopped to unlock it, and the cat came to purr loudly, and rub against them, a deserted pussy, indeed, but fat with young robins, Sylvia whispered that this was a beautiful place to live in, and she never should wish to go home.

The companions followed the shady woodroad, the cow taking slow steps and the child very fast ones. The cow stopped long at the brook to drink, as if the pasture were not half a swamp, and Sylvia stood still and waited, letting her bare feet cool themselves in the shoal water, while the great twilight moths struck softly against her. She waded on through the brook as the cow moved away, and listened to the thrushes with a heart that beat fast with pleasure. There was a stirring in the great boughs overhead. They were full of little birds and beasts that seemed to be wide awake, and going about their world, or else saying good-night to each other in sleepy twitters. Sylvia herself felt sleepy as she walked along. However, it was not much farther to the house, and the air was soft and sweet. She was not often in the woods so late as this, and it made her feel as if she were a part of the gray shadows and the moving leaves. She was just thinking how long it seemed since she first came to the farm a year ago, and wondering if everything went on in the noisy town just the same as when she was there; the thought of the great red-faced boy who used to chase and frighten her made her hurry along the path to escape from the shadow of the trees.

Suddenly this little woods-girl is horror-stricken to hear a clear whistle not very far away. Not a bird's-whistle, which would have a sort of friendliness, but a boy's whistle, determined, and somewhat aggressive. Sylvia left the cow to whatever sad fate might await her, and stepped discreetly aside into the bushes, but she was just too late. The enemy had discovered her, and called out in a very cheerful and persuasive tone, "Halloa, little girl, how far is it to the road?" and trembling Sylvia answered almost inaudibly, "A good ways."

She did not dare to look boldly at the tall young man, who carried a gun over his shoulder, but she came out of her bush and again followed the cow, while he walked alongside.

"I have been hunting for some birds," the stranger said kindly, "and I have lost my way, and need a friend very much. Don't be afraid," he added gallantly. "Speak up and tell me what your name is, and whether you think I can spend the night at your house, and go out gunning early in the morning."

Sylvia was more alarmed than before. Would not her grandmother consider her much to blame? But who could have foreseen such an accident as this? It did not seem to be her fault, and she hung her head as if the stem of it were broken, but managed to answer "Sylvy," with much effort when her companion again asked her name.

Mrs. Tilley was standing in the doorway when the trio came into view. The cow gave a loud moo by way of explanation.

"Yes, you'd better speak up for yourself, you old trial! Where'd she tuck herself away this time, Sylvy?" But Sylvia kept an awed silence; she sknew by instinct that her grandmother did not comprehend the gravity of the situation. She must be mistaking the stranger for one of the farmer-lads of the region.

The young man stood his gun beside the door, and dropped a lumpy game-bag beside it; then he bade Mrs. Tilley good-evening, and repeated his wayfarer's story, and asked if he could have a night's lodging.

"Put me anywhere you like," he said. "I must be off early in the morning, before day; but I am very hungry, indeed. You can give me some milk at any rate, that's plain."

"Dear sakes, yes," responded the hostess, whose long slumbering hospitality seemed to be easily awakened. "You might fare better if you went out to the main road a mile or so, but you're welcome to what we've got. I'll milk right off, and you make yourself at home. You can sleep on husks or feathers," she proffered graciously. "I raised them all myself. There's good pasturing for geese just below here towards the ma'sh. Now step round and set a plate for the gentleman, Sylvy!" And Sylvia promptly stepped. She was glad to have something to do, and she was hungry herself.

It was a surprise to find so clean and comfortable a dwelling in this New England wilderness. The young man had known the horrors of its most primitive housekeeping, and the dreary squalor of that level of society which does not rebel at the companionship of hens. This was the best thrift of an old-fashioned farmstead, though on such a small scale that it seemed like a hermitage. He listened eagerly to the old woman's quaint talk, he watched Sylvia's pale face and shining gray eyes with ever growing enthusiasm, and insisted that this was the best supper he had eaten for a month, and afterward the new-made friends sat down in the door-way together while the moon came up.

Soon it would be berry-time, and Sylvia was a great help at picking. The cow was a good milker, though a plaguy thing to keep track of, the hostess gossiped frankly, adding presently that she had buried four children, so Sylvia's mother, and a son (who might be dead) in California were all the children she had left. "Dan, my boy, was a great hand to go gunning," she explained sadly. "I never wanted for pa'triges or gray squer'ls while he was to home. He's been a great wand'rer, I expect, and he's no hand to write letters. There, I don't blame him, I'd ha' seen the world myself if it had been so I could."

"Sylvy takes after him," the grandmother continued affectionately, after a minute's pause. "There ain't a foot o' ground she don't know her way over, and the wild creaturs counts her one o' themselves. Squer'ls she'll tame to come an' feed right out o' her hands, and all sorts o' birds. Last winter she got the jay-birds to bangeing here, and I believe she'd 'a' scanted herself of her own meals to have plenty to throw out amongst 'em, if I had n't kep' watch. Anything but crows, I tell her, I'm willin' to help support—though Dan he had a tamed one o' them that did seem to have reason same as folks. It was round here a good spell after he went away. Dan an' his father they did n't hitch,—but he never held up his head ag'in after Dan had dared him an' gone off."

The guest did not notice this hint of family sorrows in his eager interest in something else.

"So Sylvy knows all about birds, does she?" he exclaimed, as he looked round at the little girl who sat, very demure but increasingly sleepy, in the moonlight. "I am making a collection of birds myself. I have been at it ever since I was a boy." (Mrs. Tilley smiled.) "There are two or three very rare ones I have been hunting for these five years. I mean to get them on my ground if they can be found."

"Do you cage 'em up?" asked Mrs. Tilley doubtfully, in response to this enthusiastic announcement.

"Oh no, they're stuffed and preserved, dozens and dozens of them," said the ornithologist. "And I have shot or snared every one myself. I caught a glimpse of a white heron a few miles from here on Saturday, and I have followed it in this direction. They have never been found in this district at all. The little white heron, it is," and he turned again to look at Sylvia with the hope of discovering that the rare bird was one of her acquaintances.

But Sylvia was watching a hop-toad in the narrow footpath.

"You would know the heron if you saw it," the stranger continued eagerly. "A queer tall white bird with soft feathers and long thin legs. And it would have a nest perhaps in the top of a high tree, made of sticks, something like a hawk's nest."

Sylvia's heart gave a wild beat; she knew that strange white bird, and had once stolen softly near where it stood in some bright green swamp grass, away over at the other side of the woods. There was an open place where the sunshine always seemed strangely yellow and hot, where tall, nodding rushes grew, and her grandmother had warned her that she might sink in the soft black mud underneath and never be heard of more. Not far beyond were the salt marshes just this side of the sea itself, which Sylvia wondered and dreamed much about, but never had seen, whose great voice could sometimes be heard above the noise of the woods on stormy nights.

"I can't think of anything I should like so much as to find that heron's nest," the handsome stranger was saying. "I would give ten dollars to anybody who could show it to me," he added desperately, "and I mean to spend my whole vacation hunting for it if need be. Perhaps it was only migrating, or had been chased out of its own region by some bird of prey."

Mrs. Tilley gave amazed attention to all this, but Sylvia still watched the toad, not divining, as she might have done at some calmer time, that the creature wished to get to its hole under the door-step, and was much hindered by the unusual spectators at that hour of the evening. No amount of thought, that night, could decide how many wished-for treasures the ten dollars, so lightly spoken of, would buy.

The next day the young sportsman hovered about the woods, and Sylvia kept him company, having lost her first fear of the friendly lad, who proved to be most kind and sympathetic. He told her many things about the birds and what they knew and where they lived and what they did with themselves. And he gave her a jack-knife, which she thought as great a treasure as if she were a desert-islander. All day long he did not once make her troubled or afraid except when he brought down some unsuspecting singing creature from its bough. Sylvia would have liked him vastly better without his gun; she could not understand why he killed the very birds he seemed to like so much. But as the day waned, Sylvia still watched the young man with loving admiration. She had never seen anybody so charming and delightful; the woman's heart, asleep in the child, was vaguely thrilled by a dream of love. Some premonition of that great power stirred and swayed these young creatures who traversed the solemn woodlands with soft-footed silent care. They stopped to listen to a bird's song; they pressed forward again eagerly, parting the branches—speaking to each other rarely and in whispers; the young man going first and Sylvia following, fascinated, a few steps behind, with her gray eyes dark with excitement.

She grieved because the longed-for white heron was elusive, but she did not lead the guest, she only followed, and there was no such thing as speaking first. The sound of her own unquestioned voice would have terrified her—it was hard enough to answer yes or no when there was need of that. At last evening began to fall, and they drove the cow home together, and Sylvia smiled with pleasure when they came to the place where she heard the whistle and was afraid only the night before.

II.

Half a mile from home, at the farther edge of the woods, where the land was highest, a great pine-tree stood, the last of its generation. Whether it was left for a boundary mark, or for what reason, no one could say; the wood-choppers who had felled its mates were dead and gone long ago, and a whole forest of sturdy trees, pines and oaks and maples, had grown again. But the stately head of this old pine towered above them all and made a landmark for sea and shore miles and miles away. Sylvia knew it well. She had always believed that whoever climbed to the top of it could see the ocean; and the little girl had often laid her hand on the great rough trunk and looked up wistfully at those dark boughs that the wind always stirred, no matter how hot and still the air might be below. Now she thought of the tree with a new excitement, for why, if one climbed it at break of day could not one see all the world, and easily discover from whence the white heron flew, and mark the place, and find the hidden nest?

What a spirit of adventure, what wild ambition! What fancied triumph and delight and glory for the later morning when she could make known the secret! It was almost too real and too great for the childish heart to bear.

All night the door of the little house stood open and the whippoorwills came and sang upon the very step. The young sportsman and his old hostess were sound asleep, but Sylvia's great design kept her broad awake and watching. She forgot to think of sleep. The short summer night seemed as long as the winter darkness, and at last when the whippoorwills ceased, and she was afraid the morning would after all come too soon, she stole out of the house and followed the pasture path through the woods, hastening toward the open ground beyond, listening with a sense of comfort and companionship to the drowsy twitter of a half-awakened bird, whose perch she had jarred in passing. Alas, if the great wave of human interest which flooded for the first time this dull little life should sweep away the satisfactions of an existence heart to heart with nature and the dumb life of the forest!

There was the huge tree asleep yet in the paling moonlight, and small and silly Sylvia began with utmost bravery to mount to the top of it, with tingling, eager blood coursing the channels of her whole frame, with her bare feet and fingers, that pinched and held like bird's claws to the monstrous ladder reaching up, up, almost to the sky itself. First she must mount the white oak tree that grew alongside, where she was almost lost among the dark branches and the green leaves heavy and wet with dew; a bird fluttered off its nest, and a red squirrel ran to and fro and scolded pettishly at the harmless housebreaker. Sylvia felt her way easily. She had often climbed there, and knew that higher still one of the oak's upper branches chafed against the pine trunk, just where its lower boughs were set close together. There, when she made the dangerous pass from one tree to the other, the great enterprise would really begin.

She crept out along the swaying oak limb at last, and took the daring step across into the old pine-tree. The way was harder than she thought; she must reach far and hold fast, the sharp dry twigs caught and held her and scratched her like angry talons, the pitch made her thin little fingers clumsy and stiff as she went round and round the tree's great stem, higher and higher upward. The sparrows and robins in the woods below were beginning to wake and twitter to the dawn, yet it seemed much lighter there aloft in the pine-tree, and the child knew she must hurry if her project were to be of any use.

The tree seemed to lengthen itself out as she went up, and to reach farther and farther upward. It was like a great main-mast to the voyaging earth; it must truly have been amazed that morning through all its ponderous frame as it felt this determined spark of human spirit wending its way from higher branch to branch. Who knows how steadily the least twigs held themselves to advantage this light, weak creature on her way! The old pine must have loved his new dependent. More than all the hawks, and bats, and moths, and even the sweet voiced thrushes, was the brave, beating heart of the solitary gray-eyed child. And the tree stood still and frowned away the winds that June morning while the dawn grew bright in the east.

Sylvia's face was like a pale star, if one had seen it from the ground, when the last thorny bough was past, and she stood trembling and tired but wholly triumphant, high in the tree-top. Yes, there was the sea with the dawning sun making a golden dazzle over it, and toward that glorious east flew two hawks with slow-moving pinions. How low they looked in the air from that height when one had only seen them before far up, and dark against the blue sky. Their gray feathers were as soft as moths; they seemed only a little way from the tree, and Sylvia felt as if she too could go flying away among the clouds. Westward, the woodlands and farms reached miles and miles into the distance; here and there were church steeples, and white villages, truly it was a vast and awesome world!

The birds sang louder and louder. At last the sun came up bewilderingly bright. Sylvia could see the white sails of ships out at sea, and the clouds that were purple and rose-colored and yellow at first began to fade away. Where was the white heron's nest in the sea of green branches, and was this wonderful sight and pageant of the world the only reward for having climbed to such a giddy height? Now look down again, Sylvia, where the green marsh is set among the shining birches and dark hemlocks; there where you saw the white heron once you will see him again; look, look! A white spot of him like a single floating feather comes up from the dead hemlock and grows larger, and rises, and comes close at last, and goes by the landmark pine with steady sweep of wing and outstretched slender neck and crested head. And wait! wait! do not move a foot or a finger, little girl, do not send an arrow of light and consciousness from your two eager eyes, for the heron has perched on a pine bough not far beyond yours, and cries back to his mate on the nest and plumes his feathers for the new day!

The child gives a long sigh a minute later when a company of shouting cat-birds comes also to the tree, and vexed by their fluttering and lawlessness the solemn heron goes away. She knows his secret now, the wild, light, slender bird that floats and wavers, and goes back like an arrow presently to his home in the green world beneath. Then Sylvia, well satisfied, makes her perilous way down again, not daring to look far below the branch she stands on, ready to cry sometimes because her fingers ache and her lamed feet slip. Wondering over and over again what the stranger would say to her, and what he would think when she told him how to find his way straight to the heron's nest.

"Sylvy, Sylvy!" called the busy old grandmother again and again, but nobody answered, and the small husk bed was empty and Sylvia had disappeared.

The guest waked from a dream, and remembering his day's pleasure hurried to dress himself that it might sooner begin. He was sure from the way the shy little girl looked once or twice yesterday that she had at least seen the white heron, and now she must really be made to tell. Here she comes now, paler than ever, and her worn old frock is torn and tattered, and smeared with pine pitch. The grandmother and the sportsman stand in the door together and question her, and the splendid moment has come to speak of the dead hemlock-tree by the green marsh.

But Sylvia does not speak after all, though the old grandmother fretfully rebukes her, and the young man's kind, appealing eyes are looking straight in her own. He can make them rich with money; he has promised it, and they are poor now. He is so well worth making happy, and he waits to hear the story she can tell.

No, she must keep silence! What is it that suddenly forbids her and makes her dumb? Has she been nine years and growing now, when the great world for the first time puts out a hand to her, must she thrust it aside for a bird's sake? The murmur of the pine's green branches is in her ears, she remembers how the white heron came flying through the golden air and how they watched the sea and the morning together, and Sylvia cannot speak; she cannot tell the heron's secret and give its life away.

Dear loyalty, that suffered a sharp pang as the guest went away disappointed later in the day, that could have served and followed him and loved him as a dog loves! Many a night Sylvia heard the echo of his whistle haunting the pasture path as she came home with the loitering cow. She forgot even her sorrow at the sharp report of his gun and the sight of thrushes and sparrows dropping silent to the ground, their songs hushed and their pretty feathers stained and wet with blood. Were the birds better friends than the hunter might have been,—who can tell? Whatever treasures were lost to her, woodlands and summer-time, remember! Bring your gifts and graces and tell your secrets to this lonely country child!

WINIFRED, DUCHESS OF PORTLAND

From the opening proceedings of "Protection of Bird and Animal Life"

A transaction of the *International Congress of Women*, 1899. Presented on July 3, 1899, at the Convocation Hall of Church House, Dean's Yard, Westminster. Edited by the Countess of Aberdeen, ICW President. London: T. Fisher Unwin, 1900. 235–36.

. . . It is with a certain feeling of humility that I undertake to plead a cause so simple and old-fashioned as that of the "Protection of Birds."

In an assembly like this, where many are more than suspected of being able and willing to outrun the present and forestall the future, I think we may congratulate ourselves on that immunity from criticism and misrepresentation that goes with a modest standpoint and limited aims.

Much liberal effort on the part of women suffers from the fact that they are suspected—no doubt without a particle of reason—never to mean *quite* what they say.

If they propose the removal of a pressing and admitted grievance, they are perhaps met with the retort, that what they advocate would only be

FIGURE 14 Winifred, Duchess of Portland

used as a stepping-stone to something else undesirable—if not positively dangerous.

Those of them who cannot keep politics out of education or philanthropy have made it seem that everything accomplished in these directions by others is apt to appear political to the opponents of the whole movement.

But luckily for us, our critics, if we have any, *must* stick to the point, for there is only one point to urge.

Moreover, we are a homogeneous body if a small and unimportant one.

We have none of those differences between the van and the rear that sometimes throw the main body into confusion. For instance, our friends on the Continent, who are striving for the same wider opportunities of self-improvement as we enjoy here as a matter of course, find it hard to keep up with our own dashing champions of equality, who having long since carried the universities and the medical schools, are closing their ranks for an attack upon the Senate.

Lastly, it has often been urged by critics and opponents unchivalrous enough to withhold from us the benefit of the doubt, that woman will cease to pity when she comes to power, and that, in competition with man, she will perforce borrow, or simulate, the qualities on which he relies for success in the battle of life.

If this prophecy is not to come true, then we must run with the hare and hunt with the hounds. Our presence here to-day is a sign that nothing less is the intention of a good many of us, and that if we are to learn liberty we do not mean to forget tenderheartedness and love.

I feel, therefore, that no further apology is needed for pressing upon your attention the cause of the "Protection of Birds," as one worthy to claim the best of womanly sympathy and support, even in the midst of higher themes and more urgent questions.

MRS. FRANK E. LEMON [MARGARETTA LOUISA SMITH LEMON]

"Dress in Relation to Animal Life"

Leaflet no. 33. London: Society for the Protection of Birds, 1899.

A Paper Read by Mrs. F. E. Lemon, *Hon. Sec. of the Society for the Protection of Birds, before a Sectional Meeting of the International Congress of Women, at Convocation Hall, Church House, Westminster, on July 3rd, 1899.*

The DUCHESS OF PORTLAND (President of the Society for the Protection of Birds), who was in the chair, said that the protection of birds was worthy to claim the best womanly sympathy and support, even in the midst of higher things and more urgent questions.

Mrs. F. E. LEMON read the following paper:—

The subject on which I have been asked to speak is "Dress in relation to Animal Life." I do not think there is any necessity to enter into details regarding the proper treatment which should be accorded to those animals which provide us with woollen, silken, or leathern goods. These materials are mostly obtained from domesticated animals, who in Great Britain, as well as in many other countries, are now protected by law.

I regret that I am not competent to deal with the important question of the protection of which many fur-bearing animals stand in need, and I hope that other speakers will deal with this subject. Undoubtedly, terrible abuses exist; many beautiful and useful animals are becoming extinct because they are hunted and killed without due regard to the breeding season, and we know that indescribable cruelties have been practised in the killing and skinning of the fur-bearing seals, and in the procuring of certain kinds of astrachan, which is the skin of the unborn lamb.

Surely it behooves all right-minded women who would array themselves in these costly materials to make strict enquiry as to the way in which the material is obtained. Until it has been undeniably proved that before being skinned the seal has been swiftly and mercifully killed, and that the hunting is not carried on during the breeding season, we should do well to avoid the use of that fur. If all women would thus protest, the hunters would perforce have to mend their methods. The same course of action would also doubtless bring about more humane treatment of the other creatures whose skins are obtained that we may be covered and kept warm.

With these brief allusions I now turn to my special subject, that of Bird Protection; and here I shall speak with no uncertain sound, for what I shall say is based on positive knowledge gathered during many years devoted to the question.

Unfortunately it is through women and their weak submission to the dictates of what is known as Fashion that much of the wholesale and disastrous slaughter of bird life has taken place. The question is not only a sentimental one, it is also a serious economic one. Gamekeepers and others, in ignorance, and from desire of some immediate pecuniary gain, have destroyed owls and kestrels to an alarming extent, and in consequence rats, mice, and voles unmolested are playing terrible havoc in the fields and in the farmyard. But judging by the owls' and kestrels' feathers that women display on their hats, and the numbers of these birds one has seen on their way from the London docks to the plumassiers, women cannot be held guiltless in the matter of the destruction of these most useful and necessary birds. The late Lord Lilford, when President of the British Ornithologists' Union, said that the fittest place for the wilful destroyer of any owl in this country was an asylum for idiots.

It is a disgrace to civilization that, in order to pander to the appetites of epicures, we are allowing that glad songster, the skylark, to be destroyed by millions. During the season 30,000 to 40,000 skylarks are *daily* brought into London for eating.

The rich man's demand for plovers' eggs in the spring, and for their flesh in the autumn, has meant such an increase of wireworms in some districts as to put the farmers in despair. The lapwing has been called of all birds the farmers' best friend.

These few examples hint at the practical worth of birds. They are the appointed agents for certain branches of agriculture. As such they are of paramount importance in the history of a country—indeed of the whole world. I have chosen these species as illustrations of utility because, for the purpose I have named, heavy toll has been levied on them, as well as on hundreds of others, in almost every country in Europe.

Time will not permit my even enumerating the laws which have been enacted in most civilized countries for the protection of birds—laws which, unfortunately, are nowhere enforced as they should be, owing to the laxity of public opinion with regard to them. I trouble you by alluding to this part of the subject because women so often say to me "What is the use of talking to us against wearing feathers, why don't you get laws made to protect the birds?" So I want to show that the legal aspect of the question is being constantly considered; but, unhappily, the law cannot do much, and without public opinion in its favour it can do absolutely nothing—at least with the English-speaking race!

International conferences have been held, and such steps as these are necessary. The wholesale destruction of swallows which has taken place during the last few years, and the horrors connected with the importation of live quails from Egypt and Italy call for the enactment of some stringent regulations to be observed by all nations.

I must now dwell more particularly on what has been called "Murderous Millinery," and I think you will allow that the term is a just one when I tell you that upwards of 35 millions of birds are annually imported into this country for trimmings and decorations alone. The majority of these are killed during the breeding season, as it is then that the plumage is finest and of the highest commercial value. To kill during the breeding season means the death by starvation of helpless nestlings, so that here the question of cruelty as well as that of the speedy extermination of species comes in. Lord Lilford once said to me, in referring to a Spanish proverb, Surely the cause of the birds must be safe—"entre les mains blanches." Alas! that it should not be so, and that we have to confess that women are most difficult to convince of the evil being wrought in their name and for them.

There is one kind of feather ornament which is quite innocent. The beautiful feathers of the ostrich may be obtained without any suffering or distress to the bird, and without any destruction of life. On properly conducted ostrich farms at the Cape, and in other parts of the world, every care is taken of the birds; food and all other comforts being provided for them. Just before the moult the birds are collected into a narrow passage, at the end of which they are deftly seized and held by two men, while a third quickly clips off the feathers, many of the ripe ones coming out at a touch. The process is over in a few minutes, and the bird—none the worse—is again free to roam at will.

It is a relief to know that we may wear our ostrich feathers with easy consciences; but how can tender-hearted women wear, as ornament, anything that is obtainable only at the cost of unspeakable suffering, and of the wholesale slaughter of our pretty feathered friends; and how can I possibly convey to you the cost at which the fashion of feathers and wings has been and is being complied with?

Hear what Mr. Howard Saunders, an eminently scientific man, says of gulls and seabirds:

"These birds have been slaughtered under circumstances of horrible barbarity, to provide adornments for ladies' hats. I have watched, day after day, a flotilla of boats procuring plumes for the market; one gang of men shooting, and changing their guns when too hot; another set picking up the birds, and often cutting their wings off and flinging their victims into the sea, to struggle with feet and head until death slowly came to their relief; and I have seen the cliffs absolutely "spotted" with the fledglings which had died of starvation, owing to the destruction of their parents. And it may be accounted unto me for righteousness that, in my indignation, I hove down rocks whenever such an act would interfere with the shooters."

Mr. Thomas Southwell, a well-known ornithologist, said last year, when writing of those lovely and graceful creatures, the terns, or sea swallows:

"It is these delicate and beautiful birds which are most in request—of course in their breeding plumage—to supply the "smashed birds" and groups of wings which, notwithstanding twenty years' exposure of the cruelty of the practice, still, I regret to see, are more than ever in fashion as trimmings for ladies' hats. It is quite time to speak out, and fix the blame where it is most assuredly due. After all that has been said and written, it is impossible for women to plead ignorance, and the only legitimate conclusion to which we can arrive is that they deliberately sacrifice all their finer feelings at the shrine of fashion, and care not what amount of suffering and wrong is inflicted provided their vanity is gratified."

Love of dress and fashion is leading to the extinction, complete or partial, of all the most ornamental birds in every part of the world.

. . . During the last few years the birds of paradise have been pursued so relentlessly that there is great fear of their total extermination. The bird of paradise does not reach maturity until he is four or five years old, which means that the supply is comparatively very limited. It is only the male bird who at the breeding season produces those long soft feathers known as "paradise plumes"; but the skins and heads of the females are used for trimmings also, and last year the number of female birds—mothers torn from their young—far out-numbered the males which were imported into this country. Quite apart from the cruelty exercised by the hunters, I am sure none of us could wish to be parties to the destruction of this beautiful bird, which is found nowhere outside of the Malayan and New Guinea region, and has not its peer in any other country, and which is one of the glories of creation.

I wish I had time to enumerate and describe the myriad brilliant birds which the imperious demands of women are causing to vanish:—humming birds, trogons, kingfishers, parrots, tanagers, orioles, impeyan pheasants, Victoria crowned pigeons, grebes, and many others. Even if we never have an opportunity of seeing these wonderful creatures that is no reason why we should not take a deep interest in them and delight to hear and think of them, for are we not citizens of the world? and should we not, therefore, every one of us, feel the dignity and pride of possession in *all* that this marvellous world contains, and feel it our duty to do what we can to preserve these wonders of nature which man can and does so easily and ruthlessly destroy, but which he can never again create? Says Mr. W. H. Hudson, "What an impoverished nature and earth future generations will inherit from us! God's footstool, yes; but with all the shining golden threads picked out of its embroidery."

I have mentioned figures to show the vast quantities of ornamental plumaged birds slaughtered annually. The destruction is almost incredible; but of course when the old are killed and the young are left to die of starvation, extinction is only a matter of time.

Besides beautiful tropical creatures, birds familiar to us all are killed in countless numbers. Fancy killing the robin redbreast to trim a ball dress! Fancy permitting the lovely swallows to be destroyed that their wings may trim a woman's hat!

Would that every women would take to heart Browning's incisive reproach—

She: My modiste keeps on the alert,
Owls, hawks, jays, swallows, most approve.
He: *You*—clothed with murder of His best
Of harmless beings!" [1]

1. Browning, Robert: *The Poetical Works (1888–94)*. Vol. 17. "The Lady and the Painter." ll. 14–15; 26–27. *Ed.*

For twenty years these stories have been told and retold, but we appear to preach to deaf ears, and it is the good women who are the greatest hindrances. If an out-and-out worldling declares by her words and her conduct that she will wear feathers procured only at the cost of great suffering, and that she cares nothing for the extermination of lovely species of useful beings, we fear that her heart and conscience must be non-existent; but when good women, who we *know* are in earnest in their desire that right should triumph over wrong, refuse to help our righteous cause, then we feel in despair, and ready to cry, "Let the birds perish! Let them perish! The sooner their sufferings are ended the better, and then, when it is too late, man (and woman) will discover what a poor, worthless, uninhabitable place this world is without the birds."

The statements I have made are not sensational stories, made up by sentimental women or ignorant men. Scientific men, men who would not swerve a hair's breadth from the truth to make the story sound pathetic, and who are down upon any exaggeration remorselessly, are those who have used the strongest language in condemning the wickedness, cruelty, and waste of the fashion of bird wearing.

I have quoted poets and men of science. In conclusion, may I call attention to a great artist's appeal. At the New Gallery, in Regent Street, there is exhibited a picture[2] by Mr. G. F. Watts, R.A., painted for the express purpose of pleading the cause of the birds. It is called "A Dedication to all who love the beautiful and mourn over the senseless and cruel destruction of bird life and beauty." It represents an angel with bowed head and despairing figure, bending over a marble tomb covered with birds' wings, while a spirit of evil (Fashion) grins below. While he was painting it Mr. Watts called it his "Shuddering Angel"; and as we look at it we venture to adapt the following lines, which appeared in *Punch:*—

Feathers deck the hat and bonnet;
    Though the plumage seemeth fair,
Angels as they look upon it
    See but slaughter in the air.
Many a fashion gives employment
    Unto thousands needing bread;
This to add to your enjoyment,
    Means the dying and the dead.

2. Now to be seen at Mr. Watt's Studio in Melbury Road, Kensington. [And now in the Watts Gallery, Guildford, Surrey, England. *Ed.*]

Wear the hat without the feather,
    All ye women, kind and true;
Birds enjoy the summer weather
    And the sea as much as you.
There's the riband, silk or jewel;
    Fashion's whims are oft absurd,
This is execrably cruel,
    Leave his feathers to the bird.

MARY WEBB

"The Cuckoo Clock"

Sails of Gold. Ed. Lady Cynthia Asquith. New York: Charles Scribner's Sons, 1927. 93–105.

The dreadful fate of Sam Sinnable came about in this way. First, his uncle went to a bazaar and won an egg-cabinet in a raffle. It was a beautiful cabinet. It had little drawers and big drawers, with divisions in them all, and each drawer and division was labelled with a nice, shiny, printed label, with the name of a bird on it. The people who made the cabinet seemed to think Sam would stroll out before breakfast and rob the nests of the rarest birds, and they provided a large compartment for the eggs of eagles—Sea, Spotted, and Golden.

The cabinet was varnished very plentifully, so that it shone with sticky splendour and showed finger-marks beautifully. Sam and the younger ones, even Baby, could have their thumb and finger-prints taken in the proper way, like criminals, whenever Nurse was busy. Before Sam had had it for a week, it was so covered with interesting prints and with the pudgy marks of baby's fat palm, that it seemed quite a nice, friendly piece of furniture. But it was not. It was a Temptation. It had in it two black-birds' eggs, and a sitting of thrushes. Sam thought with despair that before the great day came when he should be able to open every drawer and find every division full of the right kind of eggs he would be an old, old man, like Rip van Winkle. And he noticed that grandfathers were not really keen about these things, though they pretended they were. It was always like the games people play to amuse the children. Sam hoped very much to get his egg-cabinet full long before his beard was white, and as his age was eleven and he had not yet begun to grow it, he felt that there was still time. All the same, he must miss no chances. This was when Sam began the Downward Career, going from Bad to Worse, trespassing, playing truant, tearing his clothes, quite forgetting the golden rule his mother had taught him—One nest, one egg.

He took them all, even the tiny dozen of the Long-tailed Tit-mouse. Nests he could not reach he raked down, holding a basket to catch them. The duck pond, the dove-cote, the preserved pheasants in the wood—all these Sam robbed. The Golden Eagle's place was ingloriously filled with pigeons' eggs. But Sam's chief stand-by were the eggs of the commoner small birds, such as sparrows, thrushes, starlings and finches. He took so many of these that the garden and meadow were always full of the sound of the scolding and the mourning of the parent birds. This was what, more than anything else, brought about Sam's ruin.

Now this is what befell.

On a summer night without any moon, black and muffled and still under the leaves, the Herons came for Sam. They came to his bedside and woke him—two tall policeman herons, in sad-coloured liveries of ash grey and black. They stood there, tall and silent, looking down at Sam as if he were a very small fish, and he felt as if the long sharp swords of their beaks were already run through him.

Then they spoke in hoarse voices, both together, very solemnly.

"Oyez! Oyez! Oyez! Sam Sinnable is summoned to appear at the Birds' Assizes, on a charge of robbery, wilful cruelty and destruction. You bin a scandal in Birdland, Sam, and therefore a Round Robin was sent, with a petition to the High Judge, the great Eagle of Snowdon, and he has called the birds to the Assizes, and you mun come along of us."

Poor Sam thought the herons spoke very funnily, like people in a long-ago book. He supposed it was because birds are older than people, and can remember nothing later than Saxon. But he had no time to think of this. He was terrified by the way they eyed him—as if he were very tiny and a long way off, yet not too far for their swords to reach.

"So up you get, and away-to-go!" said the herons, speaking together, as usual.

It was terribly solemn, like the litany.

Sam got up and dressed, tears rolling down his cheeks. No sooner had he fastened his collar and tie, than the herons seized him. Spreading their great, soft, hollow wings, they plunged through the open window into the starless, damp darkness.

They went through the leaves and through the leaves, over the leaves and under the leaves, and at last they came to the Birds' Assize Court.

As the herons put him down Sam took courage to whisper a question which he had been asking himself all the way. "Shall you know the road back?" he asked anxiously. Back to bed and the kitten, and Nursery breakfast, with steaming porridge, and Nurse, cross but safe.

"There be *no* way back," said the herons.

They stood at the entrance to the Assize Court, and in the pale light left from yesterday Sam could see enormous walls of trees standing about a round glade, carpeted with cuckoopint and birds'-foot trefoil. The trees were chestnuts and firs. Every chestnut was set with white, unlit candles of flowers, and every fir was set with white, unlit candles of shoots.

It was all very solemn and still, with all the leaves neat and close on all the other leaves, like feathers, and the candles without flames standing up in the yesterday light. Sam felt as he did when his uncle took him on the scenic railway. He felt sick. He also began to be very cross with his uncle. First taking him on the scenic railway and making him sick. Then giving him the egg-cabinet and getting him into this dreadful trouble. And yet he had had to be ever so grateful for both. And now here he was. Yes, here he was, in the soft, deep, mysterious night, standing in the enormous doorway of the Assize Court!

"There's nobody there!" he whispered. "Please, Mister Herons, can't I go home?"

"There be everybody here," they answered. "A million bird-souls all told."

"But I can't see anybody."

"Folk may be here, there and everywhere, yet be not seen," said the herons.

At this moment there began the strangest, most frightening sound. It was like the rumour in the trees before thunder. It was like the first low scattered groaning or cheering of a great crowd of people. It was like the grumbling and muttering of herds on the mountains, before they break pasture and go down to the sea. Only it was soft as the soft night, muffled as a funeral bell. From every part of the huge amphitheatre the birds spoke.

"Go back? Go back? You'll never go back," cried the Grouse.

"See, see, see, see, see!" whispered the Grasshopper-Warbler, as if he wanted everybody to stare at Sam. The nightingale wept, the lapwing cried, "Eh, me! Eh, me!"

"Wicked, wicked, wicked!" cried the thrush, and the owls hooted, "It's you, you, you!"

The wood-pigeons took up the cry.

"We *knew* it was you—we *knew* it was you!" they moaned, till the sound of their soft roaring was like the sound of the sea in a dream.

Swifts screamed high above the topmost outlines of the trees, in the no-coloured sky. Ducks quacked, coots clucked, wild gees gabbled somewhere in the shadows of the heavy roots. The woodpeckers, sitting all together on a long branch, laughed nervously in a conceited manner, for they were the telegraph operators, and had to tap out messages to be sent all over Birdland. Near them were six ravens, the reporters, who kept writing absent-mindedly on their shorthand books the words "Never more."

All the birds who scream, screamed. All the birds who croak, croaked. All the birds who scold, scolded. It was as if every leaf had found a tongue.

But suddenly across the tumult a voice clanged—a wild, mighty voice, harsh, yet with something golden in it. Looking at the place it came from, Sam could dimly see, throned on a blasted tree that shone sad and grey, the great eagle from Snowdon.

At the first sound of his voice every bird was mute.

"Let the Court of Assizes be pronounced open!" said the old eagle, and the place was immediately filled with the deep, rolling boom of the bitterns sounding their gongs. Six grebes, standing stiffly in their liveries of brown and white satin stepped forward and announced in watery voices:

"Ancient eagle from Snowdon, my lords ladies and gentlemen, the Assize Court is now open!"

A long ray from the low hidden moon, which had only just risen, crept through the glade like a searchlight, streaming across from the ancient eagle to Sam, who stood with the great cliffs of trees on each side of him, seeming much too small for where he was.

The eagle lifted his head and looked full at Sam. His strong hooked face and his terrible blazing, golden eyes, made Sam feel swallowed up.

"Swear in the Jury," said the Judge.

The Clerk, a grey-headed rook, with a worried expression, began fussing about. Sam looked to see where the twelve good men and true were, and saw them very comfortable seated on a big branch, embowered in the leaves of the chestnut. At least, eleven were seated. The twelfth, whose name was Mr. Titmuss, was hanging by his feet doing gymnastics. The clerk noticed him and said:

"Contempt of court, Mr. Titmuss."

Mr. Titmuss came right side up, and explained that it had been the custom of his family from earliest times so to do, and that in no other position could he think.

"You ain't obliged to think, you silly fellow," said the Little Owl, twisting his head round several times, like a screw-top pepper-pot, without disturbing a feather.

"Well, what be I to do, then?" asked Mr. Titmuss.

"Find out what his lordship wants you to say, and say it." But Mr. Titmuss only said, "Fie, fie, fie!" and swung to and fro with such energy that Mr. Willow, from Africa (one of the numerous Warbler family) was very much annoyed. He weighed so very little that it was as easy to shake him as to shake a leaf.

"By the sun, moon, and stars, what did they put this small fry on the Jury for?" asked the old eagle.

"The robberies, your lordship, were mostly in the homes of such," replied the clerk.

At this a most tremendous twittering began. It was so loud that the frogs, swinging sweetly in the swamp, were quite alarmed and sang no more all night.

"Silence in the court!" commanded the Judge, and the twitterings died out like candles on a Christmas tree.

"A strange thing it is," said the eagle, "that I should be fetched away from my cool eyrie, where from dawn to dusk I gaze upon the sun and ponder on Eternity, where nothing troubles, and no sound is but the sound of dew distilling drop by drop and slipping into the dewpond. And behold! here is only an assemblage of wrens, robins, and what-nots. Hasten, then, for at earliest dawn I keep tryst with the sun. Bring the prisoner into the dock."

The herons led Sam to a hollow tree, ringed with dock leaves. They put Sam inside, and the court usher, a magpie in black, slashed with white, hopped forward with a bit of dock in his beak.

"The prisoner is in, my lord, and here is some of the dock," he said. His idea always was to get a bit of a thing in his beak, and things *had* been said—but chiefly by human beings, who didn't count—about petty larceny in the matter of rings and brooches. But he was always so anxious to please that the birds hushed the thing up and hoped for the best.

"Are the plaintiffs all here?" asked the Judge. "How many are there?"

"A thousand, counting the mothers, me lord, all here."

"Divide by five hundred, reduce to decimals, strike an average—in short, do anything you like so long as you get them down to five. I won't hear more than five."

So they did all those things to the plaintiffs, and there were left

Mr. Twite, Mrs. Dipper, Mr. Butcher-Bird, Miss Linnet (she was Mrs. Linnet really, only being a professional musician it was thought to be the correct thing for her to keep on being Miss, although she was Mrs.) and Mr. Fern Owl.

"Are the witnesses here?"

"Yes, my lord. Everybody living hereabouts is a witness. Everybody saw him."

"Us didna!" said the owls, who have a very countrified way of speaking, because they hang about the barns and stock yards in the evenings. "Us was asleep. Baint witnesses. Us can go to sleep again."

They all went to sleep immediately, snoring loudly, to show how annoyed they were at being hindered in their hunting.

"First plaintiff!" said the Eagle.

During the scuffling that ensued, Sam looked round in the bright moonlight, and was astonished to see, very high up on the tallest tree, a large cuckoo clock. Its round face shone with a dark lustre in the moonshine. Its long, white hands went creeping and creeping, like antennæ, which are insects' feelers, as if they were trying to get hold of poor Sam. Its fir-cone weights swung solemnly to and fro across the moon, which hung just on one side of it like a second clock face. Sam wondered what it could be there for.

The Clerk of the court called out:

"Mr. Twite!"

The court usher fussily brought him in.

"I understand you accuse the prisoner of taking, with evil intent, your whole clutch of eggs," said the Eagle.

"Quite," said Mr. Twite.

"Five, I think?"

"Quite."

"And you think he deserves the extreme penalty?"

"Quite."

"My good sir," said the Judge, "you become monotonous."

"He can't say anything else, my lord," whispered the usher.

"Miss Linnet!"

"Married woman?" asked the Eagle, frowning.

In a trilling voice she replied that she was.

"Why Miss, then?"

"A miss is as good as a mile," murmured the little owl, waking for a moment.

Miss Linnet explained about being a singer.

"Silly," said the Eagle, "but now about the prisoner?"

Miss Linnet was looking very nice in a close-fitting brown hat and dress, with touches of cream.

She immediately trilled into song.

Six eggs of palest blue
Within the hedge of yew,
Beneath blue sky,
Had I.
Where are they now, ah me?
There is the culprit. See, see, see!

"Mrs. Linnet deposes that prisoner took six eggs out of her house with intent to defraud," said the Judge, gruffly. "Next."

"Mr. Butcher-Bird."

Mr. Butcher-Bird said that he had taken a nice house with an excellent larder, and had spent a deal of time and trouble stocking the larder with everything suitable to the children, who were just ready to enter the world when Sam came and took them. So now there was all that good food, and no family to eat it.

Mrs. Butcher-Bird at this point broke down completely, and had to be taken out of court.

"Mrs. Dipper!"

Mrs. Dipper was a stout, countrified lady, very tidy in her dark dress with a white front. She curtsied to the Judge, the Jury, the Clerk, the Usher, and the whole Court. In fact, she kept on curtseying all the time.

She said that she and her husband had built a commodious residence, with a pleasant outlook over the weir pool. They had four eggs in the house. They went out early one morning for their swim, and while they were away Sam came and scooped out all the eggs with this butterfly net.

"Thanks, my good woman," said the Eagle. "Next."

Mrs. Dipper curtsied again, and withdrew.

The last plaintiff was Mr. Fern-Owl.

He said he and his wife believed in the simple life. They were camping in the wood. Late one evening he was helping his wife to churn, when he saw Sam take the eggs. Two, to be exact. And though he fled round and round Sam, and jarred as much as he could, it was of no use.

"Be there witnesses to all these sins?" asked the Judge.

A piercing silver roar of sound answered him. So many birds fluttered down into the open that they were piled up like autumn leaves.

"Gentlemen of the Jury, you have heard the evidence. Retire and consider your verdict."

"Now sirs!" said the usher, resisting the temptation to put the little owl's quill pen into his pocket. "Now sirs!"

He woke the little owl, got Mr. Titmuss right side up, and saw that Mr. Willow was not crushed by the larger birds.

"The Jury has retired, my Lord," he said.

But in less than a minute they were all back again.

"Agreed?" asked the Judge.

"Agreed, my Lord. GUILTY!"

The cheering lasted for several minutes, and poor Sam in his tree began to cry.

"Then I pass the usual sentence," said the Eagle, glad to get through so quickly, for soon now the sun would be climbing the eastern steeps of Snowdon.

"Sound the gongs of doom," said the Eagle.

The sound of the bitterns' gongs went rolling gloomily out into the forest.

"Nuthatches, do your duty!"

Twenty nuthatches, swarming up, unclosed the pulley and let down the cuckoo clock, which was received by the grey geese.

"Prisoner," said the Judge, "you have greedily and cruelly robbed the homes of the birds. People who steal from others end by losing themselves. I condemn you to perpetual imprisonment, and as the cuckoo is the only bird who steals other birds' houses, a cuckoo clock is a suitable prison for a boy who steals eggs. Herons, do your duty!"

Sam had not a moment to think or to try to escape. The herons marched him forward, the magpie officiously held open the door of the clock, the herons pushed Sam in, and shut the door. And there, to this day, poor Sam remains. Dismally, as you pass some clockmaker's on a winter evening, you may hear him calling for help. Only nobody knows it is a call for help, because all that Sam can say is "Cuckoo!" And nobody knows it is Sam, because he is dressed like a cuckoo. And the only breath of air he ever gets is when the little spring to which he is fastened with birdlime, darts forward at the hours and half hours for him to call the time. You may think how he must enjoy twelve o'clock!

So poor Sam never went home to nursery breakfast, and the kitten and Nurse. His mother called him in the flower garden, and Nurse called him in the kitchen garden. His brothers called him in the orchard, and his father called him in the wood. But all they ever had of Sam was his fingerprint on the egg-cabinet. For poor Sam Sinnable was fast in the little square parlour of the cuckoo clock, and there he is to this day.

Conservation: The Land and Its Plants

MARY RUSSELL MITFORD

"Walks in the Country: The Wood"

Our Village: Sketches of Rural Character and Scenery, volume I. London: George B. Whittaker, 1826. 73–78.

April 20th.—Spring is actually come now, with the fulness and almost the suddenness of a northern summer. To-day is completely April;—clouds and sunshine, wind and showers; blossoms on the trees, grass in the fields, swallows by the ponds, snakes in the hedge-rows, nightingales in the thickets, and cuckoos every where. My young friend Ellen G. is going with me this evening to gather wood sorrel. She never saw that most elegant plant, and is so delicate an artist that the introduction will be a mutual benefit; Ellen will gain a subject worthy of her pencil, and the pretty weed will live;—no small favour to a flower almost as transitory as the gum cistus; duration is the only charm which it wants, and that Ellen will give it. The weather is, to be sure, a little threatening, but we are not people to mind the weather when we have an object in view; we shall certainly go in quest of the wood-sorrel, and will take May,[1] provided we can escape May's followers; for, since the adventure of the lamb, Saladin has had an affair with a gander, furious in defence of his goslings, in which rencontre the gander came off conqueror; and as geese abound in the wood to which we are going (called by the country people the Pinge,) and the victory may not always incline to the right side, I should be very sorry to lead the Soldan to fight his battles over again. We will take nobody but May.

1. May is a greyhound, as is Saladin. *Ed.*

So saying, we proceeded on our way through winding lanes, between hedge-rows tenderly green, till we reached the hatch-gate, with the white cottage beside it embosomed in fruit-trees, which forms the entrance to the Pinge, and in a moment the whole scene was before our eyes.

"Is not this beautiful, Ellen?" The answer could hardly be other than a glowing rapid "Yes!"—A wood is generally a pretty place; but this wood—Imagine a smaller forest, full of glades and sheep-walks, surrounded by irregular cottages with their blooming orchards, a clear stream winding about the brakes, and a road intersecting it, and giving life and light to the picture; and you will have a faint idea of the Pinge. Every step was opening a new point of view, a fresh combination of glade and path and thicket. The accessories too were changing every moment. Ducks, geese, pigs, and children, giving way, as we advanced into the wood, to sheep and forest ponies; and they again disappearing as we became more entangled in its mazes, till we heard nothing but the song of the nightingale, and saw only the silent flowers.

What a piece of fairy land! The tall elms overhead just bursting into tender vivid leaf, with here and there a hoary oak or a silver-barked beech, every twig swelling with the brown buds, and yet not quite stripped of the tawny foliage of Autumn; tall hollies and hawthorn beneath, with their crisp brilliant leaves mixed with the white blossoms of the sloe, and woven together with garlands of woodbines and wild-briars;—what a fairy land!

Primroses, cowslips, pansies, and the regular open-eyed white blossom of the wood anemone (or to use the more elegant Hampshire name, the windflower) were set under our feet as thick as daisies in a meadow; but the pretty weed that we came to seek was coyer; and Ellen began to fear that we had mistaken the place or the season.—At last she had herself the pleasure of finding it under a brake of holly—"Oh look! look! I am sure that this is the wood-sorrel! Look at the pendent white flower, shaped like a snowdrop and veined with purple streaks, and the beautiful trefoil leaves folded like a heart,—some, the young ones, so vividly yet tenderly green that the foliage of the elm and the hawthorn would show dully at their side,—others of a deeper tint, and lined, as it were, with a rich and changeful purple!—Don't you see them?" pursued my dear young friend, who is a delightful piece of life and sunshine, and was half inclined to scold me for the calmness with which, amused by her enthusiasm, I stood listening to her ardent exclamations—"Don't you see them? Oh how beautiful! and in what quantity! what profusion! See how the dark shade of the holly sets off the light and delicate colouring of the flower!—And see that other bed of them springing from the rich moss in the roots of that old beech tree! Pray let us gather some. Here are baskets." So, quickly and carefully we began gathering, leaves, blossoms, roots and all, for the plant is so fragile that it will not brook separation!—quickly and carefully we gathered, encountering divers petty misfortunes in spite of all our care, now caught by the veil in a holly bush, now hitching our shawls in a bramble, still gathering on, in spite of scratched fingers, till we had nearly filled our baskets and began to talk of our departure:—

"But where is May? May! May! No going home without her. May! Here she comes galloping, the beauty!:—(Ellen is almost as fond of May as I am.)—"What has she got in her mouth? that rough, round, brown substance which she touches so tenderly? What can it be? A bird's nest? Naughty May!"

"No! as I live, a hedgehog! Look, Ellen, how it has coiled itself into a thorny ball! Off with it May! Don't bring it to me!"—And May, somewhat reluctant to part with her prickly prize, however troublesome of carriage, whose change of shape seemed to me to have puzzled her sagacity more than any event I ever witnessed, for in general she has perfectly the air of understanding all that is going forward—May at last dropt the hedgehog; continuing, however, to pat it with her delicate cat-like paw, cautiously and daintily applied, and caught back suddenly and rapidly after every touch, as if her poor captive had been a red-hot coal. Finding that these pats entirely failed in solving the riddle, (for the hedgehog shammed dead, like the lamb the other day, and appeared entirely motionless), she gave him so spirited a nudge with her pretty black nose, that she not only turned him over, but sent him rolling some little way along the turfy path,—an operation which that sagacious quadruped endured with the most perfect passiveness, the most admirable non-resistance. No wonder that May's discernment was at fault, I myself, if I had not been aware of the trick, should have said that the ugly rough thing which she was trundling along, like a bowl or a cricket-ball, was an inanimate substance, something devoid of sensation and of will. At last my poor pet, thoroughly perplexed and tired out, fairly relinquished the contest, and came slowly away, turning back once or twice to look at the object of her curiosity, as if half inclined to return and try the event of another shove. The sudden flight of a wood-pigeon effectually diverted her attention; and Ellen amused herself by fancying how the hedgehog was scuttling away, till our notice was also attracted by a very different object.

We had nearly threaded the wood, and were approaching an open grove of magnificent oaks on the other side, when sounds other than of nightingales burst on our ear, the deep and frequent strokes of the woodman's axe, and emerging from the Pinge we discover the havoc which that axe had committed. Above twenty of the finest trees lay stretched on the velvet turf. There they lay in every shape and form of devastation: some, bare trunks stripped ready for the timber carriage, with the bark built up in long piles at the side; some with the spoilers busy about them, stripping, hacking, hewing; others with their noble branches, their brown and fragrant shoots all fresh as if they were alive—majestic corpses, the slain of to-day! The grove was like a field of battle. The young lads who were stripping the bark, the very children who were picking up the chips, seemed awed and silent, as if conscious that death was around them. The nightingales sang faintly and interruptedly—a few low frightened notes like a requiem.

Ah! here we are at the very scene of murder, the very tree that they are felling; they have just hewn round the trunk with those slaughtering axes, and are about to saw it asunder. After all, it is a fine and thrilling operation, as the work of death usually is. Into how grand an attitude was that young man thrown as he gave the final stroke round the root; and how wonderful is the effect of that supple and apparently powerless saw, bending like a riband, and yet overmastering that giant of the woods, conquering and overthrowing that thing of life! Now it has passed half through the trunk, and the woodman has begun to calculate which way the tree will fall; he drives a wedge to direct its course;—now a few more movements of the noiseless saw; and then a larger wedge. See how the branches tremble! Hark how the trunk begins to crack! Another stroke of the huge hammer on the wedge, and the tree quivers, as with a mortal agony, shakes, reels, and falls. How slow and solemn and awful it is! How like to death, to human death in its grandest form! Cæsar in the Capitol, Seneca in the bath, could not fall more sublimely than that oak.

Even the heavens seem to sympathise with the devastation. The clouds have gathered into one thick low canopy, dark and vapoury as the smoke which overhangs London; the setting sun is just gleaming underneath with a dim and bloody glare, and the crimson rays spreading upwards with a lurid and portentous grandeur, a subdued and dusky glow like the light reflected on the sky from some vast conflagration. The deep flush fades away, and the rain begins to descend; and we hurry homeward rapidly, yet sadly, forgetful alike of the flowers, the hedgehog, and the wetting, thinking and talking only of the fallen tree.

OCTAVIA HILL

From "Our Common Land"

Our Common Land and Other Short Essays. London: MacMillan and Co., 1877. 1–17.

Probably few persons who have a choice of holidays select a Bank holiday, which falls in the spring or summer, as one on which they will travel, or stroll in the country, unless, indeed, they live in neighbourhoods very far removed from large towns. Every railway station is crowded; every booking-office thronged; every seat—nay, all standing room—is occupied in every kind of public conveyance; the roads leading out of London for miles are crowded with every description of vehicle—van, cart, chaise, gig—drawn by every size and sort of donkey, pony, or horse; if it be a dusty day, a great dull unbroken choking cloud of dust hangs over every line of road.

Yet in spite of all this, and in spite of the really bad sights to be seen at every public-house on the road, in spite of the wild songs and boisterous behaviour, and reckless driving home at night, which show how sadly intoxication is still bound up with the idea and practical use of a holiday to hundreds of our people, how much intense enjoyment the day gives! how large a part of this enjoyment is unmixed good! And the evil is kept in check very much. We may see the quiet figure of the mounted policeman as we drive home, dark in the twilight, dark amidst the dust, keeping order among the vehicles, making the drunken drivers mind what they are doing. He keeps very tolerable order. And then these days in the country ought to lessen the number of drunkards every year; and more and more we shall be able to trust to the public opinion of the quiet many to preserve order.

And watch, when at last the open spaces are reached towards which all these lines of vehicles are tending—be it Epping, or Richmond, or Greenwich, or Hampstead—every place seems swarming with an undisciplined, but heartily happy, crowd. The swings, the roundabouts, the donkeys, the stalls, are beset by dozens or even hundreds of pleasure-seekers, gay and happy, though they are not always the gentlest or most refined. Look at the happy family groups—father, and mother, and children, with their picnic dinners neatly tied up in handkerchiefs; watch the joy of eager children leaning out of vans to purchase for a halfpenny the wonderful pink paper streamers which they will stick proudly in their caps; see the merry little things running untiringly up and down the bank of sand or grass; notice the affectionate father bringing out the pot of ale to the wife as she sits comfortably tucked up in shawls in the little cart, or treating the children to sweetmeats; sympathise in the hearty energy of the great rough lads who have walked miles, as their dusty boots well show; their round, honest faces have beamed with rough mirth at every joke that has come in their way all day; they have rejoiced more in the clamber to obtain the great branches of may than even in the proud possession of them, though they are carrying them home in triumph. To all these the day brings unmixed good.

Now, have you ever paused to think what Londoners would do without this holiday, or what it would be without these open spaces? Cooped up for many weeks in close rooms, in narrow streets, compelled on their holiday to travel for miles in a crowded stream, first between houses, and then between dusty high hedges, suddenly they expand into free uncrowded space under spreading trees, or on to the wide Common from which blue distance is visible; the eye, long unrefreshed with sight of growing grass, or star-like flowers, is rejoiced by them again. To us the Common or forest looks indeed crowded with people, but to them the feeling is one of sufficient space, free air, green grass, and colour, with a life without which they might think the place dull. Every atom of open space you have left to these people is needed; take care you lose none of it; it is becoming yearly of more vital importance to save or increase it.

There is now a Bill for regulating inclosure before the House of Commons. Mr. Cross has said what he trusts will be its effect if it becomes law; but those who have been watching the history of various inclosures, and the trials respecting special Commons, are not so hopeful as Mr. Cross is as to the effect this Bill would have. It makes indeed good provisions for regulating Commons to be kept open for the public when a scheme for regulation is applied for. But the adoption of such a scheme depends in large part on the lord of the manor. Will he in nine cases out of ten ever even apply for a scheme for regulating a Common, when he knows that by doing so he shuts out from himself and his successors for ever the possibility of inclosing it, and appropriating some part of it? Do any provisions for regulating, however excellent, avail anything when no motive exists which should prompt the lord of the manor to bring the Common under them? and, as the Bill stands, it cannot be so brought without his consent.

Secondly, the Bill provides that urban sanitary authorities can purchase rights which will enable them to keep open any suburban Common, or may accept a gift of the same. But then a suburban Common is defined as one situated within six miles of the outside of a town of 5,000 inhabitants. Now, I hardly know how far out of a large town Bank-holiday excursionists go, but I know they go every year farther and farther. I am sure that a

Common twelve, nay, twenty, miles off from a large town is accessible by cheap trains to hundreds of excursionists all the summer, to whom it is an inestimable boon. Again, is the privilege of space, and light, and air, and beauty not to be considered for the small shop-keeper, for the hard-working clerk, who will probably never own a square yard of English land, but who cares to take his wife and children into the country for a fortnight in the summer? Do you not know numbers of neighbourhoods where woods, and Commons, and fields used to be open to pedestrians, and now they must walk, even in the country, on straight roads between hedges? The more that fields and woods are closed, the more does every atom of Common land, everywhere, all over England, become of importance to the people of every class, except that which owns its own parks and woods. "On the lowest computation," says the Report of the Commons Preservation Society, "5,000,000 acres of Common land have been inclosed since Queen Anne's reign; now there are but 1,000,000 acres left.[1] The right of roving over these lands has been an immense boon to our people; it becomes at once more valued and rarer year by year. Is it impossible, I would ask lawyers and statesmen, to recognise this right as a legal one acquired by custom, and not to be taken away? Mr. Lefevre suggested this in a letter to *The Times.* He says:

"The right of the public to use and enjoy Commons (which they have for centuries exercised), it must be admitted, is not distinctly recognised by law, though there is a remarkable absence of adverse testimony on the subject. The law, however, most fully recognises the right of the village to its green, and allows the establishment of such right by evidence as to playing games, &c., but it has failed as yet to recognise the analogy between the great town and its Common, and the village and its green, however complete in fact that analogy may be. But some of these rights of Common, which are now so prized as a means of keeping Commons open, had, if legal theory is correct, their origin centuries ago in custom. For long they had no legal existence, but the courts of law at last learned to recognise custom as conferring rights. The custom has altered in kind; in lieu of cattle, sheep, and pigs turned out to pasture on the Commons, human beings have taken their place, and wear down the turf instead of eating it. I can see no reason why the law, or, if the courts are too slow to move, the Legislature, should not recognise this transfer and legalise this custom. Again, it is probable that

1. The amount remaining uninclosed and subject to Common-rights is variously estimated; a report of the Inclosure Commissioners in 1874 putting it at about 2,600,000 for England and Wales, while the recent return of landowners, prepared by the Local Government Board, makes the uninclosed area little more than 1,500,000 acres.

Commons belonged originally much more to the inhabitants of a district than to the lord. Feudal theory and its subsequent development—English Real Property Law—have ridden rather roughly over the facts and the rights of the case. The first placed the lord of the manor in his position as lord, giving him certain privileges, and coupling with them many responsibilities. The second gradually removed these responsibilities, and converted into a property what was at first little more than an official trust. If these considerations are beyond the scope of the law courts, they are proper for Parliament. One step has been made. It has been proved that it is not necessary to purchase Commons for the public, but that ample means of protecting them from inclosure exist. It is also obvious that the rights which constitute these means are now in practice represented by the public user of Commons for recreation. The Legislature should, I venture to think, recognise this user as a legal right."

If the Legislature would do this, Commons all over England might be kept open, which, I venture to think, would be a great gain. Hitherto the right to keep Commons open has been maintained, even in the neighbourhood of towns, by legal questions affecting rights of pasturage, of cutting turf, or carting gravel. This is all very well if it secures the object, but it is on the large ground of public policy, for the sake of the health and enjoyment of the people, that the conscience of the nation supports the attempt to keep them open; it cares little for the defence of obsolete and often nearly valueless customs, and it would be very well if the right acquired by use could be recognised by law, and the defence put at once on its real grounds. . . .

~ E(DITH) NESBIT

From *Wings and the Child; or, The Building of Magic Cities*

New York: Hodder and Stoughton, 1913. vii–viii; 94–104.

TO THE READER

[pp. vii–viii]

When this book first came to my mind it came as a history and theory of the building of magic Cities on tables, with bricks and toys and little things

FIGURE 15 Edith Nesbit

such as a child may find and use. But as I kept the thought by me it grew and changed, as thoughts will do, until at last it took shape as an attempt to contribute something, however small and unworthy, to the science of building a magic city in the soul of a child, a city built of all things pure and fine and beautiful. As you read, it will, I hope, seem to you that something of what I say is true—in much, no doubt, it will seem to you that I am mistaken; but however you may disagree with me, you will, I trust, at least have faith in the honesty of my purpose. If I seem to you to be too dogmatic, to lay down the law too much as though I were the teacher and you the learner, I beg you to believe that it is in no such spirit that I have written. Rather it is as though you and I, spending a quiet evening by your fire, talked together of the things that matter, and as though I laid before you all the things that were in my heart—not stopping at every turn to say "Do you not think so too?" and "I hope you agree with me?" but telling you, straight from the heart, what I have felt and thought and, I humbly say, known about children and the needs of children. I have talked to you as to a friend, without the reservations and apologies which we use with strangers. And if, in anything, I shall have offended you, I entreat you to extend to me the forgiveness and the forbearance which you would exercise towards a friend who had offended you, not spoken to you as frankly and plainly as I would wish you to speak to me, were you the writer and I the reader.

THE ONE THING NEEDFUL

[pp. 94–104]

The most ardent advocate of our present civilisation, the blindest worshipper of what we call progress, can hardly fail to be aware of the steadily increasing and brutal ugliness of life. Civilisation, whatever else it is, is a state in which a few people have the chance of living beautifully—those who take that chance are fewer still—and the enormous majority live, by no choice or will of their own, lives which at the best are uncomfortable, anxious, and lacking in beauty, and at the worst are so ugly, diseased, desperate, and wretched that those who feel their condition most can hardly bear to think of them, and those who have not imagination enough to feel it fully yet cannot bear it unless they succeed in persuading themselves that the poor of this world are the heirs of the next, while hoping, at the same time, that a portion of Lazarus's heavenly legacy may, after all, be reserved for Dives.[1]

The hideous disfigurement of lovely hills and dales with factories and mines and pot banks—coal, cinder, and slag; the defilement of bright rivers with the refuse of oil and dye works; the eating up of the green country by greedy, long, creeping yellow caterpillars of streets; the smoke and fog that veil the sun in heaven; the sordid enamelled iron advertisements that scar the fields of earth—all the torn paper and straw and dirt and disorder spring from one root. And from the same root spring pride, anger, cruelty, and sycophancy, the mean subservience of the poor and the mean arrogance of the rich. As the fair face of the green country is disfigured by all this machinery which ministers to the hope of getting rich, so is the face of man marred by the fear of getting poor. Look at the faces you see in the street—old and young, gay and sad—on all there is the brand of anxiety, a terrible anxiety that never rests, a fear that never sleeps, the anxiety for the future: the fear of poverty for the rich, the fear of starvation for the poor. Think of the miles and miles of sordid squalor and suffering in the East of London—not in comfortable Whitechapel, but out Canning Town way; think of Barking and Plaistow and Plashet and Bow—then think of Park Lane and Bond

1. The rich man of Luke 16:19–31. *Ed.*

Street.[2] And if your eyes are not blinded, the West is no less terrible than the East. If you want to be sure of this, bring a hungry, ragged child from that Eastern land and set it outside a West End restaurant; let it press its dirty little face against the plate glass and gaze at the well-to-do people gorging and guzzling round the bright tables inside. The diners may be smart, the ragged child may be picturesque—but bring the two together, and consider the conjunction.

And all this ugliness springs from the same cause. As Ruskin[3] says: "We have forgotten God." We have therefore forgotten His attributes, mercy, loving-kindness, justice, truth, and beauty. Their names are still on our lips, but the great, stupid, crashing, blundering machine which we call civilisation knows them not. The Devil's gospel of *laissez-faire* still inspires the calloused heart of man. Each for himself, and Mammon for the foremost. We no longer care that life should be beautiful for all God's children—we wish it to be beautiful for us and forget who, as we wish that wish, becomes our foster-father. There can be no healing of the great wound in the body of mankind till each one of us would die rather than see the ugliness of a wound on the body of the least of these our brethren. But so dulled and stupefied is our sense of beauty, our sense of brotherhood, that our brother's wounds do not hurt us. We have not imagination enough to know how it feels to be wounded. Just as we have not imagination enough to see the green fields that lie crushed where Manchester sprawls in the smoke—the fair hills and streams on which has grown the loathsome fungus of Stockport.

Now I do believe that this insensitiveness to ugliness and misery, this blindness to wanton befouling of human life and the green world, comes less from the corruption of man's heart than from the emptiness of the teaching which man receives when he is good and little and a child. The teaching in our schools is almost wholly materialistic. The child is taught the botanical name of the orange—dissects it and its flower and perhaps learns the Latin names of the flower and fruit; but it is not taught that oranges are things you will be pleased with yourself for giving up to some one who is thirstier than you are—or that to throw orange-peel on the pavement where some one may slip on it, fall and hurt himself, is as mean a trick as stealing a penny from a blind man. We teach the children about the wonders of gases and ethers, but we do not explain to them that furnaces ought to consume their own smoke, or why. The children learn of acids and starches, but not that it is a disgraceful thing to adulterate beer and bread.

2. Fashionable sections of London. *Ed.*

3. John Ruskin (1819–1900), famous English social reformer and art critic. *Ed.*

The rules of multiplication and subtraction are taught in schools, but not the old rule, "If any will not work, neither shall he eat."

There is no dogmatical teaching. That means a diet of dry bones. It means that the child is never shown how to look for happiness in the performance of acts which do not, on the face of them, look as though they would make him happy. It is not explained to him that man's life and the will of God are like a poem—God writes a line and man must make the next line rhyme to it. When it does rhyme, then you get that happiness which can only come from harmony. And when you do your best to make your line rhyme and cannot—well, the Author of the first line knows that it was your best that you did. God is shown, when He is shown at all, to our modern children, as a sort of glorified head master, who will be tremendously down on you if you break the rules: alternatively as a sort of rich uncle who will give you things if you ask properly. He is not shown as the Father to whom you can tell everything.

If you are successful in your work you win a prize and go home to your people, and tell them that you are first in history, receiving their applause without shame.

If you are good at games or athletics you can tell your mates that you made two goals or eighty-three runs or whatever it is, and delight in their admiration. If you are an athlete the applause of the bystanders is your right and your reward.

But whom can you tell of the little intimate triumphs, the secret successes, the temptations resisted, the kind things done, the gentle refrainings, the noble darings of that struggling, bewildered, storm-tossed little thing you call your soul?

God, your Father, is the only person to whom you can talk of these. To him you can say: "Father, I wanted to pay Smith Minor out to-day for something he did last week, and I didn't because I thought You wouldn't like it. Are You pleased with Your boy?" Do they teach you this in schools or give you any hint or hope of what you will feel when your Father answers: "Yes, My son, I am pleased." Or do they teach you to say: "Father, I am sorry I was a beast to-day, and I'll try not to do it again"—and tell you that a Voice will answer, "I am sorry too, My son—but I am glad you told Me. Try again, dear lad. And let Me help you"?

As you show your Latin exes. to your master, so you should be taught to show the leaves of your life to the only One who can read and understand that blotted record. And if you learn to show that book every day there will be less and less in it that you mind showing, and more and more that will give you the glow and glory of the heart that comes to him who hears "Faithful and good, well done."

You cannot suppose that your life is rhyming with the will of God when you destroy the beauty of the country and of the lives of men so that you may get rich and you and your children may live without working.

Can you imagine a company promoter who should say: "Father, I have made a lot of money out of a company which has gone to pieces, and a lot of other people are ruined, but I know that there must always be rich and poor, and if I didn't do it some one else would"?

Or—"Father, I spoiled the green fields where children used to play and I have built a lot of streets of hideous and uncomfortable houses, but they are quite good enough for the working people. As long as they have such low wages they can't live like human beings. And Thou knowest, O Father, that wages are and must be regulated by the divine law of supply and demand."

Or—"Father, I have put sand in the sugar and poison in the beer, alum in the bread and water in the milk, all these being, as Thou knowest, Father, long-established trade customs."

Men can say these things to themselves and to each other, but there is One to whom they cannot say them. It is of Him and not only of the wonders of His Universe that I would have the children taught. But they are only taught of the wonders, not of the Wonder-worker.

. . . We shall be told how important are the telescope and the microscope, and how right it is that children should know all about their little insides. The one thing we shall not hear about will be the one thing needful.

A tottering Government may keep itself in power by such a measure, a defeated party may, but it, bring itself back to office, but such a measure will not keep the nation from perdition, nor bring back the soul of a man into the true way.

We may build up as we will schemes of Education and Instruction, add science to science, learning to learning, and facts to facts; but what we shall build will be only a dead body unless it be informed by the breath of the Spirit which maketh alive. For Education which teaches a man everything but how to live to the glory of God and the service of man is not Education, but only instruction; and it is the fruit of the tree, not of Life, but of Death.

JULIANA HORATIA EWING

"Our Field"

A Great Emergency, & Other Tales. London: G. Bell & Sons, 1911. 171–82.

There were four of us, and three of us had godfathers and godmothers. Three each. Three times three make nine, and not a fairy godmother in the lot. That was what vexed us.

It was very provoking, because we knew so well what we wanted if we had one, and she had given us three wishes each. Three times three make nine. We could have got all we wanted out of nine wishes, and have provided for Perronet into the bargain. It would not have been any good Perronet having wishes all to himself, because he was only a dog.

We never knew who it was that drowned Perronet, but it was Sandy who saved his life and brought him home. It was when he was coming home from school, and he brought Perronet with him. Perronet was not at all nice to look at when we first saw him, though we were very sorry for him. He was wet all over, and his eyes shut, and you could see his ribs, and he looked quite dark and sticky. But when he dried, he dried a lovely yellow, with two black ears like velvet. People sometimes asked us what kind of dog he was, but we never knew, except that he was the nicest possible kind.

When we had got him, we were afraid we were not going to be allowed to have him. Mother said we could not afford him, because of the tax and his keep. The tax was five shillings, but there wanted nearly a year to the time of paying it. Of course his keep began as soon as he could eat, and that was the very same evening. We were all very miserable, because we were so fond of Perronet—at least, Perronet was not his name then, but he was the same person—and at last it was settled that all three of us would give up sugar, towards saving the expense of his keep, if he might stay. It was hardest for Sandy, because he was particularly fond of sweet things; but then he was particularly fond of Perronet. So we all gave up sugar, and Perronet was allowed to remain.

About the tax, we thought we could save any pennies or half-pennies we got during the year, and it was such a long time to the time for paying, that we should be almost sure to have enough by then. We had not any money at the time, or we should have bought a savings-box; but lots of people save their money in stockings, and we settled that we would. And old stocking would not do, because of the holes, and I had not many good pairs; but we

FIGURE 16 Juliana Horatia Ewing

took one of my winter ones to use in the summer, and then we thought we could pour the money into one of my good summer ones when the winter came.

What we most of all wanted a fairy godmother for was about our "homes." There was no kind of play we liked better then playing at houses and new homes. But no matter where we made our "home," it was sure to be disturbed. If it was indoors, and we made a palace under the big table, as soon as ever we had got it nicely divided into rooms according to where the legs came, it was certain to be dinner-time, and people put their feet into it.

The nicest house we ever had was in the out-house; we had it, and kept it quite a secret, for weeks. And then a new load of wood came and covered up everything, our best oyster-shell dinner-service and all.

Any one can see that it is impossible really to fancy anything when you are constantly interrupted. You can't have any fun out of a railway train stopping at stations, when they take all your carriages to pieces because the chairs are wanted for tea; any more than you can play properly at Grace Darling[1] in a life-boat, when they say the old cradle is too good to be knocked about in that way. It was always the same. If we wanted to play at Thames Tunnel under the beds, we were not allowed; and the day we did Aladdin in the store-closet, old Jane came and would put away the soap, just when Aladdin could not possibly have got the door of the cave open.

It was one day early in May—a very hot day for the time of year, which had made us rather cross—when Sandy came in about four o'clock, smiling more broadly even than usual, and said to Richard and me: "I've got a fairy godmother, and she's given us a field."

Sandy was very fond of eating, especially sweet things. He used to keep back things from meals to enjoy afterwards, and he almost always had a piece of cake in his pocket. He brought a piece out now, and took a large mouthful, laughing at us with his eyes over the top of it.

"What's the good of a field?" said Richard.

"Splendid houses in it," said Sandy.

"I'm quite tired of fancying homes," said I. "It's no good; we always get turned out."

"It's quite a new place," Sandy continued; "you've never been there," and he took a triumphant bite of the cake.

"How did you get there?" asked Richard.

"The fairy godmother showed me," was Sandy's reply.

There is such a thing as nursery honour. We respected each other's pretendings unless we were very cross, but I didn't disbelieve in his fairy godmother. I only said, "You shouldn't talk with your mouth full," to snub him for making a secret about his field.

Sandy is very good-tempered. He only laughed and said, "Come along. It's much cooler out now. The sun's going down."

He took us along Gipsy Lane. We had been there once or twice, for walks, but not very often, for there was some horrid story about it which

1. The daughter of the keeper of a lighthouse on the Farne Islands off the coast of Northumberland. Poems have been written by Wordsworth and others about the night in September 1838 when she helped her father rescue shipwreck survivors. *Ed.*

rather frightened us. I do not know what it was, but it was a horrid one. Still we had been there, and I knew it quite well. At the end of it there is a stile, by which you go into a field, and at the other end you get over another stile, and find yourself in the high road.

"If this is our field, Sandy," said I, when we got to the first stile, "I'm very sorry, but it really won't do. I know that lots of people come through it. We should never be quiet here."

Sandy laughed. He didn't speak, and he didn't get over the stile; he went though a gate close by it leading into a little sort of bye-lane that was all mud in winter and hard cart-ruts in summer. I had never been up it, but I had seen hay and that sort of thing go in and come out of it.

He went on and we followed him. The ruts were very disagreeable to walk on, but presently he led us through a hole in the hedge, and we got into a field. It was a very bare-looking field, and went rather uphill. There was no path, but Sandy walked away up it, and we went after him. There was another hedge at the top, and a stile in it. It had very rough posts, one much longer than the other, and the cross step was gone, but there were two rails, and we all climbed over. And when we got to the other side, Sandy leaned against the big post and gave a wave with his right hand and said, "This is our field."

It sloped down hill, and the hedges round it were rather high, with awkward branches of blackthorn sticking out here and there without any leaves, and with the blossom lying white on the black twigs like snow. There were cowslips all over the field, but they were thicker at the lower end, which was damp. The great heat of the day was over. The sun shone still, but it shone low down and made such splendid shadows that we all walked about with grey giants at our feet; and it made the bright green of the grass, and the cowslips down below, and the top of the hedge, and Sandy's hair, and everything in the sun and the mist behind the elder bush which was out of the sun, so yellow—so very yellow—that just for a minute I really believed about Sandy's godmother, and thought is was a story come true, and that everything was turning into gold.

But it was only for a minute; of course I know that fairy tales are not true. But it was a lovely field, and when we had put our hands to our eyes, and had a good look at it, I said to Sandy, "I beg your pardon, Sandy, for telling you not to talk with your mouth full. It is the best field I ever heard of."

"Sit down," said Sandy, doing the honours; and we all sat under the hedge.

"There are violets just behind us," he continued. "Can't you smell them? But whatever you do, don't tell anybody of those, or we shan't keep our field to ourselves for a day. And look here." He had turned over on to his face, and Richard and I did the same, whilst Sandy fumbled among the bleached grass and brown leaves.

"Hyacinths," said Richard, as Sandy displayed the green tops of them.

"As thick as peas," said Sandy. "This bank will be blue in a few weeks; and fiddle-heads everywhere. There will be no end of ferns. May to any extent—it's only in bud yet—and there's a wren's nest in there—" At this point he rolled suddenly over on to his back and looked up.

"A lark," he explained; "there was one singing its head off, this morning. I say, Dick, this will be a good field for a kite, won't it? *But wait a bit.*"

After every fresh thing that Sandy showed us in our field, he always finished by saying, "*Wait a bit*"; and that was because there was always something else better still.

"There's a brook at the bottom there," he said, "with lots of fresh-water shrimps. I wonder whether they would boil red. *But wait a bit.* This hedge, you see, has got a very high bank, and it's worn into kind of ledges. I think we could play at 'shops' there—*but wait a bit.*"

"Its almost *too* good, Sandy dear!" said I, as we crossed the field to the opposite hedge.

"The best is to come," said Sandy. "I've a very good mind not to let it out till to-morrow." And to our distraction he sat down in the middle of the field, put his arms round his knees, as if we were playing at "Honey-pots,"[2] and rocked himself backwards and forwards with a face of brimming satisfaction.

Neither Richards nor I would have been so mean as to explore on our own account, when the field was Sandy's discovery, but we tried hard to persuade him to show us everything.

He had the most provoking way of laughing and holding his tongue, and he did that now, besides slowly turning all his pockets inside-out into his hands, and mumbling up the crumbs and odd currants, saying, "Guess!" between every mouthful.

But when there was not a crumb left in the seams of his pockets, Sandy turned them back, and jumping up, said—"One can only tell a secret once. It's a hollow oak. Come along!"

He ran and we ran, to the other side of Our Field. I had read of hollow oaks, and seen pictures of them, and once had I dreamed of one, with a

2. A children's game in which some players would crouch with their hands wrapped around their knees pretending to be honey pots, while others would come around and "weigh" them by attempting to pick them up. The children pretending to be honey pots would try not to release their position, or "break." *Ed.*

witch inside, but we had never had one to play in. We were nearly wild with delight. It looked all solid from the field, but when we pushed behind, on the hedge side, there was the door, and I crept in, and it smelt of wood, and delicious damp. There could not be a more perfect castle, and though there were no windows in the sides, the light came in from the top, where the polypody[3] hung over like a fringe. Sandy was quite right. It was the very best thing in Our Field.

Perronet was as fond of the field as we were. What he liked were the little birds. At least, I don't know that he liked them, but they were what he chiefly attended to. I think he knew that it was our field, and thought he was the watch-dog of it, and whenever a bird settled down anywhere, he barked at it, and then it flew away, and he ran barking after it till he lost it; and by that time another had settled down, and then Perronet flew at him, and so on, all up and down the hedge. He never caught a bird, and never would let one sit down, if he could see it.

We had all kinds of games in Our Field. Shops—for there were quantities of things to sell—and sometimes I was a moss-merchant, for there were ten different kinds of moss by the brook, and sometimes I was a jeweller, and sold daisy-chains and pebbles, and coral sets made of holly berries, and oak-apple necklaces; and sometimes I kept provisions, like earth-nuts, and mallow-cheeses, and mushrooms; and sometimes I kept a flower-shop, and sold nosegays and wreaths, and umbrellas made of rushes. I like that kind of shop, because I am fond of arranging flowers, and I always make our birthday wreaths. And sometimes I kept a whole lot of shops, and Richard and Sandy bought my things, and paid for them with money made of elder-pith, sliced into rounds. The first shop I kept was to sell cowslips, and Richard and Sandy lived by the brook, and were wine merchants, and made cowslip wine in a tin mug.

The elder-tree was a beauty. In July the cream-coloured flowers were so sweet, we could hardly sit under it, and in the autumn it was covered with berries; but we were always a little disappointed that they never tasted in the least like elderberry syrup. Richard used to make flutes out of the stalks, and one really did to play tunes on, but it always made Perronet bark.

Richard's every-day cap had a large hole in the top, and when we were in Our Field we always hung it on the top of the tallest of the two stile-posts, to show that we were there; just as the Queen has a flag hung out at Windsor Castle, when she is at home.

3. A type of fern. *Ed.*

We played at castles and houses, and when we were tired of the houses, we pretended to pack up, and went to the seaside for change of air by the brook. Sandy and I took off our shoes and stockings and were bathing-women, and we bathed Perronet; and Richard sat on the bank and was a "tripper," looking at us through a telescope; for when the elder-stems cracked and wouldn't do for flutes, he made them into telescopes. And before we went down to the brook we made jam of hips and haws from the hedge at the top of the field, and put it into acorn cups, and took it with us, that the children might not be short of roly-polies at the seaside.

Whatever we played at we were never disturbed. Birds, and cows, and men and horses ploughing in the distance, do not disturb you at all.

We were very happy that summer: the boys were quite happy, and the only thing that vexed me was thinking of Perronet's tax-money. For months and months went on and we did not save it. One we got as far as two-pence halfpenny, and then one day Richard came to me and said, "I must have some more string for the kite. You might lend me a penny out of Perronet's stocking, till I get some money of my own."

So I did; and the next day Sandy came and said, "You lent Dick one of Perronet's coppers; I'm sure Perronet would lend me one," and then they said it was ridiculous to leave a halfpenny there by itself, so we spent it in acid drops.

It worried me so much at last, that I began to dream horrible dreams about Perronet having to go away because we hadn't saved his tax-money. And then I used to wake up and cry, till the pillow was so wet, I had to turn it. The boys never seemed to mind, but then boys don't think about things; so that I was quite surprised when one day I found Sandy alone in our field with Perronet in his arms, crying, and feeding him with cake; and I found he was crying about the tax-money.

I cannot bear to see boys cry. I would much rather cry myself, and I begged Sandy to leave off, for I said I was quite determined to try and think of something.

It certainly was remarkable that the very next day should be the day when we heard about the flower-show.

It was in school—the village school, for mother could not afford to send us anywhere else—and the schoolmaster rapped on his desk and said, "Silence, children!" and that at the agricultural show there was to be a flower-show this year, and that an old gentleman was going to give prizes to the school-children for window-plants and for the best arranged wild flowers. There were to be nosegays and wreaths, and there was to be a first prize of five shillings, and a second prize of half-a-crown, for the best collection of wild flowers with the names put to them.

"The English names," said the schoolmaster; "and there may be—silence, children!—there may be collections of ferns, or grasses, or mosses to compete, too, for the gentleman wishes to encourage a taste for natural history."

And several of the village children said, "What's that?" and I squeezed Sandy's arm, who was sitting next to me, and whispered, "Five shillings!" and the schoolmaster said, "Silence, children!" and I thought I never should have finished my lessons that day for thinking of Perronet's tax-money.

July is not at all a good month for wild flowers; May and June are far better. However, the show was to be in the first week in July.

I said to the boys, "Look here: I'll do a collection of flowers. I know the names, and I can print. It's no good two or three people muddling with arranging flowers; but if you will get me what I want, I shall be very much obliged. If either of you will make another collection, you know there are ten kinds of mosses by the brook; and we have names for them of our own, and they are English. Perhaps they'll do. But everything must come out of Our Field."

The boys agreed, and they were very good. Richard made me a box, rather high at the back. We put sand at the bottom and damped it, and then Feather Moss, lovely clumps of it, and into that I stuck the flowers. They all came out of Our Field. I like to see the grass with flowers, and we had very pretty grasses, and between every bunch of flowers I put a bunch of grass of different kinds. I got all the flowers and all the grasses ready first, and printed the names on pieces of cardboard to stick in with them, and then I arranged them by my eye, and Sandy handed me what I called for, for Richard was busy at the brook making a tray of mosses.

Sandy knew the flowers and the names of them quite as well as I did, of course; we knew everything that lived in Our Field; so when I called, "Ox-eye daisies, cock's-foot grass, labels; meadow-sweet, fox-tail grass, labels; dog-roses, shivering grass, labels;" and so on, he gave me the right things, and I had nothing to do but to put the colours that looked best together next to each other, and to make the grass look light, and pull up bits of the moss to show well. And at the very end I put in a label, "All out of Our Field."

I did not like it when it was done; but Richard praised it so much, it cheered me up, and I thought his mosses looked lovely.

The flower-show day was very hot. I did not think it could be hotter anywhere in the world than it was in the field where the show was; but it was hotter in the tent.

We should never have got in at all—for you had to pay at the gate—but they let competitors in free, though not at first. When we got in, there were a lot of grown-up people, and it was very hard work getting along among them, and getting to see the stands with the things on. We kept seeing tickets with "1st Prize" and "2nd Prize," and struggling up; but they were sure to be dahlias in a tray, or fruit that you mightn't eat, or vegetables. The vegetables disappointed us so often, I got to hate them. I don't think I shall ever like very big potatoes (before they are boiled) again, particularly the red ones. It makes me feel sick with heat and anxiety to think of them.

We had struggled slowly all round the tent, and seen all the cucumbers, onions, lettuces, long potatoes, round potatoes, and everything else, when we saw an old gentleman, with spectacles and white hair, standing with two or three ladies. And then we saw three nosegays in jugs, with all the green picked off, and the flowers tied as tightly together as they would go, and then we saw some prettier ones, and then we saw my collection, and it had got a big label in it marked "1st Prize," and next to it came Richard's moss-tray, with the Hair-moss and the Pincushion-moss, and the Scale-mosses, and a lot of others with names of our own, and it was marked "2nd Prize." And I gripped one of Sandy's arms just as Richard seized the other, and we both cried, "Perronet is paid for!"

There was two-and-sixpence over. We never had such a feast! It was a picnic tea, and we had it in Our Field. I thought Sandy and Perronet would have died of cake, but they were none the worse.

We were very much frightened at first when the old gentleman invited himself; but he would come, and he brought a lot of nuts, and he did get inside the oak, though it is really too small for him.

I don't think there ever was anybody so kind. If he were not a man, I should really and truly believe in Sandy's fairy godmother.

Of course I don't really believe in fairies. I am not so young as that. And I know that Our Field does not exactly belong to us.

I wonder to whom it does belong? Richard says he believes it belongs to the gentleman who lives at the big red house among the trees. But he must be wrong; for we see that gentleman at church every Sunday, but we never saw him in Our Field.

And I don't believe anybody could have such a field of their very own, and never come to see it, from one end of summer to the other.

CHARLOTTE MEW

"The Trees Are Down"

The Rambling Sailor. 1929. *Charlotte Mew: Collected Poems and Prose.* Ed. Val Warner. London: Carcanet Press, 1981. 48–49.

—and he cried with a loud voice: Hurt not the earth, neither the sea, nor the trees—

Revelation

They are cutting down the great plane-trees at the end of the
gardens.
For days there has been the grate of the saw, the swish of the
branches as they fall,
The crash of trunks, the rustle of trodden leaves,
With the 'Whoops' and the 'Whoas,' the loud common talk, the
loud common laughs of the men, above it all.
I remember one evening of a long past Spring
Turning in at a gate, getting out of a cart, and finding a large dead rat
in the mud of the drive.
I remember thinking: alive or dead, a rat was a god-forsaken thing,
But at least, in May, that even a rat should be alive.

The week's work here is as good as done. There is just one bough
On the roped bole, in the fine grey rain,
Green and high
And lonely against the sky.
(Down now!—)
And but for that,
If an old dead rat
Did once, for a moment, unmake the Spring, I might never have
thought of him again.

It is not for a moment the Spring is unmade to-day;
These were great trees, it was in them from root to stem:
When the men with the 'Whoops' and the 'Whoas' have carted the
whole of the whispering loveliness away
Half the Spring, for me, will have gone with them.

It is going now, and my heart has been struck with the hearts of the
planes;
Half my life it has beat with these, in the sun, in the rains,
In the March wind, the May breeze,
In the great gales that came over to them across the roofs from the
great seas.
There was only a quiet rain when they were dying;
They must have heard the sparrows flying,
And the small creeping creatures in the earth where they were
lying—
But I, all day, I heard an angel crying:
'Hurt not the trees.'

SECTION THREE

Domesticating

In the nineteenth and early twentieth centuries, women dominated home and hearth to such an extent that words like "domestic," "domesticity," and "domesticate" still reverberate with a ring of the Victorian feminine. We speak of "domestic service," a commonplace in Victorian and Edwardian times, as service performed in and around the home, usually at the behest of or through the agency of a well-to-do woman. (In this regard one might recall the popular BBC television series *Upstairs, Downstairs* or, more recently, *The 1900 House.*) We isolate a literary form called the "domestic novel," a kind of novel that centers on domesticity, or "woman's sphere," and was also prevalent in Victorian times. One could go on, but in this section I would like to pause to look at Victorian and Edwardian women in a different kind of domestic pursuit—the domestication of animals and plants raised, fostered, or trained in and around the home. Women played an important role in this kind of domestication, just as they did in domesticating children—and even men. The women in this section transformed this kind of "home" work, often making it into a profession and/or reflecting it in professional writing. In doing so, they were following larger cultural guidelines, predominantly the guidelines of zoo or glasshouse but also those of farming or horticulture.

In 1828 the London Zoo at Regent's Park was founded as a repository for animals brought "home" to England from around the world. It exhibited the riches of empire in terms of animal species and, among other things, created an inquiring audience hungry for information about exotics (see figure 17). As people traveled more and more, animals became more readily available for private collections as well. Horticulturist Jane Loudon's fictional characters in *The Young Naturalist* (excerpted in section six), for example, marveled over a marmoset that occupied the carriage with them during their railway journey. And the poet Dante Gabriel Rossetti kept a menagerie of animal curiosities, like the wombat that slept in one of his

FIGURE 17 *Receiving Visitors on Easter Monday at the Zoological Society's Gardens, Illustrated London News,* 19 April 1873

overhead lamps. The well-to-do indulged in maintaining exotics in conservatories or cages in their homes, while people of more modest means could, in the wake of the nature "crazes," more readily raised native animals and plants. Everyone involved in such pastimes could find much to observe and even more to study. By the end of the century, not just the zoo, but institutions like the Royal Botanic Gardens at Kew, the British Museum of Natural History, and private museums flourished and fostered interest in nonhuman species, and guide books and how-to books began to abound.

Thus some women writers found themselves doubly occupied, involved not just in the raising of plants and animals but in promoting such pastimes through their writing. The animal anecdote, the animal story, the guide to herbaria or home conservatories—these and other kinds of entertainment and step-by-step "companion" books became very popular. Moreover, diffusion of knowledge through these forms came easily to many women. For centuries women had been enjoined to educate others from their homes or through science popularizations. Literary forms evolved with their times, and it was but a small step from books like Loudon's *Young Naturalist* to the animal stories and information about plant life that will be found in this section on "Domesticating." Moreover, the essentializing of women as closer to nature than men—a cultural bias that worked in women's disfavor in terms of their higher education and political clout—actually enhanced their authority in this sort of nature writing. It was easier for women to set themselves up as appropriate observers and writers about domestic situations and domesticated animals and plants than it was for men to do similarly. Their culture already expected them to be concerned over the house and its inhabitants.

The subsection "Menageries and Animal Stories" both looks at domestic menageries and traces something of the evolution of the animal story. The first writer featured in this section is the prodigious Emily Shore, who spent many of the hours of her short nineteen-year life observing nature. Birds were her special province, so much so that she had her death portrait sketched when holding a stuffed bee-eater, one of her prize possessions. In her essays for the *Penny Magazine*—a generalist magazine published every Saturday by the Society for the Diffusion of Useful Knowledge (see figure 18)—Shore writes two different kinds of accounts. The "Account of a Young Cuckoo" (1837) is an animal chronicle, a form that depicted an animal from its birth or acquisition until its death. Here Shore observes and muses over her pet cuckoo in an attempt to permit others to witness at second hand just what had fascinated her at first. By way of contrast, the piece on "The Golden-Crested Wren" informs the British bird watcher of just where to find the wren and how to observe a wild bird's behavior. Placing all this in a more personal context, the selections from Shore's journal reveal Shore's dedication to natural history and provide insights into the Shore family's 1830s menagerie of birds.

Keeping wild or tamed birds as pets was so common toward the middle of the nineteenth century that it became a frequent subject of paintings and illustrations. Walter Deverell's painting *A Pet* (1853), for example (see figure 19), depicts a woman feeding a bird with a seed held between her

THE PENNY MAGAZINE

OF THE

Society for the Diffusion of Useful Knowledge.

8.] PUBLISHED EVERY SATURDAY. [October 24, 1835

THE WHITE OR BARN OWL.

FIGURE 18 Cover, *The Penny Magazine,* 24 October 1835

teeth. A conservatory flanks the woman, and a dog rests just inside the conservatory. The painting exudes a hothouse atmosphere, the pet bird forming a contrast to the wild bird on the path outside. When exhibited at the Liverpool Academy, Deverell's painting was accompanied by a quotation from W. J. Broderip's *Leaves from the Note-Book of a Naturalist* (1852): "But after all, it is very questionable kindness to make a pet of a creature so essentially volatile." Women nevertheless did make pets of such creatures sufficiently often to warrant publication of a how-to book about them. The introduction to E. A. Maling's *Song Birds and How to Keep Them* (1867) offers its readers advice on how to nurture such pets, while her chapter on "Making Friends with Wild Birds" suggests ways in which wildlings can be enticed toward people. In the selections offered here, Maling is, however, careful to try to forestall criticism from women like those represented in "Protecting" or from men like Broderip.

FIGURE 19 Walter Deverell, *A Pet* (1853) (courtesy of the Tate Gallery, London)

Shore was primarily interested in local birds and Maling in birds like the canary that were already bred to cage or captivity. Eliza Brightwen, on the other hand, was a countrywoman of considerable means who both studied local natural history on her large estate and imported and kept a menagerie of much more exotic creatures. A long-time protectress of wild birds, she was already elderly when she began to write for publication. Her first published book, *Wild Nature Won by Kindness* (1890), was greeted by overwhelming success. Almost overnight, Brightwen became one of the most popular nature writers of the late nineteenth century. Our first selection from her work represented in this anthology comes from Brightwen's second book, *More about Wild Nature* (1892). Here Brightwen describes Impey, the exotic Indian fruit bat (see figure 26) she has recently acquired.

Through Impey she provides a look at something "other" for her British audiences; she then turns to discussing local bats in an effort to sustain reader enthusiasm for a much-maligned type of animal. The other selection reprinted here is drawn from Brightwen's 1895 book, *Inmates of My House and Garden,* and offers information about others of the acquired exotics that stalked or roamed Brightwen's house. The lemurs (see figure 27) discussed in this piece dwelt in Brightwen's beautiful conservatory. A moralist, Brightwen loved her animals but kept her Christian values intact when writing about them. Thus in *More about Wild Nature* her mongoose, Mungo, is described as "selfish" by human standards, though Brightwen is willing to forgive him for this trait.

Brightwen wrote in several forms that delighted late Victorian readers: the animal chronicle, or story of an animal from birth to death, something similar to Emily Shore's short chronicle of the cuckoo; the animal anecdote, or short vignette; and the animal biography, or longer story of the animal followed throughout a number of situations or exploits. Along the way, Brightwen leavened her work with sprinklings of popular science, giving details about the animal's biology or its habitat or peculiarities. This combination of modes kept her a popular writer for well over a decade.

If Alice Dew-Smith's writing, our next selections, offered similar kinds of animal stories, Dew-Smith's values were very different from Brightwen's (see figure 20). Brightwen had sympathy for animals but saw them as possessions, dispensable to zoos and other places when the time came to give them up. Dew-Smith tended to see from the perspective of the animals themselves, as in her account of Whishton, the marmot. Whishton was not her own pet but that of a friend, so her observations have a different tenor from those of Brightwen's more appropriative accounts. Then too, because Dew-Smith tried to imagine herself inhabiting Whishton's little body, she worked to frame thoughts for him rather than to describe him purely from the outside. In the second of her animal biographies reprinted here, "A Domestic Tragedy," she enters the world of spiders, like Brightwen deliberately choosing an often maligned group in order better to educate people to the natural world around her. We as readers enter her daily round of watching and waiting for the domestic tragedy of the spiders to unfold. In the end, however, Dew-Smith seems to be saying that no matter how close by the world of nature is and no matter how hard we look to try to figure it out, we remain outside its deepest mysteries.

Women who took up agriculture for a living could not afford to espouse this kind of attitude. Even gentlewomen farmers needed to have control over the nature that surrounded them. Two of the nonfiction prose

FIGURE 20 *Belling the Cats,* illustration from Alice Dew-Smith's *Tom Tug and Others: Sketches in a Domestic Menagerie,* opposite p. 230

selections in "Farming and Gardening" therefore reflect a distinctly different point of view. Harriet Martineau's "Poultry-Yard," from *Our Farm of Two Acres* (1865), both recounts her years poultry farming on a small plot and gives advice to women who might want to do so. Of what use is so small a plot that brings so little remuneration to its women? Martineau (figure 28) says it keeps farm workers and farm animals going, but it also helps to develop the hearts and minds of those women who are responsible for it. This kind of development seems to have been far from the mind of Annie Martin, who in the next selections discusses both the ostriches and her pets on her African ostrich farm. Martin's work thus fits into several of the categories highlighted in this section, perhaps because Martin thinks like a colonizer. Whatever lives in Africa she sees as there primarily for her pleasure, entertainment, or financial gain. Thus the wild secretary bird Jacob (figure 29) becomes a "pet," a member of a menagerie, worthy of target practice for sponges and slippers and other missiles when he comes into the house and is a "bad" bird. The ostriches can be "bad" too, as Martin's book points out, for they lack the kind of intelligence Martin seeks in animals. But they are also a crop and are interestingly described as such for an English audience's edification and entertainment in *Home Life on an Ostrich Farm* (1890). Martin's book also reveals that she returned to England and pined for the once-reviled ostriches when she attended the London Zoo and saw them there. But aside from these facts about her later life, this editor

FIGURE 21 *The Gardener,* from *Girl's Own Annual,* 1889

could find no trace of other biographical information about Martin. Alongside Martin's prose I have placed Eliza Cook's "Song of the Ostrich" to serve as a kind of corrective to Martin's sometime denigration of ostriches. More like Dew-Smith than like Martin, Cook looks at the elegant plumes of the ostrich and speaks on its behalf. If its plumes are used by humans to deck their most important people and occasions, is this not, Cook's ostrich wonders, sufficient to garner more respect for this bird of the deserts?

Today's written history has paid less attention to women agriculturalists like Martin than to women horticulturists like Gertrude Jekyll, primarily because women have themselves long been avid writers as well as readers of garden books. Trying to educate her readers to good gardening practices or innovations for trial on their own, for decades Jekyll wrote dozens of gardening columns and books. In the selections on gardening in this portion of *In Nature's Name,* I have included Jekyll to help represent a special preserve of garden writing: writing for and about children. Here a chapter from her *Children and Gardens* (1908) is coupled with two other pieces,

TABBY IN THE CERASTIUM.

FIGURE 22 *Tabby in the Cerastium,* photograph by Gertrude Jekyll

a parable from Margaret Gatty and a passage from Frances Hodgson Burnett's *Secret Garden.* All three of these selections entice children into the world of the English garden in order to introduce them to a pursuit that their culture considered especially suitable for young women (see figure 21). Intended to delight not just girls but all children, Jekyll's "Pussies in the Garden" describes some of Jekyll's cats and kittens in the context of her (and their) own environs. Tabby sets off Jekyll's cerastium (see figure 22), Pinky her garden path, and so on. In the final passage reprinted here, Jekyll reveals both her sense of humor and her designer's eye as she describes and delineates the "equicateral triangle"(see figure 32).

Home gardens were depicted by women writers as places for children not just to play but to learn, and not just about plants but about life. It is helpful to recall again, as in the section on "Protecting," that Victorian and Edwardian women bore the responsibility for the moral education for the entire family and that women writers often wrote with this kind of edification in mind. Margaret Gatty's parable "Training and Restraining" draws the parallel between good plant husbandry and good child rearing. For the sake of the young, training and restraining are necessary in both cases (see figure 33). Burnett's famous secret garden is also a training ground. There young Mary learns that the world does not revolve around her but that her talents and generosity are needed by other creatures, by plants, and by other people as well. The portion of *The Secret Garden* reprinted here occurs well into the story, when Mary makes her all-important first incursion into the

FIGURE 23 Sarah Lindley, *Interior Plants and Book Shelf*

garden that will become the source the responsibility, wonder, and transformation in her young life. By way of contrast and so that the reader can experience something of the variety of writing about gardens, the final selection on outdoor gardens moves in an opposite direction, away from childhood and toward the end of a woman's life. Mary Webb's short story "A Cedar-Rose" offers a sensitive look at the last days of a woman who has waited for seventy years for the coming of a cedar rose. Poignantly, it blooms just as her life is in final retreat.

For the last section of "Domesticating" we move indoors. Especially in Victorian times, indoor gardening was a rage. Wardian cases full of plants, window dressings, fern placement—all of these were important to women of means (see figure 23). In her *Lady's Country Companion*, horticulturist Jane Loudon describes both the culture of pot plants and appropriate plants for the ever-popular Victorian conservatory. Recall that Eliza Brightwen was a proud possessor of one such conservatory (see figure 24). To Elizabeth

FIGURE 24 Elizabeth Brightwen's conservatory (courtesy Richard Durrant)

Twining's mind, however, the impoverished were far more in need of indoor greenery than were well-to-do owners of conservatories or orangeries or even fire screens like those decorated by Anne Hassard. A botanical illustrator and author of the important *Illustrations of the Natural Order of Plants with Groups and Descriptions* (1849) (see figure 25), Twining believed that if green spaces could not be brought to everyone—particularly to people in large cities—green plants could. She wanted to make interiors not just pleasing, but more healthful. Her "A Few Words about Window-Gardens" from *What Can Window-Gardens do for our Health?* addresses two of her own deepest interests: the plant kingdom and the improvement of the lives of the impoverished. In simplest of terms, Twining rehearses the need for plants to replenish oxygen needed by human beings. She hopes that because plants need sunshine and air, the poor will be more likely to open up their windows if they tend plants. And she suggests opening homes up early in the morning, when air is freshest, to avoid the more toxic air that engulfed Victorian cities at night. Her essay also contains a short vignette about the benefits of flowers to life in a factory town and concludes with a

FIGURE 25 Elizabeth Twining, *The Ginger Tribe*

table of plants to grow in window boxes. With its varied emphases on domestication, aesthetics, and the protecting of people and environments, Twining's work shows how the categories of this book overlap one another—dealing as they do with the relationship of women to nature in its varied yet interconnected guises. The final selection in this section on indoor plants comes from Annie Hassard's *Floral Decorations for the Dwelling House* (1875). Hassard followed in the wake of the highly popular and famous *Mrs. Beeton's Book of Household Management* (1859–61). (Beeton herself was the Martha Stewart figure of her day.) Along with its illustration of the fire screen embellished with ivy in summer (figure 34), it points both to the popularity of books dealing with domestic interiors and to the lengths to which Victorian writers would go in attempting to find original ideas and natural materials for home decorators.

*M*ENAGERIES AND *A*NIMAL *S*TORIES

MARGARET EMILY SHORE

"Account of a Young Cuckoo"

The Penny Magazine, 9 December 1837: 475.

Of all the birds that visit this island, one of the most remarkable is the cuckoo. So very little is known of its habits, that the following account of a young bird of the species, which was reared in a cage for five weeks, may perhaps add somewhat to the information already possessed on the subject.

The young cuckoo is totally different in appearance from the full-grown bird; being chiefly of a dark greyish brown, the feathers barred with rust colour, and tipped with white: the under part of the body is white, with numerous transverse bars of black.[1] The plumage, unlike that of most young birds, is very thick, smooth, and close set.

The specimen, of which the following is an account, was brought to the door by a labouring boy who had found it in a meadow at the end of July. It was then about three weeks or a month old, and had just begun to fly a little. It was unable to feed itself, but ate greedily out of the hand, and had an immense appetite, which it seemed impossible to satisfy. For some days it was fed entirely on raw meat, and soaked bread, and hempseed; but its relish for this diet soon diminished, and it was then supplied with insects of various kinds, which were evidently its natural food. In less than a week from the time it was caught, it learnt to pick for itself, as well as to fly readily. Of all insects it seemed to prefer gnats and grasshoppers, especially the latter, which it would kill at a blow, and eat at one mouthful, without reject-

1. See 'Faculties of Birds,' Library of Entertaining Knowledge, p. 367. The plate there given is very like it, except that the young cuckoo rarely sits with its neck so upright and stretched out.

ing any part. Next to these it liked moths, butterflies, and caterpillars, of every species indifferently. The cabbage-caterpillar, from the facility of procuring it, was its staple-food; of these it used to eat about 200 full-grown ones in a day. The caterpillar of the buff-tip moth (*Pygæra Bucephala*), and the downy green caterpillar which feeds on the mignonette, were also given to it sometimes: the latter was perhaps its favourite food. Spiders and lady-birds it devoured greedily, and occasionally wasps and flies, though apparently without much relish. It ate large quantities of sand. From its manner of darting towards its food as it grew older, and tearing it from the hand with out-spread wings, there can be no doubt that in its natural state it finds prey on the wing as well as when stationary.

It not only had perfect command of itself on the perch and on the wing (for it had a powerful and graceful flight), but also climbed with great facility and swiftness, running dexterously up the wires of its cage. It hopped too, but not well.

At first it had two cries; one a gentle chirp, uttered incessantly when hungry, at the same time that it vehemently shook one wing (never both), so as to impart a tremulous motion to the body: the other a continued low tremulous sound, uttered while taking its food. As it grew older, it gradually discontinued this latter cry, and the first became much more loud and hoarse.

Notwithstanding the supposed stupidity of the cuckoo, which is called in Scotland "gowk," or fool, this young bird showed much intelligence and observation, and was a most amusing pet. From the first it seemed to notice everything, and was as meddlesome and fond of picking as a pie. It delighted in biting the fingers of persons who came near it; in pulling pins out of a pincushion, and in hammering at any stuffed bird which was shown to it. No creature could be more fearless and familiar. For the first fortnight it was allowed to have the range of a room during the greater part of the day; and though it was perfectly able to fly, it would sit up for hours by the side of its owner, perched on the handle of a basket, and would allow itself to be stroked, caressed, taken up, and carried about on the finger. It was impossible to drive it; if a stick were presented to it, the cuckoo would fly at it with outspread wings and attack it vigorously.

After the first fortnight it was removed from the house, and placed in a large cage out of doors, with a pair of Barbary doves. From this time a singular change took place in the creature's disposition. All gentleness and quietness of demeanour vanished: it instantly became as fierce and irritable as any young bird of prey. It did not molest the doves, except that it kept them at a distance for some time, and would strike them with his wing, and peck them sharply, if they attempted to approach him, or examine his food. Latterly they became very good friends, and would even plume each other. But it was to the human race that it showed the most dislike. If any one came near the cage, the cuckoo would raise his wings, bristle up the feathers of its head, and glare ferociously; if a finger was shown to it, it would fly at it, scream, hiss, flap its wings, and bite very hard. At the same time the expression of its face visibly altered, and it looked ill-temper personified; in short it gave every indication of being by nature a ravenous, powerful, pugnacious bird.

For five weeks the cuckoo continued healthy and flourishing, and hopes were entertained that, with care, it might be reared through the winter. This interesting experiment has generally failed, and in this instance it was unsuccessful. The cage in which it was kept was always left out of doors all night during August without the bird's receiving any injury from the exposure, and the removing it under cover was delayed a little too long; the last night of August was very cold, and the cuckoo died next day in consequence. At the time of its death it measured eighteen inches in length, not having attained either its full size or full plumage; the latter it does not acquire till the third year.

~ MARGARET EMILY SHORE

"The Golden-Crested Wren"

The Penny Magazine, December 1837: 487–88.

The golden-crested wren is the smallest and one of the most beautiful and interesting of British birds. Though it abounds in most places, its active, restless habits, and the silence of its movements, render it rather difficult to watch; and it is probably less noticed than any other common bird we possess.

The most usual haunts of the golden-crested wren are tall trees, particularly the oak, the yew, and the various species of pine and fir. In these it builds its nest, a very neat and elegant structure, the shape of which varies according to the situation in which it is placed. It is most commonly open at the top, like that of the chaffinch; but sometimes, even under the sheltering boughs of a Norway fir, it is covered with a dome, and has an opening on one side. It is always ingeniously suspended beneath the branch, like those of many tropical birds, being the only instance of the kind amongst those of Great Britain. The eggs are nine or ten in number, and are small, round, and white.

The golden-crested wren is by no means so shy of the neighbourhood of man as is generally supposed. Though it abounds in forests, yet it equally frequents gardens, occasionally even in the suburbs of large towns, and very often builds close to the house, most commonly in a yew or fir, at the height of from five to twenty or thirty feet from the ground. It will visit the plants trained round windows; and has been known, when pursued by a hawk, to fly for refuge into a room where people were sitting, and alight on the top of the bell-rope, whence it suffered itself to be taken by the hand. It is very fearless of observers, and will allow you to approach within a yard of it, while engaged, as it generally is, in hunting for insects on the stems and branches of trees. Perhaps the best time for watching it is a hot sunny day in summer or autumn. In a still and sultry noon, when not a leaf is stirring, and almost every other bird has retired from the heat of the sun into the shadiest thickets, the little solitary golden-crested wren is to be seen flitting noiselessly from spray to spray, with unwearied activity, in search of its food, paying no attention to any one who happens to be watching it, and never for a moment remaining in a state of rest. Its movements are unlike those of any other bird, except, indeed, the blue-tit—but even his do not equal in lightness and airiness this little wren. It flutters ever the slenderest twigs like a butterfly now on one side, now on the other,—sometimes above the branch, sometimes beneath, hanging with the head downwards;—often at the end of it, suspended in the air by its tiny wings, which it quivers without the slightest sound,—so that unless you see it, if it were ever so close to you, you would not be aware of its presence except for the little low chirp which it occasionally emits, and which is more like that of an insect than a bird. In shape and plumage, too, it is superior to most of the feathered inhabitants of our woods and gardens: the latter is a beautiful mixture of green and yellow, with white bars on its wings; and on its head the golden crest, bordered with black, from which it takes its name.

In the spring and summer it sings regularly, beginning about the middle of March, and continuing till the end of July. Its song is very soft and low, like a whisper, and, like that of the grasshopper-lark, is no louder at the distance of one yard than of twenty.

During the greater part of the year, it haunts tall trees, and never alights on the earth; but in the winter it is frequently seen pecking for insects in the grass, or among dead leaves, and even on a heath at some little distance from any tree; and when thus engaged will let you approach it sufficiently near to hear the little snap of its beak when it has found its prey.

The golden-crested wren remains with us all the year round: whether it is a hardy bird or not is a disputed matter.

~ EMILY SHORE

From *Journal of Emily Shore*

London: Kegan Paul, Trench, Trübner & Co., Ltd., 1891. 89; 104–5.

[p. 89]

Feb. 10 [1835], Tuesday.—. . . I shall study botany this year in a very different way from that which I have been accustomed to pursue, for I find that I have hitherto been a very superficial botanist, attending to little besides the classification, and not studying the habits, properties, and uses of plants, as I do the habits of birds. I might just as well call myself an ornithologist, if I knew only in what tribe to place a bird, as call myself at present a botanist.

[pp. 104–05]

June 11 [1835], Thursday.—. . . I am very glad to return at last to the quiet of Woodbury, much as I have liked this little excursion. We find everybody well, and the number of our bird pets somewhat increased. A cock bullfinch, shy as the species is, two days ago flew into the schoolroom; its head was bare of feathers, probably with fighting. Richard introduced him to his hen bullfinch; they live very amicably together. Mackworth is rearing a young blackbird, and Arabella and Louisa have two young chaffinches, which the mother feeds. A few days after we went to town, M. found a coal-tit's nest with six or seven young ones. He brought it to the house, and the mother came every day with food, which she brought every five minutes; she even forced her way into the cage in her anxiety to feed them. In about a fortnight the young ones were full-feathered, and flew away. The mother fed them only with small green caterpillars. The young ones had grown very tame, and perched on the heads, hands, and shoulders of the children.

June 19 [1835], Friday.—. . . As my ear gets more practised in distinguishing the songs of birds, I am surprised to find how many little differences there are between the songs of different individuals, even of species which have unvarying songs, as the chaffinch and hedge-sparrow. I observe this mostly in the chaffinch and the willow-wren. I am persuaded that, were my ear acute enough to discover it, I should find that no two individuals sang exactly alike. At present, I perceive that the chaffinches of Kent have a much softer and more liquid tone than any others I know, and even add two or three notes; those of Woodbury are very inferior performers, though they differ considerably from one another in point of excellence.

E. A. MALING

From *Song Birds and How to Keep Them*

London: Smith, Elder & Co., 1867. 1–13; 100–103.

[pp. 1–13]

CHAPTER I

Introductory

1. A great many people think that to keep birds is cruel. If it were so, indeed, few would be the cage birds one would wish to see; but happily, on the contrary, for those who, like myself, are fond of the feathered tribe, the more we know about them, the more we are content to think theirs is a happy prison. Not for all birds by any means; some would break their hearts, if they should be kept in cage. The birds of passage, all those that come and go, should never be kept from the sunny skies they seek as the winter comes. We may easily, however, find sufficient pets among our proper house-birds. The Canaries generally, and all the home-bred Finches; plenty of sweet-voiced Linnets; and amongst the foreigners, many tiny creatures, Waxbills, and Amandavas. When these are safely reared, or once have been brought to England, we have but to make them happy; it would be cruel to expose them to the misery of being loose, little shivering, trembling strangers, in an unkindly crowd. Poor little creatures, if one of them does get out, how fast it flies to seek some friendly cage: it knows not the

language, the ways and fashions of the birds around it, nor yet does it always meet with the kindest welcome from them. Besides, our home-birds want petting—they have no wish, so their gay song tells us, to seek a dirty puddle instead of a crystal bath, to hide from the rain and cower from the cold, instead of hanging singing in a pleasant room, conversing now and then with the friendly company. My Goldfinch, for instance, would he like, indeed, to go out and breakfast on his own small means? Goldie and I greatly take leave to doubt it; a flight round the room, while his mistress prepares the breakfast, is much more to Goldie's mind, and the moment it is ready, he pops back very briskly into his cage to eat it. Moreover, would he get such breakfasts every day alone if he were sent to try? And it is said goldfinches are capable of an attachment to hemp seed, that will keep them very regular in returning at proper hours, even when they are allowed to go out into the air.

2. But most people forget to reckon on the birds' social habits; nor do they give them credit for half their loving ways. I have known little pets fly all in a flutter to meet and greet me, when really I thought they would have quite forgotten that they had ever known me; and only let any one nurse a wounded bird, and see if it forgets the benefit received.

3. Besides, they are very clever. I am sure if as many people lived sociably with birds, as with dogs and cats, we should have soon a thousand proofs of their sagacious ways. Speaking for myself, I know quite well by their tones what my birds are wanting,—sometimes it may be only a kindly recognition of a passing friend; but a few days ago when two were fighting and we took no notice, there was little doubt what the conquered wanted,—she called us to her assistance as plainly as if she had spoken.

4. Birds remember, too, even if they are free, those whom they have known. We used at one time to rear many birds, half Canaries and half golden Linnets; and these birds having learnt to sing the canary notes, would be let fly away to build amongst the shrubs. It was a doubtful experiment, so many of them got caught; but it used to be very pleasant while walking amongst the trees to hear a sweet voice calling to us, and to see one of our former charges flying on before us, passing from one tree to another, bowing, and fluttering, and keeping up the talk, as long as we on our part would condescend to answer.

5. I do not know how real Canaries can be best brought to stand our cold English winters. Our own grounds were remarkably warm, and shut in amidst hills, and there were many thick belts of laurels, and dense clumps of evergreens, which certainly afforded a good deal of shelter, so that we had

no lack of English birds of all kinds, from the Wrens that built their exquisite round nest in the creepers upon the wall, to the Robin Redbreasts in their greenhouse home; the Goldfinches in the larches, the Thrushes in the laurels, and the gold-crested Wrens on an apple branch. Alas, for the cherry-trees, there were nests in them; but when seven Nightingales would be heard on a summer's evening, singing upon the lawn, we felt well repaid for any little damage that their race might do us. And thus it was, that I began to study birds, picking up those half-fledged little ones that tumbled from the nests, making daily rounds amongst those we knew, and at last, where we felt well acquainted, (as amongst those who built each year in the same place regularly), becoming very daring, we went carrying with us teacups of bread and water, and kindly volunteered our help to the old birds in their ménage. I never knew a nest deserted for us, the old birds would sit on a tree next door, and watch with much benignity while all the little things would stretch out their heads and open their mouths at once, thinking themselves very lucky because they all got fed. Living thus amongst them, it was natural by degrees to get into a birdish way of viewing things; felling the chief consideration to be not what might answer, but what was really natural; and though it is indisputable that in a cage, the state of birds is so far unnatural that they are deprived to a great degree of exercise, still they are in very frequent motion; and in a room or aviary, no one who watches them for a single day, can think they are too stationary.

[pp. 100–103]

CHAPTER XII

Making Friends with Wild Birds

1. It may seem at first as if to make friends with wild birds would be rather difficult, and also rather useless, yet it is really a pleasant branch of bird acquaintance, especially for those who live in a retired place, where they may hope to preserve their favourites from the fowler's snares, as well as from their own gardener's guns.

I cannot pretend here, however, to lay down unfailing rules; I can only mention plans which I have practised, or heard of from those on whose testimony I can depend. The simple cottage plan of feeding the birds at the door-step in winter, when the snow is swept away, or on the window-sills when the bold applicants come at our breakfast-time to mention that they have none, are certainly very good beginnings of an *entente cordiale.*

Visiting nests is also useful. I made it so much a thing of course that I am not aware of any great precautions that need to be taken: of course, one moves gently, and does not speak, except to the bird. In feeding the young it is better to begin on the third or fourth day, before they can see, as then they are used to one's voice, and to the way of feeding.

Stale bread, crumbled and scalded, the water poured off and a little cold milk poured on and beaten up, is, I think, the food that answers most generally, serving for both hard and soft-billed birds. A little finely pounded yolk of egg is an improvement, if the birds do not seem to like it without. This preparation should be made fresh each time, and the milk must not be sour, nor the egg kept more than a few hours. A quill, the end cut round, and a little notch, two or three inches higher, for admitting air, is the best thing for feeding with, a very small piece being dropped into each of the widely gaping beaks. The food should be given neither quite cold nor at all hot.

2. Birds so trained to know one grow up pretty tame. I used to take them in and out of the nests; and very often a young bird gets hurt, or a Swallow tumbles down from its own nest, and it may be nursed till it has come to be quite at home. I have brought up many and many a Swallow, though, of course, not for a cage.

In many cases a Swallow once tamed returns again, year by year, to the well-known places, and with many birds a friendship seems to be hereditary, the young pairs becoming more and more familiar. In another chapter I have alluded to birds brought up from the nest, either in a cage fed by the parents, or by hand; and also to such as having been rescued either from cold or from any accident have grown quite tame; these will hop about us, tap at the window, come in at the door, call when they see us, and be, in fact, the most amusing and bold of socially disposed birds.

3. Even London people can find some interest in the Sparrow tribe. It may be remarked that the pet cage birds are mostly themselves of the sparrow class; but at any rate friendships are sometimes struck up, which are truly amusing; and the audacity of the young Sparrow broods feeding within a yard of me, and stealing the food put down for my own birds, often affords me much entertainment: and their attitudes, basking in the sun, or taking dust baths, are very attractive while they are young and pretty.

They come too on my windows, and have great flirtations with some of my canaries—a noisy flirtation it is, both parties rattling against the window-pane—and great is my bird's excitement when she hears her sparrow.

Sparrows, though plebian, are good hearted birds. I have heard of cases where they have continually fed a cage bird, or a nest full of young hung outside a window. It is an experiment in the result of which I have but little doubt, though my fondness for feeding birds myself has deterred me from trying it. In winter it is by no means rare to find a half-starved bird, and as such a one is very likely to stay willingly indoors while the cold weather lasts; by the time that is over it is tolerably tame and accustomed to its new home.

These winter-caught birds, I think, should always be let out before the spring comes on. If the cage is then hung outside for a day or two and kept well supplied with food, it will probably induce the bird to keep up the acquaintance and to return in any trouble to the house that sheltered it. These means at any rate make the birds about a place tame and fearless, and add tenfold to the pleasure of hearing their pleasant songs.

ELIZA BRIGHTWEN

"Impey the Bat"

More about Wild Nature. London: T. Fisher Unwin, 1892. 37–41.

It is not often that such an interesting exotic creature as the Indian fruit-eating bat can be obtained in England. It was therefore with great pleasure that I heard several were to be purchased at Jamrach's, and I lost no time in sending an order for one to be forwarded to me.

There was some little excitement in opening the case which contained the illustrious stranger, as one could only know by experience whether an animal like a small fox, with leathery wings and formidable claws, possessed an amiable disposition or not. The box was therefore opened "with care," and quiet peeps taken of the inmate before he was let out.

Two lustrous black eyes set in a soft furry head, which looked timidly out of the aperture made in the box, soon disarmed all fears, for the expression was gentle, and the queer hooked wings were only used to feel about in various directions to obtain a fresh hold in order that the bat might creep out, so he was allowed to find his way into a suitable cage where he could hang comfortably from the wires at the top.

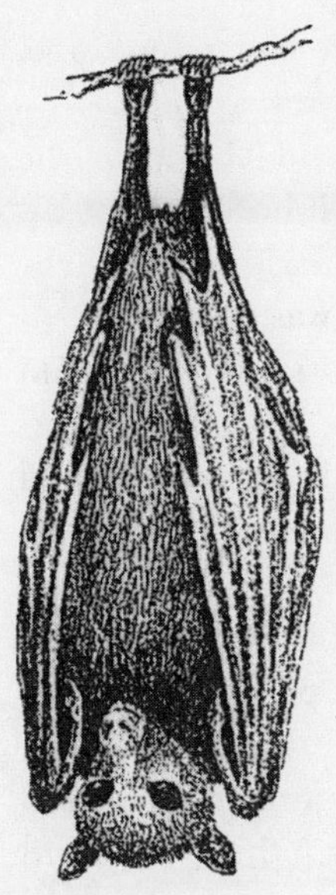

FIGURE 26 Elizabeth Brightwen, *Impey the Bat*

There was something so altogether weird and uncanny about the look of this creature that the name of Impey seemed the most appropriate that could be given. His body was clothed with very thick reddish-brown fur, the nose pointed, the ears large, formed of very thin membrane, and sensitive to the slightest sound. At night they were almost always in motion, flickering backwards and forwards. The eyes are large, and glisten like two stars if a light is brought near the cage in the evening.

The wings when expanded measure more than a yard across, and the membrane of which they are composed is somewhat like black kid.

After a time Impey was allowed to come out of his cage and creep about in the conservatory. He always made his way to some of the pillars, which were wreathed with climbing plants, and by their means he hooked himself up until he reached some wire near the roof, and from there he would hang head downwards, and taking advantage of his perfect freedom, he would thoroughly clean his fur, licking himself all over, examining his wings, and, putting himself in comfortable trim, would then wrap each wing tightly round his body, tuck his head out of sight, and go to sleep until night came on. If we paid Impey a visit about nine o'clock, we were sure to find our weird looking pet amongst the palm branches, his eyes gleaming brightly as he made his way in and out amongst the foliage. He was often in difficulties, because the plants would not sustain his weight, and he was liable to falls, so after an hour or two he was glad to return to his home, where he could suspend himself safely from the upper wires.

His food consisted of apples, grapes, and bananas, and if by chance he had too large a portion to eat conveniently, he would unhook one of his wings from above, and holding the banana against his breast with a witch-like sort of claw, he would then break pieces off until all was finished.

He never swallowed anything solid; after long mastication he would flick away grape skins, apple peel, or anything else that he could not reduce to a soft pulp. Impey was a most gentle pet; he like to be caressed and stroked, and when called by name he peered out from between his folded wings most intelligently.

I never before realised the difficulty of petting anything that would always live upside down. One longed to see how the soft, pretty face would look the other way up, but we never saw Impey either reversed or flying. Those who have known these bats in India say that they require to drop from a height of at least twenty feet in order to get the air beneath their wings and fully expand them for flight.

My specimen was *Pteropus Media,* and came from Calcutta. I felt, therefore, he would need great care through the exceptionally cold winter we have had. In the well-warmed conservatory he would hardly have felt a chill, and he had every possible variety of food, but after some months he became hopelessly diseased, a not infrequent result, I find, of these bats being in captivity, and to my great regret I was compelled to have him chloroformed to put an end to what would have been a suffering life.

I have kept our English long-eared bat as a pet for several months, until it became quite tame and seemed perfectly happy. It would take flies from my hand, and required thirty or more daily to keep it in health and vigour, and this shows how much good is done by various species of bats in clearing the air of cockchafers,[1] flies, and gnats.

When a lively bluebottle fly was offered to my bat, it would seize it eagerly, and then folding its wings over the insect, would cower down upon it so that you could not watch the process of devouring it.

On warm summer nights I am accustomed to sleep with windows open, so as to obtain as much fresh air as possible, but this allows the entrance of inquisitive bats, and thus I am often able with muslin net to capture the small visitors and keep them for a time to study their habits.

I know many people have a nervous dread of these uncanny-looking little animals, but this dread would, I think, entirely pass away if the perfectly

1. Scarablike European beetles. *Ed.*

harmless nature of the bat were better known, and certainly its great value as an insect eater should protect it from being destroyed.

It was interesting to watch the daily toilet of my small pet.

He would carefully lick his soft fur, stretch out his wings and clean them from every speck of dust, and when he considered himself in perfect order, he folded his long, delicate ears under his wings, hooked himself up on a wire at the top of the cage, and went to sleep until the dusk of evening, when he would be on the alert to be let out of his cage for a flight about the room.

Flitter-mouse seems a very appropriate name for the bat; its flight is vague and uncertain, much like that of a butterfly, quite unlike any sort of bird. On summer evenings one of the smaller species always hawks backwards and forwards on the north side of the house, keeping within a very limited space, finding, I imagine, an abundant supply of insects.

Owing to the lakes being near the house and a moat being the boundary of the garden on one side, the supply of gnats is unlimited, so that swallows, bats, and all insectivorous creatures find this place quite an earthly paradise. I have said that the bat's flight is unlike that of a bird, but one day, quite early in the spring, I saw what I took to be a large thrush flying high up above the trees in the park, and yet, as it flew in circles and at last turned somersaults in the air, I knew it must be a bat; but what species could it be that would fly thus in the bright sunshine of a spring morning? I went in search of a field-glass, and with its aid I could see that my supposed thrush was a noctule, the largest species of bat known in England. Its wings have an expansion of fifteen inches, and this must have been a full-sized specimen to look so large when high up in the air. Yarrell, writing on this bat, says that its peculiar evolutions in the air are caused by the hooks on the wings being required to manage the struggles of some large insect just captured; the bat's flight is therefore interrupted, and it drops suddenly about two feet, a manœuvre which reminds one of the odd movements of a tumbler pigeon.

On the following day a pair of noctules were seen flying in the park, so I live in hopes that some day a young one will come into my possession. I feel sure that with gentle kindness, patience, and care it would develop into a most interesting pet, for I learn from those who have kept them that they will become tame enough to fly to one's hand and take an insect from it, and if a humming noise is made with the lips, they will hover close to the face waiting for the coming dainty.

I hope I have said enough to win favour and protection for this most curious and useful creature.

ELIZA BRIGHTWEN

From *Inmates of My House and Garden*

New York: MacMillan and Co., 1895. 17–25.

Amongst the many curious animals I had kept and studied, there had never, so far, been a specimen of the monkey tribe. I had always feared that I could not meet their requirements in the way of food and temperature, and that a proper place for such creatures did not exist at the Grove.

However, the offer of a pair of lemurs tempted me into many consultations and much searching amongst the books in the library, in order to find out all that could be learned about the nature of these animals, until I found myself speculating as to whether it would not, after all, be possible to make them happy.

Lemurs are inhabitants of the island of Madagascar, where they live in the woods, feeding on fruits. All accounts agree in describing them as quiet, gentle creatures, very agile in their movements and nocturnal in their habits.

The word *lemur* was employed by the ancients to describe the unbodied sprits of men, whether beneficent or malignant; the festivals called *lemuria* were appointed for the appeasing and "laying" of ghosts. The animals received their name from their almost noiseless movements; they must, I suppose, look very ghastly and uncanny as they flit about on the tree-branches at night.

The more I read about them the more it appeared to me that I must not lightly pass by such an opportunity of obtaining rare subjects for naturalistic study. So the lemurs were accepted, and I sent a man to the other side of London to bring them, cage and all, with great care to their new home.

Until I knew their size and something about their requirements I could not very well prepare a place for them, and I reckoned on their living in the cage that they came in for a few days at least after their arrival. What, then, was my dismay when the lemurs arrived to find that they were packed in a small hamper, and that no cage had come with them, as it had been found too large to be conveyed by any cab or other sort of carriage.

Plainly the poor animals could not stay in the hamper, and I had nothing large enough to hold them. They were so timid that I was afraid to let them loose in the conservatory; they might have sprung up to the roof and remained there, where it would be cold, and as I had been very specially warned to guard them against draughts, I was puzzled indeed to know what

FIGURE 27 Elizabeth Brightwen, *Lemurs* (courtesy Richard Durrant)

to do with them. At last a large circular linen-basket was found, which made a temporary home until we could think of some better place in which to keep them.

When the hamper was opened the poor frightened creatures were seen locked in each other's arms, gazing at us with round glassy eyes. It was some days before we could really see what beautiful animals they were, since their timidity was so great that, though they would eat bananas out of my hand gently enough, nothing would induce them to come out of their hiding-place and be friendly.

As soon as possible, a bay at one end of the conservatory was wired in, some tree-branches were fixed for the lemurs to climb upon, and a large plant-case, with glass sides and top, and soft hay within, made a cosy retreat when they wished for complete retirement.

It was very enjoyable to let the new pets into their pleasant home. They instantly and fully approved of it, climbing at once to the highest branch, and gazing down at us with a far happier expression in their great eyes than they had hitherto shown. And now for the first time we could appreciate the beauty of their silky-white fur and wonderful tails.

I found out that these were specimens of the Ruffed Lemur, the most beautiful of the ten species found in Madagascar. I will try and describe them, though it will not be easy to give a very clear idea of creatures which vary so much in aspect according to the position they adopt.

Sitting on the top of their glass house, side by side, with their long furry tails coiled around them, they looked like two huge Persian cats, but standing or climbing they showed themselves to be true monkeys, although far exceeding the ordinary monkey in gracefulness.

Round the head was a full ruff of long white hairs, setting off the gentle, fox-like face, which was mostly black, as were the small, well-shaped hands and feet. Lemurs have four fingers and a thumb on the hands, and the great toe and four smaller ones, as well as the fingers, have perfect nails, which makes the creatures look very human.

The thick wooly fur was white, with large patches of black, and the tail, three-quarters of a yard in length, was precisely like a lady's black fur boa, and was used much in the same way, either laid gracefully across the back or over the feet, or wherever else warmth might be required.

When I offered food to these lemurs they had a curious way of obtaining it when not quite within their reach. The little black hand was stretched out and took a firm but very gentle grasp of my fingers, drawing them nearer until the coveted fruit could be reached, and even if the banana could have been taken direct they preferred to hold my hand, and did it so prettily that I was tempted always to make them reach out for it.

Considering the ghost-like character associated with these animals, we thought that "Spectre" and "Phantom" would be appropriate names; they do not, however, respond to any endearing epithets, and only manifest emotion when a banana is offered for their acceptance.

I fancy they are somewhat unintelligent; they differ greatly from the ordinary type of monkey, in that they sit still by the hour together, and have no idea of mischief or of helping themselves in any way; for instance, a monkey, if feeling cold, will accept a shawl and wrap it round him, finding the comfort of it; but these creatures would sit and shiver and die of cold before the idea of covering themselves would enter their dull brains.

They are masters of the art of expressing surprise and contempt. If something is offered to them that they do not like, they bridle up and turn away their heads as much as to say, "Dear me, no! nothing earthly would induce me to touch a thing like that; remove it at once!"

My greatest surprise in connection with the lemurs took place about two months after their arrival. I had carried Mungo[1] to see them, and carefully holding him by his string, I allowed him to stand and gaze up at them through the wires.

1. My pet mongoose.

He had often done this before, and beyond a few angry snorts and their usual grunting sounds they had taken no notice, but on this occasion they both at the same moment set up the most terrific roar that I ever heard. I do not exaggerate when I declare that it really seemed as loud as the roar of a lion at the Zoo. I was close to them, and it was so utterly unexpected I don't think I was ever quite so astonished in all my life. The sound was truly awful, and it lasted for half a minute or more, till I felt completely stunned, and was glad enough to retreat to a quiet room where my nerves could recover from the shock.

I think the Madagascar woods where these animals dwell must be most gruesome places at night, with these black and white creatures flitting about in the branches, abruptly uttering their terrific roars at intervals.

A family quarrel among lemurs must be a thing to remember. Besides this, they also give a loud groan now and then, which irresistibly reminds one of *Punch*'s "moaning gipsy in the back garden." Such a groan must sound additionally weird at night in the dark woods.

When I gave my friends an account of the scare I had had, one of them returned with me to the conservatory to be favoured with a special performance of "Ghosts." Mungo was brought in once more, and up rose the awful sound, with such effect that my friend turned and fled, even though she had been forewarned. Fear is quite irresistibly awakened by the strange quality of the sound given forth by these animals. Having very slight means of defending themselves, I imagine this roaring power has been bestowed upon them to enable them to scare their foes, and drive away through fear such enemies as their soft hands could never overcome in fair fight.

After keeping these lemurs about a year, I found that by no amount of kindness or coaxing could I get them to be really friendly, and I feared they were not over-happy without companions of their own kind. They were doubtless caught too old to be tamed. It was therefore deemed best to present them to the Zoo, where, under the kind and skilful treatment they receive, they are, I believe, in splendid health and spirits.

Visitors to the monkey-house can identify them from the description I have here given, and cannot fail to admire the agile movements and furry beauty of my quondam pets.

ALICE DEW-SMITH

From *Tom Tug and Others: Sketches in a Domestic Menagerie*

London: Seeley and Co., 1898. 153–60; 197–204.

[pp. 153–60]

XXI

Whishton

Whishton is known to natural history as a Mexican marmot. In appearance he is something between a small "bunnie" and a hedgehog. I first met him when paying an afternoon call. That Whishton's acquaintance should have sprung from anything so unpromising as an afternoon call, I have always looked upon as a proof that every phase of life has its possibilities.

Whishton's mistress is a genuine lover of animals. Instead of following the beaten track, and limiting her affection and interest to horses, dogs, cats and birds, she had gone off into the byeways, woods and hedges, and made friends with animals to be found outside the margin of civilization, or hovering on its border. To this latter class belongs the small four-legged bundle of fur, with character, personality, and individuality of its own, called Whishton.

When I first saw Whishton he was lying flattened out, like a very small fur rug with the head and legs and tail left on, right under the grate, in one of those old-fashioned fire-places with hobs.

"He *will* lie under the grate," said his mistress, routing him out to make him show himself. "And I know a cinder will drop on him some day and burn him. But he is dreadfully obstinate, and as soon as I take him out he goes back again."

Indeed, tenacity of purpose seemed to be the keynote of Whishton's character. No sooner was he forcibly removed than he went back and passionately flattened himself out again beneath the glowing embers. "I *will* be warm," he seemed to say, "wild horses shall not tear me from this pleasant spot." It was not till he had been dragged out half-a-dozen times that he gave it up, thinking no doubt that even warmth was dear at the price of such persistent disturbing.

Like most animals, Whishton appears to have a supreme contempt for civilization. "Bother these chairs and tables and carpets and doors!" one can almost hear him say, as he walks crossly about on the floor. "Why can't people live happily in the woods, where they can do as they like, go to bed when they like, get up when they like, and eat what and when they like; instead of in a stupid, stuffy house, where you can't go anywhere without waiting to have a door opened, and where you can't even dig a hole without having your ears boxed?"

On one occasion civilization apparently got on his nerves, and he made up his mind he could stand it no longer. He made his way up to one of the top rooms in the house where lay a roll of carpet. Into this he crept and made up his mind to stay, "far from the madding crowd." He might have remained concealed there for the rest of the winter, if it had not been for one of his little peculiarities. He always answers to his name. It is as if the mere sound "Whishton" presses a button which forces a similar cry from him. No matter in how remote a corner he has hidden himself, to call his name never fails to make an echo. So when it was discovered that the queer little creature was missing, he was called all over the house, "Whishton-Whish!" sounded from room to room, and much as he may have desired to keep his place of hiding a secret, he was forced to echo the cry.

A faint, muffled, half-plaintive cry was heard from somewhere at the top of the house. It was traced to the empty room, and once there, to the roll of carpet, in the midst of which lay Whishton warm and snug.

"Let me alone! Don't bother me!" the cry entreated. But, like other victims of domesticity, Whishton had to adapt himself to circumstances—not of his own choosing. The roll of carpet might from his point of view be most desirable as a place of residence, but from the point of view of his mistress it was undesirable in the extreme. He was promptly evicted and sent down-stairs. "One can't do a single thing!" he said petulantly as he walked down-stairs again.

Needless to say, he did not abandon his project because of a single rebuff. His mistress tells me that she believes he never will abandon the project of making his abode inside that roll of carpet. "Indeed," she said, "since we took to shutting the garret door, it has become Whishton's life-work to gnaw a hole under it and so effect an entrance. His whole soul is possessed with this desire. He thinks of nothing else all day, and as soon as an opportunity is given him by the opening of a door he makes straight for the staircase, scuttles up it, and proceeds with his gnawing."

Though Whishton's state of mind is one of placid boredom, whittled, as it were, to a point by intense concentration of purpose, I have on two occasions seen him lose his temper and give way to uncontrolled rage. The one occasion was when he was frustrated in his desire to go to this same roll of carpet. He had sat patiently at the door, waiting for it to be opened, while I talked to his mistress. Then when I got up to go, "Watch Whishton!" she said. "He is going to his roll of carpet."

No sooner was the door open than he tore down the stairs so fast that we could hardly keep him in sight, his little stand-up tail and baggy legs giving him a very quaint appearance from behind. We followed as quickly as we could, and were just in time to see him reach the bottom of the staircase and scuttle across the passage to another closed door, and wait with his nose on the ground for us to open it. Quick as lightning, when it was opened, Whishton scuttled along another passage, and we were only just in time again to see him (like the white rabbit in *Alice in Wonderland*) disappear up another staircase.

"Whishton!" called his mistress after him, and an excited answer came from the staircase up which he was tearing might and main, "I can't wait!" to be repeated louder and louder and with more intensity and passion each time he was called—"I can't and *won't* wait!!" When he reached the top he was silent, though we continued to call. He had found the door of his garret shut. If he was caught he would be brought down and put into the detestable box of straw that domesticity had assigned to him for a bed. His only safety lay in lying low. So he lay low.

But Fate was relentless. His mistress followed him up the staircase. I stayed below. The landing at the top of the staircase was pitch dark, and I could hear her feeling about in the corners for him. "Whishton! Where are you?" But answer came there none.

Suddenly "Here he is!" was followed by a scuffle and scream from the struggling Whishton; and the next minute Whishton himself, baffled and sulky, came walking slowly down the stairs. He had sense enough to see that he had lost, and there was nothing for it but to give in. Sulkily he walked along the passage at the bottom of the garret stairs, turned sulkily in at a door that opened into it, got crossly into a box that stood on the floor, and subsided with a queer little petulant gesture into the straw. His mistress followed to tuck him up and comfort him. "Don't be cross, Whishton," she said, as if she were talking to a naughty child; "I really cannot let you sleep in that roll of carpet." But he was in no mood to be comforted. With a cry of rage he flew at the comforting hand, bit, scratched, kicked, and exhibited all the signs of an ungovernable fit of temper.

On the second occasion there was, I think, more excuse for his showing temper. He was sent in a cage to a cat and rabbit show. Apparently he had not thought that life had anything so hideous in store for him as to find himself shut up in a small cage in a huge place full of other caged animals that were filling the air with a pandemonium of sounds, being glared at by strange human beings, who pushed their horrid fingers through the bars of his cage and tried to touch him. Suddenly his mistress appeared in the crowd, opened his cage door, and took him out. He clung passionately to her. "Take me away from this horrible place," he cried, "or I shall go mad!" He felt himself stroked and comforted for a moment or two, and then!—he was put back into the cage and the door shut! It was more than he could bear. He lost his self-control. He seized the bars of the cage, shook them, shrieked, and bit anything he could reach; gave way, in short, to an uncontrollable fit of rage. If Whishton could write his autobiography, what he endured at that show would, I am sure, fill many pages. If his hair had not been grey already, doubtless his mistress would have found that it had turned when she went to take him home in the evening when the show was over.

One picture I carry in my mind of Whishton, as I saw him once when I was calling on his mistress. He was sitting up on his tail looking wistfully out of the window at the trees and the garden. He sat there for about half-an-hour without moving; and I could not help feeling that he was feverishly making plans to escape from domesticity and be a little wild marmot once again.

[pp. 197–204]

XXVII

A Domestic Tragedy

If any one had told me six months ago that I should weep over the death of a spider I should have laughed them to scorn. But the, so to speak, human aspect of the little family in the screen had developed so rapidly since I had taken them under my charge that the untimely end of poor little Monsieur seemed nothing less than a tragedy. Let me tell the worst at once: he was accidentally squashed in the door of the thermometer screen.

The miserable day I had spent looking for Monsieur et Madame when they were lost, and the unexpected arrival of Bébé, seemed entirely to have swept away the "spidery" feelings with which I had formerly regarded them. They were, to me, not so much spiders as a family of very small individuals, whose doings and behaviour generally were matters of deep interest. I now visited the thermometer screen two or three times a day, with feelings of pleasant anticipation rather than horror. Madame, I think, found my visits too frequent, and objected to having the full glare of daylight flashed in upon her domestic privacy so often. For one morning when I went with

Max to pay the usual visit, she had disappeared. Monsieur and Bébé were seated side by side on the lintel, but Madame was nowhere to be seen. After a careful hunt in all the corners of the little white house, we discovered her underneath one of the thermometers that occupied a horizontal position on the floor of the screen. The little brass knobs at each end that served to attach the rings by which the thermometer could be suspended acted as supports which kept it just high enough above the floor for Madame to conceal herself with safety beneath it. After this gentle hint I made up my mind to limit my visits to two a day—one in the morning, when Max went to take the register; and one in the afternoon, after tea, just to see how they were getting on.

From his size and general behaviour I surmised that Bébé was no infant-in-arms, but a sharp youngster who had already acquired some knowledge of the world. Where his father and mother had fetched him from that day I was not prepared to say, but thought it might possibly have been from school. He was about a quarter of the size of his father, and absurdly like him in appearance. After the first day he was always to be found sitting near Monsieur, and I gathered that the latter was having an eye to his education. On one of my afternoon visits I found Bébé mounting guard in the web in the Indian corn, and surmised that he was having a lesson in hunting. For Monsieur was seated on one of the corn spikes not far off—I supposed to see how he got on. The serious business of life was, in fact, beginning for him. On another occasion I noticed near the large web an untidy, badly-made little affair, about half the size of the big one, which I took to be Bébé's first attempt.

Frequently, when we paid our evening visit, the whole family had disappeared. Nor were they always to be found in the neighbourhood of the web. We presumed, therefore, that they had other hunting-grounds besides the clump of Indian corn. Indeed, we discovered one of the family webs slung between the tall legs of the thermometer screen itself, with a goodly supply of moths and green fly in the larder. Once we found Monsieur sitting in this web apparently a good deal disturbed by a large piece of thistledown that had caught in it, and being blown backwards and forwards by the wind was creating quite a commotion. It was the more annoying since, with the exception of this innutritious obstruction, there was absolutely nothing in the web. And as it was about ten o'clock in the morning—an unusual time for Monsieur to be on the look-out for food—his presence in the web pointed to the fact that he was hungry. Max tried to remove the thistledown carefully, without destroying the web. But though he caught hold of the tip delicately and pulled it out carefully, its removal made a large hole in the web, and so alarmed Monsieur that he bolted up-stairs as hard as he could go and disappeared through the crack into the screen. We opened the screen to see if he was all right, and found him crouching in the corner, looking very small and frightened, and doubtless thinking he had had a narrow escape. Indeed, Monsieur seemed at all times to be more nervously susceptible than Madame. He would bolt into a corner at once if he were in any way interfered with, whereas Madame would allow herself to be pushed about in the most unceremonious way without even seeming to resent it. Max had occasion one morning to take up the thermometer beneath which Madame usually reposed, in order to shake it. As she clung to the underneath side of the thermometer, as a fly does to the ceiling, he was afraid the shaking might disturb her, so he pushed her off on to the floor with a pencil. Even this treatment she did not take amiss, but remained quietly where she had been deposited till the thermometer was replaced, when she crept in under it again.

On the day of the tragic occurrence we visited the screen at half-past nine, and they were all as well as possible. Bébé was asleep in his usual corner, Madame beneath the thermometer, and Monsieur had gone downstairs to see if there was anything in the larder, and was sitting on the leg, in a position that commanded the web. He came up when we opened the screen, and sat down on the lintel, just near the hinge. It was a position both he and Madame frequently occupied. We often found them there in the morning. When the panel was shut on them, we could, by stooping down, look through the crack and see them both sitting there, with plenty of room over the back of even Madame (who was an unusually large person—about twice the size of her husband) to pass a thick sheet of writing-paper. So we had always taken it for granted that they were quite able to take care of themselves, and that any position on the lintel was safe.

Just after lunch I had an unaccountable desire to break through the rule and go and pay them a mid-day visit. "Let us go and see how Monsieur, Madame, et Bébé are getting on," I said to Max, and we wandered towards the kitchen-garden. Max opened the screen in a leisurely manner, and then he took his pipe out of his mouth, and, stooping, gazed at the lintel in silence. I knew by his taking his pipe out of his mouth that something had happened. "What is the matter?" I asked, with a feeling of apprehension. "I am afraid," he said seriously, "that we have squashed poor little Monsieur." I felt a sudden pang in the region of my heart, and shrank back as one does from a horror of ordinary dimensions, not daring to go forward and see what had happened. "*Oh!*" and then to ask, with suspended breath, "Is he dead?" half hoping it might be only a slight injury. "I am afraid so," said

Max, who was investigating him carefully. And then I ventured to go forward and look.

Poor little Monsieur! He lay crumpled up, his body and one of his legs crushed by the panel. Apparently he had moved (probably while we were shutting the screen) to a part of the lintel where the joining of the wood allowed too little room for him to lie unharmed, and when the panel was shut up he had been crushed. Max was unable to say whether life was quite extinct, and so little was he mutilated that I could not help hoping it was a slight injury from which he would recover. We moved him carefully with the pencil on to the floor of the house where he would be safe from molestation and have the best chance of recovery, and then we turned to look for Madame and Bébé. Neither of them seemed to be in the least aware of the domestic misfortune that had befallen them. Madame lay apparently fast asleep under the thermometer, and Bébé sat equally unconscious in his accustomed corner, not far from the scene of the disaster. My impulse was to wake them both up and tell them what had happened, so that Madame might minister to him (make beef-tea and bind up his wounds, so to speak) if there were still life in him. But one felt a sort of delicacy about interfering with the *vie intime* of creatures of whose sphere of existence one knew so little.

I paid frequent visits during the day to Monsieur's bedside, always hoping to detect some sign of life. I even went so far as to put a very small fly quite close to his nose, so that if he felt disposed to take a little nourishment he might find it near at hand. But each visit my hope of his recovery grew fainter. The little frame lay motionless and always in the same place. Towards evening it presented a shrivelled appearance which left no doubt in my mind that Monsieur was a corpse. His death cast a gloom over the day, so that I thought of little else. My head was full of surmises as to what would become of Madame and Bébé. Would they, overwhelmed with grief, desert the thermometer screen? Who would complete Bébé's education? Would they bury Monsieur, or leave him where he was?

We visited the screen early the next morning to find that all sorts of changes had taken place. Monsieur's body had disappeared. Bébé had disappeared. Madame was no longer under the thermometer, but lying in her old position on the hinge, and not far off was—was it little Monsieur come to life again; or another husband? It was impossible to say. For the scene that was enacted in that thermometer screen during the night, was, and always will be, shrouded in complete mystery.

*F*ARMING AND *G*ARDENING

HARRIET MARTINEAU

From *Our Farm of Two Acres*

London: Cottage Farm Series, 1865. 41–48.

THE POULTRY YARD

. . . The finest young cock we had ever reared was found dead and stiff one morning. His crop, alas! was full of ivy-leaves, which he had reached and snatched from the wall of the house, by some vigorous climbing out of bounds. Chicks, and even hens, now and then are cramped by change of weather, or other mysterious causes. If observed in time, they may be recovered by warmth, friction, and apparently by the unaccountable influence of the human hand; but if they hide their trouble they will be found dead. A stray duckling may lose itself in tall grass as in a jungle. A chick may be found drowned in an inch or two of water in a pan. At one time a hawk haunted us, and we either missed a chicken occasionally, or found it dropped, with a hole in its breast. Rats are to be expected wherever a lake or river is near; but they are easily disposed of by taking up a flag, and, when their runs are traced, putting down strychnine on bread and butter. Nowhere but under pavement should that poison be placed, because it may be swallowed by some other creature than a rat: but in a subterranean way it is very useful. We have never made war in that way, as some people do, against the sparrows and chaffinches, which really are a nuisance. Where a house is covered with ivy and climbing plants, and sheltered by copses, and where fowls are fed in the open air, freebooting tribes of birds will be encroaching and audacious. We fear that a large portion of our good meal and grain goes to glut

FIGURE 28 Harriet Martineau, 1833

our enemies in the ivy and the trees. But what can we do? We make nets to cover our sprouting vegetables and ripening fruit, and that is all we can do. But about the accidents. The worst are from prowling cats. The ladies of the Four Acres lost eight chickens by cats in one night, and we have lost eight chickens by cats in one day. Such a thing as the destruction of poultry by the neighbors' cats ought never to happen when it is once known how easy prevention is. We educate our own cat, and that at the cottage; and if the neighbors would do the same, there would be an end everywhere to the loss and discontent and ill-will which arise from this cause. When a cat is seen to catch a chicken, tie it round her neck, and make her wear it for two or three days. Fasten it securely; for she will make incredible efforts to get rid of it. Be firm for that time, and the cat is cured. She will never again desire to touch a bird. This is what we do with our own cats, and what we recommend to our neighbors; and when they try the experiment, they and their pets are secure from reproach and danger henceforth. Wild, homeless, hungry, ragged, savage cats are more difficult to catch; but they are outlaws, and may be shot with the certainty that all neighbors will be thankful.

My entire poultry-yard, except a few of the old hens on the perches, was in danger of destruction by an accident one summer night, and was saved by what I cannot but consider a remarkable exercise of energy on the part of my companion, M——. Few persons in the north of England will ever forget the thunder-storm on the night of the 24th of July, 1857. At 11 P.M., the rain came down in one sheet, instantly flooding the level ground to the depth of more than a foot, and the continuous thunder seemed to crack on one's very skull, while the blue lightning never intermitted for two seconds for above an hour. The heat was almost intolerable. Our maids, however, who keep very early hours, were sleeping through it all, when M—— escorted me (very feeble from illness) up stairs, settled me with my book in my easy chair, and bade me Good-night.

Presently I drew up a window-blind, to see the lightning better from my seat. In the midst of its blue blazes there was, more than once, a yellow flicker on the window-frame which I could not understand. I went to look out, and saw a yellow light whisking about far below, sometimes in the quarry, and then mounting or descending the terrace steps. It was M——, saving the fowls. She would not allow the maids, who were stirring enough now, to go out straight from their beds into the storm; and she knew it was useless to call the man from the cottage, who was a mere encumbrance on critical occasions. In fact, he and his wife were at that moment entirely persuaded that the end of the world was come. It was no form of speech, but their real conviction; and it could not have been asked of them to care about ducks and chickens. The maids were lighting a fire in the back kitchen, and strewing the floor with straw, while M—— was out in dress which could not be spoiled, lantern, basket, and apron. Some of the hens and chickens were too cramped to move, sitting in the water. Some were taking refuge in the shrubs. Two ducklings were dead, and two more died afterwards. M—— went again and again, and to both the poultry-yards, and brought up forty fowls,—all that were in danger, every one of which would have been dead before morning. Of course she had not a dry thread about her, nor a dry hair on her head; but the wetting was a trifle in comparison with the bewildering effect of the thunder and lightning in such a midnight. She did not suffer for it more or less, and our poultry-yard was saved. The poor fowls were dried and rubbed, and made comfortable on their straw. A few were delicate for a little while, but only five died in all. It was not the pecuniary loss which M—— dreaded, but the destruction of her whole school of dependents, and the total discouragement which must have followed such a catastrophe. If the deluge had destroyed the colony that night, we should have had no more to tell of our poultry-yard. As it is, we have contemplated the proceedings of our hens and broods ever since with a stronger interest than ever before.

When a neighbor here and there said, "*I* would have let all the fowls of the air perish before I would have gone out on such a night," we think these friends of ours have yet to learn the pleasure and true interest of a rural charge, like that of a poultry-yard.

This is an impression often renewed in regard, not only to the poultry-yard, but to all the interest involved in a genuine country life. The ladies of the Four-Acre Farm tell us of a visitor of theirs who could not conceive that women who can make butter could care for books. She wondered at their subscribing to Mudie's.[1] This is, to be sure, the very worst piece of ignorance of country life and its influences that I ever read of; but it is only an exaggeration of a sentiment very common in both town and country. Some country as well as town gentry may say to us miniature farmers, "What is the use of so much doing for so little profit? A few shillings, or a few pounds, or a certain degree of domestic comfort and luxury,—this is all; and is it worth while?"

"No, this is not all," we reply. When we say what more there is, it will be for others to decide for themselves whether it is worth while to use small portions of land, or to leave them undeveloped. It is a grave and yet a cheerful consideration that the maintenance of our man and his wife is absolutely created by our plan of living; and it is worth something that the same may be said of several animals which are called into existence by it. As for ourselves and our servants, our domestic luxuries are the smallest benefit we derive from our out-door engagements. We should under no circumstances be an idle household. We have abundance of social duties and literary pleasures, in parlor and kitchen; but these are promoted, and not hindered, by our out-door interests. The amount of knowledge gained by actual handling of the earth and its productions, and by personal interest in the economy of agriculture, even on the smallest scale, is greater than any inconsiderate person would suppose; and the exercise of a whole range of faculties on practical objects, which have no sordidness in them, is a valuable and most agreeable method of adult education.

Whoever grows any thing feels a new interest in every thing that grows, and, as to the mood of mind in which the occupation is pursued, it is, to town-bred women, singularly elevating and refining. To have been reared in a farm-house, remote from society and books, and ignorant of every thing beyond the bounds of the parish, is one thing; and to pass from an indolent or a literary life in town to rural pursuits, adopted with a pur-

1. A Victorian lending library. *Ed.*

pose, is another. In the first case, the state of mind may be narrow, dull, and coarse; in the latter, it should naturally be expansive, cheery, and elevated. The genuine poetry of man and nature invests an intellectual and active life in the open universe of rural scenery. If listless young ladies from any town in England could witness the way in which hours slip by in tending the garden, and consulting about the crops, and gathering fruit and flowers, they would think there must be something in it more than they understand. If they would but try their hand at making a batch of butter, or condescend to gather eggs, and court acquaintance with hens and their broods, or assume the charge of a single nest from the hen taking her seat to the maturity of the brood, they would find that life has pleasures for them that they knew not of,—pleasures that have as much "romance" and "poetry" about them as any book in Mudie's library. "But the time!" say some. "How can you spare the time?" Well! what is it? People must have bodily exercise, in town or country, or they cannot live in health, if they can live at all. Why should country-folk have nothing better than the constitutional walk which is the duty and pleasure of townsfolk? Sometimes there is not half an hour's occupation in the field or garden in the day; and then is the occasion for an extended ramble over the hills. On other days, two, three, four hours slip away, and the morning is gone unawares: and why not? The things done are useful; the exercise is healthful and exhilarating—in every way at least as good as a walk for health's sake; and there is the rest of the day for books, pen, and needle. The fact is, the out-door amusements leave abundance of time, and ever-renewed energy for the life of books, the pen, and domestic and social offices of duty and love.

Let those ladies whose lot it is to live in the country consider whether they shall lead a town or a country life there. A town life in the country is perhaps the lowest of all. It is having eyes which see not—ears which hear not—and minds which do not understand. A lady who had lived from early childhood in a country house politely looked into my poultry-yard when it was new, and ran after me with a warm compliment.

"*What* a beautiful hen you have there;—what beautiful long feathers in its tail!"

"Why, S——," said I, "that is the cock!"

"O—oh—oh!" said she, "I did not know."

Mr. Howitt tells us somewhere of a guest of his who, seeing a goose and her fourteen goslings on a common, thought it must be very exhausting to the bird to suckle so many young ones. To women who do not know a cock from a hen, or green crops from white, or fruit-trees from forest-trees, or how to produce herb, flower, root, or fruit from the soil, it would be new life to turn up the ground which lies about them. Miniature farming would, in that very common case, not only create the material subsistence of the servants employed, but develop the mind and heart of the employer. This, and not the money made, is the true consideration when the question arises,—What shall a woman do with two or four acres?

ANNIE MARTIN

From *Home Life on an Ostrich Farm*

London: George Philip & Son, 1890. 25–31; 102–9.

[pp. 25–31]

CHAPTER II

Some of Our Pets

Friendliness of South African birds and beasts—Our secretary bird—Ungainly appearance of Jacob—His queer ways—Tragic fate of a kitten—A persecuted fowl.

South Africa is the land of pet animals. The feathered and four-footed creatures are all delightful. They have the quaintest and most amusing ways, and they are very easily tamed. The little time and attention which in a busy colonial home can be spared for the pets is always repaid a hundredfold; and often you are surprised to find how quickly the bird or beast which only a few days ago was one of the wild creatures of the *veldt*—torn suddenly from nest or burrow, and abruptly turned out from the depths of a sack or of a Hottentot's pocket into a human home—has become an intimate friend, with a clearly-marked individual character, most interesting to study, and quite different from those of all its fellows, even of the same kind. On one point, however, the whole collection is sure to be unanimous, and that is a strong feeling of rivalry, and jealousy of one another, each one striving to be first in the affections of master and mistress. A great fondness for and sympathy with animals is not the least among the many tastes which T—— and I have in common; and in our up-country home, far off as we were

FIGURE 29 *Jacob,* illustration from Annie Martin, *Home Life on an Ostrich Farm,* opposite p. 26

from human neighbours, we were always surrounded by numbers of animal and bird friends.

We began to form the nucleus of our small menagerie while still at Walmer; and one of our first acquisitions was a secretary bird. The friends near whom we lived possessed three of these creatures, which had all been found, infants together, in one nest on an ostrich farm near Port Elizabeth; and to my great delight, one of them was given to us. "Jacob," as we named him, turned out a most amusing pet. His personal appearance was decidedly comical; reminding us of a little old-fashioned man in a grey coat and tight black knee-breeches; with pale flesh-coloured stockings clothing the thinnest and most angular of legs, the joints of which might have been stiff with chronic rheumatism, so slowly and cautiously did Jacob bend them when picking anything up, or when settling himself down into his favourite squatting attitude. Not by any means a nice old man did Jacob resemble, but an old reprobate, with evil-looking eye, yellow parchment complexion, bald head, hooked nose and fiendish grin; with his shoulders shrugged up, his hands tucked away under his coat-tails, and several pens stuck behind his ear. Altogether an uncanny-looking creature, and one which, had he appeared in England some two or three centuries ago, would have stood a very fair chance of being burned alive in company with the old witches and their cats; indeed, he looked the part of a familiar spirit far better than the blackest cat could possibly do.

Yet with all his diabolical appearance, Jacob was very friendly and affectionate, and soon grew most absurdly tame—too tame, in fact. He would come running to us the moment we appeared in the verandah, and would follow us about the garden, nibbling like a puppy at our hands and clothes. He would walk, quite uninvited, into the house, where his long-legged ungainly figure looked strangely out of place, and where he was much too noisy to be allowed to remain, although the broadest of hints in the shape of wet bath-sponges, soft clothes-brushes, Moorish slippers, and what other harmless missiles came to hand, were quite unavailing to convince him he was not wanted. The noisy scuffle and indignant gruntings attendant on his forcible expulsion had hardly subsided before he would reappear, walking sedately in at the first door or window available, as if nothing had happened.

His objectionable noises were very numerous; and some of them were unpleasantly suggestive of a hospital. He would commence, for instance, with what seemed a frightful attack of asthma, and would appear to be very near the final gasp; then for about ten minutes he would have violent and alarming hiccups; the performance concluding with a repulsively realistic imitation of a consumptive cough, at the last stage. His favourite noise of all was a harsh, rasping croak, which he would keep up for any length of time, and with the regularity of a piece of clockwork; this noise was supposed to be a gentle intimation that Jacob was hungry, though the old impostor had probably had a substantial feed just before coming to pose as a starving beggar under our windows. The monotonous grating sound was exasperating; and, when driven quite beyond endurance, T—— would have recourse to extreme measures, and would fling towards Jacob a large dried puff-adder's skin, one of a collection of trophies hanging on the walls of our cottage. The sight of this always threw Jacob into a state of abject terror. He seemed quite to lose his wits, and would dance about wildly, jumping up several feet from the ground in a grotesque manner; till at last, grunting his loudest, and with the pen-like feathers on his head bristling with excitement, he would clear the little white fence, and go off at railway speed across the common, where he would remain out of sight all the rest of the day; only returning at dusk to squat solemnly for the night in his accustomed corner of the garden.

His dread of the puff-adder's skin inclined us to doubt the truth of the popular belief in the secretary's usefulness as a destroyer of snakes, on account of which a heavy fine is imposed by the Cape Government on any one found killing one of these birds. I certainly do not think Jacob would have faced a full-grown puff-adder, though we once saw him kill and eat a small young one in the garden, beating it to death with his strong feet, and then swallowing it at one gulp. He was like a boa-constrictor in his capacity for "putting himself outside" the animals on which he fed—lizards, rats, toads, frogs, fat juicy locusts, young chickens, alas! and some of the smaller pets if left incautiously within his reach, even little kittens—all went down whole. The last-named animals were his favourite delicacy, and he was fortunate enough while at Walmer to get plenty of them. His enormous appetite, and our difficulty in satisfying it, were well known in the neighbourhood, and the owners of several prolific cats, instead of drowning the superfluous progeny, bestowed them on us as offerings to Jacob. They were killed and given to him at the rate of one a day. Once, however, by an unlucky accident, one of them got into his clutches without the preliminary knock on the head; and the old barbarian swallowed it alive. For some minutes we could hear the poor thing mewing piteously in Jacob's interior, while he himself stood there listening and looking all round in a puzzled manner, to see where the noise came from. He evidently thought there was another kitten somewhere, and seemed much disappointed at not finding it.

One day, when there had been a great catch of rats, he swallowed three large ones in succession, but these were almost too much even for him; the tail of the last rat protruded from his bill, and it was a long time before it quite disappeared from view. The butcher had orders to bring liberal supplies for Jacob every day, and the greedy bird soon learned to know the hour at which he called. He would stand solemnly looking in the direction from which the cart came, and as soon as it appeared, he would run in his ungainly fashion to meet it.

Jacob was largely endowed with that quality which is best expressed by the American word "cussedness;" and though friendly enough with us, he was very spiteful and malicious towards all other creatures on the place. He grew much worse after we went to live up-country, and became at last a kind of feathered Ishmael; hated by all his fellows, and returning their dislike with interest. Some time after we settled on our farm we found that he had been systematically inflicting a cruel course of ill-treatment on one unfortunate fowl, which, having been chosen as the next victim for the table, was enclosed, with a view to fattening, in a little old packing-case with wooden bars nailed across the front. Somehow, in spite of abundant mealies and much soaked bread, that fowl never would get fat, nor had his predecessor ever done so; we had grown weary of feeding up the latter for weeks with no result, and in despair had killed and eaten him at last—a poor bag of bones, not worth a tithe of the food he had consumed. And now here was another, apparently suffering from the same kind of atrophy; the whole thing was a puzzle to us, until one day the mystery was solved, and Jacob stood revealed as the author of the mischief. He had devised an ingenious way of persecuting the poor prisoner, and on seeing it we no longer wondered at the latter's careworn looks. Jacob would come up to his box, and make defiant and insulting noises at him—none could do this better than he—until the imbecile curiosity of fowls prompted the victim to protrude his head and neck through the bars; then, before he had time to draw back, Jacob's foot would come down with a vicious dab on his head. The foolish creature never seemed to learn wisdom by experience, though he must have been nearly stunned many times, and his head all but knocked off by Jacob's great powerful foot and leg; yet as often as the foe challenged him, his poor simple face would look inquiringly out, only to meet another buffet. As he would not take care of himself, we had to move him into a safe place; where he no longer died daily, and was able at last to fulfil his destiny by becoming respectably fat.

[pp. 102–9]

. . . It is rather surprising to find how little is known in England about ostrich-farming. Any information on the subject seems quite new to the hearers; and the strangest questions are sometimes asked—as, for instance, whether ostriches fly; whether they bite; whether we ever ride or drive them, etc. It is always taken for granted that a vicious bird administers his kick backwards, like a horse; and there seems still to be a very general belief in those old popular errors of which the natural history of these creatures possesses more than the average share. If you look at the picture of an ostrich, you will be sure to find, in nine cases out of ten, that the drawing is ludicrously incorrect; the bird being almost invariably represented with three toes instead of two; and with a tail consisting of a large and magnificent bunch of *wing*-feathers, the finest and longest of "prime whites." Farmers would only be too thankful if their birds *had* such tails, instead of the short, stiff, scrubby tuft of inferior feathers which in reality forms the caudal appendage.

Each of my friends and relatives, when first told, at the time of our engagement, that T—— was "an ostrich-farmer," received the intelligence with an amused smile; and the clergyman at whose church we were married seemed quite taken aback on obtaining so novel and unexpected an answer to his question, during the vestry formalities, as to T——'s vocation in life. He hesitated, pen in hand, for some time; made T—— repeat and explain the puzzling word; and at last only with evident reluctance inscribed it in the church books.

In the early days of ostrich-farming splendid fortunes were made. Then, feathers were worth £100 per lb., the plumes of one bird at a single plucking realizing on average £25. For a good pair of breeding-birds £400, or even £500, was no uncommon price; and little chicks, only just out of the egg, were worth £10 each. Indeed, the unhatched eggs have sometimes been valued at the same amount. But, since the supply has become so much greater than the demand, things are sadly changed for the farmers; our best pair of ostriches would not now sell for more than £12, and experience has taught us to look for no higher sum than thirty shillings for the feathers of the handsomest bird at one plucking. At the same time, if a lady wishes to buy a good feather in London or Paris, she has to pay nearly the same prices as in former times.[1]

There are not many young animals prettier than a little ostrich-chick during the first few weeks of life. It has such a sweet, innocent baby-face, such large eyes, and such a plump, round little body. All its movements are comical, and there is an air of conceit and independence about the tiny creature which is most amusing. Instead of feathers, it has a little rough coat which seems all made up of narrow strips of material, of as many different shades of brown and grey as there are in a tailor's pattern-book, mixed with shreds of black; while the head and neck are apparently covered with the softest plush, striped and coloured just like a tiger's skin on a small scale. On the whole, the little fellow, on his first appearance in the world, is not unlike a hedgehog on two legs, with a long neck.

One would like these delightful little creatures to remain babies much longer than they do; but they grow quickly, and with their growth they soon lose all their prettiness and roundness; their bodies become angular and ill-proportioned, a crop of coarse, wiry feathers sprouts from the parti-coloured strips which formed their baby-clothes, and they enter on an ugly "hobbledehoy" stage, in which they remain for two or three years.

A young ostrich's rough, bristly, untidy-looking "chicken-feathers" are plucked for the first time when he is nine months old; they are stiff and narrow, with very pointed tips, and their ugly appearance gives no promise of future beauty. They do not look as if they could be used for anything but making feather brooms. In the second year they are rather more like what ostrich-feathers ought to be, though still very narrow and pointed; and not until their wearer is plucked for the third time have they attained their full width and softness.

During the first two years the sexes cannot be distinguished, the plumage of all being of a dingy drab mixed with black; the latter hue then

1. Although, since these pages were written, ostriches have somewhat increased in value it cannot, of course, be expected that they will ever again command the prices of former days.

begins to predominate more and more in the male bird with each successive moulting, until at length no drab feathers are left. At five years the bird has attained maturity; the plumage of the male is then of a beautiful glossy black, and that of the female of a soft grey, both having white wings and tails. In each wing there are twenty-four long white feathers, which, when the wing is spread out, hang gracefully round the bird like a lovely deep fringe—just as I have sometimes in Brazilian forests, seen fringes of large and delicate fern-fronds hanging, high overhead, from the branches of some giant tree.

The ostrich's body is literally "a bag of bones;" and the enormously-developed thighs, which are the only fleshy part of the bird, are quite bare, their coarse skin being of a peculiarly ugly blue-grey colour. The little flat head, much too small for the huge body, is also bald, with the exception of a few stiff bristles and scanty tufts of down; such as also redeem the neck form absolute bareness. During the breeding season the bill of the male bird, and the large scales on the fore part of his legs, assume a beautiful deep rose-colour, looking just as if they were made of the finest pink coral; in some cases the skin of the head and neck also becomes red at that time.

The North African or Barbary ostriches, several of which are to be seen at the Jardin d'Essai, in Algiers, have bright red thighs, head, and neck, and are altogether far handsomer than the Cape birds; their feathers also, being larger, softer, and possessing longer filaments, command much higher prices than those of their southern brethren.

Altogether, ostriches are queer-looking creatures; they are so awkward, so out of proportion, and everything about them, with the exception of their plumage and their big, soft, dark eyes, is so quaintly ugly as to suggest the idea that they have only by some mistake survived the Deluge, and that they would be more in their right place embedded in the fossiliferous strata of the earth than running about on its surface. And how they *do* run! Only startle an ostrich; and very little is sufficient to do this, his nerves being of the feeblest, and "his heart in his mouth" at even the smallest or most imaginary danger. What a jump he gives, and what a swerve to one side! Surely it must have dislocated some of his joints. But no; off he goes, flinging out his clumsy legs, and twisting himself about as he runs, till you almost expect to see him come to pieces, or, at any rate, fling off a leg, as a lobster casts a claw, or a frightened lizard parts from its tail. An ostrich's joints seem to be all loose, like those of a lay-figure when not properly tightened up. He rapidly disappears from view; and the last you see of him he is, as Mark Twain has it, "still running"—apparently with no intention of stopping till he has reached the very centre of Africa. But his mad scamper will most probably end a few miles off, with a tumble into a wire fence, and a broken leg.

Sometimes, however, ostriches, when they take fright, run so long and get so far away that their owner never recovers them. One we heard of, to whose tail a mischievous boy had tied a newspaper, went off at railway speed, and no tidings of it were ever received. Once, when T—— was collecting his birds for plucking, one of them was unaccountably seized with a sudden panic, and bolted; and though T—— mounted at once and rode after it, he neither saw nor heard of it again.

On a large farm, when plucking is contemplated, it is anything but an easy matter to collect the birds—the gathering together of ours was generally a work of three days. Men have to be sent out in all directions to drive the birds up, by twos and threes, from the far-off spots to which they have wandered; little troops are gradually brought together, and collected, first in a large enclosure, then in a small one, the plucking-kraal, in which they are crowded together so closely, that the most savage bird has no room to make himself disagreeable.

Besides the gate through which the ostriches are driven into the kraal, there is an outlet at the opposite end, through the "plucking-box." This latter is a most useful invention, saving much time and trouble. It is a very solid wooden box, in which, though there is just room for an ostrich to stand, he cannot possibly turn round; nor can he kick, the sides of the box being too high. At each end there is a stout door; one opening inside, the other outside the kraal. Each bird in succession is dragged up to the first door, and, after more or less of a scuffle, is pushed in and the door slammed behind him. Then the two operators, standing one on each side of the box, have him completely in their power; and with a few rapid snips of their shears his splendid wings are soon denuded of their long white plumes. These, to prevent their tips from being spoilt, are always cut before the quills are ripe. The stumps of the latter are allowed to remain some two or three months longer, until they are so ripe that they can be pulled out—generally by the teeth of the Kaffirs[2]—without hurting the bird. It is necessary to pull them; the feathers, which by their weight would have caused the stumps to fall out naturally at the right time, being gone. Some farmers, anxious to hurry on the next crop of feathers, are cruel enough to draw the stumps before they are ripe; but nature, as usual, resents the interference with her laws, and the feathers of the birds which have been thus treated soon deteriorate. It is best to pluck only once a year. The tails, and the glossy

2. Members of a South African Bantu tribe. *Ed.*

back feathers on the bodies of the birds, having small quills, are not cut, but pulled out; this, everyone says, does not hurt the birds, but there is an unpleasant tearing sound about the operation, and I think it must make their eyes water.

ELIZA COOK

"Song of the Ostrich"

The Poetical Works. London: Frederick Warne and Co., 1869. 249–51.

The minstrel ever loves to sing
Of the beautiful gloss of the raven's wing;
He tells of beauty, and seeks to compare
The pinion of jet with the maiden's hair.
The swan has a bright and goodly place
For its spotless down and stately grace;
And bards unnumbered have praised the dove,
For its gentle faith and eye of love.

The carolling lark oft wakes a tone
As rich, as sweet, and fresh as its own;
Lyres are strung for the wild sea-mew,
And the tawny night-owl hath its due.
The eagle on dark, broad wing goes by,
While we hail him and laud him as the king of the sky;
And the poet's responding echoes float
Round the knightingale's [*sic*] lay and cuckoo's note.

But, forget not, when praising the tribes of the air,
To give to the bird of the desert his share:
Though I warble not in a verdant land,
And am never leashed to a lady's hand.
Yet many a league does the traveller come,
Seeking me far in my torrid home;
To gain my plumage "rich and rare"
For the knightly train and courteous fair.

The wished-for heir to the titled line
Is worshipped and decked as a thing divine;
The helpless form and tiny face
Are swathed in purple and shaded with lace;
The mantle of velvet is richly bright,
The robe of fine lawn, soft and white;
But mine are the feathers that nod and bow
Over the first-born's baby brow.

Away on their steeds to the hostile horde
Go the warrior knight and the soldier lord;
The corselet sparkles, the baldric is gay,
And bravely they bound in their battle array.
The scarf may flutter, the steel may shine,
But a prouder and nobler place is mine!
For the gem-wrought star that may gleam on the breast
Dazzles not like the dancing plume on the crest.

The envied daughters of rank are seen
In costly garbs of lustrous sheen;
And I must be had to grace and crown
Foreheads as fair as my own soft down.
Glad and light such foreheads may seem,
And all look bright as a fairy dream;
But I have dwelt in halls of state,
While temples have throbbed beneath my weight.

Man dies and is coffined—but yet I am found
Swelling the train on the bone-strewn ground:
His race is run—his glory is past,
But I come in my pomp to mock him at last.
Then a song for the bird whose feathers wave
O'er the christening font, and the fresh-made grave—[1]
A song for the bird of the desert, whose plume
Is seen by the cradle and met at the tomb!

1. Victorian funeral corteges utilized black ostrich feathers. *Ed.*

 GERTRUDE JEKYLL

From *Children and Gardens*

London: Country Life, 1908. 164–87.

CHAPTER XII

Pussies in the Garden

My garden would not be half the pleasure it is to me without the pussies. I hope you love them as much as I do. They are perfect garden companions. When I am out at work there is sure to be one or other of them close by, lying on my jacket or on a bench if there is one near. When it is Tabby, if there is an empty basket anywhere handy he is certain to get into it. When I take one of my baskets for flowers—of the pattern that I invented and always use—if I put it down for a moment Tabby takes possession. One day I was bringing the basket home full of Hydrangeas, and put it down to see if there were any figs ripe. I did not see what was going on behind my back, but when I turned round to take up the flowers there he was established in the basket; some of the Hydrangeas were pushed out on to the grass, and Tabby had composed himself to sleep among the rest.

Another day I was doing photographs down the garden with spare plates in a palm-leaf basket. When I wanted more plates he had made himself so comfortable that I could not bear to disturb him, so I went indoors and got more plates and made his picture. When I had done one he stretched himself, gave an immense yawn, and settled himself again in a still more reposeful position.

He is particularly fond of the spring garden, where there is a patch of grass and a wooden seat, and Nut-trees and Oaks. It is sheltered and secluded, and there are banks where he can lie in the sun, and cool retreats when it is too hot, and also Yews and Hollies, under which he can always find a dry place when other parts of the ground are damp. One bank is covered with Cerastium; this he thinks is just suitable for his bed (see fig. 22). I often find him there, and though it is not quite the best thing for the Cerastium I cannot help admiring his beautiful rich tabby coat, with its large black clouds, so well set off by the velvety grey of the little downy plant. He is an old pussy now, and when you meet him coming along a path it must be confessed that he is too fat and has lost his figure. But it only shows when he is walking, for when he is sitting, or lying comfortably curled or tucked, and especially when he is on his gate-post, looking out so proud and fine, you would never call him a fat old cat. When he was younger I would hold the gate open, and he would jump from post to post. When I am near his favourite region and do not see him, I call to him; if he does not come at once and I walk on I am pretty sure to hear him asking where I am within a minute or two.

There is a little bit of turf between the two wings of the house that is another of his favourite haunts. I did his picture as he lay stretched out quite flat, asleep, with his back to me, one fine summer day. When I had done I said "Tabby." He just turned straight over, presenting his tummy, and I did the second picture.

Like most cats he is devoted to the pretty plant Catmint. It is in several places in the garden. He knows where every plant is and never passes one when we are walking together without stopping to nuzzle and nibble it. If I stop to watch him, when he has had his first taste he will push himself right into the middle of the plant and sometimes lie down and roll in it to get all he can of the sweet smell.

But you should see Blackie in the Catmint. He seems to go quite crazy with delight, jumps straight up in the air and comes down flop into the middle, dances in it and twists about, and then comes out and does it all over again. He is only an old kitten as yet, and extremely agile, but the Catmint seems to inspire him with a sort of frenzy of frantic pleasure and excitement. I wish I could have photographed him, but my camera is not quick enough, and I have to be content with giving you a sketch from recollection. He had a pretty trick when he was quite a little fellow; I would

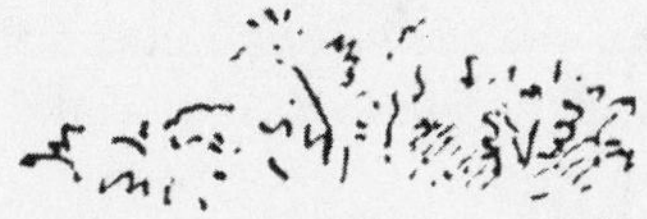

FIGURE 30 Gertrude Jekyll, *Blackie and the Catmint,* illustration from "Pussies in the Garden," p. 170

hold out my hand about a foot from the ground, say "Come, Blackie," and he would jump into my hand.

Tittlebat is only too sociable both indoors and out. When I settle myself before the fire with a book or newspaper he jumps up on my lap and insists on being petted; pushes the book away with his beautiful sleek head and nuzzles his nose into my hand again and again, and only consents to be quiet when I have given him the amount of attention that he considers his due. One day I had to go to the Rectory as it was getting dark, and did not know that he was following me. The way is across the lawn and through the region of Oaks and Hollies, then through the frame yard and all the length of the kitchen garden, past some Quince-trees and out into the main road by the gardener's cottage. It is not far beyond that to the Rectory. When I came back it was quite dark. Passing the Quince-trees I heard a disturbance in one of them, and something scrambled down to the ground. I thought it was some neighbour's cock or hen gone to roost in the tree, but the thing said May-ow, and I knew my dear Tittlebat's voice. He had followed me down and got up into the Quince to wait till I came back.

He is quite the most affectionate pussy I have ever known, and nothing, except dogs or a strange cat stalking about, has ever been known to ruffle his temper. I brought him as a kitten from the Isle of Wight, where I went one autumn to a farm lodging. I had left a family of little kittens at home, and on arriving felt rather desolate at having no small pussy playmates. But the next morning, to my delight, I saw two very shy little faces peeping out of some shrubs and garden plants that were opposite my sitting-room window, with only a narrow strip of grass between. As soon as I had finished my breakfast I went out to try and make friends, but the kittens were very wild; they had never been tamed or handled. There was a Dahlia just in front of my window at the edge of the bushes. One of its branches stuck out a little, and to this I tied a string with a bit of white paper fastened in the end, so that it swung about. Then I went in and watched. Presently the darker and more handsomely marked of the two little brothers (my future Tittlebat) came out very cautiously and examined the strange object. It moved and he made a dart at it, which made it swing still farther. He soon found out that it was a capital thing to play with. Then his brother came too, and they had a great game. Next morning at breakfast I poured a little milk into a saucer and put it on the grass near the plaything. They came to it by a little cautious advances, and lapped up the milk while I stood within sight at the open window. Then I made another plaything, the same as the Dahlia one, only on a stick, like a fishing-rod, so that I could play it from the window. After a little hesitation they came to play with it. This was a grand step, because they saw me at the window all the time. Next I put the saucer of milk on the window-sill, and great was my pleasure when Tittlebat came to it. He was the bigger and stronger of the two, and always took the lead. The next thing was to have the milk on the table put close to the window inside the room. They were attracted to it by means of the plaything, played first on the grass and then on the window-sill. They came up and on to the table. This was a great advance, and while they were lapping I just stroked them a little, very gently, taking care to bring my hand near them very slowly. A quick movement would have frightened them. Then I knew that I had got their confidence. I think this was about five days after the first offer of friendship. Then I pretended to take no notice of them, but you may be sure I was keeping a good watch out of the corner of my eye, and the next day they came up to the window and into the room of their own accord. Before my fortnight was over Tittlebat came to me as a regular thing, sitting on my lap or my shoulder and purring me his little song while I read or worked. You may imagine that when I went away I could not bear to leave him, so I begged to have him and took him home with me, where I at once gave him into the charge of Pinkie, a young pussy of my own rearing only a few months older. They took to each other at once, and very soon became quite inseparable; in fact, if they were ever apart Pinkie was miserable, and would cry most lamentably, looking about for his dear companion.

You might think from his picture that Pinkie was nearly white, but though his white tummy is very extensive all his back is tabby. The tabby comes down into the white on his sides in a way that always makes me think of geography. On the west side two large portions of the Cat-back continent,

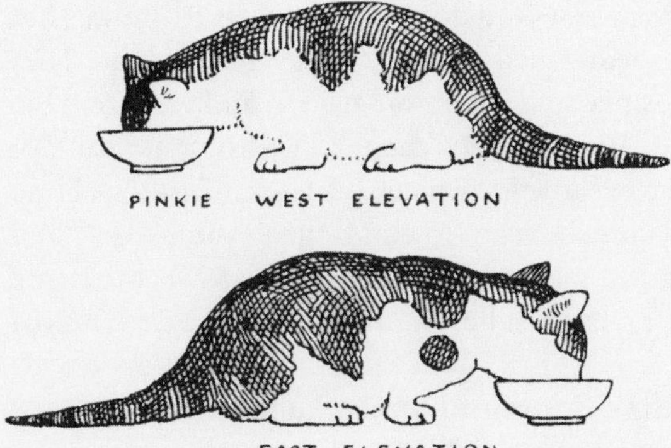

FIGURE 31 Gertrude Jekyll, *Two Side Elevations of Pinkie,* illustration from "Pussies in the Garden," p. 182

like two Indias, jut out into the white, which is the Indian Ocean. On the east side there is only one India or South Africa, extending into the Catlantic Ocean, but on his shoulder there is a large blunt promontory, and a nearly round, almost black island, which has a very handsome effect on the ground of white fur.

Tavy is very fond of that place just at the top of the steps opposite the door of the sitting-room to the garden. He likes to sit there when he knows I am near him inside, and keeps an eye on the wood close by, where there are always some objects of interest, if not in sight at least within hearing. He is red tabby and white. He does not come with me so much in the garden as the others, but indoors he is my most constant companion of all. His fur is deliciously soft and fine, and he has dainty pretty ways, quite little ladyways, we always say. He has one odd trick that I do not remember having seen in any other cat. He puffs out his tail when he is pleased—usually a short-haired cat puffs out his tail only when he is frightened, or angry, or fighting. But Tavy makes a beautiful tail when we are playing together, and he is quite pleased with himself and with me. On the rare occasions when he walks with me in the garden—he is jealous, and will never come if any other cat is present, he makes a beautiful tail and walks in a very odd way—a sort of waddling strut; we call it Tavy's ingratiating waddle; purring hard all the time and expecting a great deal of praise and attention.

Dorothea's home is a short mile away. It is a delightful house, with beautiful wild ground and garden all round it. Pussies are much loved there. A curious thing happened. One morning two tiny long-haired kittens, one black and one red, were found on the doorstep, crying with hunger and begging to be taken in. Where they came from, or how they found their way to the house will always be a mystery, for they were baby things, almost too small to have left their mother. No other house is near, and what wonderful instinct guided the little waifs to that kind door no one will ever know. They were cold and starving and bedraggled, as if they had travelled far. They were taken in and fed and cleaned and given warm beds, and very soon became quite strong and lively. When I went there a few days later, to take Dorothea a wreath of white roses, the little black kitten was frisking about, and Dorothea said, "Kitty has been trying to climb the Passion-tree." This was a Passion-Flower, with the lower part of the stem grown thick and woody, that grew against the house, just beyond the steps of the Dutch Rose garden.

I was told of a little girl who invented a beautiful word to describe a pussy purring. She said, "Puss has got the flutter-mill going."

FIGURE 32 Gertrude Jekyll, *An Equicateral Triangle,* illustration from "Pussies in the Garden," p. 187

It is amusing to see the different patterns that kittens lying in a round basket will sometimes get into. I have seen five kittens almost symmetrically arranged like cutlets in a dish, and four with their little paws all up in the middle like a pigeon pie. It was almost impossible to believe that only four small people could have so many little toes. Three at nearly equal distances round a saucer a milk make quite a pretty pattern. The architect said it was an equicateral triangle!

MARGARET GATTY

From *Parables from Nature*

London: George Bell and Sons, 1880. In *Classics of Children's Literature, 1621–1932.* New York: Garland, 1976. 36–43.

TRAINING AND RESTRAINING

"Train up a child in the way he should go."—PROV. xxii. 6.

What a fuss is made about you, my dear little friends!" murmured the Wind, one day, to the flowers in a pretty villa garden. "I am really quite surprised at your submitting so patiently and meekly to all the troublesome things that are done to you! I have been watching your friend the Gardener for some time to-day; and now that he is gone at last, I am quite curious to hear what you think and feel about your unnatural bringing up."

FIGURE 33 *Training and Restraining,* illustration for Margaret Gatty, *Parables from Nature,* opposite p. 37

"*Is* it unnatural?" inquired a beautiful Convolvulus Major, from the top of a tapering fir-pole, up which she had crept, and from which her velvet flowers hung suspended like purple gems.

"I smile at your question," was the answer of the Wind. "You surely cannot suppose that in a natural state you would be forced to climb regularly up one tall bare stick such as I see you upon now. Oh dear, no! Your cousin, the wild convolvulus, whom I left in the fields this morning, does no such thing, I assure you. She runs along and climbs about, just as the whim takes her. Sometimes she takes a turn upon the ground; sometimes she enters a hedge, and plays at bo-peep with the birds in the thorn and nut-trees—twisting here, curling there, and at last, perhaps coming out at the top, and overhanging the hedge with a canopy of green leaves and pretty white flowers. A very different sort of life from yours, with a Gardener always after you, trimming you in one place, fastening up a stray tendril in another, and fidgeting you all along—a sort of perpetual 'mustn't go here'—'mustn't go there.' Poor thing! I quite feel for you! Still I must say you make me smile; for you look so proud and self-conscious of beauty all the time, that one would think you did not know in what a ridiculous and dependent position you are placed."

Now the Convolvulus was quite abashed by the words of the Wind, for she was conscious of feeling very conceited that morning, in consequence of having heard the Gardener say something very flattering about her beauty; so she hung down her rich bell-flowers rather lower than usual, and made no reply.

But the Carnation put in her word: "What you say about the Convolvulus may be true enough, but it cannot apply to *me.* I am not aware that I have any poor relations in this country, and I myself certainly require all the care that is bestowed upon me. This climate is both too cold and too damp for me. My young plants require heat, or they would not live; and the pots we are kept in protect us from those cruel wireworms, who delight to destroy our roots."

"Oh!" cried the Wind, "our friend the Carnation is quite profound and learned in her remarks, and I admit the justice of all she says about damp and cold, and wire-worms; but,"—and here the Wind gave a low-toned whistle, as he took a turn round the flower-bed—"but what I maintain, my dear, is, that when you are once strong enough and old enough to be placed in the soil, those Gardeners ought to let you grow and flourish as nature prompts, and as you would do were you left alone. But no! forsooth, they must always be clipping, and trimming, and twisting up every leaf that strays aside out of the trim pattern they have chosen for you to grow in. Why not allow your silver tufts to luxuriate in a natural manner? Why must every single flower be tied up by its delicate neck to a stick, the moment it begins to open? Really, with your natural grace and beauty, I think you might be trusted to yourself a little more!"

And the Carnation began to think so too; and her colour turned deeper as a feeling of indignation arose within her at the childish treatment to which she had been subjected. "With my natural grace and beauty," repeated she to herself, "they might certainly trust me to myself a little more!"

Still the Rose-tree stood out that there must be some great advantages in a Gardener's care; for she could not pretend to be ignorant of her own superiority to all her wild relations in the woods. What a difference in size, in colour, and in fragrance!

Then the Wind assured the Rose he never meant to dispute the advantage of her living in a rich-soiled garden; only there was a natural way of growing, even in a garden; and he thought it a great shame for the gardeners to force the Rose-tree into an *un*natural way, curtailing all the energies of her nature. What could be more outrageous, for example, than to see one rose growing in the shape of a bush on the top of the stem of another? "Think of all the pruning necessary," cried he, "to keep the poor thing in the round shape so much admired. And what is the matter with the beautiful straggling branches, that they are to be cut off as fast as they appear? Why not allow the healthy Rose-tree its free and glorious growth? Why thwart its graceful droopings or its high aspirings? Can it be *too* large or *too* luxuriant? Can its flowers be *too* numerous? Oh, Rose-tree, you know your own surpassing merits too well to make you think this possible!"

And so she did, and a new light seemed to dawn upon her as she recollected the spring and autumnal prunings she regularly underwent, and the quantities of little branches that were yearly cut from her sides, and carried away in a wheelbarrow. "It is a cruel and a monstrous system, I fear," said she.

Then the Wind took another frolic round the garden, and made up to the large white Lily, into whose refined ear her whispered a doubt as to the necessity or advantage of her thick powerful stem being propped up against a stupid, ugly stick! He really grieved to see it! Did that lovely creature suppose that Nature, who had done so much for her that the fame of her beauty extended throughout the world, had yet left her so weak and feeble that she could not support herself in the position most calculated to give her ease and pleasure? "Always this tying up and restraint!" pursued the Wind, with an angry puff. "Perhaps I am prejudiced; but as to be deprived of freedom would be to me absolute death, so my soul revolts from every shape and phase of slavery!"

"Not more than mine does!" cried the proud white Lily, leaning as heavily as she could against the strip of matting that tied her to her stick. But it was of no use—she could not get free; and the Wind only shook his sides and laughed spitefully as he left her, and then rambled away to talk the same shallow philosophy to the Honeysuckle that was trained up against a wall. Indeed, not a flower escaped his mischievous suggestions. He murmured among them all—laughed the trim cut Box-edges to scorn—maliciously hoped the Sweet-peas enjoyed growing in a circle, and running up a quantity of crooked sticks—and told the flowers, generally, that he should report their unheard-of submission and meek obedience wherever he went.

Then the white Lily called out to him in great wrath, and told him he mistook their characters altogether. They only submitted to these degrading restraints because they could not help themselves; but if he would lend them his powerful aid, they might free themselves from at least a part of the unnatural bonds which enthralled them.

To which the wicked Wind, seeing that his temptations had succeeded, replied, in great glee, that he would do his best; and so he went away, chuckling at the discontent he had caused.

All that night the pretty silly flowers bewailed their slavish condition, and longed for release and freedom: and at last they began to be afraid that the Wind had only been jesting with them, and that he would never come to help them, as he had promised. However, they were mistaken; for, at the edge of the dawn, there began to be a sighing and a moaning in the distant woods, and by the time the sun was up, the clouds were driving fast along the sky, and the trees were bending about in all directions; for the Wind had returned,—only now he had come in his roughest and wildest mood,—knocking over everything before him. "Now is your time, pretty flowers!" shouted he, as he approached the garden; and "Now is our time!" echoed the flowers tremulously, as, with a sort of fearful pleasure, they awaited his approach.

He managed the affair very cleverly, it must be confessed. Making a sort of eddying circuit round the garden, he knocked over the Convolvulus-pole, tore the strips of bast from the stick that held up the white Lily, loosed all the Carnation flowers from their fastenings, broke the Rose-tree down, and levelled the Sweet-peas to the ground. In short, in one half-hour he desolated the pretty garden; and when his work was accomplished, he flew off to rave about his deed of destruction in other countries.

Meanwhile, how fared it with the flowers? The Wind was scarcely gone before a sudden and heavy rain followed, so that all was confusion for some time. But towards the evening the weather cleared up, and our friends began to look around them. The white Lily still stood somewhat upright, though no friendly pole supported her juicy stem; but, alas! it was only by a painful effort she could hold herself in that position. The Wind and the weight of ran had bent her forward once, beyond her strength, and there was a slight crack in one part of the stalk, which told that she must soon double over and trail upon the ground. The Convolvulus fared still worse. The garden beds sloped towards the south; and when our friend was laid on the earth—her pole having fallen—her lovely flowers were choked up by the wet soil which drained towards her. She felt the muddy weight as it soaked into her beautiful velvet bells, and could have cried for grief; she could never free herself from this nuisance. O that she were once more climbing up the friendly fir-pole! The Honeysuckle escaped no better; and the Carnation was ready to die of vexation, at finding that her coveted freedom had levelled her to the dirt.

Before the day closed, the Gardener came whistling from his farm work, to look over his pretty charges. He expected to see a few drooping flowers, and to find that one or two fastenings had given way. But for the sight that awaited him he was not prepared at all. Struck dumb with astonishment, he never spoke at first, but kept lifting up the heads of the trailing, dirtied flowers in succession. Then at last he broke out into words of absolute sorrow:—"And to think of my mistress and the young lady coming home so soon, and that nothing can be done to these poor things for a fortnight, because of the corn harvest! It's all over with them, I fear;" and the Gardener went his way.

Alas! what he said was true; and before many days had passed, the shattered Carnations were rotted with lying in the wet and dirt on the ground. The white Lily was languishing discoloured on its broken stalk; the Convolvulus' flowers could no longer be recognized, they were so coated over with mud stains; the Honeysuckle was trailing along among battered Sweet-peas, who never could succeed in shaking the soil from their fragrant heads; and though the Rose-tree had sent out a few straggling branches, she soon discovered that they were far too weak to bear flowers—nay, almost to support themselves—so that they added neither to her beauty nor her comfort. Weeds meanwhile sprang up, and a dreary confusion reigned in the once orderly and brilliant little garden.

At length, one day before the fortnight was over, the house-dog was heard to bark his noisy welcome, and servants bustled to and fro. The mistress had returned; and the young lady was with her, and hurried at once to her favourite garden. She came bounding towards the well-known spot with a song of joyous delight; but, on reaching it, suddenly stopped short, and in a minute after burst into a flood of tears! Presently, with sorrowing steps, she bent her way round the flower-beds, weeping afresh at every one she looked at; and then she say down upon the lawn, and hid her face in her hands. In this position she remained, until a gentle hand was laid upon her shoulder.

"This is a sad sight, indeed, my darling," said her mother's voice.

"I am not thinking about the garden, mamma," replied the young girl, without lifting up her face; "we can plant new flowers, and tie up even some of these afresh. I am thinking that now, at last, I understand what you say about the necessity of training, and restraint, and culture, for us as well as for flowers."

"In a fallen world;" interposed her mother.

"Yes,—because it is fallen," answered the daughter. "The wind has torn away these poor things from their fastenings, and they are growing wild whichever way they please; and I might perhaps once have argued, that if it were their *natural* way of growing it must therefore be the best. But I cannot say so, now I see the result. They are doing whatever they like, unrestrained; and the end is,—my beautiful GARDEN is turned into a WILDERNESS."

~ MARY FRANCES BURNETT

From *The Secret Garden*

1911. New York: Puffin Books, 1994. 74–82.

CHAPTER 8

. . . Mary skipped round all the gardens and round the orchard, resting every few minutes. At length she went to her own special walk and made up her mind to try if she could skip the whole length of it. It was a good long skip, and she began slowly, but before she had gone half-way down the path she was so hot and breathless that she was obliged to stop. She did not mind much, because she had already counted up to thirty. She stopped with a little laugh of pleasure, and there, lo and behold, was the robin swaying on a long branch of ivy. He had followed her, and he greeted her with a chirp. As Mary had skipped towards him she felt something heavy in her pocket strike against her at each jump, and when she saw the robin she laughed again.

'You showed me where the key was yesterday,' she said. 'You ought to show me the door today; but I don't believe you know!'

The robin flew from his swinging spray of ivy on to the top of the wall and he opened his beak and sang a loud, lovely trill, merely to show off. Nothing in the world is quite as adorably lovely as a robin when he shows off—and they are nearly always doing it.

Mary Lennox had heard a great deal about Magic in her Ayah's[1] stories, and she always said what happened almost at that moment was Magic.

One of the nice little gusts of wind rushed down the walk, and it was a stronger one than the rest. It was strong enough to wave the branches of the trees, and it was more than strong enough to sway the trailing sprays of untrimmed ivy hanging from the wall. Mary had stepped close to the robin, and suddenly the gust of wind swung aside some loose ivy trails, and more suddenly still she jumped towards it and caught it in her hand. This she did because she had seen something under it—a round knob which had been covered by the leaves hanging over it. It was the knob of a door.

She put her hands under the leaves and began to pull and push them aside. Thick as the ivy hung, it nearly all was a loose and swinging curtain, though some had crept over wood and iron. Mary's heart began to thump and her hands to shake a little in her delight and excitement. The robin kept singing and twittering away and tilting his head on one side, as if he were as excited as she was. What was this under her hands which was square and made of iron and which her fingers found a hole in?

It was the lock of the door which had been closed ten years, and she put her hand in her pocket, drew out the key, and found it fitted the keyhole. She put the key in and turned it. It took two hands to do it, but it did turn.

And then she took a long breath and looked behind her up the long walk to see if anyone was coming. No one was coming. No one ever did come, it seemed, and she took another long breath, because she could not help it, and she held back the swinging curtain of ivy and pushed back the door which opened slowly—slowly.

Then she slipped through it, and shut it behind her, and stood with her back against it, looking about her and breathing quite fast with excitement, and wonder, and delight.

She was standing *inside* the secret garden.

CHAPTER 9

It was the sweetest, most mysterious-looking place anyone could imagine. The high walls which shut it in were covered with the leafless stems of climbing roses, which were so thick that they were matted together. Mary Lennox knew they were roses because she had seen a great many roses in India. All

1. An Indian nursemaid. Mary grew up in India. *Ed.*

the ground was covered with grass of a wintry brown, and out of it grew clumps of bushes which were surely rose-bushes if they were alive. There were numbers of standard roses which had so spread their branches that they were like little trees. There were other trees in the garden, and one of the things which made the place look strangest and loveliest was that climbing roses had run all over them and swung down long tendrils which made light swaying curtains, and here and there they had caught at each other or at a far-reaching branch and had crept from one tree to another and made lovely bridges of themselves. There were neither leaves nor roses on them now, and Mary did not know whether they were dead or alive, but their thin grey or brown branches and sprays looked like a sort of hazy mantle spreading over everything, walls, and trees, and even brown grass, where they had fallen from their fastening and run along the ground. It was this hazy tangle from tree to tree which made it look so mysterious. Mary had thought it must be different from other gardens which had not been left all by themselves so long; and, indeed, it was different from any other place she had ever seen in her life.

'How still it is!' she whispered. 'How still!'

Then she waited a moment and listened at the stillness. The robin, who had flown to his tree-top, was still as all the rest. He did not even flutter his wings; he sat without stirring, and looked at Mary.

'No wonder it is still,' she whispered again. 'I am the first person who has spoken in here for ten years.'

She moved away from the door, stepping as softly as if she were afraid of awakening someone. She was glad that there was grass under her feet and that her steps made no sounds. She walked under one of the fairy-like arches between the trees and looked up at the sprays and tendrils which formed them.

'I wonder if they are all quite dead,' she said. 'Is it all a quite dead garden? I wish it wasn't.'

If she had been Ben Weatherstaff[2] she could have told whether the wood was alive by looking at it, but she could only see that there were only grey or brown sprays and branches, and none showed any signs of even a tiny leaf-bud anywhere.

But she was *inside* the wonderful garden, and she could come through the door under the ivy any time, and she felt as if she had found a world all her own.

2. The estate's gardener. *Ed.*

The sun was shining inside the four walls and the high arch of blue sky over this particular piece of Misselthwaite[3] seemed even more brilliant and soft than it was over the moor. The robin flew down from his tree-top and hopped about or flew after her from one bush to another. He chirped a good deal and had a very busy air, as if he were showing her things. Everything was strange and silent, and she seemed to be hundreds of miles away from anyone, but somehow she did not feel lonely at all. All that troubled her was her wish that she knew whether all the roses were dead, or if perhaps some of them had lived and might put out leaves and buds as the weather got warmer. She did not want it to be a quite dead garden. If it were a quite alive garden, how wonderful it would be, and what thousands of roses would grow on every side?

Her skipping-rope had hung over her arm when she came in, and after she had walked about for a while she thought she would skip round the whole garden, stopping when she wanted to look at things. There seemed to have been grass paths here and there, and in one or two corners there were alcoves of evergreen with stone seats or all moss-covered flower-urns in them.

As she came near the second of these alcoves she stopped skipping. There had once been a flower-bed in it, and she thought she saw something sticking out of the black earth—some sharp little pale green points. She remembered what Ben Weatherstaff had said, and she knelt down to look at them.

'Yes, they are tiny growing things and they *might* be crocuses or snowdrops or daffodils,' she whispered.

She bent very close to them and sniffed the fresh scent of the damp earth. She liked it very much.

'Perhaps there are some other ones coming up in the other places,' she said. 'I will go all over the garden and look.'

She did not skip, but walked. She went slowly and kept her eyes on the ground. She looked in the old border-beds and among the grass, and after she had gone round, trying to miss nothing, she had found ever so many more sharp, pale green points, and she had become quite excited again.

'It isn't a quite dead garden,' she cried out softly to herself. 'Even if the roses are dead, there are other things alive.'

She did not know anything about gardening, but the grass seemed so thick in some of the places where the green points were pushing their way through that she thought they did not seem to have room enough to grow.

3. The name of the estate. *Ed.*

She searched about until she found a rather sharp piece of wood and knelt down and dug and weeded out the weeds and grass until she made nice little clear places around them.

'Now they look as if they could breathe,' she said, after she had finished with the first ones. 'I am going to do ever so many more. I'll do all I can see. If I haven't time today I can come tomorrow.'

She went from place to place, and dug and weeded, and enjoyed herself so immensely that she was led on from bed to bed and into the grass under the trees. The exercise made her so warm that she first threw her coat off, and then her hat, and without knowing it she was smiling down on to the grass and the pale green points all the time.

The robin was tremendously busy. He was very much pleased to see gardening begun on his own estate. He had often wondered at Ben Weatherstaff. Where gardening is done all sorts of delightful things to eat are turned up with the soil. Now here was this new kind of creature who was not half Ben's size and yet had the sense to come into his garden and begin at once.

Mistress Mary worked in her garden until it was time to go to her midday dinner. In fact she was rather late in remembering, and when she put on her coat and hat and picked up her skipping-rope, she could not believe that she had been working two or three hours. She had been actually happy all the time; and dozens and dozens of the tiny, pale green points were to be seen in cleared places, looking twice as cheerful as they had looked before when the grass and weeds had been smothering them.

'I shall come back this afternoon,' she said, looking all round at her new kingdom, and speaking to the trees and rose-bushes as if they heard her.

~ MARY WEBB

"A Cedar-Rose"

Country Life. 10 July 1909: 47–48.

When you go down the lime-bordered path, jubilant with birds, to visit the Misses Amory, it is well to leave the vivid present at the garden gate, where you ring and wait like Christian for entrance. They are timid souls, and lock themselves into their fortress-like house in its enclosed garden, for fear of tramps.

Quite a little while after ringing, you hear the bell sound softly from a distance, as if it echoed down the dim passages of years.

Here the Past sleeps, still as the Sleeping Beauty, but of a relentless plainness of feature, for the youth of the Misses Amory held no romance. No gay lover ever stood in his stirrups for a glimpse into the garden, no clamorous manhood ever pealed the bell.

"How safe you are in here, Betty!" I said once to the little handmaid as she let me in.

"Too safe by far, Miss," she answered, wistfully, lingering near the gate with the look in her eyes of one who listens for a known step.

The path leads between privet hedges to the plain old house, which you enter through a glass porch all in a green haze of ferns.

No scent of dried rose leaves or lavender meets you on the threshold, for the garden never grew flowers, being too much overshadowed by an immense cedar, the pride of the old ladies' hearts. The plain rooms are permeated with the clean aroma of the spreading boughs, under which these lives came into the world, grew to womanhood, and have now grown old. Below the eastern windows is a little lawn, covered towards autumn with round, green cedar fruit.

"It is so terribly untidy, my dear," Miss Jane always says with a sigh; "but I cannot engage a boy to gather them up, for what would the birds do if a noisy boy came in here?"

It is truly an unanswerable problem, for the birds are the real owners of the house and garden; they build in the bedrooms, go to roost in the sacred cedar and have a safe home in the old ladies' hearts. The steep garden is a place of half-lights and grey rockwork, where still remain the little pools and disused fountains loved by childish imaginations, and high on the house still hangs the bell which used to call in three good little girls to bed.

Sometimes when the wind is moaning in the cedar it tolls the bell, and it is as though the spirit hands of their austere father still held the rope. There is no need now for a bedtime bell—they are quite ready for rest at the end of their busy day, and rheumatism waits to seize them in the damp garden at dusk.

Their occasional tea-parties, always limited to one guest—for they do not feel equal to entertaining more at a time—are held on the lawn only in the hottest weather, where it is restful and cool beneath the dark boughs.

One hot day we sat down to rest there after a busy and strenuous tidying of the little green fruit. We gathered it in baskets and took these down the mossy path and emptied them into the stream. How glad I should be to collect all the unnecessary little worries and cares of these two people and throw them far out into Lethe!

Miss Jane, having gone in to make the tea (it was Betty's "afternoon out") and having refused proffered help, Miss Adalia and I conversed about the usual topics, which hold an ever new delight when treated with her sweet and tender insight. We touched on the growth of "our tree," the callow brood at that moment being arranged by careful parents on a lower bough and the satisfactory improvement brought about by our afternoon's work. Then Miss Adalia looked up into the boughs and sighed.

"Ah! my dear," she said, "if it would but bear a cedar-rose!"

The very existence of such a delightful thing had been hitherto unknown to me, so I asked her to tell me about it.

"I never saw one myself, dear," she said; "but they are beautiful as they are rare. Once in a number of years one or two will appear on a cedar tree among the common fruit. They are rose-coloured, with curving petals, only in scent and substance unlike garden roses. They are like fir-cones to touch, and they have the fragrance of cedar-wood. I do not know by what law it is that they appear so seldom; Mary was our botanist, she would have told you." (Mary's footsteps having wandered thirty years ago into the garden of Eternity, the question must wait.) "Our tree has not borne one for more than seventy years," continued Miss Adalia. "Not since our mother found one when she came into the garden on her wedding day. That was before the railways, and father had brought her on a pillion[1] from her home in Cheswardine. Well, my dear, whether it was its rarity, or our mother's finding it on such an auspicious occasion, or whether it was merely the wayward imagination of a child, I cannot say, but I always thought that the finding of a cedar-rose meant a happy life for the finder. Do not think me very foolish if I confess that the happiness I dreamt of was a little romantic. We were never allowed, and rightly, to read novels, but there are beautiful stories in the Bible, and it was of a joy like Rachel's that I sometimes dreamt. Not very often, for we were sensibly brought up, and I never spoke of it to anyone but Mary. Still, that was what the blossoming of a cedar-rose meant for me."

So year by year had her gentle blue eyes looked for this blossom of joy and never found it. She had not wanted rose gardens or riotously scented parterres—only this one rather sombre flower, fit ornament of a sombre life. Such a little would have done! Some staid farmer whom she would have idolised and surrounded with comfort, and who would have giver her quiet affection: she would not have desired the tropical splendours of love; and if

1. A seat or pad behind a horse's saddle for a second rider. *Ed.*

her bliss were to be very perfect, a child to inhabit the warm house of her heart. Just one cedar-rose! Many less worthy have much more; and here was she with only the common hard fruit of little duties and cares.

"I have been very happy," she continued, as though afraid she had complained; "we had a happy life, Jane and Mary and I, while our mother lived; and even after her death—though we sadly missed her—our home was a united one and dear father ever kind, if not indulgent. He did not like society, so we saw few people and seldom went out; but Jane had her housekeeping and visiting of the poor, Mary her botany and I my painting; and then father was so clever, and would sometimes talk to us and teach us most interesting things."

The pity of it! What were the gallants of the fifties doing, what was Mother Nature doing, that this should have happened? Because Miss Adalia was plain of feature, untalented in mind and secluded in life, there was no reason why she should not have fulfilled her woman's vocation. For she was not made to be a worker like Miss Jane; even her paintings are pathetically faulty in technique, her art is not great enough to shadow forth her fluttering yearnings. The earliest are the best, reminiscences of her gala days, when she and her sisters were driven by their father in "the chaise" to some outlying farm, coming home along the winding country roads at dusk with a delightful sense of adventure accomplished. As I said good-night—Miss Jane having gone to fetch the gate key—Miss Adalia asked me gravely if I thought the blooming of a cedar flower before her death too small a thing to pray for. It was with the reiterated "why?" which we all hurl at circumstances sometimes that I went under the limes, where the dusk was piercingly sweet with the drooping flowers, and the birds were fluffing their feathers softly for the night.

It must have been about ten days later that I stood at the gate, again with a bunch of roses in my hand, listening to the distant bell, the bees in the privet and the robins.

"Oh! Miss," exclaimed Betty when she saw me. "Miss Adalia she wur main bad one mornin,' and she swounded right away, and I run to Jim, and Jim 'e run like the wind for the doctor!"

Being much concerned about the first part of the sentence, it was not until afterwards that I enquired concerning "Jim" to whom Betty so naturally fled and who possessed such a Grecian accomplishment, and lit upon an idyll in the making.

Miss Adalia was on the little lawn, as the day was very hot, and welcomed me as usual with her reserved sweetness of courtesy. The freshness of the cedar, which is more an atmosphere than a scent, encompassed us, just as the old ladies' homely goodness breathes about them. Theirs is no incense-like saintliness nor the desperate sweetness of passionate self-sacrifice; it is just natural wholesome righteousness. Sitting so, beneath the sun-resisting boughs, with a tame robin singing shrilly and gladly above, and the distant tones of Miss Jane admonishing Betty, the one miracle of Miss Adalia's life was shown to me. Her face was young again as she slowly and mysteriously unfolded her hands, which had lain in her lap one upon the other; and there, glowing on her black dress like sunrise over yew trees, was what I knew at once to be a cedar-rose. How and whence had it come so unexpectedly? Looking up into the density of foliage, I wondered how those solid branches could bear anything so fragile-looking, so delicate, as this. Looking at her transfigured face, the wonder grew.

"Oh, my dear!" she said, in a breathless tone of rapture. "On Friday morning early, when I came to feed the robins as usual, I was standing just here, and suddenly there came a little stir of wind above, and something fell softly—so softly—on the grass. And there at my feet was the cedar-rose!" Her voice quite shook with joy. "Look at it, dear; you may never see another. See the delicate petals, the faint pink colour, the lovely shape. It must have budded and blossomed on some hidden branch high up, and that was why I never saw it." Then she added softly, as if to herself: "So long in coming, but so lovely when it came." Then she turned enquiringly to me. "What can it mean? I am sure it prophesies something wonderful for me. It is childish and superstitious, I know; but I cannot help regarding it as a herald of coming joy."

"I hope so, dear Miss Adalia," was all I could say, for what bloom of youth and its happiness could come now to this tired woman of seventy? What would ease, travel or riches do for her now? Away from her sheltered nook she would be unhappy; ease she did not desire; of money she had enough. Yet here she was, with eyes alight with longing, watching my face and waiting almost with awe for the naming of the coming joy.

"What can it be?" she wondered.

A hint of wind arose, for the air was electric with coming thunder, sending down showers of green balls on our tidied lawn, and, swaying the high old bell, drew from it the echo of a sound.

"Wait and see, Miss Adalia," I said, with a laugh, though tears were nearer; and she laughed, too, and closed her hands upon her flower as Miss Jane came out to summon us to tea. Miss Jane was evidently worrying a good deal about her sister's "indisposition," to which the doctor had as yet given no name; but outwardly she was very bracing. Only after tea, when she went with me down to the stream at the foot of the garden, while we gazed down into the brown, still water, which always typifies Lethe to me, she asked anxiously if I saw any change in Miss Adalia.

"Sometimes she looks so like Mary did, and it makes me anxious, for Mary died of a decline, you know."

She was much relieved at my assurance that no change was apparent to me, and said that she hoped great things from the doctor's next visit, as it was now nearly a week since he last saw her sister on Friday, the day she fainted in the garden. When Miss Adalia said good-night to me, she told me that she meant to "confide in Jane about the rose," as she thought it only right. I wondered what that lady of sound practical sense would say to her sister's day-dreams.

My one idea was to devise some pleasure which should fitly fulfil the flower's prophecy. But the unaccustomed is not sweet to age, peace is better than intenser joys, and there seemed nothing to be done. However, one day I met the doctor by chance and, asking his advice on the subject, found that things were arranged without my feeble intervention. My schemes were unnecessary, even as my sorrow was useless. In a very little while now a wind will stir the shadowy depths of the cedar, swaying the bedtime bell into whispering vibrations, and drawing away Miss Adalia's spirit out of the silent house and garden over the river of Lethe. Then, at last, her life's dark cedar will bear its immortal flower.

Plants and Interiors

~ JANE LOUDON

From *A Lady's Country Companion*

London: Longman, Brown, Green and Longmans: 1845. 18–19; 178–81.

[pp. 18–19]

... Till your flower garden is made, I would advise you to have a few plants in pots in the east window. Remember though, you must have only a few plants, as more than five or six would give the window the appearance of being a substitute for a greenhouse, a most unpleasant idea at any time, and particularly so in the country. Two rather tall and spreading geraniums, with showy trusses of flowers, a fine well-trained Sollya heterophylla, a fine Polygala oppositifolia, and two handsome well-grown Fuchsias, will be quite enough. They should be in large handsome pots, standing in saucers for the sake of cleanliness; and care should be taken not to fill the pots with earth higher than to within about an inch from the brim, so as to leave plenty of room for watering. The space left should be filled with water every morning, and the water suffered to run through the pots into the saucers; which, after waiting about ten minutes, or more if necessary, so to allow as much water as possible to drain through the earth in the pots, should be emptied, as nothing can be more injurious to most kinds of plants in pots than to let water stand in their saucers. If a constant fire be kept in the room so that the air is always hot and dry, the pots in which the plants are kept should be set within other pots, and the space between the two filled with moss. This is also a good plan with plants in balconies, to prevent the roots of the plants becoming dry and withered. Plants in rooms always require a great deal more water than plants in a greenhouse, to counteract the dry atmosphere of a living-room; and when practicable, they should be set out in the rain or syringed over head, to wash off the dust which, from sweeping the room and other causes, will inevitably rest on the leaves and choke up their pores, thus impeding the action of these very important organs. Air also is as essential to the health of plants as it is to that of human beings, and both live by decomposing it. Thus, when plants are kept in a room, that room requires to be more carefully ventilated than would otherwise be necessary; as, though plants only absorb carbonic acid gas from the air, and set free the oxygen, which is the part required by man, that oxygen is not in a fit state to be breathed by human beings till it has been recombined with carbon.

[pp. 178–81]

As plants in the *conservatory* are grown in the free soil, they are in a much more natural state than any plants can be in pots, and consequently require much less care in their culture. There is usually a walk all round the conservatory, next the glass, and one down the middle, on each side of which are the beds containing the plants, and under which are placed the hot-water pipes that warm the house. The consequence of this arrangement is, that the beds on each side the middle walk are so planted as to have their highest shrubs in the centre, shelving down to those of lower growth on each side; and hence the centre is generally planted with tall camellias, acacias, metrosideros, eucalyptus, &c.; while near the walk are placed oleanders, myrtles, fuchsias of different kinds, together with chorozemas and many of the other most ornamental New Holland plants; and up the pillars that support the roof are trained kennedyas, begonias, ipomoeas, and passion-flowers in great variety. Clianus puniceus and Polygala oppositifolia ought to find a place in every conservatory; and a plant of Wistaria sinensis may be trained under the rafters so as to afford shade to the camellias; as, under shelter, the wistaria will flower twice in the year, and its flowers will yield a delightful, though very delicate, fragrance.

As it is of the greatest importance to the health of the plants to have the soil in a conservatory well drained, many persons form the beds by excavating pits of the proper size, about two feet and a half deep, and put at the bottom a layer of brickbats, stones, and other materials for drainage, about six inches thick. On this is deposited a thin layer of coarse rough gravel; and on that another layer of rich mould, which should be about two feet thick in the centre of the bed, where the largest shrubs are to be planted, and shelving off to about sixteen or eighteen inches at the sides next the walks. All the sashes should be made to open, and there should be large glass doors in front, that should be generally open during the day in summer, in order to admit as much air as possible. In some places a movable frame is contrived for a conservatory, into which sashes fit in winter, and which, in severe weather, is covered with tarpauling, contrived to pull down, like a blind, from a roller along the ridge of the roof; the whole frame being so contrived as to be entirely removed in summer. The upright posts are taken out, the holes may be stopped up with wooden plugs with rings attached; and the roof and horizontal pieces fit into each other, and into the uprights, the whole being kept firm by bolts. When a conservatory of this kind is to be removed for the summer, the side sashes and doors are taken away first, generally about the middle or end of April. A week or ten days after, the sashes of the roof are taken off, but the frame and tarpauling are left in case of spring frosts; and, when all danger from these is over, the whole of the framework is removed, and the orange trees, camellias, and other exotic trees that have been planted in the conservatory, appear to be growing in the open air.

The *orangery* is often contrived so as to be used as a kind of living-room during summer, as it is only intended for the reception of the orange trees, and other plants belonging to the genus Citrus, during winter. The trees are generally grown in large tubs and boxes, in a rich loamy soil, and are set out in the open air during summer, when they require but little care, provided they are frequently watered over the leaves, through they do not like much water to their roots. When young plants are raised from seed, they seldom flower till they have been budded or grafted from an old tree. Orange trees are generally put in the open air in May, and kept there till September or October; and they are very seldom shifted. They require scarcely any light or water during winter, and no heat beyond what is necessary to protect them from the frost.

~ ELIZABETH TWINING

"A Few Words about Window-Gardens"

What Can Window-Gardens do for our Health? Ladies' Sanitary Association. London: S.W. Partridge, n.d. 3–32.

Although health is one of the greatest and most valuable blessings of life, it is not always considered so much as it ought to be. But we are growing wiser in many things now, and especially in this very important matter of health. There has been formed a society especially to inquire into this subject, as regards the working classes. Medical men have had the care of the health of all classes for ages past, and all are much indebted to their skill and knowledge for the relief of our various sufferings, and the cure of many of the diseases which afflict our bodies. But in this, as in most other things, it is found that "prevention is better than cure." If we can in any way keep ourselves in good health, it is better than to be ill, even though a doctor can cure us. Now, it is surprising how many things can and do assist to keep us in health, if we only give due attention to them. How many might spare the time lost in waiting for their turn at the dispensary, had they attended to simple rules for preserving the health of which they know not the value till it is gone! The kind friends of the poor, who have united in a society to teach some useful knowledge about health, have written and published a number of very interesting little books, which have been attentively read and listened to by many a wise mother. Perhaps I may be able to give a little advice on one means of assisting to gain good health; and it shall be by speaking a few words about "window-gardens." It is to the inhabitants of London and other large cities that I am now going to speak. Those who live in country villages, and have usually a garden belonging to their house or cottage, do not care much about the small plants that can be grown in a window; though it is very pleasant to see a cottage window filled with geraniums, fuchsias, dittany, and other common flowers, closely pressed sometimes against the casement. Well, but it is concerning the effect on health that we will consider the subject of plants in the rooms of the working people. Can they in any degree assist us in preserving it? The three chief things necessary to the life and growth of a plant we find to be exactly those which human beings require—pure air, light, and water. All these are easily obtained in the country; therefore plants flourish there readily, they spring up everywhere in all possible spare places. But these things are not easily to be had pure in London, because the immense number of coal fires renders the air full of smoke, the windows of a room thick and dull. In some houses inhabited by working people in London, water is not so plentiful, and it is a labour to carry up to the second or third floor a sufficient supply for a family; therefore the plants may not get a good share. Still, although many impediments are in the way, it is quite possible to cultivate some kind of plants in London rooms with good success; and if we can prove it is of use to the health of the inhabitants of crowded houses to do so, surely it is well worth any little trouble that may be spent on them. In what way can plants assist our health? They help to purify the air, which is a very important matter. The common air surrounding us and plants is composed of different particles, so beautifully combined that we do not perceive their separate existence. By breathing one portion, we live and are kept in health. When we have taken in all this good portion, we breathe out what is no longer good. It is easy to prove this: go into a room where many persons have been shut up some hours either sleeping or waking, you will perceive a close, hot, and very disagreeable air. All the pure, good part, has been exhausted, and until the window has been opened to let in a fresh supply, the health must suffer more or less. Now, we know that the leaves of plants are covered with small pores or breathing-holes, by which they can take in air and let it out again. It has also been ascertained that they take in just that portion of the air which we do not, and that they can give out some of that good portion which we require. Thus it is clear that plants are in some degree assisting to keep us in good health, and if it be ever so little, yet all help is good in this way. Besides, as I said before, they want a good supply of air, out of which to draw in what is necessary for them; they soon begin to fade if kept shut up in bad air which has been breathed over and over again by human beings. Therefore, when a poor person, whether man, woman, or child, begins to care for a plant growing in a pot placed near the window, it seems quite natural to open the window when the sun shines on it. This is certainly good for the plant, and so also for all who live in the room. Then we have long ago found out that plants like a full bright light; so the owner of a plant will be sure to clean the windows and let all the rays of the sunshine through without being dimmed by smoke and dust on the glass-panes. Will not this be also very good for the family?—it will make it more cheerful and comfortable, and those who have any kind of sewing work to do will be enabled to do it better and longer before they need light their night lamp. The mother of little children will never be in doubt how to treat her plants, for they want exactly the same kind of treatment as her children do. She knows it is necessary to keep them clean; that they cannot be healthy if the countless small pores of the skin are allowed to be closed by dust and dirt over them. She will therefore manage the plants in the same way; wash them well all over, to keep the pores open, and thus enable them to breathe freely, and grow readily, and do their part in rendering the air around them pure. It is the smoke of our coal fires that thickens the air of London so much; it is not so from any other cause. Therefore, towards the dawn of day, when all the smoke of the day before has been dispersed and vanished from the air, it is as bright and pure as in the country. Those who do not look out and open their windows till after many thousand fires have been kindled in the morning, are not aware of this, perhaps. It is one of the very merciful arrangements made for us, and over which we have no control, that the particles of smoke or soot are so entirely dispersed or consumed during the night; else what a fearful state of accumulated smoke and fog we should live in! Well, there is an old saying, "Early to bed and early to rise is the way to be healthy, wealthy and wise." Can window-plants contribute to this happy condition? Yes, they can; for gardeners, whether in town or country, are sure to be early risers. The plants themselves are so; the little daisy opens at sunrise; many flowers and leaves which fold up at sunset, open again when the sun appears. An object to induce us to rise early in smoky London is very useful: it makes us feel for a while as if we were in some beautiful foreign city, where the air is never made foggy by coal smoke. How pleasant it is to look out about sunrise, and see a primrose, or any very little plant, outside our window looking fresh and bright in the light of morning! I was going once last summer, between six and seven, to the Charing Cross Station, for the early train to Dover. The shops were not open, very few persons about; but as I passed along a poor, narrow street, I noticed one shop open. Looking up to the house above, I spied boxes of plants at the windows, the only house in the street so adorned. Was it not a pleasant sight?—the owner had no doubt risen early to look at the flowers, and so was ready to start on his day's work in good time before his neighbours. Now, it was not a shop for milk or eatables, that must be opened early—it was a "saddler's;" so we may be sure it was some good plan connected with the "window-garden;" and doubtless it proves the truth of the old proverb, of the way "to be healthy, wealthy and wise." The outside appearance of the houses in London is very dull and dirty; but it is surprising how much cheerfulness is given to the whole front by a few green plants and coloured flowers at the windows, and then a cleaning of the window-ledge and borders is sure to follow. . . .

About two miles from one of the large wool factory towns in Yorkshire, there was a neat cottage with a garden in front—a few vegetables for use, and a few flowers for ornament, the window full of plants in pots. One summer evening the mother and children were in their little garden weeding and watering, talking the while, and wondering why "father did not come home." It was past his usual time; he never lingered by the way, but always came direct; and though he had worked hard all day in the factory, was ever ready to help or direct his children in garden work. At last, the well-known step of James Dawson was heard on the road; the youngest child knew the cheerful whistle which greeted them before he reached his garden gate. Susan went to open the gate for her husband, and kindly inquired what had made him so late.

"Well, my dear, I have some news for you—I was going to say *good* news, for so I thought it when I was told it; but as I came within sight of our pleasant cottage, and saw you and the dear children happy at work in our little garden, I feared you might not call my news *good.*"

"Dear James," said Susan, "if you think it good, I am sure we shall also; only pray tell me what it is."

"Why, just as I was putting away all my things and preparing to start for home, our master called me into his office. I thought he might wish to tell me some plan about the next week's work, but to my surprise he said he was obliged to change his foreman at the works, for his health had failed lately, and he required a place of less occupation for the mind, as well as lighter work. He thought I could undertake the situation. It was quite unexpected by me, and I did not know what to say; but the master spoke so kindly, and said he had considered the matter well, and was quite decided that I was likely to suit him as foreman. I then took courage, and assured him that I would do my best to serve him faithfully in whatever situation he thought right to place me.

"'Yes, James,' he said, 'I can trust you, and I will tell you the reason why I have chosen you for this place in my factory. You know I have often spoken to my men in their leisure half-hours, and I think you all know my mind and wishes as well as I hope I know yours. One of my desires is to help onwards those whom I perceive are trying to help themselves, and their wives and families. A few days ago I was riding along the road where you live, and observed how flourishing your garden looked. Having some business to arrange with a man in another cottage, I remarked to him that if all the cottages and gardens on that road were as well kept as James Dawson's, there would be more comfort and more health in the families. Time spent on a garden is well spent, and brings forth as much good fruit as does the seed in the ground. So, James, you see now part of the good fruit produced by your garden: it has influenced me to choose you for my foreman. If you wish to know the root of the matter still further, it is, that I believe the fact, that if a man be fond of his garden, and think it a pleasure to assist his wife and children in working in it in spare evening hours, he is safe from the evil of public-houses and bad companions.'

"Oh, Susan, I was pleased when the master said this, for that is indeed the root of the matter. I often wonder how men who work hard for their wages can be tempted to spend so much for them on what ruins the health both of body and mind. But now, dear Susan, I must tell you what, maybe, you will say is not good news. The master says, if I am foreman I must live nearer to the factory; it will be impossible for me to be so far away then. I fear it will be hard for you and the children to leave this happy, cheerful home—it will be like uprooting some of our favourite plants and seeing them wither."

Susan had already felt the same right kind of pride in the promotion of her husband from his good character; so, though it was certainly a slight check to her pleasure when she heard of the removal, she would not allow it to check her joy.

"Oh, do not think of that, James; remember how we transplanted that beautiful little honeysuckle from father's porch, when you brought me away to live here; see how that has grown up to the top of the door and around the window. It is a great satisfaction to us all that the master has such a good opinion of you. We will not regret our garden; we can have some window plants at least, even if we do remove to the smoky town."

"Well, Susan, the sun always shines in your heart wherever you are, so you will make us all cheerful, I know. I do feel glad; it is *good* news, certainly: it seems like mounting another step on the ladder. And we can send the two elder children to a better school then. It is time Jemmy was getting on more with his learning. I think if he is a good boy the master will soon take him into the factory, and when I am foreman I can see that all goes well—nothing allowed in behaviour that I should not wish our children to see or to hear."

A few days after this change in the affairs of the Dawsons, James came home and told Susan that he had found a new house for them in the town.

"Oh, father, where is it? tell us the name of the street, please," said little Lizzie, "I know the names of almost all the streets on the way to the market-place, when I go there with mother."

"Well, my dears, you will not like the name, I fear. It is called 'Gloomy Lane,' and our house is No. 5. I must say it is a true name, for the houses are indeed very dirty, the small yards in front are sadly neglected, and the whole place is gloomy."

"Never mind," said Susan, "it will be very convenient for you, James; you can come from the factory in five minutes; and then, children, you will be able to go to that nice new school which our kind minister spoke to us about some weeks ago, but then I told him it was too far off."

"Well, father," said little Mary, "may we carry away with us some of our flowers? Perhaps they will grow if we take care to wash them clean, and put them by the open window in the sunshine. We will try and make our new home look something like our old one, if we can."

Surely, there is a good result from the love of flowers and gardening; even young children learn thereby patience and perseverance. Sowing seeds and awaiting their appearance above ground, and watching the daily growth of the stem, and leaves, and flowers, does inspire an indescribable feeling of quiet pleasure; and thus, by fostering the good and pleasant thoughts, the disagreeable feelings of impatience and grumbling become checked, and often wither away altogether.

Now, we will pass over into the following year, and visit No. 5, Gloomy Lane, on Midsummer Day. Unless I could show you a sketch of the place as it was last summer, before the Dawsons moved into it, and another sketch as it is now, you would scarcely understand or believe the change that has taken place. But there are still some houses in the lane that will show you what No. 5 was. At No. 4, and others, the palings are still so broken that they are of no use in keeping out dogs or idle boys. The ground is overgrown with rough weeds; the path up to the house is just like the rest, not at all smoother. The windows are seldom opened, or the glass washed. Smoke, and soot, and dust, have been left so long that the whole front of the houses looks black and grey. The people who live in them seem determined to keep up to the character which caused the lane to have the name of "Gloomy" given to it.

But how does No. 5 look now? We will describe it. The wooden palings all repaired and painted green; the gate at the entrance has a strong latch which keeps it shut; the path up to the house is neatly paved with small flints; on each side is a bit of smooth green turf, on which are neat little borders filled with such common hardy plants as can live and grow in the smoky air of a factory town; a lilac and a laburnum stand on either side; in the front of the lower window are several plants growing in a narrow border; and in wooden boxes at the upper windows are geraniums, mignonette, and that old-fashioned favourite which will thrive almost anywhere, called Southernwood, or "old man;" a few sweetwilliams still remain, and the appearance of all the front window is bright and cheerful. Susan has been to hear a lecture on window-gardens in the winter, so was prepared with a knowledge of the plants suitable for towns. She remembered the advice given; and the children had taken long walks out into the fields and woods for primroses, creeping-jenny, and ferns. They all served the purpose of making a pleasant green border to the windows, and the children were delighted to rise early and water their little window-garden before going to school. How fresh and airy was their parlour when father and mother came in to breakfast; and how pleased was Lizzie when she set a plate of mustard-and-cress before her parents! "Why, Lizzie, have you been to market already?" said Susan. "No, dear mother, it was grown in the box at my window, and I have just cut it and washed it for you." What a relish it gave to the bread-

and-butter! and when a poor woman came to tell Susan about her sick child, Lizzie had the pleasure of giving her some of her mustard-and-cress. And what did the other inhabitants of Gloomy Lane think of this improvement in No. 5? Mrs. Watson, who lived at No. 4, often stood at her door and watched Susan as she attended to her little garden; and one day she came up to the palings for conversation. "I am glad your plants succeed so well, Mrs. Dawson; but you do take wonderful pains and trouble with them, to be sure. Well, I wish all our row looked as nice; but I do not know how you manage. Your children look as clean and healthy as your plants. Mine are always sickly; I am continually taking them to the doctor, but they get no better. And will you tell me, Mrs. Dawson, how you do contrive to get your children off so punctual to school? I can't get mine up and ready till long past the time." "I assure you, Mrs. Watson, they require no persuasion to rise early: they are so fond of their little window-gardens that they are sure to be up in time to attend to them before breakfast. I wish you had seen the nice dish of mustard-and-cress they set on the table twice last week." "Well, I never should have thought of growing anything fit to eat in Gloomy Lane. Why, it must want a deal of washing first, to get off the smuts." "Oh, no, not much: they stretch a piece of thin course muslin over it, and it is as nice as what comes out of the market-garden. Of course the children think it better, because it is their own growing." "I must say your house looks quite different from ours; your windows seem larger, and as if they were just made of new plate-glass." "They are exactly the same windows; only, you see, when we have these plants growing on the ledge, we look to the whole, and wash it all down two or three times a week. If you get a common mop and a pail of water, it is soon done; and as for clear panes of glass, you know we lived almost in the country before we came here, and were used to a clean neat cottage, and could no way bear to live in a dirty house. It is not good for the health of anybody, I am sure, especially of the children. So I think plants are very useful, for they remind us of what is good for ourselves and our children. You know, Mrs. Watson, the flowers soon fade off if we do not let them have enough fresh air and light and water; we see them droop directly. Though they cannot speak, they soon let us know what they want. Perhaps if you allow your children to keep a few plants, it will help them somehow to be more healthy than they are now. I am sure it will make them more industrious and careful, and more happy in themselves." "Thank you, Mrs. Dawson; I will tell my husband what you say, and try to persuade him to come home sooner in the evening, and to bring me a larger share of his wages; for at present I have enough to do to find food and clothes with what he gives me. And then there is a bill to pay at the doctor's as soon as I can manage it." "That is a bill I never have had to pay yet, and very thankful I am to be able to say so. God, in His mercy, has given us healthy children, and I thank Him for putting into my mind a love and care for plants, for I am sure that has led me to learn and perceive many ways of helping to keep a family in good health. Cleanliness, fresh air, and pure water, are three remedies both for plants and for ourselves. I think I can guess one thing that may be bad for the health of your children. Do you not give them odd pence now and then to spend in sweets?" "Oh, yes, to be sure, they get all my odd pence on Saturday night, and I know they spend all they can in sweets. What else can the poor children buy for a treat? And then the sweet-stalls are at the corner of all the streets they pass." "That is quite reason enough for their being sickly. Don't your remember last year some children were poisoned by eating sweets coloured by some dangerous stuff? I advise you never to give a penny to your children for that purpose; let them buy flower seeds and roots already growing. My children will be pleased to show them the part of the market where they get the cheap plants. Besides, they walk out into the woods on a holiday, and bring home ferns and many pretty things that cost no pence, and help to keep them in good health. We shall be happy to assist you whenever you are inclined to begin the plan of 'window-gardens.' Good-bye!" Let us now make one more visit to Gloomy Lane, at Michaelmas. The landlord is coming round to collect the quarter's rent. Having heard some rumours about the improvements made by one of his tenants, he resolved to go himself this time, instead of sending an agent as usual. It had been for some years so very unpleasant a place for him—so truly what its name described—that he had avoided inspecting this part of his property, thinking it a hopeless case. Before entering any of the dwellings, he walked along the whole row, and looked at ten houses and their *yards,* as they used to be called. No. 1, still in a dusty, dirty condition, palings broken, gate with broken hinges; neglected children, who evidently attended no school, throwing stones about. No. 2 and No. 3 were looking more comfortable—the paling mended, gates shut, children tidy, pulling up weeds in front of the houses; one woman washing the parlour window, a box of plants at the upper window. No. 4, still more improved, the path neatly paved, and grass growing on the space by the side. A few scarlet geraniums in pots at the windows, a sweet scent of mignonette from the border under the parlour window, which was bright and clear and wide open. He saw the mother sitting at work, and two of the children watering the plants placed in pots about the door. When he reached No. 5, he stood looking over the gate some time. At last the house door opened, and Susan came out and inquired if the gentleman wished to speak to anyone. I cannot tell you all that he said, nor what satisfaction both landlord and tenant felt and expressed. But I know that although Mr. Stewart inspected the whole house and garden, he could not find a single thing to complain of; and when Susan gave him the rent money, which was already in the desk, he left a message for James Dawson, which Susan was very much pleased to give him when he came home in the evening. Though it was Michaelmas time, and the summer passing away, yet the sun shone warm and bright in the hearts of all in No. 5. I think I may say also, what perhaps you may have already guessed, there was some glow of happy feeling in the minds of James and Susan from the consciousness of having, in their humble way, helped and encouraged their neighbors to improve their dwellings and themselves. They had been doing true Christian work, serving their Heavenly Master, as well as their earthly master. They had meekly done what was long ago set as an example for us to follow, "He lifteth the poor out of the mire." And it was done by means of the lovely green herbs which, "in the beginning," had been given to man for his service. And it was happy work too; for the first innocent work given to man in this world, was to dress and to keep the *garden* in which he was placed. This will be pleasant work as long as the seed-time and harvest of this world shall last, even though the garden be merely a small bit of ground before a house in the suburbs of a factory town, or only such as we call a "window-garden." Let us take one more look early in the following spring. No more gaps in the palings, no smoky windows, and the agent has just brought an order to John Green, the painter, who lives at No. 1, to paint the doors and window-frames of all the houses, and the palings, and to put some bright green paint over the board at the corner, and with large white letters to write the name of "Pleasant Row."

DIRECTIONS FOR WINDOW-GARDENS

Get a wooden box about two feet long, and six or eight inches wide, and paint it green. Scatter a few pebbles, or broken bits of flower-pots, at the bottom, and fill it with mould, having a little fine white sand mixed with it. Sow weeds or plant roots in it. Be careful not to pour too much water on it at one time, as it causes the wood to decay. Flower-pots do not require to be painted or stained red. It is best for the plants only to wash the outside of the pots now and then. Keep the mould about half an inch down from the top of the pot. For large plants, dahlias, and others, an old butter-tub is very suitable.

PLANTS SUITABLE FOR WINDOW-GARDENS

From Slips or Roots

Window-Balm.	Fuchsia.
Chrysanthemum.	Red Geranium.
Virginia Creeper.	Hydrangea.
Myrtle.	Begonia.
Lavender.	Cowslip.
Dahlia.	Double Daisy.
Hollyhock.	Moneywort, or
Pinks.	Creeping Jenny.
Sweetwilliam.	Coltsfoot.
Musk.	Tansy.
Bergamot.	Houseleek.
Thyme.	London Pride.
Peppermint.	Onion.
Southernwood.	Leek.
Heartsease.	Potato.
Primrose.	Watercress.

From Seeds Sown Either in November or March

Nasturtium.	Scarlet Beans.
Convolvulus.	Mustard and Cress.
Sweet Pea.	Date.
Marigold.	Plum.
Sunflower.	Cherry.
Virginia Stock.	Orange.
Lupine.	Lemon.
Stock.	Apple.
Nemophila.	Acorn.
Poppy.	Horsechesnut.
Linseed, or Flax.	Walnut.
American Corn.	

FIGURE 34 *Ivy Screen for Fire-place,* illustration for Anne Hassard, *Floral Decoration for the Dwelling House*

ANNIE HASSARD

From *Floral Decorations for the Dwelling House: A Practical Guide to the Home Arrangement of Plants and Flowers*

London: Macmillan, 1875. 65.

SCREENS FOR THE FIRE-PLACE

During the summer season, when there are no fires in the drawing-room, tastefully-decorated screens fitted into the fire-place have a charming effect. These often consist of looking-glass and specimens of dried Ferns; but, as they do not come within my range, being dried, I shall pass them over, merely remarking that, though handsome, they are expensive. The best plants with which to cover screens are the common or variegated Ivies. First, a box should be procured, the width of the fire-place, to stand inside the fender; it should be made either of zinc or wood, and should be ornamented with coloured tiles—in fact, a box such as one sees on hundreds of window-ledges; at each end, in the back corners, an upright iron rod should be fixed sufficiently high to meet the ornamental marble over the grate: between these rods a piece of fine wire netting should be strained, so as to form a screen on which to train the Ivy; this wire back should completely cover the iron or steel grate; over the holes in the bottom of the box some broken crocks should be placed, and over the crocks should be put a layer of Cocoa-nut fibre; then the box should be filled in with a mixture of rotten turf and sharp gritty sand. Some plants of Ivy should next be procured and planted firmly and rather thickly in the box, so as at once to cover the screen. Along the front of the box, set on the soil, may be pot plants, or the surface of the soil might be covered with Selaginella denticulata intermixed with cut blooms of large-sized flowers.

SECTION FOUR

Adventuring

Far from all being stay-at-homes fixed in domesticity, Victorian and Edwardian women could be a venturesome lot. In the section "Adventuring," they traverse the globe for a variety of reasons. Driven by an energy and a hunger for travel that marked their imperialist times as well as themselves, they left home to collect exotic species, to hunt and kill exotic animals, to climb exotic mountains, to accompany husbands on scientific expeditions or to government postings in the colonies and meet exotic peoples, or to search new ground for selfhood, self-improvement, or better health. "Intrepid" they were called, intrepid they often became, and in the course of their travels, many drew close to nature. Take, for example, Isabella Bird, a globe-trotter of the first order. In 1873 Bird stopped in Hawaii en route from Australia to California and stayed for seven months, in part to improve her health. This she certainly did, but at the same time fell in love with her natural surroundings. Listen as she describes a solo horseback trip into the interior of the Big Island of Hawaii in her book *Six Months in the Sandwich Islands* (1875):

> This is the height of enjoyment in travelling. I have just encamped under a *lauhala* tree, with my saddle inverted for a pillow, my horse tied by a long lariat to a guava bush, my gear, saddle-bags, and rations for two days lying about, and my saddle blanket drying in the sun. Overhead the sun blazes and casts no shadow; a few fleecy clouds hover near him, and far below, the great expanse of the Pacific gleams in a deeper blue than the sky. Far above, towers the rugged and snow-patched, but no longer mysterious dome of Mauna Kea; while everywhere ravines, woods, waterfalls, and stretches of lawn-like grass delight the eye. All green that I have ever seen, of English lawns in June, or Alpine valleys, seems poor and colourless as compared with the dazzling green of this sixty-five miles. It is a joyous green, a glory. Whenever I look up from my writing, I ask, Was there ever such green?

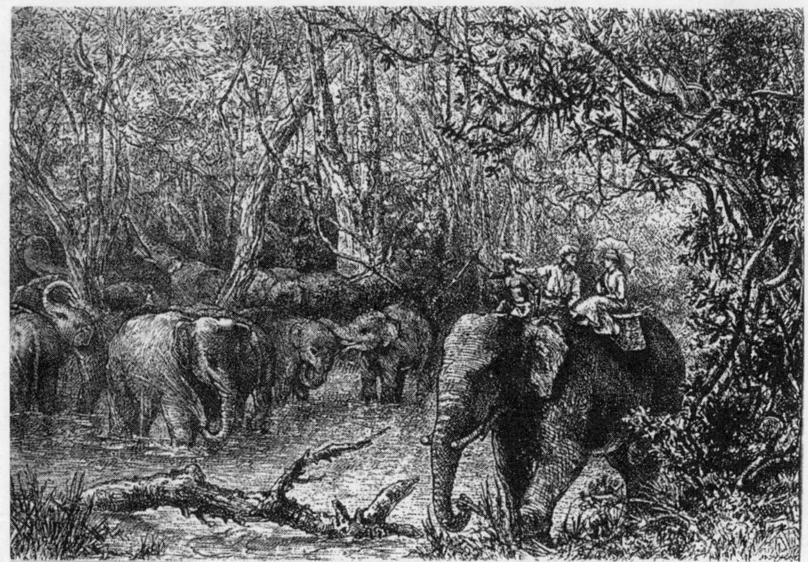

FIGURE 35 Isabella Bird riding an elephant

> Was there ever such sunshine? Was there ever such an atmosphere? Was there ever such an adventure? And Nature—for I have no other companion, and wish for none—answers, "No." (237)

A review of Isabella Bird's travel books may have remarked that "there never was anybody who had adventures so well as Miss Bird has them" (*The Spectator* 52 [8 Nov. 1879], 1412) (see figure 35), but in point of fact many women did. Their reasons for traveling were as varied as were the women themselves. The determined—she called herself unstoppable—Olivia Fanny Tonge (1858–1949) set off late in life to travel through India as a natural history illustrator. Tonge prefaced her many beautiful sketchbooks (see figure 36), now housed in the British Museum of Natural History, with these words:

> And it came to pass, that a certain Grandmother, when that she had come to nigh on two score years and ten; and had gotten long in the tooth, spake to herself thus.—Lo, will I now paint. And she took much gold, yea much fine gold, and bought her a book, and in the book, so that all men might see, painted she all the things that crawled

FIGURE 36 Olivia Fanny Tonge, *Chameleon,* from *The Sketchbooks of Mrs. O. F. Tonge* (c. 1908–12), sketchbook 8, fig. 35 (with the permission of the Trustees of The Natural History Museum, London)

> upon the face of the earth, and all things seemly, lo, that flew in the air, and all the things that swam in the waters that are under the earth . . . and no man mote stop her. (preface to "The Sketchbooks of Mrs. O. F. Tonge." Ms., British Library of Natural History)

We open the subsection "For Science" by turning to the world of natural history and what Tonge calls its "things" with selections from the writing of two famous Victorians who traveled solo, Mary Kingsley and Marianne North. A subsequent selection comes from the writing of Louisa Anne Meredith, a flower illustrator (see figure 44) who settled in Tasmania with her husband, a government officer. All three writers reveal the importance of women to the enterprise of discovering, collecting, and representing animal and plant species. Kingsley traveled in West Africa under the auspices of the British Museum of Natural History, collecting fish from rivers and lakes. During the course of three trips to that part of the world, she discovered three new species of fish that were subsequently named for her, *Ctenopoma kingsleyae, Mormyrus kingsleyae,* and *Alestes kingsleyae.* In the selection from her work excerpted here, Kingsley recounts the business and the adventure of fishing in West Africa (1897). First, there is an account of fishing by women along the shorelines of lakes; then there is a general

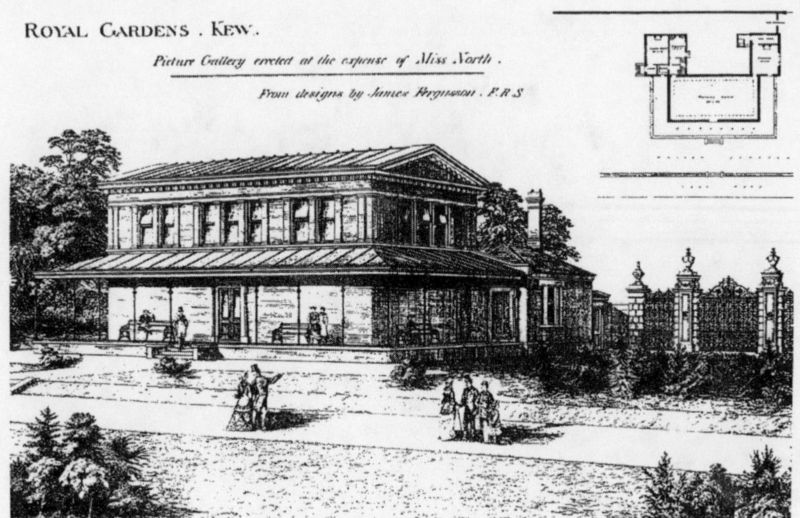

FIGURE 37 *The North Gallery, Royal Botanic Gardens, Kew,* from *The Building News,* 15 April 1881

FIGURE 38 Interior of the Marianne North Gallery, photograph by Barbara T. Gates

outline of types of lake and river fish; and then the witty description of cat-fishing on a river, where mock heroine Kingsley sinks to the muck on behalf of saving both her fish and her guidebook. Kingsley's piece concludes with a discussion of other methods of fishing and of the fish themselves. Throughout, Kingsley writes cleverly—with an aplomb and humor that also marked her lectures about the dangers and excitement of West Africa. With playful irony she manages to emerge the female adventurer, the woman who came through every adversity to triumph over both fish and environment. In Kingsley's writing we are always reminded of her stamina. Kingsley not only went to the bottoms of African rivers: she was also the first woman to climb Mount Cameroon and the woman who counseled the importance of a "good thick skirt" for those who might fall into a spiked big-game trap, as she had done.

If Kingsley promoted herself and her adventures through her writing, lecturing, and sense of fun and bravado, Marianne North promoted herself through the creation of the Marianne North Gallery at Kew Gardens (see figure 37). Still open today, the gallery features 832 of North's botanical paintings and 246 slabs of wood gathered by North on her travels throughout the world (see figure 38). North had the building designed and engineered expressly to hold these works and introduce them to what she called her "GP," or general public. Both Kingsley and North might easily have been overlooked were it not for their self-promotions in their own time and for the writings by which we still know them today. North's *Recollections of a Happy Life* (1892–94), like Kingsley's books on West Africa, was meant to offer her story to the world. A combination of travel and autobiography, it abounds in vivid word pictures like the ones excerpted from North's recollections of Brazil and reprinted here. North asks us to see for a moment through the painter's eye (see also figure 39), to know plants by their colorful details and landscapes through their botanical garnish. And we come to know the collector as well, as North anguishes over the destruction of specimens by devouring insects.

Both North and Kingsley saw with the eyes of the British imperialist. For them the world was there for the describing; its peoples existed in part to help them, rather than vice versa. Louisa Anne Meredith, née Twamley, was different. She saw through the eyes of the colonial. When she began her career as a young woman in England, Twamley produced beautiful if conventional flower books illustrating British wildflowers and seasonal blooms. But when she removed to Tasmania, Meredith began to see differently. Unlike Kingsley, North, and even Elizabeth Gould, she experienced a new con-

FIGURE 39 Marianne North, *Foliage and flowers of* Chorissa *species and double-crested humming birds, Brazil* (courtesy of the Royal Botanic Gardens at Kew)

tinent long-term. In *My Home in Tasmania, During a Residence of Nine Years* (1852), we can discern the beginnings of this longer-term vision, something that would deepen as Meredith would continue to write and illustrate books about her island home for another forty years (see figure 40). *My Home* both introduces Meredith's British readers to the strange flora and fauna of Australia and corrects for their colonialist misperceptions of the place, as when she suggests that the European condemnation of burning to improve pasturage is incorrect and that the aboriginal practice of such burning is much more in keeping with the realities of the Australian environment.

Not all women adventured abroad, of course. Jemima Blackburn painted birds at home in Scotland and had excitement enough there. The front cover for her *Birds from Moidart and Elsewhere* (see figure 41), which shows her in a barrel rowing toward some of the birds she wished to sketch, gives a sense of the perilous nature of Blackburn's pursuits. Like Kingsley's

FIGURE 40 Louisa Anne Meredith, title page, *Some of My Bush Friends in Tasmania*

ironic comments and North's own sketches of herself balanced on dangerous rocks, Blackburn's picture serves as a self-validation. "Look at how exciting and how dangerous all of this can be," she seems to be saying. "I, a woman in long skirts, can do this—mainly because I want to." It was daring, and it was sporting as well.

By the 1890s, many British women had become a different kind of sportswoman of one sort or another both at home and, if they had the mobility, abroad. Many daring New Women at the turn of the century promoted outdoor activities like bicycling, fishing, and hunting and were proud of their accomplishments (see figure 42). George Egerton's "A Cross Line" (1894), a short story excerpted here, describes such a woman: a fly-fisher who astounds her male interrogator with her knowledge of the stream and its fish and fascinates him with her bewitching difference from the other women he knows. Late Victorians who were more conventional than New Women like Egerton often viewed women who fished or hunted as

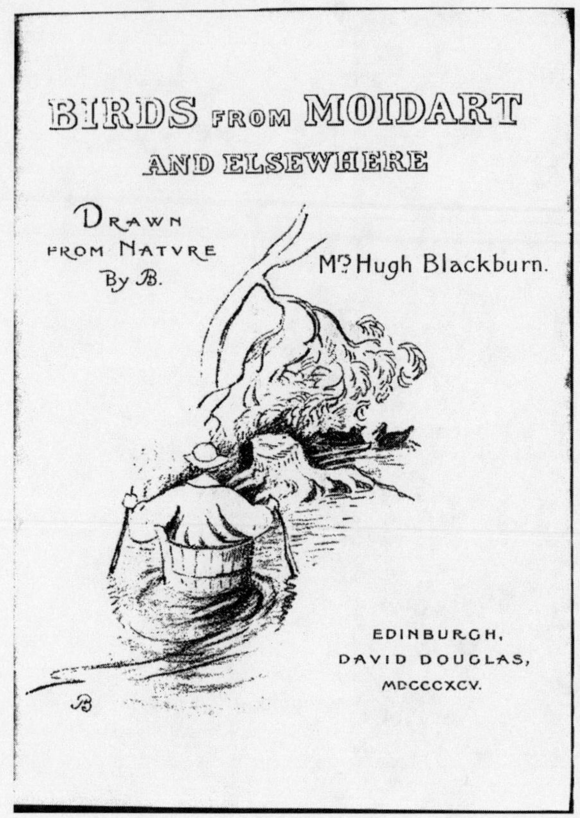

FIGURE 41 Jemima Blackburn, title page, *Birds from Moidart and Elsewhere*

dangerous, or boldly off-color. Egerton herself both exploited and took exception to such views when she used fly-fishing as a metaphor for sexual attraction. In another of her short stories, "A Little Gray Glove," her male narrator is literally hooked by a fly fisherwoman whose bait catches him by the ear.

Like fishing, hunting nonhuman species also became the preserve of the daring woman. What is more, when writers like Mrs. Tyacke and Isabel Savory describe their hunts in different parts of India, their books represent a literary genre in which men had previously excelled—the combination big-game travel book with hunting narrative. These women neither tried to whitewash this genre nor to feminize it through prettifying. Instead, they offer their own exploits as examples to other venturesome women, the implication being that women can emerge as the heroines of their own adven-

FIGURE 42 *Good Sport,* from *Illustrated London News,* 12 September 1874

ture narratives. Tyacke gives the grisly details of her "bags," the tallies of the daily slaughter perpetrated by her companions and herself. Savory presents and valorizes herself as an example—a role model, a woman who "did." Both women think nothing of the waste of animal life incurred during their hunts. In direct opposition to the many women who would work to preserve other species, they exhibit the carelessness of the tourist or short-term traveler. They also typify an Edwardian sense that the world has game aplenty—an endless resource of excitement for the well-to-do.

Although not all of the women in this book exhibited the tenderness toward animals that was considered a hallmark of their gender, most did tread more lightly than Tyacke or Savory. And many tread far and wide in search of hiking or climbing adventures. Some, like Isabella Bird and Nina Mazuchelli, quite literally tramped or rode over and across landscapes rather than stalking for the purposes of either science or sport (see figure 43). On an early trip Bird (figure 45) wrote letters home to her sister, Henrietta, who in turn read the letters to a group of friends. The group was so enthralled with what they heard that Bird was encouraged to collect her thoughts on places and people and to publish them for a wider audience.

FIGURE 43 Nina Mazuchelli, self-portrait on horseback, illustration for *The Indian Alps and How We Crossed Them,* p. 94

This she did in eleven books that described out-of-the-way places for British audiences. When in Hawaii, for example, Bird was as captivated by the volcanoes as by the lush greens of the interior. She rode on horseback to the volcanic area and climbed down into the crater of the active volcano Kilauea (see figure 46). In letter twenty-one from *Six Months in the Sandwich Islands: Among Hawai'i's Palm Groves, Coral Reefs, and Volcanoes,* excerpted here, she recaptures the danger and excitement of this vivid experience.

To Bird's readers, western North America seemed exotic—a land of Indians and rough types of people and places. Bird capitalizes on this image in her *Lady's Life in the Rocky Mountains,* from which letter seven is reprinted here. In her famous description of her ascent of Long's Peak in Colorado, through a kind of sexualized sublime, she packs her narrative full of excitement over the dangers of the ascent, her closeness to nature, and her relationship with "natural man," her guide, Rocky Mountain Jim. Women like Bird were certainly mountaineering by the 1870s, but Bird was unusual for an Englishwoman in that she did this climbing in North America. The Alps and later the Himalayas were more the norm for adventuring in her day, with the Himalayas seeming by far the more danger-fraught of these two ranges.

Nina Mazuchelli's ascent of the Himalayas was nevertheless not as raw as was Bird's of Long's Peak, although she makes it seem quite as daring in her narrative *The Indian Alps and How We Crossed Them* (1876) (see figure 47). Mainly, Mazuchelli traveled on the backs of people or of animals as she crossed the Himalayas with a party that included her husband. Excerpted here is the story of one moonlit night when she crept out of her tent and confronted nature on foot and alone. Here Mazuchelli experiences a transcendental sense of the sublime, a feeling of being transported by an overwhelming encounter with both terror and pleasure. Like the romantic poet William Wordsworth on Mount Snowdon, she is enveloped and lost in white mist, taken out of herself and into another realm entirely. Such fear and rapture at losing one's identity marks several of the passages in *The Indian Alps and How We Crossed Them.* At another point in these recollections of the Himalayas, Mazuchelli feels that she has identified closely enough with nature to have become like an eagle:

> How often from my mountain eyrie have I watched the clouds, and their marvellous and ever-changing effects, when a tempest, which has raged throughout the livelong night, has lulled and sobbed itself to rest, with the rising of the sun. (65)

Looking out through the eyes of this great bird, the poetic Mazuchelli is reminiscent of her countrywoman Eliza Cook, who saw through the eyes of a number of different birds in a series of poems attributed to the birds themselves. This section concludes with one such lyric, Cook's "Song of the Eagle," where the mountain eagle bears "limbs no trammels can bind" (line 5), like so many of the women who adventure through nature in these pages.

For Science

MARY H. KINGSLEY

From "Fishing in West Africa"

The National Review 29 (1897): 213–27.

There is one distinctive charm about fishing—its fascinations will stand any climate. You may sit crouching on ice over a hole well inside the Arctic Circle, or on a Windsor chair by the side of the River Lea in the so-called Temperate Zone; or you may squat in a canoe on an equatorial river, with the surrounding atmosphere 45 per cent. mosquito, and if you are fishing you will enjoy yourself, and what is more important than this enjoyment, is that you will not embitter your present, nor endanger your future, by going home in a bad temper, whether you have caught anything or not, provided always that you are a true fisherman.

This is not the case with other sports; I have been assured by experienced men that it "makes one feel awfully bad" when, after carrying for hours a very heavy elephant gun, for example, through a tangled forest you have got . . . a wretched bad chance of a shot at an elephant I should say, and as for football, cricket, &c., well, I need hardly speak of the unchristian feelings they engender in the minds towards umpires and successful opponents.

Being, as above demonstrated, a humble, but enthusiastic, devotee of fishing, I dare not say, as my great predecessor Dame Juliana Berners says, "with an angle," because my conscience tells me I am a born poacher—I need hardly remark that when I heard from a reliable authority at Gaboon, that there were lakes in the centre of the island of Corisco, and that these fresh-water lakes were fished annually by representative ladies from the villages on this island, and that their annual fishing was just about due, I decided that I must get there forthwith. Now, although Corisco is not more than twenty miles out to sea from the continent, it is not a particularly easy place to get at nowadays, no vessels ever calling there, so I got, through the kindness of Dr. Nassau, a little schooner and a black crew, and, forgetting my solemn resolve, formed from the fruits of previous experiences, never to go on to an Atlantic island again, off I sailed. I will not go into the adventures of that voyage here. My reputation as a navigator was great before I left Gaboon. I had a record of having once driven my bowsprit through a conservatory, and once taken all the paint off one side of a smallpox hospital to say nothing of repeatedly having made attempts to climb trees in boats I commanded, but when I returned, I had surpassed these things by having successfully got my main-mast jammed up a tap, and I had done sufficient work in discovering new sandbanks, rock shoals, &c., in Corisco Bay, and round Cape Esterias, to necessitate, or call for, a new edition of *The West African Pilot.*

. . . On arriving at Corisco Island, I "soothed with a gift, and greeted with a smile" the dusky inhabitants. "Have you got any tobacco?" said they. "I have," I responded, and a friendly feeling at once arose. I then explained that I wanted to join the fishing party. They were quite willing, and said the ladies were just finishing planting their farms before the tornado season came on, and that they would make the peculiar, necessary baskets at once. They did not do so at once in the English sense of the term, but we all know there is no time south of 40°, and so I waited patiently, walking about the island.

Corisco is locally celebrated for its beauty. Winwood Reade says, "It is a little world in miniature, with its miniature forests, miniature prairies, miniature mountains, miniature rivers, and miniature precipices on the sea-shore." In consequence partly of these things, and partly of the inhabitants' rooted idea that the proper way to any place on the island is round by the sea-shore, the paths of Corisco are as strange as several other things are in latitude 0 [zero], and, like the other things, they require understanding to get on with.

. . . At last the fishing baskets were ready, and we set off for the lakes by a path that plunged into a little ravine, crossed a dried swamp, went up a hill, and on to an open prairie, in the course of about twenty minutes. Passing over this prairie, and through a wood, we came to another prairie, like most things in Corisco just then (August), dried up, for it was the height of the dry season. On this prairie we waited for some of the representative ladies from other villages to come up; for without their presence our fishing would not have been legal. When you wait in West Africa it eats into your lifetime to a considerable extent, and we spent half-an-hour or so standing howling, in prolonged, intoned howls, for the absent ladies, notably grievously for On-gou-ta, and they came not, so we threw ourselves down on the soft-fine, golden-brown grass, in the sun, and, with the exception of myself, went asleep. After about two and a half hours I was aroused from a contemplation of the domestic habits of some beetles, by hearing a crackle, crackle, interspersed with sounds like small pistols going off, and looking round saw a fog of blue-brown smoke surmounting a rapidly-advancing wall of red fire.

I rose, and spread the news among my companions, who were sleeping, with thumps and kicks. Shouting at a sleeping African is labour lost. And then I made a bee-line for the nearest green forest wall of the prairie, followed by my companions. Yet, in spite of some very creditable sprint performances on their part, three members of the band got scorched. Fortunately, however, our activity landed us close to the lakes, so the scorched ones spent the rest of the afternoon sitting in mud-holes, comforting themselves with the balmy black slime. The other ladies turned up soon after this, and said that the fire had arisen from some man having set fire to a corner of the prairie some days previously, to make a farm, and he had thought the fire was out round his patch, whereas it was not, but smouldering in the tussocks of grass, and the wind had sprung up that afternoon from a quarter that fanned it up. I said, "People should be very careful of fire," and the scorched ladies profoundly agreed with me, and said things I will not repeat here, regarding "that fool man" and his female ancestors.

The lakes are pools of varying extent and depth, in the bed-rock of the island, and the fact that they are surrounded by thick forests on every side, and that the dry season is the cool season on the Equator, prevents them from drying up.

Most of these lakes are encircled by a rim of rock, from which you jump down into knee-deep slime, and then, if you are a representative lady, you waddle, and squeal, and grunt, and skylark generally, on your way to the water in the middle. If it is a large lake you are working, you and your companions drive in two rows of stakes, cutting each other more or less at right angles, more or less in the middle of the lake, so as to divide it up into convenient portions. Then some ladies with their specially shaped baskets form a line, with their backs to the bank, and their faces to the water-space, in the enclosure, holding the baskets with one rim under water. The others go into the water, and splash with hands, and feet, and sticks, and, needless to say, yell hard all the time. The naturally alarmed fish, fly from them, intent on getting into the mud, and are deftly scooped up by the peck by the ladies in their baskets. In little lakes the staking is not necessary, but the rest of the proceedings are the same. Some of the smaller lakes are too deep to be thus fished at all, being, I expect, clefts in the rock, such as you see in other parts of the island, sometimes 30 or 40 feet deep.

The usual result of the day's fishing is from twelve to fifteen bushels of a common mud-fish,[1] which is very good eating. The spoils are divided among the representative ladies, and they take them back to their respective villages and distribute them. Then ensues, that same evening, a tremendous fish supper, and those fish left over are smoked, and carefully kept as a delicacy, to make sauce with, &c., until the next year's fishing day comes round.

The waters of West Africa, salt, brackish, and fresh, abound with fish, and many kinds are, if properly cooked, excellent eating. For culinary purposes you may divide the fish into sea-fish, lagoon-fish, and river-fish; the first division, the sea-fish, are excellent eating, and are in enormous quantities, particularly along the windward coast on the Great West African Bank. South of this, at the mouths of the Oil rivers, they fall off, from a culinary standpoint, though scientifically they increase, in charm, as you find, hereabouts, fishes of extremely early types, whose relations have an interesting series of monuments in the shape of fossils, in the sandstone, but if primeval man had to live on them, when they were alive, I am sorry for him, for he might just as well have eaten mud and better, for then he would not have run the risk of getting choked with bones. On the south-west coast the culinary value goes up again; there are quantities of excellent deep-sea fish, and round the mouths of the rivers, shoals of bream and grey mullet.

The lagoon-fish are not particularly good, as a rule they are supremely muddy and bony; they have their uses, however, for I am informed that they indicate to Lagos when it may expect an epidemic; to this end they die, in an adjacent lagoon, and float about upon its surface, wrong side up, until decomposition does its work. Their method of prophecy is a sound one, for it demonstrates (*a*) that the lagoon drinking water is worse than usual; (*b*) if it is not already fatal they will make it so.

The river-fish of the Gold Coast are better than those of the mud-sewers of the Niger Delta, because the Gold Coast rivers are brisk sporting streams, with the exception of the Volta, and at a short distance inland they come down over rocky rapids with a stiff current. The fish of the upper

1. *Clarias laviaps.*

waters of the Delta rivers are better than those down in the mangrove-swamp region; and in the south-west coast rivers, with which I am personally well acquainted, the up-river fish are excellent in quality, on account of the swift current. I will leave culinary considerations, because cooking is a subject I am very liable to become diffuse on, and we will turn to the consideration of the sporting side of fishing.

Now, there is one thing you will always hear the Gold Coaster (white variety) grumbling about, "There is no sport." He has only got himself to blame. Let him try and introduce the Polynesian practice of swimming about in the surf, without his clothes, and with a suitable large, sharp knife, slaying sharks—there's no end of sharks on the Gold Coast, and no end of surf. The Rivermen have the same complaint, and I may recommend that they should try spearing sting-rays, things that run sometimes to six feet across the wings, and every inch of them wicked, particularly the tail. There is quite enough danger in either sport to satisfy a Sir Samuel Baker[2]; for myself, being a nervous, quiet, rational individual, a large cat-fish in a small canoe supplies sufficient excitement.

The other day I went out for a day's fishing on an African river. I and two black men, in a canoe, in company with a round net, three stout-fishing lines, three paddles, Dr. Günther's *Study of Fishes,* some bait in an old Morton's boiled-mutton tin, a little manioc, stinking awfully (as is its wont), a broken calabash bailer, a lot of dirty water to sit in, and happy and contented minds. I catalogue these things because they are either essential to or inseparable from a good day's sport in West Africa. Yes, even *I,* ask my . . . friends down there, I feel sure they will tell you that they never had such experiences before my arrival. I fear they will go on and say, "Never again!" and that it was all my fault, which it was not. When things go well they ascribe it, and their survival, to Providence or their own precautions; when things are merely usual in horror, it's my fault, which is a rank inversion of the truth, for it is only when circumstances get beyond my control, and Providence takes charge, that accidents happen. I will demonstrate this by continuing my narrative. We paddled away, far up a mangrove creek, and then went up against the black mud-bank, with its great network of grey-white roots, surmounted by the closely-interlaced black-green foliage. Absolute silence reigned, as it can only reign in Africa in a mangrove swamp. The water-laden air wrapped round us like a warm, wet blanket. The big mangrove flies came silently to feed on us and leave their progeny behind

2. Sir Samuel (White) Baker (1821–93), London-born explorer of the Nile River and its sources. *Ed.*

them in the wounds to do likewise. The stink of the mud, strong enough to break a window, mingled fraternally with that of the sour manioc.

I was reading, the negroes, always quiet enough when fishing, were silently carrying on the one great African native industry—scratching themselves—so, with our lines over side, life slid away like a dreamless sleep, until the middle man hooked a cat-fish. It came on board with an awful grunt, right in the middle of us; flop, swish, scurry, and yell followed; I tucked the study of fishes in general under my arm and attended to this individual specimen, shouting "Lef em, lef em; hev em for water one time, you sons of unsanctified house lizards,"[3] and such like valuable advice and admonition. The man in the more remote end of the canoe made an awful swipe at the 3ft.-long, grunting, flopping, yellow-grey, slimy thing, but it never reached it, owing to the paddle meeting in mid-air with the flying leg of the man in front of him, drawing blood profusely. I really fancy, about this time, that, barring the cat-fish and myself, the occupants of the canoe were standing on their heads, with a view of removing their lower limbs from the terrible pectoral and dorsal fins, which our prey made such lively play with.

"*Brevio spatio interjecto,*" as Cæsar says, in the middle of a bad battle, over went the canoe, while the cat-fish went off home with the line and hook. One black man went to the bank, whither, with a blind prescience of our fate, I had flung, a second before, the most valuable occupant of the canoe, *The Study of Fishes.* I went to investigate fluvial deposit *in situ.* When I returned to the surface—accompanied by great swirls of mud and great bubbles of the gases of decomposition I had liberated on my visit to the bottom of the river—I observed the canoe, floating bottom upwards, accompanied by Morton's tin, the calabash, and the paddles, and on the bank one black man was engaged in hauling the other out by the legs; fortunately this one's individual God had seen to it that his toes should become entangled in the net, and this floated, and so indicated to his companion where he was, when he had dived into the mud and got fairly embedded.

Now it's my belief that the most difficult thing in the world is to turn over a round-bottomed canoe that is wrong side up, when you are in the water with the canoe. The next most difficult thing is to get into the canoe, after accomplishing triumph number one, and had it not been for my black friends that afternoon, I should not have done these things successfully, and there would be by now another haunted creek in West Africa, with a mud and blood-bespattered ghost trying for ever to turn over the ghost of a little

3. Kingsley's translation: "Leave it alone! Leave it alone! Throw it into the water at once! What did you catch it for?" *Ed.*

canoe. However, all ended happily. We collected all our possessions, except the result of the day's fishing—the cat-fish—but we had had as much of him as we wanted, and so, adding a thankful mind to our contented ones, we went home.

None of us gave a verbatim report of the incident. I held my tongue for fear of not being allowed out fishing again, and I heard my men giving a fine account of a fearful fight, with accompanying prodigies of valour, that we had had with a witch crocodile. I fancy that must have been just their way of putting it, because it is not good form to be frightened by cat-fish on the West Coast, and I cannot for the life of me remember even having seen a witch crocodile that afternoon.

I must, however, own that native methods of fishing are usually safe, though I fail to see what I had to do in producing that above accident. The usual method of dealing with a cat-fish is to bang him on the head with a club, and then break the spiny fins off, for they make nasty wounds that are difficult to heal, and very painful.

The native fishing-craft is the dug-out canoe in its various local forms. The Accra canoe is a very safe and firm canoe for work of any sort except heavy cargo, and it is particularly good for surf; it is, however, slower than many other kinds. The canoe that you can get the greatest pace out of is undoubtedly the Adooma, which is narrow and flat-bottomed, and simply flies over the water. The paddles used vary also with locality, and their form is a mere matter of local fashion, for they all do their work well. There is the leaf-shaped Kru paddle, the trident-shaped Accra, the long lozenged Niger, and the long-handled, small-headed Galwa paddle, and with each of these forms the native, to the manner born, will send his canoe flying along with that unbroken sweep I consider the most luxurious and perfect form of motion on earth.

. . . The appliances for catching fish are, firstly, fish traps, sometimes made of hollow logs of trees, with one end left open and the other closed. One of these is just dropped alongside the bank, left for a week or so, until a fish family makes a home in it, and then it is removed with a jerk. Then there are fish-baskets made from split palm-stems tied together with tie tie; they are circular and conical, resembling our lobster pots and eel baskets, and they are usually baited with lumps of kank soaked in palm-oil. Then there are drag nets made of pineapple fibre, one edge weighted with stones tied in bunches at intervals; as a rule these run ten to twenty-five feet long, but in some places they are much longer. The longest I ever saw was when out fishing in the lovely harbour of San Paul de Loanda. This was over thirty feet and was weighted with bunches of clam shells, and made of European yarn, as indeed most nets are when this is procurable by the natives, and it was worked by three canoes which were being poled about, as is usual in Loanda Harbour. Then there is the universal hook and line, the hook either of European make or the simple bent pin of our youth.

But my favourite method, and the one by which I got most of my fish up rivers or in creeks is the stockade trap. These are constructed by driving in stakes close together, leaving one opening, not in the middle of the stockade, but towards the up river end. In tidal waters these stockades are visited daily, at nearly low tide, for the high tide carries the fish in behind the stockade, and leaves them there on falling. Up river, above tide water, the stockades are left for several days, in order to allow the fish to congregate. Then the opening is closed up, the fisherwomen go inside and throw out the water and collect the fish. There is another kind of stockade that gives great sport. During the wet season the terrific rush of water tears off bits of bank in such rivers as the Congo, and Ogowé, where, owing to the continual fierce current of fresh water the brackish tide waters do not come far up the river, so that the banks are not shielded by a great network of mangrove roots. In the Ogowé a good many of the banks are composed of a stout clay, and so the pieces torn off, hang together, and go often sailing out to sea, on the current, waving their bushes, and often trees, gallantly in the broad Atlantic, out of sight of land. Bits of the Congo Free State are great at seafaring too, and owing to the terrific stream of the great Zaire, spreading a belt of fresh water over the surface of the ocean 200 miles from land, ships fall in with these floating islands, their trees still flourishing. The Ogowé is not so big as the Congo, but it is a very respectable stream, even for the great continent of rivers, and it pours into the Atlantic, in the wet season, about 1,750,000 cubic feet of fresh water per second, on which float some of these islands. But by no means every island gets out to sea, many of them get into slack water round corners in the Delta region of the Ogowé and remain there, collecting all sorts of *débris* that comes down on the flood water, getting matted more and more firm by the floating grass, every joint of which grows on the smallest opportunity. In many places these floating islands are of considerable size; one I heard of was large enough to induce a friend of mine to start a coffee plantation on it; unfortunately the wretched thing came to pieces when he had cut down its trees and turned the soil up. And one I saw in the Karkola river, was a weird affair. It was in the river opposite our camp, and it very slowly, but perceptibly went round and round in an orbit, although it was about half an acre in extent. A good many of these bits of banks, do not attain to the honour of becoming islands, but get on to sand-banks in their early youth, near native town, to the joy of the inhabitants, who forthwith go off to them, and drive round them a stockade of stakes firmly anchoring them. Thousands of fishes then congregate round the little island inside the stockade, for the rich feeding in among the roots and grass, and the affair is left a certain time. Then the entrance to the stockade is firmly closed up, and the natives go inside and bale out the water, and catch the fish in baskets, tearing the island to pieces, with shouts and squeals of exultation. It's messy, but it is amusing, and you get tremendous catches.

A very large percentage of fish traps are dedicated to the capture of shrimp and craw-fish, which the natives value highly when smoked, using them to make a sauce with for their kank; among these is the shrimp-basket. These baskets are tied on sticks laid out in parallel lines of considerable extent. They run about three inches in diameter, and their length varies with the place that is being worked. The stakes are driven into the mud, and to each stake is tied a basket with a line of tie tie, the basket acting as a hat to the stake when the tide is ebbing; as the tide comes in, it lowers the basket into the current and carries into its open end large quantities of shrimps, which get entangled and packed by the force of the current into the tapering end of the basket, which is sometimes eight or ten feet from the mouth. You can always tell where there is a line of these baskets by seeing the line of attendant sea-gulls all solemnly arranged with their heads to win'ard sea-gull fashion.

Another device employed in small streams for the capture of either craw-fish or small fish is a line of calabashes, or earthen pots with narrow mouths; these are tied on to a line, I won't say with tie tie, because I have said that irritating word so often, but still you understand they are; this line is tied to a tree with more, you know what I mean, and carried across the stream, sufficiently slack to submerge the pots, and then to a tree on the other bank, where it is secured with the same material. A fetish charm is then secured to it that will see to it, that anyone who interferes with the trap, save the rightful owner, will "swell up and burst," then the trap is left for the night, the catch being collected in the morning.

Single pots, well baited with bits of fish and with a suitable stone in to keep them steady, are frequently used alongside the bank. These are left for a day or more, and then the owner with great care, crawls along the edge of the bank and claps on a lid and secures the prey.

Hand nets of many kinds are used. The most frequent form is the round net, weighted all round its outer edge. This is used by one man, and is thrown with great deftness and grace, in shallow waters. I suppose one may hardly call the long wreaths of palm branches used by the Loango and Kacongo coast natives for fishing the surf with, nets, but they are most effective. When the calemma (the surf) is not too bad, two or more men will carry this long thick wreath out into it, and then drop it and drag it towards the shore. The fish fly in front of it on to the beach, where they fall victims to the awaiting ladies, with their baskets. Another very quaint set of devices are employed by the Kru boys wherever they go to catch their beloved land and shore crabs. I remember once thinking I had providentially lighted on a beautiful bit of ju-ju; the whole stretch of mud beach had little lights dotted over it on the ground. I investigated. They were crab-traps. "Bottle of beer," "The Prince of Wales," "Jane Ann," and "Pancake" had become—by means we will not go into here—possessed of bits of candle, and had cut them up and put in front of them pieces of wood in an ingenious way. The crab, a creature whose intelligence is not sufficiently appreciated, fired with a scientific curiosity, went to see what the light was made of, and then could not escape, or perhaps did not try to escape, but stood spell-bound at the beauty of the light; anyhow, they fell victims to their spirit of enquiry. I have also seen drop-traps put for crabs round their holes. In this case the sense of the beauty of light in the crab is not relied on, and once in he is shut in, and cannot go home and communicate the result of his investigations to his family.

Yet, in spite of all these advantages and appliances above cited, I grieve to say the West African, all along the coast, descends to the unsportsmanlike trick of poisoning. Certain herbs are bruised and thrown into the water, chiefly into lagoons and river-pools. The method is effective, but I should doubt whether it is wholesome. These herbs cause the fish to rise to the surface stupefied when they are scooped up with a calabash. Other herbs cause the fish to lay at the bottom, also stupefied, and the water in the pool is thrown out, and they are collected.

More as a pastime than a sport I must class the shooting of the peculiar hopping mud-fish by the small boys with bows and arrows, but this is the only way you can secure them as they go about star-gazing with their eyes on the tops of their heads, instead of attending to baited hooks, and their hearing (or whatever it is) is so keen that they bury themselves in the mud-banks too rapidly for you to net them. Spearing is another very common method of fishing. It is carried on at night, a bright light being stuck in the bow of the canoe, and the spearer crouching, screens his eyes from the glare with a plantain leaf, and drops his long-hafted spear into the fish as they come up to look at the light. It is usually the big bream that are caught in this way out in the sea, and the carp up in fresh water.

The manners and customs of many West African fishes are quaint. I have never yet seen that fish the natives often tell me of that is as big as a man, only thicker, and which walks about on its fins at night, in the forest, so I cannot vouch for it; nor for that other fish that hates the crocodile, and follows her up and destroys her eggs, and now and again dedicates itself to its hate, and goes down her throat, and then spreads out its spiny fins and kills her.

The fish I know are interesting in quieter ways. The strange electrical fish, which sometimes have sufficient power to kill a duck, and which are much given to congregating in sunken boats, giving one much trouble when the boat is floated again, because the natives won't go near them, so as to bail her out.

Then there is that deeply trying creature the Ning Ning fish, who, when you are in some rivers in fresh water and want to have a quiet night's rest, just as you have tucked in your mosquito bar carefully and successfully, comes alongside and serenades you, until you have to get up and throw things at it with a prophetic feeling, amply supported by subsequent experience, that hordes of mosquitoes are busily ensconcing themselves inside your mosquito bar. What makes the Ning Ning—it is called after its idiotic song—so maddening is that it never seems to be where you have thrown the things at it. You could swear it was close to the bow of the canoe when you shied that empty soda-water bottle or that ball of your precious india rubber at it, but instantly comes "ning, ning, ning" from the stern of the canoe. It is a ventriloquist or goes about in shoals, I do not know which, for the latter easier explanation seems debarred by their not singing in chorus; the performance is undoubtedly a solo, and there is one thing anyone experienced in this fish soon finds out, and that is that it is not driven away or destroyed by an artillery of missiles, but merely lays low until its victim has got under his mosquito curtain, and resettled his mosquito palaver, and then back it comes with its "ning ning."

A similar affliction is the salt-water drum-fish, with its "bum-bum." Loanda Harbour abounds with these, and so does Chiloango. In the bright moonlight nights I have looked overside and seen these fish in a wreath round the canoe, with their silly noses against the side, "bum-bumming" away; whether they admire the canoe, or whether they want it to come on and fight it out, I do not know, because my knowledge of the different kinds of fishes and of their internal affairs is derived from Dr. Günther's great work, and that has not got a section on ichthyological psychology in it. The West African natives have, I may say, a great deal of very curious information on the thoughts of fishes, but, much as I like those good people, I make it a hard and fast rule to hold on to my commonsense and keep my belief for religious purposes when it comes to these deductions from natural phenomena, not that I display this mental attitude externally, and there is always in their worst and wildest fetish notions an underlying element of truth. The fetish of fish is too wide a subject to enter into here, it acts well because it gives a close season to river and lagoon fish, the natives round Lake Azingo, for example, saying that if the first fishes that come up into the lake in the great dry season are killed, the rest of the shoal turn back; so on the arrival of this vanguard they are treated most carefully, talked to with "a sweet mouth," and given things. The fishes that form these shoals are *Hemi chromis fasciatus* and *Chromis ogowensis.*

I know no more charming way of spending an afternoon than to leisurely paddle alone to the edge of an Ogowé sand bank, in the dry season, and then lie and watch the ways of the water-world below. If you keep quiet, the fishes take no notice of you, and go on with their ordinary avocations, under your eyes, hunting, and feeding, and playing, and fighting, happily and cheerily until one of the dreaded raptorial fishes appears upon the scene, and then there is a general scurry. Dreadful warriors are the little fishes that haunt sand banks (*Alestis Kingsleyæ*) and very bold, for when you put your hand down in the water, with some crumbs in, after making two or three attempts to frighten it, by sidling up at it and butting, but on finding there's no fight in the thing, they swagger into the palm of your hand and take what is to be got with an air of conquest; but, before the supply is exhausted, there always arises a row among themselves, and the gallant bulls, some two inches long, will spin round and butt at each other for a second or so, and then spin round again, and flap each other with their tails, their little red-edged fins and gill-covers growing crimson with fury. I never made out how you counted points in these fights, because no one ever seemed a scale the worse after even the most desperate duels. . . .

MARIANNE NORTH

From *Recollections of a Happy Life, Being the Autobiography of Marianne North*

Ed. Mrs. John Addington Symonds. 1892. Vol. 1: 117–19; 122–24; 128–29; 145; 150–51; 163–64; 187–88.

[pp. 117–19]

CHAPTER IV

Brazil, 1872–73

. . . Brazil offers to a stranger few inducements for spending money, except its wonderful natural curiosities, its gorgeous birds and butterflies; "Even its bugs are gems," a Yankee friend remarked to me, and these latter are set in gold as ornaments with considerable taste and fineness of workmanship. To me the hummingbirds were the great temptation. M. Bourget, one of Agassiz's late travelling companions, had a rare collection which he valued at 300 guineas, and I passed many happy mornings among his treasures hearing him talk of them and of their habits; but after the first few days I seldom went into the town.

The mule-cars passed the door of the hotel every ten minutes, and took me at six o'clock every day to the famous Botanical Gardens, about four miles off. The whole road is lovely, skirting the edges of two bays, both like small lakes, to which one sees no outlet; the mountains around them are most strangely formed—on the one side generally a sheer precipice, on the other covered with forests to the very top; and such forests! not the woolly-looking woods of Europe, but endless varieties of form and colour, from the white large-leaved trumpet-trees to the feathery palms, scarlet coral, and lilac quaresma-trees. Then the villa gardens along the roadside were full of rich flowers and fruits and noble trees; at one place a sort of marsh with masses of Indian bamboo gave the eyes a pleasant rest after the glaring gaudiness of the gardens. That drive was always charming and fresh to me, and I wished the mules had not been in such a hurry; but they were all splendid animals, and seemed to enjoy going at full gallop, after the first little scene of kicking and rearing which they considered the right thing at starting. They often went too fast, and would have arrived at the station before the appointed time if they had not been checked.

The gardens of Botofogo were a never-ending delight to me; and, as the good Austrian director allowed me to keep my easel and other things at his house, I felt quite at home there, and for some time worked every day and all day under its shady avenues, only returning at sunset to dine and rest, far too tired to pay evening visits, and thereby disgusted some of my kind friends. Of course my first work was to attempt to make a sketch of the great avenue of royal palms which has been so often described. It is half a mile long at least, and the trees are 100 feet high, though only thirty years old; they greatly resemble the cabbage-palm of the West Indies, though less graceful, having the same great green sheaths to their leaf-stalks, which peel off and drop with the leaves when ripe; about five fell in the year, and each left a distinct ring on the smooth trunk. The base of the trunk was much swollen out, and looked like a giant bulb. This huge avenue looked fine from wherever you saw it (and reminded me of the halls of Karnac).[1] There were grand specimens of other palms in the gardens: a whole row of the curious Screw-Pine, with its stilted roots and male and female trees; rows of camphor-trees, bamboos, the jack-fruit, with its monstrous pumpkin-like fruits hanging close to the rough trunks, and endless other interesting plants and trees. Beyond all rose the great blue hills. One could mount straight from the gardens to their woods and hollows, with running water everywhere.

[pp. 122–24]

I spent some days in walking and sketching on the hills behind the city; its aqueduct road was a great help to this enjoyment, being cut through the real forest about a thousand feet above the town and sea. A diligence took one half-way up to it every morning; the road itself and the grand aqueduct by its side were made two hundred years ago by the Jesuits, and the forest trees near it have never been touched, in order to help the supply of water which is collected there in a great reservoir. In this neighbourhood I saw many curious sights. One day six monkeys with long tails and gray whiskers were chattering in one tree, and allowed me to come up close underneath and watch their games through my opera-glass; the branches they were on were quite as well worth studying as themselves, loaded as they were with creeping-plants and grown over with wild bromeliads, orchids, and ferns; these bromeliads had often the most gorgeous scarlet or crimson spikes of flowers. The cecropia or trumpet-tree was always the most conspicuous one in the forest, with its huge white-lined horse-chestnut-shaped leaves, young pink shoots, and hollow stems, in which a lazy kind of ant easily found a ready-made house of many storeys. The most awkward of all animals, the

1. Part of the ruins of ancient Thebes. Located on the Nile River. *Ed.*

sloth, also spent his dull life on the branches, slowly eating up the young shoots and hugging them with his hooked feet, preferring to hang and sleep head downwards. Some of the acacia-trees grow in tufts on tall slender stems, and seem to mimic the tree-ferns with their long feathery fronds, whose stems were often twenty to thirty feet high. Mahogany, rosewood, and many less known timber-trees might be studied there; the knobby bombax, gray as the lovely butterfly which haunted them, were planted at the edge of the road in many places, and under them one got a really solid shade from the sun.

It was the favourite home of many gorgeous butterflies, and they came so fast and so cleverly that it was no easy task for a collecting maniac to make his mind which to try to catch and which to leave; before the treasure was secured more came and tempted him to drop the half-caught beauties for other, perhaps rarer ones, which he would probably miss.

One happy mortal lived up in this neighbourhood and collected calmly, with his whole heart and time in the work, thereby gaining a good livelihood; he had drawers full of the different specimens, which were worth a journey to see: alas! when I went he had just sold the whole collection to the Imperial Princess, so I kept my money, as well as a most fascinating occupation for odd hours, which would have gone if I had, as I intended, done my collecting by deputy. He lived on a lovely perch just under the Corcovado Crag, with a glorious view of the city and bay beneath, and a rare foreground of palms and cacti, one huge mamen tree in front of all, its thick umbrella of leaves supported by great pear-shaped fruit growing close to the stem. The common snail of Brazil introduced itself to me on that road; it was as large as a French roll, and its movements were very dignified. It had a considerable appetite for green leaves (as I afterwards found after keeping one as a pet in a foot-pan for a month), and its eggs were nearly as large as a pigeon's; the first I met was taking a walk on the old aqueduct amongst the begonia and fern-leaves, and moved on at least fifty yards whilst I made a two hours' sketch.

[pp. 128–29]

Such scenery! High trees draped with bougainvillea to the very tops, bushes of the same nearer the ground reminding one of the great rhododendrons in our own shrubberies in May at home, and of much the same colour, though occasionally paler and pinker. There were orange-flowered cassia-trees (whose leaves fold close together at night like the sensitive plant) and scarlet erythrinas looking like gems among the masses of rich green; exquisite peeps of the river, winding below its woody banks or rushing among great stones and rocks, came upon us, and were gone again with tantalising rapidity. My friends only laughed when I grumbled at the mules going so fast; now and then a peaked mountain-top pierced its way through the clouds for a moment and was lost again, then came a gray overhanging cliff sprinkled with bracket-like wild pines spiked with greenish flowers; the near banks were hidden by masses of large-leaved ferns and begonias and arums of many sorts, whose young fresh leaves and fronds were often tinted with crimson or copper-colour. The wild agaves too were very odd: having had their poor centre shoots twisted out, the sap accumulated in the hollow, and a wine or spirit was made from it; the wretched wounded things, sending up dwarfish flowers and prickly shoots from their other joints, formed a strange disagreeable-looking bush, several of which made a most efficient hedge. Under each of these flowers a bulb formed, which when ripe dropped and rooted itself, thus replacing the parent whose life ended at its birth. Another curious plant here abounded, the marica, like a lovely blue iris, which flowers and shoots from the ends of the leaves of the old plant, the leaf being often more than a yard in length, and weighted down to the ground by the bunch at its end. When the flower is over, a bulb forms under it which produces roots; eventually the connecting leaf rots off, so that a perfect circle of young plants succeeds round the original old one. When in flower the appearance was very peculiar; a perfect rosette of bent green leaves and a circle of delicate blue flowers outside them.

The grand coach road we went over had, of course, encouraged emigrants to settle near it; we passed miles of cultivated ground, and the long rows of tidily trimmed coffee and corn gave as much pleasure to my companions as the forest tangles gave to me.

[p. 145]

Just below the flower-garden was a perfect temple of bananas, roofed with their spreading cool green leaves, which formed an exquisite picture. Sometimes a ray of sunlight would slant in through some chink, and illuminate one of the red-purple banana flowers hanging down from its slender stem, making it look like an enchanted lamp of red flame. Masses of the large wild white ginger flowers were on the bank beyond this temple, and scented the whole air. This was a grand playground for the Hector and Morpho butterflies; here, too, I used to watch the humming-birds hovering over and under the flowers, darting from bush to bush without the slightest method—unlike their rivals, the bees, who exhaust the honey from one entire plant before they go to another. Farther down the steep path were masses of sensitive plants covering the bank with the brightest of green velvet and delicate lilac buttons. I never could resist passing the handle of my net over this, when instantly the whole bank became of a dull, dead, earthy tint, and only the dry twigs and stalks of the plants were visible, with their shrinking branchlets starting from them at most acute angles. Below this there were two or three old gray trees, on whose trunks or roots I never failed to find some new wonders of cocoons or larvæ, or odd spider's web, green, gold, or silver, as they glittered in the bright morning sun, often spangled with diamond dew. Lower still were the clear stream and rickety little bridge from which I used to watch the humming-birds and other small creatures bathing, pluming themselves afterwards on the leaves and stalks of the wild ginger or castor-oil plants. These latter grow to a height in this country, and make fine foregrounds, with their large cut leaves and purple or green heads of flowers and berries.

[pp. 150–51]

. . . collecting is one thing and preserving is another, and the difficulties of the latter process are great in so hot and damp a climate. Many of my specimens were eaten even when hung up by a string, apparently out of reach of all creeping things. Some of my collections were not pleasant to handle. One day one of the boys brought me a large black beetle in his cap which he said would bite. "Oh no, it never bites," said Mrs. G., scolding him for the very idea; then she screamed and dropped it. I got a bottle of restil to put it in, but screamed and dropped bottle and all as it hugged my fingers with its sharp-hooked feet, and Eugenio had the last word, after corking it up securely in the spirit: "He knew it *did* bite!" Another unpleasant creature was a stinging caterpillar, whose hairs were as dangerous as a scorpion's tail; a rub against them might cause the hand or arm to inflame so that amputation was necessary to save life. These dreadful things were common enough at certain seasons. I kept and fed one for a long while, hoping to see the kind of moth it turned into; but the blacks hated it to that extent that they pretended it crawled away when I was out one day—a difficult thing to accomplish with a glass shade over it! The varieties of spider were endless, and their works worthy of the old Egyptians. One huge colony formed a web from the roof of the house to the flagstaff opposite, dragging one of its sustaining ropes into an acute angle. We broke down the web, and released the rope to its old straight line. In less than a week it was again pulled towards the roof, forming a tight bridge for the enemy to cross and recross. This spider's body was no bigger than an ordinary green pea. Some of the webs were so thick and strong that they gave my face quite a cutting sensation as I rode through them.

[pp. 163–64]

CHAPTER V

Highlands of Brazil, 1873

One day we went up the big mountain whose shape is so unlike any other, sprinkled with rocks as big as houses, the two top ones, from which it takes its name, being seen from enormous distances: none but cats or Tyndall would think of climbing them, but we enjoyed our ramble at their base. The beautiful scarlet sophronitis orchids quite coloured every rock and tree-stem, shining out gloriously among their green leaves and the gray lichens round. It was difficult to make up one's mind to cease picking them, the plant came off so easily with such great satisfactory slabs of roots, and we knew how they would be valued in England if we could only get them there. There were two varieties; one, "coccinea," rather deeper-coloured and smaller than the grandiflora, which was about the size of the English peacock butterfly. A few hundred yards beneath the top there was fine pasture-ground, varied by groves of spreading trees. One wonders the rich people of Ouro Prêto do not build villas up in this lovely spot to pass their summers in; perhaps they fear the large boa constrictors which people say haunt these big rocks, occasionally attacking the cattle.

[pp. 187–88]

Did I not paint?—and wander and wonder at everything? Every rock bore a botanical collection fit to furnish any hothouse in England. Then there was a real Italian vine pergola leading down through the banana trees to the spring, with picturesque figures continually fetching water from it, and troops of mules, goats, cows, and sheep always moving about; for the grass had failed in most parts of the mountains this year, but was unusually abundant here. I found it hard to leave the next day, and lingered over my work till nearly noon, when a gentleman came down the hill leading his horse, and spoke to me about the view I was taking, then went on and spoke to my guide, arranging with him that as the inn of the place where we were to stop the night was bad, he should take me to his house, writing at the same time a few lines to his wife, to take with us and explain who we were. Who were we? And who was he? We were both ignorant on these subjects, but accepted his kind offer of hospitality in the frank spirit with which it was given, and which one only meets in remote places far from the cautious rules of civilisation, which believes every one till properly introduced to be a rogue. We descended the glorious road to Barrera (another spot for an artist to settle in), rested a few hours of the extreme heat of the day, and I worked at the view from the shady verandah. A mad river made its noisy way through great purple and gray boulders of granite from the strange group of mountains beyond, which here seemed to open themselves out like the walls of an amphitheatre, the sharp points piercing the clouds which formed its roof, and the whole in a state of quivering blue heat most difficult to represent on paper, as the intense glare of the almost perpendicular sun's rays puzzled one. Was it all shade? or all light? Flies and tiny wasps with a taste for chemistry were anxious to ascertain what my colours were made of, and carried various fancy tints into my wet sky, producing effects that were startling but not artistic. The air was heavy, and there was every appearance of a coming storm, but none came.

~ LOUISA ANNE MEREDITH

From *My Home in Tasmania, During a Residence of Nine Years*

London: John Murray, 1852. Vol. 1. 107–16, 244–60.

CHAPTER VII

Bush Fires.—Their Use.—Diamond Bird.—Robin.—Blue-Cap.—Cormorant.—Gulls.—Islands in Bass's Straits.—Pied and Black Red-Bills.—Blue Crane.

[pp. 107–16]

During the hot dry weather of the Christmas time, very extensive bush fires spread about the country, and were sometimes extremely mischievous in their destruction of fences, which are very liable to thus be burned, unless care be taken, previously to the dry season, to clear away all fallen wood and rubbish, and to burn the high grass and ferns for a breadth of three or four yards on either side. The fences of sheep-runs, which extend in lines of many miles in length, over the uncleared hills and forests, are those which most frequently suffer; but frowning crops, stacks, farm-buildings, and dwellings are likewise sometimes swept away by the rapidly-advancing fire.

FIGURE 44 Mary Morton Allport, *Louisa [Anne Meredith] at Work*, 1856 (courtesy Allport State Library of Tasmania and the Museum of Fine Arts, Hobart, Tasmania, Australia)

By day, the effect of these great conflagrations was far from pleasant, causing an increase of heat in the air, and a thick haze over the landscape generally; whilst from the various points where the fires were raging, huge columns and clouds of dense smoke were seen rising, as if from volcanoes: but at night, the scene was often very grand; sometimes the fire might be watched, on any rising ground, spreading onwards and upwards, swifter and brighter as it continually gained strength, till the whole mountain side was blazing together; and after the first fierce general flame had passed away, and the great trunks of trees alone remained burning, the effect resembled that of the scattered lights seen on approaching a distant city at night. The rocky Schoutens glittered with partial lines and trains of fire, that marked their rugged and lofty outline like burnished gold amidst the darkness. Each night showed some new change in the great illumination, until a heavy fall of rain extinguished it altogether, much to the satisfaction of all who feared its nearer approach.

A recent scientific writer (the Count Strzelecki), in treating of this colony, condemns the practice of burning, as seriously injurious to the pasturage, and seems to suppose that the custom originated with the colonists; whereas the aborigines practised it constantly, knowing the advantages of destroying the dense growth of shrubs and coarse plants which cover the country in many parts, and spring up again after the fire with young and fresh shoots, which many of the wild animals then gladly feed on. The grass also grows again immediately after the fires, and is greatly preferred by all animals to the old growth; whilst, from the destruction of tall ferns and scrub, it is rendered more accessible to them. Sheep-owners know how serviceable occasional bush fires are, and generally arrange to burn portions of their sheep-runs at different times, so as to have a new growth about every three years. Where this is neglected for a length of time, the rank luxuriance of the great brake fern and other uneatable plants, and the accumulated masses of dead wood, bark, and leaves, form such a body of fuel, that when a fire does reach it, the conflagration is thrice as mischievous in the destruction of fences as it otherwise would have been.

Although every one else perpetually complained of the heat during this glorious summer, to me it was perfectly delightful, so lasting an impression had the scorching weather of New South Wales left behind it. Sea-bathing was a great luxury, too, and a snug bath, built near the house, over a nook of the salt-water creek, sufficiently deep to afford a good plunge, enabled me to enjoy and benefit from its invigourating effects without tasking my indolence by taking a morning walk to the more distant sea-beach.

In the trees and bushes near the creek, I frequently made new acquaintances of the bird kind, but only know a few of them by name. Among these was that tiny flitting fairy called the Diamond bird: it truly is a dainty little jewel; all gold and shaded amber, with silver spots. Not less beautiful, and far more common, was my old darling robin, as exquisite a beau as ever, with his back of blackest black, and his breast a living flame of scarlet; a warm brave little heart there beats within it too, or his sparkling eye tells no true story! With him came another of Nature's marvels of beauty and brightness, dressed also partly in black, black *bird-velvet,* off the same piece as robin's coat, but with a cap and mantle of blue:—such blue! The deepest summer sky is mere dull gray to it! This wondrous little bird is called the "superb warbler" (*Malurus superbus*), and superb in truth he is. So bright, so swift, so merry, so musical as these little beings are, sure nothing else ever was! The bluecap has a domestic contrast, too, in his quiet-coloured little wife, who, like her Old-World namesake, Jenny Wren,

> Will still put on her brown gown,
> And never go too fine.

But though not dressed in as gay hues, she is as merry and sprightly as her mate; a perfect little "dot" of a bird, (I wish Dickens could see her!) quite round, like a ball set on two fine black pins, with a sweet little head at one side, and at the other, or more truly on the top, the drollest little long straight upright tail that ever was seen. The robin and Mr. Bluecap and Jenny, are all much alike in shape, and the way in which their indescribably funny little tails are so cocked up over their backs, sometimes almost touching their heads, as they hop and pop about, up and down, and in and out, cannot be imagined—it must be seen. Mr. Meredith says they seem to him to spend their whole lives in trying to prove an "*alibi,*" convincing you they are in one place, yet showing themselves in another at the same instant; whilst I, in attempting to follow with my eyes their almost invisible transits from spray to paling, and from the paling on to the rose-bush, and then back again to the cherry tree, always feel as if I were witnessing some exhibition of legerdemain or conjuring, and am prepared for surprises and mystifications without limit.

"Extremes meet," it is often said; but never can the axiom be more perfectly illustrated than when a great, heavy, ugly, stupid, gross-looking monster of a cormorant comes sousing down amongst a party of these dainty little fairy birds, as I have sometimes seen one, when attracted by the shoals of fish glancing in the bright pebbly shadows of the creek. Settling himself, after much preliminary bobbing and flapping, on a stout limb of a dead gum-tree, he sits like wooden effigy of a bird, watching his prey.

Very different are many other of the sea birds that sometimes visit the creek, but are more commonly seen on the beach and rocks. All the gulls are beautiful, whether pied, gray, or white, the latter especially; they are *so* white, and skim over the blue sea in the distant sunlight like snow-flakes, only transformed to bright-eyed birds as they near the shore; when their sweet mellow cry comes floating with them, soft as the tone of a far-away bell.

Although gulls are not generally very tempting as articles of food, I have heard Mr. Meredith recount his great delight at having once, some years ago, killed nine at one shot, when he had been ship-wrecked on an island in Bass's Straits, and had lived for some days on a miserable sort of porridge or burgoo, made of flour recovered from the wreck, and so damaged by salt water that it would not bake, mixed with water so strongly impregnated with alum that it could scarcely be drunk. After this diet, meat, even though that of a sea-bird, became valuable, and the nine gulls were a most precious acquisition; but, being shot at dusk, they were put aside until dawn, to be prepared for breakfast; and then, woful to relate, all that remained of them were two legs, the rest having been devoured during the night by rats. A species of native rat abounds on many of these islands, and snakes are numerous on all, however widely separated by the boisterous sea and strong currents that flow between them. Mr. Meredith was told by an old "Straitsman," who had for years been wandering all about them, hunting seals and mutton birds, that he never was on one, though only containing a few acres, on which he did not observe snakes; and my husband gives the same account, so far as his knowledge of them extends. On one occasion, during the sojourn on "Prime Seal Island" before mentioned, he had observed a fine "Cape Barren goose"[1] alight, and, taking his gun, was stealing warily towards it, keeping a rock between himself and the goose, when a rustling amongst the scrub caused him to look down, and he saw part of an enormous snake, which was rapidly moving across, close beneath his feet; fortunately, the loss of the goose, which he alarmed by his precipitate retreat from the snake, was the only harm done.

Among the sea-birds, the "red-bills" are great favourites of ours; they are so very sprightly and handsome in their clear brilliant black and white plumage, gaily set off by their bills and legs of the brightest coral. They run along the sands with exceeding swiftness, always running into the water to take wing, when alarmed by the approach of such terrific things as ourselves. They scarcely make anything fit to be called a nest, but lay about two eggs on the beach or sandbank, and the young ones, until able to escape danger by flight, lie close and motionless, and thus often evade destruction; but if by chance any one approaches the defenceless little ones, the old birds are extremely bold and indefatigable in their endeavours to divert his attention; flying or running close round him, and then circling away a short distance to entice pursuit; sometimes they flutter lamely along, as if hurt and incapable of flight, until they have succeeded in removing the threatened peril from the precious little babes in the sand, when, with a backward glance and a saucy cry of triumph, away they fly, as sound and swift as ever.

Besides the pied red-bills, there are some rather larger, whose plumage is wholly black; but these, although handsome, are less so than the others. Both species are sometimes eaten, but I rejoice to say their flavour is too "fishy" to be generally liked; for I love them so well whilst alive, that I grieve to have them destroyed. The wide extent of the sea beaches here requires the presence of all the birds that belong to, or are wont to visit them, to add their small items of joyous animal life to the great and grand attributes of ocean, and to people with their busy activity the otherwise lonely strand.

The figures of my favourite red-bills, under the name of "oyster-catchers," in Gould's "Birds of Australia," are less faithful than most of his

1. The "Cape Barren Goose" frequents the island from which it takes its name, and others in the Straits. It is about the same size as a common goose, the plumage a handsome mottled brown and gray, somewhat owl-like in character.

admirable plates; they are too heavy-looking, and represent the bills and feet as orange-coloured, instead of their real hue of pure brilliant coral-red.

A beautiful blue crane often came and sat in a bare tree over the creek, watching the fish: I had amused myself for some mornings in watching him with equal attention, and admiring his long elegant neck, slender legs, large bright eyes, and lovely delicate silvery-blue plumage, and I vainly hoped that we might still go on quietly together; but, alas! despite my extreme discretion in not attracting attention to my feathered companion, he was one morning seen, doomed, shot without mercy, and a day or two after appeared as a second-course roast, which was much praised. I did not taste my unlucky friend; I should, however, imagine, from what I had observed of his way of living, that the *post mortem* examination would reveal to the palates of those who did, rather strong evidence of his ichthyological researches.

[pp. 244–60]

CHAPTER XIV

As I have mentioned the kangaroo, perhaps my most systematic method will be to give a short description of the indigenous animals of Tasmania, rather than introduce stray sketches of them in the accidental manner in which I have made their acquaintance.

I commence with the largest, the Great or Forest Kangaroo (*Macropus giganteus*), the "Forester" of the colonists, which I have not yet seen in its wild state. Many years ago they were very numerous, and might constantly be observed feeding in the day-time on the open country in groups of from five to twenty. The oldest and heaviest male of the herd was called a "Boomer," probably a native term. When chased, these patriarchs of the forest, being large and heavy, were always the least swift, and consequently most frequently taken, until at length the great boomer kangaroo has become in all the inhabited districts an extinct animal. The females, and younger males, or "bucks," are much less, the elderly gentlemen alone attaining the great size described by the early settlers. So many idle vagabonds have been in the constant habit of roaming about with packs of twenty or thirty huge dogs each, to procure kangaroo skins for sale, that the forest species is now very rarely seen. An excellent Act of Council was introduced by Sir Eardley Wilmot, and passed into law, tending to the partial protection of the kangaroos, preventing persons from hunting on Crown lands without licences, which are granted by the police magistrates. If the latter always took the proper means to ascertain the characters of those who apply for licences, and conscientiously refused to grant them to men of known bad character, the benefit conferred by this Act would be very great. But as many of the so-called "kangarooers" are notorious cattle and sheep-stealers, the want of proper discrimination in the magistrates is productive of infinite evil, and in some instances not only neutralizes the effect of the Act, but adds to the mischievous power of the vagabond "kangarooers," by permitting their location on any of the Crown lands, however close to private property, thus enabling them to carry on their nefarious transactions with success and impunity.

Formerly, the size attained by the old "boomers" was enormous; the hind quarters frequently weighed (when skinned and dressed) from 70 to 90 lbs., and the whole animal from 120 to 160 lbs. These were large powerful creatures, measuring in their common position about five feet in height; but when they rise on their toes, with the strong thick tail serving as a prop and support, they stand above six feet high. When brought to bay, the old boomers fight very resolutely, and if one can take up his favourite position, in water about three feet deep, so that the dogs must swim to reach him, he can keep off a whole pack. As each dog swims up, the kangaroo lays him under water with his hand-like fore paws, holding him down until another claims his attention, and so disposes of one after another until the dogs are exhausted; and sometimes he tears them dreadfully with the long sharp solid claws of his fore feet, which he uses most adroitly, ripping and cutting in any direction with sure effect. It is, I believe, generally supposed that they inflict the most severe wounds with the hind feet, but this is not the case until they are overcome and thrown down; as, when fighting erect, they always raise themselves on their hind toes. Their general colour is dark gray, or ash colour, lighter beneath. Mr. Meredith, on one occasion, long ago, saw a pure white kangaroo, and more recently we heard of another white one having been seen: these, I imagine, are albinos, which seem to occur occasionally among all animals.

The ordinary jump of the large kangaroo is about sixteen feet; and they can clear a four-rail fence, about five feet high, in their course, without any visible alteration or exertion.

All the species of kangaroo are easily tamed, and become as familiar as any other domestic animal; but as all dogs here are accustomed and trained to hunt and kill them, pets of this kind are certain, sooner or later, to come to an untimely end. One which was reared here some time back at last stood higher than the woman it belonged to, and used to accompany her whenever she left home, just as a dog would do, hopping along by her side in a most friendly and companionable manner; but one day, meeting some strange dogs, it was unfortunately hunted and killed. The young of all species of kangaroo are commonly called Joeys, without regard to sex, but I am not aware if this is a corruption of some native name, or one bestowed by the early colonists.

The Brush Kangaroo (*Macropus Bennettii*) stands three feet high in its usual position, with the hind elbow or heels bent up. Its colour is dark iron-gray, lighter beneath. The doe, like that of the forest species, has one young one at a time, which she carries and shelters in the pouch, until the baby so much outgrows its cradle, that the long legs and tail poke out.

The sweet gentle expression of face peculiar to the kangaroo tribe is most beautiful and winning; their eyes are full, dark, and soft, and the erect, animated, widely-open ears, in perpetual motion, give at the same time a keen and yet timid expression to the head. I never had so good an opportunity of observing the different species of kangaroo, as in the collection which Sir Eardley Wilmot kept as pets in a wooded and bushy paddock close to Government House, Hobarton, where, within the paling fence, they enjoyed their liberty, and being tolerably accustomed to visitors, allowed themselves to be looked at very composedly; but in their perfectly wild state, a passing glance is all that can be obtained. The habits of the brush kangaroo are different from those of the forester; they are never seen feeding in herds by day, and if two or three chance to be started from the same vicinity, they all set off in different directions. Usually they are not seen until roused from the bush log or tussocks they have been crouching in, like a hare in her form: their common average jump is about twelve feet.

I have now (1850) two young brush kangaroos, Joey and Beppo, living in a grassy inclosure close to the house, and associating with my poultry very amicably; though they sometimes slily creep after the peacock, as if with the intention of biting his long gorgeous train, when it looks green in the sunshine, supposing it perhaps to be some new vegetable. They are fed with green food, bread, or corn, and are fond of new milk. They hold grass or leaves in their hands, and eat very daintily and elegantly, never seeming in any hurry, but helping themselves with a degree of refinement and deliberation that might offer a salutary example to some nobler animals. For a year I had only "Joey," and an old hen turkey annoyed him exceedingly at one time, in her stupid terror lest he should hurt her chickens, and chased him round the inclosure at a furious pace; but by putting the old lady under a coop, I restored poor "Joey's" peace and tranquillity. Both he and little Beppo (which we have reared this year in the house like a pet kitten) sleep some hours during the day, under the bower of boughs over their kennel, and hop about and feed chiefly in the night-time.

The Wolloby is the species next in size to the Brush Kangaroo in this colony; the name is usually spelled Wallaby, but the full native pronunciation can only be correctly represented by using the *o* instead of the *a*. In the aboriginal languages of these colonies, the vowels are sounded peculiarly full and round.

The wolloby, in its common position, stands about two feet high; the fur is gray, mingled with a brown tan colour, and is much softer than the larger kangaroo's, being more like that of the opossum. These animals frequent thickets and the dense close scrubs near rivers and watercourses, where they baffle the most active dogs by winding and popping in and out, like a rabbit in a furze-brake. In chasing kangaroos, or, as it is technically termed, "kangarooing," large powerful dogs are used; but in thickly-wooded and scrubby places, a sharp clever *little* dog is also required, to put the game out of the thickets, where the great dogs could not penetrate. The wolloby and brush kangaroo often visit gardens and fields at night, to banquet on the dainties they find there; and by far the greatest portion of those destroyed are caught in snares set for the purpose, in the tracks or "runs" they frequent. There is, it would seem, about the same difference in the habits of the forest, brush, and wolloby kangaroos, as that existing between those of the deer, the hare, and the rabbit.

The Kangaroo-Rat (*Hypsiprymnus murinus*) is a pretty little animal about thirteen inches in height, with grayish fur, harsher than that of the kangaroo, and the face has more of a *rattish* expression; nevertheless it is certainly a pretty animal, and so easily tamed as to be frequently made a pet, gambolling and frisking about the house, and following those who caress it, like a favourite dog or cat. In their natural state they eat grass, and also scratch and burrow at night for roots, and have unluckily a very clever trick of digging their own potatoes, or rather those of the settlers, which they appropriate without scruple. They form warm nests of dry grass on the ground, well-sheltered, and open at one side only. A prejudice exists against eating their flesh, which is well-flavoured and whiter than that of the true kangaroos, the latter being dark-coloured, lean, tender, and more similar to hare than any other meat I am acquainted with, and is undoubtedly excellent, when hung for a sufficient length of time, and properly dressed. A very rich gravy soup is often made from it, and a colonial dish called a "steamer," consisting of the meat and some good bacon finely minced, and stewed in rich gravy, is also good; but the hind-quarters roasted, with hare-stuffing and currant jelly, form a dish that Dr. Kitchener himself would have applauded, and which now is generally considered a dainty even here, especially by our town-friends. Yet I have had servants who looked upon our eating kangaroo as something absoluitely monstrous, and turned away in horror at the thought of partaking of what they expressively designated as "*just a wild beast!*" A haunch of tiger or a wolf-chop would, in their estimation, be quite as reasonable and proper food; but fortunately they could always find an abundance of tame mutton in our kitchen to console their outraged sensibility.

The kangaroo-rat is not by many persons considered fit to be eaten, nor have I ever had one cooked, for we partake the common prejudice—whether caused by the name, and the unpleasant association of ideas inseparable from it, I know not; but as it is a prejudice which serves to save the lives of the poor little animals, I have not the slightest desire to have it removed.

Of the Bandicoot, two species are found here: one (*Perameles Gunnii*) is of a light brownish ash-colour, half as large again as a full-sized rat, and somewhat broader in proportion; the other (*Perameles obescula*) is rather less, and its colour an ashy fawn, striped with light gray.

One of our servants lately found two young striped bandicoots, pretty little soft creatures like great mice, and brought them to the children for pets. We kept them for some weeks, feeding them on bread, milk, and raw potatoes; one was accidentally hurt, and died; the other I turned out into the garden, thinking to bestow rather a luxurious life upon him, amidst potatoes, fruit, and other good things: but I could not prevail on him to accept his liberty; he took up his abode in the parlour, and soon found a warm snug bed among the multifarious contents of a deep work-basket, where he lay coiled up all day, and grumbled and bit at any one who disturbed him until his usual time of rising, about dusk, when he regularly bounced out of the basket, ran to the corner where his saucer of fresh milk was always placed, nibbled his bread or potato, and scampered about all the evening like a great tame mouse, running under our chairs and over our feet and dresses, and up the folds of them, with confiding boldness, but not allowing any one to lay hold of him. His end, poor little fellow, was, I fear, a violent one, for I strongly suspect my demure tabby cat must have evaded our wonted vigilance and gained access to the parlour during the time poor Cooty was awake; for one morning, to the children's great regret, his bed was cold and empty, and he was no more seen amongst us.

The Porcupine (*Echidna*) is fully four times the size of an English hedgehog, covered on the back with spines three or four inches long, which protrude from a coat of thick grayish fur; its feet have long toes, with long strong claws, and, instead of a mouth and teeth, a long narrow round bill appears to complete its extraordinary visage. It usually weighs five or six pounds, being exceedingly fat. Persons who are partial to sucking pig like the flesh of the porcupine, which somewhat resembles it, but is too rich for most palates. These creatures are found in wet springy ground, where they probably feed on tadpoles, worms, and ants. They burrow in the earth, and often frequent hollows in moist rocks, and if pursued or hemmed in, make their escape by scratching a hole and sinking into it. Mr. Meredith once brought one from the Schoutens to Swan Port, and on landing put it down on the broad open beach, where, being left for a few moments, it burrowed down into the sand and vanished in an incredibly short space of time, scarcely leaving a trace behind.

On another occasion one was found by dogs on one of the rocky hills of the tier, and was safely carried down to me in a covered tin boiler. Knowing the mysterious subterranean habits of my new friend, I was not a little puzzled how to accommodate him without losing him; and, as a temporary arrangement, he was deposited at the bottom of a wooden churn, which I thought sufficiently deep to prevent his absconding. Shortly after, on going to look at my captive, I found him clinging by his long claws to the top of the churn, with his conical head peeping over. The duck-like bill is nearly as thin and round as a tobacco-pipe, and about two inches long, and gave an indescribably droll kind of pursed-up whistling expression to the strange creature's face, as his bright little eyes peered about him from out their furry nooks; the short broad tail, thickly beset with spines, like the back ad sides, being spread out in a fan shape, not unlike that of a lobster. I was very curious to watch the ways of this anomalous little animal for a while, and to keep it confined for that purpose; but there was something so pitiful, though absurd, in the pleading, helpless, puzzled look of its queer face, as it seemed prying into mine, that was to me quite irresistible, knowing, as I well did, the difficulty, not to say impossibility, of keeping it alive, far less making it happy; so I at once carried it to my garden, let it crawl away, and saw it immediately commence a sidling kind of motion, casting up a circular ridge of earth, beneath which in a few seconds it had effectually screwed itself out of sight. I hoped it would have taken up its abode there, but we never could find a sign or vestige of it afterwards.

The Wombat (*Phascolomys* ———), like the porcupine, is eaten and relished by some persons, but is fatter and coarser, with a strong rank flavour. It is a most harmless, helpless, inoffensive animal, by no means agile, and falling an easy prey to its pursuers, if cut off from its retreat to the rocky hollows and crevices in which it lives, and which it squeezes into, through a smaller opening than would be supposed capable of admitting its fat squab body. Its head resembles that of the badger, but with a rounder snout. It has very small eyes, strong bristly whiskers, very short ears, short legs, short tail, and long coarse gray hair. Its body is broad and flat, and weighs from 30 lbs. to 50 lbs., and the creature's whole aspect betokens slowness and inactivity.

The children of a settler at the river Mersey had a pet wombat, which lived with them for some time, and used to play with them, and follow them about with great docility and good temper. They made it a bed on a box, with a piece of blanket to cover it, and it was often seen to scratch the blanket snugly round it, and pull it up when slipping away, in the most cosy and civilized manner possible. Having also a *penchant* for making its way into any other bed from which a scrap of blanket or rug hung down to serve as a climbing ladder, it became an object of dislike to the servants, and the worthy farmer determined, much to the grief of the children, to part with the favourite, which, like all other favourites, was fast gaining foes. He carried it away a considerable distance, put it down in the forest, and returned home with the story of his success; but ere the evening was ended, a certain well-known scratching sound was heard at the door, and the delighted children opened it for their poor weary wombat, who had found his way home to them again. A second time he was conveyed away, and to a greater distance, but still he came back; the third time the farmer carried him across the Mersey in a boat, and left him on the opposite bank of the broad deep river, quite secure now that the business was finally settled. His poor friend was, however, still of a different opinion, and by the time the boat had touched the home shore, the creature had found a huge fallen tree, which lay half across the stream, and had crawled to the extreme end of it, wistfully gazing upon his departing friends, who, thinking it quite impossible that he could cross the intervening portion of the river, went away home. How the heavy fat thing *did* cross, no one knows, but he arrived as usual that night, and, as may be imagined, his kind-hearted master did not try again to drive him away. Unfortunately, he was at last accidentally burned, from creeping too close to the hot ashes of the hearth, and, in mercy to his sufferings, was killed.

Wombats are generally found on rocky places, especially the summits of mountains and gullies, where their haunts are mostly inaccessible. Their chief food consists of the roots of the grass-tree and other plants, to procure which they leave their rocky fastnesses at night, and visit neighbouring marshy flats, where they scratch for their living, like the porcupine and bandicoot. The skin of the wombat is so thick and tough that the teeth of large dogs are seldom strong enough to penetrate it, and are not unfrequently absolutely pulled out in the effort, so that some of the hunters of the Bush are in the habit of punishing their dogs for meddling with a wombat; and after a few such lessons, the dogs content themselves with barking round the harmless creature when they find one, and its stout natural coat befriends it like a suit of armour.

For Sport

GEORGE EGERTON [MARY CHAVELITA DUNNE BRIGHT]

From "A Cross Line"

Keynotes. Boston: Roberts Brothers; London: Elkin Mathews. 1894. 9–16.

The rather flat notes of a man's voice float out into the clear air, singing the refrain of a popular music-hall ditty. There is something incongruous between the melody and the surroundings. It seems profane, indelicate, to bring this slangy, vulgar tune, and with it the mental picture of footlight flare and fantastic dance, into the lovely freshness of this perfect spring day.

A woman sitting on a felled tree turns her head to meet its coming, and an expression flits across her face in which disgust and humorous appreciation are subtly blended. Her mind is nothing if not picturesque; her busy brain, with all its capabilities choked by a thousand vagrant fancies, is always producing pictures and finding associations between the most unlikely objects. She has been reading a little sketch written in the daintiest language of a fountain scene in Tanagra, and her vivid imagination has made it real to her. The slim, graceful maids grouped around it filling their exquisitely-formed earthen jars, the dainty poise of their classic heads, and the flowing folds of their draperies have been actually present with her; and now,—why, it is like the entrance of a half-typsy vagabond player bedizened in tawdry finery; the picture is blurred. She rests her head against the trunk of a pine-tree behind her, and awaits the singer. She is sitting on an incline in the midst of a wilderness of trees; some have blown down, some have been cut down, and the lopped branches lie about; moss and bracken and trailing bramble bushes, fir-cones, wild rose-bushes, and speckled red "fairy hats" fight for life in wild confusion. A disused quarry to the left is an ideal haunt of pike, and to the right a little river rushes along in haste to join a greater sister that is fighting a troubled way to the sea. A row of stepping-stones cross it, and if you were to stand on one you would see shoals of restless stone-loach "beardies"[1] darting from side to side. The tails of several ducks can be seen above the water, and the paddle of their balancing feet and the gurgling suction of their bills as they search for larvae can be heard distinctly between the hum of insect, twitter of bird, and rustle of stream and leaf. The singer has changed his lay to a whistle, and presently he comes down the path a cool, neat, gray-clad figure, with a fishing creel slung across his back, and a trout rod held on his shoulder. The air ceases abruptly, and his cold, gray eyes scan the seated figure with its gypsy ease of attitude, a scarlet shawl that has fallen from her shoulders forming an accentuative background to the slim roundness of her waist.

Persistent study, coupled with a varied experience of the female animal, has given the owner of the said gray eyes some facility in classing her, although it has not supplied him with any definite data as to what any one of the species may do in a given circumstance. To put it in his own words, in answer to a friend who chaffed him on his untiring pursuit of women as an interesting problem,—

"If a fellow has had much experience of his fellow-man he may divide him into types, and given a certain number of men and a certain number of circumstances, he is pretty safe on hitting on the line of action each type will strike. 'Taint so with woman. You may always look out for the unexpected; she generally upsets a fellow's calculations, and you are never safe in laying odds on her. Tell you what, old chappie, we may talk about superior intellect; but if a woman was n't handicapped by her affection or need of it, the cleverest chap in Christendom would be just a bit of putty in her hands. I find them more fascinating as problems than anything going. Never let an opportunity slip to get new data—never!"

He did not now. He met the frank, unembarrassed gaze of eyes that would have looked with just the same bright inquiry at the advent of a hare or a toad, or any other object that might cross her path, and raised his hat with respectful courtesy, saying, in the drawling tone habitual with him,—

"I hope I am not trespassing?"

" I can't say; you may be; so may I, but no one has ever told me so!"

A pause. His quick glance has noted the thick wedding-ring on her slim brown hand and the flash of a diamond in its keeper. A lady decidedly. Fast?—perhaps. Original?—undoubtedly. Worth knowing?—rather.

1. Small fish related to minnows. *Ed.*

"I am looking for a trout stream, but the directions I got were rather vague; might I—"

"It's straight ahead; but you won't catch anything now, at least not here,—sun's too glaring and water too low; a mile up you may in an hour's time."

"Oh, thanks awfully for the tip. You fish then?"

"Yes, sometimes."

"Trout run big here?" (What odd eyes the woman has! kind of magnetic.)

"No, seldom over a pound; but they are very game."

"Rare good sport, is n't it, whipping a stream? There is so much besides the mere catching of fish; the river and the trees and the quiet sets a fellow thinking; kind of sermon; makes a chap feel good, don't it?"

She smiles assentingly, and yet what the devil is she amused at, he queries mentally. An inspiration! he acts upon it, and says eagerly,—

"I wonder—I don't half like to ask, but fishing puts people on a common footing, don't it? You knowing the stream, you know, would you tell me what are the best flies to use?"

"I tie my own, but—"

"Do you? How clever of you! Wish I could;" and sitting down on the other end of the tree, he takes out his fly-book. "But I interrupted you, you were going to say—"

"Only,"—stretching out her hand, of a perfect shape but decidedly brown, for the book,—"that you might give the local fly-tyer a trial; he'll tell you. Later on, end of next month, or perhaps later, you might try the oak-fly,—the natural fly, you know. A horn is the best thing to hold them in, they get out of anything else; and put two on at a time."

"By Jove, I must try that dodge!"

He watches her as she handles his book and examines the contents critically, turning aside some with a glance, fingering others almost tenderly, holding them daintily, and noting the cock of wings and the hint of tinsel, with her head on one side,—a trick of hers, he thinks.

"Which do you like most, wet or dry fly?" She is looking at some dry flies.

"Oh," with that rare smile, "at the time I swear by whichever happens to catch the most fish,—perhaps really dry fly. I fancy most of these flies are better for Scotland or England. Up to this, March-brown has been the most killing thing. But you might try an 'orange-grouse,'—that's always good here,—with perhaps a 'hare's ear' for a change, and put on a 'coachman' for the evenings. My husband [he steals a side look at her] brought home some beauties yesterday evening."

"Lucky fellow!"

She returns the book. There is a tone in his voice as he says this that jars on her, sensitive as she is to every inflection of a voice, with an intuition that is almost second sight. She gathers up her shawl,—she has a cream-colored woollen gown on, and her skin looks duskily foreign by contrast. She is on her feet before he can regain his, and says, with a cool little bend of her head: "Good afternoon, I wish you a full basket!"

Before he can raise his cap she is down the slope, gliding with easy steps that have a strange grace, and then springing lightly from stone to stone across the stream. He feels small, snubbed someway; and he sits down on the spot where she sat, and lighting his pipe says, "Check!"

MRS. R. H. TYACKE

From *How I Shot My Bears; or Two Years' Life in Kullu and Lahoul*

London: Sampson, Low, Marston, 1893. 16–21.

CHAPTER III

The variety of game in Kullu[1] *— Our bag for one year—Small game scarce— The reasons why—Kullu's reputation as a woodcock ground— Why the cock diminish—How they could be preserved—Few snipe or duck—A suggestion for the Kullu duck-shooters.*

As may well be imagined in a country of altitudes varying from two thousand to twenty-two thousand feet above the sea, and uninhabited above nine thousand feet, there is plenty of room for sport. The game to be found in Kullu is as follows: Panther, bear (both red and black), ibex, serow, burrhel, barking deer, gooral, ounce or snow-leopard, oorial and musk-deer; of pheasants, the cheer, kalij, koklas, argus, manal; of partridge, the black, wood and chikor; also, duck, snipe, and woodcock.

1. Kullu is an area in Northwestern India about sixty miles north of Simla. *Ed.*

Our bag for one year was as follows: pheasants, 137; chikor, 321; cock, 49; snipe, 9; duck, 3; barking deer, 7; goral, 3; black bears, 6; red bears, 8; and musk-deer, 3; and this might have been considerably increased, had we cared to go in for slaughter.

With regard to some of the head, it is not more than would be shot in good coverts at home in one day. But consider the joy of shooting in these lovely mountains, in a perfect climate, where, for sporting purposes, the whole place belongs to you; where you take out no licence, pay no keepers; where the birds are *bonâ fide* wild ones, and take a lot of shooting; where you generally carry a rifle in addition to a gun, and run the chance of knocking over a bear or a panther, as well as a pheasant. All this can only be really understood and appreciated by those who have tried it.

Much is heard of the scarcity of small game in Kullu at the present time, compared to what it was a few years back, and often the European residents said to us, after we had had a good day, half in jest and half in earnest: "Why, you'll leave us nothing to shoot!" A moment's consideration, however, will convince any one, that legitimate shooting, at birds fairly on the wing, and during the season only, would tend rather to improve than to deteriorate the stock, especially in the case of *chikor,* the cock of which, when the coverts are too near together and the birds too thick, fight incessantly and *à outrance.*

But it is not difficult to account for the scarcity of game, when one takes into account the manifold enemies the poor birds have to contend with. In the first place, throughout the valley there are literally thousands of *zemidars* (small farmers) to whom are granted licences to carry a gun, nominally for the protection of their own crops from bears and birds, and their flocks from bears and panthers; but, actually, for the destruction of small game. Every evening hundreds of pheasants are potted in the trees, and scores of *chikor* are slaughtered as they sit huddled together on a rock in the cold mornings. Immense quantities are destroyed in nets, caught in traps, or shot, as they are feeding along a narrow line of corn carefully laid down in a likely spot, and watched by a concealed sportsman (?). Then, during the breeding season, numbers of eggs are taken either to be eaten or to be wantonly destroyed. The birds are captured, especially *chikor,* and sold in the different bazaars, where they are purchased for fighting purposes, to amuse fat and lazy natives, who delight in watching the poor creatures maim each other, though they would rather give up their dearest relative than fight themselves. Besides this, I regret to say, that there are some European residents in the valley, who either provide the natives with powder and shot to go and shoot for them, or else buy the birds when shot. In addition to all this, there are the birds' natural enemies, which abound—the fox, jackal, stoat, weasel, hawk, and kite. With such a host to contend against, is it surprising that the game of Kullu is diminishing? But, for all those evils, except the last named, which presents difficulties, there are remedies to be found. In the first place, licences should be granted with a more sparing hand. They are neither required, nor are they used for the ostensible purpose for which they are taken out. The price also of the licence, now only fourpence halfpenny, might be raised. With regard to the employment of natives by residents to shoot for them, the remedy is in the hands of the latter. Finally, practical measures might be taken to suppress poaching in country more poached, I believe, than any other in India.

Kullu is one of the very few places in India having a reputation for woodcock shooting. But during our first year in Kullu, D., shooting over every likely place, and bagging every bird he saw, only shot forty-nine. This was considered a good bag. But in Albania he had shot many more in one day! In years gone by in Kullu, ten or twelve couple a day was considered a good bag. That would now be thought a fair bag for a whole season. The birds have been getting less and less, and the residents, taking it for granted that the woodcock were birds of passage, have accounted for it by the difference in the severity of the different winters. If they find few birds, they argue that they have not been driven down by the snow. D., however, is strong on a theory to account for the diminution of the cock. Every likely place is walked over almost daily, and every sahib tries to get woodcock, with the result that ninety per cent. of the birds which come down the valley are shot. Thus each year there are fewer left to breed from, and if some stringent measures are not taken, Kullu will soon know them no more. Now, as an object for sport, a woodcock can hold his own against any game-bird; for among trees he is a most difficult bird to shoot, and as a table delicacy he is unrivalled. In very few places in India are they to be found at all; and it would be a thousand pities if, in any one of these places, he were to become extinct. In Kullu it would be an easy matter to save them. As they are not exactly the kind of bird to give many chances for a pot shot, and as powder and shot are too expensive articles to be wasted on the risk of shooting a bird on the wing, the cock enjoy immunity at the hands of the natives. Kullu is too far distant from a railway to suffer from an influx of winter sportsmen, and, therefore, there remains only, practically, the very few European residents, including the assistant-commissioner, forest officer, etc., to account for the cock. Should these few agree among themselves for a close period, I am convinced that Kullu would, in time, regain its old prestige as a ground for cock, and that the residents would be amply rewarded.

As regards snipe, I may mention that there are none in Kullu, except the solitary snipe. A good bag of these is twenty during the season. Duck are occasionally to be got as they pass up and down the river, to and from India and the Central Asian lakes, where they breed. The river, as it passes through Kullu, is too rapid to permit of their resting, which accounts for their being so seldom shot; but a Mr. D——, one of the residents, has now constructed a couple of ponds close to the river, and between it and his house, and the ducks settle in large quantities, and he is able to keep himself and his friends supplied during the season. If other ponds were made, above and below, there would doubtless soon be good duck shooting in the country. The land in the immediate vicinity of the river is all waste land, so that it is merely a case of flooding. I commend the suggestion to those who live in Kullu.

ISABEL SAVORY

From *A Sportswoman in India: Personal Adventures and Experiences of Travel in Known and Unknown India*

London: Hutchinson, 1900. 255–67.

CHAPTER VIII

Tiger-Shooting

. . . Such, then, is the Deccan. And it is these highlands of India which are specially connected in the mind with tigers and tiger-shooting—a theme which, I venture to hope, is not, from a woman's point of view, yet worn threadbare.

The subject is not treated here scientifically, but only as it struck a well-known Mem-sahib who has taken part in almost every variation of sport in India. It is simpler to use her own words, and I can vouch for the truth of them, at the same time gently reminding the unbelieving critic that the wildest fiction never yet eclipsed fact.

We left Bangalore one day in the middle of last April, J. and myself, in answer to a wire from Captain F. at Secunderabad, "*Arrangements for shoot complete,*" which meant getting leave from the forest authorities, police authorities, and a thousand-and-one minor details.

From Secunderabad a night journey got us to Warungal station at two in the morning. We spent the rest of the night uncomfortably in the waiting-room, and as soon as it grew light were only too glad to set off. I would impress upon every woman following our example the necessity of taking every precaution against the heat. Not only wear a large *solá topi,*[1] but have a spine pad sewn inside the coat, which should be of thin green *shikar*[2] material. I had a second pad hooked on outside. I often kept a wet rag on my head, inside my pith helmet; and I wore dogskin gloves, minus half the fingers, which enabled one to hold the burning barrels. The temperature was 104° in the shade in our tents, and later on 115°.

Our caravan really formed a most imposing train as we set off from Warungal station. Fifty-one pack-bullocks with panniers carried one hundred and sixty pounds each, which consisted of guns, ammunition, tents, beds, chairs, table, clothes, food and drink enough to last the three of us for eight weeks, corn for our ponies and the ponies of our two head *shikaris,*[3] filters, cash-box, etc., etc. Our own luggage had gone straight through from Bangalore to Warungal with our boy. It was twenty-six maunds over weight—that is, two thousand and eighty pounds! It blocked up the platform and alarmed the guard considerably.

Our whole party consisted of our three selves, our own boy for each of us, a *syce*[4] for every pony, a cook, a *mati* (or scullery-boy), a *peon* for supplies, letters, etc., ten *shikaris,* and four bullock-men to look after the bullocks. So we formed quite a camp. When on the march, we started off our fifty-one pack-bullocks at three o'clock in the morning, following ourselves at six o'clock, marching from fifteen to twenty miles a day. According to this plan, bullocks and all of us reached the new camp much about the same time; the tents were all put up; and we avoided being out in the hottest time—from twelve to four o'clock.

Up to our third camp out of Warungal we did nothing at all; we were unlucky, for at all three places we were, through some mistake, preceded by a party of the 19th Hussars, who had left Secunderabad a fortnight before. We sent on to them, and they arranged to branch off to the left, so that our next camp was on unbeaten ground.

1. A lightweight pith helmet. *Ed.*
2. Hunting. *Ed.*
3. Big-game hunters. *Ed.*
4. Attendant. *Ed.*

It *was* hot on the march. I made my *syce* carry a large kettle of cold tea or coffee wherewith to refresh myself, and J. and Captain F. supplied themselves also with something cold. The *syces* carried our guns, too, after the first day, when we saw a lot of jungle-fowl and a splendid peacock, which we would fain have shot, for they are excellent eating! Since then we stalked several when we got into camp, but they were too cunning.

Every day, as soon as the bullocks were unloaded, they were driven down to water, and there they *wallowed,* covering themselves with mud, and often only showing just their noses above the mud and water. Whenever the camp was in a likely place the *shikaris* tied up bullocks for the tigers to kill the same evening, and we went and saw what had happened the next morning. For the first two or three marches, as I said, we had no luck, and went on at once, instead of staying in one camp a week or so, as we did later on.

Our marches were all through jungle, sometimes really thick with fine trees, occasionally rough scrub and steep, rocky hills. The track was always rough and very stony, a mere path, and in many places would have been quite impossible for the roughest bullock-cart. We rode all of it at a walk, and the *syces* followed on foot.

At last we had *khubr* (news) of a tigress and two large cubs; and, full of elation, having reached the camp, six bullocks were tied up that same evening.

Next morning we started about half-past six and went out to see what had happened. We rode, two *shikaris* walking with us, till we were about half a mile from the tie-up; then, dismounting, we left the ponies with the *syces,* and crept with infinite caution up to the spot, for if the tiger has killed the bullock, he generally only drags the body a few hundred yards, and having hidden it, lies down somewhere within reach. Of course, it seems cruel to the unfortunate bullock; but, as a matter of fact, if you kill the tiger in this way, you save the lives of a number of other bullocks, for a cattle-killing tiger devours an enormous number in a year, and, in occasional cases, may take to killing men too.

Besides, how else is a tiger to be found at all? Roaming the countryside and hunting all night, they cover an enormous range of ground, and in a wild, rough scrub and jungle country, extending for hundreds of miles, without any clue to the tiger's sleeping-place during the day, one might beat perhaps for weeks and weeks, and see nothing at all.

Judged by the standard of the greatest good to the greatest number, the laws of humanity justify the working of a tiger shoot, to my mind.

Bullocks are tied up in the most likely places—always near water. The tiger, delighting in thick cover near streams, visiting the spot on his nightly beat, kills the bullock, drags the body away a few hundred yards, and hides it under a bush, or somewhere where the vultures will not see it. He makes a large meal at once, drinks at the stream, and then lies down for twelve hours or so in cool shade somewhere near at hand. If undisturbed he will sleep during the day, and returning to the carcase at night, continue his meal. One bullock will last him three or four nights.

Therefore, upon visiting cautiously in the early morning the tie-up, and finding that the bullock has been killed and dragged off, the odds are greatly in favour of the tiger's being somewhere close at hand. He is, so to speak, *located.*

And now it is worth while having a beat. And here a really good *shikari* is absolutely necessary—a first-rate man, who knows all the ground, understands exactly the right places to beat, and how to beat them, and where to post his guns.

The extraordinary, intuitive knowledge which a few *shikaris* possess, makes it almost a dead certainty as to which path a tiger will come along in a beat, and has made sportsmen complain that tiger-shooting is a well-planned, preconceived, cut-and-dried *battue.*[5] And as for danger! I have heard it compared with shooting a mad dog from the top of an omnibus. Read the rest of the chapter.

On the morning of which I speak we crept up to the first bullock and found it still unharmed; but we could track plainly where one of the tiger cubs (they were nearly full-grown) had walked up to it, and right round it, but had not seen fit to kill. We sent the reprieved bullock to water and back to camp, and crept on about a mile and a half to the next.

It was gone! We stole up to the stake. The rope was broken off short, and in the dust, close to the stake, was an enormous scratch-mark, with all the marks of the nails imprinted sharply, exactly like a gigantic cat at home might make. There was a broad trail where the body had been dragged off.

As the tiger might be lying down close to the body, it is better never to follow this up. No one who values his life should walk up to a tiger. Every one has heard how tigers which have been mortally wounded have struck down men even in their dying agonies, and almost every year some fatal accident occurs to add to the warnings, but they are still unheeded. Other animals may be dodged and avoided; but if a tiger *does* charge home, death is nearly inevitable.

Leaving two *shikaris* to arrange the general idea of the beat, we went

5. A hunt in which the woods are beaten to flush out game. *Ed.*

back to camp, four miles off. While we had breakfast, and coolies were collected for the beat, a concentrated excitement seemed in the very air.

It is best not to begin to beat till eleven or twelve o'clock; by that time the tiger is probably asleep, and is less likely to be disturbed too soon. Even should this happen, the sun and the rocks are by that time so scorchingly hot, that he is very reluctant to leave his cool sanctuary. From fifty to a hundred coolies are wanted for a beat; on this occasion we had eighty. Their pay was one rupee to eight coolies—that is barely twopence each; but it was doubled if a tiger was shot. As Furreed, the head *shikari,* remarked, "it takes very clever business" to arrange skilfully a good beat.

We beat a long nullah (a valley) on that first day, two miles long and half a mile wide. Most of the coolies and *shikaris* were sent to one end, the guns were posted at the other; but besides this, stops had to be placed all along the sides, at any point where the tiger is likely to break out. The coolies who act as stops all climb up into trees, and if they see the tiger coming their way with the idea of breaking out, they snap a twig or two, which invariably turns him back at once.

Besides this, we had brought with us about ten rolls of broad, white cloth stuff, each piece a yard wide and twenty yards long, and called "stopping cloth." This was fixed on to trees or bushes along the edge of the beat, at places where the tiger was known by the *shikaris* to be particularly likely to break out—all this with the same idea of keeping him in the desired direction of the guns, of course.

We three guns were posted in trees, seated each in a *machân,* which is, as a rule, a stout, hard, stuffed leather cushion, with straps and buckles, or else ropes, on the four corners, by means of which it is fastened up in the branches, about fifteen feet from the ground. The *machân* is reached by a little, rough ladder; and having climbed up into your perch, your gunbearer with your second gun standing or sitting on some branch near you, your *châgul* (leather water-bottle) slung below, you sit, still as death, perhaps for as long as two hours, while the beat goes on.

No. 1 place was the likeliest and best, and No. 2 second best. We changed numbers every day; and so astute are the *shikaris,* that out of seven tigers six came past No. 1.

The first morning, much to our disappointment, the tigress was never found at all. But, partly because it was the first time and all so new, it was *most* exciting; in fact, the excitement was so intense that in my heart of hearts I felt almost glad when it was all over. The *shikaris* did not think the tigress had gone far.

The next morning we had another beat, and though J. saw the tigress, he did not get a shot at her. She came back in the night and ate more of the dead body, and the *shikaris* said she was in some long, thick elephant-grass beyond either of the two preceding beats. We were up in *machâns* on one side, and by-and-by could hear her move. They set alight to one end. It did not burn very well; but after a bit, the fire and the yells of the coolies, and the blank cartridges which they kept letting off, made her move at last. She sprang up with a loud roar; but instead of coming out near any of the guns, as we hoped, she rushed off down through the grass right-handed, and I only saw her striped back for one second, only that and her tail, about sixty yards off in the grass, not enough to fire. She went right off. For more than ten miles the *shikaris* tracked her, still travelling on, and then they gave it up.

Leaving this camp, we reached that day a place called Tarwai, where we met with the first actual and sad signs of the famine, which was prevalent. We had passed across waste after waste, which should have been rice, paddy, and other grain, but now lay all uncultivated, owing to the *non est* of water.

In all the villages so far they had had rice left from last year, sufficient for a miserable pittance for this year; but at Tarwai the wailing, walking skeletons crawled up to us—heart-stirring spectacles! They clamoured for rice—with their shrunken little ones in their arms—and of course we spared them all we could, and gave them a little money to send and buy more. But it was terribly little we could do for the starving, hollow-eyed, weary suppliants, who, after we had distributed the rice, clustered over the ground where it had lain, like ants by spilled honey, searching for another grain.

The heat throughout this time could not be pictured at all by any one at home. It cannot be realised by those who have not felt it, and it gives the ordinary Britisher no adequate idea whatever to read that it was 104° in the shade. When there was any wind at all, it was generally a sort of burning, furnace-like blast. Of course, we streamed with perspiration all day and most of the night. The only cool moments were for an hour just before dawn. Captain F. and J. always slept outside, with nothing over them but their pyjama suits. The rocks would grow so hot in the sun that we could feel them all burning to our feet through boots. However, it was a healthy, dry heat, which was a blessing, and none of us were the least ill.

At last, after several days of inaction, we met with our first real excitement, and at the same time I shot my first tiger. He was well known, for three gunners who were in the same place last year had three beats after him—ineffectual beats. He was fond of killing bears—a very uncommon thing; and the villagers told us he had been seen to climb a tree after a bear which scrambled up it to get out of his clutches. He managed to reach the bear, and attacked him. Both fell out of the tree on to the ground, when the tiger promptly killed the bear.

This we did not at the time believe; it is most rare for a tiger to climb trees—in fact, almost unheard of. But it proved to be true. He was what they call a very *bobbery* (pugnacious) tiger, the first news we heard of him being that he had killed and eaten another bear six miles from our camp. We went out and had a beat, and found the remains of poor Bruin; the tiger was in the beat, but he broke out through the stops on one side without being fired at. However, the following night he killed one of our tie-ups, close to camp, and he made off it his last meal in this world.

The next morning found all three of us up in our respective *machâns.* Captain F. and myself were about eighty yards apart. The tree which he was in was not quite upright; it leaned slightly, and it had several branches at intervals up the trunk, the *machân* being fastened upon one of them. I sat on my little seat with feelings so intense and so mixed that they were absolutely painful; the strain and excitement great enough to suggest a blessed relief when all should be over. Occasionally Captain F. and I looked across at each other, as we sat, keenly alive to every leaf stirring in the dry scrub, while down upon the burning sands and rocks blazed the relentless sun.

Suddenly there was a sound—monkeys trooping through the jungle, high in the trees, grasping the pliant branches and shaking them with rage! A tiger *must* be in the neighbourhood. Another second—the jungle-grass waved and crackled, and out into the open emerged and advanced slowly—a picture of fearful beauty. A tiger seen in the Zoo gives no faint idea of what one of his species is, seen under its proper conditions. Beasts in captivity are under-fed, and have no muscle; but here before us was a specimen who had always "done himself well," was fit as a prize-fighter, every square inch of him developed to perfection. On he came, his cruel eyes lazily blinking in the sun. His long, slouching walk, suggestive of such latent strength, betrayed the vast muscle working firmly through the loose, glossy skin, which was clear red and white, with its double stripes, and the W mark on the head.

The sight of such consummate power, as he swung majestically along, licking his lips and his moustache after his feed, was one of those things not soon to be forgotten, and while it had a bracing effect on the nerves, at the same time struck rather a chilling sensation.

The tiger moved on. I sat with my rifle at full cock, but he went straight up to Captain F.'s tree, looked up, saw him, gave a fierce growl, and then stood still about ten yards off. A loud detonation followed; but Captain F. must have made a poor shot—he hit him behind, much too far back, the bullet going down almost to his hock. The tiger looked magnificent still—he stood on a little knoll, lashing his tail and looking vindictively up into the tree.

At one and the same moment Captain F. and myself fired; somehow or other we both missed him. This was rather too much. In one moment, like a flash, the tiger darted round, deliberately galloped at the tree, sprang about half-way up into its lowest branches, and, assisted by the natural oblique inclination of the trunk, swarmed up to the *machân* as quickly and easily as a cat. It was a terrible moment, one of those of which we pray that they may be few and far between; most of us can lay a finger on two or three such moments in our lives.

Poor Captain F., both barrels fired, and helpless, had in desperation sprung to his feet, his hand on the side of the *machân*. Either the tiger's teeth or his claws tore his finger all down the back of it to the bone, but the whole action took place with such lightning speed that it was hard to say which.

In my mind's eye, as the great body flew up the tree, I pictured a ghastly struggle, a heavy fall, and a sickening death; at the same instant a moment's intuition suggested a difficult but not impossible shot at the tiger's back as he clasped the tree. With my last barrel I fired. There was no time for a long and steady aim; but as the smoke cleared away—what relief!—the tiger had dropped to the ground. With nine lives—cat-like—he was not dead; he walked off and disappeared.

We dared not look for him then and there, dying and savage in such rough and dangerous cover; but next morning we found him cold and stiff. He was a magnificent male, very large and heavy, enormous paws and moustache—a splendid "great cat."

FIGURE 45 Isabella Bird

ISABELLA BIRD

From *Six Months in the Sandwich Islands: Among Hawai'i's Palm Groves, Coral Reefs, and Volcanoes*

1875. London: John Murray, 1890. 52–54.

LETTER V

. . . When I have learned more about the Hawaiian volcanoes, I shall tell you more of their phenomena, but to-night I shall only write to you my first impressions of what we actually saw on this January 31st. My highest expectations have been infinitely exceeded, and I can hardly write soberly after such a spectacle, especially while through the open door I see the fiery clouds of vapour from the pit rolling up into a sky, glowing as if itself on fire. . . .

The first descent down the terminal wall of the crater is very precipitous, but it and the slope which extends to the second descent are thickly covered with *ohias, ohelos* (a species of whortleberry), sadlerias, polypodiums, silver grass, and a great variety of bulbous plants, many of which bore clusters of berries of a brilliant turquoise blue. The "beyond" looked terrible. I could not help clinging to these vestiges of the kindlier mood of nature in which she sought to cover the horrors she had wrought. The next descent is over rough blocks and ridges of broken lava, and appears to form part of a break which extends irregularly round the whole crater, and which probably marks a tremendous subsidence of its floor. Here the last apparent vegetation was left behind, and the familiar earth. We were in a new region of blackness and awful desolation, the accustomed sights and sounds of nature all gone. Terraces, cliffs, lakes, ridges, rivers, mountain sides, whirlpools, chasms of lava surrounded us, solid, black, and shining, as if vitrified, or an ashen grey, stained yellow with sulphur here and there, or white with alum. The lava was fissured and upheaved everywhere by earthquakes, hot underneath, and emitting a hot breath.

After more than an hour of very difficult climbing we reached the lowest level of the crater, pretty nearly a mile across, presenting from above the appearance of a sea at rest, but on crossing it we found it to be an expanse of waves and convolutions of ashy-coloured lava, with great cracks filled up with black, iridescent rolls of lava, only a few weeks old. Parts of it are very rough and ridgy, jammed together like field ice, or compacted by rolls of lava which may have swelled up from beneath, but the largest part of the area presents the appearance of huge coiled hawser, the ropy formation of the lava rendering the illusion almost perfect. These are riven by deep cracks which emit hot, sulphurous vapours. Strange to say, in one of these, deep down in that black and awful region, three slender metamorphosed ferns were growing, exquisite forms, the fragile heralds of the great forest of vegetation, which probably in coming years will clothe this pit with beauty. On our right there was a precipitous ledge, and a recent flow of lava had poured over it, cooling as it fell into columnar shapes as symmetrical as those of Staffa.[6] It took us a full hour to cross this deep depression, and as long to master a steep, hot ascent of about 400 feet, formed by a recent lava-flow from Hale-mau-mau into the basin [see figure 46]. This lava hill is an extraordinary sight—a flood of molten stone, solidifying as it ran down the declivity, forming arrested waves, streams, eddies, gigantic convolutions, forms of snakes, stems of trees, gnarled roots, crooked water-pipes, all involved and contorted on a gigantic scale, a wilderness of force and dread.

6. An island off the Scottish coast, one of the Inner Hebrides. *Ed.*

Over one steeper place the lava had run in a fiery cascade about 100 feet wide. Some had reached the ground, some had been arrested midway, but all had taken the aspect of stems and trees. In some of the crevices I picked up a quantity of very curious filamentose lava, known as "Pélé's hair."[7] It resembles coarse spun glass, and is of a greenish or yellowish-brown colour. In many places the whole surface of the lava is covered with this substance seen through a glazed medium. During eruptions, when fire-fountains play to a great height, and drops of lava are thrown in all directions, the wind spins them out in clear green or yellow threads two or three feet long, which catch and adhere to projecting points.

As we ascended, the flow became hotter under our feet, as well as more porous and glistening. It was so hot that a shower of rain hissed as it fell upon it. The crust became increasingly insecure, and necessitated our walking in single file with the guide in front, to test the security of the footing. I fell through several times, and always into holes full of sulphurous steam, so malignantly acid that my strong, dog-skin gloves were burned through as I raised myself on my hands.

We had followed a lava-flow for thirty miles up to the crater's brink, and now we had toiled over recent lava for three hours, and by all calculation were close to the pit, yet there was no smoke or sign of fire, and I felt sure that the volcano had died out for once for our especial disappointment. Indeed, I had been making up my mind for disappointment since we left the crater-house, in consequence of reading seven different accounts, in which language was exhausted in describing Kilauea.

Suddenly, just above, and in front of us, gory drops were tossed in air, and springing forwards we stood on the brink of Hale-mau-mau, which was about 35 feet below us. I think we all screamed, I know we all wept, but we were speechless, for a new glory and terror had been added to the earth. It is the most unutterable of wonderful things. The words of common speech are quite useless. It is unimaginable, indescribable, a sight to remember for ever, a sight which at once took possession of every faculty of sense and soul, removing one altogether out of the range of ordinary life. Here was the real "bottomless pit"—the "fire which is not quenched"—"the place of hell"—"the lake which burneth with fire and brimstone"—the "everlasting burnings"—the fiery sea whose waves are never weary. There were groanings, rumblings, and detonations, rushings, hissings, and splashings, and

7. The Hawaiian goddess of volcanoes. *Ed.*

FIGURE 46 *Halemaumau, Jan. 31,* illustration from Isabella Bird, *Six Months in the Sandwich Islands,* p. 252

the crashing sound of breakers on the coast, but it was the surging of fiery waves upon a fiery shore. But what can I write! Such words as jets, fountains, waves, spray, convey some idea of order and regularity, but here there was none. The inner lake, while we stood there, formed a sort of crater within itself, the whole lava sea rose about three feet, a blowing cone about eight feet high was formed, it was never the same two minutes together. And what we saw had no existence a month ago, and probably will be changed in every essential feature a month hence.

ISABELLA L. BIRD

From *A Lady's Life in the Rocky Mountains*

1879. Reprint, London: Folio Society, 1988. 59–71.

[pp. 59–71]

LETTER VII

ESTES PARK, COLORADO, *October*

As this account of the ascent of Long's Peak could not be written at the time, I am much disinclined to write it, especially as no sort of description within my powers could enable another to realise the glorious sublimity, the majestic solitude, and the unspeakable awfulness and fascination of the scenes in which I spent Monday, Tuesday, and Wednesday.

Long's Peak, 14,700 feet high, blocks up one end of Estes Park, and dwarfs all the surrounding mountains. From it on this side rise, snow-born, the bright St Vrain, and the Big and Little Thompson. By sunlight or moonlight its splintered grey crest is the one object which, in spite of wapiti[1] and bighorn, skunk and grizzly, unfailingly arrests the eye. From it come all storms of snow and winds, and the forked lightnings play round its head like a glory. It is one of the noblest of mountains, but in one's imagination it grows to be much more than a mountain. It becomes invested with a personality. In its caverns and abysses one comes to fancy that it generates and chains the strong winds, to let them loose in its fury. The thunder becomes its voice, and the lightnings do it homage. Other summits blush under the morning kiss of the sun, and turn pale the next moment; but it detains the first sunlight and holds it round its head for an hour at least, till it pleases to change from rosy red to deep blue; and the sunset, as if spell-bound, lingers latest on its crest. The soft winds which hardly rustle the pine needles down here are raging rudely up there round its motionless summit. The mark of fire is upon it; and though it has passed into a grim repose, it tells of fire and upheaval as truly, though not as eloquently, as the living volcanoes of Hawaii. Here under its shadow one learns how naturally nature worship, and the propitiation of the forces of nature arose in minds which had no better light.

1. Elk. *Ed.*

Long's Peak, 'the American Matterhorn,' as some call it, was ascended five years ago for the first time. I thought I should like to attempt it, but up to Monday, when Evans left for Denver, cold water was thrown upon the project. It was too late in the season, the winds were likely to be strong, etc.; but just before leaving, Evans said that the weather was looking more settled, and if I did not get farther than the timber line it would be worth going. Soon after he left, 'Mountain Jim' came in, and said he would go up as guide, and the two youths who rode here with me from Longmount and I caught at the proposal. Mrs Edwards at once baked bread for three days, steaks were cut from the steer which hangs up conveniently, and tea, sugar, and butter were benevolently added. Our picnic was not to be a luxurious or 'well-found' one, for, in order to avoid the expense of a pack mule, we limited our luggage to what our saddle horses could carry. Behind my saddle I carried three pair of camping blankets and a quilt, which reached to my shoulders. My own boots were so much worn that it was painful to walk, even about the park, in them, so Evans had lent me a pair of his hunting boots, which hung to the horn of my saddle. The horses of the two young men were equally loaded, for we had to prepare for many degrees of frost. 'Jim' was shocking figure; he had on an old pair of high boots, with a baggy pair of old trousers made of deer hide, held on by an old scarf tucked into them; a leather shirt, with three or four ragged unbuttoned waistcoats over it; an old smashed wideawake, from under which his tawny, neglected ringlets hung; and with his one eye, his one long spur, his knife in his belt, his revolver in his waistcoat pocket, his saddle covered with an old beaver-skin, from which the paws hung down; his camping blankets behind him, his rifle laid across the saddle in front of him, and his axe, canteen, and other gear hanging to the horn, he was as awful looking a ruffian as one could see. By way of contrast he rode a small Arab mare, of exquisite beauty, skittish, high-spirited, gentle, but altogether too light for him, and he fretted her incessantly to make her display herself.

Heavily loaded as all our horses were, 'Jim' started over the half-mile of level grass at a hand-gallop, and then throwing his mare on her haunches, pulled up alongside of me, and with a grace of manner which soon made me forget his appearance, entered into a conversation which lasted for more than three hours, in spite of the manifold checks of fording streams, single file, abrupt ascents and descents, and other incidents of mountain travel. The ride was one series of glories and surprises, of 'park' and glade, of lake and stream, of mountains on mountains, culminating in the rent pinnacles of Long's Peak, which looked yet grander and ghastlier as we crossed an attendant mountain 11,000 feet high. The slanting sun added fresh beauty every hour. There were dark pines against a lemon sky, grey peaks reddening and etherealising, gorges of deep and infinite blue, floods of golden glory pouring through canyons of enormous depth, an atmosphere of absolute purity, an occasional foreground of cottonwood and aspen flaunting in red and gold to intensify the blue gloom of the pines, the trickle and murmur of streams fringed with icicles, the strange *sough* of gusts moving among the pine tops—sights and sounds not of the lower earth, but of the solitary, beast-haunted, frozen upper altitudes. From the dry, buff grass of Estes Park we turned off up a trail on the side of a pine-hung gorge, up a steep pine-clothed hill, down to a small valley, rich in fine, sun-cured hay about eighteen inches high, and enclosed by high mountains whose deepest hollow contains a lily-covered lake, fitly named 'The Lake of the Lilies.' Ah, how magical its beauty was, as it slept in silence, while *there* the dark pines were mirrored motionless in its pale gold, and *here* the great white lily cups and dark green leaves rested on amethyst-coloured water!

From this we ascended into the purple gloom of great pine forests which clothe the skirts of the mountains up to a height of about 11,000 feet, and from their chill and solitary depths we had glimpses of golden atmosphere and rose-lit summits, not of 'the land very far off,' but of the land nearer now in all its grandeur, gaining in sublimity by nearness—glimpses, too, through a broken vista of purple gorges, of the illimitable Plains lying idealised in the late sunlight, their baked, brown expanse transfigured into the likeness of a sunset sea rolling infinitely in waves of misty gold.

We rode upwards through the gloom on a steep trail blazed through the forest, all my intellect concentrated on avoiding being dragged off my horse by impending branches, or having the blankets badly torn, as those of my companions were, by sharp dead limbs, between which there was hardly room to pass—the horses breathless, and requiring to stop every few yards, though their riders, except myself, were afoot. The gloom of the dense, ancient, silent forest is to me awe-inspiring. On such an evening it is soundless, except for the branches creaking in the soft wind, the frequent snap of decayed timber, and a murmur in the pine tops as of a not distant waterfall, all tending to produce *eeriness* and a sadness 'hardly akin to pain.' There no lumberer's axe has ever rung. The trees die when they have attained their prime, and stand there, dead and bare, till the fierce mountain winds lay them prostrate. The pines grew smaller and more sparse as we ascended, and the last stragglers wore a tortured, warring look. The timber line was passed, but yet a little higher a slope of mountain meadow dipped to the south-west towards a bright stream trickling under ice and icicles, and there a grove of the beautiful silver spruce marked our camping ground. The trees were in miniature, but so exquisitely arranged that one might well ask what artist's hand had planted them, scattering them here, clumping them there, and training their slim spires towards heaven. Hereafter, when I call up memories of the glorious, the view from this camping ground will come up. Looking east, gorges opened to the distant Plains, then fading into purple grey. Mountains with pine-clothed skirts rose in ranges, or, solitary, uplifted their grey summits, while close behind, but nearly 3000 feet above us, towered the bald white crest of Long's Peak, its huge precipices red with the light of a sun long lost to our eyes. Close to us, in the caverned side of the Peak, was snow that, owing to its position, is eternal. Soon the afterglow came on, and before it faded a big half-moon hung out of the heavens, shining through the silver blue foliage of the pines on the frigid background of snow, and turning the whole into fairyland. A courageous Denver artist attempted the ascent just before I arrived, but, after camping out at the timber line for a week, was foiled by the perpetual storms, and was driven down again, leaving some very valuable apparatus about 3000 feet from the summit.

Unsaddling and picketing the horses securely, making the beds of pine shoots, and dragging up logs for fuel, warmed us all. 'Jim' built up a great fire, and before long we were all sitting round it at supper. It didn't matter much that we had to drink our tea out of the battered meat-tins in which it was boiled, and eat strips of beef reeking with pine smoke without plates or forks.

'Treat Jim as a gentleman and you'll find him one,' I had been told; and though his manner was certainly bolder and freer than that of gentlemen generally, no imaginary fault could be found. He was very agreeable as a man of culture as well as a child of nature; the desperado was altogether out of sight. He was very courteous and even kind to me, which was fortunate, as the young men had little idea of showing even ordinary civilities. That night I made the acquaintance of his dog 'Ring,' said to be the best hunting-dog in Colorado, with the body and legs of a collie, but a head approaching that of a mastiff, a noble face with a wistful human expression, and the most truthful eyes I ever saw in an animal. His master loves him if he loves anything, but in his savage moods ill-treats him. Ring's devotion never swerves, and his truthful eyes are rarely taken off his master's face. He is almost human in his intelligence, and, unless he is told to do so, he never takes notice of anyone but 'Jim.' In a tone as if speaking to a human being, his master, pointing to me, said, 'Ring, go to that lady, and don't leave her again tonight.' Ring at once came to me, looked into my face, laid his head on my shoulder, and then lay down beside me with his head on my lap, but never taking his eyes from 'Jim's' face.

The long shadows of the pines lay upon the frosted grass, an aurora leaped fitfully, and the moonlight, though intensely bright, was pale beside the red, leaping flames of our pine logs and their red glow on our gear, ourselves, and Ring's truthful face. One of the young men sang a Latin student's song and two negro melodies; the other, 'Sweet Spirit, Hear my Prayer.' 'Jim' sang one of Moore's[2] melodies in a singular falsetto, and all together sang 'The Star-spangled Banner' and 'The Red, White, and Blue.' Then 'Jim' recited a very clever poem of his own composition, and told some fearful Indian stories. A group of small silver spruces away from the fire was my sleeping-place. The artist who had been up there had so woven and interlaced their lower branches as to form a bower, affording at once shelter from the wind and a most agreeable privacy. It was thickly strewn with young pine shoots, and these, when covered with a blanket, with an inverted saddle for a pillow, made a luxurious bed. The mercury at 9 p.m. was 12 degrees below the freezing point. 'Jim,' after a last look at the horses, made a huge fire, and stretched himself out beside it, but Ring lay at my back to keep me warm. I could not sleep, but the night passed rapidly. I was anxious about the ascent, for gusts of ominous sound swept through the pines at intervals. Then wild animals howled, and Ring was perturbed in spirit about them. Then it was strange to see the notorious desperado, a red-handed man, sleeping as quietly as innocence sleeps. But, above all, it was exciting to lie there, with no better shelter than a bower of pines, on a mountain 11,000 feet high, in the very heart of the Rocky Range, under twelve degrees of frost, hearing sounds of wolves, with shivering stars looking through the fragrant canopy, with arrowy pines for bed-posts, and for a night lamp the red flames of a camp fire.

Day dawned long before the sun rose, pure and lemon-coloured. The rest were looking after the horses, when one of the students came running to tell me that I must come farther down the slope, for 'Jim' said he had never seen such a sunrise. From the chill, grey Peak above, from the everlasting snows, from the silvered pines, down through the mountain ranges with their depths of Tyrian purple, we looked to where the Plains lay cold, in blue grey, like a morning sea against a far horizon. Suddenly, as a dazzling streak at first, but enlarging rapidly into a dazzling sphere, the sun wheeled

2. Thomas Moore (1799–1852), an Irish poet famous for his songs and ballads. *Ed.*

above the grey line, a light and glory as when it was first created. 'Jim' involuntarily and reverently uncovered his head, and exclaimed, 'I believe there is a God!' I felt as if, Parsee-like, I must worship. The grey of the Plains changed to purple, the sky was all one rose-red flush, on which vermilion cloud-streaks rested; the ghastly peaks gleamed like rubies, the earth and heavens were new-created. Surely 'the Most High dwelleth not in temples made with hands'! For a full hour those Plains simulated the ocean, down to whose limitless expanse of purple, cliffs, rocks, and promontories swept down.

By 7 we had finished breakfast, and passed into the ghastlier solitudes above, I riding as far as what, rightly or wrongly, are called the 'Lava Beds,' an expanse of large and small boulders, with snow in their crevices. It was very cold; some water which we crossed was frozen hard enough to bear the horse. 'Jim' had advised me against taking any wraps, and my thin Hawaiian riding-dress, only fit for the tropics, was penetrated by the keen air. The rarefied atmosphere soon began to oppress our breathing, and I found that Evans's boots were so large that I had no foothold. Fortunately, before the real difficulty of the ascent began, we found, under a rock, a pair of small over-shoes, probably left by the Hayden[3] exploring expedition, which just lasted for the day. As we were leaping from rock to rock, 'Jim' said, 'I was thinking in the night about your travelling alone, and wondering where you carried your Derringer, for I could see no signs of it.' On my telling him that I travelled unarmed, he could hardly believe it, and adjured me to get a revolver at once.

On arriving at the 'Notch' (a literal gate of rock), we found ourselves absolutely on the knife-like ridge or backbone of Long's Peak, only a few feet wide, covered with colossal boulders and fragments, and on the other side shelving in one precipitous, snow-patched sweep of 3000 feet to a picturesque hollow, containing a lake of pure green water. Other lakes, hidden among dense pine woods, were farther off, while close above us rose the Peak, which, for about 500 feet, is a smooth, gaunt, inaccessible-looking pile of granite. Passing through the Notch, we looked along the nearly inaccessible side of the Peak, composed of boulders and débris of all shapes and sizes, through which appeared broad, smooth ribs of reddish-coloured granite, looking as if they upheld the towering rock-mass above. I usually dislike bird's-eye and panoramic views, but, though from a mountain, this was not one. Serrated ridges, not much lower than that on which we stood, rose, one beyond another, far as that pure atmosphere could carry the vi-

3. Ferdinand Hayden (1829–87), an American geologist and explorer of Yellowstone country and the Grand Tetons who led a number of definitive expeditions into the American West. *Ed.*

sion, broken into awful chasms deep with ice and snow, rising into pinnacles piercing the heavenly blue with their cold, barren grey, on, on for ever, till the most distant range upbore unsullied snow alone. There were fair lakes mirroring the dark pine woods, canyons dark and blue-black with unbroken expanses of pines, snow-slashed pinnacles, wintry heights frowning upon lovely parks, watered and wooded, lying in the lap of summer; North Park floating off into the blue distance, Middle Park closed till another season, the sunny slopes of Estes Park, and winding down among the mountains the snowy ridge of the Divide, whose bright waters seek both the Atlantic and Pacific Oceans. There, far below, links of diamonds showed where the Grand River takes its rise to seek the mysterious Colorado, with its still unsolved enigma, and lose itself in the waters of the Pacific; and nearer the snow-born Thompson bursts forth from the ice to begin its journey to the Gulf of Mexico. Nature, rioting in her grandest mood, exclaimed with voices of grandeur, solitude, sublimity, beauty, and infinity, 'Lord, what is man, that Thou art mindful of him? or the son of man, that Thou visitest him?' Never-to-be-forgotten glories they were, burnt in upon my memory by six succeeding hours of terror. You know I have no head and no ankles, and never ought to dream of mountaineering; and had I known that the ascent was a real mountaineering feat I should not have felt the slightest ambition to perform it. As it is, I am only humiliated by my success, for 'Jim' dragged me up, like a bale of goods, by sheer force of muscle. At the Notch the real business of the ascent began. 2000 feet of solid rock towered above us, 4000 feet of broken rock shelved precipitously below; smooth granite ribs, with barely foothold, stood out here and there; melted snow, refrozen several times, presented a more serious obstacle; many of the rocks were loose, and tumbled down when touched. To me it was a time of extreme terror. I was roped to 'Jim,' but it was of no use, my feet were paralysed and slipped on the bare rock, and he said it was useless to try to go that way, and we retraced our steps. I wanted to return to the Notch, knowing that my incompetence would detain the party, and one of the young men said almost plainly that a woman was a dangerous encumbrance, but the trapper replied shortly that if it were not to take a lady up he would not go up at all. He went on to explore, and reported that further progress on the correct line of ascent was blocked by ice; and then for two hours we descended, lowering ourselves by our hands from rock to rock along a boulder-strewn sweep of 4000 feet, patched with ice and snow, and perilous from rolling stones. My fatigue, giddiness, and pain from bruised ankles, and arms half pulled out of their sockets, were so great that I should never have gone half-way had not 'Jim,' *nolens volens,* dragged me along with a patience and skill, and withal a determination that I should ascend the Peak, which never failed. After descending about 2000 feet to avoid the ice, we got into a deep ravine with inaccessible sides, partly filled with ice and snow and partly with large and small fragments of rock, which were constantly giving way, rendering the footing very insecure. That part to me was two hours of painful and unwilling submission to the inevitable; of trembling, slipping, straining, of smooth ice appearing when it was least expected, and of weak entreaties to be left behind while the others went on. 'Jim' always said that there was no danger, that there was only a short bad bit ahead, and that I should go up even in he carried me!

Slipping, faltering, gasping from the exhausting toil in the rarefied air, with throbbing hearts and panting lungs, we reached the top of the gorge and squeezed ourselves between two gigantic fragments of rock by a passage called the 'Dog's Lift,' when I climbed on the shoulders of one man and then was hauled up. This introduced us by an abrupt turn round the south-west angle of the Peak to a narrow shelf of considerable length, rugged, uneven, and so overhung by the cliff in some places that it is necessary to crouch to pass at all. Above, the Peak looks nearly vertical for 400 feet; and below, the most tremendous precipice I have ever seen descends in one unbroken fall. This is usually considered the most dangerous part of the ascent, but it does not seem so to me, for such foothold as there is is secure, and one fancies that it is possible to hold on with the hands. But there, and on the final, and, to my thinking, the worst part of the climb, one slip, and a breathing, thinking, human being would lie 3000 feet below, a shapeless, bloody heap! Ring refused to traverse the Ledge, and remained at the 'Lift' howling piteously.

From thence the view is more magnificent even than that from the Notch. At the foot of the precipice below us lay a lovely lake, wood-embosomed, from or near which the bright St Vrain and other streams take their rise. I thought how their clear cold waters, growing turbid in the affluent flats, would heat under the tropic sun, and eventually form part of that great ocean river which renders our far-off islands habitable by impinging on their shores. Snowy ranges, one behind the other, extended to the distant horizon, folding in their wintry embrace the beauties of Middle Park. Pike's Peak, more than one hundred miles off, lifted that vast but shapeless summit which is the landmark of Southern Colorado. There were snow patches, snow slashes, snow abysses, snow forlorn and soiled-looking, snow pure and dazzling, snow glistening above the purple robe of pine worn by all the mountains; while away to the east, in limitless breadth, stretched the green-grey of the endless Plains. Giants everywhere reared their splintered crests. From thence, with a single sweep, the eye takes in a distance of 300 miles—that distance to the west, north, and south being made up of mountains 10, 11, 12, and 13,000 feet in height, dominated by Long's Peak, Gray's Peak, and Pike's Peak, all nearly the height of Mont Blanc! On the Plains we traced the rivers by their fringe of cottonwoods to the distant Platte, and between us and them lay glories of mountain, canyon, and lake, sleeping in depths of blue and purple most ravishing to the eye.

As we crept from the lodge round a horn of rock, I beheld what made me perfectly sick and dizzy to look at—the terminal Peak itself—a smooth, cracked face or wall of pink granite, as nearly perpendicular as anything could well be up which it was possible to climb, well deserving the name of the 'American Matterhorn.'[4]

Scaling, not climbing, is the correct term for this last ascent. It took one hour to accomplish 500 feet, pausing for breath every minute or two. The only foothold was in narrow cracks or on minute projections on the granite. To get a toe in these cracks, or here and there on a scarcely obvious projection, while crawling on hands and knees, all the while tortured with thirst and gasping and struggling for breath, this was the climb; but at last the Peak was won. A grand, well-defined mountain-top it is, a nearly level acre of boulders, with precipitous sides all round, the one we came up being the only accessible one.

It was not possible to remain long. One of the young men was seriously alarmed by bleeding from the lungs, and the intense dryness of the day and the rarefaction of the air, at a height of nearly 15,000 feet, made respiration very painful. There is always water on the Peak, but it was frozen as hard as a rock, and the sucking of ice and snow increases thirst. We all suffered severely from the want of water, and the gasping for breath made our mouths and tongues so dry that articulation was difficult, and the speech of all unnatural.

From the summit were seen in unrivalled combination all the views which had rejoiced our eyes during the ascent. It was something at last to stand upon the storm-rent crown of this lonely sentinel of the Rocky Range, on one of the mightiest of the vertebrae of the backbone of the North American continent, and to see the waters start for both oceans. Uplifted above love and hate and storms of passion, calm amidst the eternal silences, fanned by zephyrs and bathed in living blue, peace rested for that one bright day on the Peak, as if it were some region

4. Let no practical mountaineer be allured by my description into the ascent of Long's Peak. Truly terrible as it was to me, to a member of the Alpine Club it would not be a feat worth performing.

Where falls not rain, or hail, or any snow,
Or ever wind blows loudly.[5]

We placed our names, with the date of ascent, in a tin within a crevice, and descended to the Ledge, sitting on the smooth granite, getting our feet into cracks and against projections, and letting ourselves down by our hands, 'Jim' going before me, so that I might steady my feet against his powerful shoulders. I was no longer giddy, and faced the precipice of 3500 feet without a shiver. Repassing the Ledge and Lift, we accomplished the descent through 1500 feet of ice and snow, with many falls and bruises, but no worse mishap, and there separated, the young men taking the steepest but the most direct way to the Notch, with the intention of getting ready for the march home, and 'Jim' and I taking what he thought the safer route for me—a descent over boulders for 2000 feet, and then a tremendous ascent to the Notch. I had various falls, and once hung by my frock, which caught on a rock, and 'Jim' severed it with his hunting-knife, upon which I fell into a crevice full of soft snow. We were driven lower down the mountains than he had intended by impassable tracts of ice, and the ascent was tremendous. For the last 200 feet the boulders were of enormous size, and the steepness fearful. Sometimes I drew myself up on hands and knees, sometimes crawled; sometimes 'Jim' pulled me up by my arms or a lariat, and sometimes I stood on his shoulders, or he made steps for me of his feet and hands, but at six we stood on the Notch in the splendour of the sinking sun, all colour deepening, all peaks glorifying, all shadows purpling, all peril past.

'Jim' had parted with his *brusquerie* when we parted from the students, and was gentle and considerate beyond anything, though I knew that he must be grievously disappointed, both in my courage and strength. Water was an object of earnest desire. My tongue rattled in my mouth, and I could hardly articulate. It is good for one's sympathies to have for once a severe experience of thirst. Truly, there was

Water, water, everywhere,
But not a drop to drink.[6]

Three times its apparent gleam deceived even the mountaineer's practised eye, but we found only a foot of 'glare ice.' At last, in a deep hole, he succeeded in breaking the ice, and by putting one's arm far down one could scoop up a little water in one's hand, but it was tormentingly insufficient.

5. Alfred Lord Tennyson, "Morte d'Arthur," lines 260–61. *Ed.*

6. Samuel Taylor Coleridge, "Rime of the Ancient Mariner," part 2, lines 121–22. *Ed.*

With great difficulty and much assistance I recrossed the Lava Beds, was carried to the horse and lifted upon him, and when we reached the camping ground I was lifted off him, and laid on the ground wrapped up in blankets, a humiliating termination of a great exploit. The horses were saddled, and the young men were all ready to start, but 'Jim' quietly said, 'Now, gentlemen, I want a good night's rest, and we shan't stir from here tonight.' I believe they were really glad to have it so, as one of them was quite 'finished.' I retired to my arbour, wrapped myself in a roll of blankets, and was soon asleep. When I woke, the moon was high shining through the silvery branches, whitening the bald Peak above, and glittering on the great abyss of snow behind, and pine logs were blazing like a bonfire in the cold still air. My feet were so icy cold that I could not sleep again, and getting some blankets to sit in, and making a roll of them for my back, I sat for two hours by the camp fire. It was weird and gloriously beautiful. The students were asleep not far off in their blankets with their feet towards the fire. Ring lay on one side of me with his fine head on my arm, and his master sat smoking, with the fire lighting up the handsome side of his face, and except for the tones of our voices, and an occasional crackle and splutter, as a pine-knot blazed up, there was no sound on the mountain side. The beloved stars of my far-off home were overhead, the Plough and Pole Star, with their steady light; the glittering Pleiades, looking larger than I ever saw them, and 'Orion's studded belt' shining gloriously. Once only some wild animals prowled near the camp, when Ring, with one bound, disappeared from my side; and the horses, which were picketed by the stream, broke their lariats, stampeded, and came rushing wildly towards the fire, and it was fully half an hour before they were caught and quiet was restored. 'Jim,' or Mr Nugent, as I always scrupulously called him, told stories of his early youth, and of a great sorrow which had led him to embark on a lawless and desperate life. His voice trembled, and tears rolled down his cheek. Was it semiconscious acting, I wondered, or was his dark soul really stirred to its depths by the silence, the beauty, and the memories of youth?

We reached Estes Park at noon on the following day. A more successful ascent of the Peak was never made, and I would not now exchange my memories of its perfect beauty and extraordinary sublimity for any other experience of mountaineering in any part of the world. Yesterday snow fell on the summit, and it will be inaccessible for eight months to come.

NINA MAZUCHELLI

From *The Indian Alps and How We Crossed Them: Being a Narrative of Two Years' Residence in the Eastern Himalaya and Two Months' Tour into the Interior*

New York: Dodd, Mead, and Company, 1876. 5–8; 275–81.

[pp. 5–8]

. . . Would you see Nature in all her savage grandeur? Then follow me to her wildest solitudes—the home of the yâk, and the wild deer, the land of the citron, and the orange, the arctic lichen, and the pine—where, in deep Alpine valley, rivers cradled in gigantic precipices, and fed by icy peaks, either thunder over tempest-shattered rock, or sleep to the music of their own lullaby—even to the far East, amongst the Indian Alps. . . .

It has been said that nothing can be more grand and majestic than the Alps of Switzerland, and that size is a phantom of the brain, an optical illusion, grandeur consisting rather in form than size. As a rule it may be so; but they are 'minute philosophers' who sometimes argue thus. Not that I would disparage the Swiss Alps, which were my first loves, and which, it must be acknowledged, do possess more of picturesque beauty than the greater, vaster mountains of the East; but the stupendous Himalaya—in their great loneliness and vast magnificence, impossible alike to pen and pencil adequately to portray, their height, and depth, and length, and breadth of snow appealing to the emotions—impress one as nothing else can, and seem to expand one's very soul.

We were sitting at dinner one evening beneath a punkah in one of the cities of the plains of India, feeling languid and flabby and miserable, the thermometer standing at anything you like to mention, when the 'khansamah' (butler) presented F—— with a letter, the envelope of which bore the words, 'On Her Majesty's Service'; and on opening it he found himself under orders for two years' service at Darjeeling, one of the lovely settlements in the Himalaya, the 'Abode of Snow'—*Him,* in Sanscrit, signifying 'Snow,' and *alaya* 'Abode'—the *Imaus* of the ancients.

Were the 'Powers that be' ever so transcendently gracious? Imagine, if you can, what such an announcement conveyed to our minds. Emancipation from the depleting influences of heat almost unbearable, for the bracing and life-giving breezes which blow over regions of eternal ice and snow.

THE

INDIAN ALPS

AND

HOW WE CROSSED THEM

BEING A NARRATIVE OF

TWO YEARS' RESIDENCE IN THE EASTERN HIMALAYA
AND TWO MONTHS' TOUR INTO THE INTERIOR

BY

A LADY PIONEER

ILLUSTRATED BY HERSELF

NEW YORK
DODD, MEAD, AND COMPANY
PUBLISHERS

FIGURE 47 Nina Mazuchelli, title page, *The Indian Alps and How We Crossed Them*

But even in these days it is wonderful to what an extent ignorance prevails about the more unfrequented parts of India; for it is not generally known, except as a mere abstract truth, that in this vast continent—associated as it is in the purely English mind with scorching heat and arid plains, stretching from horizon to horizon, relieved by naught save belts of palm-girt jungle, the habitat of the elephant, the tiger, and the deadly snake—every variety of climate may be found, from the sultry heat and miasma of the tropical valley, to the temperature of the Poles.

Is not India, indeed, almost exclusively regarded as a land of songless birds arrayed in brightest plumage; of gorgeous butterflies and 'atlas' moths; of cacao-nuts, and dates, and pines more luscious than anything of which the classic Pomona could boast?—a land also where snakes sit corkscrew-like at the foot of one's bed, and wild beasts take shelter in one's 'bungalow'; and where her Majesty's liege subjects, whose fate it is to be exiled there, are exposed to the alternate processes of roasting under a tropical sun, and melting beneath a punkah?

To the feminine mind, again, is it not a land of Cashmere shawls—'such loves'—and fans, and sandalwood boxes, and diaphanous muslins?—presents sent over at too infrequent intervals from uncles and cousins, about whom, vegetating in that far-off land, there is always a halo of pleasant mystery, and arriving, redolent of 'cuscus' and spicy odours and a whole bouquet of Indian fragrance, which wafts one away in spirit across the desert and the sunlit ocean to that wonderland in an instant.

A region there is, however, of countless bright oases in these vast plains, where the cuckoo's plaintive note recalls sweet memories of our island home, and mingles with the soft melody of other birds; where the stately oak—monarch of our English woods—spreading its branches, blends them with those of the chestnut, the walnut, and the birch; where in mossy slopes the 'nodding violet blows,' and wild strawberries deck the green bank's side, like rubies set in emerald. I allude of course to the noble snow-capped Himalaya, the loftiest mountains in the world, with whose *existence* everyone is acquainted, but about which brains even saturated with geographical knowledge are yet as ignorant, so far as their topographical aspect and wondrous hidden beauty are concerned, as they are about the mountains in the moon.

[pp. 275–81]

At half-past ten o'clock, peeping forth from my tent, the moon was still shining brilliantly, but clouds that almost appeared to touch me were scurrying past. The snows too were veiled by a semi-transparent mist which half hid them, so that, my ardour somewhat abating, I subsided beneath the canvas, and sat on the foot of my little camp bed reading. At length extinguishing the light, I threw myself down without undressing, and was soon fast asleep, and the moonlight and the snows and my hoped-for picture were alike forgotten. But the evening's impressions must have been strong upon me still, causing my sleep to be uneasy and intermittent, for two hours later I awoke, and a little moonbeam was shining on my bed through a crack in the canvas. This induced me to get up to see how all was looking outside.

Noiselessly untying the flaps which enclosed the entrance, I crept out. The moon was shining so brightly that I could have read the smallest print by its aid, and the snows were positively dazzling. The sky was of that exquisite violet blue, or rather, what I think describes it better, *sapphire,* which one sees on clear moonlight nights in Italy—that land so favoured by heaven with tender beauteous skies.

Now I have no wish to make myself out to be a heroine, being on the contrary the veriest coward; never, *entre nous,* having yet been able to go into a dark room alone, or pass an open doorway at night, without seeing faces peering at me out of the darkness; but somehow I can go through a great deal for a picture.

It was the thought of a moment; I never dreamt of possibilities. Once more groping my way under the 'kernaughts,' I felt for my block and chalks, which I had prepared in readiness early in the evening, knowing that I could not use colours on this occasion, and throwing a cloak over my shoulders and a fur hood over my head, I sallied forth, closing the aperture as well as I could from the outside, and then pausing, held my breath to listen whether F—— was stirring; but no! he still breathed heavily. Passing C——'s tent, I could hear that he too was fast asleep.

I had now to make my way past the camp, under the lee of the rhododendron bushes. The fires still burnt brightly, and the poor tired fellows were lying prostrate around them, wrapped in deepest slumber, their gay-coloured gaberdines paled in the moonlight, except here and there, when a fire, gleaming forth with a sudden flash, lighted up patches of red and amber, which stood out prominently where all else was colourless.

No one observed me, or, if they did, probably mistook me for some erratic member of their own fraternity. Amongst the number I recognised the Herculean form of Hatti, lying with his face upwards, and I could not help thinking, as I passed close to him with stealthy footsteps, how easy it would have been to drive a nail into his head, had *I* been Jael the wife of Heber, and *he* Sisera! [1]

I dared not arouse him; to have awakened one, would have been to awaken all. Otherwise I should have done so, as I needed someone to carry my block, which, though no encumbrance to me at present, I knew would be so further on, when I should require both hands free to help myself along.

The ground, which had thawed in the vicinity of the fires, was here

1. Jael killed Sisera as he slept, after Sisera had fled when his chariots were destroyed. Judges 4:12–22. *Ed.*

thickly coated with frost, which crunched beneath each footfall; yet no one moved. Nor was there even a breath of air stirring, to bear me company as I walked onwards, and it was not long before I found myself starting at my own shadow. The very beauty of the scene made me afraid, it was all so supernatural, so pale, so still, so passionless, so spectral. I grew cowardly, and, stopping short, I felt I could not face it alone. Retracing my steps as far as Fanchyng's sleeping-place on the outskirts of the camp, I stooped till my lips almost touched the covering of the tilt.

"Fanchyng," I whispered—"Fanchyng, I want you,—come out!"

But there was no answer, though I waited long; she was sleeping too heavily to be awakened by a call so gentle, yet I dare not speak more loudly.

At last, despising myself for my cowardice, I determined to be brave, and go on alone. I was soon under the shelter of the copse, having taken care to enter it by the way which F—— and I had previously taken together, as a pathway had already been made for me there; whilst the moon shining through the branches afforded quite sufficient light to enable me to trace it by the fallen trees, that had been cut down as we passed early in the evening. I was about halfway through, when something rose at my feet with a whr-r-r, which startled me greatly. I had no doubt flushed a bird, a moonāl (hill pheasant), probably. On I went, the thick rhododendron leaves through which I brushed covering me with a shower of hoar frost. Then arriving at the rock I before mentioned, which I climbed on hands and knees, throwing my block before me at every few steps, I succeeded in reaching the top.

What a spectacle now presented itself to my view! In the valley lay a white lake of transparent mist, and rising out of it, the snows, shrouded in unearthly vapour, looked mysterious and ghost-like. To the right, rocky mountains, shattered and riven, appeared like battlements for giant soldiery, whilst to the left were the beetling crags and swelling buttresses of the Singaleelah range. Dotted about the lesser and unsnow-clad mountains, where the moonlight fell, were portions of 'mica schist,' which, sparkling brilliantly, looked like stars fallen to earth. Stars seemed not only twinkling above, but below me, and this glittering 'mica' produced the most extraordinary effect imaginable; whilst the dead pines standing with their trunks blanched, looked like phantom guardians of the whole.

It was altogether such a spectral and unearthly scene, that I realised in an instant how utterly hopeless it would be to attempt to portray it, and simply stood entranced, losing for awhile even my own individuality, feeling that I had almost entered some new world.

I do not know how long I had been standing there, when a sensation came over me as though some one behind were softly enveloping me in a wet sheet. Looking over my shoulder, I found that the rhododendron copse had vanished; the gleam of the many camp-fires was visible no longer, and the rock at my feet, with every other object, was shut out by a white ocean of mist.

My position was by no means a dangerous one. I knew that I had only to remain quietly where I stood, till the cloud had passed over, and all would be well; but my heart beat fast and thick notwithstanding. My limbs were getting numb and frozen, and I knew not how long I could hold out. My first impulse was to call for help; but trying to reason calmly with myself, I saw how futile that would be, for no one *could* possibly find his way through the copse in the mist, even if he tried, while I should be exposing many to the risk of falling over the ridge into the abyss beneath.

As I reasoned thus with myself, the vapour grew gradually more dense, while the thickest part of the cloud passed over me, and I was surrounded by almost total darkness. A death-like stillness prevailed, the only thing audible being the thumping of my own heart.

Drawing my cloak more closely round me, I struggled to be brave. After a short time the mist became thinner, shining vapour succeeded in darkness, and the moon asserting its supremacy gradually shone out brightly as before, whilst a stratum of vapour which had just arisen from the valley seemed floating beneath my very feet. In stooping to pick up my block, I became conscious of the appearance of a dark shadow or figure opposite; and on standing erect, a phantom of gigantic dimensions was before me. Terribly frightened, my heart this time stopped beating altogether, and a deadly faintness crept over me. I had grown nervous and superstitious. But summoning up all my courage, which rarely forsakes me utterly in times of need, I felt sure it must be only one of those phenomena, which I had heard of as occasionally to be met with in these altitudes.

The moon was shining obliquely *behind* me, and what I saw might be nothing more than my own shadow, greatly exaggerated, thrown upon the lake of white mist at my feet. Without tarrying to convince myself of the truth or otherwise of this hypothesis, I descended the rock as quickly as I could, and retraced my steps; nor did I stop even to take breath till I reached the tent, when, for an instant pressing my ear to the canvas to ascertain whether F—— slept, I softly entered.

For one moment only I thought he was waking, as the open 'kernaughts' admitted a flood of light; in addition to which I must, forsooth, catch my foot in the dhurrie,[2] and overturn one of the baggage baskets lean-

2. A thick woolen or cotton rug. *Ed.*

ing against the wall of the tent; but he only turned over on the other side, and I could hear by his stertorous breathing that he was sleeping soundly as before.

ELIZA COOK

"Song of the Eagle"

The Poetical Works. London: Frederick Warne and Co., 1869. 581–82.

My home is made in the mountain land,
Where the chasms yawn and the torrents leap;
Where no coward race can hold a place,
But forms are as free as the winds that sweep.
Mine are the limbs no trammels can bind;
Mine is the course no foot can track;
Wide is my range, and lonely my flight;
The vulture may gaze, but he will not dare
To ruffle my feathers, or challenge my right,
For the Eagle, the Eagle is King of Air.

Let the dazzling sun rise clear and high
In the warmth and blaze of a southern day,
But the light that dwells in an Eagle's eye,
Can flash back again with as fierce a ray.
When the storm comes on with its thunder loud,
As the Bird of Jove I keep my fame;
My broad wings flap through the blackest cloud,
And my talons cleave through the bluest flame.
My speed is as fast as the hurricane's blast,
And curbless and wild as the ocean tide.
To the north or the west, no hand can arrest;
I am free in my will, and supreme in my pride.

Whene'er I take my place below,
    No green or bloom-wreathed perch is mine;
For I rest on the pathless peak of snow,
    Or swing on the dark and giant pine.
The shot or the barb may bid me die,
    But I know the stroke and aim must be
From the mighty arm and the steady eye,
    That can only be found 'mid the bold and free.
I live with glory—I fall with the same;—
    And though earth may have creatures strong and fair,
Though the fearless and brave fill the wood and the wave,
    None can shadow the Eagle—the King of the Air.

SECTION FIVE

Appreciating

The beauties of nature as witnessed and represented by Victorian and Edwardian women have been a part of this book from its first pages and will continue to be until its last. The beauty of things destroyed tore at the hearts and minds of nature's protectresses; the majesty of mountains and large animals affected adventurers; the variety and detail of individual species dazzled collectors; and the wonders of nature and the romance of natural history touched the women who wrote to popularize or explain science. Nevertheless, aesthetic appreciation is so significant a factor in Victorian and Edwardian women's representations of nature as to demand a category unto itself. Women's contributions in this area call out for recognition, particularly since the major aesthetic movements in nineteenth- and early twentieth-century Britain were for so long defined almost exclusively in terms of men. For example, until recent decades English romanticism has been read as the province of six male poets—Blake, Wordsworth, Coleridge, Keats, Shelley and Byron—with some attention to their family members like Mary Shelley. Aestheticism, too, has belonged to a coterie of gentlemen, some not always so gentlemanly, gathered around Oxford University, its dons and ideas men, and its poets and artists. The Pre-Raphaelites also used to come to us packaged as a brotherhood that deliberately excluded women like Christina Rossetti from its midst rather than as the center of a larger movement that included women other than those married to, related to, or taught by its practitioners. More recently, women's important contributions to all of these areas have been brought to the fore and reassessed in numbers of collections and studies that have compelled sensitive readers to totally rethink these fields.[1] But only in the last decade has the continuity of women's writ-

1. In terms of English romanticism, Anne K. Mellor's *Romanticism and Gender* (New York: Routledge, 1992) and Stuart Curran's many essays on women and romanticism are especially noteworthy. So are *Revisioning Romanticism: British Women Writers, 1776–1837,* ed. Carol Shine Wilson and Joel Haefner (Philadelphia: University of Pennsylvania Press, 1994); *Romantic Women Poets: An Anthology* (Oxford: Basil Blackwell, 1997), ed. Duncan Wu; and Elizabeth Fay's *A Feminist Introduction to Romanticism* (Oxford: Basil Blackwell,

ing from the late eighteenth century through modernism been more fully acknowledged in terms of the "long centuries" I mentioned in my preface. As readers of this book will see, recuperating nature writing by women not only enhances this sense of continuity; it also points to the need for continuing reassessments of female traditions in the context of larger literary moments.

In *Kindred Nature* I attempted to revise the limitations placed upon Victorian women in terms of the aesthetic category of the sublime. There I posed a special category, the "Victorian female sublime," to suggest that like many romantic women, a number of Victorian women perceived sublimity differently from men. Nina Mazuchelli, for example, when she becomes the eagle in the passage reprinted in the section "Adventuring," represents herself as a part of nature, not simply as its beholder, as might William Wordsworth,[2] and certainly not as its master or conqueror, as would Lord Byron's Manfred. In *Kindred Nature* I also included garden writing by Jekyll in an attempt to show that the aestheticism of the late nineteenth century encompassed far more genres than we allow ourselves when we limit to traditional, male-dominated forms like poetry. What is more, if looked at from a female perspective, aestheticism was not anti-nature, but in part a continuation of the romanticism of nature. In this section, "Appreciation," women writers also force us to push the envelope of earlier aesthetic categories. For example, at the opening of her *Alfoxden Journal* (1798) Dorothy Wordsworth, writing in a quotidian form long considered traditional to women, forces us to redefine the idea of the early romantic mıovement as characterized by the ego of the male poet. In the selections reprinted here, Wordsworth's persona is all but absent from her texts. Her journal entries read like Chinese poems, with nature presented through word and image with no sense of a human

1998). Corresponding volumes on Victorian women, *Victorian Women Poets: An Anthology* (Oxford: Basil Blackwell, 1995), ed. Angela Leighton and Margaret Reynolds, and Leighton's *Victorian Women Poets: Writing against the Heart* (New York: Harvester, 1992), have also helped resculpt their fields. Recent feminist revisionist work on British aestheticism has included *Women and British Aestheticism,* ed. Talia Schaffer and Kathy Alexis Psomiades (Charlottesville: University Press of Virginia, 1999) and Schaffer's *The Forgotten Female Aesthetes: Literary Culture in Late Victorian England* (Charlottesville: University Press of Virginia, 2000). The Pre-Raphaelites have had a consistent reviser in Jan Marsh, most recently in the catalogue *Pre-Raphaelite Women Artists,* ed. Jan Marsh and Pamela Gerrish Nunn (Manchester: Manchester Art Galleries, 1997). These are only a few of the authors and books this editor has found most useful in her own reappraisals of these fields.

2. Throughout this section I have deliberately chosen to compare the women writers I discuss with William Wordsworth, since for so long he has been considered the epitome of the English romantic poet of nature. My comparisons are not intended to minimize Wordsworth's accomplishments but to help relocate some aspects of romantic nature writing.

ego intervening. (A related kind of imagism also pervades the selection of poems on color at the end of "Appreciation.")

The remainder of the subsection entitled "Romanticism" illustrates how deeply what we have come to identify as romantic attitudes toward nature—love of nature, interest in the insights and homely wisdom of childhood and the people who live close to nature, and deepened sense of the self's relationship to the natural world—were embedded in women's writing throughout the period covered in this anthology. Emily Brontë's haunting 1836 tribute to movement and changeability as witnessed on her beloved moors is captured in flawless rimes studded with verbals that indicate the inexorable pace of nature's mutability. Brontë inspired latter-day writers like Charlotte Mew, whose deep appreciation of Brontë is reflected here in her tribute to this literary foremother, just as it is in her own poetry included in this section. Mary Howitt, on the other hand, sings the praises of the wild, free dorhawk (whippoorwill), so difficult to see but easy to hear, and prizes the elusive bird far above any stuffed bird she might be able to examine more closely. Florence Dixie's 1901 "With Nature," which originally appeared in *Songs of a Child* (published when Dixie was nineteen and under the pseudonym "Darling"), indicates that Dixie's passionate "love" of nature extends to what have been considered traditional Wordsworthian pursuits for the boy-child of nature. But if Dixie's poem seems full of Wordsworthian pastimes—deer chasing, and mountain climbing, and pony riding—why was a woman, forty years into the Victorian era, still writing in such a way? And did/do her subjects strike readers differently because projected by a woman's voice? I do not believe that the answers to the first of these questions lie simply in pointing up the time lag between men writers and women followers and implying that women's writing was derivative because women were slow to catch on. In a time like our own, when novelty comes so highly prized in the arts, such speculation perpetuates an unjust ignoring or denigration of women's writing. I would posit instead that an answer to this first question may be enfolded in the second question: perhaps women writers spoke to women readers about lives lived as potentially close to nature as they were to the domestic because female audiences desired to visualize women in roles like the ones described by Dixie. And perhaps they needed to do so until well into the twentieth century.

In working with the biographies and autobiographies of many of the women in this book—Emily Brontë, Octavia Hill, Beatrix Potter, and Eleanor Ormerod, to name just a few—I have found frequent descriptions of powerful, indelible one-on-one encounters with nature. These were not individual moments as in the case of Wordsworth's "spots of time"—single moments lived in a younger life and then later recaptured for all time in poetry. Instead they were recurrent, familiar experiences that through their very repetition insisted themselves upon those who knew them. Rethinking and replaying such experiences seems to have been one way the women who experienced them gained strength and credibility as nature writers, acquiring a vigor of voice and becoming inspirational to other women. This could be another reason why women nature writers became such excellent writers of so much of the children's literature reproduced in this anthology: they often revisited their own girlhood in nature and grafted it to their writing.

By confining ourselves to a nature romanticism of the early nineteenth century and to poets, most of whom died young or stopped writing nature poetry early in their lives, we may have overlooked older age as being central to British romantic literature. The remaining writers chosen for this section on "Romanticism" represent thoughts not just about childhood but about growing old alongside the valued aspects of the natural world. For a late example of this, we might turn back to Mary Webb's "A Cedar-Rose," reprinted in the section "Domesticating." Here is a short story about the ending of a life in the presence of a desired for cedar rose, but its narrator is herself sifting through the implications of her tale for her own life. Eliza Cook's two 1869 poems included in "Appreciation" are also full of reminiscences about earlier life in nature. "The Old Green Lane" may at first seem to be "recollected in tranquillity"—to use a famous phrase from Wordsworth's Preface to his *Lyrical Ballads*—but its narrator reveals that she is nowhere near tranquillity but far closer to pain as she muses and remembers. If nature seems the same to her, the people with whom she lived close to nature in younger days are all gone, as is her former self. This idea looms even larger in "Not as I Used to Do," where suffering and loss of color haunt the eye that now gazes at the natural world.

Our section on "Romanticism" concludes with an unpublished meditation by Beatrix Potter (see figure 48), "Elder flowers." Here Potter contemplates the complexities of the flowers of this tree, grasping for poetical metaphors and descriptors to capture them. In her final questioning, Potter posits the possibility of an "Elder-mother." In this piece she seems to move effortlessly from natural object to its personification, something she must frequently have done when imagining her animal characters as she conceived and wrote her "little" books for children. But "Elder flowers" also al-

FIGURE 48 Beatrix Potter

lows us to place Potter in relation to other women writers in this book. Potter here realizes a kind of mother-nature figure like those that mark science popularization by women and an older woman figure in some ways akin to those of Cook and Webb.

To turn now to "Aestheticism" and a movement usually considered to encompass "art for art's sake": in this anthology the closeness of aspects of this movement to nature will also become evident. The aesthetic movement took shape in the middle of the nineteenth century, partly under the aegis of the famous art critic, John Ruskin (1819–1900). Ruskin counseled the need for beautifying life in all its aspects and fostered the Pre-Raphaelite painters and writers. He also believed in art for the sake of society and influenced Octavia Hill by giving her a grant to try to improve housing for the poor. Aestheticism as a literary movement grades from romanticism, and male aesthetes have been called "the last romantics,"[3] though with the possible exception of Gerard Manley Hopkins they were not really the last nature romantics. Women were, and the remainder of this book is devoted to female aestheticism as an offshoot of romanticism. Though their routes varied, most of the women represented here believed that the aesthetic could in one way or another lead to the transcendental, that beauty contained within it a spiritual component, something they held in common with early romantic poets. The first section on aestheticism opens with a different kind of selection from Eliza Brightwen's *More about Wild Nature.* Unlike the selections from Brightwen chosen for "Domesticating," "Dame Nature" is a meditation, one both more general and more colorful than Potter's on elder flowers. Brightwen, so often the moralist, reminds us that nature is long and art short and that nature's art is there to be enjoyed while we may. In this 1892 piece, however, nature is not only beautiful but kindly, revealing Brightwen's frequent recourse to what is called "natural theology," the seeing of godhead in nature, an idea more prevalent in the late eighteenth than in the late nineteenth century.

Vernon Lee presents a different sort of spirituality, one more intellectualized and more in keeping with her time. Her poetic prose set out to capture the genius loci, the spirit of place, for her late Victorian generation. In the selection "Among the Marble Mountains," the mountains are daunting not so much in their sublime majesty (as in the section on "Adventuring") but as a source of great art through the ages. For Lee, capturing place in words also means capturing something of the abiding link between art and nature. By way of contrast, in her short piece "Asphodels," we see the beautiful represented in a kind of minute detail that characterized Victorian seeing—Ruskin's, for example, or, again, the poet Gerard Manley Hopkins's. Lee brings us to her asphodels slowly, however: first through a train window and a book, then across a landscape on a bicycle, and finally we achieve the desired closeness. Again, art—in this case a photograph—and nature complement each other. Similarly, in "The Lizard in the Abbey Church," the hulking Abbey Church and its history offset the tiny living creature found within, but both will enter the cycle of life and death. Lee's own work may be tribute enough to her sensitivity toward both art and nature, but I have

3. See Graham Hough, *The Last Romantics* (London: Duckworth, 1949).

included Amy Levy's "To Vernon Lee" as a final homage to this remarkable spirit. Levy looks upon Lee with adulation, catching the closeness of art and life that marked Lee's mind and recalling an exchange of flowers that has created an indelible memory for Levy, the slightly younger woman. Levy reminds us that like aesthetic men, aesthetic women participated in creating their own influences and traditions.

The last piece in "Aestheticism" is Alice Meynell's quiet appreciation of rain, another instance of the importance of the visual to the nature writer. Seeing even more than hearing, smelling, and feeling dominates much of romantic, Victorian, and modernist writing. Even the nearly invisible rain, so evident to us through its sound, its feel, and the odors it extracts from the ground, is in Meynell's essay apprehended as it "flashes" on our real eye and on what Meynell calls our "meditative eyes." Again the unseen is reintroduced into this section otherwise so deeply imbued with representations of physical perception.

Because seeing was so significant to the aesthetics of our time frame, I have chosen "The Color of Life" as the concluding section. Color delighted Gertrude Jekyll, first when she was a painter and later when her eyesight began to fail her and she was forced to take up gardening in order to work in larger blocks of color. Jekyll wrote an entire book on color, *Colour Schemes for the Flower Garden,* one section of which, "Gardens of Special Colouring," is included here to reveal the subtleties of Jekyll's painterly vision (see figure 49). But color was important to Victorians and Edwardians of many stripes, as Octavia Hill's "Colour, Space, and Music for the People" suggests. Hill's essay complements Twining's on window boxes in the section "Domesticating" in that both try to explain how to improve lives by beautifying environments. Color here is contrasted to "dinginess," which Hill thought marked the environs of the poor. I have included Hill's essay to enable contemporary readers to realize ideas of Victorian benevolence at work alongside aesthetics. Hill's "lady bountiful" approach to the poor may seem demeaning to some today, but Hill was an impassioned and important reformer in her day, a woman absolutely dedicated both to beauty and to the improvement of the lives of her contemporaries. Among other things, through her preservationist ideals and devotion to the National Trust, she helped save the very landscape of the British Isles.

Like Alice Meynell, Mary Webb could wax eloquent over sight, and like Vernon Lee, she could move effortlessly from nature to art. In "The Beauty of Colour," another delicate work of nonfiction, she reflects on color as manifested in the natural world, concluding with the description of a sunset intended to encompass all color. Webb's essay here sets the stage for a series of short, imagistic poems that each center on color in nature. Each is by a different writer and each finds its primary focus in a different color. Collectively they yield a kaleidoscope of aesthetic responses to the beauty of color.

ROMANTICISM

DOROTHY WORDSWORTH

From *The Alfoxden Journal*

Oxford: Oxford University Press, 1971. 1, 9.

Alfoxden, *20th January, 1798.* The green paths down the hillsides are channels for streams. The young wheat is streaked by silver lines of water running between the ridges, the sheep are gathered together on the slopes. After the wet dark days, the country seems more populous. It peoples itself in the sunbeams. The garden, mimic of spring, is gay with flowers. The purple-starred hepatica spreads itself in the sun, and the clustering snow-drops put forth their white heads, at first upright, ribbed with green, and like a rose-bud; when completely opened, hanging their heads downwards, but slowly lengthening their slender stems. The slanting woods of an unvarying brown, showing the light through the thin net-work of their upper boughs. Upon the highest ridge of that round hill covered with planted oaks, the shafts of the trees show in the light like the columns of a ruin.

1st March. We rose early. A thick fog obscured the distant prospect entirely, but the shapes of the nearer trees and the dome of the wood dimly seen and dilated. It cleared away between ten and eleven. The shapes of the mist, slowly moving along, exquisitely beautiful: passing over the sheep they almost seemed to have more of life than those quiet creatures. The unseen birds singing in the mist.

EMILY BRONTË

"High Waving Heather"

December 13, 1836. *The Complete Poems of Emily Jane Brontë.* Ed. C. W. Hatfield. New York: Columbia University Press, 1941. 31.

High waving heather, 'neath stormy blasts bending,
Midnight and moonlight and bright shining stars;
Darkness and glory rejoicingly blending,
Earth rising to heaven and heaven descending,
Man's spirit away from its drear dongeon sending,
Bursting the fetters and breaking the bars.

All down the mountain sides, wild forests lending
One mighty voice to the life-giving wind;
Rivers their banks in the jubilee rending,
Fast through the valleys a reckless course wending,
Wider and deeper their waters extending,
Leaving a desolate desert behind.

Shining and lowering and swelling and dying,
Changing for ever from midnight to noon;
Roaring like thunder, like soft music sighing,
Shadows on shadows advancing and flying,
Lightning-bright flashes the deep gloom defying,
Coming as swiftly and fading as soon.

CHARLOTTE MEW

From "The Poems of Emily Brontë"

Temple Bar 130 (1904): 153–67.

The earth—her passionate and only love—was peopled for her by spirits of storm and cloud, of sun and darkness. These were the sole companions of those boding or ministering spirits within her soul. Fancy—that 'fairy love'—was her chosen playfellow and perhaps the only child she ever knew. Seldom, if ever, seeking intercourse with those around her, and impervious to the influence of other minds, she was mainly dependent on the material her own imagination could supply. Throughout these ideal and impersonal lyrics the individual note is everywhere discernible. They are melodies, rather than a sweeping and mournful music peculiarly her own.

MARY HOWITT

"The Dor-Hawk"

Sketches of Natural History: or Songs of Animal Life. 1834. London, Edinburgh, and New York: T. Nelson and Sons, 1872. 146–49.

In the dark brown wood beyond us,
    Where the night lies dusk and deep;
Where the fox his burrow maketh,
Where the tawny owl awaketh
    Nightly from his day-long sleep;

There, Dor-hawk, is thy abiding,
    Meadow green is not for thee;
While the aspen branches shiver,
'Mid the roaring of the river,
    Comes thy chirring voice to me.

Bird, thy form I never looked on,
    And to see it do not care;
Thou hast been and thou art only
As a voice of forests lonely,
    Heard and dwelling only there.

Bringing thoughts of dusk and shadow;
    Trees huge-branched in ceaseless change;
Pallid night-moths, spectre-seeming;
All a silent land of dreaming,
    Indistinct and large and strange.

Be thou thus, and thus I prize thee
    More than knowing thee face to face,
Head and beak and leg and feather,
Kept from harm of touch and weather,
    Underneath a fine glass-case.

I can read of thee, and find out
    Of thy flight, if fast or slow;
Of thee in the north and south too,
Of thy great moustachioed mouth too,
    And thy Latin name also.

But, Dor-hawk, I love thee better
    While thy voice unto me seems
Coming o'er the evening meadows,
From a dark brown land of shadows,
    Like a pleasant voice of dreams!

FLORENCE DIXIE

"With Nature"

Songs of a Child, and other Poems by "Darling." London, Leadenhalt Press, 1901. 45–46.

I love to wander in the fields alone,
    Or drift in silence down the river stream,
To harken to the boom, and buzz, and drone
    Of flies and busy bees. To lie and dream
Of golden sunlight and of azure skies,
    Of singing birds and many coloured flow'rs,
To listen to the zephyrs' gentle sighs
    Flitting throughout the green trees nestling bow'rs.

I love to climb the rugged mountain sides
    And peer into their precipices deep,
To clamber where the silver cloudlet hides

Many a tow'ring, sky aspiring peak;
Or follow in the torrent's winding track,
As serpent-like it twists first here then there,
And watch the grouse rise up in serried pack
To sweep away upon the sunlit air.

I love to follow where the red deer roam,
Amidst their straths[1] and corries[2] far on high,
To visit them within their "forest" home
And hear therein the golden eagle's cry.
Here in its haunts the snow-white ptarmigan,
With gentle dove-like flight, flits o'er the brae,[3]
It never wanders in the path of man,
But loves the misty heights and chasms grey.

I love to mount my pony and to make
A point to point excursion through the fields,
Each obstacle encountered he does take
With ready nerve, and prompt obedience yields
To ev'ry touch of rein. No truer friend
Has man than his good horse save the dear hound,
Who clings to him unto the very end;
Than these, no better comrades can be found.

I love to sail upon the rolling sea
And mark the wonders of its vasty deep,
To watch the seagulls swooping in the lee
On moveless wing with gliding, graceful sweep.
I love to see the billows tempest tossed,
Green featured rise and fall in sportive play,
To mark their crests with creamy foam embossed,
Go wand'ring on upon their forward way.

Where Nature is, 'tis there I love to be,
I loathe those man-made buildings men call towns,
With all their suff'ring and their cruelty,

1. Open valleys. *Ed.*
2. Circular valleys. *Ed.*
3. A bank or hillside. *Ed.*

Their unwashed features and their ugly frowns.
Where Nature is unfettered she is fair,
Be it in sunlight or in rugged storm,
Her ev'ry breath casts fragrance on the air,
She is a being of divinest form.

ELIZA COOK

"The Old Green Lane"

The Poetical Works. London: Frederick Warne and Co., 1869. 442–43.

'Twas the very, merry, summer time
That garlands hills and dells,
And the south wind rang a mystic chime
Upon the foxglove bells;
The Cuckoo stood on the lady-birch
To bid her last good-bye—
The lark sprang o'er the village church,
And whistled to the sky;
And we had come from the harvest sheaves,
A blithe and tawny train,
And tracked our path with poppy leaves
Along the Old, green lane.

'Twas a pleasant way on a sunny day,
And we were a happy set,
As we idly bent where the streamlet went
To get our fingers wet;
With the dog-rose here, and the orchis there,
And the woodbine, twining through;
With the broad trees meeting everywhere,
And the fern still dank with dew.
Ah! we all forgot in that blissful spot,
The names of Care and Pain,
As we lay on the bank by the shepherd's cot
To rest in the Old, green lane.

Oh, days gone by! I can but sigh
As I think of that rich hour,
When my heart in its glee, but seemed to be
Another wood-side flower;
For though the trees be still as fair,
And the hedge bloom still as gay,—
Though the south wind sends as sweet an air,
And Heaven as bright a day;
Yet the merry set are far and wide,
And we never shall meet again;—
We shall never ramble, side by side,
Along that Old, green lane.

ELIZA COOK

"Not as I Used to Do"

The Poetical Works. London: Frederick Warne and Co., 1869. 549–50.

I look on the chestnut blossom
As it points to the cloudless sky,
On the daisy's golden bosom,
And the hyacinth's deep blue eye.
I see the lime-tree flinging
Its delicate green arms out,
The fragrant jasmine clinging,
And the woodbine running about;
The lilac hiding the paling
With clusters of purple and white,
And the graceful laburnum trailing
Its tresses of radiant light.
But for me the garlanded bowers
Have lost their dazzling hue:
I look on the fields and flowers,
But not as I used to do.

I hear the bird boy's rattle
Chime in with the cawing rook;
I hear the low of the cattle,
And the plash of the rippling brook.
I hear the shepherd singing,
And the bleat of the sportive lamb;
I hear the loud flail swinging,
And the barn-door's creaking slam;
I hear the swallows darting,
Like arrows, in chase of the fly,
And the tawny leveret starting
At play in the copse just by;
I hear the broad flags quiver
Where the wind and tide rush through;
I listen to mill-wheel and river,
But not as I used to do.

I hear the blackbird telling
His love tale to his mate,
And the merry skylark swelling
The choir at "heaven's gate."
The cuckoo away in the thicket
Is giving his two, old notes,
And the pet-doves hung by the wicket
Are talking with ruffled throats;
The honey-bee hums as he lingers
Where shadows on clover heads fall,
And the wind with leaf-tipped fingers,
Is playing in concert with all.
I know the music that gushes
Is melody sweet and true,
And I listen to zephyrs and thrushes,
But not as I used to do.

No more can my footsteps wander
Through woodlands loved and dear;
I gaze on the hill-tops yonder,
Through the mist of a hopeless tear.
My spirit is worn and weary,
With waiting for health and rest;

My long, long night is dreary,
    And my summer day unblest:
My suffering darkens the noonlight,
    My anguish embitters the balm,
My loneliness weeps in the moonlight,
    And sighs in the evening calm.
Oh, Suffering's mournful story
    Must be wofully long and true,
When it finds me noting God's glory,
    But not as I used to do.

BEATRIX POTTER

"Elder flowers"

Ms. BP 1296. Victoria and Albert Museum Library, London. (Reproduced by kind permission of Frederick Warne & Co.)

Aug. 28.

Elder flowers, elder flowers; pale disks that shine in level tiers: pale, sweet, unstirring, breathlessly still. Arched branches "duskily green that darkly hem in the orchard garth:" tall pithy shoots motionless in the twilight; silence darkness, stoney and mysterious underneath the bowr [*sic*] trees.

Elder flowers, myriads of cream flowrets, loading the summer night with heavy sweetness. There are three sweetneses, different yet alike: the breath of kine, the scent of hawthorn, and the smell of elder flowers.

Why do they seem so still—so very still? Is it that Elder-mother sits in the heart of the arching branches? ~~motionless, shadowy, darkly clothed in green?~~[1] Her skin is colourless; her wimple, her ruff, her fan, are the cream elder flowers. Her gown is green, and her apron is brownish green; with her white hands she holds it outspread. The flowrets fall into her lap. Without wind, without sound, in the sweet smelling darkness they pass in a night.

1. Text that was deleted by Potter on her handwritten manuscript is shown here by strikethrough. *Ed.*

They fall from her softly; the stoney ground is powdered with sweetness. Then silently slowly she draws into the bowr [*sic*] tree. Not for her the cloying juice of the luscious berries ripened by September thunder. She dwells in dreams within the hollow elder stems, withdrawn until another summer's summer night.

Aesthéticism

ELIZA BRIGHTWEN

"Dame Nature"

More About Wild Nature. London: T. Fisher Unwin. 1892. 173–76.

What a charming beautifier Dame Nature is! She likes that things should harmonise, she knows which colours will go together better than do all the artists in creation, and, what is more, she will not have discordant tints in her domain if she can possibly help it. If, for instance, man chooses to erect a staring new wall of an excruciating brick-red, out of all keeping with its surroundings, then the old dame rises to the occasion, and with a gentle murmur of pity for his lack of taste, off she goes to her stores, and empties out of the next soft zephyr that is going that way, a whole lapful of seeds of lichens and mosses; they fall into the cracks and crannies in the wall, finding, it may be, only a little dust to root into, but they are patient and hopeful and do their best. They drink in the morning and evening dews, the life within them begins to stir, and soon we see tender films of grey and green beginning to tone down the fiery red bricks. A few months pass by, and we find these films have grown into patches of lichen spreading in circles here and there, soft as velvet, and of all shades of delicate colour. Some of these lichens are like a mouse's coat, others pale creamy green shading into buff and grey; all have some form of fruitfulness in tiny shields or cups strewn over the crinkled surface. Then in the crevices of the brickwork are the vivid green mosses bearing their little brownish-crimson urns with waterproof covers, which little beakers will in due time bend downwards and empty their stores to enrich still further the bare and barren wall. The zephyr came again later on bringing with it a supply of the seeds of wallflowers, willow-herb, whitlowgrass and many other plants, which seeds were given into the keeping of the mosses and from out their rounded cushions young plants, laden with flower-buds, are quietly growing up, and soon sweet blossoms will give their odours to the zephyr to be carried far and wide.

Thus Nature, dear old beautifier! will have attained her end and given man's ugly work a beauty of her own, so that as the eye wanders down the lane past many a tree-trunk mantled with ivy, the tinge of red in the wall, softened as it is by its veil of lichens and mosses, comes in harmoniously, and no longer strikes a jarring note in the scale of colour.

Each year only adds to these beauties until a time-worn wall with crumbling bricks held together by masses of ivy, decked with the crimson leaves of herb robert and masses of yellow and brown wallflower, becomes a thing of real beauty.

The grey lichen-stained wall which forms the boundary of many of England's stately homes has a voice of its own. It speaks of a long-ago time when those who perhaps now lie peacefully sleeping in the churchyard were young and strong and used to climb over it in their youthful rambles; yes, it *has* its lesson for those who will listen.

Man lives his short life and passes away; would that his aim were always to make life more beautiful for all who live around him. Added years only enhance the venerable beauty of trees and rocks and hills, they gain touches of colour and picturesque beauty of form by the slow corroding touch of age, and we can recall many a place where

"Cushioned mosses to the stone
Their quaint embroidery lent."

All these things speak of the harmonious power of beneficent Nature, and make us grateful to her for the silent work she is ever carrying on. May we, like her, veiling with tender loving charity the harsh and rugged things that meet us in our daily life, do all that in us lies to make this world of ours fairer, brighter, and happier for all who dwell in it!

VERNON LEE

"Among the Marble Mountains"

Genius Loci. London: Grant Richards, 1898. 63–71.

This is the heart of the marble mountains, of those peaks and crags which bound the grass plains of Lucca and Pisa like a group of giants reclining on their elbow at table, and which, from the bridges of Florence and the heights above Siena, loom fitfully, a spectral wreath, so faint and immaterial as to be distinguished from storm-clouds only by their sharp and flame-like forms. I am seated under sparse yellowing chestnuts on the hillside, above the quarry forge, smelling of dry balm and of myrrh. High up, so high that if I turn round I look across a series of descending ridges, not into the valleys, but down on to the sea. And close opposite, in front, abrupt, like the house facing one in a street, rises the great Monte Altissimo, serrated like a broken crystal, pure marble rock from crags to base. Bare marble rock, of faintest lilac where the weather has toned it, striped here and there with fainter cinnamon brown, on which my climbing friend and the two quarrymen look like pins' heads.

They are climbing up to the highest quarry, the famous Tacca Bianca, the White Scar. You see it from miles and miles away, like a great patch of snow with jagged outline against the sky: the stratum of whitest, most crystalline marble; the innermost core of the mountain, not excavated like the other quarries by the hand of man, but laid bare by the unceasing labour of sun and frost and storm. Up there, above and below the narrow ledges of road, iron wedges are driven into the rock, planks laid across them or slung by ropes, and the mountain-side cut away into blocks by the quarrymen hanging on its face. The great White Scar faces me if I raise my eyes, white, hazy, in the blinding sunlight. And from the whole of the great mountain, mingled with the clear voice of the well-head below, comes a faint clink of chisel; and every now and then the rattle of an avalanche of white quarry refuse, bounding from ledge to ledge.

The quarries of Monte Altissimo are only the highest and most wonderful among innumerable others of the twin valleys of Seravezza. They hang everywhere on the mountain sides, above the autumnal woods of chestnut and beech scrub, mere distant snow-like patches when high up; and lower down great scoopings, wonderful crumblings of white marble shale, and loose deep scarlet earth, runs of flaky débris, like overblown chrysanthemums among the thick groves of olive. Two torrents, glacier white with marble dust, twist through the double valley, and make their way, a shallow quiet stream, among the yellowing poplars to the sands. And as they go they turn the sawmills, which grind quartz sand into the marble blocks and cut them into slabs.

The roads are deep in marble dust, furrowed into enormous ruts by the strings of bullocks, sometimes as many as four yoke, carting the great slabs and rough-hewn blocks. Arrived at their destination, sawmill or storehouse, the drivers dismount from between the huge horns of the oxen, and prise the block round on steel levers, chanting as they move. The block slowly turns on itself, balances on the brink of the cart, sways, topples, leaps down into the slush of pounded marble, heaves on its point, and steadies itself on its side.

The quite primitive labour of this carting and quarrying of marble is very interesting and beautiful. No two blocks seem ever to be alike, and they act as if alive, moving as the result not of brute force, but of extraordinarily distributed skilful touch. Hence the men also seem alive, dealing with things which have a will. This struck me particularly in one of the lowest quarries of the valley, which we called the Red Quarry. It is a circular amphitheatre, cut in crimson, *carmine* earth, a few big olives and white walls of marble débris overhanging it, its entrance guarded by huge rough-hewn blocks. These blocks are covered on one side by a network of what looks like orange crystal or lichen, wherever the water has trickled; the other side is toned and stained a golden rosy flesh colour, compared with which Giorgione's nudes and the Subiaco Niobide are pale and cold. Above the quarry chasm of brilliant red earth another quarry, half hidden among the olives; and below immense, almost vertical, runs of white and pinkish refuse, perpetually slipping and clattering into the river pools of the valley. It was down one of these rubbish slides that the men were preparing to launch a colossal block of marble. The block was being lifted on to rollers made of undressed chestnut wood, in a sort of little square at the quarry brink, a few huts of leafage, and some strange primitive hand-saws, like those on obelisks, all round. About a dozen men, some really beautiful, and all with beautiful movements, were raising the block with their crowbars, singing like sailors as they pushed it along and eased it. At last it rushed along, like a boat on rollers, to the edge of the platform, all the men shouting as they ran. Then the pieces of wood, all but one, were picked away, and the block was raised on its point with the levers. The foreman, having got it eased all round, gave the signal, and it was launched. It ran down the steep shoot, some hundred feet long, gathering as it went the dust of the marble shale, till it was enveloped in what seemed a cloud of smoke, which continued along its course. The hillside *shook;* the block had arrived at the bottom. "How it smoked!" remarked the foreman.

These quarries of the valleys of the Serra and the Vezza do not appear to have been known in Antiquity, which quarried marble, ever since the time of Augustus, in the other valleys, nearer the Gulf of Spezia, of Luni, or, as we now call them, of Carrara. Michelangelo seems to have been the first to recognize that the Florentines possessed in their own territory (what he calls the mountains of Pietrasanta) marble as fine as any they could obtain from the Marquises of Lunigiana; and as a result he was, as we all know, employed for years to make roads and open quarries for Clement VII. He is said to have quarried even on Monte Altissimo: perhaps—who knows?—to have reached the wonderful Tacca Bianca at its summit. The quarry smith at the foot of the Altissimo, with whom I had a long talk under the chestnut trees, informed me that before our hospitable French friends, the Henraux, had attacked the wonderful White Scar in 1870, attempts to quarry it had been made, many, many years ago, by "a certain Buonarroti";[1] but that might be merely an old woman's tale, a *favola.* Be this as it may, and despite the complaints in his letters, I cannot help feeling that the great marble peaks and the narrow gorges were a fitter place for Michelangelo than the ante-rooms of the Vatican. And I would willingly forget all those studio vexations and intrigues, and think of his real life as up here, watching the storms smoking along the crags, or the ships sailing in the sunset in the sea, far, far away across the mountain ridges—a fit successor of Dante's mysterious soothsayer Aruns, who

> Had once a cave, among the snowy marbles,
> For his abode, whence, when he scanned the
> stars there,
> And scanned the sea, his view was not impeded.[2]

Certainly, the marble mountains, seen from the hills of Florence or from their own seaboard, seem to have haunted Michelangelo's imagination. And if he never put real mountains into his backgrounds, he caught, nevertheless, their attitude and, so to speak, their gesture: the weary repose of some, the uneasy leaning on elbow and shoulder of others, the twisting of neck and straining of back and loins, the whole primeval tragedy of effort,

1. Michelangelo (1475–1564). *Ed.*
2. *Inferno* 2. 46–51. *Ed.*

and triumph, and failure of the marble giants; and copied them into his prophets, and sibyls, and tragic allegoric men and women.

And this—who knows?—is perhaps the greatest service which the marble mountains, which this great Monte Altissimo, rising in front of me with pinnacles like a weather-worn cathedral, have done to art. For, alas! the marble—the finest, purest, almost Grecian marble—has come too late in the day. Niccolo and Giovanni Pisano, Donatello and Jacopo della Quercia,[3] when they could not get some fragment of an antique column, had only veined, spotty, easily-decaying marble to work in; and Michelangelo himself does not seem to have employed the finest marble of these valleys, certainly never the marble of the Tacca Bianca. That was reserved for the benefit of contemporary salons and academies. And, meanwhile, there are the men hanging from the crags by ropes, cutting the blocks from the perpendicular face of the mountain. . . . As regards myself, I feel, as I hear the faint click of invisible chisels from across the ravine, and the rattle of marble débris, and occasional distant rumble of blasting, that the works of modern sculpture, all this dead and dreary art, will have in future a living and wonderful side for me; in the fact of the marble in which they are carved, and the remembrance of the scent of sun-dried herbs, of the sound of the well-head at the base of the Altissimo, and the sight of the eagle circling above its spectral white crags.

VERNON LEE

"Asphodels"

The Spirit of Rome: Leaves from a Diary. London: John Lane, 1906. 70–71.

Like Johnson and his wall-fruit,[1] I have never had as many asphodels to look at as I wanted. Ever since I saw them first, rushing by train through the

3. All famous sculptors or architects. *Ed.*

1. Possible reference to Ben Jonson's (1572–1637) poem, "To Penshurst," lines 41–44:

The early cherry, with the later plum,
Fig, grape, and quince, each in his own time doth come;
The blushing apricot and the wooly peach
Hang on thy walls, that every child may reach.

Lee might also be referring to a passage from Boswell's *Life of Johnson. Ed.*

Maremma, nay ever since I saw them in a photograph of a Sicilian temple, nay perhaps, secretly, since hearing their name, I have felt a longing for them, and a secret sense that I was never going to be shown as many as I want. Here I have. Yesterday morning bicycling in land, along a rising road along which alternate green pastures and sea, and woods of dense myrtle and lentisk scrub overtopped by ilexes and cork trees, *there were asphodels enough:* deep plantations, little fields, like those of cultivated narcissus, compact masses of their pale salmon and grey shot colours and greyish-green leaves, or fringes, each flower distinct against field or sky, on the ledges of rock and the high earth banks. The flowers are rarely perfect when you pick them, some of the starry blossoms having withered and left an untidy fringe instead; but at a distance this half-decay gives them a singular distinction, makes the light fall on the very tips, the silvery buds, sinking the stretching out branches and picking out the pale rose colour with grey. The beauty of the plant is in the candlestick thrust of the branches. The flower has a faint oniony smell, but fresh like box hedge.

ANZIO, EASTER DAY.

~ VERNON LEE

"The Lizard in the Abbey Church"

The Tower of the Mirrors and Other Essays on the Spirit of Places. London: John Lane, 1914. 7–12.

. . . I have been sitting on a tree stump (last winter's floods have thrown some poplars across the stream, uprooted) by the river Serein; Serenus, the monks of the abbey called him, or the Romans before them, and they named him well: pale jade water moving slowly under pollard willows, between rustling poplars, into whose greyish-green autumn is mingling the first yellow. And serene also is this country of the Burgundian marches: the sweep of low horizon under a pale sunny sky, enfolding in luminous mists the vast plains, the whole great continent one feels unseen beyond. The wind in the poplars mimics a missing weir. A flock of geese rise from the stream, shake wings, and disappear in the grass; and some ducks are moored, asleep, where the fallen trees have dammed and deepened the current.

Up there, beyond the scrubby apple-trees on the stubble, and the low vineyards, rises the white hulk of the Abbey church, like a huge prowless ship, keel upwards. Of that great Burgundian monastery—nay, of those four great Cistercian foundations: Citeaux and Clairvaux and Morimont and Pontigny—it alone remains intact, itself vast as a cathedral. It, and the huge monastic granary; and, beyond the orchard, some Louis XV. pavilions, on what must once have been the monastery's fortified walls. With their steep roofs velveted over with moss and long bright windows and dainty shallow fireplaces in the panelled rooms, their terraces and balustrades reminding you of the places where Dives[1] takes his pleasure in Venetian pictures with dwarfs and bass-viol players and stomacher'd ladies, these little buildings are discreet yet not at all furtive, little *maisons du péché,* one might say, but of sins venial, graceful, and unhidden. One shudders to think of St. Bernard's feelings, if he looks down upon these only remaining habitations of his Cistercians! But facing their eighteenth-century windows, at the end of a neglected avenue of lime-trees, looms the tall white gauntness of the abbey-church and the penthouse of its narthex. *That* has not altered since St. Bernard saw it, and must have seen in it the expression of his austere and poetic ardour.

That great white church! Entering from the narthex, or vestibule, into its soaring emptiness, the stillness of the place, the up-lift of those congregated columns, the fugued vistas of the pointed, turning aisles and choir, catch at one's heart and make the breath stop. The autumn sunlight lies in broad gashes across the pale pure gloom; and in it flit the shadows of the swallows gathering round the roof and turrets outside. Conformably to St. Bernard's austerity, which growled and railed at the splendours of the neighbouring abbey of Vézelay, this church of Pontigny is totally unadorned. The outside is in truth little more than a colossal barn, the buttressed apse even having but little shape, the narthex being but a huge shed, and the only beauty about the thing being the work of Time, which has tarnished its whiteness to silver. St. Bernard wanted a mere shell for the human souls within. But where there is soul, there will needs be art, whether saints like it or not. And the Gothic art of the thirteenth century, sternly forbidden the sculpture which sprouts like vine and ivy in these Burgundian valleys, shaped that bleak bare church-emptiness into a figure more divine than any of its sculptors ever carved in the image of man. There is now a crucified Christ over the rood-screen; and a saint, a saint great, Edmund of

1. The rich man of Luke 16:19–31. *Ed.*

Canterbury, lies enshrined in the high altar. But these are poor, paltry excuses! The real divinity is the white, vast emptiness itself, the pale sunlight gathered up into great clustered pillars and bent like beech-wood into hooped white vaultings; the building is a phantom, a dead and haunting Godhead who draws you to his secret heart.

Nowadays it has become the parish church of a tiny village, half of whose inhabitants are unbelievers, and I had never found it otherwise than empty. But Sunday afternoon, wandering around, I thought I heard sounds issuing faintly. And, pushing the door from the narthex, I was met by the voice of the church. It was only a dozen schoolboys and villagers, in shabby holiday finery, occupying a few of the oak stalls which some seventeenth-century abbot, forgetful of St. Bernard, ornamented with cherubs and garlands. These people and the priest were singing, and it could scarcely be called music. But, as I stood in the door, the chaunts in their archaic nakedness seemed the voice of the nude white building, the audible chorus adding a part to the visible counterpoint of the many-vista'd piers and vaultings.

Thc following morning, when the abbey church was once more deserted, I spent most of my time there in dealings with a lizard. I found it between the steps leading down from the narthex and the first pier of the left aisle, lying against the stone wainscoting, a flattish brown thing, which I took at first for one of those creatures haunting old masonry, and falsely called tarantula in Italy, where they are reputed to be venomous. I expected it to disappear into some hole, and prodded it idly to hasten its retreat. But it moved slowly, stopping to take note of possible crannies, without making for any one of them. Then I noticed that it had caught its hind legs and tail in a kind of string hindering its progress, trying to loosen which I became aware that the creature was wrapped round and trammelled by a mantle of dusty cobwebs. It proved to be a field lizard, greenish, which must have entered on Sunday while the doors stood open, and was now vainly seeking an exit. I pushed it slowly in the direction of the door, which I had set ajar; and then, seeing its inability to get up the two steps into the narthex, and, indeed, its utter weariness, I took it in my handkerchief and set it down in the grass outside. But whether from fright, or fatigue, or the clinging wrapper of clerical cobwebs, the poor little brute, Apollo's nimble playfellow (for the Praxitelian Sauroktonos[2] is not slaying, only taming it with his pipings!), merely slipped behind some weeds and lay there like dead. This morning, however, returning to the church, I turned the grass over without finding a

2. Lee here describes a statue, Apollo, the Lizard Slayer, by Praxiteles, a Greek sculptor, c. 350 B.C. The statue is currently in the Louvre. *Ed.*

trace of it, so I hope that it washed the monastic foulness off in the dew and returned to the vineyards; unless, indeed, it was put to death mercifully by one of the swallows in their autumn hoverings.

The day, which after that radiant morning had become covered and sad, is ending with a clear sky once more. The vapours have dropped back on to the horizon faintly reddened by the invisible sunset. From the river meadows and the stubblefields rise white gauzes of mist, in which mingles the smoke of supper and of burning weeds. Above a red farm-roof, the moon, nearly full, floats white in the thin blue air. The great abbey church seems asleep, its high brown roof and turrets and buttresses unsubstantial among the poplars. An hour hence it will have vanished back into the distant ages.

AMY LEVY

"To Vernon Lee"

A London Plane-Tree and Other Poems. 1889. *Complete Novels and Selected Writings of Amy Levy, 1861–1889.* Ed. Melvyn New. Gainesville: University Press of Florida, 1993. 398.

On Bellosguardo,[1] when the year was young,
We wandered, seeking for the daffodil
And dark anemone, whose purples fill
The peasant's plot, between the corn-shoots sprung.

Over the grey, low wall the olive flung
Her deeper greyness; far off, hill on hill
Sloped to the sky, which, pearly-pale and still,
Above the large and luminous landscape hung.

A snowy blackthorn flowered beyond my reach;
You broke a branch and gave it to me there;
I found for you a scarlet blossom rare.

1. A hill in Florence. *Ed.*

Thereby ran on of Art and Life our speech;
And of the gifts the gods had given to each—
Hope unto you, and unto me Despair.

ALICE MEYNELL

"Rain"

Essays by Alice Meynell. New York: Charles Scribner's Sons, 1914. 12–14.

Not excepting the falling stars—for they are far less sudden—there is nothing in nature that so outstrips our unready eyes as the familiar rain. The rods that thinly stripe our landscape, long shafts from the clouds, if we had but agility to make the arrowy downward journey with them by the glancing of our eyes, would be infinitely separate, units, an innumerable flight of single things, and the simple movement of intricate points.

The long stroke of the raindrop, which is the drop and its path at once, being our impression of a shower, shows us how certainly our impression is the effect of the lagging, and not of the haste, of our senses. What we are apt to call our quick impression is rather our sensibly tardy, unprepared, surprised, outrun, lightly bewildered sense of things that flash and fall, wink, and are overpast and renewed, while the gentle eyes of man hesitate and mingle the beginning with the close. These inexpert eyes, delicately baffled, detain for an instant the image that puzzles them, and so dally with the bright progress of a meteor, and part slowly from the slender course of the already fallen raindrop, whose moments are not theirs. There seems to be such a difference of instants as invests all swift movement with mystery in man's eyes, and causes the past, a moment old, to be written, vanishing, upon the skies.

The visible world is etched and engraved with the signs and records of our halting apprehension; and the pause between the distant woodman's stroke with the axe and its sound upon our ears is repeated in the impressions of our clinging sight. The round wheel dazzles it, and the stroke of the bird's wing shakes it off like a captivity evaded. Everywhere the natural haste is impatient of these timid senses; and their perception, outrun by the shower, shaken by the light, denied by the shadow, eluded by the distance, makes the lingering picture that is all our art. One of the most constant causes of all the mystery and beauty of that art is surely not that we see by flashes, but that nature flashes on our meditative eyes. There is no need for the impressionist to make haste, nor would haste avail him, for mobile nature doubles upon him, and plays with his delays the exquisite game of visibility.

Momently visible in a shower, invisible within the earth, the ministration of water is so manifest in the coming rain-cloud that the husbandman is allowed to see the rain of his own land, yet unclaimed in the arms of the rainy wind. It is an eager lien that he binds the shower withal, and the grasp of his anxiety is on the coming cloud. His sense of property takes aim and reckons distance and speed, and even as he shoots a little ahead of the equally uncertain ground-game, he knows approximately how to hit the cloud of his possession. So much is the rain bound to the earth that, unable to compel it, man has yet found a way, by lying in wait, to put his price upon it. The exhaustible cloud "outweeps its rain,"[1] and only the inexhaustible sun seems to repeat and to enforce his cumulative fires upon every span of ground, innumerable.

Baby of the cloud, rain is carried long enough within that troubled breast to make all the multitude of days unlike each other. Rain, as the end of the cloud, divides light and withholds it; in its flight warning away the sun, and in its final fall dismissing shadow. It is a threat and a reconciliation; it removes mountains compared with which the Alps are hillocks, and makes a childlike peace between opposed heights and battlements of heaven.

1. Meynell may be referring to Algernon Charles Swinburne's (1837–1909) "outweep heaven at rainiest" from his *Atalanta in Calydon: A Tragedy. Ed.*

*T*HE *C*OLOR OF *L*IFE

OCTAVIA HILL

From "Colour, Space, and Music for the People"[1]

Nineteenth Century 15 (1884): 741–52.

I believe I may assume that many Londoners have a general idea of the objects and ways of action of the Kyrle Society,[2] and have seen enough of the poorer inhabitants of their city to realise that they need the gifts it brings them; but the work of the Society increases year by year, and the Committee feel that it is now necessary to secure if possible a larger measure of public support. I propose, therefore, here to indicate what forms of useful action this might take.

Before I enter upon this, the main subject of my paper, let me say, once for all, that I am not among those who have any tendency to exaggerate the importance of beauty. The Kyrle Society might be described as one formed for giving pleasure to the poor, but its founders certainly have no idea that it brings to them the principal sources of joy. The certainty of loving guidance, the near presence of a Father by us day by day, form so immeasurably the greatest joy in life that it seems to me both sad and extraordinary to hear people talk as if music and painting filled so large a part of their horizon, and assume that under what they call 'wretched circumstances'; life is necessarily cheerless. To any one who knows the way in which a thought of God transcends all sorrow and subdues all fear, the idea of there being *any* life which need be forlorn sounds strange. Again, the second great source

1. Adapted from a paper read before the Kyrle Society at Grosvenor House on the 24th of March last.

2. Founded by Hill's sister Miranda and named after Alexander Pope's John Kyrle, the Kyrle Society strove to improve outdoor spaces used by the working class by adding fountains, aviaries, flowers, and the like. *Ed.*

of human joy lies in family ties: these exist in all classes, and circumstances, however trying, only bring out more strongly the blessing of this family life to every man and woman who enters into the inheritance of love by the fulfillment of duty. These two primary blessings, the power of entering into divine and human love, we all possess—high and low, rich and poor.

But how about the secondary gifts—music, colour, art, nature, space, quiet? Let us pause for a moment to reflect how unequally are these divided. In late years, I suppose, many of us have tried to share them with those who have least of them, but how far—how very far—are they yet from reaching with any sort of frequency thousands upon thousands of our fellow-citizens! Can we do more than alter this state of things? That is the question I propose to consider here. Can this little society help any one to do more, can it expand to anything like the extent which is needed?

I said I would certainly not exaggerate the value of the things it provides. I believe I would rather ask my readers to pause and consider whether they should not try to supply these things, not because they are large gifts, but because they are small; or, to speak more precisely, to give them not because they are magnificent gifts, but because they should be so common. Think, those of you who have had any country life as children, how early the wild flowers formed your delight; remember, those of you who can, what the bright colour of flag, or dress, or picture was; recall the impression of concerted music when first its harmonies reached you; live over again the glad burst out of doors into any open space where you could breathe and move freely; trace onward from earliest childhood what, in developed forms, these gifts of nature, colour, painting, music, and open space have been, and then, summoning before you the scene you best remember in poor London—I will not describe any—picture it for yourselves this time—resolve whether you will try for your part henceforward silently, but steadily, to send there something of all the splendour, brightness, harmony, you gather round you in your London homes.

For instance, there are doubtless on your own walls pretty papers, various and harmonious colours, and probably something in the way of pictures. I went the other day to see the Hospital for Accidents at Poplar, which has applied to the Society for decorations which cannot be completed without more money. The hospital is mainly for men. It is close to the docks, where there are many accidents. Most of the patients are strong men, or big lads, suddenly struck down, bread-winners cut short in their work—many of them crippled for life. Tedious enough at best will be to them the six weeks' idleness till the broken leg or arm is healed. It is little enough, but will those of you who can paint give them anything more cheerful to look at than the distempered wall? 'He will never get up again,' said the nurse to me as she looked towards the bed of a man whose spine was injured. 'How long shall you keep him here?' I asked. 'As long as ever we can spare a bed,' she replied. While he pauses there, before going back to the cramped room at home, or to the hopeless workhouse, what shall his surroundings be? Can you carry his thoughts anywhere away from his own blasted life? Can you do so through his eyes, by means of those vivid and abiding images which penetrate deep through organs formed to be links between God's visible world and our minds? Shall any picture of our Lord's life recall the Great Healer? Shall any cottage scene carry the man's mind back to his child-life in the country? Shall story in form make him forget himself, even for a few minutes, in some other life, the illustration of an incident transporting him into other scenes and times? You think a good deal of an amusing book if time drags when you lie ill, and books are much needed in hospitals too, but to those who are not accustomed to read much, to many who are more used to *things* than to books, a picture is more living, and easier to look at, than a book.

Again, colour is intended to be a perpetual source of delight. From the early pleasure in a scarlet dress for dolly, and a gilt top, on to the glow and splendour of Venetian art, from the buttercup to the sunrise, all bright colour exhilarates and gives a sense of gladness. Till you stay a little in the colourless, forlorn desolation of the houses in the worst courts, till you have lived among the monotonous, dirty tints of the poor districts of London, you little know what the colours of your curtains, carpets, and wall-papers are to you. See how the first thing the Irishwoman does when she gets any affection for her tiny room is to pin up a coloured print, or put a gay quilt on her bed. Notice the effort of the prosaic English workman to procure pictures in gilt frames, wax flowers, or a red or green table cover. Instantly, if we come upon these little signs of care and taste, however rude, we feel a sense of relief if we have been wading through the multitudes of monotonous, colourless, dreary rooms, approached by staircases as desolate, which disgrace our courts and alleys. Let the room we enter be small, low, even dark, if but one touch of colour strike the eye it rests there thankful. So instantly, so strangely, does the human soul recognise, and rest in, one of God's gifts even when surrounded by the degradation man has too often brought into his Father's bright world of beauty.

In their own little homes we may trust the human heart, which is the same everywhere, wherever it has a chance of scope for the elasticity which is in it, to teach the inhabitants to provide these natural sources of simple pleasure. When not quite oppressed by toil and poverty, the father makes window-boxes for his nasturtiums, the girl puts on her bright ribbon, the mother hangs up the red curtain. But there are certain rooms where we ask the poor to come in to see us, or to enjoy entertainments. Call them school-rooms, mission-rooms, parish-rooms, what you will. Thanks to the better understanding of the wants of those who work all day, these are increasingly used for parties and amusements. I asked you just now to consider what your own London sitting-rooms would be if you withdrew all colour from them; I will ask you now to think what you would feel if you were giving a party and all the colour were suddenly to disappear. You feel at once that, though your guests come from bright homes and will return to them, the loss would be depressing. Do you not think we ought to be ashamed if we any longer leave in their present ugliness the parish-rooms which are the only drawing-rooms where our various hard-working clergy and ministers can entertain their poor neighbours, and our fellow citizens, for us? I have visited many a one for the Kyrle Society when decorations have been asked for, I have accepted the loan of many, kindly lent me for parties of my own tenants, and I must say my heart has sunk at the forlorn look. Dirty distemper, or at best of a pale, dingy, yellowy brown if quite new; flat ceilings often blackened with gas and smoke; heavy, long, comfortless benches, frequently without backs; old dusty cords to the windows; no mantel-piece, bracket, or pillar where one can put a glass of flowers; not a picture on the walls unless some wretched rolled glazed print or map; not a curtain to introduce colour, or break the line of square, flat windows; draughts under the doors; black coal-scuttles, broken fenders—everything ugly, everything dingy. If there are any tea-things, they are sure to be of the commonest; if there are any urns they probably leak. Bare and hideous, their surfaces broken with nothing but holes made by nails torn out from the plaster, the walls stare at one. Cleanliness and good repair are the primary needs, and these the Kyrle Society does not profess to supply. But when these are secured, the place still looks cheerless without colour or decoration. Many such rooms have been put in order by their owners, encouraged by the promise of the Society that decoration would then be supplied. Many such now await treatment. More volunteers to paint, more money to buy what is needed, are now asked for, for fresh applications reach us continually; there are some hundreds of such rooms which ought to be done. When from the bare homes, when out of the streets, when from the dark courts, you ask your poor neighbours to turn in to their parish-parlour, I am sure you do not wish this to be your preparation to receive them, you, whose walls blaze with gold and mirrors, and who put down red cloth to step from carriage to hall. Paint the walls, lighten them, brighten them, for the love of colour is a human instinct.

We often have to lend from our store of flags and mottoes, coloured table-covers, and pretty vases, a number of things for evening parties in rooms such as these. Increase our stock of such if you can; they are borrowed continually by workers in poor districts, and transform the ugliest rooms for the time, and make pleasant variety in those which are not dreary. If you send scrap-books or illustrated books, try, so far as is easily possible, to send them in bright covers.

The workers who live habitually in a dingy, shabby district feel this need of colour quite as much as the poor. We ought to think of them; they are leading a forlorn hope against enemies we only fight from a distance. It would strike you very much to hear many of them speak, as they have often done to us, as if the ugliness of the eastern districts were almost unbearable after a time; and I remember well happening to be present at a Committee of the House of Commons when a deputation of hardy working men, representing sixty-eight trades, came up to speak about model lodging-houses. There was no sentiment or nonsense about them, but it was evident from every sentence how painfully the ugliness oppressed them: 'dreadful sameness,' 'dreary whitewash,' 'miserable monotony,' and similar expressions occurred over and over again from them as they protested against the uniform, barrack-like look of many blocks of buildings. . . .

~ GERTRUDE JEKYLL

"Gardens of Special Colouring"

Colour Schemes for the Flower Garden. London: Country Life, Ltd., 1908. 98–114.

It is extremely interesting to work out gardens in which some special colouring predominates, and to those who, by natural endowment or careful eye-cultivation, possess or have acquired what artists understand by an eye for colour, it opens out a whole new range of garden delights.

Arrangements of this kind are sometimes attempted, for occasionally I hear of a garden for blue plants, or a white garden, but I think such ideas are but rarely worked out with the best aims. I have in mind a whole series of gardens of restricted colouring, though I have not, alas, either room or means enough to work them out for myself, and have to be satisfied with an all-too-short length of double border for a grey scheme. But besides my small grey garden I badly want others, and especially a gold garden, a blue garden and a green garden; though the number of these desires might easily be multiplied.

It is a curious thing that people will sometimes spoil some garden project for the sake of a word. For instance, a blue garden, for beauty's sake, may be hungering for a group of white Lilies, or for something of palest lemon-yellow, but it is not allowed to have it because it is called the blue garden, and there must be no flowers in it but blue flowers. I can see no sense in this; it seems to me like fetters foolishly self-imposed. Surely the business of the blue garden is to be beautiful as well as to be blue. My own idea is that it should be beautiful first, and then just as blue as may be consistent with its best possible beauty. Moreover, any experienced colourist knows that the blues will be more telling—more purely blue—by the juxtaposition of rightly placed complementary colour. How it may be done is shown in the plan, for, as I cannot have these gardens myself, it will be some consolation to suggest to those who may be in sympathy with my views, how they may be made.

The Grey garden is so called because most of its plants have grey foliage, and all the carpeting and bordering plants are grey or whitish. The flowers are white, lilac, purple and pink. It is a garden mostly for August, because August is the time when the greater number of suitable plants are in bloom; but a Grey garden could also be made for September, or ever October, because of the number of Michaelmas Daisies that can be brought into use.

A plan is given of a connected series of gardens of special colouring. For the sake of clearness they are shown in as simple a form as possible, but the same colour scheme could be adapted to others of more important design and larger extent.

The Gold garden is chosen for the middle, partly because it contains the greater number of permanent shrubs and is bright and cheerful all the year round, and partly because it is the best preparation, according to natural colour law, for the enjoyment of the compartments on either side. It is supposed that the house is a little way away to the north, with such a garden scheme close to it as may best suit its style and calibre. Then I would have a plantation of shrubs and trees. The shade and solidity of this would rest and refresh the eye and mind, making them the more ready to enjoy the colour garden. Suddenly entering the Gold garden, even on the dullest day, will be like coming into sunshine. Through the shrub-wood there is also a path to right and left parallel to the long axis of the colour garden, with paths turning south at its two ends, joining the ends of the colour-garden paths. This has been taken into account in arranging the sequence of the compartments.

The hedges that back the borders and form the partitions are for the most part of Yew, grown and clipped to a height of seven feet. But in the case of the Gold garden, where the form is larger and more free than in the others, there is no definite hedge, but a planting of unclipped larger gold Hollies, and the beautiful golden Plane, so cut back and regulated as to keep within the desired bounds. This absence of a stiff hedge gives more freedom of aspect and a better cohesion with the shrub-wood.

In the case of the Grey garden the hedge is of Tamarisk (*Tamarix gallica*), whose feathery grey-green is in delightful harmony with the other foliage greys. It will be seen on the plan that where this joins the Gold garden the hedge is double, for it must be of gold Holly on one side and of Tamarisk on the other. At the entrances and partition where the path passes, the hedge shrubs are allowed to grow higher, and are eventually trained to form arches over the path.

In the Gold and Green gardens the shrubs, which form the chief part of the planting, are shown as they will be after some years' growth. It is best to have them so from the first. If, in order to fill the space at once, several are planted where one only should eventually stand, the extra ones being removed later, the one left probably does not stand quite right. I strongly counsel the placing of them singly at first, and that until they have grown, the space should be filled with temporary plants. Of these, in the Gold garden, the most useful will be *Œnothera lamarckiana, Verbascum olympicum* and *V. phlomoides* with more Spanish Broom than the plan shows till the gold Hollies are grown; and yellow-flowered annuals, such as the several kinds of *Chrysanthemum coronarium,* both single and double, and *Coreopsis Drummondi;* also a larger quantity of African Marigolds, the pale primrose and the lemon-coloured. The fine tall yellow Snapdragons will also be invaluable. Flowers of a deep orange colour, such as the orange African Marigold, so excellent for their own use, are here out of place, only those of pale and middle yellow being suitable.

In such a garden it will be best to have, next the path, either a whole edging of dwarf, gold-variegated Box-bushes about eighteen inches to two feet high, or a mixed planting of these and small bushes of gold-variegated Euonymus clipped down to not much over two feet. The edge next the path would be kept trimmed to a line.

The strength of colour and degree of variation are so great that it is well worth going to a nursery to pick out all these gold-variegated plants. It is not enough to tell the gardener to get them. There should be fervour on the part of the garden's owner such as will take him on a gold-plant pilgrimage to all good nurseries within reach, or even to some rather out of reach. No good gardening comes of not taking pains. All good gardening is the reward of well-directed and strongly sustained effort.

Where, in the Gold garden, the paths meet and swing round in a circle, there may be some accentuating ornament—a sundial, a stone vase for flowers, or a tank for a yellow Water-lily. If a sundial, and there should be some incised lettering, do not have the letters gilt because it is the Gold garden; the colour and texture of gilding are quite out of place. If there is a tank, do not have goldfish; their colour is quite wrong. Never hurt the garden for the sake of the tempting word.

The word "gold" in itself is, of course, an absurdity; no growing leaf or flower has the least resemblance to the colour of gold. But the word may be used because it has passed into the language with a commonly accepted meaning.

I have always felt a certain hesitation in using the free-growing perennial Sunflowers. For one thing, the kinds with the running roots are difficult to keep in check, and their yearly transplantation among other established perennials is likely to cause disturbance and injury to their neighbours. Then, in so many neglected gardens they have been let run wild, surviving when other plants have been choked, that, half unconsciously, one has come to hold them cheap and unworthy of the best use. I take it that my own impression is not mine alone, for often when I have been desired to do planting-plans for flower borders, I have been asked not to put in any of these Sunflowers, because "they are so common."

But nothing is "common" in the sense of base or unworthy if it is rightly used, and it seems to me that this Gold garden is just the place where these bright autumn flowers may be employed to great advantage. I have therefore shown *Helianthus rigidus* and its tall-growing variety *Miss Mellish,* although the colour of both is quite the deepest I should care to advise. . . .

The golden Planes, where the path comes in from the north, are of course deciduous, and it might be well to have gold Hollies again at the back of these, or gold Yews, to help the winter effect.

In some places in the plan the word "gold" has been omitted, but the yellow-leaved or yellow-variegated form of the shrub is always intended. There is a graceful cut-leaved Golden Elder that is desirable, as well as the common one.

Perhaps the Grey garden [figure 49] is seen at its best by reaching it through the orange borders. Here the eye becomes filled and saturated with the strong red and yellow colouring. D on the plan stands for Dahlia; the other plant names are written in full. This filling with the strong, rich colouring has the natural effect of making the eye eagerly desirous for the complementary colour, so that, standing by the inner Yew arch and suddenly turning to look into the Grey garden, the effect is surprisingly—quite astonishingly—luminous and refeshing. One never knew before how vividly bright Ageratum could be, or Lavendar or Nepeta; even the grey-purple of Echinops appears to have more positive colour than one's expectation would assign to it. The purple of the Clematises of the Jackmani class becomes piercingly brilliant, while the grey and glaucous foliage looks strangely cool and clear.

The plan shows the disposition of the plants, with grey-white edging of *Cineraria maritima,* Stachys and Santolina. There are groups of Lavender with large-flowered Clematises (C in the plan) placed so that they may be trained close to them and partly over them. There are the monumental forms of the taller Yuccas, *Y. gloriosa* and its variety *recurva* towards the far angles, and, nearer the front (marked Yucca in plan), the free-blooming *Yucca filamentosa* of smaller size. The flower-colouring is of purple, pink and white. Besides the Yuccas, the other white flowers are *Lilium longiflorum* and *Lilium candidum* (L C on plan), the clear white Achillea The Pearl and the grey-white clouds of *Gypsophila paniculata.* The pink flowers are Sutton's Godetia Double Rose, sown in place early in May, the beautiful clear pink Hollyhock Pink Beauty and the pale pink Double Soapwort. Clematis and white Everlasting Pea are planted so that they can be trained to cover the Gypsophila when its bloom is done and the seed-pods are turning brown. As soon as it loses its grey colouring the flowering tops are cut off, and the Pea and Clematis, already brought near, are trained over. When the Gypsophila is making its strong growth in May, the shoots are regulated and supported by some stiff branching spray that is stuck among it. A little later this is quite hidden, but it remains as a firm substructure when the top of the Gypsophila is cut back and the other plants are brought over.

Elymus is the blue-green Lyme-grass, a garden form of the handsome blue-leaved grass that grows on the seaward edges of many of our sea-shore sandhills. The Soapwort next to it is the double form of *Saponaria officinalis,* found wild in many places.

Of Ageratum two kinds are used—a brightly coloured one of the dwarf kinds for places near the front, where it tells as a close mass of colour, and the tall *A. mexicanum* for filling up further back in the border, where it

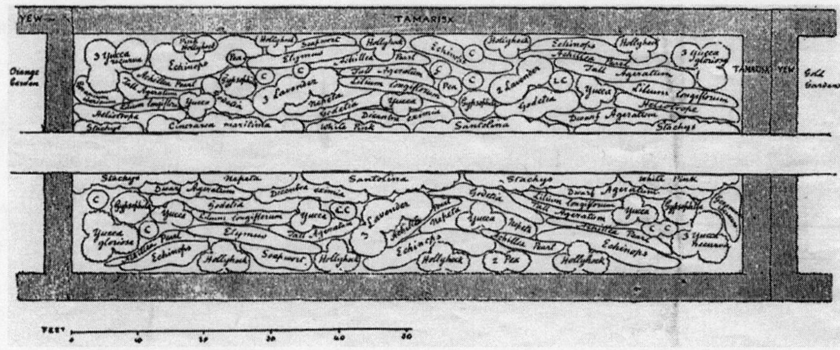

FIGURE 49 Gertrude Jekyll, *The Grey Garden*, from *Colour Schemes for the Flower Garden*, p. 105

shows as a diffuse purple cloud. The Nepeta is the good garden Catmint (*N. Mussini*). Its normal flowering-time is June, but it is cut half back, removing the first bloom, by the middle of the month, when it at once makes new flowering shoots.

Now, after the grey plants, the Gold garden looks extremely bright and sunny. A few minutes suffice to fill the eye with the yellow influence, and then we pass to the Blue garden, where there is another delightful shock of eye-pleasure. The brilliancy and purity of colour are almost incredible. Surely no blue flowers were ever so blue before! That is the impression received. For one thing, all the blue flowers used, with the exception of Eryngium and *Clematis davidiana*, are quite pure blues; these two are grey-blues. There are no purple-blues, such as the bluest of the Campanulas and the perennial Lupines; they would not be admissible. With the blues are a few white and palest yellow flower; the foam-white *Clematis recta*, a delightful foil to Delphinium Belladonna; white perennial Lupine with an almond-like softness of white; *Spiræa Aruncus*, another foam-coloured flower. Then milk-white Tree Lupine, in its carefully decreed place near the bluish foliage of Rue and Yucca. Then there is the tender citron of Lupine Somerset and the full canary of the tall yellow Snapdragon, the diffused pale yellow of the soft plumy Thalictrum and the strong canary of *Lilium szovitzianum*, with white Everlasting Pea and white Hollyhock at the back. White-striped Maize grows up to cover the space left empty by the Delphiniums when their bloom is over, and pots of *Plumbago capense* are dropped in to fill empty spaces. One group of this is trained over the bluish-leaved *Clematis recta*, which goes out of flower with the third week of July.

Yuccas, both of the large and small kinds, are also used in the Blue garden, and white Lilies, *candidum* and *longiflorum.* There is foliage both of glaucous and of bright green colour, besides an occasional patch of the silvery *Eryngium giganteum.* At the front edge are the two best Funkias, *F. grandiflora,* with leaves of bright yellow-green, and *F. Sieboldi,* whose leaves are glaucous. The variegated Coltsfoot is a valuable edge-plant where the yellowish white of its bold parti-colouring is in place, and I find good use for the variegated form of the handsome Grass *Glyceria* or *Poa aquatica.* Though this is a plant whose proper places is in wet ground, it will accommodate itself to the flower border, but it is well to keep it on the side away from the sun. It harmonises well in colour with the Coltsfoot; as a garden plant it is of the same class as the old Ribbon Grass, but is very much better. It is a good plan to replant it late in spring in order to give it a check; if this is not done it has a rather worn-out appearance before the end of the summer; but if it is replanted or divided late in April it stands well throughout the season. The great white-striped Japanese grass, *Eulalia japonica striata,* is planted behind the Delphiniums at the angles, and groups well with the Maize just in front.

From the Blue garden, passing eastward, we come to the Green garden. Shrubs of bright and deep green colouring and polished leaf-surface predominate. Here are green Aucubas and Skimmias, with *Ruscus racemosus,* the beautiful Alexandrian or Victory Laurel, and more polished foliage of *Acanthus, Funkia, Asarum, Lilium candidum* and *longiflorum,* and *Iris fœtidissima.* Then feathery masses of paler green, Male Fern and Lady Fern and *Myrrhis odorata,* the handsome fern-like Sweet Cicely of old English gardens. In the angles are again Eulalias, but these are the variety *zebrina* with the leaves barred across with yellow.

In the Green garden the flowers are fewer and nearly all white—Campanulas *macrantha alba* and *persicifolia,* Lilies, Tulips, Foxgloves, Snapdragons, Peonies, Hellebores—giving just a little bloom for each season to accompany the general scheme of polished and fern-like foliage. A little bloom of palest yellow shows in the front in May and June, with the flowers of Uvularia and Epimedium. But the Green garden, for proper development, should be on a much larger scale.

MARY WEBB

"The Beauty of Colour"

The Spring of Joy: A Little Book of Healing. 1917. New York: E. P. Dutton, 1937. 186–93.

The Sunne shone
Upon my bed with bright bemes,
With many glad gilden stremes,
And eke the welkin was so faire,
Blew, bright, clere was the air.

Chaucer

A rose that flushes in the bud grows pure white in maturity; a sycamore leaf, from the moment of its soft uncurling, changes a little day by day until the final flame of the year; so the colours of all things fluctuate continually. They seem to float round material forms, migratory, never a changeless possession of any. Nightly the darkness washes them out with her dusky brush, and in the strong hands of the seasons they are ephemeral. When the hazy freshness thickens daily round an alder-trunk, one can hardly believe that anything so ethereal emanates from the black bark; it is like a green gossamer from the evening west caught in the branches. Blossoming time in a damson country, when the whiteness foams over valley and ridge, has the same effect of clouds resting on the trees. To the eye of imagination all things stand haloed in colour that flickers and quickens mysteriously.

However much we may learn of chlorophyll, chromogen, and colour-cells—the pigments of nature that are made from earth and rain, air and sun, somewhere in the dark habitation of the roots and airy galleries of the leaves—we do not know why the same ingredients should clothe one petal with flame and another with blue. We do not know what impulse sends up the water-lily from the stagnant ooze in glistening white, and lays a mauve mantle over the wistaria that feeds upon corruption; nor why two plants of the same genus in the same conditions should be so differently coloured as are the blue and yellow gentian. Colour, like fragrance, is intimately connected with light; and between the different rays of the spectrum and the colour-cells of plants there is a strange telepathy. These processes, so little explored, seem in their deep secrecy and earthly spirituality more marvellous than the most radiant visions of the mystics.

Of all colours, brown is the most satisfying. It is the deep, fertile tint of the earth itself; it lies hidden beneath every field and garden; it is the garment of multitudes of earth's children, from the mouse to the eagle; the men of the fields are russet-clad and russet-complexioned; thousands of seeds, from the heavy burr to the breeze-blown thistle-fluff, are brown as the soil from which they come, to which they return; and of the same fruitful colour are the rushing streams, the pillars of the forest, and the buttresses of the hills. It is dim with antiquity, full of the magic that lurks within reality; and just as one stands in an ancient hall, gazing into the duskiness and waiting for the coming of departed inhabitants, so one watches and listens in, the tawny furrowlands for the tread of the myriads whose lives have gone to the making of them. There is that in brown which surely speaks to all who are ever born into the world.

Green is the fresh emblem of well-founded hopes. In blue the spirit can wander, but in green it can rest. A picture of vivid contrasts could be painted in green alone; there are a hundred shades of it in one field—malachite, beryl, emerald, and all the intermediate tints. Uncurling oak leaves have a dash of blue and a great deal of sienna; daffodil leaves and holly are blue-green: young larches are sky and gamboge; there is a great deal of red in the tender young leaves of birches; fir-needles have a whitish line on the underside; yews are black-green; the laburnum is toned with grey. Because it is so plentifully mixed with other colours, it is never crude. It also has endless variations of transparency and opacity; beech leaves in May are so pellucid that you can almost see through them; rhododendrons are so solidly coloured that they reflect the light. The best of all greens are in the tender plants of spring woods and meadows—the anemone, the red-spotted sorrel, ferns of fine texture, glaucous mosses, sedges even cooler to look upon than water. Not a place on earth need be destitute of green; the desert has its cactus, the sea its translucent weed. However poor a man may be, he can have a sprig of green by his door, even if it is only a trail of ivy in a broken jar. The saddest place can have its green shoot of hope, the same hope that irradiates the burgeoning forest. Deep in men's hearts there lives this spirit of hope—or religion—renewed each spring. Over churches of the sternest creeds the ivy is not afraid to climb; and when the church has crumbled with its dogma, the ivy covers all with its kindly curtain and speaks of a life greater than these, and an evergreen love that embraces all.

Those hot splendours of sunrise and sunset, of first and last things—red and gold—are the colours of all man loves—wealth and the blood that is poured to gain it, scarlet lips and yellow hair, the sacramental chalice and the wine within. Nature is prodigal of them, and autumn is their festival, with its shining pavements of harvest, its sierras of flaming bracken, its burning woods and smouldering hedges and trees like tongues of orange and red flame. No coolness of the blue above, no liquidness of silver nights can quench their fierceness until they have consumed their prey. They are the colours of crises; in stormy dawns they put the darkness to flight with their bright scimitars, and stain the streams and possess the sky. To them belongs ripeness—apple and pomegranate and the tree of the knowledge of good and evil. To them belong the haughty beauty of tropical flowers and the terrible loveliness of fire, and a blood-red blossom with a golden heart is the ancient emblem of passion.

Mauve has a delicate artificiality, something neither of earth nor heaven. It is like the temperament which can express in sheer artistic pleasure heights and depths which it can never touch. Whether it is sultry, as in lilac, or cool, as in lady's-smocks, this mingling of fierce red and saintly blue has an elfin quality. Hence comes the eeriness of a field of autumn crocuses at twilight, when every folded flower is growing invisible, and doubtless there is a fairy curled up in each. Children look for the Little People in mauve flowers—Canterbury bells and hyacinths—and, though they never find them, they know them there. Mauve enchants the mind, lures it to open its amethyst door, and behold! nothing but emptiness and eldritch moonshine. It is a Vivian crowned with nightshade and helleborine, leading with soft allurements to a country whose shores are of vanishing mist.

Silver is akin to mauve. Foam and icicles, dandelion clocks in the sun, the moon and stars, white flowers under the moon—all have this pristine tint that is more a radiance than a colour, that is without depth or shadow, with a fleetingness like that of dreams. It is the colour of the undersides of things. White-willow and poplar leaves are lined with it; watching them, one is reminded of the moment when a friend unexpectedly turns his remoter self toward one—his white self that is so easily transfigured. When the wind is in a plane-tree, the multitudes of leaves are suddenly ruffled, so that the whole tree shines; it is like watching a crowd of people under some soul-stirring emotion. Half the charm of silver in nature is due to its remoteness; no ore of man's refining can attain the sparkle of a raindrop; we cannot distil the radiance from a white narcissus, nor rob the stars of their silver fleeces. There is a perfect harmony of mauve and silver in a birch wood a little while before the leaves come. The shining stems rise out of a faint purple mist which deepens in the distance. Above, all the twigs are softly purple too, and, being very fine and numerous, they make another haze higher up. The straight silver rods gleam in long perspective in their setting of cloudy violet, lost in it above and below. Any face might look out from that mist, any white feet of nymph of hamadryad pass among the glimmering aisles; in the dim, lilac-tinted distance it may be that Merlin still sleeps in his vaporous magic circle.

Blue is the rarest colour, the one which least often imprisons itself in material things. There are few blue flowers, and most of them are small and fragile, like love-in-a-mist and speedwell. Gentian is never so lavishly outspread as it is upon the heights, symbolically near the sky. Blue expanses—reflections in water, the cobalt of distance, are only lent to earth. If we want endless, satisfying blue, we must look up to where it dwells in impalpable space, shining like solid enamel, or liquid and vague. There is the roaming-place of the mystic; through the dissolving azure of a summer day he tries to probe; into the impenetrable heavens of night he launches his spirit like a coracle[1] among the stars. Blue is a holy colour; the Sufis wore it with this significance, and it is fitly used for Madonnas' robes and temple hangings, since the temple of our conscious and unconscious worship is canopied with it. Often a flash of sapphire in water, a shade of turquoise in the sky, will strike across the heart with an inexplicable pang. It is not sorrow; it is more than joy; it is at once the realisation of a perfect thing, the fear that we may never see it again, and the instinct that urges us to ascend through the known beauty to the unknown which is both the veil and the voice that summons beyond it.

Though winter may wear a sad-coloured garment, it is shot with bright threads of reminiscence and prophecy. Orange oak-leaves, lingering seed-vessels on ash and lime, crimson blackberry trails, are recollections of past splendour. The sere and broken reeds and rushes—golden and russet—are like the piled trophies of some fairy warfare; spear and sword and bulrush-banner recall the time when conquering summer led forth his legions. There are dreams and dawnings of another summer also. The twigs that look so lifeless have minute buds on them, vivid points of colour. The alder's purple buds and dripping gold of catkins, the red knobs on larches, the sticky, brown chestnut-buds, the green buds of the sycamore, are all brilliant and warm with sleeping summer. The purple osier is already set with green points from which are to emerge fluffy catkins, and the sallow is preparing its gold and silver blossoms which are to be the early palm, drip-

1. A small boat. *Ed.*

ping with honey and humming with insects. There are pale blooms of box and ivy; fir-cones rich as pine-apples in the sun, with flashes of blue-tits' wings about them; red-pine trunks; shining greys of ash and beech bole; vivid green of elder-trees; holly (Robin Hood of the woods) flames in red and green; blue-grey birds scud across the dim, tufted meadows. The distant woods grow auburn as the leaf-buds swell, and in their folds the shadows are like dwale.[2] After the turn of the year the tops of the poplars and aspens take the colour of ripe oats. Wildfire runs along the elms as the red buds push out. In February is the bridal of the yew, when one tree is covered with small wax cups—the future berries—and another is thick with honey-coloured flowers; then, at the least breeze, the air is full of the gold dust of pollen. In dark November comes the heyday of the mother-tree. She flushes into young rose, tender as pink hawthorn, but deeper; all her sombre recesses of ancient green are transfigured by this surprise of beauty, by these multitudes of japonica-tinted berries. At each spray's end flutter missel-thrushes, their spread wings lined with silver. Upon the dark-green background this harmony of rose and pearl glows like an old illumination; its unobtrusiveness deepens the charm. Only the undersides of the branches glimmer with colour, only the underwings have a moonlit look; yet it is enough, since we know that the dark wings can be transfigured, that the melancholy trees can sometimes stand beneath the pale sky in a rosy haze, as if ethereal dew had distilled upon them. The spirit of the picture is reminiscent of Orcagna's[3] *Assumption of the Virgin* in alabaster, where angels hover round a berry-shaped mandorla in which Mary is throned.

Atmosphere, that whimsical artist, transforms the already brilliant world by clothing things in tints other than their own. A wide sweep of country fascinates us not only by its innate beauty but by the airy blue of the far plain, the smoking woods, the hills like wet violets. The haze that clings in the hearts of autumn trees, that foams like a white sea round the stems in a larch copse, and hangs—pale lavender—in the recesses of beech woods, lends the trees more loveliness than their own. Brimming the valleys, dimpling the fields, it is the magic of a March morning; looming over hills, it adds mystery to their strength of outline. Near sunset, soft films gather imperceptibly, stealing over everything, so that all colours, while keeping their

2. A deadly nightshade plant. *Ed.*

3. Orcagna (c.1308–c.1368), an Italian painter, sculptor, and architect, noted for his Florentine frescoes. *Ed.*

individuality, are mixed with gold medium. The clearest atmosphere throws a veil over actual things; upon even a near horizon trees seldom look green, but are etched upon the clouds in pale peacock and silver-grey, flaming at the sun's pleasure into bronze and copper. Often the most ordinary scenery puts on such colours as no painter would dare to imitate; whoever cares to look may see his neighbour's barn standing in the celestial radiance of *Revelations* or the fantastic brilliance of elfdom. They can see ploughland red in the sunset, as though stained with the blood of generations; topaz pastures; hedges of the blue of Gobelin tapestry; valleys sheeted in silver, when the rising mist and the descending moonlight are interfused. In heavy, thunderous weather the earth returns to the iron age; everything is sombre, hard and grey until the sky grows hot for the melting and gives things the metallic look of lustre-ware. Sometimes in snow a miracle of air and light transforms the world into a great glowing rose. Atmosphere has no abiding place, no set rules for its coming and going; when you walk upon the hills, their watchet raiment fades, and you cannot carry home the primrose mist of morning. All the more appealing is this vagrant glamour, because it only brushes the solid earth with swallow wings.

The best way of seeing colour unallied with material form is to watch the sky; and when everything else is gone, it shines still above us. Once on a December evening the clouds were in three distinct layers of colour, each moving independently, blown by a different wind. First came ebony; beyond that, moving more slowly, a long, straight cloud of geranium; above that again, a soft stratum of brown; and through one tremendous gash in all three shone the kingfisher-blue sky. Low in the west, safe and far from the tempestuous masses, stood Hesperus; around him, ivory and crocus splashed the blue, and just above the distant hills lay a line of green.

On a November morning, when the sky was faint and clear, and a lake of light widened momentarily along the horizon, the moon stood high up with a star at her feet—pale silver. Another star, not so near, was soon merged in the oncoming tawny flood, which softly inundated every little crevice of the bare trees on the skyline. Then in plunged the sun, swimming strongly, bent on reaching her, who thought herself so safe up there in the great expanses; and she paled and slid away with her attendant star, while he swam on with the tide of light that washed the sky.

Winter sunrise gives the impression that all colours have been drawn from the earth and set in the treasury of the heavens. There are the wild roses of summer hedges, the young green leaves of spring; there gold quickens, reminding us that the sun has not forgotten his daffodils; and the world warms her frozen breast in the reflected glory. Often in the life of the mind also the sky brightens as the earth fades. When the forlorn soul lies under a black frost and hears the long sigh of the snow-wind; when it seems that no shoot of hope can ever rise from an exception so bound and burdened, reduced to almost imbecile passivity—then across the eternal heavens trail the essential colours of life, and the frozen spirit flushes into rose.

CHRISTINA ROSSETTI

"Where innocent bright-eyed daisies are"

Sing-Song: A Nursery Rhyme Book. 1872. London: Macmillan, 1893. 59.

Where innocent, bright-eyed daisies are,
    With blades of grass between,
Each daisy stands up like a star
    Out of a sky of green.

MICHAEL FIELD (KATHERINE BRADLEY AND EDITH COOPER)

"Noon"

Underneath the Bough: A Book of Verses by Michael Field. London: George Bell and Sons, 1893. 103–4.

Full summer and at noon; from a waste bed
Convolvulus, musk-mallow, poppies spread
The triumph of the sunshine overhead.

Blue on refulgent ash-trees lies the heart;
It tingles on the hedge-rows; the young wheat
Sleeps, warm in golden verdure, at my feet.

The pale, sweet grasses of the hayfield blink;
The heath-moors, as the bees of the honey drink,
Suck the deep bosom of the day. To think

Of all that beauty by the light defined
None shares my vision! Sharply on my mind
Presses the sorrow: fern and flower are blind.

MICHAEL FIELD (KATHERINE BRADLEY AND EDITH COOPER)

"Cyclamens"

Underneath the Bough: A Book of Verses by Michael Field. London: George Bell and Sons, 1893. 108.

They are terribly white:
There is snow on the ground,
And a moon on the snow at night;
The sky is cut by the winter light;
Yet I, who have all these things in ken,
Am struck to the heart by the chiselled white
Of this handful of cyclamen.

MARY WEBB

"The White Moth"

Written in June 1902.

Over the fields at the fall of dusk,
Glamour is far and near.
Grasshopper-warblers are whispering
Close in the ear.

Delicate lavender ladysmocks
Shimmer along the way;
Eerie and wan in the afterglow
They bend and sway.

Down by the stream in the deepening night
Magical odours creep,
Breath of basil and mallow and musk
Falling asleep.

Under the moon, when the world is hushed,
If you were there to see,
Wonderful things are happening
In the willow-tree.

The furry white moth has a cradle there,
Hid in the silver bark.
She wakens and stirs at the rise of the moon,
And wings through the dark.

The sweet white campion is calling her
With fragrant voice in the night:
Deep in the heart of the glimmering cup
She tastes delight.

MARY E. COLERIDGE

"L'Oiseau Bleu"

Poems by Mary E. Coleridge. 1907. London: Elkin Matthews and Marrot, 1927. 52.

The lake lay blue below the hill.
    O'er it, as I looked, there flew
Across the waters, cold and still,
    A bird whose wings were palest blue.

The sky above was blue at last,
    The sky beneath me blue in blue.
A moment, ere the bird had passed,
    It caught his image as he flew.

CHARLOTTE MEW

"The Sunlit House"

Charlotte Mew: Collected Poems and Prose. 1915. Ed. Val Warner. London: Carcanet Press, 1981. 30–31.

White through the gate it gleamed and slept
    In shuttered sunshine: the parched garden flowers
Their fallen petals from the beds unswept,
    Like children unloved and ill-kept,
    Dreamed through the hours.
Two blue hydrangeas by the blistered door, burned brown,
    Watched there and no one in the town
Cared to go past, it night or day,
    Though why this was they wouldn't say.
But, I the stranger, knew that I must stay,
    Pace up the weed-grown paths and down,
    Till one afternoon—there is just a doubt—
    But I fancy I heard a tiny shout—
    From an upper window a bird flew out—
    And I went my way.

ALICE MEYNELL

"A Dead Harvest: In Kensington Gardens"

The Poems of Alice Meynell. 1901. New York: Charles Scribner's Sons, 1923. 55.

Along the graceless grass of town
They rake the rows of red and brown,—
Dead leaves, unlike the rows of hay
Delicate, touched with gold and grey,
Raked long ago and far away.

A narrow silence in the park,
Between the lights a narrow dark,
One street rolls on the north; and one,
Muffled, upon the south doth run;
Amid the mist the work is done.

A futile crop!—for it the fire
Smoulders, and, for a stack, a pyre.
So go the town's lives on the breeze,
Even as the sheddings of the trees;
Bosom nor barn is filled with these.

SECTION SIX

Popularizing Science

Lydia Becker's plea for women to be permitted to study science, featured in the first section, "Speaking Out," can be misleading without sufficient context. Becker was concerned about the increasing professionalization of science and its effect on the women of the late 1860s, when most women were still excluded from formal tertiary science education and from membership in the influential scientific societies of their day. She knew that the understanding of science had come to require technical knowledge. The gulf between men's and women's learning was increasing despite the opening of schools like Queen's College in 1848 and Bedford in 1849, both of which catered to women. Becker was certainly correct in her diagnosis. As we shall see in this section, women had more and more reasons to feel excluded from the ranks of professional scientists as the nineteenth century wore on. Nevertheless, I would like to emphasize that many women had been studying science from the seventeenth century until the time of Becker's essay. They attended lectures and discussions, went to science museums, bought nature atlases, and collected and observed natural phenomena—especially during the nature "crazes" of the 1830s and 1840s, when all manner of people were out collecting. So far as was possible in their culture, numbers of women educated themselves to the current state of science. Moreover, many writers had also set about devising ways to disseminate scientific knowledge in popular magazines and books geared especially for the general reader, hoping to make science accessible to women, to members of the working classes, and even to children (see figure 50).

These popularizers, whose ranks certainly included numerous women, did not intend to be originators of science but knowledgeable purveyors of scientific information. Creating popular science required their translating scientific language and theory into the vernacular (see figure 51), and the forms taken by their work were many: lectures, printed dialogues,

FIGURE 50 *Entomology,* children's playing card, c. 1843

conversations, letters, children's fairy stories, and parables, to name just a few. Underlying all these forms was one overriding purpose of popularization: to enable others to grasp basic, and sometimes complex, scientific phenomena. A secondary purpose was to interpret the larger social, political, and religious significance of scientific theories. In order to give some sense of the spectrum of this writing, in this section I have endeavored to reproduce a cross-section of popular science as written by a variety of Victorian and Edwardian women. It is important to remember that the art of popularization afforded many of them a living and all of them a voice in their culture, two attainments that were often very difficult for women in their day.

FIGURE 51 Louisa Anne Meredith, *Superb Dragon and Ostracian,* from *Tasmanian Friends and Foes,* opposite p. 196.

We begin with Jane Marcet (see figure 52), who in the early years of the nineteenth century wrote in a form called "conversations." Marcet's best-known book was *Conversations on Chemistry: in which the elements of that science are familiarly explained and illustrated by experiments* (1806), a groundbreaking work written after Marcet had heard a series of lectures on chemistry delivered by the famous chemist, Sir Humphry Davy. Marcet felt impelled to reproduce her newly found knowledge for others—particularly, as her subtitle suggests, for other women. Her conversations belonged to a category of discourses known as "familiar formats," all of which offered fictional representations of informal discussions on learned subjects. Familiar formats included both letters and dialogues and were popular from the seventeenth until the middle of the nineteenth century. In her *Letters for Literary Ladies* (1795), writer Maria Edgeworth (1768–1849) found them ideal for conveying subjects thought to be difficult for women or "unsuited to their sex." In Marcet's conversations, the dialogues take the form of discussions among three females: one older and two younger, the youngest being the most naïve and therefore most in need of instruction and points of clarification. In keeping with the focus on natural history and the human body that prevails in this text, I have here excerpted Marcet's *Conversations on Natural Philosophy* (1819), where her characters discuss the functioning of the human eye, rather than one of her books devoted exclusively to physical science. As here, in Mrs. B's last speech, the eye was often linked to natural theology, the idea that nature was a book through which one could visualize godhead.

Marcet was well respected in her own day. Her *Conversations on Chemistry* sold 160,000 copies in its day and went through sixty editions in less than forty years. But no woman popularizer was more respected than Mary Somerville (see figure 56). Somerville was an exception to the rule that popularizers were not usually experimenters or initiators of theory, although she was occasionally criticized on the second count. Beginning in 1826, she produced a number of scientific papers and by the time of the publication of her most famous book, *On the Connexion of the Physical Sciences* (1834), was well known in the scientific community. Excerpted here, the *Connexion* was written deliberately to disseminate science and was dedicated to the queen in hopes of making "the laws by which the material world is governed more familiar to my countrywomen" (*Connexion*, preface).

Alongside the work of Somerville, a more playful, fictional kind of science writing evolved. It was developed by women like Jane Loudon, who began her writing career as the writer of the futuristic thriller *The Mummy* (1827). Along with other approaches to science popularization and horticultural writing like that found in the section "Domesticating," Loudon instituted the "journey" for children. By delineating fictional trips that exposed its characters to new places as well as new plants and animals, this format set out to capture more than one aspect of a child's imagination. In *The Young Naturalist; or, The Travels of Agnes Merton and Her Mamma*, the journey is a railway journey meant to open the child's mind both to adaptation in the animal world and to awareness of parts of the United Kingdom made accessible by the burgeoning railway system. Spirited and clever, Loudon's episodic "journeys" writing stems from a desire to make learning enjoyable.

No one, however, could have been more eager in such a desire than Arabella Buckley. Former secretary to the eminent geologist Sir Charles Lyell (1797–1875), Buckley was a Darwinian who began producing scientific popularizations after Lyell's death. She was highly adept at this art, appealing directly to the senses in hopes of offering her readers what would become a characteristic "you-are-there" approach to her chosen subjects. By Buckley's time, the dialogue was no longer felt to be a viable form for teaching science, and Buckley's *Fairy-land of Science* instead compares the wonders of science to the wonders of a fairyland (see figure 57). In choosing this analogy, Buckley drew upon a late Victorian fascination with fairies and their imagined world, a fascination that would itself become a kind of "craze" of the late nineteenth century. In its direct address to the reader and its attempts to draw her or him immediately into the text, *Fairy-land* provides an interesting contrast with Marcet's conversations, which are meant to be dialogues overheard.

Analogy, like Buckley's to fairies, was another popular way to inform the uninformed. It was, for example, widely used when framing plant and animal parallels to human sexual reproduction in order to avoid what might have been considered the bad taste of directness and explicitness. Essays, books, and monographs utilizing this sort of analogy were so popular that they have given us a cliché still used today when we speak of "the birds and the bees." Ellis Ethelmer's *Baby Buds,* reprinted in part here, offers a description of human sexual reproduction as conveyed through analogy to plant life. Driven by a sincere earnestness that even the youngest of readers should not be misinformed about its serious subject, Ethelmer's work provides an interesting example of the Victorian bowdlerizing of the rites of human reproduction. It also concocts an unusual blend of sex education with altruism: proper, "pure" lovemaking is here discussed as a tribute to "Mother Nature," just as are love and kindness for all of nature's other creatures.

A final subsection of "Popularizing Science" is devoted entirely to women who wrote on the subject of Darwinism. The publication of Darwin's *Origin of Species* in 1859 certainly created a major upheaval in Victorian culture. Humanity's place in the scheme of evolution became a vexed question, as did the nature of survival itself. Not just religious ideas seemed challenged; so did people's very perceptions of the humanity of humankind. Many thinkers and writers therefore joined in explaining to others just what Darwin meant by natural selection and what the implications of such an idea were for their time. Most of these were highly serious, but some of these, too, were playful. For example, in March of 1862 a humorous writer for *Cornhill Magazine* posited a fictionalized, middle-aged woman visiting the zoo dressed in a "blue dress and sober bonnet." When queried as to who she is by the narrator—who himself seems to be in the midst of a doze—she presents him with a calling card reading, "Natural Selection! Originator of Species!"[1] and frightens him with her underlying ferocity masquerading as sober innocence. Darwin had, of course, personified his Nature as female in the first edition of the *Origin.* But here the association of women with Darwin's ideas, although it is clearly satirical, nevertheless feeds myths about women's nature as being subversively dangerous or destructive to men, an idea prevalent in mid-Victorian times.

In reality, far from being dangerous forces of nature masquerading as sober spinsters or matrons in unfashionable clothing, many women were themselves intellectuals fascinated by Darwinism. They explained, reexamined, and themselves satirized Darwinists. This subsection is intended to offer some of the women popularizers' diverse points of view on topics like natural selection and survival of species. It is important to remember that most of the women encountered in this book in one way or another were rocked in the wake of Darwinism. Frances Power Cobbe felt Darwinism was leading to vivisection and other undesirable forms of "science" making; Rosa Frances Swiney found "Darwin's man, a super-evolved woman, and Spencer's woman, an arrested man!" (*Woman and Natural Law* 400); Vernon Lee posited a kind of aesthetic evolution; and Mary Webb schooled herself in Darwin, Thomas Henry Huxley (1825–95, a biologist who was known as "Darwin's bulldog"), and Ernst Haeckel (1834–1919, a German zoologist and latter-day Darwinian). Arabella Buckley herself neither radically challenged nor fully appropriated Darwin; instead she attempted to extend his view of altruism. The central aim of much of her writing was to set out current theories of evolution for lay audiences and to do so just as clearly as possible. In two vivid books in particular, *Life and Her Children* (1880) and *Winners in Life's Race* (1883), she carefully sketched the seven divisions of life. The first book covers the first six divisions, the invertebrates—from the amoebas to the insects—and the second, the "backboned family." The heroine of both books is Life, or the life force, the moving force of the evolutionary process. For the purposes of this anthology, I have excerpted Buckley's beautiful description of Life from the first chapter of *Life and Her Children* and her resounding statement of belief that the animal kingdom moves in the direction of greater altruism from *Winners.* The latter section also reveals the sweep of Buckley's prose when she brings her

1. E. S. Dixon, "A Vision of Animal Existences," *Cornhill Magazine* 5 (March 1862), 311–18.

highly visual, panoramic "you-are-there" imagination to bear on the subject of evolution.

Appreciation and lyricism were, as we have seen, not the only responses to Darwinism at the end of the nineteenth century. Poet Mary Robinson did follow in some of Buckley's pathways, but Alice Bodington and May Kendall veered in quite other directions. Bodington offered an update on Darwin for the 1890s. According to her—and as Darwin himself eventually realized—a study of natural selection needed to be counterweighted with a study of the influence of environment on evolution. Alice Bodington's piece on mammalia grapples with this. A longer selection of Bodington might have admitted more of her humor as well as her clarity in updating Darwin. Often with tongue in cheek, Bodington seems to have enjoyed spoofing science fiction, contemporary obsessions with Darwinism, and contemporary customs, and she embedded such spoofs in her text on evolution. For example, in a passage that precedes the one excerpted here, she suggests that it would be interesting to imagine a world "where everyone had their mouths in the middle of their bodies . . . and their eyes at the ends of their fingers and toes." She then adds an aside suggesting what havoc such adaptations might wreak on a Victorian dinner party (*Studies in Evolution and Biology* 20). Poet May Kendall exhibited a similar sense of humor toward what her culture might make of Darwinism. In her satirical "Lay of the Trilobite" and "The Lower Life" she makes light of the human striving for both intellectual and physical prowess by setting these desires in the context of evolution. In the bargain she manages to deflate famous poets, philosophers, and even the irrepressible Huxley.

Readers of the entirety of this book will realize that this section explicitly devoted to science popularization gives only a sampling of this type of writing by women. This art form is found elsewhere in this text, particularly in some of the writing on behalf of other species and in the next section, on what constitutes a professional. One might ask then in what sense all of the women just mentioned in this introduction would have thought themselves professionals. Was it as writers? as scientists? Most of them received money for their books and essays and would have considered themselves literary women or educators—education and diffusion of their culture's norms and ideas having always been a primary concern of women. Yet only one of them, Mary Somerville, for whom a women's college at Oxford was named, received the acclaim of a professional scientist. Most of the others opened their books with prefaces and careful disclaimers about their own knowledge, suggesting that they were interpreters, not scientists, and were reliant on others' authority for their science. But then, as the next section will show, the business of just who had the right to be considered a scientific "professional" was a gray area indeed, especially so far as women were concerned.

*K*INDS OF *S*CIENCE *P*OPULARIZATION

JANE MARCET

From *Conversations on Natural Philosophy*

1819. London: Longman, Rees, Orme, Brown, Green, & Longman, 1836. 434–55.

CONVERSATION XVIII

Optics

On the Structure of the Eye, and Optical Instruments

Description of the Eye.— Of the Image on the Retina.—Refraction of the Humours of the Eye.— Of the use of Spectacles.— Of the Single Microscope.— Of the Double Microscope.— Of the Solar Microscope.— Magic Lanthorn.—Refracting Telescope.—Reflecting Telescope.

Mrs. B

I shall this morning give you some account of the structure of the eye; you have hitherto considered it only as a simple camera obscura, in which the representation of objects is made on the retina; but I must now tell you, that this camera obscura is furnished with a variety of substances, all of which contribute to the perfection of vision, and enclosed in a double covering to guard it from injury.

The body of the eye is of a spherical form [figure 52.1]; it has two membranous coverings; the external one, *a a a,* is called the sclerotica: this has a projection in that part of the eye which is exposed to view, *b b,* which is called the cornea, because, when dried, it has nearly the consistence of very fine horn, and is sufficiently transparent for the light to obtain free passage through it.

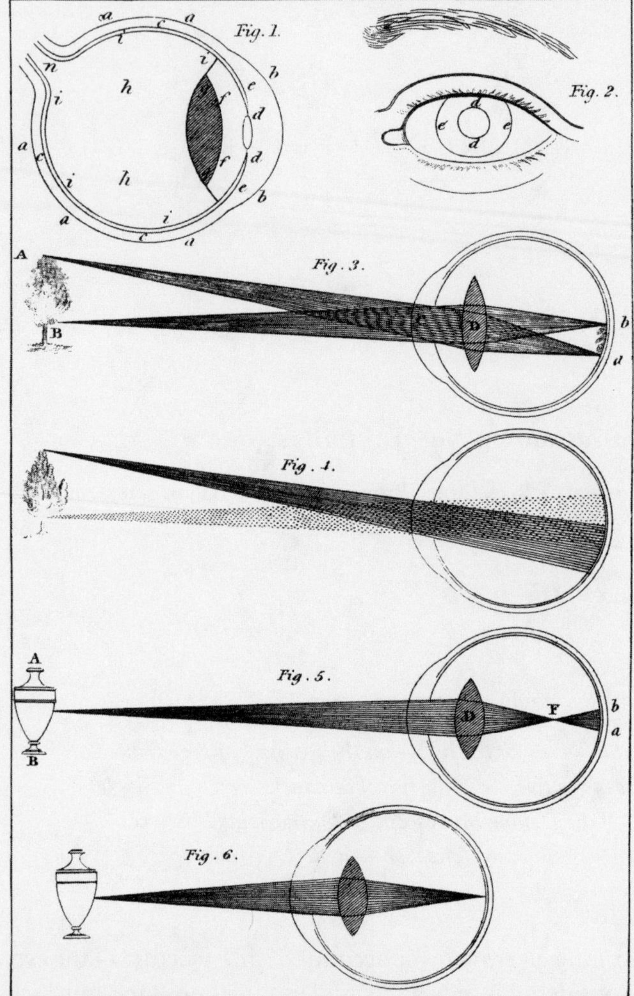

FIGURE 52 The body of the eye, from Jane Marcet, *Conversations on Natural Philosophy*, opposite p. 435

The second membrane, which lines the cornea, and envelopes the eye, is called the choroid, *c c c;* this has an opening in front just beneath the cornea, which forms the pupil, *d d,* through which the rays of light pass into the eye. The pupil is surrounded by a coloured border of fibres, called the iris, *e e,* which, by its motion, always preserves the pupil of a circular form, whether it be expanded in the dark, or contracted by a strong light.

FIGURE 53 Jane Marcet

Emily

I did not know that the pupil was susceptible of varying its dimensions.

Mrs. B

The construction of the eye is so admirable, that it is capable of adapting itself, more or less, to the circumstances in which it is placed. In a faint light the pupil dilates so as to receive an additional quantity of rays, and in a strong light it contracts, in order to prevent the intensity of the light from injuring the optic nerve. Observe Emily's eyes, as she sits looking toward the windows: the pupils appear very small, and the iris large. Now, Emily, turn from the light, and cover your eyes with your hand, so as entirely to exclude it for a few moments.

Caroline

How very much the pupils of her eyes are now enlarged, and the iris diminished. This is, no doubt, the reason why the eyes suffer pain, when from darkness they suddenly come into a strong light; for the pupil being dilated, a quantity of rays must rush in before it has time to contract.

Emily

And when we go from a strong light into obscurity, we at first imagine ourselves in total darkness; for a sufficient number of rays cannot gain admittance into the contracted pupil to enable us to distinguish objects: but in a few minutes it dilates, and we clearly perceive objects which were before invisible.

Mrs. B

It is just so. The choroid, *c c,* is lined with a black paint, which serves to absorb all the rays that are irregularly reflected, and to convert the body of the eye into a more perfect camera obscura. When the pupil is expanded to its utmost extent, it is capable of admitting ten times the quantity of light that it does when most contracted. In cats, and animals which are said to see in the dark, the power of dilatation and contraction of the pupil is still greater: it is computed that their pupils may admit one hundred times more light at one time than at another.

Within these coverings of the eye-ball are contained three transparent substances, called humours. The first occupies the space immediately behind the cornea, and is called the aqueous humour, *f f,* from its liquidity and its resemblance to water. Beyond this is situated the crystalline humour, *g g,* so called from its clearness and transparency: it has the form of a lens, and refracts the rays of light in a greater degree of perfection than any that have been constructed by art; it is attached by fibres to each side of the choroid. The back part of the eye between the crystalline humour and the retina, is filled by the vitreous humour, *h h,* which derives its name from an apparent resemblance to glass or vitrified substances.

The membraneous coverings of the eye are intended chiefly for the preservation of the retina, *i i,* which is by far the most important part of the eye, as it is that which receives the impression of the objects of sight, and conveys it to the mind. The retina consists of an expansion of the optic nerve, which proceeds from the brain, enters the eye at *n,* on the side next the nose, and is finely spread over the interior surface of the choroid.

The rays of light which enter the eye by the pupil are refracted by the several humours in their passage through them, each pencil uniting in a focus on the retina.

Caroline

I do not understand the use of these refracting humours: the images of objects is represented in the camera obscura, without any such assistance.

Mrs. B

That is true; but the representation would be much more strong and distinct, if we enlarged the opening of the camera obscura, and received the rays into it through a lens.

I have told you that rays proceed from bodies in all possible directions. We must, therefore, consider every part of an object which sends rays to our eyes as points from which the rays diverge, as from a centre.

Emily

These divergent rays, issuing from a single point, I believe you told us, were called a pencil of rays?

Mrs. B

Yes. Now divergent rays, on entering the pupil do not cross each other; the pupil, however, is sufficiently large to admit a small pencil of them; and these, if not refracted to a focus by the humours, would continue diverging after they had passed the pupil, would fall dispersed upon the retina, and thus the image of a single point would be expanded over a large portion of the retina. The divergent rays from every other point of the object would be spread over a similar extent of space, and would interfere and be confounded with the first; so that no distinct image could be formed, and the retina would represent total confusion both of figure and colour. Fig. 52.3. represents two pencils of rays issuing from two points of the tree A B, and entering the pupil C, refracted by the crystalline humour D, and forming distinct images of the spot they proceed from, on the retina, at *a b*. Fig. 52.4. differs from the preceding, merely from not being supplied with a lens; in consequence of which the pencils of rays are not refracted to a focus, and no distinct image is formed on the retina. I have delineated only the rays issuing from two points of an object, and distinguished the two pencils in fig. 52.4 by describing one of them with dotted lines: the interference of these two pencils of rays on the retina will enable you to form an idea of the confusion which would arise, from thousands and millions of points at the same instant pouring their divergent rays upon the retina.

Emily

True; but I do not yet well understand how the refracting humours remedy this imperfection.

Mrs. B

The refraction of these several humours unite the whole of a pencil of rays, proceeding from any one point of an object, to a corresponding point on the retina, and the image is thus rendered distinct and strong. If you conceive, in fig. 52.3, every point of the tree to send forth a pencil of rays similar to those, A B, every part of the tree will be as accurately represented on the retina as the points *a b*.

Emily

How admirably, how wonderfully, this is contrived!

Caroline

But since the eye requires refracting humours in order to have a distinct representation formed on the retina, why is not the same refraction necessary for the image formed in the camera obscura?

Mrs. B

Because the aperture through which we received the rays into the camera obscura is extremely small; so that but very few of the rays diverging from a point gain admittance: but we shall now enlarge the aperture, and furnish it with a lens, and you will find the landscape to be more perfectly represented.

Caroline

How obscure and confused the image is now that you have enlarged the opening, without putting in the lens.

Mrs. B

Such, or very similar, would be the representation on the retina, unassisted by the refracting humours. But see what a difference is produced by the introduction of the lens, which collects each pencil of divergent rays into their several foci.

Caroline

The alteration is wonderful; the representation is more clear, vivid, and beautiful than ever.

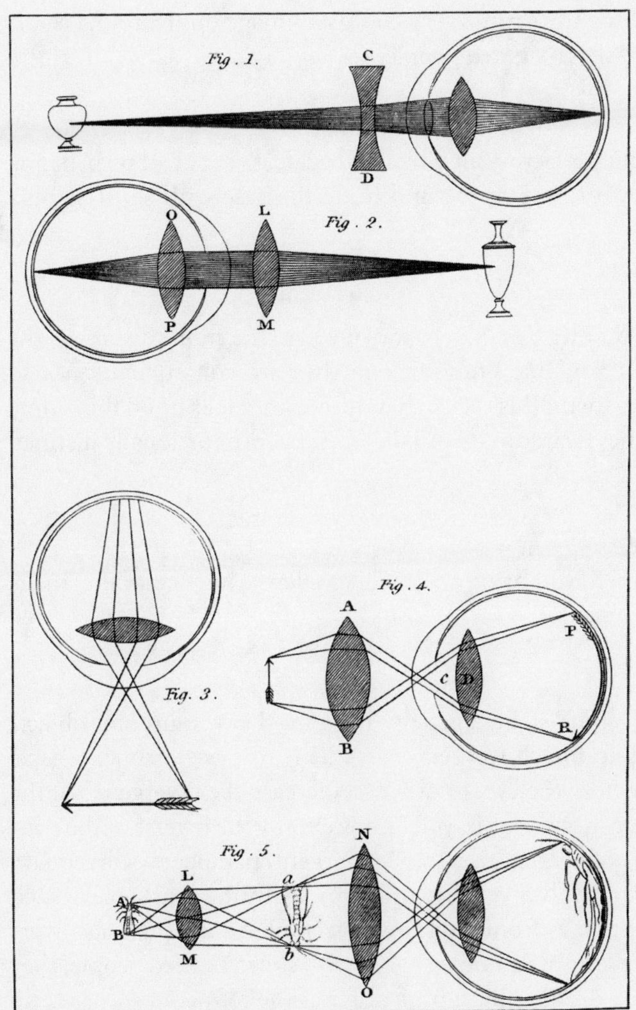

FIGURE 54 Concave lens, from Jane Marcet, *Conversations on Natural Philosophy,* opposite p. 442

Mrs. B

You will now be able to understand the nature of that imperfection of sight, which arises from the eyes being too prominent. In such cases the crystalline humour, D (fig. 52.5), being extremely convex, refracts the rays too much, and collects a pencil, proceeding from the object A B, into a focus, F, before they reach the retina. From this focus, the rays proceed diverging, and consequently form a very confused image on the retina at *a b*. This is the defect of short-sighted people.

Emily

I understand it perfectly. But why is this defect remedied by bringing the object nearer to the eye, as we find to be the case with short-sighted people?

Mrs. B

The nearer you bring an object to your eye, the more divergent the rays fall upon the crystalline humour, and they are consequently not so soon converged to a focus: this focus, therefore, either falls upon the retina, or at least approaches nearer to it, and the object is proportionally distinct, as in fig. 52.6.

Emily

The nearer, then, you bring an object to a lens, the further the image recedes behind it.

Mrs. B

Certainly. But short-sighted persons have another resource for objects which they cannot approach to their eyes; this is to place a concave lens, C D [figure 54.1], before the eye, in order to increase the divergence of the rays. The effect of a concave lens is, you know, exactly the reverse of the convex one; it renders convergent rays less convergent, parallel rays divergent, and those which are already divergent, still more so. By the assistance of such glasses, therefore, the rays from a distant object fall on the pupil as divergent as those from a less distant object; and, with short-sighted people, they throw the image of a distant object back as far as the retina.

Caroline

This is an excellent contrivance, indeed.

Mrs. B

And tell me, what remedy would you devise for such persons as have a contrary defect in their sight; that is to say, in whom the crystalline humour, being too flat, does not refract the rays sufficiently, so that they reach the retina before they are converged to a point?

Caroline

I suppose that a contrary remedy must be applied to this defect; that is to say, a convex lens, L M, fig. 54.2, to make up for the deficiency of convexity of the crystalline humour, O P. For the convex lens would bring the rays nearer together, so that they would fall either less divergent, or parallel on the crystalline humour; and, by being sooner converged to a focus, would fall on the retina.

Mrs. B

Very well, Caroline. This is the reason why elderly people, the humours of whose eyes are decayed by age, are under necessity of using convex spectacles. And when deprived of that resource, they hold the object at a distance from their eyes.

Caroline

I have often been surprised when my grandfather reads without his spectacles, to see him hold the book at a considerable distance from his eyes. But I now understand it; for the more distant the object is from the crystalline humour, the nearer the image will be to it.

Emily

I comprehend the nature of these two opposite defects very well; but I cannot now conceive, how any sight can be perfect; for if the crystalline humour is of a proper degree of convexity, to bring the image of distant objects to a focus on the retina, it will not represent near objects distinctly; and if, on the contrary, it is adapted to give a clear image of near objects, it will produce a very imperfect one of distant objects.

Mrs. B

Your observation is very good, Emily; and it is true, that every person would be subject to one of these two defects, if they had it not in their power to increase or diminish, in some degree, the convexity of the crystalline humour, and to project it towards, or draw it back from the object, as circumstances require. In a young well-constructed eye, the fibres to which the crystalline humour is attached have so perfect a command over it, that the focus of the rays constantly falls on the retina, and an image is formed equally distinct both of distant objects and of those which are near.

Caroline

In the eyes of fishes, which are the only eyes I have ever seen separate from the head, the cornea does not protrude, in that part of the eye which is exposed to view.

Mrs. B

The cornea of the eye of a fish is not more convex than the rest of the ball of the eye; but to supply this deficiency, their crystalline humour is spherical, and refracts the rays so much, that it does not require the assistance of the cornea to bring them to a focus on the retina.

Emily

Pray what is the reason that we cannot see an object distinctly, if we place it very near to the eye?

Mrs. B

Because the rays fall on the crystalline humour too divergent to be refracted to a focus on the retina; the confusion, therefore, arising from viewing an object too near the eye, is similar to that which proceeds from a flattened crystalline humour; the rays reach the retina before they are collected to a focus (fig. 54.3) If it were not for this imperfection, we should be able to see and distinguish the parts of objects which are now invisible to us from their minuteness; for could we approach them very near the eye, their image on the retina would be so much magnified as to render them visible.

Emily

And could there be no contrivance to convey the rays of objects viewed close to the eye, so that they should be refracted to a focus on the retina?

Mrs. B

The microscope is constructed for this purpose. The single microscope (fig. 54.4), consists simply of a convex lens, commonly called a magnifying glass; in the focus of which the object is placed, and through which it is viewed; by this means, you are enabled to approach your eye very near the object; for the lens A B, by diminishing the divergency of the rays before

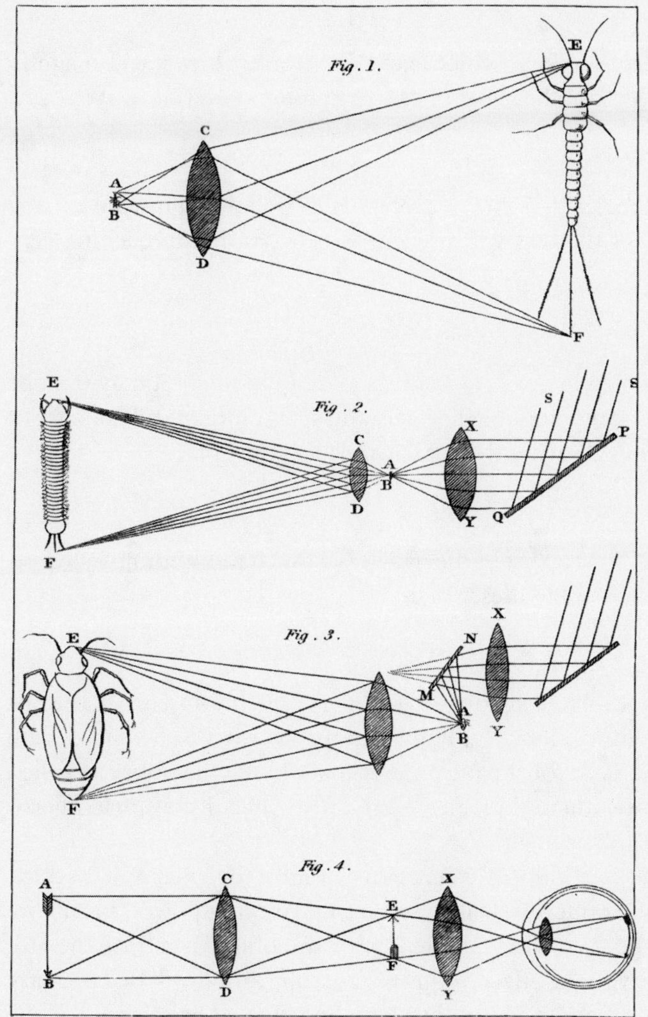

FIGURE 55 Small insect and solar microscope, from Jane Marcet, *Conversations on Natural Philosophy,* opposite p. 448

they enter the pupil C, makes them fall parallel on the crystalline humour D, by which they are refracted to a focus on the retina at R R.

Emily

This is a most admirable invention, and nothing can be more simple, for the lens magnifies the object merely by allowing us to bring it nearer to the eye.

Mrs. B

Those lenses, therefore, which have the shortest focus, will magnify the object most, because they enable us to bring the object nearest the eye.

Emily

But a lens, that has the shortest focus, is most bulging or convex; and the protuberance of the lens will prevent the eye from approaching very near to the object.

Mrs. B

This is remedied by making the lens extremely small: it may then be spherical without occupying much space, and thus unite the advantages of a short focus, and of allowing the eye to approach the object.

Caroline

We have a microscope at home which is a much more complicated instrument than that you have described.

Mrs. B

It is a compound microscope (fig. 54.5) in which you see, not the object A B, but a magnified image of it, *a b*. In this microscope, two lenses are employed; the one L M, for the purpose of magnifying the object, is called the object-glass; the other, N O, acts on the principle of the single microscope, and is called the eye-glass.

There is another kind of microscope, called the solar microscope, which is the most wonderful, from its great magnifying power: in this we also view an image formed by the lens, not the object itself. As the sun shines, I can show you the effect of this microscope; but it will be necessary to close the shutters, and admit only a small portion of light, through the hole in the window-shutter, which we used for the camera obscura. We shall now place the object A B [figure 55.1], which is a small insect, before the lens, C D, and nearly at its focus; the image E F will then be represented on the opposite wall in the same manner as the landscape was in the camera obscura; with this difference, that it will be magnified instead of being diminished. I shall leave you to account for this by examining the figure.

Emily

I see it at once. The image E F is magnified, because it is further from the lens than the object A B; while the representation of the landscape was diminished, because it was nearer the lens than the landscape was. A lens, then, answers the purpose equally well, either for magnifying or diminishing objects?

Mrs. B

Yes. If you wish to magnify the image, you place the object near the focus of the lens; if you wish to produce a diminished image, you place the object at a distance from the lens, in order that the image may be formed in, or near, the focus.

Caroline

The magnifying power of this microscope is prodigious: but the indistinctness of the image, for want of light, is a great imperfection. Would it not be clearer, if the opening in the shutter were enlarged, so as to admit more light?

Mrs. B

If the whole of the light admitted does not fall upon the object, the effect will only be to make the room lighter, and the image consequently less distinct.

Emily

But could you not, by means of another lens, bring a large pencil of rays to a focus on the object, and thus concentrate the whole of the light admitted upon it?

Mrs. B

Very well. We shall enlarge the opening, and place the lens X Y (fig. 55.2) in it, to converge the rays to a focus on the object A B. There is but one thing more wanting to complete the solar microscope, which I shall leave to Caroline's sagacity to discover.

Caroline

Our microscope has a small mirror attached to it, upon a moveable joint, which can be so adjusted as to receive the sun's rays, and reflect them upon the object. If a similar mirror were placed to reflect light upon the lens, would it not be a means of illuminating the object more perfectly?

Mrs. B

You are quite right. P Q (fig. 55.2) is a small mirror, placed on the outside of the window-shutter, which receives the incident rays S S, and reflects them on the lens X Y. Now that we have completed the apparatus, let us examine the mites on this piece of cheese, which I place near the focus of the lens.

Caroline

Oh, how much more distinct the image now is! and how wonderfully magnified! The mites on the cheese look like a drove of pigs scrambling over rocks.

Emily

I never saw any thing so curious. Now, an immense piece of cheese has fallen: one would imagine it an earthquake. Some of the poor mites must have been crushed; how fast they run,—they absolutely seem to gallop.

But this microscope can be used only for transparent objects; as the light must pass through them to form the image on the wall.

Mrs. B

Very minute objects, such as are viewed in a microscope, are generally transparent; but when opaque objects are to be exhibited, a mirror, M N (fig. 55.3), is used to reflect the light on the side of the object next the wall: the image is then formed by light reflected from the object, instead of being formed by rays transmitted by it.

Emily

Pray, is not a magic lanthorn constructed on the same principles?

Mrs. B

Yes; with this difference, that the light is supplied by a lamp, instead of the sun.

The microscope is an excellent invention, to enable us to see and distinguish objects, which are too small to be visible to the naked eye. But there are objects, which, though not really small, appear so to us, from their distance; to these we cannot apply the same remedy; for when a house is so far distant as to be seen under the same angle as a mite which is close to us, the effect produced on the retina is the same: the angle it subtends is not large enough for it to form a distinct image on the retina.

Emily

Since it is impossible, in this case, to approach the object to the eyes, cannot we by means of a lens bring an image of it nearer to us?

Mrs. B

Yes; but then, the object being very distant from the focus of the lens, its image would always appear much smaller than the object itself.

Emily

Then, why not look at the image through another lens, which will act as a microscope, enable us to bring the image close to the eye, and thus magnify it?

Mrs. B

Very well, Emily; I congratulate you on having invented a telescope. In fig. 55.4 the lens C D forms an image, E F, of the object A B; and the lens X Y serves the purpose of magnifying that image; and this is all that is required in a common refracting telescope.

Emily

But in fig. 55.4 the image is not inverted on the retina, as it usually is: the object should, therefore, appear to us inverted: and that is not the case in the telescopes I have looked through.

Mrs. B

When it is necessary to represent the image erect, two other lenses are required; by which means a second image is formed, the inverse of the first, and consequently upright. These additional glasses are used to view terrestrial objects; for no inconvenience arises from seeing the celestial bodies inverted.

Emily

The difference between a microscope and a telescope seems to be this:—a microscope produces a magnified image, because the object is nearest the lens; and a telescope produces a diminished image, because the object is furthest from the lens.

Mrs. B

Your observation applies only to the lens C D, or object-glass, which serves to bring an image of the object nearer the eye; for the lens X Y, or eye-glass, is, in fact, a microscope, as its purpose is to magnify the image. But it was found, in constructing telescopes, that the object glass, instead of bringing the rays to a perfect focus, slightly dispersed them, and produced a confused coloured image. This defect was remedied by substituting two lenses in contact, one of flint glass, the other of crown glass, of such forms and proportions as to counteract each other's dispersive powers, so that a well defined and colourless image is produced. This is called the *achromatic telescope.*

Emily

I have observed this defect in an opera glass, when the actor I was looking at appeared to be surrounded by a coloured fringe of the dispersed rays.

Mrs. B

The two surfaces of the edges of the lens not being parallel, disperse the coloured rays nearly as much as a prism, and produce this effect.

When a very great magnifying power is required, telescopes are constructed with concave mirrors, instead of lenses. Concave mirrors, you know, produce, by reflection, an effect similar to that of convex lenses by refraction. In reflecting telescopes, therefore, mirrors are used in order to bring the image nearer the eye; and a lens or eye-glass, the same as in the refracting telescope, to magnify the image.[1]

The great advantage of the reflecting telescope consists in its producing no dispersion whatever of the rays: and the images, consequently, are much more distinct and perfect, and will bear to be magnified to a much greater extent: for you recollect that the rays of light are never dispersed by reflection, but only by refraction.

Caroline

But I thought it was the eye-glass only which magnified the image; and that the other lens served to bring a diminished image nearer to the eye.

Mrs. B

This image is diminished in comparison to the object, it is true; but it is larger than it would appear to the naked eye without the intervention of any optical instrument; the object-glass, therefore, serves to magnify the object, as well as the eye-glass, and it is this magnifying power which is greater in reflecting than in refracting telescopes.

1. It would have been difficult to have explained to the pupils the principles which have enabled opticians to shorten refracting telescopes.

We must now bring our observations to a conclusion, for I have communicated to you the whole of my very limited stock of knowledge of Natural Philosophy. If it will enable you to make further progress in that science, my wishes will be satisfied; but remember that, in order that the study of nature may be productive of happiness, it must lead to an entire confidence in the wisdom and goodness of its bounteous Author.

MARY SOMERVILLE

From *On the Connexion of the Physical Sciences*

1834. London: J. Murray, 1846. 1–4; 173–76; 434–35.

To the Queen.

MADAM,

If I have succeeded in my endeavour to make the laws by which the material world is governed more familiar to my countrywomen, I shall have the gratification of thinking, that the gracious permission to dedicate my book to your Majesty has not been misplaced.

I am,
With the greatest respect,
YOUR MAJESTY'S
Obedient and Humble Servant,
MARY SOMERVILLE

[pp. 1–4]

INTRODUCTION

. . . Astronomy affords the most extensive example of the connection of the physical sciences. In it are combined the sciences of number and quantity, of rest and motion. In it we perceive the operation of a force which is mixed up with everything that exists in the heavens or on earth; which pervades every atom, rules the motions of animate and inanimate beings, and is as sensible in the descent of a rain drop as in the falls of Niagara; in the weight of the air, as in the periods of the moon. Gravitation not only binds satellites to their planet, and planets to the sun, but it connects sun with sun throughout the wide extent of creation, and is the cause of the disturbances,

FIGURE 56 Mary Somerville, from *Personal Recollections from Early Life to Old Age of Mary Somerville* (Boston: Roberts, 1874), opposite title page

as well as of the order of nature: since every tremour it excites in any one planet is immediately transmitted to the farthest limits of the system, in oscillations, which correspond in their periods with the cause producing them, like sympathetic notes in music, or vibrations from the deep tones of an organ.

The heavens afford the most sublime subject of study which can be derived from science. The magnitude and splendour of the objects, the inconceivable rapidity with which they move, and the enormous distances between them, impress the mind with some notion of the energy that maintains them in their motions, with a durability to which we can see no limit. Equally conspicuous is the goodness of the great First Cause, in having endowed man with faculties, by which he can not only appreciate the magnificence of His works, but trace, with precision, the operation of His laws, use the globe he inhabits as a base wherewith to measure the magnitude and distance of the sun and planets, and make the diameter of the earth's orbit the first step of a scale by which he may ascend to the starry firmament. Such pursuits, while they ennoble the mind, at the same time inculcate humility, by showing that there is a barrier which no energy, mental or physical, can ever enable us to pass: that, however profoundly we may penetrate the depths of space, there still remain innumerable systems, compared with which, those apparently so vast must dwindle into insignificance, or even become invisible; and that not only man, but the globe he inhabits—nay, the whole system of which it forms so small a part—might be annihilated, and its extinction be unperceived in the immensity of creation.

A complete acquaintance with physical astronomy can be attained by those only who are well versed in the higher branches of mathematical and mechanical science, and they alone can appreciate the extreme beauty of the results, and of the means by which these results are obtained. It is nevertheless true, that a sufficient skill in analysis to follow the general outline—to see the mutual dependence of the different parts of the system, and to comprehend by what means the most extraordinary conclusions have been arrived at,—is within the reach of many who shrink from the task, appalled by difficulties, not more formidable than those incident to the study of the elements of every branch of knowledge. There is a wide distinction between the degree of mathematical acquirement necessary for making discoveries, and that which is requisite for understanding what others have done.

Our knowledge of external objects is founded upon experience, which furnishes facts; the comparison of these facts establishes relations, from which the belief that like causes will produce like effects, leads to general laws. Thus, experience teaches that bodies fall at the surface of the earth with an accelerated velocity, and with a force proportional to their masses. By comparison, Newton proved that the force which occasions the fall of bodies at the earth's surface is identical with that which retains the moon in her orbit; and he concluded, that as the moon is kept in her orbit by the attraction of the earth, so the planets might be retained in their orbits by the attraction of the sun. By such steps he was led to the discovery of one of those powers, with which the Creator has ordained, that matter should reciprocally act upon matter.

Physical astronomy is the science which compares and identifies the laws of motion observed on earth, with the motions that take place in the heavens; and which traces, by an uninterrupted chain of deduction from the great principle that governs the universe, the revolutions and rotations of the planets, and the oscillations of the fluids at their surfaces; and which estimates the changes the system has hitherto undergone, or may hereafter experience—changes which require millions of years for their accomplishment.

The accumulated efforts of astronomers, from the earliest dawn of civilization, have been necessary to establish the mechanical theory of astronomy. The courses of the planets have been observed for ages, with a degree of perseverance that is astonishing, if we consider the imperfection and even the want of instruments. The real motions of the earth have been separated from the apparent motions of the planets; the laws of the planetary revolutions have been discovered; and the discovery of these laws has led to the knowledge of the gravitation of matter. On the other hand, descending from the principle of gravitation, every motion in the solar system has been so completely explained, that the laws of any astronomical phenomena that may hereafter occur, are already determined.

[pp. 173–76]

SECTION XIX

The Constitution of Light

It is impossible thus to trace the path of a sunbeam through our atmosphere without feeling a desire to know its nature, by what power it traverses the immensity of space, and the various modifications it undergoes at the surfaces and in the interior of terrestrial substances.

Sir Isaac Newton proved the compound nature of white light as emitted from the sun, by passing a sunbeam through a glass prism, which separating the rays by refraction, formed a spectrum or oblong image of the sun, consisting of seven colours, red, orange, yellow, green, blue, indigo, and violet; of which the red is the least refrangible and the violet the most. But when he re-united these seven rays by means of a lens, the compound beam became pure white as before. He insulated each coloured ray; and finding that it was no longer capable of decomposition by refraction, concluded that white light consists of seven kinds of homogeneous light, and that to the same colour the same refrangibility ever belongs, and to the same refrangibility the same colour. Since the discovery of absorbent media, however, it appears that this is not the constitution of the solar spectrum.

We know of no substance that is either perfectly opaque or perfectly transparent. Even gold may be beaten so thin as to be pervious to light. On the contrary, the clearest crystal, the purest air or water, stops or absorbs its rays when transmitted, and gradually extinguishes them as they penetrate to greater depths. On this account objects cannot be seen at the bottom of very deep water, and many more stars are visible to the naked eye from the tops of mountains than from the valleys. The quantity of light that is incident on any transparent substance is always greater than the sum of the reflected and refracted rays. A small quantity is irregularly reflected in all directions by the imperfections of the polish by which we are enabled to see the surface; but a much greater portion is absorbed by the body. Bodies that reflect all the rays appear white, those that absorb them all seem black; but most substances, after decomposing the white light which falls upon them, reflect some colours and absorb the rest. A violet reflects the violet rays alone and absorbs the others. Scarlet cloth absorbs almost all the colours except red. Yellow cloth reflects the yellow rays most abundantly, and blue cloth those that are blue. Consequently colour is not a property of matter, but arises from the action of matter upon light. Thus a white riband reflects all the rays, but when dyed red the particles of the silk acquire the property of reflecting the red rays most abundantly and of absorbing the others. Upon this property of unequal absorption, the colours of transparent media depend. For they also receive their colour from their power of stopping or absorbing some of the colours of white light and transmitting others. As for example, black and red inks, though equally homogeneous, absorb different kinds of rays; and when exposed to the sun, they become heated in different degrees; while pure water seems to transmit all rays equally, and it is not sensibly heated by the passing light of the sun. The rich dark light transmitted by a smalt-blue finger-glass is not a homogeneous colour like the blue or indigo of the spectrum, but is a mixture of all the colours of white light which the glass has not absorbed. The colours absorbed are such as mixed with the blue tint would form white light. When the spectrum of seven colours is viewed through a thin plate of this glass they are all visible; and when the plate is very thick, every colour is absorbed between the extreme red and the extreme violet, the interval being perfectly black: but if the spectrum be viewed through a certain thickness of the glass intermediate between the two, it will be found that the middle of the red space, the whole of the orange, a great part of the green, a considerable part of the blue, a little of the indigo, and a very little of the violet, vanish, being absorbed by the blue glass: and that the yellow rays occupy a larger space, covering part of that formerly occupied by the orange on one side, and by the green on the other. So that the blue glass absorbs the red light, which when mixed with the yellow constitutes orange; and also absorbs the blue light, which when mixed with the yellow forms part of the green space next to the yellow. Hence by absorption, green light is decomposed into yellow and blue, and orange light into yellow and red. Consequently the orange and green rays, though incapable of decomposition by refraction, can be resolved by absorption, and actually consist of two different colours possessing the same degree of refrangibility. Difference of colour, therefore, is not a test of difference or refrangibility, and the conclusion deduced by Newton is no longer admissible as a general truth. By this analysis of the spectrum, not only with blue glass, but with a variety of coloured media, Sir David Brewster,[1] so justly celebrated for his optical discoveries, has proved that the solar spectrum consists of three primary colours, red, yellow, and blue, each of which exists throughout its whole extent, but with different degrees of intensity in different parts; and that the superposition of these three produces all the seven hues according as each primary colour is an excess or defect. Since a certain portion of red, yellow, and blue rays constitute white light, the colour of any point of the spectrum may be considered as consisting of the predominating colour at that point mixed with white light. Consequently, by absorbing the excess of any colour at any point of the spectrum above what is necessary to form white light, such white light will appear at that point as never mortal eye looked upon before this experiment, since it possesses the remarkable property of remaining the same after any number of refractions and of being capable of decomposition by absorption alone.

In addition to the seven colours of the Newtonian spectrum, Sir John Herschel[2] has discovered a set of very dark red rays beyond the red extremity of the spectrum which can only be seen when the eye is defended from the glare of the other colours by a dark blue cobalt glass. He has also found that beyond the extreme violet there are visible rays of a lavender gray colour which may be seen by throwing the spectrum on a sheet of paper moistened by the carbonate of soda. The illuminating power of the different rays of the spectrum varies with the colour. The most intense light is in the mean yellow ray.

[pp. 434–35]

CONCLUSION

. . . In the work now brought to a conclusion, it has been necessary to select from the whole circle of the sciences a few of the most obvious of those

1. Scottish physicist (1787–1863), best known for his work in optics and polarized light. *Ed.*

2. Sir John Herschel (1792–1871), English astronomer, well known for his work in stellar and nebular observation. *Ed.*

proximate links which connect them together, and to pass over innumerable cases both of evident and occult alliance. Any one branch traced through its ramifications would alone have occupied a volume; it is hoped, nevertheless, that the view here given will suffice to show the extent to which a consideration of the reciprocal influence of even a few of these subjects may ultimately lead. It thus appears that the theory of dynamics, founded upon terrestrial phenomena, is indispensable for acquiring a knowledge of the revolutions of the celestial bodies and their reciprocal influences. The motions of the satellites are affected by the forms of their primaries, and the figures of the planets themselves depend upon their rotations. The symmetry of their internal structure proves the stability of these rotatory motions, and the immutability of the length of the day, which furnishes an invariable standard of time; and the actual size of the terrestrial spheroid affords the means of ascertaining the dimensions of the solar system, and provides an invariable foundation for a system of weights and measures. The mutual attraction of the celestial bodies disturbs the fluids at their surfaces, whence the theory of thc tides and of the oscillations of the atmosphere. The density and elasticity of the air, varying with every alternation of temperature, lead to the consideration of barometrical changes, the measurement of heights, and capillary attraction; and the doctrine of sound, including the theory of music, is to be referred to the small undulations of the aërial medium. A knowledge of the action of matter upon light is requisite for tracing the curved path of its rays through the atmosphere, by which the true places of distant objects are determined, whether in the heavens or on the earth. By this we learn the nature and properties of the sunbeam, the mode of its propagation through the ethereal fluid, or in the interior of material bodies, and the origin of colour. By the eclipses of Jupiter's satellites, the velocity of light is ascertained; and that velocity, in the aberration of the fixed stars, furnishes the only direct proof of the real motion of the earth. The effects of the invisible rays of light are immediately connected with chemical action; and heat, forming a part of the solar ray, so essential to animated and inanimated existence, whether considered as invisible light or as a distinct quality, is too important an agent in the economy of creation, not to hold a principal place in the connexion of physical sciences. Whence the globe, its power on the geological convulsions of our planet, its influence on the atmosphere and on climate, and its effects on vegetable and animal life, evinced in the localities of organized beings on the earth, in the waters, and in the air. The connexion of heat with electrical phenomena, and the electricity of the atmosphere, together with all its energetic effects, its identity with magnetism and the phenomena of terrestrial polarity, can only be understood from the theories of these invisible agents, and are, probably, identical with, or at least the principle causes of, chemical affinities. Innumerable instances might be given in illustration of the immediate connexion of the physical sciences, most of which are united still more closely by the common bond of analysis, which is daily extending its empire, and will ultimately embrace almost every subject in nature in its formulæ.

These formulæ, emblematic of Omniscience, condense into a few symbols the immutable laws of the universe. This mighty instrument of human power itself originates in the primitive constitution of the human mind, and rests upon a few fundamental axioms, which have eternally existed in Him who implanted them in the breast of man when He created him after His own image.

JANE LOUDON

From *The Young Naturalist; or, The Travels of Agnes Merton and Her Mamma*

1840. London: Routledge, Warne, and Routledge, 1863. iii–vi; 1–13.

[pp. iii–vi]

PREFACE TO THE SECOND EDITION

Natural history has always appeared to me a particularly suitable study for young people; as it excites the youthful mind to the contemplation of the infinite wisdom which has been shown in making all creatures form one vast whole; every part of which is in some way connected with, and dependent on, the rest. Nothing has been made in vain. Earth, air, and sea, are all peopled with living things, suited to the different situations in which they are to exist, and to the functions which they are destined to fulfil. The mole, for example, was intended to live underground; and how wisely and how wonderfully it is suited for this purpose! Its long snout pierces into and loosens the earth, which its paws, armed as they are with strong nails, scrape away; it has no visible eyes—for eyes would be useless in the narrow cell which serves for its habitation; and its thick velvety coat, while its softness, joined to the tapering form of the body, enables the mole to glide through the long galleries in which it resides, prevents it from being hurt by any stones or hard substances which it may meet with in its way. The animals of very hot and of very cold climates are both generally covered with a thick coating of hair or fur, which protects them alike from extreme heat or extreme cold, by preventing them from being sensibly affected by the atmospheric temperature. The birds which are intended to live principally in the air, are gifted with extraordinary strength of pinion, while their legs are short, so as not to impede their flying; their bodies are also of extraordinary lightness, and they are furnished with long slender claws to enable them to grasp the branch on which they perch. The duck, on the contrary, has broad webbed feet, which act as paddles in the water to assist its swimming; and the ostrich has long strong legs, each armed with a single toe in front, to enable it to make its way through deserts of moving sand. When the works of man are long and closely examined, some trifling fault or error never fails to be discovered in them; but with the works of God, the longest and most minute examinations only convince us more and more of their excellence and perfection.

Feelings of the above nature having often arisen in my mind when I have been turning over the volumes of the *Magazine of Natural History,* the idea struck me, that many of the papers contained in the earlier volumes of that work (while it was under the superintendence of my late husband) might, if stripped of their technicalities, be rendered both interesting and amusing to children. This was the origin of the present work; though the papers taken from the *Magazine of Natural History* have been so changed in fitting them for the comprehension of children, that, in most cases, it would be difficult for those who may have read them before to recognise them. The adaptation of them has, indeed, cost me quite as much time and labour as the writing of an entirely new work; and the principal advantage I have reaped from the *Magazine,* is the power it affords me of assuring my young readers that all the anecdotes here related of the animals are strictly true; though the incidents of the journey, and the persons introduced, are partly imaginary.

Some alterations have been made in the present edition; but they are only such as have appeared to me necessary to bring the work down to the present time.

J. W. L.

Bayswater, Dec. 17th, 1850.

[pp. 1–13]

CHAPTER I

The Mamozeet Monkey, and the Mangouste

Agnes Merton's mamma having to make a long journey through several of the counties of England, determined to take with her her little girl, who was then about seven years old, and who was very fond of travelling. The first place they were to go to was Birmingham, and as Mrs. Merton had decided on travelling by the railroad, she and her little daughter went on the appointed day to the terminus in Euston-square.

Agnes, who had never travelled by a railroad before, was very much struck with, and almost frightened at, the number of carriages; and still more so at the crowd of people who bustled about, all eager to secure their places, and all seeming in the greatest hurry and confusion; while the porters passed to and fro, each with a kind of wheelbarrow, loaded with almost innumerable trunks and carpetbags. Agnes clung close to her mamma, and was very glad when one of the men showed them a carriage in which there was room for them. They had scarcely taken their places when a lady came on the platform, followed by a servant carrying a Mamozeet monkey, and Agnes soon became quite absorbed in watching the antics of this curious little animal. The monkey was very small, not larger than a squirrel, and it was quite as active as one of those nimble little creatures. It was never still a moment; one instant it was peeping under the servant's arm, then it was on his shoulder, and then twisting round his body; the servant, during all these movements, keeping fast hold of a chain which was attached to a black-leather belt, fastened round the animal's body. Agnes was delighted with watching this monkey, which was, indeed, a very curious little creature. It was covered with long light brown hair, edged with grey, which made it look as though it were striped: its tail was very long, and distinctly marked with black and white rings; and its face was one of the sharpest and most cunning-looking that can possibly be conceived. Its little twinkling black eyes were set off by a tuft of a long white hair behind each; and its ears, which were very large, went flapping up and down among this hair, as if it were listening to everything that was said. The lady appeared a long time in doubt where to go, but at last, to Agnes's great delight, the porter opened the door of the carriage in which they sat, and the lady having entered it, the servant gave her the monkey and retired.

"Did you ever see a monkey like this before?" asked the lady of Agnes, as soon as she had seated herself, observing how intently the little girl was watching the antics of her pet.

"Never," said Agnes. "He looks just like a little old man."

"That," said the lady, "is what the sailors called him on board the ship in which we brought him from his native country, Brazil. His curious tricks made him the favourite of everybody on board."

"Oh! how I should like to hear all about them," cried Agnes.

"With your mamma's permission," returned the lady, "I will tell you all I remember."

Mrs. Merton gladly consented, and thanked the lady, who began as follows:—

"I had long wished for a Mamozeet monkey, but though they are generally common enough in Brazil, they happened to be scarce when we were there, and we did not succeed in getting one till a few days before we sailed for England. One day, however, my husband happened to go into the market-place in Bahia, the town in which we resided, and there he saw a slave offering this monkey, and several other wild animals, for sale."

"What, was this monkey ever wild?" asked Agnes.

"Yes," returned the lady. "There are a great many monkeys wild in the woods in Brazil; and many persons make the catching of them a kind of trade."

"Then I suppose the monkey was frightened at you at first, and would not let you stroke him as he does now?"

"He would not let me touch him; but I had not much time to try, for he was taken on board the very day after we bought him. The monkey, never having seen a ship before, was very much terrified at everything, and was at first so wild and fierce that everybody was afraid of going near him. He had a nice little kennel made on purpose for him, and placed on the deck; but he would never remain still in it a single moment. By degrees, however, our little old man, as the sailors called him, became less savage, though he never lost his activity and wildness. Even when he was being fed or caressed, if he saw a cockroach, he would dart away after it like lightning, whisking his long tail about, and springing from side to side, like a cat at a fly, till he had caught his prey. The ship abounded with cockroaches, and some of them were above two inches long. When the little old man had caught one of these large insects, he would glance his keen little eyes about from side to side, and if he was satisfied that he was not observed, he would sit down and begin to prepare the cockroach for his meal. He was very particular in his manner of doing this: first, he bit the head off; then he drew out the inside, and threw it on one side; then he carefully stripped the insect of its wings, its wing-cases, and its legs, which are covered with short stiff bristles; and at last finished by devouring the body with every appearance of satisfaction."

"I think he could not have been very hungry," said Agnes, "to take so much time in preparing such a little creature as a cockroach. He would have hardly anything left to eat when he had done."

"You forget," said the lady, "that I told you some of the cockroaches were very large; and it was with these only that he took so much trouble. With the smaller cockroaches he was not so particular, and his appetite for them was so keen, that he would frequently eat a score or two of them in a day. Nothing could exceed the vigilance and activity of this Mamozeet as long as he remained in a warm climate. When he saw on the deck, his little head was turning incessantly from side to side, his keen sparkling eyes were always on the watch, and his large ears were raised so as to catch the slightest sound. Whenever he saw any stranger approaching him he would dart off, uttering those shrill disagreeable cries which have procured for this monkey, in Brazil, the name of Ouistiti."

"What a frightful name!" said Agnes.

"It is at any rate an expressive one," said Mrs. Merton; and then, turning to the lady, she asked what they fed the monkey with on board the ship?

"His ordinary food," replied the lady, "consisted of oranges, bananas, mangoes, and Indian corn; but as the supply of these articles was limited, he was fed, during the latter part of the voyage, with milk, sugar, raisins, and crumbs of bread. As the ship approached England, and the climate grew colder, the poor Mamozeet seemed to suffer exceedingly. The cockroaches were now unheeded, and their once indefatigable and active enemy kept constantly in his kennel, muffled up in a piece of flannel which had been put in to keep him warm, and in which he rolled himself, only venturing out when the sun shone brightly enough for him to bask in its beams; and hurrying back to his den at the first breath of cold wind."

"Poor little fellow!" said Agnes.

"When our little old man arrived in England, and was put into a warm room," continued the lady, "he gradually recovered some of his former liveliness, and would run about, dragging his kennel after him. He did not like, however, to be noticed, and was very indignant when any one attempted to touch or caress him; and he never recovered his appetite for cockroaches. I then began to feed him myself, and found that he was particularly fond of jelly and ripe fruit; I also gave him so much milk and crumbs of bread, that he soon became plump and healthy. He grew tolerably tame, and he was so fond of me that he would eat out of my hand, and would come to me when I called him; but he was still very violent with strangers. Even after he had been long domesticated, if any one attempted to handle or play with him, his eyes sparkled, the long white hairs on each side of his face stood erect, his nostrils dilated, and he grinned and showed his teeth, while his little wrinkled features assumed a most ludicrous expression of rage. He was, however, very fond of playing with the cat, which is very remarkable, as these monkeys are generally said to be great enemies to cats."

"That is very remarkable, indeed," said Mrs. Merton; "but animals in a domesticated state often appear to lose their natural antipathies. Do you think it safe to allow my little girl to touch your monkey?" continued she, observing that Agnes wished very much to stroke it.

"Oh!" replied the lady, "there is not the slightest danger. Since my husband's death, Jacopo has been my constant companion, and he is very fond of children."

"I remember to have read," observed Mrs. Merton, "that these monkeys are very attentive to their young. A pair of them, which were kept in Paris, had three young ones, which I believe were the first born in Europe. The mother was rather careless, and seemed soon to get tired of carrying them about; and when this was the case, she would hold out the little creatures to their father, or would playfully put them on his back. The male monkey generally took them in his hands and nursed and played with them, till they became restless for food, when he gave them back to their mother."

"How delighted I should have been to see them!" exclaimed Agnes.

"As your daughter seems so pleased with what I have been able to tell her about my monkey," said the lady, addressing Mrs. Merton, "perhaps she will like to hear something of another very curious animal, called a Mangouste, that my brother brought over from the East Indies, some years since, and that he still keeps, and is very fond of."

"I should, indeed," replied Agnes; "though I don't exactly know what a Mangouste is."

"The Mangouste," said the lady, "is a ferret-like looking animal, about two feet long, a native of the East Indies, but covered with as thick a coating of shaggy hair as though it came from a cold country. The one I allude to, which is a female, was brought to England from Madras. Her colour is apparently a silvery grey, but on a nearer inspection every one of her hairs (which are long and coarse) will be found to be marked with bars of black, brown, and white, like the quills of a porcupine; her head is small; her legs are short and strong; and her tail is long and very thick near the body, but tapering at the end."

"Is she intelligent?" asked Agnes.

"She is very inquisitive," replied the lady; "and she runs about the house of her master searching into every corner and devouring all the insects she can find. She is very light and active, and after she has examined every part of the floor, she jumps upon the chairs and tables, springing lightly from chair to chair, and poking her nose into the pockets of those who are sitting upon them. She uses her fore-paws like hands, and with great dexterity pulls clothes and other things about, turning them over and seeming to be examining them. Her tail seems to assist her in leaping and turning; and in so doing, she frequently strikes it against hard objects with such force as to make it bleed at the extremity."

"Does the Mangouste play with the cat like your little Jacopo?" inquired Mrs. Merton.

"No," replied the lady; "but she has formed an acquaintance with the dog. When she was first brought to my brother's cottage, she growled, and set up her hair, as a cat does, at the sight of the dog kept there. They had afterwards a slight contest; but after the Mangouste had given the dog a bite on the face, they became good friends, and have continued ever since. The Mangouste possesses great strength and activity, and she is as playful as a kitten, twisting her long body about into the most curious attitudes, one of the most remarkable of which is, her standing upon her tail and hind legs, and leaping like a kangaroo."

"I suppose this creature is too cat-like to live on bread and milk?" said Mrs. Merton.

"You are quite right," returned the lady, "in calling the Mangouste cat-like; for the change that takes place in her when she is fed is very striking. At other times she is mild and docile, but the moment she sees food, especially if a live bird be given to her, she becomes fierce and ravenous; her eyes glare, she utters a low, savage growl, and, if any one approaches, gnashes her teeth and attempts to bite. One day a basin of water was offered to her, in which was an egg; when she eagerly dived for it, up to her shoulders, as she did when some minnows were substituted for the egg; but when a larger vessel was presented to her, the water seemed to deprive her of sight; and after a few ineffectual attempts to dive for the minnows, she contented herself with sitting close to the edge of the tub, and watching till they came to the surface, when she pounced upon them. She was very fond of birds, and used to climb dexterously into bushes in search of them. She was also very fond of mice, rats, lizards, and frogs, playing with them a long time before killing them, and only giving their *coup-de-grace* when there appeared some chance of their making their escape."

ARABELLA B. BUCKLEY

From *The Fairy-land of Science*

London: Edward Stanford, 1879. 1–25.

LECTURE I

How to Enter It; How to Use It; and How to Enjoy It

I have promised to introduce you today to the fairy-land of science,—a somewhat bold promise, seeing that most of you probably look upon science as a bundle of dry facts, while fairy-land is all that is beautiful, and full of poetry and imagination. But I thoroughly believe myself, and hope to prove to you, that science is full of beautiful pictures, of real poetry, and of wonder-working fairies; and what is more, I promise you they shall be true fairies, whom you will love just as much when you are old and greyheaded as when you are young; for you will be able to call them up wherever you wander by land or by sea, through meadow or through wood, through water or through air; and though they themselves will always remain invisible, yet you will see their wonderful power at work everywhere around you.

Let us first see for a moment what kind of tales science has to tell, and how far they are equal to the old fairy tales we all know so well. Who does not remember the tale of the "Sleeping Beauty in the Wood," and how under the spell of the angry fairy the maiden pricked herself with the spindle and slept a hundred years? How the horses in the stall, the dogs in the courtyard, the doves on the roof, the cook who was boxing the scullery boy's ears in the kitchen, and the king and queen with all their courtiers in the hall remained spell-bound, while a thick hedge grew up all round the castle and all within was still as death. But when the hundred years had passed the valiant prince came, the thorny hedge opened before him bearing beautiful flowers; and he, entering the castle, reached the room where the princess lay, and with one sweet kiss raised her and all around her to life again.

Can science bring any tale to match this?

Tell me, is there anything in this world more busy and active than water, as it rushes along in the swift brook, or dashes over the stones, or spouts up in the fountain, or trickles down from the roof, or shakes itself into ripples on the surface of the pond as the wind blows over it? But have you never seen this water spell-bound and motionless? Look out of the window some cold frosty morning in winter, at the little brook which yesterday was flowing gently past the house, and see how still it lies, with the stones over which

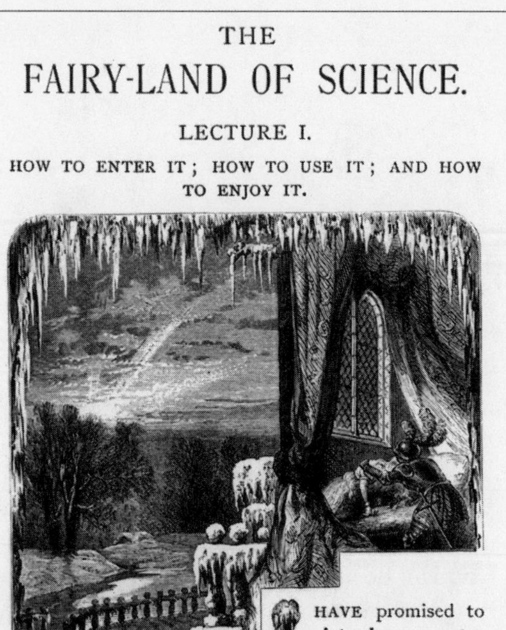

THE

FAIRY-LAND OF SCIENCE.

LECTURE I.

HOW TO ENTER IT; HOW TO USE IT; AND HOW TO ENJOY IT.

I HAVE promised to introduce you to-day to the fairy-land of science,—a somewhat bold promise, seeing that most of you probably look upon science as a bundle of dry facts, while fairy-land is all that is beautiful, and full of

FIGURE 57 First page, Arabella Buckley, *Fairy-land of Science*

it was dashing now held tightly in its icy grasp. Notice the wind-ripples on the pond; they have become fixed and motionless. Look up at the roof of the house. There, instead of living doves merely charmed to sleep, we have running water caught in the very act of falling and turned into transparent icicles, decorating the eaves with a beautiful crystal fringe. On every tree and bush you will catch the water-drops napping, in the form of tiny crystals; while the fountain looks like a tree of glass with long down-hanging pointed leaves. Even the damp of your own breath lies rigid and still on the window-pane frozen into delicate patterns like fern-leaves of ice.

All this water was yesterday flowing busily, or falling drop by drop, or floating invisibly in the air; now it is all caught and spell-bound—by whom? By the enchantments of the frost-giant who holds it fast in his grip and will not let it go.

But wait awhile, the deliverer is coming. In a few weeks or days, or it may be in a few hours, the brave sun will shine down; the dull-grey, leaden sky will melt before him, as the hedge gave way before the prince in the fairy-tale, and when the sunbeam gently kisses the frozen water it will be set free. Then the brook will flow rippling on again; the frost-drops will be shaken down from the trees, the icicles fall from the roof, the moisture trickles down the window-pane, and in the bright, warm sunshine all will be alive again.

Is not this a fairy tale of nature? and such as these it is which science tells.

Again, who has not heard of Catskin, who came out of a hollow tree, bringing a walnut containing three beautiful dresses—the first glowing as the sun, the second pale and beautiful as the moon, the third spangled like the star-lit sky, and each so fine and delicate that all three could be packed in a nut? But science can tell of shells so tiny that a whole group of them will lie on the point of a pin, and many thousands be packed into a walnut-shell; and each one of these tiny structures is not the mere dress but the home of the living animal. It is a tiny, tiny shell-palace made of the most delicate lacework, each pattern being more beautiful than the last; and what is more, the minute creature that lives in it has built it out of the foam of the sea, though he himself appears to be merely a drop of jelly.

Lastly, anyone who has read the 'Wonderful Travellers' must recollect the man whose sight was so keen that he could hit the eye of a fly sitting on a tree two miles away. But tell me, can you see gas before it is lighted, even when it is coming out of the gas-jet close to your eyes? Yet, if you learn to use that wonderful instrument the spectroscope, it will enable you to tell one kind of gas from another, even when they are both ninety-one millions of miles away on the face of the sun; nay more, it will read for you the nature of the different gases in the far distant stars, billions of miles away, and actually tell you whether you could find there any of the same metals which we have on the earth.

We might find hundreds of such fairy tales in the domain of science, but these three will serve as examples, and we must pass on to make the acquaintance of the science-fairies themselves, and see if they are as real as our old friends.

Tell me, why do you love fairy-land? what is its charm? Is it not that things happen so suddenly, so mysteriously, and without man having anything to do with it? In fairy-land, flowers blow, houses spring up like Aladdin's palace in a single night, and people are carried hundreds of miles in an instant by the touch of a fairy wand.

And then this land is not some distant country to which *we* can never hope to travel. It is here in the midst of us, only our eyes must be opened or we cannot see it. Ariel and Puck did not live in some unknown region. On the contrary, Ariel's song is

> "Where the bee sucks, there suck I;
> In a cowslip's bell I lie;
> There I couch when owls do cry.
> On the bat's back I do fly,
> After summer, merrily." [1]

The peasant falls asleep some evening in a wood, and his eyes are opened by a fairy wand, so that he sees the little goblins and imps dancing round him on the green sward, sitting on mushrooms, or in the heads of the flowers, drinking out of acorn-cups, fighting with blades of grass, and riding on grass-hoppers.

So, too, the gallant knight, riding to save some poor oppressed maiden, dashes across the foaming torrent; and just in the middle, as he is being swept away, his eyes are opened, and he sees fairy water-nymphs soothing his terrified horse and guiding him gently to the opposite shore. They are close at hand, these sprites, to the simple peasant or the gallant knight, or to anyone who has the gift of the fairies and can see them. But the man who scoffs at them, and does not believe in them or care for them, he *never* sees them. Only now and then they play him an ugly trick, leading him into some treacherous bog and leaving him to get out as he may.

Now, exactly all this which is true of the fairies of our childhood is true too of the fairies of science. There are *forces* around us, and among us, which I shall ask you to allow me to call *fairies,* and these are ten thousand times more wonderful, more magical, and more beautiful in their work, than those of the old fairy tales. They, too, are invisible, and many people live and die without ever seeing them or caring to see them. These people go about with their eyes shut, either because they will not open them, or because no one has taught them how to see. They fret and worry over their own little work and their own petty troubles, and do not know how to rest and refresh them-

1. From Shakespeare's *Tempest:* 5.1.88–94. *Ed.*

selves, by letting the fairies open their eyes and show them the calm sweet pictures of nature. They are like Peter Bell of whom Wordsworth wrote:—

> "A primrose by a river's brim
> A yellow primrose was to him,
> And it was nothing more."[2]

But we will not be like these, we will open our eyes, and ask, "What are these forces or fairies, and how can we see them?"

Just go out into the country, and sit down quietly and watch nature at work. Listen to the wind as it blows, look at the clouds rolling overhead, and the waves rippling on the pond at your feet. Hearken to the brook as it flows by, watch the flower-buds opening one by one, and then ask yourself, "How all this is done?" Go out in the evening and see the dew gather drop by drop upon the grass, or trace the delicate hoar-frost crystals which bespangle every blade on a winter's morning. Look at the vivid flashes of lightning in a storm, and listen to the pealing thunder: and then tell me, by what machinery is all this wonderful work done? Man does none of it, neither could he stop it if he were to try; for it is all the work of those invisible *forces* or *fairies* whose acquaintance I wish you to make. Day and night, summer and winter, storm or calm, these fairies are at work, and we may hear them and know them, and make friends of them if we will.

There is only one gift we must have before we can learn to know them —we must have *imagination.* I do not mean mere fancy, which creates unreal images and impossible monsters, but imagination, the power of making pictures or *images* in our mind, of that which *is,* though it is invisible to us. Most children have this glorious gift, and love to picture to themselves all that is told them, and to hear the same tale over and over again till they see every bit of it as if it were real. This is why they are sure to love science if its tales are told them aright; and I, for one, hope the day may never come when we may lose that childish clearness of vision, which enables us through the temporal things which are seen, to realize those eternal truths which are unseen.

If you have this gift of imagination come with me, and in these lectures we will look for the invisible fairies of nature.

Watch a shower of rain. Where do the drops come from? and why are

2. William Wordsworth, *Peter Bell: A Tale,* part 1, lines 58–60. *Ed.*

they round, or rather slightly oval? In our fourth lecture we shall see that the little particles of water of which the rain-drops are made, were held apart and invisible in the air by *heat,* one of the most wonderful of our forces[3] or fairies, till the cold wind passed by and chilled the air. Then, when there was no longer so much heat, another invisible force, *cohesion,* which is always ready and waiting, seized on the tiny particles at once, and locked them together in a drop, the closest form in which they could lie. Then as the drops became larger and larger they fell into the grasp of another invisible force, *gravitation,* which dragged them down to the earth, drop by drop, till they made a shower of rain. Pause for a moment and think. You have surely heard of gravitation, by which the sun holds the earth and the planets, and keeps them moving round him in regular order? Well, it is this same gravitation which is at work also whenever a shower of rain falls to the earth. Who can say that he is not a great invisible giant, always silently and invisibly toiling in great things and small whether we wake or sleep?

Now the shower is over, the sun comes out, and the ground is soon as dry as though no rain had fallen. Tell me, what has become of the rain-drops? Part no doubt have sunk into the ground, and as for the rest, why you will say the sun has dried them up. Yes, but how? The sun is more than ninety-one millions of miles away; how has he touched the rain-drops? Have you ever heard that invisible waves are travelling every instant over the space between the sun and us? We shall see in the next lecture how these waves are the sun's messengers to the earth, and how they tear asunder the rain-drops on the ground, scattering them in tiny particles too small for us to see, and bearing them away to the clouds. Here are more invisible fairies working every moment around you, and you cannot even look out of the window without seeing the work they are doing.

If, however, the day is cold and frosty, the water does not fall in a shower of rain; it comes down in the shape of noiseless snow. Go out after such a snow-shower, on a calm day, and look at some of the flakes which have fallen; you will see, if you choose good specimens, that they are not mere masses of frozen water, but that each one is a beautiful six-pointed crystal star. How have these crystals been built up? What power has been at work arranging their delicate forms? In the fourth lecture we shall see that

3. I am quite aware of the danger incurred by using this word "force," especially in the plural; and how even the most modest little book may suffer at the hands of scientific purists by employing it rashly. As, however, the better term "energy" would not serve here, I hope I may be forgiven for retaining the much-abused term, especially as I sin in very good company.

up in the clouds another of our invisible fairies, which, for want of a better name, we call the "force of crystallization," has caught hold of the tiny particles of water before "cohesion" had made them into round drops, and there silently but rapidly, has moulded them into those delicate crystal stars knows as "snowflakes."

And now, suppose that this snow-shower has fallen early in February; turn aside for a moment from examining the flakes, and clear the newly-fallen snow from off the flower-bed on the lawn. What is this little green tip peeping up out of the ground under the snowy covering? It is a young snowdrop plant. Can you tell me why it grows? where it finds its food? what makes it spread out its leaves and add to its stalk day by day? What fairies are at work here?

First there is the hidden fairy "life," and of her even our wisest men know but little. But they know something of her way of working, and in Lecture VII. we shall learn how the invisible fairy sunbeams have been busy here also; how last year's snowdrop plant caught them and stored them up in its bulb, and how now in the spring, as soon as warmth and moisture creep down into the earth, these little imprisoned sun-waves begin to be active, stirring up the matter in the bulb, and making it swell and burst upwards till it sends out a little shoot through the surface of the soil. Then the sun-waves above-ground take up the work, and form green granules in the tiny leaves, helping them to take food out of the air, while the little rootlets below are drinking water out of the ground. The invisible life and invisible sunbeams are busy here, setting actively to work another fairy, the force of "chemical attraction," and so the little snowdrop plant grows and blossoms, without any help from you or me.

One picture more, and then I hope you will believe in my fairies. From the cold garden, you run into the house, and find the fire laid indeed in the grate, but the wood dead and the coals black, waiting to be lighted. You strike a match, and soon there is a blazing fire. Where does the heat come from? Why do the coals burn and give out a glowing light? Have you not read of gnomes buried down deep in the earth, in mines, and held fast there until some fairy wand has released them, and allowed them to come to earth again? Well, thousands and millions of years ago, those coals were plants; and, like the snowdrop in the garden of to-day, they caught the sunbeams and worked them into their leaves. Then the plants died and were buried deep in the earth and the sunbeams with them; and like the gnomes they lay imprisoned till the coals were dug out by the miners, and brought to your grate; and just now you yourself took hold of the fairy wand which was to release them. You struck a match, and its atoms clashing with atoms of oxygen in the air, set the invisible fairies "heat" and "chemical attraction" to work, and they were soon busy within the wood and the coals causing their atoms too to clash; and the sunbeams, so long imprisoned, leapt into flame. Then you spread out your hands and cried, "Oh, how nice and warm!" and little thought that you were warming yourself with the sunbeams of ages and ages ago.

This is no fancy tale; it is literally true, as we shall see in Lecture VIII., that the warmth of a coal fire could not exist if the plants of long ago had not used the sunbeams to make their leaves, holding them ready to give up their warmth again whenever those crushed leaves are consumed.

Now, do you believe in, and care for, my fairy-land? Can you see in your imagination fairy *Cohesion* ever ready to lock atoms together when they draw very near to each other: or fairy *Gravitation* dragging rain-drops down to the earth; or the fairy *Crystallization* building up the snow-flakes in the clouds? Can you picture tiny sunbeam-waves of light and heat travelling from the sun to the earth? Do you care to know how another strange fairy, *Electricity,* flings the lightning across the sky and causes the rumbling thunder? Would you like to learn how the sun makes pictures of the world on which he shines, so that we can carry about with us photographs or sun-pictures of all the beautiful scenery of the earth? And have you any curiosity about *Chemical action,* which works such wonders in air, and land, and sea? If you have any wish to know and make friends of these invisible forces, the next question is

How are you to enter the fairy-land of science?

There is but one way. Like the knight or peasant in the fairy tales, you must open your eyes. There is no lack of objects, everything around you will tell some history if touched with the fairy wand of imagination. I have often thought, when seeing some sickly child drawn along the street, lying on its back while other children romp and play, how much happiness might be given to sick children at home or in hospitals, if only they were told the stories which lie hidden in the things around them. They need not even move from their beds, for sunbeams can fall on them there, and in a sunbeam there are stories enough to occupy a month. The fire in the grate, the lamp by the bedside, the water in the tumbler, the fly on the ceiling above, the flower in the vase on the table, anything, everything, has its history, and can reveal to us nature's invisible fairies.

Only you must wish to see them. If you go through the world looking upon everything only as so much to eat, to drink, and to use, you will never see the fairies of science. But if you ask yourself why things happen, and how the great God above us has made and governs this world of ours; if you listen to the wind, and care to learn why it blows; if you ask the little flower why it opens in the sunshine and closes in the storm; and if when you find questions you cannot answer, you will take the trouble to hunt out in books, or make experiments, to solve your own questions, then you will learn to know and love those fairies.

Mind, I do not advise you to be constantly asking questions of other people; for often a question quickly answered is quickly forgotten, but a difficulty really hunted down is a triumph for ever. For example, if you ask why the rain dries up from the ground, most likely you will be answered, "that the sun dries it," and you will rest satisfied with the sound of the words. But if you hold a wet handkerchief before the fire and see the damp rising out of it, then you have some real idea how moisture may be drawn up by heat from the earth.

A little foreign niece of mine, only four years old, who could scarcely speak English plainly, was standing one morning near the bedroom window and she noticed the damp trickling down the window-pane. "Auntie," she said, "what for it rain inside?" It was quite useless to explain to her in words, how our breath had condensed into drops of water upon the cold glass; but I wiped the pane clear, and breathed on it several times. When new drops were formed, I said, "Cissy and auntie have done like this all night in the room." She nodded her little head and amused herself for a long time breathing on the window-pane and watching the tiny drops; and about a month later, when we were travelling back to Italy, I saw her following the drops on the carriage window with her little finger, and heard her say quietly to herself, "Cissy and auntie made you." Had not even this little child some real picture in her mind of invisible water coming from her mouth, and making drops upon the window-pane?

Then again, you must learn something of the language of science. If you travel in a country with no knowledge of its language, you can learn very little about it: and in the same way if you are to go to books to find answers to your questions, you must know something of the language they speak. You need not learn hard scientific names, for the best books have the fewest of these, but you must really understand what is meant by ordinary words.

For example, how few people can really explain the difference between a *solid,* such as the wood of the table; a *liquid,* as water; and a *gas,* such as I can let off from this gas-jet by turning the tap. And yet any child can make a picture of this in his mind if only it has been properly put before him.

All matter in the world is made up of minute parts or particles; in a *solid* these particles are locked together so tightly that you must tear them forcibly apart if you wish to alter the shape of the solid piece. If I break or bend this wood I have to force the particles to move round each other, and I have great difficulty in doing it. But in a *liquid,* though the particles are still held together, they do not cling so tightly, but are able to roll or glide round each other, so that when you pour water out of a cup on to a table, it loses its cuplike shape and spreads itself out flat. Lastly, in a *gas* the particles are no longer held together at all, but they try to fly away from each other; and unless you shut a gas in tightly and safely, it will soon have spread all over the room.

A solid, therefore, will retain the same bulk and shape unless you forcibly alter it; a liquid will retain the same bulk, but not the same shape if it be left free; a gas will not retain either the same bulk or the same shape, but will spread over as large a space as it can find wherever it can penetrate. Such simple things as these you must learn from books and by experiment.

Then you must understand what is meant by *chemical attraction;* and though I can explain this roughly here, you will have to make many interesting experiments before you will really learn to know this wonderful fairy power. If I dissolve sugar in water, though it disappears it still remains sugar, and does not join itself to the water. I have only to let the cup stand till the water dries, and the sugar will remain at the bottom. There has been no chemical attraction here.

But now I will put something else in water which will call up the fairy power. Here is a little piece of the metal potassium, one of the simple substances of the earth; that is to say, we cannot split it up into other substances, wherever we find it, it is always the same. Now if I put this piece of potassium on the water it does not disappear quietly like the sugar. See how it rolls round and round, fizzing violently, with a blue flame burning round it, and at last goes off with a pop.

What has been happening here?

You must first know that water is made of two substances, hydrogen and oxygen, and these are not merely held together, but are joined so completely that they have lost themselves and have become water; and each atom of water is made of two atoms of hydrogen and one of oxygen.

Now the metal potassium is devotedly fond of oxygen, and the moment I threw it on the water it called the fairy "chemical attraction" to help it, and dragged the atoms of oxygen out of the water and joined them to itself. In doing this it also caught part of the hydrogen, but only half, and so the rest was left out in the cold. No, not in the cold! for the potassium and oxygen made such a great heat in clashing together that the rest of the hydrogen became very hot indeed, and sprang into the air to find some other companion to make up for what it had lost. Here it found some free oxygen in the air, and it seized upon it so violently, that they made a burning flame, while the potassium with its newly found oxygen and hydrogen sank down quietly into the water as *potash.* And so you see we have got quite a new substance *potash* in the basin; made with a great deal of fuss by *chemical attraction* drawing different atoms together.

When you can really picture this power to yourself it will help you very much to understand what you read and observe about nature.

Next, as plants grow around you on every side, and are of so much importance in the world, you must also learn something of the names of the different parts of a flower, so that you may understand those books which explain how a plant grows and lives and forms its seeds. You must also know the common names of the parts of an animal, and of your own body, so that you may be interested in understanding the use of the different organs; how you breathe, and how your blood flows; how one animal walks, another flies, and another swims. Then you must learn something of the various parts of the world, so that you may know what is meant by a river, a plain, a valley, or a delta. All these things are not difficult, you can learn them pleasantly from simple books on physics, chemistry, botany, physiology, and physical geography; and when you understand a few plain scientific terms, then all by yourself, if you will open your eyes and ears, you may wander happily in the fairy-land of science. Then wherever you go you will find

> "Tongues in trees, books in the running brooks,
> Sermons in stones, and good in everything."[4]

And now we come to the last part of our subject. When you have reached and entered the gates of science, how are you to use and enjoy this new and beautiful land?

This is a very important question, for you may make a twofold use of it. If you are only ambitious to shine in the world, you may use it chiefly to get prizes, to be at the top of your class, or to pass in examinations; but if you also enjoy discovering its secrets, and desire to learn more and more of

4. Shakespeare's *As You Like It:* 2.2.16–17. *Ed.*

nature, and to revel in dreams of its beauty, then you will study science for its own sake as well. Now it is a good thing to win prizes and be at the top of your class, for it shows that you are industrious; it is a good thing to pass well in examinations, for it shows that you are accurate; but if you study science for this reason *only,* do not complain if you find it dull, and dry, and hard to master. You may learn a great deal that is useful, and nature will answer you truthfully if you ask your questions accurately, but she will give you dry facts, just such as you ask for. If you do not love her for herself she will never take you to her heart.

This is the reason why so many complain that science is dry and uninteresting. They forget that though it is necessary to learn accurately, for so only can we arrive at truth, it is equally necessary to love knowledge and make it lovely to those who learn, and to do this we must get at the spirit which lies under the facts. What child which loves its mother's face is content to know only that she has brown eyes, a straight nose, a small mouth, and hair arranged in such and such a manner? No, it knows that its mother has the sweetest smile of any woman living; that her eyes are loving, her kiss is sweet, and that when she looks grave, then something is wrong which must be put right. And it is in this way that those who wish to enjoy the fairy-land of science must love nature. . . .

~ ELLIS ETHELMER (ELIZABETH WOLSTENHOLME ELMY)

From *Baby Buds*

Congleton: Buxton House, 1895. 26–27; 37–40; 46–47.

[pp. 26–27]

You will perhaps ask—"Then, are the male flowers of a vegetable marrow plant needless, or do they lead a useless life; seeing that they bear no fruit?"

Not so, my child; neither the male flowers of the vegetable marrow, nor of any other plant, are useless; for they produce the peculiar yellowish dust, or grains, called pollen, about which I have already said a few words.

And, indeed, if you will notice one of the vegetable marrow male flowers attentively, you will see inside it a thickish white stalk, whose top is covered with this yellow dust, of which some must find its way to the female flower and to each of the ovules in her ovary; or if any ovule misses being mingled with the contents of a grain of the pollen, that particular ovule will not become a really living seed, capable of growing into a plant.

"But how does the pollen get from the male flower to the female flower, since they cannot move near and touch one another?"

You may learn how this comes about if you will look carefully inside the female flower. For there you will see also a stalk from her ovary, reaching outwards until it is exposed to the air.

It looks somewhat similar to the stalk inside the male flower, but does not produce any pollen. Its top, however, is rough, and moist with a sticky fluid; so that, if there were wind enough to blow some of the pollen off the male flower, and a grain or two chanced to drop on this female stalk, it would be caught and kept.

And this is actually the way in which the pollen is carried from the male to the female in many kinds of flowers; it is so, for instance, with the hazel and the willow and the yew, as also with grasses and corn.

But with most flowers the method is that which you will see, if it happens to be a dry sunny morning like this, and you will wait and notice.

[pp. 37–40]

We shall now, darling, be more able to trace and perceive the further resemblances and differences in the method by which plants and animals (including human beings) come into existence.

For animals have parts or organs somewhat similar in formation, and the same in purpose, as those we have noticed in flowers.

Thus, in a full grown female mammal or bird there is an ovary, somewhat as in a flower, and containing ovules which, under certain circumstances, will develop into young. There is not, however, any outward form of a flower, for the animal's flower-like organs are contained inside the lower part of her body, so as to be little exposed to chance of harm.

So also, the male animal or bird, when fully grown, produces a substance of a similar nature to the pollen of a flower, and equally needful before an ovule can become capable of growing into a young animal.

Mammals or birds have no need of bees or moths to transfer the pollen substance from the male to the female; for they can approach one another for that purpose, when they are grown up and strong. Indeed they do so approach at certain times, that the ovules of the female may receive some of the pollen substance.

How this fully comes about, you can scarcely understand till you are older; but you may understand even now that the action of the ovules is very similar to what takes place in a flower.

In a bird we see that the ovule very rapidly grows larger, and becomes an egg, with a hard shell; which the bird at once puts out of its body, and then hatches into full life.

But in a mammal the ovule does not increase so quickly, nor does a hard shell form around it; but it is retained in the mother's body in a further receptacle or chamber, called the womb. Here the ovule lies, and is cherished by the mother's warmth, and nourished by her blood flowing through it, till it is entirely formed as a young animal; and it is then put out of her body, or "born."

As in the seeding of flowers, so here again, the time of the young within the mother's body varies according to the species of animal. In a tiny puppy it is only nine weeks; but in a little human baby it is the same number of months.

So, alike in plants, in animals, and in human beings, the young one exists first as an ovule within the mother, and receives nourishment and development from her body, till fitted for the outward early conditions of the different life each will have to fill.

I have said that some part of all this will be clearer to you as you grow older, and the necessity for that further knowledge arises. For though the important flower-like organs, male or female—according as you are a boy or a girl—are already developing in you, they make no special claim to notice while you are still young. And, when they gradually grow, so that you do become somewhat conscious of them, you will readily understand, from what you have already learnt, to be most daintily cautious that no playing or meddling with them ever takes place. For, till you are fully grown up, these parts are as a delicate bud to the coming flower; and you know if harm were done to a bud, how the flower would be injured.

Such care is needful in all children and young persons; and not for the sake of their own health only, but because with them, in the future, will be—as a good man has written—"the solemn duty and privilege of continuing the life of the nation, and adding to its well-being and greatness by becoming the parents of healthy children."

So may you too, my darling, grow up strong and clean in body and in act; and be fair and sweet as a flower in the fragrance of a pure mind and heart.

[pp. 46–47]

In his quest for yet fuller truer life, man will not be swayed by meaner desires, but will guide his actions and his very passions by his ever-growing knowledge and observation of Nature's ways. It lies in the power of each one of us thus to raise himself or herself higher in the scale of intelligence and wisdom; and, in so doing, to become not only worthier ourselves, but to add likewise to the good of all around us.

Deeply, too, is borne in on us the lesson that as our amount of intellect and power is greater, so also the more urgent is our duty of causing what happiness we can, and not pain, to these less favoured brothers and sisters of ours in the family of Life,—be they beast, or bird, or lower animals, or plants.

We may at least strive to make easy and healthy and pleasant the lives and surroundings of the animals that are our helpers; no wild creature shall suffer torture or imprisonment at our hands, or be needlessly slain; and not even a little flower will we recklessly pull and cast away, but choose rather to leave it unmolested, and tenderly watch it live on, to "enjoy the air it breathes." [1]

Nor may we doubt, darling, that in so caring for Nature's offspring, "both great and small," the gentle Mother will smile on us in return; and will make our own lives richer and sweeter, as she teaches us to know ever more and more of her beauty, of her wonder, of her happiness, and of her love.

1. See William Wordsworth, "Lines Written in Early Spring," line 12. *Ed.*

Women and Darwin

ARABELLA B. BUCKLEY

From *Life and Her Children*

London: Edward Stanford, 1880. v; 1–13.

[p. v]

PREFACE

The plan of this work is so fully explained in the Introductory Chapter that but little preface is needed. Its main object is to acquaint young people with the structure and habits of the lower forms of life; and to do this in a more systematic way than is usual in ordinary works on Natural History, and more simply than in text-books on Zoology.

For this reason I have adopted the title "Life and her Children," to express the family bond uniting all *living* things, as we use the term, "Nature and her Works," to embrace all organic and inorganic phenomena; and I have been more careful to sketch in bold outline the leading features of each division, than to dwell upon the minor differences by which it is separated into groups.

I have made use of British examples in illustration wherever it was possible, and small specimens of most of the marine animals figured may be found upon our coasts at low tide.

ARABELLA B. BUCKLEY.
LONDON, *November* 1880.

[pp. 1–13]

CHAPTER I

Wisdom and Spirit of the Universe!
Thou Soul, that art the Eternity of Thought!
And giv'st to forms and images a breath
And everlasting motion!—WORDSWORTH.[1]

I wonder whether it ever occurs to most people to consider how brimful our world is of life, and what a different place it would be if no living thing had ever been upon it? From the time we are born till we die, there is scarcely a waking moment of our lives in which our eyes do not rest either upon some living thing, or upon things which have once been alive. Even in our rooms, the wood of our furniture and our doors could never have been without the action of life; the paper on our walls, the carpet on our floors, the clothes on our back, the cloth upon the table, are all made of materials which life has produced for us; nay, the very marble of our mantelpiece is the work of once living animals, and is composed of their broken shells. The air we breathe is full of invisible germs of life; nor need we leave the town and go to the country in search of other living beings than man. There is scarcely a street or alley where, if it be neglected for a time, some blade of grass or struggling weed does not make its appearance, pushing its way through chinks in the pavement or the mortar in the wall; no spot from which we cannot see some insect creeping, or flying, or spinning its web, so long as the hand of man does not destroy it.

And when we go into the quiet country, leaving man and his works behind, how actively we find life employed! Covering every inch of the ground with tiny plants, rearing tall trees in the forest, filling the stagnant pools full of eager restless beings; anywhere, everywhere, life is at work. Look at the little water-beetles skimming on the surface of the shady wayside pool, watch the snails feeding on the muddy bank, notice the newts putting their heads above water to take breath, and then remember that, besides these and innumerable other animals visible to the naked eye, the fairy-shrimp and the water-flea, and other minute creatures, are probably darting across the pond, or floating lazily near its surface; while the very scum which is blown

1. Printed in *The Friend* (28 December 1809), a journal edited by Samuel Taylor Coleridge. Probably written in 1798. *Ed.*

in ridges towards one corner of the pool is made up of microscopic animals and plants.

Then, as we pass over plain, and valley, and mountain, we find things creeping innumerable, both small and great; some hidden in the moss or the thick grass, rolled up in the leaves, boring into the stems and trunks of trees, eating their way underground or into even the strongest rock; while others, such as the lion, the tiger, and the elephant, roaming over Africa and India, rule a world of their own where man counts for very little. Even in our own thickly peopled country rabbits multiply by thousands in their burrows, and come to frolic in the dusk of evening when all is still. The field-mice, land and water rats, squirrels, weasels, and badgers, have their houses above and below ground, while countless insects swarm everywhere, testifying to the abundance of life. Not content, moreover, with filling the water and covering the land, this same silent power peoples the atmosphere, where bats, butterflies, bees, and winged insects of all forms, shapes, and colours, fight their way through the ocean of air; while birds, large and small, sail among its invisible waves.

And when by and by we reach the sea, we find there masses of tangled seaweed, the plants of the salt water, while all along the shores myriads of living creatures are left by the receding tide. In the rocky pools we find active life busily at work. Thousands of acorn-shells, many of them scarcely larger than the head of a good-sized pin, cover the rocks and wave their delicate fringes in search of food. Small crabs scramble along, or swim across the pools, sand-skippers dart through the water, feeding on the delicate green seaweed, which in its turn is covered with minute shells not visible to the naked eye, and yet each containing a living being.

Wherever we go, living creatures are to be found, and even if we sail away over the deep silent ocean and seek what is in its depths, there again we find abundance of life, from the large fish and other monsters which glide noiselessly along, lords of the ocean, down to the jelly-masses floating on the surface, and the banks of rocky coral built by jelly-animals in the midst of the dashing waves. There is no spot on the surface of the earth, in the depths of the ocean, or in the lower currents of the air, which is not filled with life whenever and wherever there is room. The one great law which all living beings obey is to "increase, multiply, and replenish the earth;" and there has been no halting in this work from the day when first into our planet from the bosom of the great Creator was breathed the breath of life,—the invisible mother ever taking shape in her children.

No matter whether there is room for more living forms or not, still they are launched into the world. The little seed, which will be stifled by other plants before it can put forth its leaves, nevertheless thrusts its tiny root into the ground and tries to send a feeble shoot upwards. Thousands and millions of insects are born into the world every moment, which can never live because there is not food enough for all. If there were only one single plant in the whole world to-day, and it produced fifty seeds in a year and could multiply unchecked, its descendants would cover the whole globe in nine years.[2] But, since other plants prevent it from spreading, thousands and thousands of its seeds and young plants must be formed only to perish. In the same way one pair of birds having four young ones each year, would, if all their children and descendants lived and multiplied, produce *two thousand million* in fifteen years,[3] but since there is not room for them, all but a very few must die.

What can be the use of this terrible overcrowding in our little world? Why does this irresistible living breath go on so madly, urging one little being after another into existence? Would it not be better if only enough were born to have plenty of room and to live comfortably?

Wait a while before you decide, and think what every creature needs to keep it alive. Plants, it is true, can live on water and air, but animals cannot; and if there were not myriads of plants to spare in the world, there would not be enough for food. Then consider again how many animals live upon each other; if worms, snails, and insects, were not over-abundant, how would the birds live? upon what would lions, and tigers, and wolves feed if other animals were not plentiful; while, on the other hand, if a great number of larger animals did not die and decay, what would the flesh-feeding snails, and maggots, and other insects find to eat? And so we see that for this reason alone there is some excuse for the over-abundance of creatures which life thrusts into the world.

But there is something deeper than this to consider. If in a large school every boy had a prize at the end of the half-year, whether he had worked or not, do you think all the boys would work as hard as they do or learn as well? If every man had all he required, and could live comfortably, and bring up his children to enjoy life without working for it, do you think people would take such trouble to learn trades and professions, and to improve themselves so as to be more able than others? Would they work hard day and night to make new inventions, or discover new lands, and found fresh colonies, or be in any way so useful, or learn so much as they do now?

No, it is the struggle for life and the necessity for work which makes

2. Huxley.

3. Wallace.

people invent, and plan, and improve themselves and things around them. And so it is also with plants and animals. Life has to educate all her children, and she does it by giving the prize of success, health, strength, and enjoyment to those who can best fight the battle of existence, and do their work best in the world.

Every plant and every animal which is born upon the earth has to get its own food and earn its own livelihood, and to protect itself from the attacks of others. Would the spider toil so industriously to spin her web if food came to her without any exertion on her part? Would the caddis worm have learnt to build a tube of sand and shells to protect its soft body, or the oyster to take lime from the sea-water to form a strong shell for its home, if they had no enemies to struggle against, and needed no protection? Would the bird have learnt to build her nest or the beaver his house if there was no need for their industry?

But as it is, since the whole world is teeming with life, and countless numbers of seeds and eggs and young beginnings of creatures are only waiting for the chance to fill any vacant nook or corner, every living thing must learn to do its best and to find the place where it can succeed best and is least likely to be destroyed by others. And so it comes to pass that the whole planet is used to the best advantage, and life teaches her children to get all the good out of it that they can.

If the ocean and the rivers be full, then some must learn to live on the land, and so we have for example sea-snails and land-snails; and whereas the one kind can only breathe by gills in the water, the other breathes air by means of air-chambers, while between these are some marsh-snails of the tropics, which combine both, and can breathe in both water and air. We have large whales sailing as monarchs of the ocean, and walruses and seals fishing in its depths for their food, while all other animals of the mammalian class live on the land.

Then, again, while many creatures love the bright light, others take advantage of the dark corners where room is left for them to live. You can scarcely lift a stone by the seaside without finding some living thing under it, nor turn up a spadeful of earth without disturbing some little creature which is content to find its home and its food in the dark ground. Nay, many animals for whom there is no chance of life on the earth, in the water, or in the air, find a refuge in the bodies of other animals and feed on them.

But in order that all these creatures may live, each in its different way, they must have their own particular tools to work with, and weapons with which to defend themselves. Now all the tools and weapons of an animal grow upon its body. It works and fights with its teeth, its claws, its tail, its sting, or its feelers; or it constructs cunning traps by means of material which it gives out from its own body, like the spider. It hides from its enemies by having a shape or colour like the rocks or the leaves, the grass or the water, which surround it. It provides for its young ones either by getting food for them, or by putting them, even before they come out of the egg, into places where their food is ready for them as soon as they are born.

So that the whole life of an animal depends upon the way in which its body is made; and it will lead quite a different existence according to the kind of tools with which life provides it, and the instincts which a long education has been teaching to its ancestors for ages past. It will have its own peculiar struggles, and difficulties, and successes, and enjoyments, according to the kind of bodily powers which it possesses, and the study of these helps us to understand its manner of existence.

And now, since we live in the world with all these numerous companions, which lead, many of them, such curious lives, trying like ourselves to make the best of their short time here, is it not worth while to learn something about them? May we not gain some useful hints by watching their contrivances, sympathising with their difficulties, and studying their history? And above all, shall we not have something more to love and to care for when we have made acquaintance with some of Life's other children besides ourselves?

The one great difficulty, however, in our way, is how to make acquaintance with such a vast multitude. Most of us have read anecdotes about one animal or another, but this does not give us any clue to the history of the whole animal world; and without some such clue, the few observations we can make for ourselves are very unsatisfactory. On the other hand, most people will confess that books on zoology, where accounts are given of the structure of different classes of animals, though very necessary, are rather dull, and do not seem to help us much towards understanding and loving these our fellow-creatures.

What we most want to learn is something of the *lives* of the different classes of animals, so that when we see some creature running away from us in the woods, or swimming in a pond, or darting through the air, or creeping on the ground, we may have an idea what its object is in life—how it is enjoying itself, what food it is seeking, or from what enemy it is flying.

And fortunately for us there is an order and arrangement in this immense multitude, and in the same way as we can read and understand the history of the different nations which form the great human family spread over the earth, and can enter into their feelings and their struggles though we cannot know all the people themselves; so with a little trouble we may learn to picture to ourselves the general life and habits of the different branches of the still greater family of Life, so as to be ready, by and by, to make personal acquaintance with any particular creature if he comes in our way.

This is what we propose to do in the following chapters, and we must first consider what are the chief divisions of our subject, and over what ground we have to travel. It is clear that both plants and animals are the children of Life, and indeed among the simplest living forms it is often difficult to say whether they are plants or animals.

But it is impossible for us to follow out the history of both these great branches of *Kingdoms*, as naturalists call them, so we must reluctantly turn our backs for the present upon the wonderful secrets of plant life, and give ourselves up in this work to the study of animals.

First we meet with those simple forms which manage so cleverly to live without any separate parts with which to do their work. Marvellous little beings these, which live, and move, and multiply in a way quite incomprehensible as yet to us. Next we pass on to the slightly higher forms of the *second* division of life, in which the members have some simple weapons of attack and defence. Here we come first upon the wonderful living sponge, building its numerous canals, which are swept by special scavengers; these form a sort of separate group, hovering between the *first* and *second* division, and from them we go on to the travelling jelly-fish, with their rudiments of eyes and ears, and their benumbing sting, and then to the sea-anemones with their lasso-cells, and to the wondrous coral-builders. Already we are beginning to find that the need of defence causes life to arm her children.

The *third* division is a small, yet most curious one, containing the star-fish with their countless sucker-feet, the sea-urchins with their delicate sharp spines and curious teeth, and the sea-cucumbers with their power of throwing away the inside of their body and growing it afresh. This division goes off in one direction, while the next, or *fourth,* though starting with creatures almost as simple as the coral-builders, takes quite a different line, having for its members mussels and snails, cuttle-fish and oysters, and dividing into two curious groups: the one of the shell-fish with heads, and the other of those without any.

The *fifth* division, starting also in its own line by the side of the third and fourth, includes the creeping worms provided with quite a different set of weapons, and working in their own peculiar fashion, some living in the water, some on the earth, and some in the flesh of other beings, feeding upon their living tissues. An ugly division this, and yet when we come to study it we shall find it full of curious forms showing strange habits and ways.

The *sixth* division is a vast army in itself, with four chief groups all agreeing in their members having jointed feet, and subdivided into smaller groups almost without number. The first group, including the crabs and their companions, live in the water, and their weapons are so varied and numerous that it will be difficult for us even to gain some general idea of them. The other three groups, the centipedes, spiders, and six-legged insects, breathe only in the air. This sixth or jointed-legged division contains more than four-fifths of the whole of the living beings on our globe, and it forms a world of its own, full of interest and wonders. In it we have all the strange facts of metamorphosis, the wondrous contrivances and constructions of insect-life, and at the head of it those clever societies of wasps, bees, and ants, with laws sometimes even nearer to perfection than those of man himself.

Lastly we come to the *seventh* and vast division of back-boned animals which will claim a separate volume to itself. This division has struggled side by side with the other six till it has won a position in many respects above them all. Nearly all the animals which we know best belong to it,—the fishes, toads, newts (amphibia), the reptiles, the birds, and the mammalia, including all our four-footed animals, as well as the whales, seals, monkeys, and man himself.

Under these seven divisions then are grouped the whole of the living animals as they are spread over the earth to fight the battle of life. Though in many places the battle is fierce, and each one must fight remorselessly for himself and his little ones, yet the struggle consists chiefly in all the members of the various brigades doing their work in life to the best of their power, so that all, while they live, may lead a healthy, active existence.

The little bird is fighting his battle when he builds his nest and seeks food for his mate and his little ones; and though in doing this he must kill the worm, and may perhaps by and by fall a victim himself to the hungry hawk, yet the worm heeds nothing of its danger till its life comes to an end, and the bird trills his merry song after his breakfast and enjoys his life without thinking of perils to come.

> While ravening death of slaughter ne'er grows weary,
> Life multiplies the immortal meal as fast.
> All are devourers, all in turn devoured,
> Yet every unit in the uncounted sum

Of victims has its share of bliss—its pang,
And but a pang of dissolution: each
Is happy till its moment comes, and then
Its first, last suffering, unforeseen, unfear'd,
Ends with one struggle pain and life for ever.[4]

So life sends her children forth, and it remains for us to learn something of their history. If we could but know it all, and the thousands of different ways in which the beings around us struggle and live, we should be overwhelmed with wonder. Even as it is we may perhaps hope to gain such a glimpse of the labours of this great multitude as may lead us to wish to fight our own battle bravely, and to work, and strive, and bear patiently, if only that we may be worthy to stand at the head of the vast family of Life's children.

ARABELLA B. BUCKLEY

From *Winners in Life's Race*

London: Edward Stanford, 1883. 334–53.

. . . We have seen also that, as in all families of long standing, many branches have become extinct altogether; the great enamel-plated fish, the large armour-covered newts, the flying, swimming, and huge erect-walking reptiles, the toothed and long-tailed birds, the gigantic marsupials, the enormous ground-loving sloths, and many others, have lived out their day and disappeared; their place being filled either by smaller descendants of other branches of the group, or by new forms in the great armies of fish, birds, and milk-givers which now have chiefly possession of the earth.

Still, on the whole, the history has been one of a gradual rise from lower to higher forms of life; and if we put aside for a moment all details, and, forgetting the enormous lapse of time required, allow the shifting scene to pass like a panorama before us, we shall have a grand view indeed of the progress of the great backboned family.

4. James Montgomery, "The Pelican Island: A Poem in Nine Cantos" 3:43–44, 46–52. *The Poetical Works.* 1850. *Ed.*

First, passing by that long series of geological formations in which no remains of life have been found, or only those of boneless or invertebrate animals, we find ourselves in a sea abounding in stone-lilies and huge crustaceans, having among them the small forms of the earliest fish known to us, those having gristly skeletons. Then as the scene passes on, and forests clothe the land, we behold the descendants of these small fish becoming large and important, wearing heavy enamelled plates or sharp defensive spines; some of them with enormous jaws, two or three feet in length, wandering in the swamps and muddy waters, and using their air-bladder as a lung. But these did not turn their air-breathing discovery to account; they remained in the water, and their descendants are fish down to the present day.

It is in the next scene, when already the age of the huge extinct fishes is beginning to pass away, and tree ferns and coal forest plants are flourishing luxuriantly, that we find the first land animals, which have been growing up side by side with the fish, and gradually learning to undergo a change, marvellous indeed, yet similar to one which goes on under our eyes each year in every country pond. For now, mingling with the fish, we behold an altogether new type of creatures which, beginning life as water-breathers, learn to come out upon the land and live as air-breathers in the swamps of the coal forests.

A marvellous change this is, as we can judge by watching our common tadpole, and seeing how during its youth its whole breathing organs are remade on a totally different principle, its heart is remodelled from an organ of two chambers into one of three, the whole course of its blood is altered, some channels being destroyed and others multiplied and enlarged, a sucking mouth is converted into a gaping bony jaw, and legs with all their bones and joints are produced where none were before, while the fish's tail, its office abandoned, is gradually absorbed and lost.

The only reason why this completely new creation, taking place in one and the same animal, does not fill us with wonder is, that it goes on in the water where generally we do not see it, and because the most wonderful changes are worked out *inside* the tadpole, and are only understood by physiologists. But in truth the real alteration in bodily structure is much greater than if a seal could be changed into a monkey.

Now this complete development which the tadpole goes through in one summer is, after all, but a rapid repetition, as it were, of that slow and gradual development which must have taken place in past ages, when water-breathing animals first became adapted to air-breathing. Any one, therefore, who will take the spawn of a frog from a pond, and watch it through all its stages, may rehearse for himself that marvellous chapter in the history of the growth and development of higher life.

And he will gain much by this study, for all nature teaches us that this is the mode in which the Great Power works. Not "in the whirlwind," or by sudden and violent new creations, but by the "still small voice" of gentle and gradual change, ordering so the laws of being that each part shall model and remodel itself as occasion requires. Could we but see the whole, we should surely bend in reverence and awe before a scheme so grand, so immutable, so irresistible in its action, and yet so still, so silent, and so imperceptible, because everywhere and always at work. Even now to those who study nature, broken and partial as their knowledge must be, it is incomprehensible how men can seek and long for marvels of spasmodic power, when there lies before them the greatest proof of a mighty wisdom in an all-embracing and never-wavering scheme, the scope of which is indeed beyond our intelligence, but the partial working of which is daily shown before our very eyes.

But to return to our shifting scene where the dense forests of the Coal Period next come before us. There, while numerous fish, small and great, fill the waters, huge Newts have begun their reign (*Labyrinthodonts*), wandering in the marshy swamps or swimming in the pools, while smaller forms run about among the trees, or, snake-like in form, wriggle among the ferns and mosses; and one and all of these lead the double-breathing or amphibian life.

In the next scene the coal forests are passing away, though still the strange forms of the trees and the gigantic ferns tell us we have not left them quite behind; and now upon the land are true air-breathers, no longer beginning life in the water, but born alive, as the young ones of the black salamander are now. The Reptiles have begun their reign, and they show that, though still cold-blooded animals, they have entered upon a successful line of life, for they increase in size and number till the world is filled with them.

Meanwhile other remarkable forms now appear leading off to two new branches of backboned life. On the one hand, little insect-eating warm-blooded marsupials scamper through the woods, having started we scarcely yet know when or where, except that we learn from their structure that they probably branched off from the amphibians in quite a different line from the reptiles, and certainly gained a footing upon the earth in very early times. On the other hand, birds come upon the scene having teeth in their mouths, long-jointed tails, and many other reptilian characters. We have indeed far more clue to the relationship of the birds than we have of the marsupials, for while we have these reptile-like birds, we have also the bird-like reptiles such as the little Compsognathus, which hopped on two feet, had a long neck, bird-like head and many other bird-like characters, though no wings or feathers.

The birds, however, even though reptile-like in their beginning, must soon have branched out on a completely new line. They for the first time among this group of animals,[1] have the perfect four-chambered heart with its quick circulation and warm blood; while not only do they use their fore limbs for flying (for this some reptiles did before them), but they use them in quite a new fashion, putting forth a clothing of feathers of wondrous beauty and construction, and with true wings taking possession of the air, where from this time their history is one of continued success.

And now we have before us all the great groups of the backboned family—fish, amphibia, reptiles, birds and mammalia; but in what strange proportions! As the scenery of the Chalk Period with its fan-palms and pines comes before us, we find that the gristly fish, except the sharks and a few solitary types, are fast dying out, while the bony fish are but just beginning their career. The large amphibians are all gone long ago; they have run their race, enjoyed their life and finished their course, leaving only the small newts and salamanders, and later on the frogs and toads, to keep up the traditions of the race. The land-birds are still in their earliest stage; they have probably scarcely lost their lizard-like tail, and have not yet perfected their horny beak, but are only feeling their way as conquerors of the air. And as for the milk-givers, though we have met with them in small early forms, yet now for a time we lose sight of them again altogether.

It is the reptiles—the cold-blooded monster reptiles—which seem at this time to be carrying all before them. We find them everywhere—in the water, with paddles for swimming; in the air, with membranes for flying; on the land hopping or running on their hind feet. From small creatures not bigger than two feet high, to huge monsters thirty feet in height, feeding on the tops of trees which our giraffes and elephants could not reach, they fill the land; while flesh-eating reptiles, quite their match in size and strength, prey upon them as lions and tigers do upon the grassfeeders now. This is no fancy picture, for in our museums, and especially in Professor Marsh's wonderful collection in Yale Museum in America, you may see the skeletons of these large reptiles, and build them up again in imagination as they stood in those ancient days when they looked down upon the primitive birds and tiny marsupials, little dreaming that their own race, then so powerful, would dwindle away, while these were to take possession in their stead.

And now in our series of changing scenes comes all at once that strange blank which we hope one day to fill up; and when we look again the large reptiles are gone, the birds are spreading far and wide, and we come

1. Sauropsida.

upon those early and primitive forms of insect-eaters, gnawers, monkeys, grass-feeders, and large flesh-eaters, whose descendants, together with those of the earlier marsupials, are henceforward to spread over the earth. We need scarcely carry our pictures much farther. We have seen how, in these early times, the flesh-feeders and grass-feeders were far less perfectly fitted for their lives than they are now; how the horse has only gradually acquired his elegant form; the stag his branching antlers; and the cat tribe their scissor-like teeth, powerful jaws, and muscular limbs; while the same history of gradual improvement applies to nearly all the many forms of milk-givers.

But there is another kind of change which we must not forget, which has been going on all though this long history, namely, alterations in the level and shape of the continents and islands, as coasts have been worn away in some places and raised up or added to in others, so that different countries have been separated from or joined to each other. Thus Australia, now standing alone, with its curious animal life, must at some very distant time have been joined to the mainland of Asia, from which it received its low forms of milk-givers, and since then, having become separated from the great battlefield of the Eastern Continent, has been keeping for us, as it were in a natural isolated zoological garden, the strange primitive Platypus and Echidna, and Marsupials of all kinds and habits.

So too, Africa, no doubt for a long time cut off by a wide sea which prevented the larger and fiercer animals from entering it, harboured the large wingless ostriches, the gentle lemurs, the chattering monkeys, the scaly manis, and a whole host of insect-eaters; while South America, also standing alone, gave the sloths and armadilloes, the ant-bears, opossums, monkeys, rheas, and a number of other forms, the chance of establishing themselves firmly before stronger enemies came to molest them. These are only a few striking examples which help us to see how, if we could only trace them out, there are reasons to be found why each animal or group of animals now lives where we find it, and has escaped destruction in one part of the world when it has altogether disappeared in others.

So, wandering hither and thither, the backboned family, and especially the milk-givers, took possession of plans and mountain ranges, of forests and valleys, of deserts and fertile regions. But still another question remains—How has it come to pass that large animals which once ranged over all Europe and Northern Asia,—mastodons, tusked tapirs, rhinoceroses, elephants, sabre-toothed tigers, cave-lions, and hippopotamuses in Europe, gigantic sloths and llamas in North America, and even many huge forms in South America, have either been entirely destroyed or are represented now only by scattered groups here and there in southern lands? What put an end to the "reign of the milk-givers," and why have they too diminished on the earth as the large fish, the large newts, and the large lizards did before them?

. . . We know that gradually from the time of tropical Europe, when all the larger animals flourished in our country, a change was creeping very slowly and during long ages over the whole northern hemisphere. The climate grew colder and colder, the tropical plants and animals were driven back or died away, glaciers grew larger and snow deeper and more lasting, till large sheets of ice covered Norway and Sweden, the northern parts of Russia, Germany, England, Holland, and Belgium, and in American the whole of the country as far south as New York. Then was what geologists call the "Glacial Period;" and whether the whole country was buried in ice, or large separate glaciers and thick coverings of snow filled the land, in either case the animals, large and small, must have had a bad time of it.

True, there were probably warmer intervals in this intense cold, when the more southern animals came and went, for we find bones of the hippopotamus, hyæna, and others buried between glacial beds in the south of England. But there is no doubt at this time numbers of land animals must have perished, for in England alone, out of fifty-three known species which lived in warmer times, only twelve survived the great cold, while others were driven southwards never to return, and the descendants of others came back as new forms, only distantly related to those which had once covered the land.

Moreover, when the cold passed away and the country began again to be covered with oak and pine forests where animals might feed and flourish, we find that a new enemy had made his appearance. Man—active, thinking, tool-making man—had begun to take possession of the caves and holes of the rocks, making weapons out of large flints bound into handles of wood, and lighting fires by rubbing wood together, so as to protect himself from wild beasts and inclement weather.

In America and in England alike, as well as in Northern Africa, Asia Minor, and India, we know that man was living at this time among animals, many of them species which have since become extinct, and with his rude weapons of jagged flint was conquering for himself a place in the world.

He must have had a hard struggle, for we find these flint implements now lying among the bones of hyænas, sabre-toothed tigers, cave-lions, cave-bears, rhinoceroses, elephants, and hippopotamuses, showing that it was in a land full of wild beasts that he had to make good his ground.

By the swamp in the forest
The oak-branches groan,
As the savage primeval,
With his russet hair thrown
O'er his huge naked limbs, swings his hatchet of stone.

And now, hark! as he drives with
A last mighty swing,
The stone blade of the axe through
The oak's central ring,
From his blanched lips what screams of wild agony spring!

There's a rush through the fern-fronds,
A yell of affright,
And the Savage and Sabre-tooth
Close in fierce fight,
As the red sunset smoulders and blackens the night.[2]

Many and fierce these conflicts must have been, for the wild beasts were still strong and numerous, and man had not yet the skill and weapons which he has since acquired. But rough and savage though he may have been, he had powers which made him superior to all around him. For already he knew how to make and use weapons to defend himself, and how to cover himself at least with skins as protection from cold and damp. Moreover, he had a brain which could devise and invent, a memory which enabled him to accumulate experience, and a strong power of sympathy which made him a highly social being, combining with others in the struggle for life.

And so from that early time till now, man, the last and greatest winner in life's race, has been taking possession of the earth. With more and more powerful weapons he has fought against the wild beasts in their native haunts; and by clearing away the large forests, cutting up the broad prairies and pastures, and cultivating the land, he has turned them out of their old feeding grounds, till now we must go to the centre of Africa, the wild parts

2. From "A Legend of a Stone Axe," a clever and suggestive poem in the *New Quarterly*, April 1879. The text is slightly altered.

of Asia, or the boundless forests of South America, to visit in their homes the large wild animals of the great army of milk-givers.

Since, therefore, these forms are growing rarer every century, and some of them, such as the Dodo, Epyornis, and Moa among birds, and the northern sea-cow or Rhytina among milk-givers, have already disappeared since the times of history, we must endeavour, before others are gone for ever, to study their structure and their habits. For we are fast learning that it is only by catching at these links in nature's chain that we can hope to unravel the history of life upon the earth.

At one time naturalists never even thought that there was anything to unravel, for they looked upon the animal kingdom as upon a building put together brick by brick, each in its place from the beginning. To them, therefore, the fact that a fish's fin, a bird's wing, a horse's leg, a man's arm and hand, and the flipper of a whale, were all somewhat akin, had no other meaning than that they seemed to have been formed upon the same plan; and when it became certain that different kinds of animals had appeared from time to time upon the earth, the naturalists of fifty years ago could have no grander conception than that new creatures were separately made (they scarcely asked themselves how) and put into the world as they were wanted.

But a higher and better explanation was soon to be found, for there was growing up among us the greatest naturalist and thinker of our day, that patient lover and searcher after truth, Charles Darwin, whose genius and earnest labours opened our eyes gradually to a conception so deep, so true, and so grand, that side by side with it the idea of making an animal from time to time, as a sculptor makes a model of clay, seems too weak and paltry ever to have been attributed to an Almighty Power.

By means of the facts collected by our great countryman and the careful conclusions which he drew from them, we have learned to see that there has been a gradual unfolding of life upon the globe, just as a plant unfolds first the seed-leaves, then the stem, then the leaves, then the bud, the flower, and the fruit; so that though each part has its own beauties and its own appointed work, we cannot say that any stands alone, or could exist without the whole. Surely then Natural History acquires quite a new charm for us when we see that our task is to study among living forms, and among the remains of those that are gone, what has been the education and the development of all the different branches, so as to lead to the greatest amount of widespreading life upon the globe, each having its own duty to perform. With the great thought before us that every bone, every hair, every small peculiarity, every tint of colour, has its meaning, and has, or has had, its use in the life of each animal or those that have gone before it, a lifelong study even can never weary us in thus tracing out the working of Nature's laws, which are but the expression to us of the mind of the great Creator.

When we once realise that whether in attacking or avoiding an enemy it is in most cases a great advantage to all animals to be hidden from view, and that each creature has arrived at this advantage by slow inheritance, so that their colours often exactly answer the purpose, how wonderful becomes the gray tint of the slug, the imitation of bark in the wings of the buff-tip moth, the green and brown hues of the eatable caterpillars, the white coat of the polar bear, and the changing colour of the arctic fox, the ermine, and the ptarmigan, as winter comes on! And when, on the other hand, we find badly-tasting creatures such as ladybirds and some butterflies, or stinging animals like bees and wasps, having bright colours, because it is an actual advantage to them to be known and avoided, we see that in studying colour alone we might spend a lifetime learning how the winners in life's race are those best fitted for the circumstances under which they live, so that in ever-changing variety the most beautifully-adapted forms flourish and multiply.

Then if we turn to the skeleton and the less conspicuous framework of the body, the flippers of the whale, the manatee, or the seal, doing the work of a fish's fin and yet having the bones of a hand and arm, reveal a whole history to us when we have once learned the secret that in the attempt to increase and multiply no device is left untried by any group of animals, and so every possible advantage is turned to account.

Next, the wonderful instincts taught by long experience give us a whole field of study. We see how frogs and reptiles, and even higher animals such as marmots, squirrels, shrews and bears, escape the cold and scarcity of food in winter by burying themselves in mud, or in holes of trees or caves of the earth till spring returns; and while we find alligators burying themselves in cold weather in America, we find crocodiles, on the contrary, taking their sleep in the hot dry weather in Egypt because then is their time of scarcity.

Then we learn that the birds avoid this difficulty of change of climate in quite another manner. They with their power of flight have learned to migrate, sometimes for short distances, sometimes for more than a thousand miles, so that they bring up their young ones in the cool north in summer, when caterpillars and soft young insects are at hand for their prey, and lead them in the winter to the sunny south where food and shelter in green trees are always to be found. So long indeed has this instinct of migration been at work, that often we are quite baffled in trying to understand why they take this or that particular route for their flight, because probably, when the first stragglers chose it, even the areas of land and water were not divided as now, so that we must study the whole history of the changing geography of the earth to understand the yearly route of the swallow or the stork.

And last but not least, when we look upon the whole animal creation as the result of the long working out of nature's laws as laid down from the first by the Great Power of the Universe, what new pleasure we find in every sign of intelligence, affection, and devotion in the lower creatures! For these show that the difficulties and dangers of animal life have not only led to wonderfully-formed bodies, but also to higher and more sensitive natures; and that intelligence and love are often as useful weapons in fighting the battle of life as brute force and ferocity.

Even among the fish, which, as a rule, drop their eggs and leave them to their fate, we have exceptions in the nest-building sticklebacks and the snake-headed fish of Asia, which watch over and defend their fry till they are strong, in the pipe-fish where the fathers carry the young in a pouch, and in sharks which travel in pairs; while a pike has been known to watch for days at the spot where his mate was caught and taken away, and mackerel and herrings live in shoals and probably call to each other across the sea.

Among the other cold-blooded animals—the frogs, newts, and reptiles—it is true we find less show of feeling, but we must remember that these are only poor remaining fragments of large groups which have disappeared from the earth. Even among the amphibia however a tame toad will become attached to one person; while among reptiles, lizards are full of intelligence and affection, and snakes are well-known for their fondness for their owners. The case of the snake which died by its master's side when he fell down insensible,[3] if it can be relied upon, would show that even cold-blooded animals have tender hearts.

Yet these are all instances of affection of lower animals to man. We must turn to the birds, that group which has gone on increasing in strength and numbers down to our day, to find that tender devotion which watches over the helpless nursling, defends the young at the risk of life, nay, like the peewit with the dragging wing, will even run in the face of death to lure the cruel destroyer away from the hidden nest. Natural history teems with examples of birds faithful to each other and pining even till death for the loss

3. *Animal Intelligence*, Romanes, p. 261.

of a mate; while many birds, such as rooks, starlings, wild geese, swans, and cranes, not only live in companies and exact obedience from their members, but even set sentinels to watch, the duties of the office being faithfully fulfilled.

Then again it is to the higher animals, those nearer to ourselves, that we must look for the truest affection, and the strongest proofs of that obedience and sympathy which lead them to unite and so become strong in the face of danger. Among the beasts of prey it is true that, except the wolves and jackals, none herd together; but family love is strong and true. No tiger is so dangerous as is the mother tigress if any one approaches her young ones, or the lioness whose cubs are attacked, and in our own homes we all know the tenderness and devotion of a cat to her kittens. Nevertheless, these animals have very little social feeling; theirs are the narrower virtues of courage and fidelity to home, and to the duty of providing food for wife and children. It is among the gentler vegetable-feeders,—the antelopes and gazelles, the buffaloes, horses, elephants, and monkeys,—that we find the instinct of herding together for protection, and with this the consciousness of the duty of obedience and fidelity to the herd and to one another.

It is easy to see how this was necessary to protect these feebler animals from the attacks of their ferocious neighbours, and also what an advantage they had when they had once learned to set sentinels who understood the duty of watching while others fed, as in the case of the chamois and seals, of obeying the signal of a leader like the young baboons on the march, or of putting the mothers and children in the centre for protection, as horses and buffaloes do.

And there is a real significance in this gradual education in duty to others which we must not overlook, for it shows that one of the laws of life which is as strong, if not stronger, than the law of force and selfishness, *is that of mutual help and dependence.* Many good people have shrunk from the idea that we owe the beautiful diversity of animal life on our earth to the struggle for existence, or to the necessity that the best fitted should live, and the feeblest and least protected must die. They have felt that this makes life a cruelty, and the world a battlefield. This is true to a certain extent, for who will deny that in every life there is pain and suffering and struggle? But with this there is also love and gentleness, devotion and sacrifice for others, tender motherly and fatherly affection, true friendship, and a pleasure which consists in making others happy.

This we might have thought was a gift only to ourselves—an exception only found in the human race; now we see that it has been gradually developing throughout the whole animal world, and that the love of fathers and mothers for their young is one of the first and greatest weapons in fighting life's battle. So we learn that after all, the struggle is not entirely one of cruelty or ferocity, but that the higher the animal life becomes, the more important is family love and the sense of affection for others, so that at last a fierce beast of prey with strength and sharp tools at his command, is foiled in attacking a weak young calf, because the elders of the herd gather round him, and the destroyer is kept at bay.

Surely then we have here a proof that, after all, the highest and most successful education which Life has given her children to fit them for winning the race is that "unity is strength;" while the law of love and duty beginning with parent and child and the ties of home life, and developing into the mutual affection of social animals, has been throughout a golden thread, strengthened by constant use in contending with the fiercer and more lawless instincts.

So it becomes evident that the beautiful virtue of self-devotion, one of the highest man can practise, has its roots in the very existence of life upon the earth. It may appear dimly at first,—it may take a hard mechanical form in such lowly creatures as insects, where we saw the bees and ants sacrificing all tender feelings to the good of the community. But in the backboned family it exists from the very first as the tender love of mother for child, of the father for his mate and her young ones, and so upwards to the defence of the tender ones of the herd by the strong and well-armed elders, till it has found its highest development in man himself.

Thus we arrive at the greatest and most important lesson that the study of nature affords us. It is interesting, most interesting, to trace the gradual evolution of numberless different forms, and see how each has become fitted for the life it has to live. It gives us courage to struggle on under difficulties when we see how patiently the lower animals meet the dangers and anxieties of their lives, and conquer or die in the struggle for existence. But far beyond all these is the great moral lesson taught at every step in the history of the development of the animal world, that amidst toil and suffering, struggle and death, the supreme law of life is the law of SELF-DEVOTION AND LOVE.

A. MARY F. ROBINSON

"Darwinism"

The Collected Poems, Lyrical and Narrative. 1888. London: T. Fisher Unwin, 1902. 144.

When first the unflowering Fern-forest
Shadowed the dim lagoons of old,
A vague, unconscious, long unrest
Swayed the great fronds of green and gold.

Until the flexible stem grew rude,
The fronds began to branch and bower,
And lo! upon the unblossoming wood
There breaks a dawn of apple-flower.

Then on the fruitful forest-boughs
For ages long the unquiet ape
Swung happy in his airy house
And plucked the apple, and sucked the grape.

Until at length in him there stirred
The old, unchanged, remote distress,
That pierced his world of wind and bird
With some divine unhappiness.

Not love, nor the wild fruits he sought,
Nor the fierce battles of his clan
Could still the unborn and aching thought,
Until the brute became the man.

Long since; and now the same unrest
Goads to the same invisible goal,
Till some new gift, undream'd, unguess'd,
End the new travail of the soul.

ALICE BODINGTON

From *Studies in Evolution and Biology*

London: Elliot Stock, 1890. 22–28.

THE MAMMALIA: EXTINCT SPECIES AND SURVIVING FORMS

The lovers of zoology find their favourite study become ever increasingly fascinating, as the discoveries of modern palæontology more and more triumphantly vindicate the theory of evolution. Although that theory received its greatest impetus in England and on the continent from the works of Darwin, yet it is evident that the great master himself had only grasped one form of the law governing evolution. He sought, at least in his earlier works, to account for all changes in animals and plants by natural selection; whereas we now see that the infinite, delicate variations in the world of organic beings are owing to the intense irritability and susceptibility to molecular changes of protoplasm, and the consequent action of the environment upon it. Natural selection evoked some unknown force vaguely of the nature of will. The action of the environment upon protoplasm requires nothing but ordinary and well-known phenomena of organic chemistry.

In 1861 Darwin thought the 'direct action of the conditions of life cannot but have played an extremely small part in producing all the numerous and beautiful variations in every living creature.' But in one of his later letters we see how much he had seen reason to change his views on this point, for he says: 'In my opinion, *the greatest error I have committed* [the italics are Bodington's] has been in not allowing sufficient weight to the direct action of the environment, independently of natural selection.' Natural selection is by no means excluded, but plays only a subordinate part in the great drama of development.

The zoologist can now trace pedigrees to which the longest human pedigree is but as the flash of a second; a pedigree showing the most delicate and gradual changes: a cusp of a tooth disappearing here, a joint becoming anchylosed there, yet by slight, constant variations effecting the most startling changes of structure. He can trace the camel, the horse, the dog, the cat, to their primitive, or rather to their more simple forms. For the truly primitive forms from which the higher animals are descended are as yet undiscovered—possibly buried for ever beneath the ocean, but ever sought with unwearied skill and patience.

The labours of the embryologist and the comparative anatomist enable us, through the 'scientific imagination,' more or less imperfectly, to reconstruct these ancient forms. But the oldest mammals known, though almost reptilian in development in comparison with the mammalia of the present day, are yet highly differentiated, and must have had long lines of ancestors.

The problem to which I chiefly desire to attract attention in this article is that of the extinction of species. It is usually assumed that some catastrophe must have led to the destruction of any given species. The Glacial period accounts conveniently for the disappearance of many forms. It is gravely stated that the oceans are now not large enough for all the whales that formerly flourished; and a general drying up of swamps is supposed to account for the disappearance of the earlier pachyderms. But we have every reason to doubt a theory which requires constant catastrophes to make it tenable.

Another theory, which has an undoubted mingling of fact to support it, is that the lower animals necessarily die out in the struggle for existence before the higher ones. But, as I hope to be able to show, though the lower orders of mammals tend to disappear before the higher ones, yet species, and even orders, die out where *there has been no competition with higher forms.*

It will make the difficulties of the question to be solved appear more clearly if we go through the main orders of mammals, and see how few species, comparatively speaking, survive, and how mysterious are the laws governing their appearance and disappearance. We will consider the marsupials first. In this order, as is well known, no placenta is developed, and the mother animal transfers the embryo in a very immature condition to an external pouch. Until lately it was thought that the marsupials made their earliest appearance in Europe, and it was plausibly urged that they had necessarily died out before the higher placental forms. In the Miocene period they had become extinct, both in Europe and in North America.

This theory is highly satisfactory till we examine into the history of the marsupials in their own island-continent, Australia. Australia was cut off from the rest of the world before the Cretaceous period, and before the placental mammals had had time to arrive on its soil. Here the marsupials were the masters of all they surveyed. What happened? They flourished and developed in all possible ways. They became differentiated into vegetable-feeders, into insect and root-eaters, into formidable carnivorous animals; they lived in trees, flew after the fashion of bats, burrowed in holes; and, in short, mimicked most of the great animal orders in other parts of the world. Some attained a gigantic size, and must have been as much as sixteen feet high, the largest existing kangaroo measuring about five feet. The living genus *Macropus* (the kangaroo) was represented in the Post-Tertiary deposits by species in all essential respects agreeing with the recent forms, but of immense size, one species being as large as the rhinoceros. *Diprotodon* had a skull more than a yard in length, and was about sixteen feet in height. 'It was,' says Owen, 'a giant kangaroo, but without the power of leaping.' *Thylacoleo* was named by Owen the 'Marsupial Lion,' which animal it rivalled in size. The dentition was not the same as that of the carnivorous marsupials of the present day, but was of so powerful and formidable a character as irresistibly to suggest the habits of a beast of prey.

The wombats are represented by fossil species, partly corresponding with them in size and partly far exceeding them. *Nototherium,* for instance, far exceeded the living species in size, and had the most hideous skull imaginable—very nearly as broad as it was long. The living marsupials of Australia are evidently, therefore, but diminished and scattered survivals of the marsupials of the past.[1] All these fossil marsupials, too, belong to the most recent geological period. On the Darling Downs, Leichhard collected bones which were so little like fossils that he expressed a hope that he would find living specimens of the same animals further in the interior of the continent. Here, in Australia, the marsupials had no rivals. There was no glacial epoch which has so conveniently killed off all sorts of animals in Europe. Things have gone on in Australia since Post-Tertiary times much as they are going on now. Man himself has probably only recently become a denizen of this 'fifth quarter' of the globe. He appears in the rudest and most primitive state, and was unable to kill off even the diminished kangaroos of the present day. Therefore, it seems safe to say that there is a *law governing the duration of species.* As a man may die by accident or disease after a longer or shorter life, yet must at last die of old age, so it seems to be with species and even orders of animals. They may be *prematurely* destroyed by glacial epochs, or drying up of marshes, or inundations of the sea, but if they are exposed to no possibility of perishing by external accidents, *the species dies out of old age.*

The Liberal-Conservative animals, if I may be allowed to borrow a term from politics, seem to have the best chance of comparatively long duration: those which do not change too quickly or too slowly. The frogs have outlived the enterprising *Deinosaurs*[2] by long ages, and the elephant has persisted longer than the much bigger and more formidably tusked

1. Schmidt.
2. The highest type ever attained by a reptile.

mammoth. *Deinoceras* (whose reptilian brain could suggest no method of making a mark in the world except by growing six horns on the top of his nose) was doomed to a particularly speedy extinction.

MAY KENDALL

"The Lower Life"

Dreams to Sell. London: Longmans Green, 1887. 23–25.

It might seem matter for regret
That Evolution has not yet
    Fulfilled our wishes.
The birds soar higher far than we,
The fish outswim us in the sea,
    The simple fishes.

But, evolutionists reflect,
We have the pull in intellect,
    And that's undoubted:
Yet still we cry: 'Can this atone
For fins or pinions of our own,
    Not to be scouted?'

We hold that Evolution's plan,
To give as little as she can,
    Is sometimes trying.
Fair share of brains, indeed, we win;
But why not throw the swimming in,
    Why not the flying?

But ah, she gives not more or less.
We pay for all that we possess,
    We weep and waver,
While Evolution, still the same,
With knights or pawns pursues the game,
    And shows no favour.

As onward yet life's currents roll,
The gaining of a higher goal
    Increaseth sorrow;
And what we win at its own cost
We win; and what we lose is lost,
    Nor can we borrow.

If we have freedom, we lose peace.
If self-renunciation, cease
    To care for pleasure.
If we have Truth—important prize!
We wholly must away with lies,
    Or in a measure.

Is wisdom, then, the only test,
Of lot superlatively blest?
    There have been others.
Our aeon too will pass, and then
Are monads so much less than men?
    Alas, my brothers!

This higher life is curious stuff,
Too high, yet not quite high enough,
    A mingled vial!
This higher life is sold too dear—
Would I could give a lower sphere
        An equal trial!

Ah, could I be a fish indeed,
Of lucky horoscope, and creed
    Utilitarian,
'Mong blissful waves to glide or rest,
I'd choose the lot I found the best,
    Or fish or Aryan!

Or could I be a bird and fly
Through forests all unhaunted by
    The shooting season,
I'd tell you which I voted for,
The flight of airy pinions, or
    The March of Reason!

MAY KENDALL

"Lay of the Trilobite"

Dreams to Sell. London: Longmans Green, 1887. 7–10.

A mountain's giddy height I sought,
    Because I could not find
Sufficient vague and mighty thought
    To fill my mighty mind;
And as I wandered ill at ease,
    There chanced upon my sight
A native of Silurian[1] seas,
    An ancient Trilobite.[2]

So calm, so peacefully he lay,
    I watched him even with tears;
I thought of Monads[3] far away
    In the forgotten years.
How wonderful it seemed and right,
    The providential plan,
That he should be a Trilobite,
    And I should be a Man!

And then, quite natural and free
    Out of his rocky bed,
That Trilobite he spoke to me,
    And this is what he said:
'I don't know how the thing was done,
    Although I cannot doubt it;
But Huxley—he if anyone
    Can tell you all about it;

1. A paleozoic geological period.
2. An extinct marine arthropod.
3. A single-celled organism.

'How all your faiths are ghosts and dreams,
How in the silent sea
Your ancestors were Monotremes—[4]
Whatever these may be;
How you evolved your shining lights
Of wisdom and perfection
From Jelly-fish and Trilobites
By Natural Selection.

'You've Kant to make your brains go round,
Hegel you have to clear them,
You've Mr. Browning to confound,
And Mr. Punch to cheer them!
The native of an alien land
You call a man a brother,
And greet with hymn-book in one hand
And pistol in the other!

'You've Politics to make you fight
As if you were possessed:
You've cannon and you've dynamite
To give the nations rest:
The side that makes the loudest din
Is surest to be right,
And oh, a pretty fix you're in!'
Remarked the Trilobite.

'But gentle, stupid, free from woe
I lived among my nation,
I didn't care—I didn't know
That I was a Crustacean.[5]
I didn't grumble, didn't steal,
I *never* took to rhyme:
Salt water was my frugal meal,
And carbonate of lime.'

4. The lowest order of mammals.

5. "He was not a Crustacean. He has since discovered that he was an Arachnid, or something similar. But he says it does not matter. He says they told him wrong once, and they may again." (This amusing note by Kendall.)

Reluctantly I turned away,
    No other word he said;
An ancient Trilobite, he lay
    Within his rocky bed.
I did not answer him, for that
    Would have annoyed my pride:
I merely bowed, and raised my hat,
    But in my heart I cried:—

'I wish our brains were not so good,
    I wish our skulls were thicker,
I wish that Evolution could
    Have stopped a little quicker;
For oh, it was a happy plight,
    Of liberty and ease,
To be a simple Trilobite
    In the Silurian seas!'

SECTION SEVEN

Amateurs or Professionals?

Contemporary historians of science are reviewing women's place in science culture as they rethink just what has constituted being an amateur and what a professional.[1] When it comes to the time frame represented in this anthology, these questions become especially vexed. The one clear thing is that we cannot judge nineteenth- and early twentieth-century notions of professionalism exclusively from twenty-first-century vantage points. We must try to reenter the older contexts, as will the section "Amateurs or Professionals?" It plunges into and complicates the debate over amateurism versus professionalism by providing an often-ignored context—selections from women's work that illustrate different possible definitions and different types of professionalism.

In the eighteenth and early nineteenth centuries, the boundaries between amateur and professional natural historians had been fluid, if not blurred. For example, country dwellers, men, women, and children alike, contributed widely to natural history as they explored and collected specimens in their local areas (see figure 58). But as the nineteenth century grew, so too did a new professionalism in the biological sciences, a situation that made it harder and harder for people not trained by universities or associated with laboratories or museums to enter scientific fields. The numbers of learned journals increased as did exclusive learned societies. Science moved to the cities and university centers, and scientists began to close ranks, to break into discreet experimentalist disciplines, and to denigrate amateurs as having a lower status than theirs. As a result, natural history, for example, was eventually assumed by biology.

Women who desired what we would today consider scientific careers found this entire situation especially difficult. Not until the later decades of

1. For an excellent summary of this reconceptualizing, see Adrian Desmond, "Redefining the X Axis: 'Professionals,' 'Amateurs,' and the Making of Mid-Victorian Biology—A Progress Report," *Journal of the History of Biology* 34 (2001): 3–50.

FIGURE 58 Goleman's *Nature Study,* ca. 1860

the century were they admitted to tertiary educational programs in science and then only in small numbers. Even after the establishment of women's colleges at Cambridge, women tended to become part of a subculture of women scientists who were educated to become instructors in the more elementary subjects. Also, by midcentury, some previously woman-friendly scientific associations, like the Ethnological Society, rethought their policies. And because so many scientific societies continued to deny women membership, when women managed to produce scientific research on their own, it was difficult for them to get a hearing. Beatrix Potter was well on her way to becoming a pioneering, if self-taught, mycologist when, in the late 1890s, she was prevented from reading a paper on fungi before the august Linnean Society. The Linnean did not permit women members until 1905. Connections and social standing—like Mary Somerville's, for example—were far more likely to allow women access to scientific circles than was merit or desire, but even these did not work for Potter. In general, women remained eager members of the audience for science but found it difficult to be practitioners.

Nevertheless, women like Mary Kingsley and Marianne North, whose work we previewed in "Adventuring," did serve as foot soldiers in the march toward biological knowledge and recently have been acknowledged for their work. And there were many such women. Among their ranks were field-workers, collectors, illustrators, and observers (see figure 59) who were of enormous value to the sciences with which they were connected. Among their ranks too were women who aspired to the status of professionals in allied fields like agriculture. The section "Who/What Was a Professional?" offers the work of some of those women in order to show both how varied was their endeavor and how difficult, perhaps even irrelevant, it is for us today to make determinations as to whether they were in fact "only" amateurs. Virginia Woolf catches something of their importance—and their modesty—in her novel *Mrs. Dalloway,* when she has her main character, Clarissa Dalloway, introduce an elderly scientific aunt to a guest at her home. Mrs. Dalloway begins the introduction by saying that the guest has been to Burma. Then her aunt falls into a reverie: "Ah. She could not resist recalling what Charles Darwin had said about her little book on the orchids of Burma. . . . No doubt it was forgotten now, her book on the orchids of Burma, but it went into three editions before 1870."[2] In this section we go in search of such aunts and their status in their culture.

We begin with an essay from the 1899 International Congress of Women by Henrietta Margaret White, principal at Alexandra College, Dublin (see figure 60). The congress (also attended by the Duchess of Portland and Margaretta Lemon, whose speeches appear in "Protecting") was convened by the International Council of Women. The 1899 meeting was held in London, with subsequent meetings offered in The Hague in 1915, in Zurich in 1919, and in Vienna in 1921. All of the meetings resulted in publications, one of which is White's 1899 discussion of the merits of professional training for women horticulturists. White troubles over the increasing degree of book knowledge required for female horticulturists and discusses the value of such learning vis-à-vis hands-on learning for women. White was hoping to prepare the way for professional gardeners like Gertrude Jekyll, who earned her living by planning and writing about gardens and by selling plants. Known especially for introducing complex and satisfying color arrangements into Victorian gardening, in her essays (two of which are reprinted elsewhere in this anthology) Jekyll hoped to train still other gardeners in the nuances of her art.

"Who/What Was a Professional?" continues with further tributes to field-workers. Careful fieldwork was crucial to the scientific enterprise in the nineteenth century, but as laboratory and theoretical work became

2. *Mrs. Dalloway* (New York: Harcourt, Brace and World, 1925), 272.

FIGURE 59 John Dillwyn Llewelyn, *Thereza,* ca. 1853 (courtesy Gilman Paper Company, New York)

increasingly valued, the status of field-workers was increasingly devalued. Nevertheless, no one, amateur or professional, could collect without both know-how and proper tools and techniques. George Eliot and her companion George Henry Lewes found this out the hard way when they set off as novice collectors of seaside specimens in Ilfracombe and soon realized that without good equipment, they were hampered right and left. Lewes was working on the book that would become *Sea-side Studies* (1858), and the two had come from London with "deep well-like jars" which turned out to be quite "unfit for our purpose,"[3] says Eliot in her "Ilfracombe Journal." Likewise, Mary Kingsley, when she collected fish in West Africa for the British Museum of Natural History in London, discovered that many of her first lot of specimens were spoiled by improper preparation in the field.

It was in Africa, too, that Sarah Bowdich Lee became well attuned to the need for proper treatment of biological specimens. Lee's husband died on a natural history expedition to that country, and she remained to write up and illustrate the results of that trip. After Thomas Bowdich's death, Lee was forced to make a living for her family and turned to professional writing and illustration to do so. Among a variety of books she produced was a volume on taxidermy, excerpted here, where she offers Charles Waterton's method of preparing mammals. The piece reveals that in the 1840s there was a market for information useful to collectors in need of advice largely unavailable to those traveling the borderlands of amateurism and professionalism.

Certainly ornithologists Elizabeth Gould and her husband, John, knew about the art of taxidermy when they worked on their series of books on the birds of the world and were able to preserve their own specimens. Elizabeth was a skilled illustrator and mother of eight who toiled over the Gould books for little recompense other than the acknowledgement "J and E Gould del et lith" [drew and put on stone] on the plates of her birds. Elizabeth Gould is represented here by an excerpt from a letter written to her mother when Elizabeth was in Australia working on the *Birds of Australia* in 1838. In today's era of increased ecological consciousness, the letter's contents may not sound fresh or intellectually innovative. But in early Victorian times, for Gould to practice drawing plants in order to represent the Australian birds in their native habitat would have taken a special sensitivity to the interconnections of species and environment. It reveals Elizabeth to have been as seriously dedicated a professional as was John Gould, the highly acclaimed "bird man." The letter, with its concern about her health,

3. *Selected Essays, Poems, and Other Writings* (London and New York: Penguin Books, 1990), 219–20.

is touching. Gould's health did break, and she died young—some speculate from the hard work on the books coupled with frequent childbearing. Because illustrators traditionally received little credit for their insights (Elizabeth's breathtaking birds from Australia have often been credited to her husband), I have included in this book one of the thoroughly professional illustrations from *The Birds of Australia* that was executed by Elizabeth Gould (see figure 61).

Throughout the Victorian era, bird observations were commonly recorded by both amateurs and professionals. In his own work, Charles Darwin utilized observations made by numerous amateurs. And Emily Shore's two pieces of observation, written for amateurs and published in the *Penny Magazine* (see the section "Protecting") have counterparts later in the century in various magazines read by professionals and amateurs alike. Jemima Blackburn's careful observations of the behavior of cuckoo (see figure 62) chicks, included here in the form of a letter to the journal *Nature* in 1872, actually served to correct a misapprehension of the nature of these birds printed by John Gould in his *Birds of Great Britain.* Although an artist prized for her accuracy and knowledge of ornithology (and one who published several distinguished books), *Birds Drawn from Nature* and *Birds from Moidart,* Blackburn would certainly not have considered herself a professional scientist. All the same, her intent to produce the best possible representations of the birds she knew locally in her native Scotland resulted in two distinguished books and many more journals, in part detailing observations of bird behavior.

The first part of this section closes with another unpublished essay by Beatrix Potter. Potter's first professional desire was to be a scientific illustrator and experimental scientist. A dedicated student of fungi, Potter wrote a scientific paper on the germination of a fungus called *Agaricinea.* She also produced dozens of anatomically correct illustrations of fungi and other natural history subjects, including fossils she found and others studied in the British Museum of Natural History. Recently the Linnean Society has apologized to Potter for its treatment of her in the 1890s and has issued a number of its *The Linnean* (16, no. 1, January 2000), attempting to explain Potter's contributions to the science of mycology. Over one hundred years after her paper was presented—by one of its members, and not by Potter herself—Potter has been commended for her activities in "(1) biorecording, (2) germination of fungal and lichen spores, (3) the role of algae in lichenized fungi, (4) asexual stages in the life-cycle of macromycetes and (5) questioning whether there were such things as hybrids in this last group" (24).

In her own time, her exclusion from the ranks of the botanists discouraged Potter from further professional scientific pursuits, and eventually she turned to the writing and illustration of the "little" books for which she is so widely known today. Unfortunately, Potter's scientific paper has disappeared over time and cannot be reprinted in this book. Included instead is a short, more informal essay on hedgehogs that Potter did not publish but kept among her papers. Potter had a pet hedgehog that she constantly observed and reobserved (see figure 63), as would any good natural historian or science illustrator. In the course of this study, she developed her essay simply called "Hedgehogs." Today it is informative both as an example of Victorian field notes and observations and as a gloss on Potter's hedgehog tales like that of Mrs. Tiggy-Winkle.

The next section, "Seaweeds, Zoophytes, and Women," offers a cameo look at one area of great interest to Victorian amateur and professional naturalists alike and is meant to show ways in which both these groups were drawn to study the sea. The ocean was one focus for students of evolution, and England's island status allowed its easy access for many Victorians. "Crazes" for plant and animal collection could therefore take place at the edge of the sea, much as they did on land. To set the scene, this section opens with an excerpt from Eliza Cook's "Song of the Sea-weed," an 1869 poem narrated by a seaweed. As we have already seen, Victorian women delighted in identifying with something other, especially another species with greater mobility than their own—a bird, for example. What is different here is that Cook's "Song" suggests the seaweed's relative freedom from the onslaught of nature study that must have marked the lives of the much-studied and much-trampled land plants that amused and delighted so many Victorian amateurs during "pteridomania," the "fern craze." In comparison, Cook's seaweed inhabits a fluid, borderless world.

This world was beautifully represented in the cyanotypes Anna Atkins (1799–1871) created for her book, *British Algae* (1843). Cyanotypes were blue-toned photograms created by exposing specimens to the sun on light-sensitive paper (see figure 64). No negatives or cameras were required in the work, which Atkins performed fastidiously. In this process, the specimen was placed on paper that had been coated with ferric ammonium citrate and potassium ferricyanide and after exposure was washed with water, then dried. Extensive and beautiful as it was, Atkins's collection proved, however, of little value to professional scientists for several reasons. First, it consisted of individual specimens that were not necessarily representative or typical of their kind. Second, the blue tones, rather than multicolored drawings, could mislead collectors as to the alga's real color. And third, Atkins did not always note where her algae were collected, so that the collection was not a guide to species' whereabouts.

Atkins's work nevertheless gives a sense of the importance of sea life to women as collectors and aspiring scientists, as do Anne Pratt's thoughts about zoophytes. During the Victorian period the zoophyte, an animal belonging to the family of corals and sea anemones, was an object of wonder. For decades, the classification of these animals was debated. How could an animal be so much like a plant? Were there borderland plants/animals and was this one of them? Popular seaside books like Pratt's, George Henry Lewes's, Charles Kingsley's *Glaucus* (1855), and Philip Gosse's *Aquarium* (1854) all dealt with "wonders" of the sea like the zoophytes and were meant to be studied at home and then carried to the seaside when closer study was possible. Best known for her popular studies and beautifully executed illustrations of various plants, Pratt herself could hardly skirt this subject when she came to examine common things of the seaside (see figure 65). Nor did Margaret Gatty (see figure 66) in her popular moral tales about nature, *Parables from Nature,* a book that went into print in the 1850s and stayed in print through the nineteenth century. In the selection from *Parables* reprinted here, a zoophyte, a plant, a zoologist, and a bookworm debate the zoophyte's proper classification. The naturalist ends the debate by demonstrating that the zoophyte is indeed an animal. In a nod to the authority of science in her day, Gatty gives her professional the last word.

Of course Gatty was herself a professional in several senses of the word, skilled and valued both as a children's writer and popularizer of science, as was Pratt. But Gatty worked science like a professional too. For fourteen years she researched and studied seaweeds in order to write and publish her *British Sea-weeds* in 1863. The book was a supplement to William Harvey's *Manual of British Algae* (1841), an authoritative but incomplete volume. In the selection from *British Sea-weeds* reprinted here, I have included a number of passages from Gatty's introduction, hoping to reveal something about her sense of audience. Gatty appears to have expected an audience of women and amateurs who needed to know not just what to look for but how to dress and how to use her book. This is therefore a nuts-and-bolts handbook as well as a guide to the seaweeds themselves. Interesting are the various ways she introduces one species or family of seaweeds to her readers. She traced them throughout her plates, her description of her plates, her guide to "arrangement in the herbarium," and her "Amateur's Synopsis." This variety of approaches to one plant assured Gatty of a more diverse audience for her book.

Gatty would not have minimized the importance of work like hers, but she did not really aspire to the status of a professional scientist herself. Interesting from this point of view are Gatty's reflections here on others rising from amateur to professional status, something she clearly thinks is possible, once interest is piqued through study of the seaweeds via her book. Diffusion of knowledge and education of others remained of primary importance to Gatty, as they were to earlier women who had popularized science, a number of whom are found in the previous section.

In "Professionals," the final part of this section, we look at the work of three women of a later generation, all of whom qualified for their fields of study in different ways. The first is Margaret Fountaine, a lepidopterist who has often received more notoriety than admiration for her tireless work collecting, breeding, and studying the behavior of butterflies. In recent decades, Fountaine's journals have been excerpted in two volumes edited by W. F. Cater, *Love among the Butterflies: The Travels and Adventures of a Victorian Lady* (1980) and *Butterflies and Late Loves: The Further Travels and Adventures of a Victorian Lady* (1986). As their titles indicate, these handsome books emphasize Fountaine's affair with her fellow collector Charles Neimy as much as her contributions to her field (see figure 68). Nevertheless, Fountaine spent a lifetime in search of rare butterflies and collected over twenty-two thousand, which have been preserved in mahogany cases and reside in the Norwich Museum. She also wrote a number of scientific papers, like the one reprinted here, where the degree of her technical knowledge becomes clear. Beginning with an introduction to the places in which butterflies were collected, this particular paper has the flavor of a travel book but goes on to discuss in detail a genus of butterflies resident in the Philippines. The paper—published, unlike Potter's on the hedgehog—offers a rethinking of Fountaine's field notes, making her knowledge available to future collectors.

Fountaine was self-taught, as was Eleanor Ormerod (see figure 69), a noted economic entomologist, some of whose reminiscences are found here. The two selections are from Robert Wallace's edition of her autobiographical musings. In the first, Ormerod searches her memory for the source of her interest in her field. In the second, she goes on to detail just how she got started as an economic entomologist: by personally acting as a clearinghouse for data on harmful insects. Unlike Fountaine, Ormerod's work gained widespread acclaim in her own day. She was elected to the Entomological Society of London, became an official consultant to the Royal Agricultural Society of England, and lectured for the Royal Agricultural College. But Ormerod refused to take money for her work because she felt this might be seen to compromise her standards. If from our own contemporary vantage point we choose to confer the name professional only upon people performing paid work like John Gould's, she remained an amateur, despite her expertise and high honors. Viewed from another perspective, that of her pioneering contributions to economic entomology, Ormerod was one of the very first professionals in her chosen field.

The final woman represented in this section is Marie Stopes, better known as an advocate for birth control than as a paleobotanist. Yet Stopes is the one woman in our last grouping to have earned a doctoral degree. (Ormerod had the degree conferred upon her by the University of Edinburgh toward the end of her career.) Stopes studied fossil plants and took her degree from the University College, London, in 1904. For several years she pursued this career, teaching at the University of Manchester and writing scientific papers, like the one reprinted here from the *New Phytologist.* Unlike Potter, Stopes gained entry into the Linnean and Geographical Societies. But her career as a natural scientist was never her exclusive interest. A true professional in every sense of the word, Stopes nevertheless chose to broaden her horizons to include science popularization, as the excerpts from *The Study of Plant Life for Young People* (1906) reveal. In doing so she followed in the footsteps of earlier women who wanted to make natural history available to larger audiences—to be educators in a broader sense of the word. From there Stopes made the leap into birth-control education, a decision that nearly destroyed her. Written as a guide to women and men who had little knowledge of human sexuality, her *Married Love* appeared in 1918. Immediately Stopes was reviled for her discussions of sexuality—even by formerly respectful colleagues in paleobotany. Stopes could be a professional when it came to fossilized plants, but when it came to sexology, she found herself in the wrong century. People still expected work like Ellis Ethelmer's *Baby Buds* and not a more comprehensive and graphic discussion of menstruation, copulation, and female desire, the twentieth-century topics that conclude this final section.

Who/What Was a Professional?

MISS [HENRIETTA MARGARET] WHITE, OF THE INTERNATIONAL CONGRESS OF WOMEN

"The Training of Women as Gardeners"

Women in Professions, Being the Professional Section of the International Congress of Women, July 1899. London: T. Fisher Unwin, 1900.

I am afraid that an exceedingly unfortunate selection was made, when I was asked to speak on the "Training of Women as Gardeners," I, who at best am but an untrained amateur, and who, unfortunately, have further increased my disqualifications by straying from the paths of horticulture into those of higher education, a journey by no means beneficial to a gardener. Much therefore that I am about to say will, I fear, seem to many of my hearers unprofessional and unorthodox; it can scarcely be otherwise . . . nothing, alas! can come from me except the views of a very humble working gardener.

On one ground only do I feel that I have a right to speak on this subject, and it is that of a life-long interest in it. Nearly twenty years ago, before I was perplexed, as now, by the problem of finding "openings for women," I had arrived at the conclusion that women ought to be gardeners, and a friend of mine and I drew up, and had printed, a short paper embodying our views on the subject.

This paper was, as far as I know, one of the first, if not the first attempt definitely to formulate the theory that gardening was a suitable profession for women, and that they ought to be regularly trained and prepared to enter it.

From my childhood women gardeners have appeared to me to belong to the natural order of things, for one of my earliest recollections is that of

FIGURE 60 Miss Henrietta White (courtesy Alexandra College, Dublin)

a garden managed and tended by my mother, assisted by her forewoman. It was only as my knowledge of gardens extended that I learnt that this was not the usual arrangement.

I take it for granted that we are all agreed that gardening is a suitable profession for women, and that we need not therefore discuss this point, but may proceed at once to examine the question how the best preparation and training for the work can be given. In order to do this it will be necessary for us to consider for a little the nature of the work that is to be undertaken, and the kind of candidate that it is desirable to train for it.

There are many different branches of gardening, which include market gardening, nursery gardening, job gardening, and gardening in a private situation. It is to the latter branch that I shall chiefly direct attention, for, in the first place, I am best acquainted with the qualifications needed for it, and further, it seems to me that this is the direction in which employment is most likely afterwards to be found.

In speaking of training I shall therefore assume that the special post for which preparation is being given is that of head gardener in a private situation. I should start with an entrance examination, the important function of which, to my mind, would be to discover whether the candidate had any genuine taste or liking for horticulture. I should reject all whose enthusiasm reached no higher point than that of "not disliking the subject" or "knowing nothing better to take up," or, worst of all, taking it "because it was easy and they had failed at everything else." Whatever road candidates of this kind take, it is not likely to bring them anywhere near success, but I can think of none that would bring them with more fatal directness to the abyss of failure than gardening. A tradition exists among gardeners that their craft can only be worthily practised by those whose hearts have been touched by gardening fire; be this as it may, we may at all events feel certain that no one will ever garden well who is without the suspicion of a spark of any such fire.

The entrance examination should also test such knowledge of chemistry, botany, and geology as it is thought desirable that an intelligent gardener should possess, but once a student has entered a horticultural college her all-too-limited time should be devoted almost exclusively to the subject that she has come there specially to learn.

Some of the time-tables which I have seen, and which are mapped out with the intention, I presume, of preparing practical gardeners, fill me, I must confess, with feelings akin to dismay. In one I find four hours a day devoted to practical work; in another, two. As I read this allocation of time, the advice of the botanist de Candolle[1] to Mrs. Somerville[2] comes forcibly to my mind, and she, be it remembered, was not being prepared to be a professional gardener. "I advise you above all things to see the plants at all their ages, to follow their growth, to describe them in detail, in a word, to live with them more than with books." If such an apportionment of time to practical work as I have mentioned is intended merely to arouse an interest in horticulture and to give amateurs an idea of its possibilities, I do not quarrel with it; but if, on the other hand, there is any idea that at the end of a course such as this students will be fit to be head-gardeners in good places, it can have, it seems to me, but one end, that of bitter disappointment. Think for a moment what the requirements are for such a post as this. The supply of vegetables, fruit, and cut flowers must be continuously kept up all the year round, and not only this, but crops must be ready for a given day—the early fruit and vegetables for a race meeting perhaps, the late supply for an autumn shoot. Good gardeners have told me that the growing of crops for a particular date is one of the most difficult branches of their work, and they have also added that in large places more gardeners have lost their

1. Augustin-Pyrame de Candolle (1778–1841) offered a natural system of plant classification that supplanted Linnaeus's. *Ed.*

2. Mary Somerville (1780–1872), whose *On the Connexion of the Physical Sciences* (1834) is excerpted in this book. *Ed.*

situations through inability to comply with these requirements than from any other cause.

Much knowledge is required to attend properly to the stove house, for any negligence or ignorance would be attended there by serious if not irreparable loss. The flower-beds near the house must be gay during the greater part of the year, the shrubberies well kept, the herbaceous border, planted with well harmonised colours, must be flowery at most seasons, and if the owner is interested in gardening there will be, in addition, the rock garden with its collection of miffy Alpines, the bog garden with its marsh and water plants, and doubtless some specialty, onocyclus, irises, or the like.

There may be some of my hearers who see nothing formidable in this; to them I can but say that it is only those who have had practical experience of the work who have any idea of the knowledge, care, foresight, and observation that are required for its successful accomplishment. I am afraid that the most copious notes, which might even have been supplemented by two-hour trips to the garden, would avail but little in grappling with requirements such as these.

In the garden the press of present work is generally so great that there is much danger in forgetting the future, and to do so is fatal. To guard against this I think it essential that the student should during her training get some idea of the strain that she will afterwards have to meet, and also that she should become fully conversant with the sequence of garden work. This she cannot possible do unless she lives in the garden. In my own gardening days, at busy times, twelve hours a day practical work was often insufficient, and I fancy that my experience is common to most women who manage their gardens.

I find it said of Miss Hope,[3] a great Scotch gardener, that "she was in her garden early and at work there late, working as hard as her men, and doing everything much better than they did."

The owner of the best English garden I know is a woman. She is in her garden before the men, and she works on after time with them till late in the summer evenings. Women cannot possibly hope to make their way in any profession unless they receive as good and thorough a training for it as that which is given to men. Let us consider for a moment the preparation that is deemed necessary to equip a man for the post of head-gardener.

Mr. Moore, the Curator of the Royal Botanic Gardens at Glasnevin, has kindly furnished me with the following particulars of the training given

3. Frances Hope (d.1880), author of *Notes and Thoughts on Gardens and Woodlands* (1881). *Ed.*

in good gardens to men. We assume that we start with an intelligent lad. The course extends over a period of from five to six years, during which time the hours of practical work in the summer months are from 6 a.m. to 6 p.m. The pupil begins as a garden-boy, when he crocks and cleans pots, and carries potting material to the sheds, and does rough watering under direction. After six months or so he will be allowed to do coarse jobs himself. After a year, if he goes on well, he will be given the charge of a house, and will be taught to thin fruit and to stake and tie plants. In the third year he will be shown how fruit is borne, and will be allowed to follow the pruner as nailer and tier, he will also be given better class work outside to do, and he will have to attend to the kitchen gardens and pleasure-grounds. During this year he may also be given charge of a small department, and he will have to look after the forcing and heating and he is allowed to handle the orchids and choicer stove plants. During the fourth year he has the grapes and the pruning. He is also shown how to arrange plants and cut-flowers in the house. At the beginning of this year he will probably have been made assistant foreman, when he will be responsible to see that others carry out properly the operations that he himself has learnt in the previous years. In the fifth year he is ready to take a foreman's place, and when he has had a year's experience as foreman he will then be ready for a place as head-gardener.

This is what is thought necessary for men. What approximation do we make to it in the training we give our girls? We are careful to teach them botany, chemistry, geology, and physics, with such a modicum of horticulture as can be compressed into from two to four hours; practical work a day for one or two years; and from this we expect the same results as from the training that I have sketched. Comment is needless, unless indeed we allow Professor Huxley to speak, and to say, as he did to the boys of our public schools, "There you shall toil, or be supposed to toil, and yet you shall fail to learn what you will most want to know directly you leave school, and enter the practical business of life."

I am apprehensive lest the expression of my convictions on this subject should give rise to misunderstanding, and that I might be supposed to be antagonistic to women's horticultural colleges. Nothing could possibly be further from being the case. I feel that we are under the deepest obligations to them, for it is mainly through their instrumentality that the gardening profession has been opened to women. They have had the hard task of hewing through the thicket of convention and prejudice, and if all is not yet perfect, the defects are largely due to the difficulties that they have had to contend with. In illustration of this, I may mention that entirely practical courses would not, as I am told, meet the requirements of the county councils, whose scholars are sent to horticultural colleges, nor, if they were adopted, could grants be earned from the Science and Art Department, which are so important to the finances of the colleges. We can only hope that horticulturists may in time be able to get the county councils and the Science and Art Department to recognise the claims of their science, and the need of having it taught practically, and, above all, to see that a practical knowledge of it does not come as a natural consequence of an elementary acquaintance with five or six other sciences. Sir Michael Foster speaks truly when, in his paper on Irises, he says, "There are more things in the plant and in the soil than are dreamt of in the latest philosophy of the newest botany." This is so. There are things that books cannot teach, which must be learnt from constant association with, and observation of, plants.

Some published examination papers that I have come across, headed "Science of Horticulture" have caused me no little surprise. I find in them such questions as these:—

By what characteristics are the following orders of plants distinguished: Cruciferæ, Leguminosæ, Umbelliferæ? Give the names of three common genera belonging to each.

To what order would a plant with the following description belong: "A complete flowered polypetalous plant with five petals and numerous stamens inserted upon the calyx, a pistil of numerous free carpels, and a juicy fruit?"

By what experiments would you show the extreme sensitiveness of root tips to gravitation?

If these questions had been given under the heading Elementary Botany I should have no quarrel with them, but I ask any gardener in the room what on earth they have got to do with horticulture? Horticulture means, as we all know, the culture of a garden.

I showed these papers to a botanical friend of mine and enlarged on my grievance against them as a horticulturist, to which he replied, "After all, it doesn't so much matter about horticulture, but the really annoying thing is to have botany hocus-pocussed in this fashion." Apparently then, this so-called Science of Horticulture is as little pleasing to the botanist as to the gardener. It has always struck me as anomalous that an intimate knowledge of the best books on gardening would give little or no help in answering most of the examination papers on horticulture that I have come across. We neglect garden literature far too much in our horticultural education. I was glad to see that in an American horticultural college garden literature forms part of the course, but I have found nothing corresponding to this in the English syllabuses that I have looked through. I am jealous for horticulture.

Those of us who realise, even in some small degree, all that a knowledge of it implies must resent this serving up of snippets of another science, and calling them by its name.

Horticulture seems to me to be somewhat in the position of certain authors who are so surrounded by commentators that they are in danger of being lost sight of themselves. We make most careful and elaborate scientific preparations for coming to the garden, and then we seem to get little, if at all, beyond the gate, and yet it is abundantly worth while to enter and to tarry.

"A garden," it has been truly said, "is a beautiful book writ by the finger of God." The object of this paper has been to urge that in the pages of that book the future gardener will find the best preparation for her work, and to ask that she should give to them the study they so richly merit, and which they will so amply repay.

SARAH BOWDICH LEE

Taxidermy; or, The Art of Collecting, Preparing, and Mounting Objects of Natural History

London: Longman, Brown, Green, and Longmans, 1843. iii–iv; 20–21; 219–33.

[pp. iii–iv]

ADVERTISEMENT

In the year 1821, when Mr. Bowdich and myself were studying Natural History in Paris, in order to prepare ourselves for again travelling in Africa, we became aware, that no English work on Taxidermy existed, and finding it absolutely necessary to understand the Art ourselves, it occurred to us, that in the progress of learning, we might not only supply the deficiency, but by so doing, impress our studies still more forcibly on our own minds. The higher branches of science, however, in which Mr. Bowdich was deeply engaged, soon absorbed his time so entirely, that the task devolved upon me alone, and for the better execution of it, I not only read the best writings on the subject, and consulted those most skilled in the Art, but verified all my instructions in the laboratories of the Museum in Paris. Several of the following pages are mere translations from printed memoirs, chiefly that of M. Dufresne, others are noted down from explanations given *vivâ voce;* but these are so mingled with original matter, that after this lapse of time, it is impossible to separate them from each other; it is, however, advisable that I should establish my claims to the work, as, owned or unowned, it forms the basis of all modern treatises on Taxidermy, and in some instances, the very words are copied without an acknowledgment, as if an anonymous author were a fairer object for piracy than one whose name stands on the title page.

As each edition has gone through the press, every improvement has been noticed, and much added in the shape of notes; but in the present, these notes are, as far as possible, incorporated with the work itself. There will also be found in it, an account of Mr. Waterton's[1] system, which is not contained in any other work on the subject.

Before closing this Advertisement, I beg to offer my grateful thanks to those who, by their contributions or suggestions, have given so much additional value to my labors.

S. LEE

[pp. 20–21]

PREPARATION OF MAMMALIA

Of Man

All the efforts of man to restore the skin of his fellow-creature to its natural form and beauty have hitherto been fruitless; the trials which have been made have only produced mis-shapen, hideous objects, and so unlike nature, that they have never found a place in our collections. We have only some parts of man, either dried or preserved in spirits of wine, sufficiently entire to be recognised, unless we except two dried bodies in the Museum of the College of Surgeons, one of which is that of the first wife of Mr. Van Butchell. In several Museums we see human heads injected, and preserved in oil of turpentine. The anatomical collection of the Museum of Natural History in Paris possesses a head prepared in this way more than a hundred years ago, by the celebrated Ruitch, a Dutch physician. It still preserves all the vivacity of its colours, but the cold so far affects the liquor in which it is contained, as to hide it completely during the winter, and not till the

1. Charles Waterton (1782–1865), British natural historian noted especially for his ornithology. *Ed.*

return of spring, when the liquor becomes clear, can we perfectly distinguish the object.

Without doubt all these preparations are very useful to science, and are even necessary to the demonstrations of professors. Human skeletons are more so; and since the bony part of our body is the only one which we are able to preserve entire and in its natural position, we will try to describe the different methods employed for this purpose in the present day.

[pp. 219–33]

MR. WATERTON'S METHOD OF PRESERVING ANIMALS

The foregoing pages were preparing for the press when Messrs. Longman suggested to me, that the value of my work would be much enhanced, if I could obtain from Mr. Waterton, of Walton Hall, a description of his mode of preserving objects of Natural History. I accordingly wrote to that gentleman, requesting he would favour me with a description of his proceedings. He replied, that all he could write on the subject had been published in his "Wanderings in South America," and in a volume of Essays on Natural History, to which I was welcome; provided that those who possess the copyright of those books would give me permission to make use of the information. He, however, urged me to visit him at Walton Hall, and witness his operations, as he felt it impossible to convey a correct idea of them by means of pen and ink. This in a measure disheartened me; for if the inventor himself could not enlighten the world at large, how could I hope to do so? Still I thought it my duty to profit by so kind an invitation, and I proceeded to Yorkshire, where, in the hospitable mansion of my instructor, I, for eight days, received a lesson of more than three hours' duration, and saw the art practised on two birds and a quadruped. It is true, that I became fully convinced of the inadequacy of language to give an idea of the nice touches, the delicate handling of the tools, or the extreme beauty of the specimens when finished; still the outline may be traced for those whose genius and feeling will lead them to adopt it, and who, possessing these requisites, will be afterwards capable of supplying my deficiencies from their own resources. In giving this outline, partly from Mr. Waterton's own lips, and partly from my own observations, it will be impossible to avoid certain and unintentional coincidences between my expressions and those contained in the before mentioned books; and all I can do is to apologise for them to the proprietors, and to state, that whatever I do must be rendered more complete by consulting Mr Waterton himself in these volumes. There is one thing, however, which duty to myself obliges me to declare; it is, that in the present description are to be found all the improvements and minor changes which experience on the part of the talented operator has suggested, and which give so much facility to practice.

The implements have been reduced to the most simple form, in order to make them portable, and consist of several slender sticks, like knitting needles, but pointed at one end; a quantity of well-carded, urspun cotton, horsehair, chaff, fine sand, a sharp penknife, needles of many sizes, some of which have been again passed through the fire to make them pliant, and others three-sided, like those used by glovers, pieces of cork of various dimensions, eyes of different kinds, a hard and a soft brush, thread, wooden pegs, wire nippers, modelling irons, the tops of which are bent, and varying in size from a knitting needle to a ramrod, or even larger, common wax, corrosive sublimate, spirits of wine, varnish, a central support to be hereafter described, and a stand made in the shape of a long stool, with four legs, the top of which is perforated with holes at various distances, some of which form a horizontal line, and others right angles to it, but which may be made as required. These tools will serve for every purpose; and I shall now exhibit their application, beginning with birds.

Dissolve the corrosive sublimate in spirits of wine, in the proportion of half an ounce to a quart, but which may be increased to any strength, which will not leave a white deposit upon a black feather when dipped into it. In this poisonous solution immerse the bird, and let it lie till completely saturated; then take it out and dry it before a fire, or in a hot sun, constantly shaking it, in order to accelerate the drying, and bring out the feathers. When dry, fill the beak and nostrils with cotton, and proceed to take the skin from the body. As Mr. Waterton's process of skinning differs in some degree from that usually adopted, I shall give the whole. Place the bird with its head next to you, and hold your knife in nearly a horizontal position, the handle towards you, and make an incision from the sternum to the anus; loosen the skin on each side with your fingers, and as it comes off, tuck plenty of cotton between it and the body; cut the tail off far into the flesh, hold the skin back, always inserting cotton as you proceed; disjoint the legs and wings from the body, and leave them to be attended to afterwards; go on towards the head, push the skin down over the neck and skull, and cut away the whole of the latter as far as the beak, except the bones of the lower jaw; take especial care to cut through the nictitating membrane, or it will tear open the orbits, and also be sure not to cut through the commissure, or angle of the mouth. In performing this, cotton should be plentifully used; the fingers should always be preferred to the knife, and, in fact, much more must be done by pushing than cutting; pieces of muscle or fat adhering to the skin must be removed, and the latter must never dangle from the hand while attending to the head and neck, but always rest either on the knee or a table. Clean the jaws from all flesh, touch the bones with the solution, and then return the skin to its proper position without stretching it. When properly arranged, and the feathers of the neck and back are put straight, remove all the dirty cotton used in skinning, and take the skin off the wings to the last joint; make an incision in the last joint, outside, and touch it with the solution, which quickly spreads to the surrounding parts; entirely cut off the first joint, clean the second from the flesh, touch the bones with the solution, then pass a thread round the head of each, and tie these threads together, inside, so as to bring them to the same distance from each other as they would occupy in life; impregnate the whole of the upper part of the skin with the solution, which is best done by twisting some cotton round the top of one of the sticks, dipping it into the liquid, and applying it in this manner where required. Stuff this upper part with fresh cotton, and then attend to the thighs; push the skin off them as far as the tarsus, take away the first joint, clean the second from the adhering muscles and tendons; if the bone be large, bore a hole in the top with a large needle, by which means the marrow is pumped out; dip the bone in the solution; but if a small bone it may be merely touched with the poison; twist some cotton round it to make a false thigh; wash the skin with solution, and return the bones to their proper places. Having lost their upper joint, the legs would hang perpendicularly were there not some precaution taken to avoid it. For this purpose, let the legs lie towards the head, pass a thread round the head of each bone, and convey it with a needle through the skin, at the place which it would touch if the bird were standing; then fasten it there with two or three stitches. Anoint the skin of the body as far as the thighs, stuff it with cotton, and then attend to the tail. Take away every vestige of flesh and oil gland, till the roots of the feathers are visible; touch them with solution as well as the rest of the skin, and put in all the cotton required to complete the body. Take three small pellets of horse-hair; place one on each side, just where the leg is fastened to the skin, and the third in the middle, which pellets give firmness and elasticity. Sew up the slit, beginning from the centre of the anus, and proceeding towards the sternum. It may be well to mention here, that birds sooner putrefy at the lower extremity of the body than elsewhere, in consequence of which the skin is often destroyed. When this has taken place, Mr. Waterton cuts away all the putrid parts, removes the bowels, and washes the inside of the body with water before he steeps it in the solution, and this being accomplished, he substitutes a piece of thin kid leather for the skin, which is easily hidden by the feathers, and is sewn on with a needle and thread. The body being done, the head and throat must be attended to. Take out the cotton first put in, free the mandibles entirely from the flesh, take hold of the lower beak, and hold the mouth open while you wash the skin well inside with the solution, reaching down the throat with the cotton dipped in the poison; push some cotton in so as to form the throat, guiding it with a stick; stuff the head; make the mandibles fit exactly, and fasten them together with a needle, which must project for about half an inch below the beak. The quantity of cotton introduced ought to make the bird about a sixth larger than life; and an additional pad should be placed at the sternum to mark that bone: the whole should be firm, but not hard. The attitude to the legs must then be given, which is done in two ways; if the leg be of that nature which would show the impression of the needle, the latter must be driven through the joints, and the ends nipped off; but if not, a burnt needle is inserted into the false thigh, and bound to the leg below the knee by strong thread, which will allow of bending in any direction, and is a much less troublesome operation. Pass a needle and thread through the skin of the legs, and pulling them towards each other, secure them at their proper distance; then a needle into the sole of each foot; and insert this needle into any of the holes of the stand which will suit the purpose, and secure the needles by putting your hand underneath the stool, and pushing a peg up the hole by the side of it; the bird will then stand, and the posture be given to the legs and hinder part of the body. Further apparatus is required for the head and neck, for which, run one of the sticks through a piece of cork, and through that cork put two long needles; fix the stick upright into any one of the holes which suits the purpose, the cork at the top, and the whole secured by pegs; warm a small lump of wax, and envelope the beak with it, covering the needle, which is left in order to prevent the wax from slipping off; insert the needles into the wax, slipping the cork up or down till the proper position be given to the head. If the bird is to look forward, let the stick be fastened in front; if the head is to turn round, place the stick on one side, &c.; and if the weight of the bird should pull the stick forward, pass a thread round it, and fasten it to the edge of the stand. The bird is now ready for those daily finishing touches on which the beauty of the whole so much depends. All the feathers must be constantly placed in order; if they appear to be drying flat, they must be gently pulled, so as to raise the skin to which they are attached, and all must be constantly lifted up by running a needle under them; the shape of the head is finished by working with a small modelling iron through the orbits, raising the brow, and throwing out the muscles of the throat, as they appear in life; and each touch may be supported by an additional quantity of cotton. The orbits during this part of the operation are very apt to get stretched. It is therefore necessary to tie them at the corner next to the back of the head, by running a fine thread through the upper and lower edges, and fastening it in a knot: they themselves require the nicest attention, that too much of them may not be seen; and the feathers round them should be delicately picked into their places with the point of the needle, like stippling in painting. If the nostrils be fleshy, they must be raised with a modelling iron, that they may not become flat and shrivelled. The eyes are placed in when the bird is left; and the whole is to be kept out of the reach of the sun, the fire, or wind. To these general rules there must be certain modifications; for instance, if the bird have a crest, and it be desirable to erect that crest, the feathers should be daily placed, over and over again, in an erect position; if the wings are to be stretched, they must be pulled out till they form the proper arch, and then supported by props, which are either large needles, the points of which are pushed into the stand, or little sticks stuck into lumps of wax put on to the stand; if the tail is to expand, each feather must be so placed as to have the wrong edge uppermost; if the bird lean on one side by some accident, it must be propped into an erect posture; if the legs be large, an incision must be made in them, and the blunt head of a needle passed frequently between the skin and the bone; if it be web-footed, the webs must be stretched out, and kept in their proper places by fine needles, and daily rubbed with a modelling-iron; if the bird is to stand upon the finger, or a round stick, raise the needles which are inserted into the sole of the foot, wet the claws daily with one part of olive oil and three of spirits of turpentine, and bend them into their proper position. If the beaks be large and coloured, as in the Toucan, they must be well cleaned, and painted inside with water colours; the caruncles of the Gallinaceæ must be modelled by making an incision with a knife, touching them with the poison, and running the irons inside, and when they are dry must be painted their natural colour with oil paint; the necks of vultures, &c. must be restored to their natural tints with colours in powder rubbed on in a dry state. Besides these additional and individual instructions, many others must be left to the genius and experience of the operator.

I cannot too forcibly impress the necessity of a daily portion of attention to those parts which require modelling, or which impart roundness to the object, for if once the skin be suffered to dry in a wrong position, nothing can ever restore it. In about a week or ten days it will, however, obey every touch, and finish by remaining as you have put it; at the end of three weeks, the whole will probably be dry, the upright stick may be removed, and the head will remain in its posture; if the wings have been spread, they will retain their natural arch; if the crest has been erected, it will stand as in life; if the tail has been extended, one knock of the hand, and the feathers will fall into their natural positions, and display themselves like a fan; the eyes which have been daily removed, in order to model the head from the inside, may be finally placed by the shanks sticking in the cotton, taking care to fix them with the utmost precision, the needles pulled out, the threads untied, the wax removed from the beak, and the bird will appear alive.

More than twenty years have elapsed since the greater part of Mr. Waterton's unrivalled preparations have been done, and they are as fresh as ever, an incontrovertible proof that the corrosive sublimate and spirits of wine perfectly answer as a preservative, and there is none of that sickly smell which generally prevails in other collections. Objections may be made to the time which this method takes, but they are obviated by having a number preparing at the same time, for after the first placing on the stand, an hour or two each day for working at them will be quite sufficient. They may be unstuffed at pleasure, and packed close in boxes for transportation, and when they are to be set up again, the skins are softened in cold water for twenty-four hours, and restuffed in a very short period, for the skin having dried in its proper form, will for ever retain it, and requires little or no fresh modelling.

~ ELIZABETH GOULD

From a letter of 9 January 1838

Addressed from Government House, Hobarton. From Alec H. Chisholm, *The Story of Elizabeth Gould* (Melbourne: Hawthorne Press, 1944), 49–50.

My dear Mother,

. . . Just now during John's absence I find amusement and employment in drawing some of the plants of the colony, which will help to render the work on Birds of Australia more interesting. All our sketches are much approved of and highly complimented by our friends. I wish you could

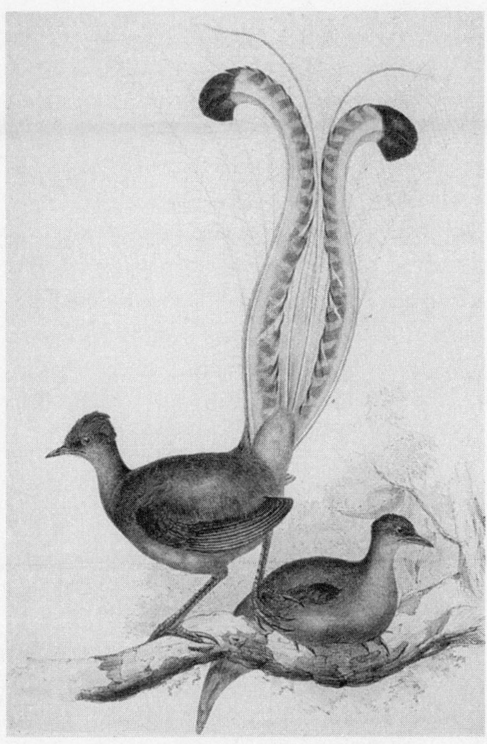

FIGURE 61 Elizabeth Gould, *Superb Lyre Bird,* from *The Birds of Australia*

hear some of the magnificent speeches that are frequently made us, because I know you like dearly to hear your daughter praised. But at the end of all I sigh and think if I could but see old England again, and the dear dear treasures it contains, I would contentedly sit down at my working table and *stroke, stroke* away to the end of the chapter, that is health permitting.

I trust we shall be enabled to make our contemplated work of sufficient interest to ensure it a good sale. Certainly a perfect work could [not] have been made by us without visiting the colony. While John's attention is principally directed to the ornithological department, he does not neglect the other branches as far as he can obtain specimens without interfering with the primary object. . . .

Your affectionate daughter,

ELIZA GOULD

JEMIMA BLACKBURN

Letter to *Nature* 5 (14 March 1872): 383.

Several well-known naturalists who have seen my sketch from life of the young cuckoo ejecting the young pipit . . . have expressed a wish that the details of my observations of the scene should be published. I therefore send you the facts though the sketch itself seems to me to be the only important addition I have made to the admirably accurate description given by Dr Jenner in his letter to John Hunter, which is printed in the "Philosophical Transactions" for 1788 (vol. lxxviii., pp. 225, 226), and which I have read with pleasure since putting down my own notes.

The nest which we watched last June, after finding the cuckoo's egg in it, was that of the common meadow pipit (Titlark, Mosscheeper), and had two pipit's eggs besides that of the cuckoo. It was below a heather bush, on the declivity of a low abrupt bank on a Highland hill-side in Moidart.

At one visit the pipits were found to be hatched, but not the cuckoo. At the next visit, which was after an interval of forty-eight hours, we found the young cuckoo alone in the nest and both the young pipits lying down the bank, about ten inches from the margin of the nest, but quite lively after being warmed in the hand. They were replaced in the nest beside the cuckoo, which struggled about till it got its back under one of them, when it climbed backwards directly up the open side of the nest, and hitched the Pipit from its back on to the edge. It then stood quite upright on its legs, which were straddled wide apart, with the claws firmly fixed half-way down the inside of the nest among the interlacing fibres of which the nest was woven; and, stretching its wings apart and backwards, it elbowed the pipit fairly over the margin so far that its struggles took it down the bank instead of back into the nest.

After this the cuckoo stood for a minute or two, feeling back with its wings, as if to make sure that the pipit was fairly overboard, and then subsided into the bottom of the nest.

As it was getting late, and the cuckoo did not immediately set to work on the other nestling, I replaced the ejected one, and went home. On returning next day, both nestlings were found, dead and cold, out of the nest. I replaced one of them, but the cuckoo made no effort to get under and eject it, but settled itself contentedly on the top of it. All this, I find, accords accurately with Jenner's description of what he saw. But what struck me most

FIGURE 62 Jemima Blackburn, *Cuckoo,* illustration from *Birds from Moidart and Elsewhere*

was this: The cuckoo was perfectly naked, without a vestige of a feather or even a hint of future feathers; its eyes were not yet opened, and its neck seemed too weak to support the weight of its head. The pipits had well-developed quills on the wings and back, and had bright eyes, partially open; yet they seemed quite helpless under the manipulations of the cuckoo, which looked a much less developed creature. The cuckoo's legs, however, seemed very muscular, and it appeared to feel about with its wings, which were absolutely featherless, as with hands, the "spurious wing" (unusually large in proportion) looking like a spread-out thumb. The most singular thing of all was the direct purpose with which the blind little monster made for the open side of the nest, the only part where it could throw its burthen down the bank. I think all the spectators felt the sort of horror and awe at the apparent inadequacy of the creature's intelligence to its acts that one might have felt at seeing a toothless hag raise a ghost by an incantation. It was horribly "uncanny" and "grewsome."

FIGURE 63 Beatrix Potter, *Studies of a Pet Hedgehog* (reproduced by kind permission of Frederick Warne & Co.)

BEATRIX POTTER

"Hedgehogs"

Ms. BP 1306. Victoria and Albert Museum Library, London. (Reproduced by kind permission of Frederick Warne & Co.)

Although sufficiently common animals, hedgehogs appear to have been very little studied by naturalists, judging by the letters that occasionally appear in the Field. The animal moults about ⅓ of its spines every spring, ~~following on the~~ <the spines being>[1] moulted ~~of the~~ <after the> rest of the fur. It will be noticed that the fur and spines pass from one form to the other—stiff bristly hair <gradating into> ~~and~~ their spines at the borders of the prickly jacket. The spines are attached to the skin by a slight knob. I believe that they fall out, I do not think that they are pushed out by a new spine growing in the old socket. This is a point of interest because new spines grown at odd times to replace broken ones, are I think grown from the old ~~socket~~ root; and they are white and soft like those of a young hedgehog.

1. Text that was deleted or added by Potter on her handwritten manuscript is shown here by strikethrough and angle brackets, respectively. *Ed.*

The spines which are grown in the ordinary course of moulting, are dark coloured and hard when they first pierce the skin. They grow very rapidly and cause the animal extreme irritation; it scratches itself with its hind claws like a dog. A few <new> spines are scattered all over the prickle jacket, but the main crop grows in bands. One season it is along the top of the back, another season in a stripe along either side; (but a healthy animal is never without a sufficient coat for protection.) (I think the animal completes a new coat about every third year, but a few ~~old~~ <individual> spines may stick in for several years longer.) ~~No doubt~~ <Probably> the bald hedgehog described in the Field was unable to grow new spines through some physical deficiency; it is no more remarkable than a bald Skye-terrier.

The generally received idea that hibernation—(like the freezing of water)—depends directly upon a given low temperature is not borne out by intimate acquaintance with <the> habits of hedgehogs, wild or tame. Their footprints may be seen in the snow, & there is nothing mysterious in the fact.

The <hibernating trance> cataleptic state is intirely [*sic*] under the animal's own control, and only in a secondary degree dependant on the weather. My tame hedgehog could rouse herself at half an hour's notice at any time, even during severe frost; and conversely she could "go off" at will on a merely ~~chilly~~ <wet> day in August, or upon the hearthrug in front of a hot fire.

I have watched the somewhat ghastly process on several occasions. The first time I saw it I administered brandy, being under the impression that the animal was dying. The trick is done by swallowing the breath, like Stevenson's 'Secundra Das' in the Master of Ballantrae. The hedgehog composes itself comfortably, usually after a large meal & an evening of extra livelyness [*sic*].[2] It closes its eyes & holds its breath, occasionally it catches a breath in spite of itself with a sobbing gasp. The process looks difficult and highly uncomfortable; and the animal is very cross if interrupted. <Gradually> the involuntary ~~breaths~~ <gasps> come at longer intervals, the extremities grow cold and the nose becomes quite dry. In ~~about~~ <less than> an hour the cataleptic trance is complete. When the hedgehog wants to return to the world the process is reversed, the breathing which has been ~~exceedingly~~ slow & ~~slight~~ <faint> during the trance is quickened tremendously. I <think I> have counted 120 respirations to the minute. The first visible result of this vigorous consumption of <air> oxygen is a trickling <wetness> of the hitherto dry nose. The heat reaches the paws last. The waking up is a much slower process than the going off, and the animal is often painfully weak & nervous for several hours.

2. At this point in the text, Potter has inserted an illegible half line over her existing text. *Ed.*

Seaweeds, Zoophytes, and Women

ELIZA COOK

From "Song of the Sea-weed"

The Poetical Works. London: Frederick Warne and Co., 1869. 309.

I am born in crystal bower
Where the despot hath no power
To trail and turn the oozy fern,
Or trample down the fair sea-flower.
I am born where human skill
Cannot bend me to its will;
None can delve about my root,
And nurse me for my bloom and fruit;
I am left to spread and grow
In my rifted bed below,
Till I break my slender hold,
    As the porpoise tumbleth o'er me;
And on I go—now high—now low—
    With the ocean world before me.

FIGURE 64 Anna Atkins, *Sargassum bacciferum*, from *Photographs of British Algae: cyanotype impressions* (Seven Oaks: Halstead Place, 1843) (courtesy New York Public Library)

ANNE PRATT

"Zoophytes"

Chapters on the Common Things of the Sea-side. London: Society for Promoting Christian Knowledge, 1850. 237–41.

There are many who are not aware that on our own shores, delicate and beautiful zoophytes, many of them like plants, are brought up by the waves to their feet continually, and are lying on almost every beach, or grow among our rocks, or creep by entangling fibres or sand-coloured patches, over our sea-weeds, or are dredged up by the fishermen in multitudes. It is true, that the corals of the British coast are few and inconsiderable, but the skeleton of zoophytes from which the polypes which made them have died away, are among its commonest objects; and picked up often, and looking like plants, they puzzle the inexperienced marine botanist, who wonders that he cannot find their description in his work on sea-weeds. Nor is it much more than a century since, that men of science thought these zoophytes were vegetables, and led by their plant-like appearance, their fixed place of growth, the discs or tubular fibres which constitute their point of attachment, they hesitated not to describe them as sea-weeds or mosses.

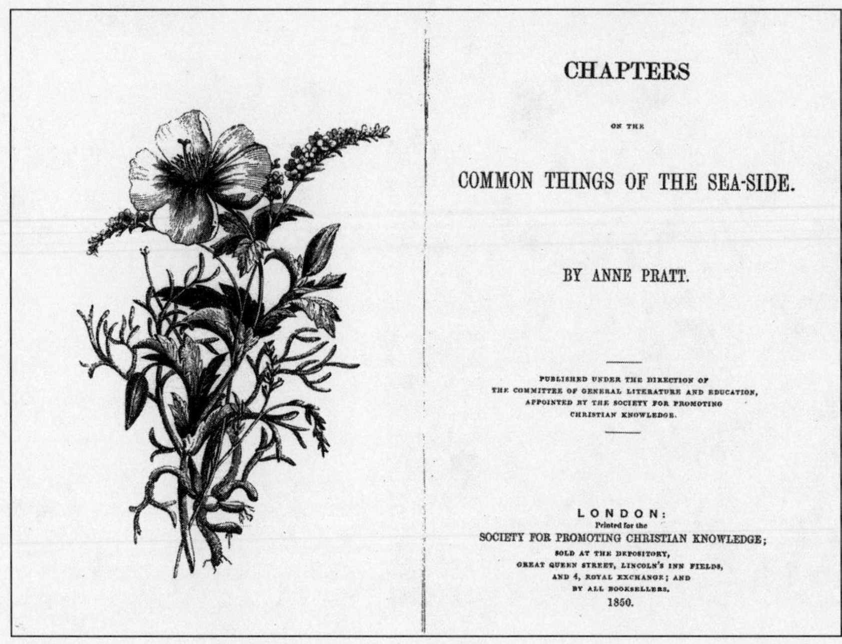

CHAPTERS

ON THE

COMMON THINGS OF THE SEA-SIDE.

BY ANNE PRATT.

PUBLISHED UNDER THE DIRECTION OF
THE COMMITTEE OF GENERAL LITERATURE AND EDUCATION,
APPOINTED BY THE SOCIETY FOR PROMOTING
CHRISTIAN KNOWLEDGE.

LONDON:
Printed for the
SOCIETY FOR PROMOTING CHRISTIAN KNOWLEDGE;
SOLD AT THE DEPOSITORY,
GREAT QUEEN STREET, LINCOLN'S INN FIELDS,
AND 4, ROYAL EXCHANGE; AND
BY ALL BOOKSELLERS.
1850.

FIGURE 65 Anne Pratt, title page, *Chapters on the Common Things of the Sea-side*

They could discover in their leaf-like expansions, in their graceful sprays, no similarity to any living creature yet known as the resident of earth or air, or of the deep waters; and they had not as yet unfolded that page of Nature's book, which, after a series of patient and diligent investigation, has revealed to modern observers a new world of wonders, a new lesson of Almighty skill and design, as indicative to the thoughtful mind of the work of God, and as sublime in its influence over our spirits, as are the teachings of the stars and suns of the lofty skies.

In the few pages to which we must limit our remarks, little can be done beyond describing some few of the commonest zoophytes of our shores, and naming such facts respecting them as may awaken an interest in the subject, and lead the reader to seek for further information. The zoophytes are well described as plant-like animals, the greater number of them being also compound animals. Thus when we speak of a zoophyte, we usually include the stony, or horny, or membranous fabric or case, and the polypes, the little living creature which dwells in these structures, which make them, and are indeed a part of them. In these skeletons or polypidoms, it may be that thousands of individuals exist, all united by a living thread, running through every part, and constituting a common circulation. Different individuals are they, and yet the same; their feelings, their interests, and labours all under the influence of one harmonious instinct; and yet each flower-like polype having so far independent consciousness, as to shrink if touched, while the other polypes seem quite unaffected by the movement, and fearless of harm. It is these cases, or polypidoms, which so often attract us on the beach or sands, where they lie; blown about by every wind, or finding a resting-place in some hollow among the stones. Beautiful horn-coloured sprays, like little fir-trees, or resembling brittle withered leaves, or forming crusts on sea-weeds, we see them every day in our summer rambles on the shore, and perhaps admire their graceful forms, and see how they are adapted to bend before the wave; but when we behold them through the microscope, and discover their wondrous living inmates, their active star-like polypes, all instinct with life and vigour; their beautiful cup-like, or bell-shaped, cells; their vesicles, now resembling a pomegranate flower, now shaped like some antique model of a vase, we feel how much there is of beauty lying unperceived by us even in common things, and bow in humble reverence before the Almighty maker, to whom the little and great seem alike deserving of his wondrous skill, alike the objects of his constant care.

Interesting as are the permanent fabrics of the zoophytes, the sea-fans, of far distant seas, the corals of commerce, or the white stony mushroom-like corals which greet us in museums; and elegant as are the horny branches on our sands, yet the little polypes, unseen by the naked eye, are no less beautiful, and present a far more wondrous structure than the skeletons themselves. Let us gather up from the beach one of those horny sprays, which the wind blows hither and thither, and place it under a good microscope, and down the side of every branch, or in some species on both sides, we see a number of little horny cups, some close to the branch, others raised on stalks, and constituting, it may be, some hundreds or even thousands of cells. If our specimen is fresh and living, we may see, at the opening of these cups, the tentacles of the active polypes, arranged like rays around the centre, looking like so many daisies or other rayed blossoms, and, in fact, forming so many mouths and stomachs to feed one common body, placed within the horny spray, and each retiring, if alarmed, within its own cell. Every little thread-like branch, and every stem, is hollow; and the pink fleshy substance of the zoophyte, like a mere thread, may be seen filling up every part, and this is the living portion to which so many mouths are furnishing the needful food, when moving their active feelers about in the water, they catch the living prey which every drop of ocean contains.

If we gather up our specimen in spring-time we may in some species, easily, with the naked eye, discover a number of clear little vesicles, which look like seed-vessels; and are quite distinct from the cells in which the polypes reside. These contain the germ of the polypes, and from these proceed new structures; each horny fabric originating in a single polype. When viewed beneath a microscope, even these minute objects are found to be most beautifully varied; each species having vesicles of a form peculiar to itself. Thus in one common coralline we find them ovate or pear-shaped; in another they resemble an oblong pouch, marked with numerous and crested ribs. One species has vesicles reminding us of a swollen pod, girded round with from five to nine bands, and rising into short spines; another has them covered over, at top, with a rounded lid. The germs within these vesicles, or seed-vessels, are seen by the aid of the microscope to be very small granules, their surfaces covered with minute hairs (ciliæ), and actively floating within these vases. They are extremely irritable, and if they come in contact with a hair, a grain of sand, or other small substance, they are capable of contracting their bodies into various forms. They whirl about in constant motion, until they select some point of attachment, where they fix themselves, and thence, in course of time, arises the goodly spray which delights our eye.

~ MARGARET GATTY (MRS. ALFRED GATTY)

From *British Sea-weeds*

1863. Vol. I. London: Bell and Daldy, 1872. vii; viii; x; xvii–xix; xxviii–xxix.

[p. vii]

INTRODUCTION

It was once prettily said by a lady who cultivated flowers, that she had "buried many a care in her garden;" and the sea-weed collector can often say the same of his garden—the shore; as many a loving disciple could testify, who, having taken up the pursuit originally as a resource against weariness, or a light possible occupation during hours of sickness, has ended by an enthusiastic love, which throws a charm over every sea-place on the coast, however dull and ugly to the world in general; makes every day spent there too short, and every visit too quickly ended. Only let there be sea, and

FIGURE 66 Margaret Gatty

plenty of low, dark rocks stretching out, peninsular-like, into it; and only let the dinner-hour be fixed for high-water time,—and the loving disciple asks no more of fate. Turn him out on that flat, and, to you (O Gentile of the outer courts), *uninteresting* shore, with a basket, a bottle, a stick, a strong pair of boots (oiled, not polished with blacking), and, let us add, to crown the comfort, a strong, friendly, and willing, if not learned companion; and all the crowned heads of Europe may be shaken without his being able to feel that he cares. When the returning tide has driven him backwards from his best hunting grounds, and sent him home at last to dinner and things of the earth, earthy, the squabbles of nations may come in for a share of his attention perhaps; but, even then, only imperfectly, for the collected treasures have to be examined and preserved, and the heart of the collector yearns after them. . . .

[p. viii–ix]

Next to boots comes the question of petticoats; and if anything could excuse a woman for imitating the costume of a man, it would be what she suffers as a sea-weed collector from those necessary draperies! But to make the best of a bad matter, let woollen be in the ascendant as much as possible; and let the petticoats never come below the ankle. A ladies' yachting costume has come into fashion of late, which is, perhaps, as near perfection for shore-work as anything that could be devised. It is a suit consisting of a full short skirt of blue flannel or serge (like very fine bathing-gown material), with waistcoat and jacket to match. Cloaks and shawls, which necessarily hamper the arms, besides having long ends and corners which cannot fail to get soaked, are, of course, very inconvenient, and should be as much avoided as possible; but where this cannot be, a good deal may be done towards tucking them neatly up out of the way. In conclusion, a hat is preferable to a bonnet, merino stockings to cotton ones, and a strong pair of gloves is indispensable. All millinery work—silks, satins, lace, bracelets, and other jewellery, &c. must, and will, be laid aside by every rational being who attempts to shore-hunt.

A stick was alluded to before, and is a very desirable appendage, both as a balance in rock-clambering and for drawing floating sea-weeds from the water. It should have a crook for a handle therefore. But about these sort of matters, people should amuse themselves by devising ingenious varieties. The basket may be lined with gutta percha,[1] or exchanged, by those who care to invest in it, for an Indian-rubber bag, which can be strapped round the waist, and into an inside pocket of which a bottle or two for the more delicate sea-weeds may be easily stowed away. But the common basket which has served the bygone generation will do very well for any one who is in earnest in this. Few tools come amiss to a good workman, and it argues a rather *dilettante* state of mind to insist on having everything the perfection of convenience. Into which question comes also that of expenditure; and the reader is here assured, once for all, that it is quite possible to go shore-hunting for life quite comfortably without any extra expense whatever; that *very* strong-soled pair of boots perhaps alone excepted, and they will be found quite as useful in country walks afterwards, as on the sands. . . .

[p. x]

And once on the beach under the favourable circumstances of a fine day, a receding tide, sufficient refection in the basket to prevent an inglorious retreat for lack of food—what is the wisest course to pursue? To go straight down at once to as low-water as the tide admits of, and so gradually follow its retreat; or to indulge the very natural inclination to stop and gather the wash-up (*wreck*, or *wrack*) which may possibly be scattered at your feet? The answer depends upon circumstances, but, as a general rule, the first is decidedly the better plan for a sea-weed collector. Sunshine so quickly injures

1. A rubberlike material, made from the juice of Malayan trees. *Ed.*

the greater number of the finer plants (fading them to yellow and white), that they are scarcely worth picking up after a few hours' exposure. But if a rough sea has brought an unusually profuse and thick deposit, they are well worth a turn over or two from your stick just to see that you are not leaving pearls behind you unaware; and if you are one of those who patronise zoophytes as well as algæ, you are pretty sure to find something worth stopping a few minutes for. Very good zoophytes are sometimes washed up to the very last high-water mark line, an instance of which once occurred at Filey, where a layer of the scarce *Thuiaria articulata* was left round one side of the bay, close under the cliffs. . . .

[pp. xvii–xix]

A few words remain to be said about the descriptions of the Plates which follow; the most important being an assurance to the reader that he is secured from the danger of meeting with serious errors, by the fact that private friendship has enabled me to consult Dr. Harvey[2] from first to last throughout, as also to make use of his various works. Those works are intended for scientific or, certainly, *advanced* students, and any one who will compare his descriptions with mine will discover that what I have done—or rather what I have attempted to do—is to bring his scientific statements within the range of general comprehension by such alterations of language as might soften the technical difficulties which are such a stumbling-block to amateur beginners.

Should any one, from looking at these descriptions, desire to rise out of amateurship into science, he will seek and find his proper food elsewhere. The books are open for those who can understand them, and those will understand them who care sufficiently to try, and will find the pursuit a charmed one. So that to have assisted in whetting the appetite of any worthy disciple in favour of it would be a fact to reflect upon with pleasure, and make the labour bestowed on these pages seem well employed. And who can doubt that those who desire to take the higher flight, will be all the better able to do so from having condescended to begin as children, and work upwards by childish steps?

They may laugh hereafter, perhaps, at ever having looked at a book which translates *ramuli* into *branchlets,* and *ramelli* into *branchleteens;* but it will be in the same way that grown-up people smile at the spelling-book which enabled them to begin literature by stories of one-syllabled words. By

2. Gatty here refers to William Harvey's *Manual of British Algae* (1841), a standard work that she is supplementing here. *Ed.*

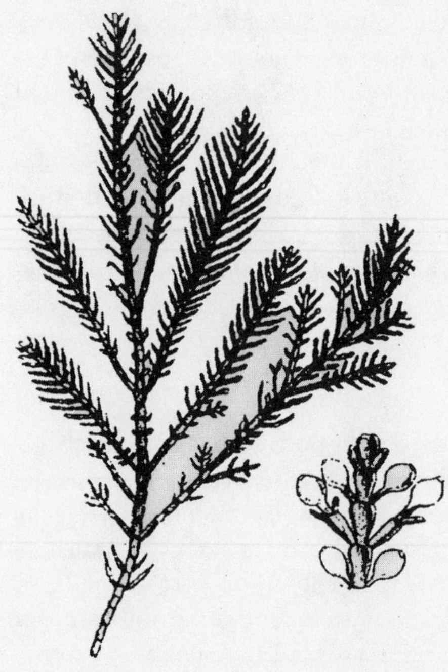

FIGURE 67 *Corralina officinalis,* illustration for Margaret Gatty, *British Sea-weeds*

the time my amateur beginners have learnt to know that *ramelli,* as *branchleteens,* are distinct from *ramuli,* as *branchlets*—have seen *threads* explained as *filaments* so often, that to forget what *filaments* mean is impossible, with other similar lessons—they will look at the pages of Phycologias,[3] British and Foreign, with comparatively open eyes, and on their own heads will it be if they do not persevere further!

Moreover, it is believed that the plan here adopted, of arranging the *subjects* of observation in separate lines and in uniform order, will facilitate the necessary comparison of species with species. Thus, at a glance, *colour* can be matched with *colour, substance* with *substance, form* with *form* (under the title *Character of Frond*), &c., and a plant referred to the one with which it proves to agree.

It is true, the absence of scientific *generic* classification and headings makes it difficult at first to discover to which *set of species* a plant may belong; but, to meet this difficulty, two attempts are now made; one of which is to throw brief *generic* and *specific* distinctions together in the descriptions. Thus, on the first page, in the account of the *Sargassums,* the statement that

3. Books dealing with seaweeds or algae. *Ed.*

they have "branches bearing distinct leaves" is made of both, and is followed in both cases by a more particular description of the leaves. Now the fact of "bearing distinct leaves" is a *generic* character, and separates the *Sargassums* from all the other plants that follow; whereas the minute differences as to *width,* the presence of *pores* in the leaves, &c., are among the *specific* ones which distinguish *S. vulgare* from *S. bacciferum.* . . .

But, besides this, in the second place, there will be found appended to this volume a *Synopsis of Sea-weed Appearances,* which it is hoped will be a great assistance to the collector in tracing any plant he may meet with to its *generic,* and finally, its *specific,* home. In this the *first* step towards algological classification is as clearly marked as in the most scientific works, viz. the division of algæ into three chief colour-groups,—olive, red, and grass-green:[4] but this stage over, scientific classification is laid aside, and the plants are grouped together by the more obvious characters of form and habit of growth. To begin at the beginning, however. The first inquiry of a collector must still be—Is my plant olive, red, or grass-green? And this he must find out whenever he wishes to ascertain its name. In most cases it will be easy enough to do so, but in others he can only accomplish it by holding up the plant to the light, or by examining through a pocket lens (a magnifying-glass used by all botanists, and to be carried in the pocket); or, better still, under the microscope. And here he must bear in mind that all algæ are coloured one of the three colours named, unless faded by exposure. The tempting white bits so common on the shore near high-water mark, therefore, are worthless, except to make a variety of appearance in a sea-weed picture or basket.

The colour ascertained, he now knows in which of the three colour-groups to look for his plant, and may proceed next to consider to which of the principal *divisions* of its group it belongs; whether to the FLATS, the CYLINDRICALS (*i.e.* those *shaped* like a thread, whether coarse or slender), the INCRUSTATIONS, OR IRREGULAR LUMPS. Then—if flat, for instance—he must go on to observe whether it is *with* or *without a midrib;* whether *leaf-like* or *irregular* in shape; whether *branched* or *unbranched,* &c.; for it is impossible to do more here than give a general ideal of *how* the investigations are to be pursued. They will need patient labour and careful observation; but if these are given they will probably be successful. What the *Synopsis* fails to give, the specific descriptions and plates will probably supply; and

4. Not that the colour-groups are so arranged *because* of colour, but because of structure; consequently, in a few cases where colour and structure clash, colour gives way. Hence the exceptional *red* cases in the grass-green group, where the structure is strictly that of grass-green plants.

the List of *Families, Genera, and Species,* which follows, will enable the student to reduce his scattered materials into their proper order, and arrange his plants in the herbarium according to their scientific classification.

It is true the difficulties increase as the inquiry proceeds. It is easier to find the generic than the *specific* name of a plant; to trace it home to its family, than to identify it as an individual. But those who have accomplished the one are little likely to rest satisfied without attempting the other. And if a real difficulty occurs, surely some more advanced naturalist-friend can always be got hold of to throw light on the subject. For brotherhood is strong among them—especially among the highest—whose readiness to help the ignorant, even at the expense of much valuable time and trouble, is an example which all will do well to imitate. On the other hand, the "*ignorant*" should carefully guard from presuming on such good nature. A habit of recklessly sending unexamined specimens to be named—a dozen of one sort, perhaps—cannot be too strongly deprecated. But a real difficulty, which the possessor of a plant has tried in vain to surmount, is sure to be kindly and considerately met by any one to whom reference is made.

[pp. xxviii–xxix]

HOW TO MAKE SECTIONS OF ALGÆ FOR MICROSCOPIC EXAMINATION

For making sections or *durchschnitts* it is necessary to have a small working microscope, a few glass slides and thin cell-covers, and a delicately fine knife.

An excellent microscope of the proper sort is to be had for a few shillings; and if the knife it contains be not sufficiently fine, an infant's gum lancet, well sharpened, answers the purpose.

The little instrument has, of course, a stem on which the eye-glass runs up and down; and this being fastened to the wood-work of the box, can be shut in or turned out at will. When turned out, the box itself forms a small stage or platform to work upon; the student looking down upon it through the glass. Note here, that it is well to gum a piece of white paper on the stage to begin with, as the operations to be performed are thus more easily seen. On this stage place a glass slide, and on the slide place a morsel of the plant to be examined, say a quarter of an inch or so of a stem or branch. Hold this scrap firmly down to the slide by the first finger of your left hand, pressing the nail against its extreme end, so that as you look through the eye-glass you can only see the *merest edge* of the plant. Then, with the knife or lancet in your right hand, slice off this *mere edge* (the thinner the slice the better), and drawing the left nail very slightly back, leave another *mere edge*, which cut off in a similar way; and so another, and another, and another, till you have six or eight slices on your slide.

Now wet the tip of a finger in clean water, and let down one *small* drop thereof upon the centre of the slide; into which minute pool coax your little *durchschnitts*, by the aid of the small *pointer* contained in your microscope box, and then—replacing the slide on the stage—give yourself the pleasure of watching the magnified slices expand in the liquid.

With fresh-gathered plants there is no difficulty, of course, but sections of dried specimens are occasionally troublesome, by refusing to resume their natural shape. A drop of muriatic acid will sometimes induce them to open, but not always. Nevertheless, it is so rarely possible to mend the matter by moistening the dried specimen before it is cut, and clean, good sections are so much more easily made of dried plants than of remoistened ones, that the *rule* is, to cut them in their dried state, as a first effort, and resort to other expedients, if necessary afterwards.

But to proceed. The sections being more [or] less expanded, take one of the thin cell-covers (ascertaining that it is clean and bright), and let it gently down upon the slide over the little pool and its contents, and you have at once a *microscopic slide* ready for examination under your compound microscope.

Troublesome as this operation may seem to be, when read of, it is a very amusing one in practice, and by no means hard of accomplishment. *Longitudinal* sections are made in the same way; but it is always well then to secure a *fork* in the branching, as the one stem can be held down quite firmly while the other is being cut; whereas one only, if very slender, cannot be thoroughly secured during the process of cutting.

Were the mechanical part now described the worst difficulty in the examination of sea-weed structure, all the world might be made learned by algological *durchschnitts;* but the delicacy of eye and judgement requisite for understanding the meaning of what is seen, is a part of the matter not so easily taught or acquired. Courage, however! A comparison of fresh-gathered and dried *durchschnitts* of the same *genera;* a habit, if possible, of making drawings of everything one sees; and a patient acquiescence with the necessity of being twenty times mistaken at first for every once one is right, will go a long way towards making a *scholar* in its secondary sense, out of a mere scholar or amateur.

~ MARGARET GATTY

"Knowledge Not the Limit of Belief"

Parables from Nature. First published 1855, added to until 1871. *Classics of Children's Literature, 1621–1932.* Ed. Diane Johnson. New York: Garland, 1976. 27–35.

"Canst thou by searching find out God?"

JOB xi. 7.

It was but the banging of the door, blown to by a current of wind from the open window, that made that great noise, and shook the room so much!

The room was a Naturalist's library, and it was a pity that some folio books of specimens had been left so near the edge of the great table, for, when the door clapt to, they fell down; and many plants, seaweeds, &c, were scattered on the floor.

And, "Do we meet once again?" said a Zoophyte to a Seaweed (a *Corallina*) in whose company he had been thrown ashore,—"Do we meet once again? This is a real pleasure. What strange adventures we have gone through since the waves flung us on the sands together!"

"Ay, indeed," replied the Seaweed, "and what a queer place we have come to at last! Well, well—but let me first ask you how you are this morning, after all the washing, and drying, and squeezing, and gumming, we have undergone?"

"Oh, pretty well in health, Seaweed, but very, very sad. You know there is a great difference between you and me. You have little or no cause to be sad. You are just the same now that you ever were, excepting that you can never grow any more. But *I!* ah, I am only the skeleton of what I once was! All the merry little creatures that inhabited me are dead and dried up. They died by hundreds at a time soon after I left the sea; and even if they had survived longer, the nasty fresh water we were soaked in by the horrid being who picked us up, would have killed them at once. What are you smiling at?"

"I am smiling," said the Seaweed, "at your calling our new master a horrid being, and also at your speaking so positively about the little creatures that inhabited you."

"And why may I not speak positively of what I know so well?" asked the other.

"Oh, of what you *know,* Zoophyte, by all means! But I wonder what we *do* know! People get very obstinate over what they think they know, and then, lo and behold! it turns out to be a mistake."

"What makes you say this?" inquired the Zoophyte; and the Seaweed answered, "I have learnt it from a very curious creature I have made acquaintance with here—a Bookworm. He walks through all the books in this library just as he pleases, and picks up a quantity of information, and knows a great deal. And he's a mere nothing, he says, compared to the creature who picked us up—the 'horrid being,' as you call him. Why, my dear friend, the Bookworm tells me that he who found us is a man, and that a man is the most wonderful creature in all the world; that there is nothing in the least like him. And this particular one here is a Naturalist; that is, he knows all about living creatures, and plants, and stones, and I don't know what besides. Now, wouldn't you say that it was a great honour to belong to him, and to have made acquaintance with his friend the Bookworm?"

"Of course I should, and do—" the Zoophyte replied.

"Very well," continued his companion, "I knew you would; and yet I can tell you that this Naturalist and his Bookworm are just instances of what I have been saying. They fancy that betwixt them they know nearly everything, and get as obstinate as possible over the most ridiculous mistakes."

"My good friend Seaweed, are you a competent judge in such matters as these?"

"Oh, am I not!" the Seaweed rejoined. "Why now, for instance, what do you think the Bookworm and I have been quarrelling about half the morning? Actually as to whether *I* am an animal or a vegetable. He declares that I am an animal full of little living creatures like yours, and that there is a long account of all this written on the page opposite the one on which I am gummed!"

"Of all the nonsense I ever listened to!" began the Zoophyte, angrily, yet amused—but he was interrupted by the Seaweed—

"And as for *you*—I am almost ashamed to tell you—that you and all your family and connections were, for generations and generations, considered as vegetables. It is only lately that these Naturalists found out that you were an animal. May I not well say that people get very obstinate about what they think they know, and after all it turns out to be a mistake? As for me, I am quite confused with these blunders."

"O dear, how disappointed I am!" murmured the Zoophyte. "I thought we had really fallen into the hands of some very interesting creatures. I am very, very sorry! It seemed so nice that there should be wonderful, wise beings, who spend their time in finding out all about animals, and plants, and such things, and keep us all in these beautiful books so carefully. I liked it so much; and now I find the wonderfully wise creatures are wonderfully stupid ones instead."

"Very much so," laughed the Seaweed, "though our learned friend, the Bookworm, would tell you quite otherwise; but he gets quite muddled when he talks about them, poor fellow!"

"It is very easy to ridicule your betters," said a strange voice; and the Bookworm, who had just then eaten his way through the back of Lord Bacon's *Advancement of Learning,* appeared sitting outside, listening to the conversation. "I shall be sorry that I have told you anything, if you make such a bad use of the little bit of knowledge you have acquired."

"Oh, I beg your pardon, dear friend!" cried the Seaweed. "I meant no harm. You see it is quite new to us to learn anything; and, really, if I laughed, you must excuse me. I meant no harm—only I *do* happen to know—really for a fact—that I never was alive with little creatures like my friend the Zoophyte; and he happens to know—really for a fact—that he never was a vegetable; and so you see it made us smile to think of your wonderful creature, man, making such wonderfully odd mistakes."

At this the Bookworm smiled; but he soon shook his head gravely, and said—"All the mistakes man makes, man can discover and correct—I mean, of course, all the mistakes he makes about creatures inferior to himself, whom he learns to know from his own observation. He may not observe quite carefully enough one day, but he may put all right when he looks the next time. I never give up a statement when I know it is true: and so I tell you again—laugh as much as you please—that, in spite of all his mistakes, man is, without exception, the most wonderful and the most clever of all the creatures upon earth!"

"You will be a clever creature yourself if you can prove it!" cried both the Zoophyte and Seaweed at once.

"The idea of taking me with my hundreds of living inhabitants for a vegetable!" sneered the Zoophyte.

"And me with my vegetable inside, covered over with lime, for an animal!" smiled the Seaweed.

Bookworm. "Ah! have your laugh out, and then listen. But, my good friends, if you had worked your way through as many wise books as I have done, you would laugh less and know more."

Zoophyte. "Nay, don't be angry, Bookworm."

Bookworm. "Oh, I'm not angry a bit. I know too well the cause of all the folly you are talking, so I excuse you. And I am now puzzling my head to find out how I am to prove what I have said about the superiority of man, so as to make you understand it."

Seaweed. "Then you admit there is a little difficulty in proving it? Even *you* confess it to be rather puzzling."

Bookworm. "I do; but the difficulty does not lie where you think it does. I am sorry to say it—but the only thing that prevents your *understanding* the superiority of man, is your own immeasurable inferiority to him! However many mistakes he may make about *you*, he can correct them all by a little closer or more patient observation. But no observation can make you understand what man is. *You* are quite within the grasp of *his* powers, but *he* is quite beyond the reach of *yours*."

Seaweed. "You are not over-civil, with all your learning, Mr. Bookworm."

Bookworm. "I do not mean to be rude, I assure you. You are both of you very beautiful creatures, and, I dare say, very useful too. But you should not fancy either that you *do* know everything, or that you are *able* to know everything. And, above all, you should not dispute the superiority and powers of another creature merely because you cannot understand them."

Seaweed. "And am I then to believe all the long stories anybody may choose to come and tell me about the wonderful powers of other creatures?—and, when I inquire what those wonderful powers are, am I to be told that I can't understand them, but am to believe them all the same as if I did?"

Bookworm. "Certainly not, unless the wonderful powers are proved by wonderful results; but if they are, I advise you to believe in them, whether you understand them or not."

Seaweed. "I should like to know how I am to believe what I don't understand."

Bookworm. "Very well, then, don't! and remain an ignorant fool all your life. Of course, you can't *really* understand anything but what is within the narrow limits of your own powers; so, if you choose to make those powers the limits of your belief, I wish you joy, for you certainly won't be overburdened with knowledge."

Seaweed. "I will retort upon you that it is very easy to be contemptuous to your inferiors, Mr. Bookworm. You would do much better to try and explain to me those wonderful powers themselves, and so remove all the difficulties that stand in the way of my belief."

Bookworm. "If I were to try ever so much, I should not succeed. You can't understand even *my* superiority."

Seaweed. "Oh, Bookworm! now you are growing conceited."

Bookworm. "Indeed I am not; but you shall judge for yourself. I can do many things you can't do; among others, I can *see*."

Seaweed. "What is that?"

Bookworm. "There, now! I knew I should puzzle you directly! Why, seeing is something that I do with a very curious machine in my head, called an eye. But as you have not got an eye, and therefore cannot see, how am I to make you understand what seeing is?"

Seaweed. "Why, you can tell us, to be sure."

Bookworm. "Tell you what? I can tell you I see. I can say, *Now I see, now I see,* as I walk over you, and see the little bits of you that fall under my small eye. Indeed, I can also tell you *what* I see; but how will that teach you what seeing is? You have got no eye, and therefore you can't see, and therefore also you can never know what seeing is."

Zoophyte. "Then why need we believe there is such a thing as seeing?"

Bookworm. "Oh, pray, don't believe it! I don't know why you should, I am sure! There's no harm at all in being ignorant and narrow-minded. I am sure I had much rather you took no further trouble in the matter; for you are, both of you, very testy and tiresome. It is from nothing but pride and vanity, too, after all. You want to be in a higher place in creation than you are put in, and no good ever comes of that. If you would be content to learn wonderful things in the only way that is open to you, I should have a great deal of pleasure in telling you more."

Zoophyte. "And pray what way is that?"

Bookworm. "Why, from the effects produced by them. As I said before, even where you cannot *understand* the wonderful powers themselves, you may have the grace to believe in their existence, from their wonderful results."

Seaweed. "And the results of what you call 'seeing' are—"

"In man," interrupted the Bookworm, "that he gets to know everything about you, and all the creatures, and plants, and stones he looks at; so that he knows your shape, and growth, and colour, and all about the cells of the little creatures that live in you—how many feelers these have, what they live upon, how they catch their food, how the eggs come out of the egg-cells, where you live, where you are to be found, what other Zoophytes are related to you, *i.e.,* which are most like you—in short, the most minute particulars;—so that he puts you into his collections, not among strange creatures, but near to those you are most nearly connected with; and he describes you, and makes pictures of you, and gives you a name so that you are known for the same creature, wherever you are found, all over the world. And now, I'm quite out of breath with telling you all these wonderful results of seeing."

"But he once took me for a vegetable," mused the Zoophyte.

"Yes; as I said before, he had not observed quite close enough, nor had he then invented a curious instrument which enables his great big eye to see such little fellows as your inhabitants are. But when he made that instrument, and looked very carefully, he saw all about you."

"Ay, but he still calls me an animal," observed the Seaweed.

"I know he does, but I am certain he will not do so long! If you are a vegetable, I will warrant him to find it out when he examines you a little more."

"You expect us to believe strange things, Bookworm," observed the Zoophyte.

"To be sure, because there is no end of strange things for you to believe! And what you can't find out for yourself, you must take upon trust from your betters," laughed the Bookworm. "It's the only plan. *Observation and Revelation are the sole means of acquiring knowledge.*"

Just at that moment the door opened, and two gentlemen entered the room.

"Ah, my new specimens on the floor!" observed the Naturalist; "but never mind," added he, as he picked them up, "here is the very one we wanted; it will serve admirably for our purpose. I shall only sacrifice a small branch of it, though."

And the Naturalist cut off a little piece of the Seaweed and laid it in a saucer, and poured upon it some liquid from a bottle, and an effervescence began to take place forthwith, and the Seaweed's limy coat began to give way; and the two gentlemen sat watching the result.

"Now," whispered the Bookworm to the Zoophyte, "those two men are looking closely at your Seaweed friend, and trying what they call experiments, that they may find out what he is; and if they do not succeed, I will give up all my arguments in despair."

But they *did* succeed!

The gentlemen watched on till all the lime was dissolved, and there was nothing left in the saucer but a delicate red branch with little round things upon it, that looked like tiny apples.

"This is the fruit decidedly," remarked the Naturalist; "and now we will proceed to examine it through the microscope."

And they did so.

And an hour or more passed, and a sort of sleepy forgetfulness came over the Bookworm and his two friends; for they had waited till they were tired for further remarks from the Naturalist. And, therefore, it was with a start they were aroused at last by hearing him exclaim, "It is impossible to entertain the slightest doubt. If I ever had any, I have none now; and the *Corallinas* must be removed back once more to their position among vegetables!"

The Naturalist laughed as he loosened the gum from the specimen, which he placed on a fresh paper, and classed among Red Seaweeds. And soon after, the two gentlemen left the room once more.

"So he has really found our friend out!" cried the Zoophyte; "and he was right about the fruit too! Oh, Bookworm, Bookworm, would that I could know what *seeing* is!"

"Oh, Zoophyte, Zoophyte! I wish you would not waste your time in struggling after the unattainable! You know what *feeling* is. Well, I would tell you that *seeing* is something of the same sort as feeling, only that it is quite different. Will that do?"

"It sounds like nonsense."

"It *is* nonsense. There *can* be no answer but nonsense, if you want to understand 'really for a fact,' as you call it, powers that are above you. Explain to the rock on which you grow, what *feeling* is!"

"How could I?" said the Zoophyte; "it has no sensation."

"No more than you have sight," rejoined the Bookworm.

"That is true indeed," cried the Zoophyte. "Bookworm! I am satisfied—humbled, I must confess, but satisfied. And now I will rejoice in our position here, glory in our new master, and admire his wonderful powers, even while I cannot understand them."

"I am proud of my disciple," returned the Bookworm kindly.

"I also am one of them," murmured the Seaweed; "but tell me now, are there any other strange powers in man?"

"Several," was the Bookworm's answer; "but to be really known they must be possessed. A lower power cannot compass the full understanding of a higher. But to limit one's belief to the bounds of one's own small powers, would be to tie oneself down to the foot of a tree, and deny the existence of its upper branches."

"There are no powers beyond those that man possesses, I suppose," mused the Zoophyte.

"I am far from saying that," replied the Bookworm; "on the contrary—"

But what he would have said further no one knows, for once more the door opened, and the Naturalist, who now returned alone, spent his evening in putting by the specimens in their separate volumes on the shelves. And it was a long, long time before the Bookworm saw them again; for the volumes in which they were kept were bound in Russia leather, to the smell of which he had a particular dislike, so that he could never make his way to them for a friendly chat, and they could only meet henceforth by accident.

PROFESSIONALS

MARGARET E. FOUNTAINE, F.E.S.

"Amongst the Rhopalocera of the Philippines"

Entomologist 58 (1925): 235–39, 263–65.

When these wonderful islands were taken over by the Americans about the year 1898 a certain amount of work had been already accomplished, notably amongst the Rhopalocera,[1] but at the same time a far greater amount had been left undone, still at the present day leaving a good deal yet to do. The fauna is an exceptionally rich one, many of the different islands frequently presenting forms peculiar to themselves; and the conditions for the working of these islands are sometimes (where the Americans have established themselves) exceptionally desirable; but more often than not the entomological collector will find himself confronted with much really hard work, to be carried on under somewhat adverse circumstances. As there was, when we were there, a lot of trouble going on with the Moros,[2] on Mindanao, it appeared scarcely desirable to go there to collect, and having been told that it would be most inadvisable for us to leave the immediate vicinity of the town of Surigao to penetrate any distance into the surrounding country, where much of the fighting was in progress, I need hardly say this idea did not appeal either to Mr. Neimy or myself. We were therefore obliged to give up our visit to that island, with much regret, and confine our operations to a few localities on Luzon and the small but exceedingly interesting island of Polillo. This island lies off the east coast of Luzon, and, with the exception of a few rocks, is not in a group, but lies alone, not, however, more

1. A genus of butterflies collected and studied by Fountaine. *Ed.*
2. Members of a Muslim Malay tribe of the southern Philippines. *Ed.*

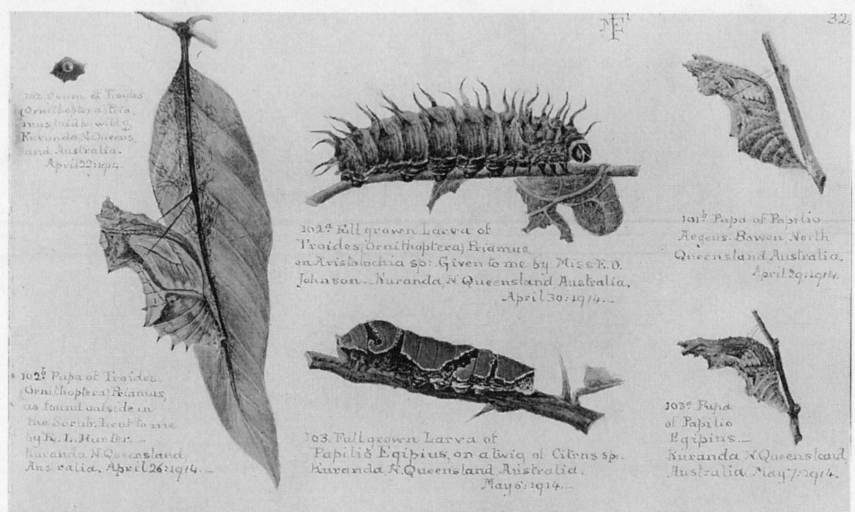

FIGURE 68 Margaret Fountaine, Lepidoptera larvae from Queensland, Australia, from manuscript notebook, vol. 2, 1910–26 (courtesy Natural History Museum, London)

than 18 miles from "the mainland" (*i.e.* the big island of Luzon) "as the crow files," but for the greater part of the year, in fact throughout the typhoon season, is practically inaccessible, except by a small coasting steamer, which plies fortnightly, back and forth, between Polillo (pueblo) and Hondagua, calling at other almost equally isolated ports *en route,* and often the voyage, supposed to occupy 14 hours, would really take 16 or 17 hours to accomplish.

Our first move after landing at Manila, on August 7th, 1923, was to go to Los Baños, acting on the excellent advice of Mr. W. Schultze, of the Bureau of Science in Manila; and at Los Baños we had the pleasure and good fortune to make the acquaintance of Dr. C. F. Baker, Dean of the Agricultural College at that place, who not only gave us much useful information regarding that immediate neighbourhood, but also enabled us later on to visit Polillo, by recommending us to a native family living on that island, who were willing to accommodate strangers.

The wet season of 1923 was still very much in progress during the first month or two while we were in Los Baños; nearly every morning would appear gloriously fine, but dark storm-clouds would soon be seen gathering over Mr. Mackling, and deluges of rain would fall every day; but conditions gradually improved, and we soon found the neighbourhood of Los Baños to be all Mr. Schultze had said of it.

However, the very best time was much later on, right in the dry season, during February and March, when butterflies, especially on the way to the Waterfall (not more than a mile or so from the Los Baños Hotel) were sufficiently in evidence to rejoice the heart of any collector.

At Baguio (4800 feet) during the month of November and early in December it was quite cold, especially at night, and there did not seem to be many butterflies about. But Antipolo (700 feet), a place about 25 kilometres from Manila, afforded quite good collecting about Christmas time. At Hondagua (on the east coast of Luzon) the country was for miles entirely given over to the cultivation of cocoa-nuts; and through Dalagang, a few stations farther down the line, was surrounded by a huge and most magnificent native jungle, the collecting there was on the whole very disappointing, affording only two or three rather good species, and very little else besides.

No doubt Polillo was far the most interesting place we visited, and also much the most difficult to work. In the immediate vicinity of the pueblo rice-fields extended for some distance, and as these were always under water and at least knee-deep in mud, the jungle beyond seemed almost unapproachable; and when we did reach it, it would only be to find that there was practically no way into it, except, perhaps, by walking along a river-bed, which though probably not more than about a foot deep in water, and with a clean sandy bottom, was scarcely conducive to making rapid progress, and never seemed to get you anywhere either. Down, or up the coast, in either direction, jungle was also accessible to a certain extent, but even this meant having to wade across the mouths of several small rivers and streams—easy enough at low tide, but when the tide was in there was nothing for it but to plunge boldly through a depth of some 2 or 3 feet of water at least, hoping to encounter no jelly-fish on the way; or trust yourself to the precarious assistance afforded by some chance boat, scooped out of the trunk of a tree, which was liable to upset at any minute, unless equipped with bamboo appendages, which rendered the chances of such a catastrophe at least much less likely (I always preferred to wade if possible). And even when at last the outskirts of these jungles were reached it again soon became very evident that there was no way into them except indeed to follow the ill-defined trail of some hunter, when you would have to creep along with considerable difficulty through thorny undergrowth, alike disastrous to clothes and nets, while whatever butterflies there were would be quite happily besporting themselves some 30 or 40 feet above where you were groping below, flying outside over the tops of the trees. However, up the coast, in a westerly direction, there was a narrow strip of jungle all the way running parallel with the coast-line, and this had a regular trail cut through it, so that it was here that we did most of our collecting.

The Dean had put us in touch with a native collector, a "wild man of the woods," who, however, spoke a Spanish dialect sufficiently well to make himself intelligible, and also to understand us; so occasionally we took Mariano with us, but for some reason, best known to himself, he invariably managed that these "personally conducted" expeditions were never productive of good results. His own methods when stalking his quarry were most interesting to watch, for to see Mariano after a butterfly was to see the primitive man hunting his prey. With no more clothing than decency demanded, he would glide with astonishing rapidity through the densest undergrowth, quite regardless of snakes, thorns, leeches or any other evils liable to be encountered under such conditions; he always kept well below the object of his chase, every movement rapid, though stealthy, and very much on the alert. He generally succeeded in capturing his "game," but always in a manner that rendered the specimen unfit for use from the vigour of his attack.

I will now proceed to give what information I can while enumerating the different species taken, which, owing to the kind and most invaluable assistance obtained at the British Museum (Nat. Hist.), I have been enabled in every instance to identify.

1. *Papilio daedalus,* Feld.—This magnificent insect occurred fairly commonly at Los Baños, and was also observed not infrequently on Polillo. It was most commonly on the wing in February and March, especially on the way to the Waterfall, near Los Baños. This butterfly is, without exception, the most rapid flier and the most shy and difficult to catch of any I have ever encountered. The only way I did at last succeed in taking some half-dozen good specimens was either by having to resort to the methods prevalent amongst the natives of using a decoy (a *modus operandi* which does not appeal to me), or, when the lovely blue-green blossoms of a rare leguminous creeper were to be found hanging gracefully over the bed of a stream, to stand quite still on a slippery rock and await results, which would probably mean that the first *daedalus* to pass that way would soon be plunging his whole head right into one of those beautiful blossoms, and become so engrossed in sipping the delicious nectar that he would for the moment be heedless of the close proximity of danger, and thus fall an easy prey to my net. But this leguminous creeper was rare, and its clusters of flowers so attractive in their appearance that no sooner would some festoon be in full bloom than you might be sure it would be plucked by the first Filipino who happened to pass that way, more especially if he found out the use it was being put to by me.

2. *P. agamemnon,* Linn.—Fairly common in most low-lying districts. The larvae were to be found, if searched for, on the fresh green leaves of the sour-sop.

3. *P. euphrates*, Feld.—Occurred rather sparingly at Los Baños; rather more abundantly on Polillo, especially in April and May, where I was fortunate enough one day to see a [female] lay two eggs on *Uvaria rufa*, and subsequently found larvae of this and of the two following species on these shrubs, which grew fairly abundantly in jungle clearings all round Polillo, in some places quite close to the pueblo. The ova were laid on the extreme edge of the large but tender leaves of the food-plant, and the young larva is of a deep cream colour when first hatched, gradually assuming the black streaks and markings usual in this class of *Papilio*, as it passes through its various moults, till in the last skin it becomes a soft willow-green, with the strongly marked lines and short spines on the thorax of a dull brown colour. The pupa is remarkable for the long projection at the upper end of it, and is entirely without the reddish markings which appear so conspicuously in the blunt pupa of *P. antiphates*, the outlines in *euphrates* being indicated by creamy yellow only.

4. *P. antiphates*, Cram.—Flew at the same time as the preceding species, but as far as my experience went, on Polillo Island only. The eggs are laid on the young shoots of *Uvaria rufa*, and the young larva is at once distinguishable from that of *euphrates* by having the indication of black markings from the very first strongly visible, even to the naked eye. It was easily found outside concealed in the very young shoots of its food-plant, unless a most evilly stinking little bug was present there in its stead. I found quite a number of them in this early stage of their development, besides ova, and also some larger caterpillars, and should no doubt have bred a long series of this as well as of the preceding species, but unfortunately it was not a great while before we were leaving Polillo, in the middle of May, that we first discovered them, and thus many that were still in the larval stage perished in consequence of my having to place them on sour-sop at Los Baños, till we had discovered there one fine shrub (only) of *Uvaria rufa*, by which time there were but few survivors left; these, however, now fed up well, one or two only preferring to remain on the sour-sop. The full-grown larva was also easily distinguishable from *euphrates*, being of a pale, dull pinkish colour, streaked and dusted over with yellowish green, the short spines on the thorax being of a brick-red, the two farthest away from the head having a spot of bright sky-blue at the base.

5. *P. gordion*, Feld.—Flew round Los Baños and on Polillo, but was never at all common anywhere. We found a few of its larvae on *Uvaria rufa* while searching that plant for those of the two preceding species.

6. *P. codrus*, Cram.—One specimen only, taken at Polillo in May. It was rather damaged, so, believing it to be a [female], I put it in a cage, supplied

with sprigs of the *Anonaceae* most likely to appeal to that class of *Papilio;* but it died in a few days, having laid nothing, and then I discovered that I had, quite unknowingly, made a prisoner of a poor [male].

7. *P. alphenor,* Cram.—Common everywhere, except in the high mountains. I bred numbers of them, either on wild or garden citrus of any description, from ova and larvae found outside, and thus got a fine lot of varieties amongst the [females]. The larva is only slightly distinct from that of *P. polytes,* but the points of difference are absolutely constant, the young larva always being much more broadly marked with white, especially on the posterior segment, while in the adult the whitish and russet-coloured bands breaking up the green both meet like a saddle over the back, whereas in *polytes* they break off suddenly on either side, the dorsal area being green throughout.

8. *P. rumanzovia,* Esch.—I caught and bred a good many of this species, including some good varieties in the [females], amongst which the form described in Seitz as *semperinus.* Haase, was much the most common, while the one which is considered to be typical was seen only at Polillo, and very rarely there; in fact I have but two specimens, having failed to capture a third, and these three were all we ever saw. The other two forms also both occurred on Polillo, but this butterfly was always much less common there than at Los Baños, where in September and October I bred quite a number of them on citrus from larvae found outside, and also from ova laid by captive [females], a very large proportion of [males] when the butterflies emerged causing me to wish we had bred many more of them, which we could easily have done. The larva in every moult differs notable from that of *P. memnon* by having all the white markings very much broader and more distinct. Fifteen ova laid by a captive [female], late in the afternoon of September 14th, hatched on September 19th, and began hanging up for pupation on October 10th, when just three weeks old, and the first to emerge (a [male]) was on October 29th, while all the other broods we had occupied approximately the same periods in passing through their early stages. The *semperinus* form in the [female] was always much the most largely represented; however, the form approaching most nearly to the [male] in colour also appeared once or twice, though all the parents had been *semperinus;* but in these bred specimens a typical one never showed up at all, nor did we ever see any in the neighbourhood of Los Baños or Pagsanjan.

9. *P. palephates,* Westw.—Occurred very sparingly near Los Baños, in fact it seemed to be most common in the immediate neighbourhood of Manila, from which place we bred a few from larvae found on *Litsea glutinosa* in Mr. Schultze's garden. This same shrub grew on the College Cam-

pus and other places near Los Baños, but I never found there but one larva, which for no obvious reason, died. However, we occasionally saw an imago, though generally in such poor condition as to be not worth netting. I tried once to obtain ova from a captive [female], but without success.

10. *P. kotzebuea,* Esch.—Very common everywhere round Los Baños. We bred numbers of them on *Aristolochia,* mostly from ova laid by captive [females], the larva, of course, being of the type usual to the class of *Aristolochia*-feeding Papilios, which in all their stages bear a far greater resemblance to the *Ornithoptera* than to any of the other Papilios, this similarity to the former being noticeable even in the flight of the imago. At Polillo I bred from a [female] which had a well-defined light-coloured patch on the upper side of her hind wings, but few of her offspring showed any inclination to perpetuate this variety, and none so markedly so as the parent.

11. *P. semperi,* Feld.—Always in my experience a very rare species. It is said to occur at Los Baños, and I believe I once saw one on the wing in that neighbourhood. On Pollilo, however, it was possible to come across it, especially during our first visit to that island in the month of January, when, two days after our arrival on December 30th. Mr. Neimy was fortunate in capturing a [female] which, not being quite perfect, we decided to put up for eggs. She soon began to lay freely on *Aristolochia tagala,* depositing in all 62 eggs, and then died. The larvae, unlike those of most rare species, were easy enough to rear, especially as this Aristolochid grew profusely all round Polillo, both near the pueblo and in the depths of the jungle; but unluckily they were just beginning to think about pupating when we were leaving the island at the end of January, and for this reason several of them failed to pupate successfully, and therefore subsequently produced deformed specimens; but in spite of this we did breed quite a number of this extremely rare insect—I believe previously unknown in its early stages. The full-grown larva is an exceedingly handsome creature, very dark velvety brown, conspicuously ornamented with a number of bright vermilion-red spines, tapering to a point tipped with black. We scarcely ever saw *semperi* on our return visit to Polillo, from mid-March to mid-May, but I chanced to find one full-grown larva outside, which eventually produced a fine [male].

12. *P. almae,* Semper.—Not very uncommon in January, but we got no opportunity to breed it, and the specimens captured were always more or less worn. It appeared again in the spring months, but was then extremely rare.

13. *Ornithoptera rhadamantus,* v. *nephereus,* Gray.—Fairly common round Los Baños and at Pagsanjan, but very much more so on Polillo in April and May. Like all members of this genus, a very strong and high flyer,

therefore rather hard to catch. However, we soon found there was no difficulty in obtaining ova from captive [females]; one especially, caught by Mr. Neimy on October 2nd, laid very freely, in fact she deposited no less than 24 eggs that same afternoon in a cage on the verandah of the hotel, well supplied with *Aristolochia tagala,* and not only was it after 5 p.m., but also raining heavily outside nearly all the time; the next day she laid 17 more and was then liberated. These ova all hatched out, and did remarkably well, though it was quite a big proposition to keep them supplied with sufficient food when in their last skins, there being so many of them, all with enormous appetites. The summing up of the life-cycle of this butterfly is as follows: The ovum hatches in 6 days, the larva takes only 17 days to feed up, and the pupal stage lasts just 3 weeks; thus from the day the egg is laid till the emergence of the perfect insect a period of 6 weeks and 2 days is occupied. The marriage flight of *O. rhadamantus* is a sight once seen never to be forgotten; I saw it on one occasion at Polillo. It was rather late in the afternoon; both butterflies were flying together at the same time, never attempting to settle at all, but soaring 30 feet above the ground, and as I watched them there hovering though the warm palpating air, in that jungle clearing, it brought to my mind those lines of Rogers:

> Child of the Sun! pursue thy rapturous flight,
> Mingle with her thou lovest, in fields of light.
> And where the flowers of Paradise unfold,
> Quaff fragrant nectar from their cups of gold.
> There shall thy wings, rich as an evening sky,
> Expand and shut with silent ecstasy.[3]
>
> Rogers.

14. *O. magellanus,* Feld.—My record of this most magnificent butterfly more or less spells failure. It was not so very rare at Polillo in January, and I secured 2 very fine [males], and one damaged specimen of the same sex. The [females] were (unfortunately) rather more easily obtained than the [males], owing, I suppose, to their less continuous flight. I say *un*fortunately, as the result was that no less than 3 [females] of this rare and valuable butterfly were brought in to me at different times by Filipino children not only so damaged as to be useless for cabinet specimens, but also so much injured that any attempts to obtain ova from them were quite in vain. Thus the misplaced energies of these children proved nothing but a nuisance, till

3. From Samuel Rogers's "To the Butterfly" (1806). *Ed.*

we gave up giving them any more centavos or accepting their captures. However, later on, when I caught 2 of this sex myself (one very worn, the other quite fresh), we still failed to procure so much as a single egg from either of them. The only possible solution to which I can attribute this failure is that maybe *magellanus,* for reasons best known to herself, does not favour *Aristolochia tagala,* but prefers some other much rarer species of the genus growing in less accessible situations. All this was during the month of January, and on returning to Polillo in the spring our anticipations were doomed to the utmost disappointment. One [male] *magellanus* only was seen on the 1st of May—a very fresh waiting and cautious stalking, finally fell a victim to my net. This lovely Ornithoptera is a gorgeous sight when seen flying in brilliant sunshine, the iridescence on the lower wings being most conspicuous.

15. *Leptocircus meges,* Link.—Very common, and in fine condition on the way to the Waterfall near Los Baños in February and March; nearly always found near water, and very fond of settling on wet, sandy places between the rocks and on the edge of streams. Rather rare in the autumn months. Not seen anywhere else but at Los Baños.

16. *Hebomoia glaucippe,* Linn.—Flew on Polillo Island and at Los Baños; a very high and rapid flyer.

ELEANOR ORMEROD

From *Eleanor Ormerod, LL.D.*

Robert Wallace, ed. New York: E. P. Dutton, 1904. 53–56; 59–67.

Note: All of the footnotes to this excerpt are from Wallace's edition. *Ed.*

[pp. 53–56]

CHAPTER XIII

Beginning the Study of Entomology, Collections of Economic Entomological Specimens, and Family Dispersal

So far as a date can be given to what has been the absorbing interest of the work of my life, the 12th of March, 1852, would be about the beginning

FIGURE 69 Eleanor Ormerod

of my real study of Entomology. I fancy I attended to it more than I knew myself, for little things come back to memory connected with specimens being brought to me to name or look at, one in particular regarding a rare locust. The date was some time before coaches were discontinued, and the usual gathering of people in those days had collected at the door of the George Hotel in Chepstow to see the coach change horses, when, to the astonishment of all, a fine rose-underwinged locust appeared amongst them. Chepstow is on a steep hill, and the "George" about half a mile from the bridge. Down the hill set off the locust, pursued by a party from the George, until it was captured at the bridge, and our family doctor conveyed it alive and uninjured to me. On my father sending it up to Oxford to Professor Daubeney as a probable curiosity, he identified it as being the first of the kind which had been taken so far west. If he gave us the name, I have forgotten it. In March I began my studies by buying my first entomological book, and I chose beetles for the subject, and Stephens's "Manual of British Beetles"[1] for my teacher. Those who know the book will understand my difficulties. It has no illustrations, glossary, nor convenient abstracts to help

1. *Manual of British Coleoptera, or Beetles,* published by Longmans, Green & Co., 1839. In Miss Ormerod's copy is a pencil note: "J. F. S., died 1853."

beginners, and, if such things existed in those days, they were not accessible to me. But I made up my mind that I was going to learn, and as *palpi, maxillæ,* and names of all the smaller parts of the insects were wholly unknown to me, I struck out a plan of my own. From time to time I got one of the very largest beetles that I could find, something that I was quite sure of, and turned it into my teacher. I carefully dissected it and matched the parts to the details of the description given by Stephens. The process was very tedious and required great care, but I got a sound foundation, and by making a kind of synopsis of the chief points of classification I got a start. To this day (1891) I have my old Stephens's Manual with my own pencil markings, that started me on my unaided course. Identification was very difficult for a long time, but I "looked out" my beetles laboriously till I thought I was sure of the name, and then, to make quite certain, I took the subject the other way forward—worked back systematically from the species till I found that there was no other kind that it could be. Killing my specimens was another difficulty. I had been told that if beetles were dropped into hot water death was instantaneous. I was not aware that it should be boiling. So into the kitchen I went with a water-beetle, which in after years I found must have been *Dytiscus marginalis*—a large water-beetle which has great powers of rapid swimming—got a tumbler of hot water, and dropped my specimen in. But to my perfect horror, instead of being killed instantaneously, it skimmed round and round on the water for perhaps a minute as if in the greatest agony. This was my second lesson; thenceforward I supplied myself with chloroform.

My first experience in the use of the microscope was gained by helping my brother William to prepare botanical specimens for examination under his microscope. I thus had useful practice early in life, 1849 (?), in the management of a good instrument. I bought my own about 1864, after my brother John's death—one of Pillischer's—a good working instrument with excellent 1-inch and ¼-inch lenses on a nose-piece. I first studied with it the hairs of different animals. I also worked preparations of teeth, showing the fluid contents when in a fresh state.

In the number of the "Gardeners' Chronicle and Agricultural Gazette" for August 1, 1868, the announcement was made that "Throughout the month of August there will be open in the Palace of Industry, in the Champs Elysées, Paris, an Exhibition which we conceive cannot fail to be of great service in extending a knowledge of the destructive or beneficial habits of various species of insects. . . . The Exhibition is organised by the 'Société d'Insectologie Agricole' under the Presidency of Dr. Boisduval, one of the

Vice-Presidents of the Horticultural Society of Paris, and under the auspices of the Minister of Agriculture, Commerce, and Public Works. The object of this Society (and consequently of the Exhibition itself) is twofold: firstly, to investigate the economy and to extend the benefits resulting from insects serviceable to mankind; and secondly, to study the habits of those species which affect our gardens, orchards, farms or forests, in order to arrest their ravages or destroy them individually."

Details were given at some length of the classes of subjects to be represented, in the hope that it might attract the attention of the Council of our own Horticultural Society to the desirability of arranging some similar exhibition, and, on the 22nd of August following, the public were informed (again in the "Gardeners' Chronicle," p. 893) that "the desideratum lately pointed out as falling within the province of the Royal Horticultural Society to supply, viz., a Collection of Insects (and their products), is now in a fair way to be made good." A short sketch was given of the plan on which it was proposed to deal with the subject, in which the "insect friends" of the horticulturist were the division to be placed first. Following these were to be "gardeners' enemies," and the plants on which they feed; next to these again, "insects beneficial or injurious to man." Negotiations on the part of the Council of the Royal Horticultural Society with the Science with the Science and Art Department resulted in the agreement that, if the Society would form the Collection, the Department would house, care for, and display it. The eminently qualified Fellows of the Society, Mr. Wilson Saunders, Mr. Andrew Murray,[2] and Mr. M. J. Berkeley, agreed to lend their best assistance in the matter, and Mr. Murray, at the request of the Council, undertook the most laborious part of the task—that of receiving, arranging, and putting in order the various specimens that might be sent from time to time. All collectors and observers who might be willing to help were requested to communicate with Mr. Murray, and without delay I availed myself of the opportunity, in pleasant anticipation of the entomological co-operation, giving a use to what had been previously somewhat desultory observation.

I was singularly well situated for the collection of ordinary kinds of injurious insects, and for the observation of their workings, as I then resided on my father's Gloucestershire property. The extent was not very great, only about 800 acres, but the nature of both the land and the cultivation afforded wonderful variety of material for commencing a collection. The wood- and

2. Secretary of the Royal Horticultural Society, who did excellent work in Economic Entomology for the Bethnal Green and South Kensington Museums. Miss Ormerod described him as a "profoundly scientific and intellectual man."

park-land included old timber trees in some instances dating back to the time of the Edwards, and also plenty of ordinary deciduous woodland and coppice. The fir plantations supplied conifer-loving forest pests; the ordinary insects of crop and garden were of course plentiful; the woodland and field pools added their quota; and the diversity in exposure from the salt pasturage by the Severn to the various growths up the face of the cliffs to about 140 feet probably had something to do also with the great variety of insect life. I had willing helpers in the agricultural labourers—when they had not made up their minds whether they would assist or not. They had always helped, for we were on very friendly terms, and some of them or their children, like myself, had been born on the estate. But, though I did not know it at the time, I heard afterwards that when I asked for such special help they held a sort of informal meeting to consult whether it should be granted. Happily they settled that I was to be helped because the rural council stated I made use of what I got. The verdict was satisfactory in practical results, but I had my own private opinion that what were sometimes called "Miss Eleanor's shillings" helped the cause of collection. From the commencement of work until my father's death, when I ceased to have command of the large area of ground, I collected and sent the results to the charge of Mr. Murray. Communication was entirely carried on by letter.

[pp. 59–67]

CHAPTER IX

Commencement and Progress of Annual Reports of Observations and Injurious Insects

In the spring of 1877 I issued a short pamphlet of seven pages, entitled "Notes for Observations of Injurious Insects,"[3] in which I suggested how much a series of observations in relation to insect ravages on food crops was to be desired; this not merely for scientific purposes, but with a view to finding means of lessening the amount of yearly loss which tells so heavily on individual growers, and also on the country at large. I pointed out shortly that many insect attacks could be remedied, if attention were directed to the subject; and also that many would probably be found, if reliable information could be procured, to be coincident with multiplication or diminution

3. Miss Ormerod had been a contributor to scientific literature for some years before this date. Writing in 1900 she says:—"My first regular paper was printed in the Journal of Linn. Soc., vol. xi., No. 56, Zoology, July 18, 1873, on *The Cutaneous Exudation of the 'Triton cristatus.'* I think it is sound and unusual!"

of insect life. On the way in which this increase and decrease were affected by surroundings, such as plants, &c., suitable for food or shelter; by agricultural conditions, such as drainage, nature of the soil and of manures; and also by the state of the weather—I gave some guiding notes, and requested information from agriculturists and entomologists, who were both practically and scientifically qualified to aid in the matter. I also added some short remarks as to the nature of the entomological observations desired; as of date, and amount of appearance of larvæ (grubs); amount of injury caused; and any other points of use and interest that might occur to the observer. And further (as some sort of assistance in the commencement of the plan of campaign) I gave a list of about eighteen of our commonest crop, fruit, and forest insects, with short descriptions in the very plainest words I could use, in most cases accompanied by illustrations.

As my name was then little before the public, although I had worked on entomology for a good many years, I requested permission of two of my scientific friends, the Rev. T. A. Preston, one of the masters of Marlborough College, and much interested in phenology (*i.e.,* observation of natural phenomena); and Mr. E. A. Fitch, Secretary of the Entomological Society, to allow me to add their names as referees. To this they kindly consented, but with the stipulation from Mr. Preston that he did not wish to co-operate further. I believe I may say with regard to Mr. Fitch such a very small amount of communication took place that it would not have been worth while to mention the matter, excepting *pro forma,* on account of the names being recorded. These were soon removed from succeeding reports as unnecessary. The pamphlet was widely circulated and the request for observations was responded to far more cordially than could have been expected. Notes regarding insect appearances, together with observations of their habits, and of practicable methods of prevention, were forwarded by observers—who were qualified both as technically scientific and practical workers—from localities scattered over the country as far north as Aberdeenshire in Scotland and south to Hants and Devonshire in England. In fact the communications were quite sufficient to show that the plan was approved of from an agricultural point of view, and might be continued hopefully. In after years I was told that it was very well received by the press. I have been greatly indebted since both to the agricultural and general press, but at the time it did not seem to me to be peculiarly warmly welcomed, nor I think was it likely to be, until it had more to say for itself. The pamphlet was not of many pages; the knowledge of the great mischief caused by insect pests, and the need of prevention of their ravages, was not spread abroad as at the present day, and I was not able at first to utilise to the best advantage the information sent as I had no working reports of my own to help me as to examples of the best methods of arrangement.[4]

From the first I had excellent contributions. Various members of our Entomological Societies were good enough to send me notes on insects to which they devoted special study, and so also were members of the Meteorological Society, regarding points of natural history, bird life, weather, &c., connected with entomological considerations, and regarding which they were special observers. Agriculturally I had good help also from other quarters, and amongst many who assisted me, I will take leave to especially give the name of the late Mr. Malcolm Dunn, the Duke of Buccleuch's superintendent at the Palace Gardens, Dalkeith, N.B. We never met, but whenever I applied to him he was unfailing in prompt and serviceable reply. As a commencement, the introductions with which he favoured me to the leading foresters and horticulturists of North Britain, were of such invaluable aid that I should be ungrateful not mention his name as of one to whom I owe a deep debt of gratitude.

In the report for the year 1881 I altered the plan of arrangement to one which so far as I can judge met all that was needed for practical as well as scientific service so conveniently that I have since adhered to it. The information was classed under headings of (*a*) farm crops, (*b*) orchard and bush fruits, and (*c*) forest trees, regarding which observations of insect attack were forwarded. These headings were arranged alphabetically, for instance: Apple, Bean, Corn and Grass, Hop, Oak, Peas, Pine, Turnip, &c., &c. Any information as to live-stock or animal insect pests was similarly placed (that is, alphabetically) amongst the other attacks, under the headings of Deer, Grouse, Horses, &c., &c., as the case might be; but beyond what was absolutely necessary, as in the case of Ox warble, I endeavoured to avoid entering on stock infestations as leading to investigations very unpleasant to myself either to make or to discuss, and very much better left in the hands of

4. To such of my readers as possess some portion only of the early series, it may be of interest to point out that the observations, up to those for 1880 inclusive, were arranged, not as afterwards, as detached papers, placed alphabetically under the heading of the names of the crops to which they referred, but under the numbers given in the successive preceding guide lists issued for the use of observers—as for instance, "6, *Anthomyia ceparum,* Onion fly;" or "25, *Abraxas grossulariata,* Magpie moth."

These were arranged numerically, from "I" onwards, all the observations on one kind of insect attack being arranged successively in a long unbroken paragraph under the selected number, together with the name of the pest. For want of better knowledge of the requisites for a readable as well as useful report, I condensed the information into as few words as possible, with few, if any, breaks in the long paragraphs, and so, until 1880, the results (excepting to technical readers) could not be considered "taking." If any of my entomological readers will turn to a very useful work, the *Forst Zoologie,* of Dr. Bernard Altum, they will see in the second division of the "Insecten" at pp. 36, 37, and again at pp. 162, 163, the difficulties that are thrown in the way of comfortably grasping the subject, by the matter being printed continuously without breaks. This, however, as well as many other things, I had then still to learn. (E.A.O.)

veterinary surgeons. Following each heading, the observations were placed which had been contributed during the season, and which appeared to be of sufficient interest to be recorded, regarding the special crop, or fruit, &c., referred to, these being given with locality and date, as far as possible in the contributor's words, and over his own name, unless by request, or for some special reason. This plan of giving the very fullest recognition possible of the source of the information, I, for three very special reasons, most strongly recommend to the consideration of all my readers not fully accustomed to practical reporting:

1. That thus the information may very often carry conviction with it by the name of some well-known agriculturist or cattle-breeder being appended.
2. That to do otherwise is a robbery of the credit of the contributor, and a false appropriation of it by the reporter, wholly unbecoming an honest worker.
3. That the full recognition is a great protection to the reporter or compiler of the reports from plagiarism of his own work. There are people who think nothing of appropriating the credit of true workers, and who absorb also rewards in the shape of salaries and official position based on their own questionable conduct.

In the year 1881 it seemed desirable to change the running heading at the top of the pages. The name of the crop, fruit, or other subject to which the paper referred was henceforward placed at the top of the left-hand page, and the name of each successive attack to it at the top of the right-hand page; as, for instance, Cabbage at the left side, and the different kinds of infestations recorded during the year which might occur to Cabbage, as Cabbage butterfly (large white), Cabbage-root fly, Cabbage moth, on the right-hand heading. At the beginning of each paper, the name of the crop, or fruit, was given in large capitals, and beneath and at the heading of each successive paper, the name of the injurious insect to be referred to, also in English, with the scientific name, and authority for the same following. The observations of contributors were inserted unbroken, so that the methods of prevention and remedy noted as successful by each observer were thus recorded in connection with the accompanying peculiarities of cultivation, soil, manure, weather, &c. The whole life-history of the insect, so far as known or accessible, was given, and sometimes, as in great attacks or in special circumstances, a "summary" of the preceding recorded information; this being, wherever possible, followed by some paragraphs or pages of "Methods of Prevention and Remedy."

In matters of phraseology, selection of the very plainest and shortest words that I could choose was part of my plan, and after the first few years I exchanged the short table of contents for a plain working index.

Illustration always appeared to me a very important part of the work, so that readers might start with the knowledge of the appearance of the insects under consideration, gained by a glance at the accompanying figure, without having the trouble of trying to form a kind of "mind picture" from the descriptions given, often very unlike the true object.[5] At first—in the small beginning—the numbers needed were also small, and I think the little stock of figure blocks with which I started, and for which I was indebted to the kind courtesy of a friend, amounted to *one dozen!* This matter, however, I set right as soon as possible by the purchase from Messrs. Blackie & Sons, of Glasgow, of electros of most of the beautiful wood engravings given in Curtis's "Farm Insects," under an agreement that the accommodation was granted on condition of my using the figures only in my own publications. Some of the illustrations I drew myself on the blocks, and as time went on, and infestations, little or not at all entered on before, required illustration, I engaged the valuable assistance of two brothers,[6] which was continued thenceforward throughout the work. It appears to me that it is hardly possible to exceed the beauty of their work, whether in characteristic representation or in precise and accurate details. I have had great pleasure in the entomological approval which has been bestowed upon it. Illustrations from other sources have of course been used, always, so far as I am aware, most carefully acknowledged; and so far as has been in my power, I have endeavoured that the illustration of each infestation should show the insect (where it was possible to do so) in each of its successive stages of life, as of the caterpillar or maggot (scientifically the *larva*); the chrysalis (*pupa*); and the perfect insect, butterfly, beetle, sawfly, &c., as the case might be. This matter is of great importance agriculturally, for how else (it may be asked) in common circumstances, excepting by a good, plain illustration, is a farmer or fruit-grower to know what the connection is between the grubs and maggots which he finds underground or on his trees and the moths or beetles which he may notice in his fields or orchards. To give a single instance, how seldom the grey, cylindrical, legless grubs of the Daddy Longlegs are known to have anything to do with the large, gnat-like, two-winged

5. This consideration induced the Editor to introduce many figures of insects into the chapters of correspondence in the present volume.

6. Messrs. Horace Knight and E. C. Knight, of the staff of Messrs. West, Newman & Co., 54, Hatton Garden, London.

flies which are to be seen floating over our grass-fields in legions where the larvæ have been destroying underground. And so the work went on, and I believe that I may say that—from the great amount of useful information contributed, together with my own co-operation in entomological verification, adding requisite details, publishing the year's communications, and distributing them to my contributors—it answered fairly the purpose for which it was set on foot. And year by year we gained knowledge till we possessed serviceable information on the main points, both of habits and means of prevention of the greater number of our really seriously injurious farm, orchard, and forest pests of Britain.

Those who wish to investigate in detail the various kinds of infestation noticed during the first twenty-two years of my observations will find them in "The General Index to my Annual Reports on Injurious Insects, 1877–1898," compiled at my request by Mr. Robert Newstead.[7] In this index the insects are arranged alphabetically under their popular and also under their scientific names, with references to the various Annual Reports in which notices of their observation are recorded, or papers given on them, and also of the pages in each paper containing information on their habits and history and means of prevention. Lists are also given of crops and plants, stock, &c., affected. The index thus affords a fair summary of the advance of our knowledge of crop infestation during the years referred to.[8]

In the year 1881 I published a digest of the information sent in up to date in an octavo volume of 323 pages, very fully illustrated, entitled "Manual of Injurious Insects, with Methods of Prevention and Remedy"; and in 1890 I followed this by a much enlarged demy-octavo second edition of 450 pages, bearing the same title. In 1898, under the title of "Handbook of Insects Injurious to Orchard and Bush Fruits, with Means of Prevention and Remedy," pp. 280, I included the special observations on fruit infestations which had been sent me. In 1900 I published a pamphlet (also illustrated) entitled "Flies Injurious to Stock" (pp. 80), giving reports of observations of life history and habits, and also of means of prevention of a few kinds of infestation. These were given as shortly as they could serviceably be dealt with, excepting in the case of the Warble fly, *Hypoderma bovis*. Into

7. Curator of the Grosvenor Museum, Chester.

8. On November 26, 1899, Miss Ormerod wrote to Mr. Newstead:—"I am delighted with our index—the more I examine it the better I like it. Some acknowledgments have come in already, and they are most pleasantly cordial. All are delighted to have such a good reference work . . . One recipient suggests the index would be more serviceable to him if he had a complete set of my reports! He absolutely enclosed a list of deficiencies, but I thought he had best buy, and only sent him that for 1896."

Other letters she wrote about the index "were on much the same lines, and one refers to the cordial letter received from the Board of Agriculture." (R.W.).

this it appeared desirable to enter more fully, it having been under my observation since the year 1884, and having been carefully written on in every detail of habits and means of prevention, as observed by my contributors and myself in this country.

Besides the above publications, I arranged, for gratuitous circulation, various four-page leaflets on our commonest farm pests. Each contained an illustration and as much information as I could manage to condense into the limited space. Among the subjects discussed were the widely destructive Wireworm and equally destructive grubs of the Daddy Longlegs or Crane-fly, the Mangold-leaf maggot, the Mustard beetle, the minute Stem eel-worm (which causes the malformed growth of cereal plants known as "tulip root" and does much harm in clover shoots), the Warble fly and the troublesome Forest fly. Our recent investigations have proved this last to be present in two other districts at least, besides the New Forest and its vicinity in Hampshire, to which previously it had been supposed to be almost limited. For the leaflet on the Warble fly, its history, and easily practicable methods of prevention and remedy, there has been such a large demand that various issues have been successively printed amounting to 170,000 copies, including 15,000 copies which the Messrs. Murray, of Aberdeen, requested permission to print at their own cost.

The original plan (or rather that which gradually formed in the first few years) of arrangement of the Annual Reports appeared to meet all requirements, so long as the requirements of the case remain unaltered. Year after year such information as had been asked for was sent, gradually completing most of the histories of our seriously injurious crop and orchard insects, but in the report for 1899 it was requisite to make some arrangement for insertion of disconnected additional observations of appearance, habits, &c., of insects, previously referred to. These I gave accordingly in an appendix under the heading of "Short Notices," not to encumber the report with repetitions that could be avoided.

In 1901, when about to publish my report of observations of the preceding year, it appeared to me that a large proportion of the new information contributed bore on points of scientific entomological interest, or on occasional appearance of little observed attacks of very little interest or use to the majority of our agriculturists and orchard growers, and quite foreign to the broad scale consideration of pests, which was the object of these reports. It seemed something more than *un*necessary to continue this work, and I, therefore, inserted the following notice in the preface of my Annual Report for 1900, thus closing the series with the closing century:—

"*But now, although with much regret, I am obliged to say that I feel the time has come for discontinuing this series of Annual Reports.* When I commenced the work in 1877, comparatively little was known of the habits and means of prevention of insects seriously injurious to our crops, and of this little a very small amount was accessible for public service, and I undertook the series of reports in the hope (so far as in my power lay) of doing something to meet both these difficulties. Firstly, by endeavouring to gain reliable information of the kind needed; and secondly, by publishing this, with all requisite additions, and especially with illustrations, at a price far below the publication expenses, so that it might be accessible to all who wished to purchase, but especially by sending a copy of each Annual Report to each contributor who had favoured me with useful information. It seemed to be but right and fair that those who kindly helped in the work should have their courtesy acknowledged to the best of my power, and I have continued the reciprocation throughout. But the work was hard; for many years for about five or six months all the time I could give to the subject was devoted to arranging the contributions of the season for the Annual Report of the year, with the addition of the best information I could procure from other sources (in every case, whether of contributors or otherwise, *fully acknowledged*). As the consultation enquiries were kept up during winter as well as summer, I found the work, carried on single-handed, at times very fatiguing. But so long as there appeared to be a call for it, I have tried to do what I could. Now, however, the necessities of the case have (as a matter of course) been gradually changing. Year after year information has been sent, gradually completing the histories of most of our worst insect pests, and now additional information is rare (as is to be expected after twenty-four years' observations) on points of great agricultural importance.

"I claim no credit to myself in the work; but those who will look over the names of the contributors, given with their information, will see how deeply indebted I am to them, and to other good friends, who have placed their experience and great knowledge at the public service. To them, and to all who have assisted me, and to some who have allowed what began as agricultural communications to ripen into valuable friendship, I offer my grateful thanks and my deep appreciation of their goodness, and I trust they will believe that if, as I well know, much of my work has not been so well done as it would have been in better qualified hands, at least I have earnestly tried to do my very best."[9]

9. Preface to "Twenty-fourth Report of Observations of Injurious Insects." By E. A. Ormerod, LL.D., p. vii.

MARIE C. STOPES

"The 'Xerophytic' Character of the Gymnosperms: Is It an Ecological Adaptation?"

New Phytologist 6 (1907): 46–50.

That the living Coniferales, almost without exception, are xerophytic[1] in their structure, is a statement of morphological and anatomical facts which are so well known as to require no illustration.

Nevertheless, the distribution of the group at the present day, though wide, is in the main coincident with areas where the rainfall is plentiful, or at least sufficient to allow less protected plants to flourish. Frequently the marked protection of the gymnosperms seems out of place and superfluous, as it appears in the lives of many species of *Abies,* the large American forest trees, and in the various species commonly found growing in a mixed deciduous forest.

The explanation of this apparent anomaly which has been offered, and is widely accepted, is that the present day Coniferales are descended from plants which had grown under conditions demanding special protection, and that many of them have retained the ancestral character in spite of the fact that they no longer need it in their individual lives. In short, that their xerophily is inherited. To quote Schimper[2] "die xerophile Structur der Coniferen eine erbliche Eigenthümlichkeit darstellt, welche den gegenwärtigen Existenzbedingungen nicht immer zu entsprechen scheint."

As the Ecologists are now showing what wonders can be worked in the life of even a single generation of xerophytic plants, one is forced to believe that there must be something much stronger than an ancient inheritance underlying the well developed, but apparently useless, xerophily of so many Gymnosperms.

Let us first see what grounds there are for assuming that it is a character depending on the environment of past ancestors. Both from the botanical evidence and judging from analogy with animals it would be extremely unlikely that many living species have come down from the Eocene to the present day, but for the sake of the argument let us look back as far as the Cretaceous.

Coniferales are recognised as playing an important part in the Tertiary

1. Adapted for growth under damp conditions. *Ed.*
2. Schimper, A. W. "Pflanzengeographie." Jena, 1898, p. 595.

floras of which we have any knowledge. The many impressions of stems and foliage which have been preserved show that their morphology was exceedingly similar to that of the recent species. Hence these Tertiary Conifers may be the ancestors which have imprinted their habit on those living to-day. But when we look at the fossil impressions of the flowering plants associated with these Gymnosperms, we find many forms resembling our Maples, Beeches and Magnolias, which do not pre-suppose any excessively xerophytic character in the environment, with others indicating a warm and even protected habitat. Further, it is known from the plants found in the Tertiary deposits of such places as Spitzbergen that similar conditions prevailed even far north, and they point to a widely spread mild climate and luxuriant flora. Also in the Cretaceous we find a similar relation between the plants, the Coniferales resembling the recent ones in their xerophytic character, but living associated with mesophilous plants which apparently flourished under no excessive drought conditions.

We are therefore left with the Cretaceous and Tertiary Gymnosperms in just the same position as with regard to the modern ones, *viz.*, that their environment offers no apparent explanation of their xerophilous structure. It is true that the earlier Gymnosperms, right back to the earliest known Palæozoic, also show xerophytic structure; but to consider that a purely *Ecological* adaptation should have been transmitted through the many changing species which lie between these ancient Gymnosperms and even their Cretaceous descendants, is a position that seems utterly untenable.

For an explanation of their structure let us turn to the living plants themselves. We see numbers of Gymnosperms choosing to live among the deciduous forest trees, though they are apparently qualified to inhabit more arid regions. The explanation of inherited xerophily does not seem to bear looking into closely. Are there any other factors apart from environment which might necessitate xerophily in a group of plants?

The great influence of the surroundings and climatic conditions on plant structure is so universally recognised that we are liable to forget the still stronger influence on its form of the specific possibilities of the plant itself.

If, as I now suggest, the Gymnospermic "xerophily" is not the result of even inherited adaptations to dry conditions, is not in fact an Ecological adaptation in the usual sense, but is a result of their histological structure (which is incapable of allowing a rapid flow of water through the wood), then the plants must set strict limits to their leaf surface and transpiration. Hence, even though they are growing with leafy deciduous trees in a mesophytic community well supplied with water, they are in individual want of a sufficient flow of water to allow of anything but what we call a typical "xerophytic" foliage.

We must, it appears, distinguish between a xerophily which is the result of environment or of a past environment, and that which is the result of the individual limitations of the plant.

Let us turn to some phylogenetic and physiological facts which bear on the special case of the Gymnosperms.

From the study of Fossils we know that the Gymnosperms are a very ancient group, immensely older than the flowering plants. We also know that they are a more primitive group, and come in systematic position between the ferns and the flowering plants (properly above the Pteridosperms). Histologically we know that they have characteristic wood, entirely consisting of tracheides, which are usually pierced by "bordered pits"; the diameter of the tracheides is less than that of the vessels of the flowering plants, and the whole structure of the wood[3] is simpler and more uniform. Gymnosperms in fact represent plants in which the woody conducting system had not reached the state of specialisation and efficiency which was afterwards attained by Angiosperms.

The work of plant physiologists has shown the relative capacities for water transportation in various woods. It is found that the amount of flow in vessels of the same length is roughly proportional to the square of the radius of the vessels. Hence the advantage in large wood vessels.

To abstract some figures from Ewart's[4] tables:—

PLANT	**Rate of Flow in centimetres per hour**	**Internal radius of larger tracheæ**	**Squares of Internal radius, × 10³**	**Relative volume passing through each trachea**
Yew	26	0.0006 cm.	36 cm.	28 cm.
B. Currant	58	0.0025″	635″	210″
Elm	50	0.0033″	1,099″	400″
Elder	155	0.0034″	1,156″	1,200″
Marrow	1,180	0.0200″	40,000″	90,000″

And when dealing with the average radius of the vessels and the maximal rate of the transpiration current we get:—

3. "Wood" is taken to cover the parenchyma, medullary rays, tracheides, vessels, and all accessory tissues of the xylem.

4. Ewart, A. J. "The Ascent of Water in Trees." Phil. Trans. Roy. Soc., 1905. B., p.52

PLANT	Rate of Transpiration Current	Average Radius of Vessels × 10^4
Yew	16 cm.	6 cm.
Apple	92″	18″
B. Currant	121″	22″
Elder	130″	24″
Pear	158″	25″

Furthermore the length of the tracheal elements has a certain influence on the flow, though not in a simple ratio. In this respect also the Gymnospermic wood stands low in the scale.

PLANT	Greatest Length of Tracheal Element in Centimetres	Average Length of Larger Elements in Centimetres
Yew	0.5	0.25
Raspberry	15.0	12.0
Pear	25	18
Elder	24	21
Apple	34	24
Wych Elm	48	36

Strasburger[5] found that in the *Taxus* and *Tsuga,* with which he experimented, in order to drive a current of water through the stem at the transpiration rate, a head of water was required several times the length of the stem, while in *Acacia* a head of 12 cm. sufficed for a piece of stem 10 cm. long.

These figures, which represent but a minute fraction of the work done on water transmission in stems, yet illustrates the fact that physiologically the wood of the Gymnosperms is not by any means so effective as that of the average Angiosperm. In this fact we may now see the fundamental explanation of the figures illustrating the amounts transpired by different trees.

The following are taken from Schimper's quotation of Von Höhnel's work, as the original was not available. The *relative* amount of water transpired from June 1st to November 30th per 100 grammes dry weight of leaf:—

Birch	...	67.9	Oak	...	28.3
Lime	...	61.5	Red Spruce	...	5.3

5. Strasburger, E. Hist. Beitr. III. "Leitungsbahnen," Jena, 1891, p. 779.

Beech	...	56.6	White Pine	...	5.8
Maple	...	46.2	Silver Fir	...	4.4
Elm	...	40.7	Austrian Pine	...	3.2

This is immediately correlated with the size of the leaves, and their protected form in the Gymnosperms, but it appears that their leaf-structure is the result of the necessity for economy in transpiration enforced by the structure (not the quantity, for the woody stems of Conifers are relatively thick for the amount of foliage-bearing branches) of their wood, which is a family character uninfluenced by environment.

As we know from the study of the evolution of plants, the potentialities of adaptation, and generic, even specific, change and evolution, do not remain indefinitely in any given group. The Gymnosperms, being so ancient a group, did not *as such* retain their adaptability till they had completed the efficiency of their wood, but stopped, and still stop short at tracheides with bordered pits, just as in their fructifications they have stopped short of evolving closed carpels. Corresponding to their lower systematic position is their less efficient woody stem, and as a necessary result of this the "xerophilous" character of their leaves, even when the plants are growing with a good water-supply.

This would explain the almost universal occurrence of xerophytic structures in the higher Gymnosperms from the Palæozoic upwards.

It appears then that the xerophytic characters of the Coniferales in very many cases are not adaptations to xerophytic conditions in their own lines, nor are they "inherited" from the remote past as vestigial characters no longer in touch with present day necessities, but are the result of physiological limitations of the type of wood in this ancient and incompletely evolved group. In other words their "xerophytism" is not ecological, but phylogenetic.

The University, Manchester. M. C. STOPES.

M. C. STOPES

From *The Study of Plant Life for Young People*

London: Alexander Moring, Ltd. 1906. 1–3; 194–96.

[pp. 1–3]

CHAPTER I

Introductory

Many people do not realise that plants are alive. This mistake is due to the fact that plants are not so noisy and quick in their ways as animals, and therefore do not attract so much attention to themselves, their lives, and their occupations.

When we look at a sunflower, surrounded by its leaves and standing still and upright in the sunlight, we do not realise at first that it is doing work; we do not connect the idea of work with such a thing of beauty, but look on it as we should on a picture or a statue. Yet all the time that plant is not only living its own life, but is doing work of a kind which animals cannot do. Its green leaves in the light are manufacturing food for the whole plant out of such simple materials that an animal could not use them at all as food. Even its beautiful flower is creating and building up the seeds which will form the sunflowers of the future. All animals directly or indirectly make use of the work done by plants in manufacturing food, for they either live on plants themselves, or eat other animals which do so.

Plants are living, and therefore require food of some kind as well as air and water in the same way, and for the same purposes as do animals. We cannot see them breathing and eating as a rule, but that is because we do not look in the right way. In our study of plants we must first learn how to see and question them properly, and when we have done this they will show themselves to us and tell us stories of their lives which are quite as interesting as any animal stories.

Now the sunflower we have just thought of is probably growing in a garden well looked after by a gardener, who sees that it gets all the light and water and just the kind of soil it needs. It is therefore protected and cared for to a certain extent, but who looks after the wild plants which manage to grow everywhere? These have not only their own life to live, but by their own efforts must overcome difficulties which are not even felt by the cultivated ones.

They succeed in a wonderful way, and some plants manage to grow under very difficult conditions, even in places where they get no water for months under a burning sun, or in forests where the overshadowing trees cut off the light, or in ponds under the water where they get no direct air. They have to do all the usual work of plants, and at the same time struggle against the hardships of their surroundings. They are like men fighting for their lives with one hand and doing a piece of work with the other.

The result of this is that they sometimes make themselves strange-looking objects, and in some plants which have had a very hard struggle it is difficult to know which part of the plant is which. Look, for example, at a Cactus, which grows in the desert; it appears to have neither stem nor leaves like an ordinary plant, and to consist merely of a roundish green mass covered with needle-like prickles. Yet when you come to study the Cactus you will find out that the thick, fleshy mass is really its stem, and the prickles its leaves which have taken on these strange shapes. By means of its unusual form the Cactus can live where our common plants would die of the dry heat in a day or two. The power plants have of changing their bodies so as to fit themselves to live under all kinds of conditions is one of the strongest proofs that they are alive.

All the parts of plants have some special life-work, just as we have legs and arms for different purposes, and every part is formed in some way to suit the needs of the plant and help it to get on well in its home.

The main thing to realise at the beginning of the study of plants is that they are living things, and therefore to try to discover the importance of the shape and arrangement of all their parts and their relation to the life of each plant as a whole.

We will begin by looking carefully for all the signs of life in them, and noting how often these are the same as those of the animals, even though the whole plant-body is so different from that of an animal.

[pp. 194–96]

CHAPTER XXXVI

Excursions and Collecting

When you plan an excursion do not take your collecting tin and a "Flora" in which to look up the names of all you find, and then imagine that you are fully prepared for a day's botanising. It is, of course, a very useful thing to learn the names of the flowers you find, because you cannot even speak of a plant if you do not know its name, but the *mere* naming is in reality the least interesting and important thing about them, as you will know if you have followed the study of plants in the way suggested in this book.

In arranging an excursion, or what is far better, a series of excursions into the country, *the most important thing to have is a plan of action.* Do not wander aimlessly in the woods, attracted from side to side by all that comes your way; choose rather some special set of things to collect and study. If there are several of you together, then each one should have a particular subject about which to make notes and collections; then afterwards all the members of the excursion party should meet together and compare their results, and show each other any interesting specimens obtained.

Each person should be provided with:—A tin collecting-box, a strong knife or digger, a note-book, pencil, and magnifying glass, some string, and a fine knife.

In case you find it difficult to decide on special things to do, here is a list of a few of the many suitable subjects which may be chosen. The list is not at all complete, but it may give you a few ideas at the beginning of your field-work.

1. In the early spring, study particularly all the plants which are flowering. Dig up complete specimens of all the smaller plants, and notice how many of them have some special means of storing food underground through the winter, such as *bulbs, tubers,* and so on. This stored food makes it possible for the flowers to bloom before the leaves have done any work, a thing which would be impossible in the case of ordinary young plants. Our "early" spring flowers are really *late* flowerers, as they bloom on the result of the food made in the previous year. Make drawings, or press a series of these.
2. Collect buds and opening buds, getting series of scales from the outer hard ones to the inner developed leaves, and press them.
3. Notice, and make sketches of, the different ways in which leaves are folded in buds: the fan-like beech, the coiled fern, and so on.
4. Collect seedlings; notice specially those of trees. Study the form of their earlier leaves, which are generally simpler than the mature ones.
5. In summer, collect as many forms as possible of full-grown leaves. Compare and classify them according to their nature and shape: those which are simple or compound, and then in more detail. Dry and mount a series of representative ones.

6. Study very particularly flowers in relation to their insect visitors. For this it is better to remain a long time in one place, so that it is not so good for a general excursion, but is splendid if you can get of for an early excursion by yourself, or with one or two companions.
7. Make collections and lists of all climbing plants, noting by what means they climb.
8. Keep a list for the whole year of the colours of the flowers as they come out, noting in general which are the most characteristic for the different seasons.
9. Collect fruits, and arrange them according to the way they scatter the seeds.
10. When the leaves are falling, notice where they break away, and what form of scars they leave. In the case of compound leaves, whether they fall off whole or in parts.
11. Collect series of plants which are growing together in different places, e.g., those in a woodland glade, those at the edge of a pond, those on a sandy hill, and so on. Dry them by pressure between sheets of paper, and mount them, noting how their forms correspond to their surroundings.
12. Go to the same spot in a wood in spring, summer, autumn, and winter; make notes and drawings of what you see each time. In the spring there will be a carpet of flowers under the bare trees, note what happens in the summer, and later on.

These suggestions are only a beginning, and special problems will arise of their own accord in connection with the work you are doing, till you find that the real excursion becomes the most interesting and important part of your work. If we go to the plants themselves and ask them to teach us, they will never fail to give us the chance of learning lessons of ever-increasing interest.

MARIE CARMICHAEL STOPES

From *Married Love: A New Contribution to the Solution of Sex Difficulties*

1918. New York: Eugenics, 1931. 25–36.

CHAPTER III

Woman's "Contrariness"

. . . Many writers, novelists, poets and dramatists have represented the uttermost tragedy of human life as due to the incomprehensible contrariness of the feminine nature. The kindly ones smile, perhaps a little patronisingly, and tell us that women are more instinctive, more childlike, less reasonable than men. The bitter ones sneer or reproach or laugh at this in women they do not understand, and which, baffling *their* intellect, appears to them to be irrational folly.

It seems strange that those who search for natural law in every province of our universe should have neglected the most vital subject, the one which concerns us all infinitely more than the naming of planets or the collecting of insects. Woman is *not* essentially capricious; some of the laws of her being might have been discovered long ago had the existence of law been suspected. But it has suited the general structure of society much better for men to shrug their shoulders and smile at women as irrational and capricious creatures, to be courted when it suited them, not to be studied.

Vaguely, perhaps, men have realised that much of the charm of life lies in the sex-*differences* between men and women; so they have snatched at the easy theory that women differ from themselves by being capricious. Moreover, by attributing to mere caprice the coldness which at times comes over the most ardent woman, man was unconsciously justifying himself for at any time coercing her to suit himself.

Circumstances have so contrived that hitherto the explorers and scientific investigators, the historians and statisticians, the poets and artists have been mostly men. Consequently woman's side of the joint life has found little or no expression. Woman, so long coerced by economic dependence, and the need for protection while she bore her children, has had to be content to mould herself to the shape desired by man wherever possible, and she has stifled her natural feelings and her own deep thoughts as they welled up.

Most women have never realised intellectually, but many have been dimly half-conscious, that woman's nature is set to rhythms over which man has no more control than he has over the tides of the sea. While the ocean can subdue and dominate man and laugh at his attempted restrictions, woman has bowed to man's desire over her body, and, regardless of its pulses, he approaches her or not as is his will. Some of her rhythms defy him—the moon-month tide of menstruation, the cycle of ten moon-months of bearing the growing child and its birth at the end of the tenth wave—these are essentials too strong to be mastered by man. But the subtler ebb and flow of woman's sex has escaped man's observation or his care.

If a swimmer comes to a sandy beach when the tide is out and the waves have receded, leaving sand where he had expected deep blue water—does he, baulked of his bathe, angrily call the sea "capricious"?

But the tenderest bridegroom finds only caprice in his bride's coldness when she yields her sacrificial body while her sex-tide is at the ebb.

There is another side to this problem, one perhaps even less considered by society. There is the tragic figure of the loving woman whose love-tide is at the highest, and whose husband does not recognise the delicate signs of her ardour. In our anæmic artificial days it often happens that the man's desire is a surface need, quickly satisfied, colourless, and lacking beauty, and that he has no knowledge of the rich complexities of love-making which an initiate of love's mysteries enjoys. To such a man his wife may indeed seem petulant, capricious, or resentful without reason.

Welling up in her are the wonderful tides, scented and enriched by the myriad experiences of the human race from its ancient days of leisure and flower-wreathed love-making, urging her to transports and to self-expressions, were the man but ready to take the first step in the initiative or to recognise and welcome it in her. Seldom dare any woman, still more seldom dare a wife, risk the blow at her heart which would be given were she to offer charming love-play to which the man did not respond. To the initiate she will be able to reveal that the tide is up by a hundred subtle signs, upon which he will seize with delight. But if her husband is blind to them there is for her nothing but silence, self-suppression, and their inevitable sequence of self-scorn, followed by resentment towards the man who places her in such a position of humiliation while talking of his "love."

So unaware of the elements of the physiological reactions of women are many modern men that the case of Mrs. G. is not exceptional. Her husband was accustomed to pet her and have relations with her frequently, but yet he never took any trouble to rouse in her the necessary preliminary feeling for mutual union. She had married as a very ignorant girl, but often vaguely felt a sense of something lacking in her husband's love. Her husband had never kissed her except on the lips and cheek, but once at the crest of the wave of her sex-tide (all unconscious that it was so) she felt a yearning to feel his head, his lips, pressed against her bosom. The sensitive interrelation between a woman's breasts and the rest of her sex-life is not only a bodily thrill, but there is a world of poetic beauty in the longing of a loving woman for the unconceived child which melts in mists of tenderness toward her lover, the soft touch of whose lips can thus rouse her mingled joy. Because she shyly asked him, Mrs. G.'s husband gave her one swift unrepeated kiss upon her bosom. He was so ignorant that he did not know that her husband's lips upon her breast melt a wife to tenderness and are one of a husband's first and surest ways to make her physically ready for complete union. In this way he inhibited her natural desire, and as he never did anything to stir it, she never had any physical pleasure in their relation. Such prudish or careless husbands, content with their own satisfaction, little know the pent-up aching, or even resentment, which may eat into a wife's heart, and ultimately may affect her whole health.

Often the man is also the victim of the purblind social customs which make sex-knowledge taboo.

It has become a tradition of our social life that the ignorance of woman about her own body and that of her future husband is a flower-like innocence. And to such an extreme is this sometimes pushed, that not seldom is a girl married unaware that married life will bring her into physical relations with her husband fundamentally different from those with her brother. When she discovers the true nature of his body, and learns the part she has to play as a wife, she may refuse utterly to agree to her husband's wishes. I know one pair of which the husband, chivalrous and loving, had to wait years before his bride recovered from the shock of the discovery of the meaning of marriage and was able to allow him a natural relation. There have been not a few brides whom the horror of the first night of marriage with a man less considerate has driven to suicide or insanity.

That girls can reach a marriageable age without some knowledge of the realities of marriage would seem incredible were it not a fact. One highly educated lady intimately known to me told me that when she was about eighteen she suffered many months of agonising apprehension that she was about to have a baby because a man had snatched a kiss from her lips at a dance. And another girl told me she also not only suffered in the same way mentally, but that this fear of the results of a mere kiss so affected her that menstruation was suppressed for months.

When girls so brought up are married it is a *rape* for the husband to insist on his "marital rights" at once. It will be difficult or impossible for such a bride ever after to experience the joys of sex-union, for such a beginning must imprint upon her consciousness the view that the man's animal nature dominates him.

In a magazine I came across a poem which vividly expresses this peculiarly feminine sorrow:

> . . . To mate with men who have no soul above
> Earth grubbing; who, the bridal night, forsooth,
> Killed sparks that rise from instinct fires of life,
> And left us frozen things, alone to fashion
> Our souls to dust, masked with the name of wife—
> Long years of youth—love years—the years of passion
> Yawning before us. So, shamming to the end,
> All shrivelled by the side of him we wed,
> Hoping that peace may riper years attend,
> Mere odalisques are we—well housed, well fed.
>
> KATHARINE NELSON.

Many men who enter marriage sincerely and tenderly may yet have some previous experience of bought "love." It is then not unlikely that they may fall into the error of explaining their wife's experiences in terms of the reactions of the prostitute. They argue that, because the prostitute showed physical excitement and pleasure in union, if the bride or wife does not do so, then she is "cold" or "undersexed." They may not realise that often all the bodily movements which the prostitute makes are studied and simulated because her client enjoys his climax best when the woman in his arms simultaneously thrills.

As Forel[1] says ("The Sexual Question," Engl. Trans. 1908): "The company of prostitutes often renders men incapable of understanding feminine psychology, for prostitutes are hardly more than automata trained for the use of male sensuality. When men look among these for the sexual psychology of woman they find only their own mirror."

Yet the simulated transports of the prostitute have their meretricious value only because they imitate something real, something which should sweep over every wife each time she and her husband unite. The key which

1. Auguste-Henri Forel (1848–1931), a Swiss entomologist and psychologist who actively lobbied for reforms that would prevent the spread of venereal diseases. *Ed.*

unlocks this electric force in his wife must reverently be sought by every husband, and its place varies in different women.

Fate is often cruel to men, too. More high-spirited young men than the world imagines strive for and keep their purity to give their brides; if such a man then marries a woman who is soiled and has lost her reverence for love, or, on the other hand, one who is so "pure" and prudish that she denies him union with her body, his noble achievement seems bitterly vain. On the other hand, it may be that after years of fighting with his hot young blood a man has given up and gone now and again for relief to prostitutes, and then later in life has met the woman who is his mate, and whom, after remorse for his soiled past, and after winning her forgiveness for it, he married. Then, unwittingly, he may make the wife suffer either by interpreting her in the light of the other women or perhaps (though this happens less frequently) by setting her absolutely apart from them. I know of a man who, after a loose life, met a woman whom he reverenced and adored. He married her, but to preserve her "purity," her difference from the others, he never consummated his marriage with her. She was strangely unhappy, for she loved him passionately and longed for children. She appeared to him to be pining "capriciously" when she became thin and neurotic.

Perhaps this man might have seen his own behaviour in a truer light had he known that some creatures simply *die* if unmated.

The idea that woman is lowered by sex-intercourse is very deeply rooted in our present society. Many sources have contributed to this mistaken idea, not the least powerful being the ascetic ideal of the early Church and the fact that man has *used* woman as his instrument so often regardless of her wishes. Women's education, therefore, and the trend of social feeling have largely been in the direction of freeing her from this, and thus mistakenly encouraging the idea that sex-life is a low, physical, and degrading necessity which a pure woman is above enjoying.

In marriage the husband has used his "marital right"[2] of intercourse

2. "Conjugal Rights," *Notes and Queries,* May 16, 1891, p. 383. "S. writes from the Probate Registry, Somerset House: 'Previous to 1733 legal proceedings were recorded in Latin, and the word then used where we now speak of *rights* was *obsequies.* For some time after the substitution of English for Latin the term *rites* was usually, if not invariably adopted; *rights* would appear to be a comparatively modern error.'"

"Mr. T. E. Paget writes (*Romeo and Juliet,* Act. V., Scene III.):

> "What cursed foot wanders this way to-night
> To cross my obsequies, and true lovers rite?

"Well may Lord Esher say he has never been able to make out what the phrase 'conjugal rights' means. The origin of the term is now clear, and a blunder, which was first made, perhaps, by a type-setter in the early part of the last century, and never exposed until now, has led to a vast amount of apprehension. Here, too, is another proof that Shakespeare was exceedingly familiar with 'legal language.'"

when *he* wished it. Both law and custom have strengthened the view that he has the right to approach his wife whenever he wishes, and that she has no wishes and no fundamental needs in the matter at all.

That woman has a rhythmic sex-tide which, if its indications were obeyed, would ensure not only her enjoyment and an accession of health and vitality, and would explode the myth of her capriciousness, seems not to be suspected. We have studied the wave-lengths of water, of sound, of light; but when will the sons and daughters of men study the sex-tide in woman and learn the laws of her Periodicity of Recurrence of desire?

POSTLUDE

This book's ultimate selection, like one of its two opening selections, "The Secret Joy," is a tribute to the versatility of the little-heralded Mary Webb. Here Webb looks at nature in one more guise—not for its inexorability, its closeness to death, or its poetry, but for its healing powers. Her "*Vis Medicatrix Naturæ*" from *The Spring of Joy* (1917) demonstrates Webb's own belief, garnered from personal experience as she tried to weather Graves' disease. "Earth," she tells us, "is not just the mother of the strong" but of all, and nature is present everywhere in the smallest of creatures and scenes. In this late piece, we return one last time to the religious dimension that so persistently marks the nature writing of Victorian and Edwardian women and that threads its way through this section. In Webb's essay, Beauty is paired with Joy and Laughter, and all three flow as gifts from some larger power.

~ MARY WEBB

From "*Vis Medicatrix Naturæ*"

The Spring of Joy: A Little Book of Healing. 1917. New York: E. P. Dutton, 1937. 1–18.

We live the life of plants, the life of animals, the life of men, and at last the life of spirits.

SIR THOMAS BROWNE

On some day of late January, when the honey-coloured west is full of soft grey cloud, when one lone minstrel thrush is chanting to the dying light, what is the thrill that shakes us? It is not only that the delicate traceries of silver birches are tenderly dark on the illumined sky, that a star springs out of it like darting quick-silver, that the music of tone and tint has echoed last April's song. It is something deeper than these. It is the sudden sense—keen and startling—of oneness with all beauty, seen and unseen. This sense is so misted over that it only comes clearly at such times. When it does come, we are in complete communion with the universal life. The winds are our playfellows; Sirius is our fellow-traveller; we are swept up into the wild heart of the wild. Then we know that we are not merely built up physically out of flower, feather and light, but are one with them in every fibre of our being.

Then only do we have our full share in the passion of life that fills all nature; then only do we possess perfect vitality. Then we are caught into the primal beauty of earth, and life flows in upon us like an eagre.[1] Life—the unknown quantity, the guarded secret—circles from an infinite ocean through all created things, and turns again to the ocean. This miracle that we eternally question and desire and adore dwells in the comet, in the heart of a bird, and the flying dust of pollen. It glows upon us from the blazing sun and from a little bush of broom, unveiled and yet mysterious, guarded only by its own light—more impenetrable than darkness.

The power of this life, if men will open their hearts to it, will heal them, will create them anew, physically and spiritually. Here is the gospel of earth, ringing with hope, like May mornings with bird-song, fresh and healthy as fields of young grain. But those who would be healed must absorb it not only into their bodies in daily food and warmth but into their minds, because its spiritual power is more intense. It is not reasonable to suppose that an essence so divine and mysterious as life can be confined to material things; therefore, if our bodies need to be in touch with it so do our minds. The joy of a spring day revives a man's spirit, reacting healthily on the bone and the blood, just as the wholesome juices of plants cleanse the body, reacting on the mind. Let us join in the abundant sacrament—for our bodies the crushed gold of harvest and ripe vine-clusters, for our souls the purple fruit of evening with its innumerable seed of stars.

We need no great gifts—the most ignorant of us can draw deep breaths of inspiration from the soil. The way is through love of beauty and reality, and through absorbed preoccupation with those signs of divinity that are like faint, miraculous footprints across the world. We need no passports in the freemasonry of earth as we do in the company of men; the only indispensable gifts are a humble mind and a receptive heart. We must go softly if we desire the butterfly's confidence; we must walk humbly if we dare to ask for an interpretation of this dream of God.

No accident of environment or circumstance need cut us off from Nature. Her spirit stirs the flowers in a town window-box, looks up from the eyes of a dog, sounds in the chirp of grimy city sparrows. From an observation hive in a London flat the bee passes out with the same dumb and unfathomable instinct that drove her from her home on Hybla of old. We may pry into her daily life, but her innermost secrets are as inviolable and as fascinating to us as they were to Virgil, watching from the beech-tree shade.

1. A sudden flood of tide in an estuary. *Ed.*

It does not matter how shut in we are. Opportunity for wide experience is of small account in this as in other things; it is depth that brings understanding and life. Dawn, seen through a sick woman's window, however narrow, pulses with the same fresh wonder as it does over the whole width of the sea. A branch of flushed wild-apple brings the same joy as the mauve trumpet-flower of the tropics. One violet is as sweet as an acre of them. And it often happens—as if by a kindly law of compensation—that those who have only one violet find the way through its narrow, purple gate into the land of God, while many who walk over dewy carpets of them do not so much as know that there is a land or a way.

The primal instincts can seldom be so dead that no pleasure or kinship wakens at the thronging of these vivid colours and mysterious sounds. Here is a kingdom of wonder and of secrecy into which we can step at will, where dwell nations whose very language is for ever unknown to us, whose laws are not our laws, yet with whom we have a bond, because we are another expression of the life that created them. Here we find beauty that takes away the breath, romance that tingles to the fingertips. We think that there is some deep meaning in it all, if we could only find it; sometimes we catch an echo of it—in a plover's cry, in the silence before a storm. So we listen, hearing a faint call from afar. It is this sense of mystery—unfading, because the veil is never lifted—that gives glory to the countryside, tenderness to atmosphere. It is this that sends one man to the wilds, another to dig a garden; that sings in a musician's brain; that inspires the pagan to build an altar and the child to make a cowslip-ball. For in each of us is implanted the triune capacity for loving his fellow and nature and the Creator of them. These loves may be latent, but they are there; and unless they are all developed we cannot reach perfect manhood or womanhood. For the complete character is that which is in communion with most sides of life—which sees, hears, and feels most—which has for its fellows the sympathy of understanding, for nature the love that is without entire comprehension, and for the mystery beyond them the inexhaustible desire which surely prophesies fulfilment somewhere.

Earth is not only the mother of the young, the strong, the magnificent, whose tried muscles and long-limbed grace are the embodiment of her physical life, in whose eager glance burns the vitality of her spirit: she is also the pitiful mother of those who have lost all; she will sing lullabies to them instead of battlesongs; she will pour her life into them through long blue days and silver nights; she will give back the mirth and beauty that have slipped through their fingers. When participation in man's keen life is denied, it is not strange if laughter dies. In the sirocco of pain it is not surprising if joy and faith are carried away. So many sit by the wayside begging, unconscious that the great Giver is continually passing down the highways and hedges of nature, where each weed is wonderful. So many are blind and hopeless, yet they have only to desire vision, and they will see that through His coming the thickets are quickened into leaf and touched with glory. Out in this world the spirit that was so desolate, lost in the strange atmosphere of physical inferiority, may once more feel the zest that he thought was gone for ever. And this zest is health: sweeping into the mind and into those recesses of being beyond the conscious self, it overflows into the body. Very often this great rush of joy, this drinking of the freshets of the divine, brings back perfect health. Even in diseases that are at present called incurable, and that are purely physical, no one will deny the immense alleviation resulting from this new life. It is possible that, as the spiritual ties between man and Nature grow stronger, all disease may vanish before the vitality that will stream into us so swiftly, so easily, because it will not be confined to one channel. A man who holds direct intercourse with the cosmic life through his heart and mind knows a glad comradeship with cloud and tree; there dwells with him a consciousness of surrounding splendour—of swift currents, marvel underfoot and overhead; he has a purpose in waking each morning, a reason for existing—he clings to the beauty of earth as to a garment, and he feels that the wearer of the garment is God.

Beauty and Joy and Laughter are necessities of our being, and nature brims with them. There are some things that always bring joy—a ripple of song in winter, the blue flash of a kingfisher down-stream, a subtle scent that startles and waylays. The coming of spring brings it—the first crocus pricking up, dawn a moment earlier day by day, the mist of green on honeysuckle hedges in February, the early arabis, spicily warm, with the bees' hum about it. The flawless days of May bring it—when big white clouds sail leisurely over the sky, when the 'burning bush' is in the height of its beauty, and white lilac is out, and purple lilac is breaking from the bud, and chestnut spires are lengthening, and the hawthorn will not be long. Out in the fresh, green world, where thrushes sing so madly, the sweets of the morning are waiting to be gathered—more than enough for all, low at our feet, higher than we can reach, wide enough even for the travelling soul. Joy rushes in with the rain-washed air, when you fling the window wide to the dawn and lean out into the clear purity before the light, listening to the early 'chuck-chuck' of the blackbird, watching the pulse of colour beat higher in the east. Joy is your talisman, when you slip out from the sleeping house, down wet and gleaming paths into the fields, where dense canopies of cobwebs are lightly swung from blade to blade of grass. Then the air is full of wings; birds fly in and out of the trees, scattering showers of raindrops as they dash from a leafy chestnut or disappear among the inner fastnesses of a fir. Pinions of dark and pinions of day share the sky, and over all are the brooding wings of unknown presences. The east burns; the hearts of the birds flame into music; the wild singing rises in a swelling rhythm until, as the first long line of light creeps across the meadows, the surging chorus seems to shake the treetops.

Laughter need not be lost to those that are cut off from their fellows. The little creatures of earth are the court jesters of all that dwell in the hall of sorrow. And although more insight and love are needed to enjoy their subtle humour than to enjoy our own, we have an ample reward of unfailing and spontaneous laughter. As vicarious grief is the keenest of all, so is vicarious laughter. Anyone who has watched the farcical solemnities of a rookery, the carefully thought-out inanities of wagtails, the drunken decorum of bees in full honey-flow, will not mind being cut off from human gatherings, where the laughter is sometimes a little mirthless. Anyone who has pondered on the ways of the meadow-ant—that influential dairy-farmer, with her prosperous herds of aphides, cared for with the same transparently self-interested devotion as the cottager's pig; and on the mind of the aphis—which allows itself to be milked and driven with such cowlike placidity; and on the hill-ants—who surreptitiously milk each other's cows—need never be dull.

There are many to whom all beauty seems denied; they hunger for it dumbly, unconsciously. Is their life to be a stricken tree, colourless and silent? Surely not. It may be all illumined, like a sombre pine at the advent of wood-pigeons—when there are low, contented croonings instead of silence; soft, iridescent breasts against the harsh spines; widespread opal wings irradiating the tree. The flawless forms and colours of nature are an especial consolation to those who are oppressed by that dark tragedy, deformity of body or unloveliness of face. How deep is the desolation, when a sad soul looks out anxiously, through eyes that cannot reflect its beauty, watching for an answering smile, and meeting only a look of swiftly concealed repulsion! Startled and ill at ease in the ruinous mortal dwelling, reminded of it continually, this soul leads a life of torture. I saw one of these look from her windows and weep bitterly, finding no comfort. Then a voice came in the long sigh of the dawn breeze:

'I know, inhabitant of eternity, how strait and comfortless your home is. Go out into my garden and forget. The skies are clear; see where I lead out my sidereal flocks! The tall young larches are dreaming of green; there is moonlight in the primrose woods. There is a fit dwelling for you; go, and be at peace.'

She rose and went, and her laugh came back on the wind. The leaves do not hesitate to finger and kiss any face, however marred, that looks up into their dwelling. No distortion of body frightens the birds, if the heart within loves them.

One flower of germander speedwell may be the magic robe that clothes us with the beauty of the earth. As the maiden found her bridal garment in the fairy nut, so we may find in the folded speedwell-bud glimmering raiment to cover our homespun. It has the same strength of structure, wonder of tint and mystery of shadow as all natural things. Awakened by its minute perfection, the mind travels softly away through chequered woods, over the swinging sea, to mountains gleaming like a medieval paradise, forests of sumach, lakes of pink and blue lilies. Returning as from a trance, weary with splendour, it realizes that nature's beauty can never be perfectly grasped. Yet, since in essence it is the same wherever a blade of grass appears or a bird's shadow passes over; since the fact of seeing it, in whatever degree, is the precious thing—let us go out along the lovely ways that lead from our doors into the heart of enchantment. Ceasing for a time to question and strive, let us dare to be merely receptive—stepping lightly over the dewy meadows, brushing no blue dust from the butterfly's wing. Then, if life is suddenly simplified by the removal of all that we hold most dear, we shall know the way to other things, not less precious. We shall know of long, green vistas, carpeted with speedwell, ascending to a place of comfort, and the blue butterfly will lead us into peace.

These three—Joy, Laughter, and Beauty—are the broadest riverways down which may flow the essential life which itself is health and youth—beyond thought, beyond time, a sea that fills eternity—yet nearer than the air we breathe, immanent in the humblest creature, making material things transparent as a beech-leaf in the sun. And because those who most need its influx have only the least of earth's graces to watch, this book is concerned with muted skies, minute miracles, songs of the night, and the proud humility of the germ that holds in its littleness the Lord of Immortality.

Chronology

Date	Work in Anthology	Other Literary/ Artistic Works	Events of Significance to British History and Politics	Events in Women's History and Feminist Politics[1]	Events of Significance to the History of Science, Technology, and Medicine
					Invention of the power loom
1786	Sarah Trimmer, *Fabulous Histories*				
1789		Jeremy Bentham, *Introduction to the Principles of Morals;* William Blake, *Songs of Innocence*	French Revolution		
1791		Thomas Paine, *The Rights of Man;* James Boswell, *Life of Johnson*		Olympe de Gouges, *Declaration of the Rights of Women*	
1792				Mary Wollstonecraft, *A Vindication of the Rights of Women*	Coal gas first used for lighting
1793		Maria Edgeworth, *Letters to Literary Ladies*			Erasmus Darwin, *Zoönomia*
1794		William Blake, *Songs of Experience*			
1795			Methodist secession from Church of England; Speenhamland system of outdoor relief introduced		
1796		Fanny Burney, *Camilla*			Jenner develops smallpox vaccine

1. The editor is indebted to Kristin Olsen's *Chronology of Women's History* (Westport, CT: Greenwood Press, 1994) for much of the information found in this column.

1797					Buffon's *Natural History* translated into English (1797–1807)
1798	Dorothy Wordsworth, *Alfoxden Journal*	William Wordsworth and Samuel Taylor Coleridge, *Lyrical Ballads;* Thomas Malthus, *Essay on . . . Population*			
1799			Combination Acts		Discovery of nitrous oxide, first effective anesthetic; mammoth discovered in Siberia
1801			Union with Ireland		
1802					William Paley, *Natural Theology*
1803		Mary Hay, six-volume *Dictionary of Female Biography*		Abortion made criminal in England	Erasmus Darwin, *The Temple of Nature*
1805			Battle of Trafalgar		
1806		Margaret Bryan, *Lectures on Natural Philosophy*			
1811		Jane Austen, *Sense and Sensibility*	Luddite riots		Marry Anning discovers the first complete ichthyosaur skeleton
1812		Lord Byron, "Childe Harold's Pilgrimage," cantos I and II			

Date	Work in Anthology	Other Literary/ Artistic Works	Events of Significance to British History and Politics	Events in Women's History and Feminist Politics	Events of Significance to the History of Science, Technology, and Medicine
1813		Jane Austen, *Pride and Prejudice;* Percy Bysshe Shelley, "Queen Mab"		English Lady Hester Stanhope journeys with a Bedouin tribe through the desert to Palmyra	
1814		Jane Austen, *Mansfield Park;* Sir Walter Scott, *Waverley;* Lord Byron, "The Corsair"			
1815			Battle of Waterloo; Congress of Vienna; Corn Laws passed	German physician Josepha Siebold becomes the first woman in Germany to earn a doctorate in obstetrics	
1816		Jane Austen, *Emma;* Sir Walter Scott, *The Antiquary;* Lord Byron, "Childe Harold's Pilgrimage," canto III			
1817		Samuel Taylor Coleridge, *Biographia Literaria;* Sir Walter Scott, *Rob Roy*			
1818		Jane Austen, *Northanger Abbey, Persuasion;* Lord Byron, "Childe Harold's Pilgrimage," canto IV; Mary Shelley, *Frankenstein*			

1819	Jane Haldimand Marcet, *Conversations on Natural Philosophy*	Sir Walter Scott, *Ivanhoe;* Lord Byron, *Don Juan,* 1819–24	Peterloo massacre	German obstetrician Charlotte Siebold (daughter of Josepha) assists at the birth of Queen Victoria	
1821		Sir Walter Scott, *Kenilworth*			
1823				In Britain, *The King vs. the Inhabitants of St. Faith,* determines that a married woman may legally keep her maiden name	
1824		James Hogg, *Confessions of a Justified Sinner*	Repeal of Combination Acts; founding of Royal Society for the Prevention of Cruelty to Animals		
1826	Mary Russell Mitford, *Our Village: Sketches of Rural Character and Scenery*	Benjamin Disraeli, *Vivian Grey*			
1827					Discovery of the mammalian ovum
1828	Mary Sherwood, *Saffrona and Her Cat Muff*				Mary Anning discovers a pterodactyl skeleton

Date	Work in Anthology	Other Literary/ Artistic Works	Events of Significance to British History and Politics	Events in Women's History and Feminist Politics	Events of Significance to the History of Science, Technology, and Medicine
1829			Catholic Emancipation Act	Suttee banned in British India; in America "petticoat war" causes a rift between U.S. president Andrew Jackson and vice president John Calhoun	Development of Braille
1830		Alfred Lord Tennyson, *Poems, Chiefly Lyrical*	George III dies; William IV succeeds; first major cholera epidemic (1830–1832)		Charles Lyell, *Principles of Geology, I;* Faraday discovers electromagnetic induction
1831					Darwin begins voyage on *Beagle*
1832			First Reform Bill		
1833		Thomas Carlyle, *Sartor Resartus*	Abolition of slavery throughout the empire; Factory Act; beginning of Oxford Movement	Oberlin College accepts women students	
1834	Mary Somerville, *On the Connexion of the Physical Sciences;* Mary Howitt, "The Dor-Hawk," "The Cry of the Suffering Creatures"		New Poor Law; Robert Peel's first government	Part of the New Poor Law makes it illegal for unwed mothers to sue the fathers of their children for support; Marie Tussaud founds her wax museum	First photographs produced by Fox Talbot; Babbage invents first computer
1836	Emily Brontë, "High Waving Heather"	Dickens, *Sketches by Boz, Pickwick Papers*			Botanical Society founded

1837	Emily Shore, "Golden-Crested Wren," "Account of a Young Cuckoo"	Dickens, *Oliver Twist*	William IV dies; succeeded by Victoria		Telegraph
1838	Elizabeth Gould, letter to her mother		Anti–Corn Law League established; People's Charter drafted		Morse code
1839		Thomas Carlyle, *Chartism*	Chartist riots; Eglinton tournament		Daguerreotype process discovered
1840	Jane Loudon, *The Young Naturalist*	Charles Dickens, *Old Curiosity Shop*	Queen Victoria marries Prince Albert		William Whewell, *Philosophy of Inductive Sciences;* John Gould, *Birds of Australia* (1840–48)
1841		Charles Dickens, *Barnaby Rudge; Punch* founded	Peel's second government		Chemical Society founded
1842			Mudie's Circulating Library founded	Ashley's Act (women and children in mines)	Ether used in a minor operation
1843	Anne Brontë, "The Captive Dove"; Anna Atkins, *British Algae;* Sarah Bowdich Lee, *Taxidermy*	Thomas Carlyle, *Past and Present;* John Ruskin, *Modern Painters;* Charles Dickens, *A Christmas Carol*	Wordsworth made poet laureate		
1844		Benjamin Disraeli, *Coningsby;* Harriet Martineau, *Life in the Sickroom*	John Henry Newman converts to Roman Catholicism	Factory Act (women and children in factories)	Robert Chambers, *Vestiges of the Natural History of Creation;* Charles Darwin, *Voyage of the H.M.S. Beagle*

Date	Work in Anthology	Other Literary/ Artistic Works	Events of Significance to British History and Politics	Events in Women's History and Feminist Politics	Events of Significance to the History of Science, Technology, and Medicine
1845	Jane Loudon, *A Lady's Country Companion*		Potato famine		
1846		George Eliot, translation of Strauss's *The Life of Jesus*	Repeal of Corn Laws; free trade triumphs		Railway boom begins
1847	Anne Brontë, *Agnes Grey*	Charlotte Brontë, *Jane Eyre;* Emily Brontë, *Wuthering Heights;* Alfred Lord Tennyson, *The Princess*			Chloroform first used in operating room
1848	Cecil Frances Alexander, "All things bright and beauteous"	Anne Brontë, *Tenant of Wildfell Hall;* Elizabeth Gaskell, *Mary Barton;* William Makepeace Thackeray, *Pendennis;* Karl Marx and Friedrich Engels, *The Communist Manifesto*	Founding of the Pre-Raphaelite Brotherhood; revolutions in Europe; Public Health Act	Queen's College (for women) founded in London; Seneca Falls Women's Rights Convention in America	Mary Somerville, *Physical Geography;* Alexander von Humboldt, *Kosmos*
1849		Charlotte Brontë, *Shirley;* Charles Dickens, *David Copperfield;* Dante Gabriel Rossetti paints *Girlhood of Mary Virgin*		Elizabeth Blackwell becomes the first American woman MD; Bedford College for Women founded	

1850	Anne Pratt, *Chapters on the Common Things of the Sea-side*	Alfred Lord Tennyson, *In Memoriam;* William Wordsworth, *The Prelude;* Nathaniel Hawthorne, *The Scarlet Letter;* Elizabeth Barrett Browning, *Sonnets from the Portuguese;* Dante Gabriel Rossetti founds *The Germ;* John Millais paints *Christ in the House of His Parents*	Wordsworth dies; Tennyson made poet laureate; restoration of Roman Catholic hierarchy in England; Public Libraries Act		Gasoline refinement process; Oxford institutes degrees in science (Cambridge, 1851)
1851		Herman Melville, *Moby Dick;* John Ruskin, *Pre-Raphaelitism, Stones of Venice*	Great Exhibition at Crystal Palace; census reveals that half of British population lives in towns	Women's Suffrage Petition presented to the House of Lords; Second Women's Rights Convention, where Sojourner Truth gives her "Ain't I a Woman?" speech	Singer introduces the sewing machine; natural sciences tripos begins at Cambridge
1852	Louisa Anne Meredith, *My Home in Tasmania*	Charles Dickens, *Bleak House;* William Makepeace Thackeray, *The History of Henry Esmond;* Harriet Beecher Stowe, *Uncle Tom's Cabin;* Florence Nightingale, *Cassandra;* John Henry Newman, *The Idea of a University*	Duke of Wellington dies		Spencer coins term "evolution"

Date	Work in Anthology	Other Literary/ Artistic Works	Events of Significance to British History and Politics	Events in Women's History and Feminist Politics	Events of Significance to the History of Science, Technology, and Medicine
1853		Charlotte Brontë, *Villette*		Queen Victoria given chloroform during childbirth	Photographic Society founded; Joseph Hooker, *Flora Novae Zelandiae*
1854		Charles Dickens, *Hard Times;* Thoreau, *Walden*	London Workingmen's College founded; Crimean War	Elizabeth Cady Stanton founds NY Suffrage Society	Bessemer invents steel converter
1855	Margaret Gatty, "Training and Restraining"; Margaret Gatty, "Knowledge Not the Limit of Belief"	Elizabeth Gaskell, *North and South;* Whitman, *Leaves of Grass;* Henry Wadsworth Longfellow, *Hiawatha;* Robert Browning, *Men and Women*	Palmerston's first government; newspaper tax abolished		Livingstone discovers Victoria Falls
1857		Elizabeth Barrett Browning, *Aurora Leigh*	Indian Mutiny; Second Opium War	Matrimonial Causes Act	Neanderthal man discovered; Science Museum established; Louis Agasiz, *Essay on Classification*
1858		William Morris, "Defense of Guenevere"		Elizabeth Blackwell placed on British Medical Register	
1859		Wilkie Collins, *Woman in White;* Charles Dickens, *A Tale of Two Cites;* George Eliot, *Adam Bede;* Alfred Lord Tennyson, *Idylls of*	Palmerston's second government	Society for Promoting the Employment of Women founded	Charles Darwin, *The Origin of Species;* first oil well drilled in U.S.

		the King (first parts); Samuel Smiles, *Self-Help*			
1860		Charles Dickens, *Great Expectations;* John Ruskin, *Unto this Last;* George Eliot, *The Mill on the Floss;* Nathaniel Hawthorne, *The Marble Faun*	Food and Drugs Act		Huxley-Wilberforce debate at Oxford; source of the Nile discovered
1861		George Eliot, *Silas Marner*	Prince Albert dies; American Civil War begins	Isabella Beeton, *Beeton's Book of Household Management*	The ovum is discovered to be a generative cell
1862	Jemima Blackburn, *Birds Drawn from Nature*	Christina Rossetti, *Goblin Market and Other Poems;* Mary Elizabeth Braddon, *Lady Audley's Secret;* Victor Hugo, *Les Miserables;* George Eliot, *Romola*		U.S. bans polygamy; Frances Power Cobbe urges university education and examinations for women at the Association for the Promotion of Social Science	
1863	Margaret Gatty, *British Sea-weeds*	Charles Kingsley, *Water-Babies;* D. G. Rossetti paints *Beata Beatrix*	John Stuart Mill, *Utilitarianism*		Thomas Henry Huxley, *Man's Place in Nature*
1864		Charles Dickens, *Our Mutual Friend;* John Henry Newman, *Apologia Pro Vita Sua;* Elizabeth Gaskell, *Wives and Daughters;* Richard Wagner composes *Tristan and Isolde*	Schools inquiry mission (Taunton Commission)	First of Contagious Diseases Acts	Invention of pasteurization

Date	Work in Anthology	Other Literary/ Artistic Works	Events of Significance to British History and Politics	Events in Women's History and Feminist Politics	Events of Significance to the History of Science, Technology, and Medicine
1865	Harriet Martineau, *Our Farm of Two Acres*	Matthew Arnold, *Essays in Criticism;* Lewis Carroll, *Alice's Adventures in Wonderland;* John Ruskin, *Sesame and Lilies;* Algernon Charles Swinburne, *Atalanta in Calydon*		University of Zurich is the first European university to admit women; Elizabeth Garrett receives the licentiate of the Society of Apothecaries	Antiseptic surgery (Lister); transatlantic cable
1866		John Ruskin, *Crown of Wild Olive*	Hyde Park riots over franchise	1,498 women establish a committee to legalize women's suffrage in Britain and present Britain's first women's, suffrage petition to Parliament through J. S. Mill	Ernst Haeckel, *Generelle Morphologie der Organismen*
1867	E. A. Maling, *Song Birds and How to Keep Them*	Karl Marx, *Das Kapital,* vol. 1	Second Reform Bill; Dominion of Canada Act; Fenian movement revives in Ireland		Typewriter invented
1868	Lydia Becker, "Is There Any Specific Distinction Between Male and Female Intellect?"	Robert Browning, *The Ring and the Book;* Wilkie Collins, *The Moonstone*	Abolition of public executions; Disraeli's first government (Feb.); W. E. Gladstone's first government (Dec.)	Susan B. Anthony begins publishing *The Revolution;* the term "Shrieking Sisterhood" is coined by British journalist Eliza Lynn Linton	

1869	Eliza Cook, *The Poetical Works;* Lydia Becker, "Study of Science by Women"	John Stuart Mill, *On the Subjection of Women;* Matthew Arnold, *Culture and Anarchy;* Louisa May Alcott, *Little Women*	Opening of the Suez Canal; Metaphysical Society founded	Girton College, Cambridge, established for women; Women's "Manifesto" (for repeal of Contagious Diseases Acts); first female medical students enter the University of Edinburgh	Mendeleev produces the periodic table
1870		Charles Dickens, *The Mystery of Edwin Drood*	Irish Land Act; Franco-Prussian War; Forster's Education Act	Married Women's Property Act; 251 women, including Josephine Butler, Harriet Martineau, and Florence Nightingale, protest the Contagious Diseases Act	First Caesarean operation performed; Devonshire Commission on Scientific Education; Anthropological Institute formed
1871		George Eliot, *Middlemarch;* Anthony Trollope, *The Eustace Diamonds*	Trade unions legalized; religious tests for university teachers abolished; civil service exams instituted	Newnham College opened (as Merton Hall)	Charles Darwin, *The Descent of Man;* John Tyndall, *Fragments of Science*
1872	Christina Rossetti, *Sing-Song;* Jemima Blackburn, letter to *Nature*	Friedrich Nietzsche, *The Birth of Tragedy*	Secret ballot adopted	New Hospital for Women founded; Girl's Public Day School founded	Edison perfects electric telegraph; Charles Darwin, *The Expression of Emotions in Man and Animals*

Date	Work in Anthology	Other Literary/ Artistic Works	Events of Significance to British History and Politics	Events in Women's History and Feminist Politics	Events of Significance to the History of Science, Technology, and Medicine
1873		Anthony Trollope, *Phineas Redux;* Leo Tolstoy, *Anna Karenina*	Gladstone resigns after defeat of Irish Universities Bill; agricultural depression	Elizabeth Garrett Anderson becomes the first female member of the British Medical Association	Cavendish Laboratory set up in Cambridge
1874	Emma Wallington, "The Physical and Intellectual Capacities of Woman Equal to Those of Men"	Thomas Hardy, *Far From the Madding Crowd*	Disraeli's second government	London School of Medicine for Women opened	
1875	Isabella Bird, *Six Months in the Sandwich Islands;* Annie Hassard, *Floral Decorations for the Dwelling House*	Thomas Hardy, *The Hand of Ethelberta;* Anthony Trollope, *The Prime Minister*	Founding of the Theosophical Society; Artisans' Dwelling Act (public housing)	Annie Besant is arrested for distributing tracts on birth control	Alfred Russel Wallace, *Natural Selection*
1876	Nina Mazuchelli, *The Indian Alps and How We Crossed Them*	George Eliot, *Daniel Deronda*	Victoria proclaimed Empress of India; Victoria Street Society (antivivisection) founded	Parliament allows English universities to grant medical degrees to women	Bell invents telephone; invention of carpet sweeper
1877	Anna Sewell, *Black Beauty;* Octavia Hill, *Our Common Land and Other Short Essays*		Confederation of British and Boer States in South Africa; Society for the Protection of Ancient Buildings founded		Edison invents the phonograph

1878		Thomas Hardy, *The Return of the Native;* William Gilbert and Arthur Sullivan, *H.M.S. Pinafore*	Ruskin-Whistler libel trial; Salvation Army founded	University of London approves all degrees open to women	Invention of the microphone
1879	Isabella Bird, *A Lady's Life in the Rocky Mountains;* Arabella Buckley, *Fairy-land of Science*	George Meredith, *The Egoist;* Henry James, *Daisy Miller;* Henrik Ibsen, *A Doll's House;* Gilbert and Sullivan, *Pirates of Penzance*	Zulu War	First women's colleges at Oxford (Lady Margaret Hall and Somerville)	Edison invents the incandescent lamp
1880	Arabella Buckley, *Life and Her Children*	Thomas Hardy, *The Trumpet Major;* Henry James, *The Portrait of a Lady*	Gladstone's second government; First Boer War	Compulsory elementary education	
1881	Marianne North's Gallery opens at Kew	Henry George, *Progress and Poverty*	Irish Coercion Acts		British Museum of Natural History opens in South Kensington (moved from Bloomsbury)
1882	Vernon Lee, "Vivisection"	Algernon Charles Swinburne, *Tristram of Lyonesse;* Robert Louis Stevenson, *Treasure Island*	Triple Alliance (Germany, Austria, Italy)	Aletta Jacobs, Holland's first female physician, opens the world's first birth control clinic in Amsterdam; Married Women's Property Act	Tuberculosis bacillus isolated; invention of the electric iron
1883	Anna Kingsford, *Spiritual Therapeutics;* Arabella Buckley, *Winners in Life's Race*	Mark Twain, *Life on the Mississippi*	Britain occupies Egypt		

Date	Work in Anthology	Other Literary/ Artistic Works	Events of Significance to British History and Politics	Events in Women's History and Feminist Politics	Events of Significance to the History of Science, Technology, and Medicine
1884	Octavia Hill, "Colour, Space, and Music for the People"	Sarah Orne Jewett, *A Country Doctor;* George Bernard Shaw, *An Unsocial Socialist*	Fabian Society founded; Third Reform Bill; National Socialist League founded		
1885		Gilbert and Sullivan, *The Mikado*	Fall of Khartoum; death of Charles Gordon	Britain raises the age of consent for girls from 13 to 16	Daimler invents first automobile with internal-combustion engine; Pasteur develops hydrophobia vaccine
1886	Sarah Orne Jewett, *"A White Heron" and Other Stories*	Thomas Hardy, *The Mayor of Casterbridge, The Woodlanders;* Robert Louis Stevenson, *Dr. Jekyll and Mr. Hyde*	Gladstone's third government; First Irish Home Rule Bill; Liberal Party splits	Physician Sofia Jex-Blake establishes the Edinburgh School of Medicine for Women; repeal of Contagious Diseases Acts	American Josephine Cochrane invents first dishwashing machine
1887	May Kendall, *Dreams to Sell*	Arthur Conan Doyle, *A Study in Scarlet*	Bloody Sunday (socialist demonstration); Queen's golden jubilee		
1888	A. Mary F. Robinson, "Darwinism"	Oscar Wilde, *The Happy Prince and Other Tales*			Hertz produces radio waves; Kodak box camera invented
1889	Frances Power Cobbe, "Science in Excelsis"; Amy Levy, "To Vernon Lee"; Mathilde Blind, "On a Forsaken Lark's Nest"		London dock strike; British South Africa company chartered; Society for the Protection of Birds founded		

1890	Annie Martin, *Home Life on an Ostrich Farm;* Florence Dixie, *Gloriana;* Alice Bodington, *Studies in Evolution and Biology*	William James, *Principles of Psychology;* James McNeill Whistler, *The Gentle Art of Making Enemies;* Arthur Conan Doyle, *The Sign of Four;* Emily Dickinson, post-humous *Poems;* Founding of the Kelmscott Press			Invention of the electric stove; first underground railway (London)
1891	Emily Shore, journal issued by her sisters	Thomas Hardy, *Tess of the D'Urbervilles;* Oscar Wilde, *The Picture of Dorian Gray;* William Morris, *News From Nowhere*		In Britain, husbands can no longer legally force their wives to have sexual relations	
1892	Florence Dixie, "The Horrors of Sport"; Eliza Brightwen, *More About Wild Nature;* Mona Caird, "A Defence of the So-called 'Wild Women'"; Marianne North, *Recollections of a Happy Life*	W. B. Yeats, *The Countess Cathleen;* Arthur Conan Doyle, *The Adventures of Sherlock Holmes*	Gladstone's fourth government	Physical education director of Smith College in Massachu-setts, Senda Berenson, organizes the first women's basketball game	Invention of diesel fuel
1893	Mrs. R. H. Tyacke, *How I Shot My Bears;* Michael Field, "Noon," "Cyclamens"		Second Irish Home Rule Bill	New Zealand becomes the first nation to grant women the vote; Mary Kingsley travels to Africa	

Date	Work in Anthology	Other Literary/ Artistic Works	Events of Significance to British History and Politics	Events in Women's History and Feminist Politics	Events of Significance to the History of Science, Technology, and Medicine
1894	George Egerton, "A Cross Line"	*The Yellow Book* founded; Rudyard Kipling, *The Jungle Book;* Oscar Wilde, *Salome*			
1895	Eliza Brightwen, *Inmates of My House and Garden;* Jemima Blackburn, *Birds from Moidart and Elsewhere;* Ellis Ethelmer, *Baby Buds*	H. G. Wells, *The Time Machine*		Lilian Murray becomes the first woman dentist in the UK	Discovery of X-rays
1896		Thomas Hardy, *Jude the Obscure; Kelmscott Chaucer* printed by William Morris	Sudan conquered; *Daily Mail* founded		Wireless telegraph
1897	Mary Kingsley, "Fishing in West Africa"		Opening of the Tate Gallery; Queen's diamond jubilee		
1898	Alice Dew-Smith, *Tom Tug and Others: Sketches in a Domestic Menagerie;* Vernon Lee, "Among the Marble Mountains"				The Curies discover radium

1899	Winifred, Duchess of Portland, “Protection of Bird and Animal Life”; Margaretta Lemon, “Dress in Relation to Animal Life”; Miss White, “The Training of Women as Gardeners”	H. G. Wells, *The War of the Worlds;* Oscar Wilde, *The Ballad of Reading Gaol;* Hardy, *Wessex Poems*	Second Boer War	International Congress of Women	Invention of aspirin
1900	Isabel Savory, *A Sportswoman in India*	Sigmund Freud, *The Interpretation of Dreams;* Conrad, *Lord Jim*	Commonwealth of Australia Act		Development of quantum theory
1901	Florence Dixie, “With Nature”; Alice Meynell, “A Dead Harvest: In Kensington Gardens”	Rudyard Kipling, *Kim;* Arthur Conan Doyle, *The Hound of the Baskervilles*	Queen Victoria dies		First transatlantic radio message; invention of the vacuum cleaner
1902	Mary Webb, “The White Moth”	J. A. Hobson, *Imperialism;* Claude Debussy composes *Pelléas and Mélisande*	Balfour’s Unionist government		Peter Kropotkin, *Mutual Aid*
1903	Louise Lind-af-Hageby and Liese Schartau, *The Shambles of Science*	Henry James, *The Ambassadors*		Emmeline Pankhurst founds the Women’s Social and Political Union	Wright brothers’ flight

Date	Work in Anthology	Other Literary/ Artistic Works	Events of Significance to British History and Politics	Events in Women's History and Feminist Politics	Events of Significance to the History of Science, Technology, and Medicine
1904	Charlotte Mew, "Emily Brontë"; Eleanor Ormerod, *Eleanor Ormerod, LL.D.*	Max Weber, *The Protestant Ethic and the Spirit of Capitalism*	Anglo-French entente		
1905		J. M. Synge, *Riders to the Sea;* Mary Cassatt paints *Mother and Child*		Hertha Ayrton, physicist, is the first woman to present a paper to the Royal Society	Albert Einstein, *Special Theory of Relativity;* Havelock Ellis, *Studies in the Psychology of Sex;* Alfred Russel Wallace, *My Life*
1906	Vernon Lee, "Asphodels"; Marie Stopes, *The Study of Plant Life for Young People*		Labour Party formed		
1907	Mary E. Coleridge, "*L'Oiseau Bleu*"; Frances Swiney, "Man's Necessity"; Marie Stopes, "The 'Xerophytic' Character of the Gymnosperms"	Joseph Conrad, *The Secret Agent;* John Millington Synge, *The Playboy of the Western World*	Anglo-Russian entente; Old Brown Dog riots in Battersea		
1908	Gertrude Jekyll, "Pussies in the Garden," "Gardens of Special Colouring"	Lucy Maud Montgomery, *Anne of Green Gables*	Asquith's government; Old Age Pensions Plan introduced	Emmeline Pankhurst is arrested for the first time and jailed with her daughter, Christabel	Ford, mass-production of the Model T

1909	Mary Webb, "A Cedar-Rose"			
1911	Juliana Ewing, *A Great Emergency, & Other Tales;* Frances Hodgson Burnett, *The Secret Garden*	D. H. Lawrence, *The White Peacock*	National Health Insurance Bill	Asquith orders force-feeding of hunger-striking suffragists
1912	Frances Swiney, *Woman and Natural Law*		Third Irish Home Rule Act; sinking of the *Titanic*	
1913	Edith Nesbit, *Wings and the Child; or, The Building of Magic Cities*	D. H. Lawrence, *Sons and Lovers*		"Cat and Mouse Act" enacted to sabotage hunger-striking suffragists; Juliette Low founds the Girl Scouts
1914	Vernon Lee, "The Lizard in the Abbey Church"; Alice Meynell, "Rain"	James Joyce, *Dubliners*	Assassination of Archduke Ferdinand at Sarajevo (June); British Empire enters WWI (Aug.)	Mother's Day becomes a U.S. holiday
1915	Charlotte Mew, "The Sunlit House"	D. H. Lawrence, *The Rainbow*		
1916		James Joyce, *A Portrait of the Artist as a Young Man*	Lloyd George, first government; Easter Rising in Ireland	
1917	Mary Webb, *Gone to Earth, The Spring of Joy, The Secret Joy*	T. S. Eliot, "The Love Song of J. Alfred Prufrock"	Russian Revolution	Margaret Sanger opens first birth control clinic in New York
1918	Marie Stopes, *Married Love*	Lytton Strachey, *Eminent Victorians*		Voting Act

Date	Work in Anthology	Other Literary/ Artistic Works	Events of Significance to British History and Politics	Events in Women's History and Feminist Politics	Events of Significance to the History of Science, Technology, and Medicine
1919			Treaty of Versailles		Beginning of regular London-to-Paris air service
1920		D. H. Lawrence, *Women in Love*	Mussolini forms fascist government in Italy	Soviet Union becomes the first country in the world to legalize abortion; Oxford awards degrees to women	Electric typewriter
1921				Marie Stopes opens England's first birth control clinic	
1922		James Joyce, *Ulysses;* T. S. Eliot, "The Wasteland"		Cambridge awards degrees to women	Radio broadcasting
1923			Baldwin, first government	Marie Stopes, *Contraception: Its History, Theory, and Practice*	
1924		E. M. Forster, *A Passage to India*			
1925	Margaret Fountaine, "Amongst the Rhopalocera of the Philippines"	Virginia Woolf, *Mrs. Dalloway;* Adolf Hitler, *Mein Kampf*			
1926		Ernest Hemingway, *The Sun Also Rises*			

1927	Mary Webb, *Sails of Gold*			Gertrude Ederle swims the English Channel	Lindbergh flies solo over the Atlantic; sound films start to replace silent films
1928		Virginia Woolf, *Orlando;* Lawrence, *Lady Chatterley's Lover*		Equal Franchise Act	Discovery of penicillin
1929	Charlotte Mew, "The Trees Are Down"	Virginia Woolf, *A Room of One's Own;* William Faulkner, *The Sound and the Fury*			

Biographical Sketches

Cecil Frances Alexander, née Humphreys (1818–95)

Alexander, an Anglo-Irish poet and hymn writer married to an archbishop of the Established Church, is best known today for "All things bright and beauteous." The poem is reprinted here from her 1848 volume, *Hymns for Little Children,* a volume that sold a quarter million copies in its day. Its sentiments hark back to the philosophy of William Paley (1743–1805), whose "natural theology" suggested that one can argue for the presence of God based on the design of nature. In this poem, Alexander followed Paley's argument into the sphere of human nature, arguing for the appropriateness of rank as well. Despite outmoded thinking, the poem stands at the beginning of this volume as one of the world's most famous hymns in praise of nature.

Lydia Ernestine Becker (1827–90)

Herself an amateur botanist and a correspondent with Charles Darwin, Lydia Becker was a pioneer in promoting scientific education for women. In 1865 she founded the Ladies Literary Society in Manchester, an organization dedicated to the study of science. A year earlier she had published *Botany for Novices: A Short Outline of the Natural System of the Classification of Plants.* An early activist and pamphleteer in the votes-for-women campaign, Becker was also the founder and editor (1870–90) of the *Woman's Suffrage Journal* and secretary of both the Manchester Women's Suffrage Committee and the London Central Committee for Women's Suffrage.

Isabella Lucy Bird Bishop (1831–1904)

"There never was anybody who had adventures so well as Miss Bird," wrote the *Spectator* of this talented and prolific travel writer. Bird traveled the world—America, Japan, Hawaii, Persia, Kurdistan, Korea, and China—and produced eleven books describing such off-the-beaten-path places for a home audience in Great Britain. She began publishing her travel books after she found that a circle of women surrounding her sister, Henrietta, had developed an appetite for letters she had sent home. Only after being encouraged by this reception did Bird turn professional. With an intrepid thirst for traveling, she continued her journeying into her seventieth year and eventually became the first woman Fellow of the Royal Geographical Society. The selections offered in this anthology are drawn from *Six Months in the Sandwich Islands* (1875) and *A Lady's Life in the Rocky Mountains* (1879), where Bird first describes the hardships of lives lived in Colorado and then her now-famous ascent of Long's Peak, in the company of a rough frontiersman called "Rocky Mountain Jim."

Jemima Blackburn (1823–1909)

Highly skilled both as a watercolorist and ornithological painter, Blackburn was praised by such notables as the critic John Ruskin and animal painter Edwin Landseer. Like others of the women in this volume, she was keenly enthusiastic about natural history from the time of her childhood and not only observed but also dissected animals and birds in order better to understand their anatomy. She prided herself in drawing "from nature." Her books include *Illustrations from Scripture by an Animal Painter* (1854), *Birds Drawn from Nature* (1862), *The Pipits* and *Caw! Caw!* (1871), both children's books, and *Birds from Moidart and Elsewhere* (1895). Blackburn's cover for *Birds from Moidart* is placed at the beginning of the section on adventuring.

Blackburn was meticulous both in her representations and her careful observation of bird life. Her *Pipits* was based on knowledge she gained through such observation. Although so powerful a scientific authority as John Gould had contended that parent birds accidentally destroyed their young when trying to feed an interloping cuckoo chick whose egg had been deposited in their nest, Blackburn had witnessed young cuckoos themselves ejecting the host hatchlings. Blackburn's letter, reprinted in this volume, was sent to the journal *Nature* in 1872, detailing what she knew to be the facts of this matter. It is included in order to show the importance of field observers to the still-changing field of biology.

Mathilde Blind [Claude Lake] (1841–96)

Born in Germany, Blind was brought to England when her family fled in the wake of the 1848–49 Baden insurrection. In her adopted country, Blind was closely associated with the Pre-Raphaelite Brotherhood of painters and with the New Woman movement, becoming a good friend of Mona Caird's. Always interested in social reform, she wrote a long poem, *The Fire on the Heather* (1886), in protest against Highland land clearances and the eviction of Scottish peasants. Like May Kendall, she knew both literature and science, using Darwin's theories to critique her own society. In 1888 she produced another long poem, *The Ascent of Man* (1888), an epic of Darwinism that was introduced by leading evolutionist, Alfred Russel Wallace (1823–1913). In addition to writing poetry, Blind produced a biography of the poet Shelley and several biographies for the Eminent Women Series, George Eliot's among them. She was also a keen admirer of Christina Rossetti's poetry for young people. As a tribute to both poets, Blind's "On a Forsaken Lark's Nest" has been deliberately placed alongside Rossetti's

"Hurt No Living Thing," "Frog," and "Hear What the Mournful Linnets Say" in this anthology.

Alice Bodington (1841–97)

Little is known about Alice Bodington. From facts listed on her death certificate, she seems to have been born in Rome. For much of her life she lived in Suffolk. About ten years before her death, she migrated to British Columbia, where her husband became superintendent of an asylum for the insane in Vancouver. In addition to her *Studies in Evolution and Biology,* which was printed in England, she published four papers in the field of psychology and one on the parasitic protozoa that are found in cancerous diseases. All of these papers appeared in the *American Naturalist* between the years 1892 and 1896. Her work was also published in *The Popular Science Review* and the *International Journal of Microscopy.*

Eliza Elder Brightwen (1830–1906)

All her life, Brightwen studied natural history and kept copious notes on what she observed. In her sixtieth year, she began to write for publication. The literary result was *Wild Nature Won by Kindness* (1890), which earned her immediate acclaim and an audience eager for more. Brightwen went on to produce six more popular books of natural history. In her later years, she rarely left her estate at Stanmore, where she continued to study natural history both outdoors and in. The excerpts from her work included here are drawn from *More About Wild Nature* (1892) and *Inmates of My House and Garden* (1895) and describe some of the many animals Brightwen raised in her home—a lemur, a mongoose, and several bats—all of which she kept in her menageries and/or conservatory.

Anne Brontë [Acton Bell] (1820–42)

The youngest of the three Brontë sisters, Anne was, like her sisters, both a poet and a novelist. Her first novel, *Agnes Grey* (1847), was a governess novel about a young woman and her troubled appointments as governess to difficult children. In the passage selected here, the heroine deals with an unruly boy who has been encouraged by an insensitive uncle to rob birds' nests. It suggests the firmness Agnes was prompted to show in the face of juvenile protests—firmness that usually went unrewarded by the children's parents. In both this novel and in her *Tenant of Wildfell Hall* (1848), Brontë also expressed concern over differing standards for rearing boys and girls that often marked the child raising of her day.

Emily Brontë [Ellis Bell] (1818–48)

Best known for her novel *Wuthering Heights* (1848), Emily Brontë was also a poet whose work reveals a fine sonority and an exquisite eye for nature. First published by her sister Charlotte in 1846—in a volume published under the sisters' pseudonyms and entitled *Poems by Currer, Ellis and Acton Bell*—Ellis Bell, or Emily Brontë, was immediately recognized as a poet of talent, one with a distinctive voice. Not published until 1902, long after her death, "High Waving Heather" displays these gifts and Brontë's remarkable ability to catch a fleeting moment on her beloved Yorkshire moors.

Arabella Burton Buckley (Mrs. Fisher) (1840–1929)

An authoritative popularizer of science and secretary to Sir Charles Lyell from 1864 to 1875, Arabella Buckley was personally familiar with the leading scientists and scientific theories of her day. A lecturer from 1876 to 1888, Buckley was also editor of Mary Somerville's *On the Connexion of the Physical Sciences* (1877), a portion of which appears in this anthology. In her own first book, *A Short History of Natural Science* (1876), she recalled that she "often felt very forcibly how many important facts and generalizations of science, which are of great value . . . in giving a true estimate of life and its conditions, [were] totally unknown to the majority of otherwise well-educated persons" (vii–viii).

Grounded in evolutionary theory and in all aspects of the new geology, Buckley re-created this knowledge in two popular books whose narratives are highly imaginative, *Life and Her Children* (1881) and *Winners in Life's Race* (1883). Here Buckley presented seven divisions of life: *Life and Her Children* covers the first six, from the amoebas to the insects, and *Winners in Life's Race* is entirely devoted to seventh, the "great backboned family." Buckley was equally aware of the nature of science writing itself and realized that science, though based in fact or experiment, was transmitted as a literary construction. Two other books, *The Fairy-land of Science* (1879, reissued in a number of late nineteenth-century editions) and its sequel, *Through Magic Glasses* (1890), demonstrate her skill at telling the stories of science. In *Fairy-land,* Buckley generated interest in her scientific subjects by borrowing the language of fairy stories and wizardry to reinforce her ultimate belief that the wonders of science not only paralleled but surpassed the wonders of fairyland. In its sequel, *Through Magic Glasses,* Buckley would focus more closely on what childlike eyes can see, here with the help of the telescope, stereoscope, photo camera, microscope, and a fictional guide, a magician whose chamber—and eyes—we enter with the first pages of the book.

Frances Hodgson Burnett (1849–1924)

Author of both *Little Lord Fauntleroy* (1886) and *The Secret Garden* (1911), Burnett needs little introduction to avid readers of children's classics. Burnett was a woman of two continents, having moved from England to Tennessee in 1865. In addition to her two best-known novels—one of which has given us bywords for overly charming and effeminately dressed boys and both of which have been dramatized for stage and television—Burnett wrote many others. The passage included in this anthology shows Mary, of *The Secret Garden,* in the process of discovering the mysterious, hidden garden at Misselthwaite Manor, where she has been brought after the death of her parents in India. This secret garden will soon become central to her own, and others', health and well-being.

(Alice) Mona Caird [G. Noel Hatton] (1854–1932)

Mona Caird was a novelist, antivivisectionist, and avid feminist who championed unconventional women. She is best known today for novels like *The Daughters of Danaus* (1894), the story of a failed marriage and the price it exacted from its heroine. In her book of essays, *The Morality of Marriage and Other Essays* (1891), as in the essay included here, Caird takes on Eliza Lynn Linton (1822–98), an antisuffragist and proponent of women as homebodies. Here Caird enters a discussion that had raged in the pages of the *Nineteenth Century.* In 1890, Lady Jersey (1849–1945) had initiated what has come to be called the "wild woman" debate by simply arguing that women's free choice of mental or physical activity did not make them unfit for motherhood. Linton had argued the other side, suggesting that separate male and female spheres needed to be maintained and that motherhood was women's primary role. Infuriated by Linton, Caird cleverly attacked her lapses of logic, suggesting that the time-honored appeals to "nature" and "woman's nature" were simply utilized to keep women in their place and needed to be seen for the cultural constructions they were.

Frances Power Cobbe (1822–1904)

Social reformer and crusader on behalf of both women and animals, Cobbe was one of the best-known women journalists of her time. The *Daily News,* the *Standard,* the *Spectator, Fraser's Magazine,* the *Quarterly Review,* and the *Contemporary Review*—these are just a few of the newspapers and magazines for which she wrote. A tireless worker on behalf of women's suffrage and the passage of the Married Women's Property Act (which would enable women to inherit and keep their own property), Cobbe was an equally avid antivivisectionist and a founder of the Victoria Street Society, organized in 1876 to protest vivisection. The essay on this topic reprinted here soundly challenges the ethics of vivisection. Others of her essays would expose vivisecting experiments in even more graphic terms, incorporating pictures like the one reproduced in this text.

Mary E. (Elizabeth) Coleridge [Anodos] (1861–1907)

Educated at home by a scholar and poet who had resigned from Eton, Coleridge herself became a poet, an essayist, a novelist, and a teacher—in her case a teacher at the Working Women's College. Descended from the line of poets stemming from Samuel Taylor Coleridge and including his daughter, Sara, Mary Coleridge showed considerable poetic talent from a young age. Nevertheless, she did not publish any of her work until the 1890s and most of her poems were published posthumously. Many have female personae and reflect on women's losses and longings. *L'Oiseau Bleu,* reprinted here, is atypical in this sense, but it shows Coleridge's remarkable talent as a colorist in words.

Eliza Cook (1818–89)

A self-educated poet and journalist, Cook began writing at fifteen, publishing her *Lays of a Wild Harp* (1835) two years later. Considerable in its range, her poetry was immensely popular in her own day. The poems of the natural world, a number of which are included in this volume, show close observation and attention to the behaviors of nonhuman species; the poems about women are remarkable for their interest in women across classes and age groups. As a journalist, Cook was editor of *Eliza Cook's Journal,* a miscellany of reviews, poems, and social essays intended for a female audience, published from 1849 to 1854, and written mainly by herself. Aimed at ordinary readers, the journal was affordable (one and a half pence per issue) and sold extremely well.

Alice Dew-Smith, née Murray

Alice Dew-Smith was a feminist and professional journalist, contributing regularly to the column "The Wares of Autolycus" in the *Pall Mall Gazette.* From this column stemmed her two books of plant and animal anecdotes, *Confidences of an Amateur Gardener* (1897) and *Tom Tug and Others: Sketches in a Domestic Menagerie* (1898). Dew-Smith was radical among late Victorian animal writers in her nonhierarchical view of animals. To her all were deserving of human admiration and/or empathy. In *Confidences* she reflected, "[I]n Nature one's sympathies are continually being divided. One is sorry for the hungry spider, who must go without his dinner for want of a fly, and extremely sorry for the fly whose lot it is to provide the much-wished-for meal" (59).

Lady Florence Dixie, née Florence Caroline Douglas [Darling] (1857–1905)

Feminist, traveler, novelist, and poet, the polymath Lady Florence Dixie is best known today as a champion of women's suffrage. A onetime big game hunter, Dixie is, however, represented in this anthology by "The Horrors of Sport" (1892), an essay condemning hunting, a position she eventually came to understand and then to encourage. Her feminist utopia, *Gloriana; or The Revolution of 1900* (1890), is represented in the section "Speaking Out" both by its preface and by a selection in which its heroine, cross-dressed, speaks to the parliament of her country on behalf of women's suffrage. Dixie's heroine is careful to point out that society, not nature, is what has dictated women's secondary social status. "With Nature," one of Dixie's poems and included in the section "Appreciating," reveals that Dixie—under the pseudonym "Darling"—had developed her attachment to the natural world before the age of nineteen.

George Egerton (pseud of. Mary Chavelita Dunne Bright) (1859–1945)

Egerton is best known for her collections of short stories, *Discords* (1894) and *Keynotes* (1894), from which the selection included here was taken. A brilliant story writer and exponent of the New Woman, Egerton allowed her publisher, John Lane, to take her title, *Keynotes,* as the name for an entire series of new works of fiction by women.

Open to discussion of women's ambitions and sexual needs in her stories, Egerton was also attacked by the press. But she and her heroines maintained that Victorian culture, not their own nature, was what held women back.

Ellis Ethelmer (pseud. of Elizabeth Wolstenholme Elmy) (1837–1918)

Under her maiden name, Elizabeth Wolstenholme was an outspoken advocate on behalf of women's rights. Friend to Josephine Butler (1828–1906), who crusaded for an end to the Contagious Diseases Acts (which inspected the bodies of women suspected of being involved in prostitution), Wolstenholme Elmy was an activist for the same cause. Under the name "Ellis Ethelmer," and probably along with her husband, Ben Elmy, Wolstenholme Elmy was a sex educator who informed her audience through birds-and-bees primers about sexuality. She wrote a series of such books, addressing different audiences from young children to adults. The example included here is from *Baby Buds* (1895), in which a fictional mother explains sexual reproduction to a child just over four years of age.

Juliana Horatia Ewing, née Gatty (1841–85)

Daughter of Margaret Gatty, who is also found in this volume, Ewing was an amateur botanist who often utilized her knowledge of the plant kingdom in her literature for children. The "Judy" of *Aunt Judy's Magazine,* founded by Gatty and later continued by Ewing and her husband, Ewing published many of her children's stories in her own magazine. Her love of plants extended to their preservation, and she kept notebooks observing which wild plants disappeared and which survived when their habitat was disturbed. In "Our Field," reprinted here, Ewing projects a young narrator who reflects her own cherished beliefs that no person can truly "own" land and that we must all work to be its stewards.

Michael Field (pseud. of Katherine Bradley [1846–1914] and Edith Cooper [1862–1913])

From the mid-1880s onward, Bradley and Cooper—an aunt and her niece and acknowledged lovers—published most of their poetry together under the pseudonym of "Michael Field." Bradley had published earlier under another pseudonym, Arran Leigh, and Cooper had worked as Isla Leigh—both probably in tribute to Elizabeth Barrett Browning's poetic heroine, Aurora Leigh. Both women were feminists and antivivisectionists, and both openly acknowledged their lesbianism. Friends of Vernon Lee, Walter Pater, and other aesthetes, the two traveled widely and for years cultivated a distinguished circle of literary friends. Later in life they became more reclusive. Their nature poetry is often entwined with the sense of a powerful Darwinian life force—insistent and inescapable. "Cyclamens," however, which is included here, shows their wedding of nature to a more precious and purer aestheticism of color, more like that of Oscar Wilde's shorter verse.

Margaret Fountaine (1862–1940)

Margaret Fountaine was a dedicated entomologist whose specialty was butterflies. Her published work included scientific papers for the *Entomologist,* such as the one included here. Since Fountaine has recently been more celebrated for her private love life than for her science, it is offered as an example of the seriousness involved in her fieldwork and writing. During her lifetime, Fountaine also developed a collection of over twenty-two thousand butterflies, which she preserved in mahogany cases and willed to the Norwich Museum, and produced a series of beautiful and scientifically accurate watercolors showing the life cycles of the many butterflies she raised and observed.

Margaret Gatty (1809–73)

Margaret Gatty had two prepossessing professional interests: writing for children and the study of marine algae. After fourteen years of intensive research, she published her *British Sea-weeds* (1863), a two-volume supplement to William Harvey's authoritative *Manual of British Algae* (1841). For decades, too, she published—and republished in multiple reprints—one of the most popular books of the second half of the nineteenth century: *Parables from Nature* (1855–71). Aimed at the education of children, this series of short, simple tales—several of which are reproduced in this anthology—was based in science but meant to inculcate morality. In 1866, Gatty founded *Aunt Judy's Magazine,* a children's magazine she named after her daughter, Juliana Horatia Ewing, who is also represented in this anthology.

Elizabeth Gould (1804–41)

One of the finest bird illustrators of her time, Elizabeth Gould accompanied her husband, John (1804–81), on expeditions to gather ornithological information for their famous series of books. The Gould bird books would become authoritative reference tools for ornithologists and amateurs alike, eventually earning John Gould the nickname "the bird man." The selection included here is writing in another vein—Gould's letter to her mother in England. Gould had had to leave several of her eight children behind while she traveled to Australia to illustrate what would become the seven-volume *Birds of Australia* (1840–48). Of special interest here is her early fascination with what we would now call the "ecology" of the Australian bush. Because of their intimate interconnection, birds and plants had begun to form a dual interest for Elizabeth Gould. Overworked, Gould died young, even before the completion of the Australian series.

Annie Hassard

Other than the fact that Hassard's *Floral Decorations for the Dwelling House: A Practical Guide to the Home Arrangement of Plants and Flowers* was popular enough to go through a number of editions, little is known about Annie Hassard.

Octavia Hill (1838–1912)

Hill was a social reformer and educator, interested both in improving the lives of urban poor and in preserving land for their use. Throughout her long association with reform causes—working conditions, urban housing, land preservation, and crime prevention, to name a few—she wrote frequently for periodicals, trying always to inform a larger public of the pressing issues that absorbed her. With her sister, Miranda, she became an officer of the Kyrle Society, an organization dedicated to beautifying human environments through such activities as planting and distributing flowers, providing clean water, and erecting aviaries. Beauty, she believed, was essential to mental health. Hill was also one of the founders of the National Trust and a member of the Royal Commission on the Poor Laws.

Mary Howitt, née Botham (1799–1888)

Even to posterity, Mary Howitt is most often associated with her husband, William. The two were often humorously designated "William and Mary," after the monarchs. Together the two worked out a joint career, beginning with *The Forest Minstrel* (1823), a collection of their early poems. Both then continued to earn their living entirely through literary pursuits, among other things editing *Howitt's Journal,* a literary magazine that published many luminaries of their day. A disciplined writer who wrote daily, Mary Howitt, who was a religious person all of her life, also found time to espouse the causes of antivivisection, antislavery and women's rights. Her "Cry of the Suffering Creatures"—written as a modified ballad, a form for which she was known—sounds the cry of animal voices, all begging for compassion. Its final lines may refer to Howitt's Quaker upbringing and the idea of a Peaceable Kingdom of all God's creatures on earth. Her "Dor-Hawk" reveals Howitt's exquisite senses of beauty and otherness.

Gertrude Jekyll (1843–1932)

Jekyll was one of the foremost gardeners of her time. Professional in every sense of the word, she both studied her calling assiduously and depended upon it for income. A regular contributor to the *Guardian,* she wrote a twice-monthly garden column for years. Over a lifetime committed to gardening, she wrote fourteen books and more than two thousand notes and articles on the subject, designed dozens of gardens, and sold plants from her home. Having begun as an artist but having had to give up painting because of poor eyesight, Jekyll remained a specialist in color, as the selection from her *Colour Schemes for the Flower Garden* (1908) in the section "Appreciating" amply illustrates. Her written works also encompass books on water gardens, rose gardens, and wall gardens, and special books for children, like *Children and Gardens* (1908), from which "Pussies in the Garden" in the section "Domesticating" was taken. Jekyll enjoyed observing her own pet cats, which were allowed to roam her garden, and produced this whimsical piece to celebrate both the garden and its feline inhabitants.

Sara Orne Jewett (1849–1909)

Jewett lived in Maine and wrote haunting stories about the people and places there, among them the justly well-known *Country of the Pointed Firs* (1896). Her sensitive story, "A White Heron," has been included here to remind readers that the protection of birds was not simply a British phenomenon and that murderous millinery was not the only lure for hunters of bird skins. They were also used in scientific collections like John Gould's and John James Audubon's (1785–1851) and therefore hunted by young men like the one in this story.

May Kendall, née Emma Goldworth (1861–1943)

Poet, novelist, social activist, and humorist, May Kendall published many of her poems in the magazines of the 1880s. Her two volumes of poetry, *Dreams to Sell* (1887) and *Songs from the Dreamland* (1894), show a considerable range of tone and form. All three of Kendall's novels espoused the cause of women; the first, *From a Garret* (1887), was part of the "New Women Novels" series. Kendall was also devoted to social improvement for the poor and collaborated with B. Seebohm Rowntree, a prominent Quaker reformer, on two books describing the needs of the laboring class, *How the Labourer Lives* (1913) and *The Human Needs of Labour* (1919). In terms of science, Kendall was herself a Darwinian, but she did not allow this to interfere with her satirical sense of humor towards Darwinism, as in the delightful spoofs included in this volume.

Anna Bonus Kingsford [Mary; Hermes] (1846–88)

Practicing physician, spiritualist writer, and mystic, Kingsford was a woman of many talents. A journalist as well, she edited the *Lady's Own Paper: A Journal of Progress, Taste, and Art.* Best known for her books on spiritualism, Kingsford had her first exposure to this popular belief (that the dead communicate with the living) when she met a medium as she canvassed for the Married Women's Property Act in the late 1860s. Much of her later life was devoted to producing spiritualist books like *Perfect Way* (1881), written with the man she called her "co-religionist," Edward Maitland. Kingsford's other abiding interest was antivivisection. In her case the passion to protect animals stemmed from her years as a medical student in Paris, where she was so moved by the plight of vivisected animals that she decided to write her thesis on vegetarianism. "Unscientific Science" (1883), excerpted in this anthology, offers a spiritualist interpretation of the vivisection that Kingsford so abhorred.

Mary Henrietta Kingsley (1862–1900)

A member of the famous Kingsley family that included the writer, Charles (her uncle), Kingsley first went to Africa to further the research of her father, George Kingsley, who had died while writing a book on African religion and law. On her expeditions, Kingsley also collected fish for the British Museum of Natural History. Her first trip took her to the Congo Basin, her second to the Ogooué (Ogowé) River, where her guides, the Fang, were reputed to be cannibals. In two highly authoritative and even more highly amusing books, *Travels in West Africa* (1897) and *West African Studies* (1899), Kingsley described some of her findings and exploits in those areas. During her travels, she not only met with adventures, she also brought home sixty-five species of fish, including three never before catalogued that now bear her name. "Fishing in West Africa," excerpted here, was first published independently in the *National Review* (1897) and later placed in her collection *West African Studies.*

Sarah Bowdich Lee (1791–1856)

Widowed when her husband, Thomas Bowdich (1791–1824), died of a fever on a scientific expedition for which she was illustrator, Sarah Bowdich Lee supported herself and her family through illustration and writing. She completed the volume Thomas Bowdich was writing at his death, *Excursions in Madeira and Porto Santo* (1825) and went on to work on a beautiful *Fresh-Water Fishes of Great Britain, Drawn and Described by Mrs. T. Edward Bowdich* (1828). She then turned to more lucrative writing: fiction, a biography of the geologist Baron Cuvier, and a book on taxidermy, intended to draw a popular audience and excerpted here.

Vernon Lee (pseud. of Violet Paget) (1856–1935)

A prolific critic and essayist and a fiction writer as well, Vernon Lee was one of the key voices in the field of aesthetics at the end of the nineteenth century. A New Woman and enfant terrible, unconventional in her behavior as in her thinking, Lee moved in many of the literary and artistic circles of her day. Much of her life was lived in Italy, the source of inspiration for many of her books of criticism and travel. Her novel, *Miss Brown* (1884) was a satire of Pre-Raphaelite aesthetics. Lee's own brand of aestheticism was different, inspired in part by the *genius loci,* or spirit of place, which she redefined for her generation. All of the selections from her writing reprinted in this anthology reveal Lee's hypersensitivity to place and thing as well as to culture. Thus the piece on vivisection, little known to readers today, is not uncharacteristic of Lee's concern for life in all its variety.

Margaretta Louisa Smith Lemon (Mrs. Frank E. Lemon) (1860–1953)

Margaretta Lemon was the first honorary secretary of the Society for the Protection of Birds, a title her lawyer husband took over when the organization received a royal charter in 1904. Women could not hold such positions once such a charter was granted. Nevertheless, Margaretta Lemon continued virtually to run the organization for years, serving as its correspondent, the secretary of its publications, and its historian. Lemon attributed her early interest in saving birds to a reading of Eliza Brightwen's *Wild Things Won by Kindness* (1890). She later enlisted Brightwen (also represented in this anthology) in the cause of the SPB, and Brightwen contributed a pamphlet condemning the slaughter of breeding egrets to *Bird Notes and News.* Reprinted here is Lemon's own haunting plea for an end to bird use in apparel, delivered at the International Congress of Women in 1899.

Amy Levy (1861–89)

Amy Levy's short life, which ended in suicide, was a life dedicated to writing. From her days at Newnham College, Cambridge (where she was the first Jewish student admitted), until her death, Levy published widely in journals and magazines and produced several volumes of poetry. She also wrote three novels and numerous essays and short stories, many about Jewish life in London. Levy herself lived there and, along with her father, worked toward providing educational opportunities for people living in the East End. Her best-known novel, *Reuben Sachs: A Sketch* (1888), derives from her Jewish heritage and satirizes the aloofness of well-to-do London Jewry. Levy met Vernon Lee in Florence, when she stayed at Lee's home during a visit to Italy. Paying tribute both to Lee's beloved landscape and to Lee as observer of color and space, Levy's "To Vernon Lee" nostalgically recalls that visit and a walk in the hills surrounding Florence.

Louise Lind-af-Hageby and Liese Schartau

Louise Lind-af-Hageby and Liese Schartau were two Swedish women from affluent families who enrolled in the London School of Medicine for Women for the purpose of furthering the cause of antivivisection. Their goals were to acquire the physiological knowledge necessary to argue against vivisection from a position of authority and to gather evidence against practitioners of vivisection. They came to oppose vivisection after visiting the Pasteur Institute in Paris, where they had witnessed the suffering of many vivisected animals. During the course of their studies, they kept journals, which they later converted into a series of vignettes and published as a book with the help of Stephen Coleridge of the Victoria Street Anti-Vivisection Society (later known simply as the Victoria Street Society). The vignettes recount in vivid detail the gruesome procedures of individual vivisection as the women witnessed them and describe the callous attitude with which physiologists treated the subjects of their vivisections.

Lind-af-Hageby and Schartau are important figures in women's history as well as in the history of humane activism, for they moved beyond the accepted sphere in which women were expected to function as reformers. The existence of female antivivisectionists who knew little if anything about science could be explained away by their opponents as a manifestation of well-meaning but ignorant and overblown female sentimentality. Lind-af-Hageby and Schartau educated themselves so that they could not be so easily dismissed by advocates of vivisection. Their method of rousing public interest was certainly effective, for their book, *The Shambles of Science: Extracts from the Diary of Two Students of Physiology* (1903), eventually led to the riots over vivisection in Battersea, London, in 1907.

Jane Loudon, née Webb (1807–58)

Jane Webb was both a botanist and a novelist. Her career began with the publication of *The Mummy, A Tale of the Twenty-Second Century* in 1827. This potboiler was read by John Claudius Loudon (1783–1843), a well-known landscape gardener and horticultural writer, who desired to meet its author and then to marry her. As companion and secretary to Loudon, Jane learned and came to share in his business and worked with him on his important *Encyclopedia of Gardening* (1834). Her own books on botany and gardening, such as *The Ladies' Companion to the Flower Garden* (1841) and *The Lady's Country Companion* (1845) sold extremely well. Loudon also founded and edited a large-format Saturday weekly, *The Ladies' Companion at Home and Abroad.* These and other publications based on her knowledge of the natural world supported her and her daughter after the death of John Loudon, just as the *Mummy* had helped her to make a living after the earlier death of her father. The selection from *The Young Naturalist* (1863), included here, is an example of Loudon's combining her knowledge of natural history with science popularization and children's literature.

E. A. Maling

Like Elizabeth Twining, E. A. Maling held plants and their domestication as a primary interest. In the 1860s she wrote a number of books intended to instruct women about plants and flowers and their appropriateness for the Victorian home. Among them were *Flowers for Ornament and Decoration and How to Arrange Them* (1862), *The Indoor Gardener* (1863), *Indoor Plants and How to Grow Them for the Drawing Room, Balcony, and Greenhouse* (1865), and *Handbook for Ladies: on Indoor Plants, Flowers for Ornament, and Song Birds* (1867). The selection on keeping song birds, included in this anthology, would later become part of Maling's *Handbook for Ladies.*

Jane Haldimand Marcet (1769–1858)

Jane Marcet produced a number of popular science books called *Conversations,* volumes that utilized the dialogue form to introduce subjects like chemistry and natural philosophy to women, working people, and children. Having attended lectures by Sir Humphry Davy (1778–1829) and having herself been fascinated by science prompted desire to present science to the uninformed in some easily accessible form. In her dialogues, a knowledgeable older woman talks with a somewhat informed young woman and a child, listening and then teaching the two what they need to know. Her *Conversations on Chemistry* (1806) would serve as a primer text for Michael Faraday (1791–1867), an apprentice bookbinder who would become one of the world's most famous electrochemists.

Annie Martin

After writing her *Home Life on an Ostrich Farm* (1890), Annie Martin returned to London from Africa and, filled with nostalgia, paid a visit to the ostriches at the London Zoo. No further information on Annie Martin has been found.

Harriet Martineau (1802–76)

Martineau was a political writer, novelist, travel writer, and essayist who is sometimes called the "first sociologist." Well known for her *Illustrations of Political Economy* (1832–34) and her studies of America, she was also deeply concerned over the role of women in her day. She eulogized women like Jane Marcet and Charlotte Brontë in her book *Biographical Sketches* (1864), a collection of pieces she had published in various Victorian journals. Like the Brontës and Sherwood, she also produced a novel on the plight of the governess, *Deerbrook,* published in 1839, as well as three other novels. Her nonfictional *Our Farm of Two Acres* (1865), excerpted here, describes her short venture into farming.

Nina Elizabeth Mazuchelli (1832–1914)

Nina Mazuchelli went to India with her husband, Francis, an army chaplain. They were first posted in the plains and then in Darjeeling, where Mazuchelli was smitten with the Himalaya Mountains. Along with several guides, the Mazuchellis made a life-threatening trip across the mountains, mainly to satisfy Nina's curiosity. Represented in the form of a travel narrative—*The Indian Alps and How We Crossed Them: Being a Narrative of Two Years' Residence in the Eastern Himalaya and Two Months' Tour into the Interior* (1876) by a "Lady Pioneer"—Mazuchelli's life in upland India becomes a half-serious, half-comic, and altogether absorbing story. Mazuchelli was the first British woman ever to have penetrated so far into the high peaks area of the eastern Himalayas.

Louisa Anne Meredith (Mrs. Charles Meredith), née Twamley (1812–95)

Louisa Meredith began her career as a poet and artist and soon became a botanical illustrator and expert on British wildflowers, producing two books, *The Romance of Nature; or, The Flower Seasons Illustrated* (1836) and *Our Wildflowers Familiarly Described and Illustrated* (1839) as Louisa Twamley. She then married a young cousin who was posted to Tasmania and spent the rest of her life there. In Australia, she continued writing and illustrating for a "home" audience in Britain, beginning with a series of travel books and culminating in a number of books concentrating on the flora and fauna of Tasmania. *My Home in Tasmania* (1852), one of the earlier books on Tasmania and the one excerpted here, describes the perils as well as the animals and plants of the island. Increasingly, Meredith's books came to represent her adopted continent in greater detail and with deeper fondness.

Charlotte Mew (1869–1928)

A fine poet and a great dramatic monologist, Mew is in many respects the last of a line that included earlier Victorian women poets, Christina Rossetti and Emily Brontë among them. Her "The Trees Are Down," in the section "Protecting," shows Mew's deep love of the green world and her anger at its destruction. Her sensitive appraisal of Brontë's voice in the section "Appreciating" also reveals her to be an excellent critic. This essay serves not only as a gloss on the earlier poet's "High Waving Heather" but as a fitting tribute from woman poet to woman poet. Mew's own "The Sunlit House," also found in "Appreciating," in its haunting simplicity hints at the complexities of her dramatic monologues. Here Mew is unwilling to keep us in a world of personification and pathetic fallacy—whereby nature takes on human characteristics. Her final image in this poem can be read simply for what it is—a fleeting glimpse of a bird leaving an empty house.

Alice (Christiana Gertrude) Meynell, née A. C. Thompson (1847–1922)

Poet, prose writer, journalist, and supporter of the suffrage movement and pacifist causes, Alice Meynell excelled in many media. Married at age thirty, she bore eight children but continued writing and editing. She and her husband, Wilfred Meynell, edited the *Weekly Register* from 1881 to 1888 and *Merry England* from 1883 to 1895. Beginning in 1875, Alice published collections of poems, the first of which was *Preludes,* written under her maiden name. Twice nominated for the poet laureateship, in 1895 and again in 1913, Meynell garnered the respect of notable poets and critics for most of her writing life. The essay "Rain" reveals how Meynell's prose was often colored by her poetic sensibility. Like other pieces in the section "Appreciating," it celebrates the momentariness of things natural. "A Dead Harvest: In Kensington Gardens," also reprinted here, possesses the lyrical melancholy that marks much of her poetry.

Mary Russell Mitford (1787–1855)

Poet, writer of fiction, avid letter-writer, and dramatist, Mitford is best-known today for her remarkable *Our Village* (1824–32), a five-volume work that established her as an international celebrity. She herself categorized this work as "a series of sketches of country manners, scenery, and character, with some story intermixed, and connected by unity of locality and of purpose." The whole is narrated by one central female persona, who leads the reader through landscapes and introduces her or him to a deepening sense of place. The section reprinted here takes the reader on a spring walk. What begins as an idyll ends in a scene of destruction, as the narrator mourns the loss of a grove of trees. Mitford's is an early work on a subject far more typical of later Victorian and early Edwardian writers.

E. (Edith) Nesbit (Mrs. Hubert Bland) (1858–1924)

A socialist and one of the founders of the Fabian Society, Nesbit was also a prolific novelist and children's writer. Wife to Hubert Bland, who could not support his family and was something of a philanderer as well, Nesbit wrote to live, producing nine novels, fifteen children's novels, and over forty other books. Her two trilogies, *The Treasure Seekers* (1899) and *The Wouldbegoods* (1902), and her book *The Railway Children* (1906) are justly famous as novels for young people. Whereas most of Nesbit's children's books are more fanciful than didactic, "The One Thing Needful," with its deep concern over the befouling of the green world, is atypical and owes more to her socialist beliefs than to her love of magic and sense of the comic.

Marianne North (1830–90)

A self-financed traveler and painter, Marianne North roamed the globe in search of botanical subjects. Her wide-ranging collection of paintings was eventually housed in a gallery she herself sponsored at Kew Gardens, where it may still be viewed today. Her autobiographical reminiscences were published under the title *Recollections of a Happy Life* (1892–94). During her wanderings, North, like Mary Kingsley, discovered species previously unknown, in her case five new species that were named after her. The selections from *Recollections* reprinted here, about her time in Brazil, suggest the power of North's painterly eye.

Eleanor Anne Ormerod (1828–1901)

Self-taught, Eleanor Ormerod became a leading economic entomologist. Curious about insects from an early age, at her own expense Ormerod published a significant pamphlet in 1877, "Notes for Observations of Injurious Insects." This led her to issue a series of *Annual Reports of Observations of Injurious Insects* from 1877 to 1900, documents that gleaned information from a number of informants and were widely used by agriculturalists and entomologists. Eventually her service to her field garnered her an honorary doctorate from the University of Edinburgh, the first such degree ever awarded to a woman. A professional in every other sense of the word, Ormerod would not accept remuneration for her work, for she felt this might somehow undermine the credibility of a woman working in a man's field. Nevertheless, she was an acknowledged expert on such species as the botfly and Hessian fly, on the uses of pesticides, and on the ecology of birds and insects.

Winifred, Duchess of Portland (1863–1954)

The Duchess of Portland was the first president of the Society for the Protection of Birds and held that position for over sixty-five years. Her work with the society began at the beginning, in 1891, when members of the Fur, Fin and Feather Society of Croydon joined with a group of women from Manchester to form the SPB. Known as a gracious benefactor, the duchess was also vice president of the Royal Society for the Prevention of Cruelty to Animals and an advocate for the mining population of Nottinghamshire. As president of the SPB and benefactress of the RSPB, she opened the proceedings for the discussion of bird and animal life at the International Congress of Women.

(Helen) Beatrix Potter (1866–1943)

Beatrix Potter needs no introduction to most audiences. Her "little books" like *The Tale of Peter Rabbit* (1902) are known worldwide. Less well known is Potter's penchant for scientific study. As children, Potter and her brother drew from nature long before she began to write her famous books for children. The two selections printed here are examples of Potter's poetic and scientific talents at work in documents previously unpublished. The piece on the elder-flowers is contemplative, dealing with personification and the kind of transformation of plant into character that foreshadows Potter's interest in fictionalizing the natural world more poetically. The essay on the hedgehog shows Potter studying a pet closely to learn and explain its precise behavior. Later, she would portray such a creature in her tales of the hedgehog-washerwoman, Mrs. Tiggy-Winkle.

Anne Pratt (1806–93)

From childhood, Anne Pratt studied plants of every sort. From 1828 onward, she wrote, illustrated, and published book after book about flowers, fields, woodlands, sedges, ferns, and sea plants. There were nearly twenty in all, and all were about native British plants. Among the most important was *Flowering Plants and Ferns of Great Britain,* a five-volume text first published in 1855 and intended to guide her reader through every order of British plants. Pratt was a popularizer of science of the first order who reached an eager audience for accessible botanical texts. Her most popular volume was *Wild Flowers* (1852–53), a work illustrated in block prints and intended for children. The selection in this text is from *Chapters on the Common Things of the Sea-side* (1850), where Pratt explores not only plants but the shells and marine animals of seashores.

A. (Agnes) Mary F. (Frances) Robinson (Mrs. James Darmesteter; Madame Duclaux) (1857–1944)

Mary Robinson was a graduate of University College, London, and a friend of Vernon Lee's. Her interests in poetry bloomed early: her first volume, *A Handful of Honeysuckle* (1878) was privately printed by her parents in lieu of a coming-out party and launched her as a poet. In addition to several subsequent volumes of poetry, Robinson wrote a biography of Emily Brontë (1883) for the Eminent Women Series and a novel, *Arden.* Her *Collected Poems, Lyrical and Narrative,* appeared in 1902 and argued in its preface for "women's forms" of poetry like the ballad, of which "Darwinism" is an example—although one unconventional in its subject matter.

Christina Rossetti [Ellen Alleyn; Christian Rossetti] (1830–94)

Youngest child of the famous Rossetti family of poets, artists, and critics, Christina Rossetti was herself a poet of the first order. Her poetic ear was exquisite, and her range extended from religious verse, to children's poetry, to the sonnet sequence *Monna Innominata,* spoken in the voice of a woman, to remarkable and uncategorizable works like *Goblin Market* (1862), about two sisters tempted by goblin men and their magical and deadly fruit. *Sing-Song* (1872), the source of the poems reprinted in this anthology, is a volume for children, one full of rhymes about the natural world as well as famous lullabies and nonsense rhymes.

Isabel Savory (b. 1869)

Isabel Savory was a turn-of-the-century travel writer. In addition to her hunting narrative, *A Sportswoman in India* (1900), excerpted here, she published two other books:

In the Tail of the Peacock (1903), a study of Morocco, and *The Romantic Roussillon: In the French Pyrenees* (1919). Her *Sportswoman* set out to capture an audience of women by romanticizing hunting as a sport suitable for women. The book capitalized on the popularity of hunting narratives of the 1880s and 1890s, most of which were written by men and for men. No protectress of animals, Savory recommended to other women adventures similar to hers.

Anna Sewell (1820–78)

Sewell produced only one published book, the justly famous *Black Beauty: His Grooms and Companions: The Autobiography of a Horse* (1877). Injured as a young girl, Sewell had become a rider to increase her limited mobility and kept a horse most of her life. At fifty-one, when she was finally forced by ill health to give up her horse, she began *Black Beauty* to repay what she felt was a lifelong debt to the species. The hero of her story is a thoroughbred who falls upon hard times and witnesses the worst atrocities committed against his kind. Black Beauty's story was couched as an autobiography and spoken in the voice of an animal. Sewell died within three months of the novel's publication, but by then ninety-one thousand copies had already been sold.

Mary Martha Sherwood (1775–1851)

Sherwood was a highly prolific fiction writer, producing such socially significant works as *Caroline Mordaunt; or The Governess* (1835), a book that paved the way for a host of "governess novels," including Charlotte Brontë's *Jane Eyre* (1848). In her day she was a favorite with child readers, for whom she produced dozens of stories throughout a fifty-five-year career. A didactic writer, Sherwood often wrote in the tradition of Mary Wollstonecraft and Sarah Trimmer, producing tales intended to teach children gentleness toward other species. *Soffrona and Her Cat Muff* (1828) is typical of such tales and clearly links kindness to animals with a Christian respect for other human beings.

Margaret Emily Shore (1819–39)

Emily Shore was a child prodigy. Despite a life cut very short by tuberculosis, she nevertheless managed to write natural histories, histories of the Jews, the Greeks, and the Romans, two novels, three epics, many poems, and a translation of Xenophon's *Anabasis.* We know of these achievements through her surviving sisters, Arabella and Louisa, themselves authors and the editors of Shore's remarkable *Journal of Emily Shore,* first published in 1891, almost sixty years after her death. In her journal we come face to face both with Shore's deep learning and with her keen sense of observation.

Two of the selections on bird life offered here were published in Shore's lifetime in the *Penny Magazine,* a popular magazine sponsored by the Society for the Diffusion of Useful Knowledge. Other passages from her journal describe Shore's intense interest in ornithology and the kinds of domestication of birds attempted by the Shore family.

Mary (Fairfax Greig) Somerville (1780–1872)

Mary Somerville, like Jane Marcet, contributed enormously to science popularization in the early nineteenth century. Her work was primarily in the physical sciences, one of her two most famous volumes being *On the Connexion of the Physical Sciences* (1834, with nine subsequent editions), excerpted here. Somerville had earlier translated Laplace's *The Mechanism of the Heavens* (1831), which served as a college textbook for close to one hundred years. There followed important books on physical geography and molecular and microscopic science. Like many women in this volume, Somerville intended her work to be useful to other women, as the dedication to *Connexion* suggests. But unlike some of the women reprinted here, Somerville was highly acclaimed in her own day. The Royal Society placed her bust in its Great Hall, and Somerville College, one of the first two colleges for women at Oxford, was named after her.

Marie Carmichael Stopes (1880–1958)

Marie Stopes was a paleobotanist who earned a doctorate from University College, London, in 1904 and became a fellow of both the Linnean Society and the Geological Society and the first woman scientist on the faculty of the University of Manchester. Well-respected for her work in paleobotany, Stopes published not only scientific papers, but science popularizations intended for young audiences, such as *The Study of Plant Life for Young People* (1906).

Stopes is best known today as the author of the best-selling *Married Love* (1918), a sexual primer for adults. As a scientist and as a woman, Stopes was appalled that adults, herself included when she was first married, would "search for natural law in every province of our universe" and yet neglect "the most vital subject, the one which concerns us all infinitely more than the naming of planets or the collecting of insects" (*Married Love* 25–26). For espousing such a view Stopes incurred the disapproval of many of her scientific colleagues. Despite opposition, Stopes persisted with her efforts toward promoting sex education, eventually founding the first instructional clinic for contraception in Britain. *In Nature's Name* offers selections from each of the categories that marked Stopes's public writing: paleobotany, science popularization for children, and the explanation of human sexuality.

Rosa Frances Swiney (1847–1922)

Frances Swiney was what has been called a "hyperfeminist," a woman who believed in the innate superiority of women. A respectable matron living in Cheltenham, Swiney was fiery when she took up her pen. This she did in a number of pamphlets, books, and letters written from the 1890s until the First World War. She founded what she called the League of Isis to promote her unique kind of theosophy, one that championed women as more highly evolved than men and that counseled sexual relations only for the purposes of procreation. A feminist activist as well as writer, Swiney was president of the Women's Suffrage Society of Cheltenham and a contributor to the *Awakener*, an anti–white slavery paper.

Sarah Kirby Trimmer (1741–1810)

Trimmer was an early children's writer and popularizer of science, a woman who raised ten children to adulthood and found a way of uniting her motherly responsibilities with her desire to write. Her first book, *An Easy Introduction to the Knowledge of Nature* (1780) was written expressly to educate children to the wonders of the natural world. A moralist who believed in kindness to all living things, she was the first woman to be published by the influential Society for Promoting Christian Knowledge. *Fabulous Histories, Designed for the Instruction of Children, Respecting Their Treatment of Animals* (1786), excerpted here, is famous for its story of a human family—the Bensons—their wise mother, and their learning relationship to a family of robins.

Elizabeth Twining (1805–89)

Elizabeth Twining, a member of the famous tea-growing family, dedicated much of her life to two different pursuits: flower illustration and philanthropy. As a young woman, Twining pored over copies of *Curtis's Botanical Magazine,* studying and copying the pictures and learning about plant anatomy and physiology. Fascinated by drawings of exotic plants, she was a frequent visitor to botanical gardens, where she lingered to study living specimens. In 1849 she published her *Illustrations of the Natural Order of Plants with Groups and Descriptions,* based in part on plants she had seen displayed at the Royal Botanic Gardens at Kew. Respected and authoritative, it went through a number of editions. Twining devoted many of her later years to her second major pursuit, philanthropy. She refurbished the almshouse at Twickenham, and established a hospital for the poor (St. James) and the Bedford Home for Destitute Girls. The selection offered in this anthology was chosen to show how Twining's writing could combine her interest in plant life with the improvement of the lives of the poor.

Mrs. R. H. (Richard) Tyacke

Mrs. Tyacke and her husband both hunted avidly in Kashmir, in Albania, and in the western Himalayas, and both wrote books about their hunting adventures. Richard Tyacke's was entitled *The Sportsman's Manual in Quest of Game* (1893). Mrs. Tyacke's book on hunting in India, a small portion of which is excerpted here, shows a love of animals strangely coupled with the ruthlessness necessary to hunt them down after admiring their maternal qualities.

Emma Wallington

No further information on Wallington has been found. She may well, however, have been the author of another paper from the 1870s, one delivered to the Victoria Discussion Society in 1870 and printed in *Victoria Magazine* in September of 1870. This paper, "Women as They Are Supposed to Be and Women as They Are," espouses many of the same ideas about women and nature as the paper reprinted here. It was met with applause, according to the printed version of the discussion afterward, and supported by the able feminist Emily Faithfull.

(Gladys) Mary Webb (1881–1927)

Mary Webb was a fiction writer who wrote in the time frame between Victorian and modernist literature. For Webb, nature was always central, both in her life and in her writing, beginning with the volume of essays *Spring of Joy* (1917), written between 1909 and 1912. Here, as in her novel *Gone to Earth* (1917)—both of these works are excerpted in this anthology—, Webb espouses a kind of nature pantheism: all nature is imbued with spirit and human nature's well-being depends on realizing this. In "A Cedar-Rose," reprinted here in its entirety, Webb looks at an important moment in the life of an elderly woman, a woman waiting for a sign from a cedar tree. I have chosen Webb's writing for both the opening and closing sections of *In Nature's Name* because her work is so closely tied to the scope and intents of this book.

Henrietta Margaret White (1856–1936)

Henrietta White was the Principal of Alexandra College, Dublin, a women's college founded in 1866. She held a LL.D. from that institution and was also a graduate of Newnham College, Cambridge. A suffragist and an important advocate of higher education for women, Dr. White wrote articles on various social and educational subjects. At Alexandra College she is noteworthy for having established the College Guild in 1897; its aim was (and still is) to teach students social responsibility for the disadvantaged. Dr. White was also an avid gardener, collected sweet-scented pelargoniums, and corresponded with important botanists and horticulturists. The paper included here demonstrates White's combined interest in women's education and gardening.

Dorothy Wordsworth (1771–1855)

Dorothy Wordsworth, once best known as "Wordsworth's exquisite sister" and the inspirer of his poetry, is now recognized as a skilled literary woman and one of the finest writers of nature journals of all time. Her *Alfoxden Journal* and her *Grasmere Journal* each detail, with utter precision and poetic flair, Dorothy Wordsworth's piercing insights into the world around her. In these journals natural observations, like those embedded in the two selections printed here, are often complemented with insights into daily life and into the people and places the Wordsworths were likely to encounter in their rambles.

For Further Reading

Speaking Out (Including Gender Studies)

Anderson, Elizabeth Garrett. "Sex in Mind and Education: A Reply." *Fortnightly Review.* 15 (1874): 582–94.

Ardis, Ann. "'The Journey from Fantasy to Politics': Representations of Socialism and Feminism in *Gloriana* and *The Image-Breakers.*" *Rediscovering Forgotten Radicals: British Women Writers, 1889–1939.* Ed. Angela Ingram and Daphne Patai. Chapel Hill: University of North Carolina Press, 1993. 43–56.

———. *New Women, New Novels: Feminism and Early Modernism.* New Brunswick: Rutgers University Press, 1990.

Auerbach, Nina. *Woman and the Demon: The Life of a Victorian Myth.* Cambridge: Harvard University Press, 1982.

Bauer, Carol, and Lawrence Ritt, eds. *Free and Ennobled: Source Readings in Victorian Feminism.* Oxford: Pergamon, 1979.

Bernard, H. M., and M. Bernard. *Woman and Evolution.* London: Frank Palmer, 1909.

Birke, Lynda. *Women, Feminism, and Biology.* New York: Methuen, 1986.

Bleier, Ruth. *Science and Gender: A Critique of Biology and Its Theories on Women.* New York: Pergamon 1984.

Bonavia, E. M., M. D. "Women's Frontal Lobes. A Biological and Social Question." *Provincial Medical Journal* 1 July 1892: 358–62.

Boyd, Nancy. *Josephine Butler, Octavia Hill, Florence Nightingale: Three Victorian Women Who Changed the World.* London: Macmillan, 1982.

Brown, Penelope, and L. J. Jordanova. "Oppressive Dichotomies: The Nature/Culture Debate." *Women in Society: Interdisciplinary Essays Compiled and Edited by the Cambridge Women's Studies Group.* London: Virago Press, 1981. 224–41.

Burstyn, Joan. "Education and Sex: The Medical Case against Higher Education for Women in England, 1870–1900." *Proceedings of the American Philosophical Society* 117 (1973): 79–89.

Butler, Josephine. *Personal Reminiscences of a Great Crusade.* London: Horace Marshall and Son, 1898.

Caird, Mona. "A Defence of the So-Called 'Wild Women.'" *Nineteenth Century* 31 (1892): 811–29.

Carpenter, Edward. *Love's Coming of Age: A Series of Papers on the Relations of the Sexes.* Manchester: Labour Press, 1896.

Chant, Laura Ormiston. "Woman As An Athlete: A Reply to Dr. Arabella Kenealy." *Nineteenth Century* 45 (1899): 745–54.

Chesser, Elizabeth Sloan. *Women, Marriage, and Motherhood.* London: Cassell and Co., 1913.

Dixie, Florence. *Gloriana; or The Revolution of 1900.* London: Henry and Co., 1890.

———. *Isola; or, The Disinherited, a Revolt for Woman and All the Disinherited.* London: Leadenhall Press, 1903.

Drysdale, Alice Vickery. "Discussion on Restrictions in Marriage and on Studies in National Eugenics." *Sociological Papers* 2 (1906): 21–22.

Duffin, Lorna. "Prisoners of Progress: Women and Evolution." *The Nineteenth-Century Woman: Her Cultural and Physical World.* Ed. Sara Delamont and Lorna Duffin. London: Croom Helm, 1978. 57–91.

Eastlea, Brian. *Science and Sexual Oppression: Patriarchy's Confrontation with Women and Nature.* London: Weidenfeld and Nicolson, 1981.

Ellis, Havelock. *Man and Woman: A Study of Secondary Sexual Characters.* London: Walter Scott, 1894.

Fausto-Sterling, Anne. *Myths of Gender: Biological Theories about Women and Men.* New York: Basic Books, 1985.

Fee, Elizabeth. "The Sexual Politics of Victorian Anthropology." *Clio's Consciousness Raised: New Perspectives on the History of Women.* Ed. Mary S. Hartman and Lois Banner. New York: Harper and Row, 1974. 86–102.

Fox-Keller, Evelyn. *Reflections on Gender and Science.* New Haven: Yale University Press, 1985.

Geddes, Patrick, and J. Arthur Thompson. *The Evolution of Sex.* London: Walter Scott, 1890.

Grand, Sarah [Frances McFall]. *The Beth Book.* London: Virago Press, 1980.

Holton, Sandra Stanley. "Free Love and Victorian Feminism: The Divers Matrimonials of Elizabeth Wolstenholme and Ben Elmy." *Victorian Studies* 37 (1994): 199–222.

Jameson, Anna. *Sisters of Charity and the Communion of Labour. Two Lectures on the Social Employment of Women.* London: Longman, Brown, Green, Longmans, and Roberts, 1859.

Jann, Rosemary. "Darwin and the Anthropologists: Sexual Selection and Its Discontents." *Victorian Studies* 37 (1994): 287–306.

Jeffreys, Sheila. *The Spinster and Her Enemies: Feminism and Sexuality 1880–1930.* London: Pandora, 1985.

Jersey, M. E. [Lady Jersey]. "Ourselves and Our Foremothers." *Nineteenth Century* 27 (1890): 56–64.

Jex-Blake, Sophia. *Medical Women: A Thesis and a History.* Edinburgh: Oliphant, Anderson and Ferrier, 1886.

Kenealy, Arabella. "Woman as Athlete." *Nineteenth Century* 45 (1899): 636–54.

Kestner, Joseph. *Mythology and Misogyny.* Madison: University of Wisconsin Press, 1989.

Levine, Phillipa. *Feminist Lives in Victorian England: Private Roles and Public Commitment.* Oxford: Basil Blackwell, 1990.

Linton, Elizabeth Lynn. "Wild Women as Politicians." *Nineteenth Century* 30 (1891): 79–88.

———. "Wild Women as Social Insurgents." *Nineteenth Century* 30 (1891): 596–605.

Manton, Jo. *Elizabeth Garrett Anderson.* London: Methuen, 1965.

Maudsley, Henry. "Sex in Mind and Education." *Fortnightly Review* 15 (1874): 466–83.

Moscucci, Ornella. *The Science of Woman.* Cambridge: Cambridge University Press, 1990.

Mosedale, Susan Sleeth. "Science Corrupted: Victorian Biologists Consider 'The Woman Question.'" *Journal of the History of Biology* 2 (1978): 1–55.

Ortner, Sherry B. "Is Female to Male as Nature Is to Culture?" *Woman and Values: Readings in Recent Feminist Philosophy.* Ed. Marilyn Pearsall. Belmont, CA: Wadsworth, 1985. 62–75.

Poovey, Mary. *Uneven Developments: The Ideological Work of Gender in Mid-Victorian England.* Chicago: University of Chicago Press, 1988.

Porter, Roy, and Leslie Hall. *The Facts of Life: The Creation of Sexual Knowledge in Britain, 1650–1950.* New Haven: Yale University Press, 1995.

Richards, Eveleen. "Darwin and the Descent of Woman." *The Wider Domain of Evolutionary Thought.* Ed. David Oldroyd and Ian Langham. London: D. Reidel, 1983. 57–111.

Romanes, George. "Mental Differences between Men and Women." *Nineteenth Century* 21 (1887): 654–72.

Rowald, Katharina, ed. *Gender and Science: Late Nineteenth-Century Debates on the Female Mind and Biology.* Bristol: Thoemmes Press, 1996.

Russett, Cynthia Eagle. *Sexual Science: The Victorian Construction of Womanhood.* Cambridge: Harvard University Press, 1989.

Saleeby, C. W. *Woman and Womanhood.* London: William Heinemann, 1912.

Schiebinger, Londa. *Nature's Body: Gender in the Making of Modern Science.* Boston: Beacon Press, 1993.

Soloway, Richard Allen. "Feminism, Fertility, and Eugenics in Victorian and Edwardian England." *Political Symbolism in Modern Europe: Essays in Honor of George L. Mosse.* Ed. Seymour Drescher, David Sabean, and Allan Sharlin. London: Transaction Books, 1982. 121–45.

Spencer, Herbert. *Education: Intellectual, Moral, and Physical.* London: Williams and Norgate, 1861.

———. *The Principles of Ethics.* 2 vols. London: Williams and Norgate, 1892–93.

———. *Study of Sociology.* New York: Appleton, 1873.

Stopes, Marie. *Married Love: A New Contribution to the Solution of Sex Difficulties.* 1918. New York: Eugenics Publishing Company, 1931.

Swiney, Rosa Frances. *The Ancient Road: or the Development of the Soul.* London: G. Bell and Sons, 1918.

———. *The Bar of Isis or The Law of the Mother.* London: C. W. Daniel, Ltd., 1912.

———. *The Cosmic Procession or the Feminine Principle in Evolution.* London: Ernest Bell, 1906.

———. *The League of Isis. Rules (of observance).* London: National Union of Women's Suffrage Societies, n.d.

———. *Science and Women: The Missing Factor.* London: National Union of Women's Suffrage Societies, n.d.

———. "The Tender Mercies of the Vicious." *Awakener* 26 July 1913, 5, 8.

———. *Woman and Natural Law.* London: C. W. Daniel, 1912.

Tuana, Nancy. *Feminism and Science.* Bloomington: Indiana University Press, 1989.

———. *The Less Noble Sex: Scientific, Religious, and Philosophical Conceptions of Woman's Nature.* Bloomington: Indiana University Press, 1993.

Weeks, Jeffrey. *Sex, Politics, and Society: The Regulation of Sexuality since 1800.* London: Longman, 1981.

"Woman in her Psychological Relations." *Journal of Psychological Medicine and Mental Pathology* 4 (1851): 8–50.

Protecting

Bell, E. Moberly. *Octavia Hill: A Biography.* London: Constable, 1942.

Bostock, Stephen St. C. *Zoos and Animal Rights: The Ethics of Keeping Animals.* London: Routledge, 1993.

Briggs, Julia. *A Woman of Passion: The Life of E. Nesbit, 1858–1924.* London: Hutchinson, 1987.

Cobbe, Frances Power. "Dogs Whom I Have Met." *Cornhill Magazine* 26 (1872): 662–78.

———. "The Ethics of Zoophily." *Contemporary Review* 68 (1895): 497–508.

———. *Life of Frances Power Cobbe by Herself.* Boston: Houghton Mifflin, 1894.

———. *The Modern Rack: Papers on Vivisection.* London: Swan Sonnenschein and Co., 1889.

Coles, Gladys Mary. *The Flower of Light: A Biography of Mary Webb.* London: Duckworth, 1978.

Doughty, Robin, W. *Feather Fashions and Bird Preservation: A Study in Nature Protection.* Berkeley: University of California Press, 1975.

Eden, K. F. *Juliana Horatia Ewing and Her Books.* Detroit: Gale Research Co., 1969.

Ewing, Juliana Horatia. *A Great Emergency and Other Tales.* London: Bell and Son, 1911.

———. *Mary's Meadow and Letters from a Little Garden.* London: Society for Promoting Christian Knowledge, 1886.

Ferguson, Moira. *Animal Advocacy and Englishwomen, 1780–1900.* Ann Arbor: University of Michigan Press, 1998.

Gaard, Greta, ed. *Ecofeminism: Women, Animals, Nature.* Philadelphia: Temple University Press, 1993.

Gould, Peter C. *Early Green Politics; Back to Nature, Back to the Land, and Socialism in Britain 1880–1900.* New York: St. Martin's Press, 1988.

Hill, Octavia. *The Life of Octavia Hill as Told in Her Letters.* Ed. C. Edmund Maurice. London: Macmillan, 1913.

———. "Natural Beauty as a National Asset." *Nineteenth Century and After* 58 (1905): 935–41.

———. *Our Common Land and Other Short Essays.* London: Macmillan, 1877.

Hudson, W. H. *Feathered Women.* London: Society for the Protection of Birds, 1902.

———. *Green Mansions: A Romance of the Tropical Forest.* London: Duckworth, 1904.

Keith, Thomas. *Man and the Natural World: Changing Attitudes in England, 1500–1800.* London: Allen Lane, 1983.

Kingsford, Anna. *Spiritual Therapeutics.* Ed. William Colville Jr. 1883. Chicago: Educator Pub. Co., 1890. 290–308.

———, and Edward Maitland. *The Perfect Way; or, The Finding of Christ.* London: John M. Watkins, 1923.

Lansbury, Coral. *The Old Brown Dog: Women, Workers, and Vivisection in Edwardian England.* Madison: University of Wisconsin Press, 1985.

Lemon, Mrs. Frank E. *The Bird of Paradise.* London: Society for the Protection of Birds, 1899.

———. *Dress in Relation to Animal Life.* London: Society for the Protection of Birds, 1899.

———. "The Story of the R.S.P.B." *Bird Notes and News* 20, nos. 5–8 (1943): 67–68, 84–87, 100–102, 116–18.

Maitland, Edward. *Anna Kingsford: Her Life, Letters, Diary, and Work.* Vol 1. London: George Redway, 1896.

Malchow, H. L. "Public Gardens and Social Action in Late Victorian London." *Victorian Studies* 29 (1985): 97–124.

Matthews, L. H. "The Zoo: 150 Years of Research." *Zoos and Animal Rights: the Ethics of Keeping Animals.* Ed. Stephen St. C. Bostock. London: Routledge, 1993.

Merchant, Carolyn. *The Death of Nature: Women, Ecology, and the Scientific Revolution.* San Francisco: Harper and Row, 1980.

———. *Earthcare: Women and the Environment.* New York: Routledge, 1996.

Phillips, Mrs. E. *Destruction of Ornamental-Plumaged Birds.* London: Society for the Protection of Birds, 1897.

———. *Mixed Plumes.* London: Society for the Protection of Birds, 1895.

Philpot, Mrs. J. H. *The Sacred Tree.* London: Macmillan, 1897.

Ritvo, Harriet. *The Animal Estate: The English and Other Creatures in the Victorian Age.* Cambridge: Harvard University Press, 1987.

Trimmer, Sarah. See "Popularizing Science."

Turner, James. *Reckoning with the Beast: Animals, Pain, and Humanity in the Victorian Mind.* Baltimore: Johns Hopkins University Press, 1980.

Webb, Mary. *Gone to Earth.* New York: Dutton, 1917.

Domesticating

Beeton, Isabella Mary. *The Book of Household Management.* London: Ward, Lock and Tyler, 1869.

Bennett, Jennifer. *Lilies of the Hearth: The Historical Relationship between Women and Plants.* Camden, Ontario: Camden House, 1991.

Bixler, Phyllis. "Gardens, Houses, and Nurturant Power." *Romanticism and Children's Literature in Nineteenth-Century England.* Ed. James Holt McGavran Jr. Athens: University Press of Georgia, 1991. 208–24.

Blunt, Wilfrid. *The Ark in the Park: The Zoo in the Nineteenth Century.* London: Hamish Hamilton, 1976.

Bostock, Stephen St. C. *Zoos and Animal Rights: The Ethics of Keeping Animals.* London: Routledge, 1993.

Branca, Patricia. *Silent Sisterhood: Middle Class Women in Victorian Homes.* Pittsburgh: Carnegie Mellon Press, 1975.

Briggs, Asa. *Victorian Things.* London: B. T. Batsford, 1988.

Broderip, W. J. *Zoological Recreations.* London: Henry Colburn, 1847.

Brookshaw, George. *A New Treatise on Flower Painting or Every Lady Her Own Drawing Master.* London: Longman, Hurst, Rees, Orme and Brown, 1816.

Dew-Smith, Alice. *Confidences of an Amateur Gardener.* London: Seely and Co., 1897.

———. *Tom Tug and Others: Sketches in a Domestic Menagerie.* London: Seely and Co., 1898.

Fitch, Walter. "Botanical Drawing." *Gardeners' Chronicle.* 1869. *The Art of Botanical Illustration.* Ed. Wilfrid Blunt. London: Collins, 1950.

Grey, Maria, and Emily Shirreff. *Thoughts on Self-Culture, Addressed to Women.* Boston: Crosby and Nichols, 1851.

Holden, Edith. *Country Diary of an Edwardian Lady.* New York: Holt, Rinehart and Winston, 1977.

Hope, Frances. *Notes and Thoughts on Gardens and Woodlands.* London: Macmillan and Co., 1881.

Horn, Pamela. *Victorian Countrywomen.* Oxford: Basil Blackwell, 1991.

Loudon, Jane. *The Ladies' Flower-Garden of Ornamental Annuals.* London: W. S. Orr, 1849.

———. *The Lady's Country Companion.* London: Longman, Brown, Green and Longmans, 1845.

Malamud, Randy. *Reading Zoos: Representations of Animals and Captivity.* New York: New York University Press, 1998.

Martin, Annie. *Home Life on an Ostrich Farm.* London: George Philip and Son, 1890.

Martineau, Harriet. *Our Farm of Two Acres.* London: Cottage Farm Series, 1865.

Seaton, Beverly. *The Language of Flowers: A History.* Charlottesville: University Press of Virginia, 1995.

Adventuring

Allen, Charles. *A Glimpse of the Burning Plain: Leaves from the Indian Journals of Charlotte Canning.* London: Michael Joseph, 1986.

Barr, Pat. *A Curious Life for a Lady: The Story of Isabella Bird.* London: Macmillan, 1970.

Bird, Isabella. *A Lady's Life in the Rocky Mountains.* 1879. London: Folio Society, 1988.

———. *Six Months in the Sandwich Islands: Among Hawai'i's Palm Groves, Coral Reefs, and Volcanoes.* 1875. London: John Murray, 1890.

Bohls, Elizabeth A. *Women Travel Writers and the Language of Aesthetics, 1716–1818.* Cambridge: Cambridge University Press, 1995.

Brantlinger, Patrick. *The Rule of Darkness: British Literature and Imperialism, 1830–1914.* Ithaca: Cornell University Press, 1988.

Buckland, Frank. *Logbook of a Fisherman and Zoologist.* London: Chapman and Hall, 1875.

Chrisman, Laura. "Empire, Race, and Feminism at the *Fin de Siècle.*" *Cultural Politics at the Fin de Siècle.* Ed. Sally Ledger and Scott McCracken. Cambridge: Cambridge University Press, 1995. 45–65.

Early, Julie English. "The Spectacle of Science and Self: Mary Kingsley." *Natural Eloquence: Women Reinscribe Science.* Ed. Barbara T. Gates and Ann B. Shteir. Madison: University of Wisconsin Press, 1997. 215–36.

Egerton, George (Mary Chavelita Dunne). *Keynotes.* London: Elkin Matthews, 1894.

Ellis, Vivienne Rae. *Louisa Anne Meredith: A Tigress in Exile.* Sandy Bay, Tasmania: Blubber Head Press, 1979.

Foster, Muriel. *Muriel Foster's Fishing Diary.* New York: Viking, 1980.

Fountaine, Margaret. *Butterflies and Late Loves: The Further Travels and Adventures of a Victorian Lady.* Ed. W. F. Cater. London: Collins, 1986.

———. *Love among the Butterflies: The Travels and Adventures of a Victorian Lady.* Ed. W. F. Cater. Boston: Little Brown, 1980.

Frank, Katherine. *The Voyager Out: The Life of Mary Kinglsey.* Boston: Houghton Mifflin, 1986.

Frawley, Maria. *A Wider Range: Travel Writing by Women in Victorian England.* Rutherford, NJ: Fairleigh Dickinson University Press, 1991.

Fulford, Tim, and Peter J. Kitson, eds. *Travels, Explorations, and Empires, 1770–1835.* 2 vols. London: Pickering and Chatto, 2001–2.

Green, Martin. *Dreams of Adventure, Deeds of Empire.* New York: Basic Books, 1979.

Gwynn, Stephen. *The Life of Mary Kingsley.* London: Macmillan, 1932.

Havely, Cicely Palser. *This Grand Beyond: The Travels of Isabella Bird Bishop.* London: Century, 1984.

Hobusch, Erich. *Fair Game: A History of Hunting, Shooting, and Animal Conservation.* New York: Arco Publishing Co., 1980.

Kaye, Evelyn. *Amazing Traveller: Isabella Bird.* Boulder: Blue Penguin Press, 1994.

Kingsley, Mary H. *Travels in West Africa.* 1897. Boston: Beacon Press, 1982.

———. *West African Studies.* New York: Barnes and Noble, 1964.

MacKenzie, John M. *The Empire of Nature: Hunting, Conservation, and British Imperialism.* Manchester: Manchester University Press, 1988.

Mazuchelli, Nina. *The Indian Alps and How We Crossed Them: Being a Narrative of Two Years' Residence in the Eastern Himalaya and Two Months' Tour into the Interior.* New York: Dodd, Mead, and Company, 1876.

Meredith, Louisa. See "Popularizing Science."

Mills, Sara. *Discourses of Difference: An Analysis of Women's Travel Writing and Colonialism.* New York: Routledge, 1991.

———. "Knowledge, Gender, and Empire." *Writing Women and Space: Colonial and Postcolonial Geographies.* Ed. Alison Blunt and Gillian Rose. London: Guilford Press, 1994. 29–50.

"Miss North's Paintings of Plants." *The Times* 8 June 1882, 4.

Morgan, Susan. *Place Matters: Gendered Geography in Victorian Women's Travel Books about Southeast Asia.* New Brunswick: Rutgers University Press, 1996.

North, Marianne. *Recollections of a Happy Life.* 3 vols. London: Macmillan and Co., 1890.

Parks, Fanny. *Wanderings of a Pilgrim in Search of the Picturesque.* 2 vols. London: Pelham Richardson, 1850. London: Oxford University Press, 1975.

Pfeiffer, Ida. *A Lady's Voyage Round the World.* London: Longman, Brown, Green, and Longmans, 1851.

Pratt, Mary Louise. *Imperial Eyes: Travel Writing and Transculturation.* New York: Routledge, 1992.

Rigby, Elizabeth [Lady Eastlake]. "Lady Travelers." *Quarterly Review* 76 (1844): 98–137.

Robinson, Jane. *Wayward Women: A Guide to Women Travellers.* Oxford: Oxford University Press, 1990.

Savory, Isabel. *A Sportswoman in India: Personal Adventures and Experiences of Travel in Known and Unknown India.* London: Hutchinson, 1900.

Selous, Frederick Courteney. *Travel and Adventure in South-East Africa.* 1893. London: Century Publishing, 1984.

Stevenson, Catherine Barnes. *Victorian Women Travel Writers in Africa.* Boston: Twayne, 1982.

Stopes, Marie Carmichael. *Journal from Japan: A Daily Record as Seen by a Scientist.* London: Blackie and Son, 1910.

Suleri, Sara. *The Rhetoric of English India.* Chicago: University of Chicago Press, 1992.

Tyacke, Mrs. R. H. *How I Shot My Bears; or Two Years' Tent Life in Kullu and Lahoul.* London: Sampson, Low, Marston, 1893.

Ware, Vron. *Beyond the Pale: White Women, Racism, and History.* London: Verso, 1992.

Appreciating

Allen, Grant. *Physiological Aesthetics.* London: Henry S. King and Co., 1877.

Armstrong, Nancy. *Desire and Domestic Fiction: A Political History of the Novel.* Oxford: Oxford University Press, 1987.

Auerbach, Nina, and U. C. Knoepflmacher. *Forbidden Journeys: Fairy Tales and Fantasies by Victorian Women Writers.* Chicago: University of Chicago Press, 1992.

Burke, Edmund. *A Philosophical Enquiry into the Origin of Our Ideas of the Sublime and the Beautiful.* 2d ed., 1759. Menston: Scolar Books, 1970.

Cavaliero, Glen. *The Rural Tradition in the English Novel, 1900–1939.* Totowa, NJ: Rowman and Littlefield, 1977.

Dixie, Florence. *Songs of a Child.* London: Leadenhall Press, 1902.

Freeman, Barbara Claire. *The Feminine Sublime: Gender and Excess in Women's Fiction.* Berkeley: University of California Press, 1995.

Jekyll, Gertrude. *Children and Gardens.* London: Country Life, 1908.

———. *Colour Schemes for the Flower Garden.* London: Country Life, 1908.

———. *Wall and Water Gardens.* 1901. Salem, NH: Ayer Company, 1983.

———. *Wood and Garden.* 1899. Salem, NH: Ayer Company, 1983.

Lee, Vernon [Violet Paget]. *Genius Loci.* London: Grant Richards, 1899.

———. *The Handling of Words and Other Studies in Literary Psychology.* London: Bodley Head, 1923.

———. *Laurus Nobilis: Chapters on Art and Life.* London: John Lane, 1909.

———. *Renaissance Fancies and Studies, Being a Sequel to Euphorion.* London: Smith, Elder and Co., 1896.

———. *The Sentimental Traveller: Notes on Places.* London: John Lane, 1908.

———. *The Spirit of Rome: Leaves from a Diary.* London: John Lane, 1906.

———. *The Tower of Mirrors and Other Essays on the Spirit of Place.* London: John Lane, 1914.

———, and Clementina Anstruther-Thomson. *Beauty and Ugliness and Other Studies in Psychological Aesthetics.* London: John Lane, 1912.

Manos, Nikki Lee, and Meri-Jane Rochelson, eds. *Transforming Genres: New Approaches to British Fiction of the 1890s.* New York: St. Martins's Press, 1994.

Mellor, Anne. *Romanticism and Gender.* New York: Routledge, 1993.

Morton, Peter. *The Vital Science: Biology and the Literary Imagination, 1860–1900.* London: George Allen and Unwin, 1984.

Murphy, Patrick D. *Farther Afield: In the Study of Nature-Oriented Literature.* Charlottesville: University of Virginia Press, 2000.

Murray, Heather. "Frances Hodgson Burnett's *The Secret Garden:* The Organ(ic)ized World." *Touchstones: Reflections on the Best in Children's Literature.* Ed. Perry Nodleman. Vol. 1. West Lafayette, IN: Children's Literature Association, 1985. 30–43.

Pratt, Annis. *Archetypal Patterns in Women's Fiction.* Bloomington: Indiana University Press, 1981.

Schaffer, Talia, and Katy Alexis Psomiades, eds. *Women and British Aestheticsim.* Charlottesville: University P of Virigina, 1999.

Webb, Mary. *Mary Webb: The Spring of Joy.* Intro. by Walter De La Mer and Martin Armstrong. New York: Dutton, 1937.

Wilson, Carol Shiner, and Joel Haefner, eds. *Re-Visioning Romanticism: British Women Writers, 1776–1837.* Philadelphia: University of Pennsylvania Press, 1994.

Popularizing Science

Allen, David Elliston. "Natural History and Visual Taste: Some Parallel Tendencies." *The Natural Sciences and the Arts: Aspects of Interaction from the Renaissance to the Twentieth Century: An International Symposium.* Stockholm: Almquist and Wiksell, 1985. 32–45.

———. "The Women Members of the Botanical Society of London." *British Journal for the History of Science* 13 (1980): 240–54.

Barber, Lynn. *The Heyday of Natural History, 1820–1870.* London: J. Cape, 1980.

Barton, Ruth. "The Purposes of Science and the Purposes of Popularization." Paper Presented to the Australasian Victorian Studies Association. Adelaide, Australia, February 1996.

Blum, Ann Shelby. *Picturing Nature: American Nineteenth-Century Zoological Illustration.* Princeton: Princeton University Press, 1993.

Blunt, Wilfred. *The Art of Botanical Illustration.* London: Collins, 1950.

Bodington, Alice. *Studies in Evolution and Biology.* London: Elliot Stock, 1890.

Bridson, Gavin D. R. *Plant, Animal, and Anatomical Illustration in Art and Science: A Bibliographical Guide from the Sixteenth Century to the Present Day.* Detroit: Omnigraphics, 1990.

Brightwen, Eliza. *Eliza Brightwen: The Life and Thoughts of a Naturalist.* Ed. W. H. Chesson. Intro. by Edmund Gosse. London: T. Fisher Unwin, 1909.

———. *Glimpses of Plant Life; an Easy Guide.* London: T. Fisher Unwin, 1897.

———. *Inmates of My House and Garden.* New York: Macmillan, 1895.

———. *More about Wild Nature.* London: T. Fisher Unwin, 1892.

———. *A Talk about Birds.* London: Society for the Protection of Birds, n.d.

Brock, W. H. "*Glaucus:* Kingsley and the Seaside Naturalists." *Cahiers Victoriens et Edouardiens* 3 (1976): 25–36.

———. *Science for All: Studies in the History of Victorian Science and Education.* Aldershot: Ashgate Press, 1996.

Bryan, Margaret. *Lectures of Natural Philosophy, the Result of Many Years' Practical Experience of the Facts Elucidated.* London: J. Murray, 1806.

Buckley, Arabella. *The Fairy-land of Science.* London: Edward Stanford, 1879.

———. *Life and Her Children: Glimpses of Animal Life from the Amoeba to the Insects.* London: Edward Stanford, 1880.

———. *Moral Teachings of Science.* London: Edward Stanford, 1891.

———. *A Short History of Natural Science.* London: John Murray, 1876.

———. *Winners in Life's Race.* London: Edward Stanford, 1883.

Cooter, Roger, and Stephen Pumfrey. "Separate Spheres and Public Places: Reflections of the History of Science Popularization and Science in Popular Culture." *History of Science* 32 (1994): 237–67.

Crary, Jonathan. *Techniques of the Observer: On Vision and Modernity in the Nineteenth Century.* Cambridge: MIT Press, 1990.

Dance, Peter. *The Art of Natural History: Animal Illustrators and Their Work.* Woodstock, NY: Overlook Press, 1978.

Darwin, Erasmus. *Plan for the Conduct of Female Education in Boarding Schools.* 1797. New York: S.R. Publishers, Ltd., 1968.

Desmond, Ray. *Dictionary of British and Irish Botanists and Horticulturalists Including Plant Collectors and Botanical Artists.* London: Taylor and Francis, 1977.

Early, Julie English. "The Science of Work, Life, and Text: Margaret Fountaine's Captures/Capturing Margaret Fountaine." *Women's Writing: The Elizabethan to Victorian Period* 2 (1995): 183–97.

Elmy, Elizabeth Wolstenholme. *The Human Flower: A Simple Statement of the Physiology of Birth and the Relations of the Sexes.* London: Buxton House, 1895.

———. *Phases of Love.* London: Buxton House, 1897.

———. *Woman Free.* Congleton: Women's Emancipation Press, 1893.

Gates, Barbara T., ed. *Journal of Emily Shore.* Charlottesville: University P of Virginia, 1991.

———. *Kindred Nature: Victorian and Edwardian Women Embrace the Living World.* Chicago: University of Chicago Press, 1998.

Gates, Barbara T., and Ann B. Shteir, eds. *Natural Eloquence: Women Reinscribe Science.* Madison: University of Wisconsin Press, 1997.

Gatty, Margaret. *Parables from Nature.* London: George Bell, 1880. Reprinted in *Classics of Children's Literature 1621–1932.* New York: Garland Pub. Co., 1976.

Gosse, Philip Henry. *The Aquarium: An Unveiling of the Wonders of the Deep Sea.* London: J. Van Voorst, 1854.

Johnston, Judith. "The 'Very Poetry of Frogs': Louisa Anne Meredith." *Natural Eloquence: Women Reinscribe Science.* Ed. Barbara T. Gates and Ann B. Shteir. Madison: University of Wisconsin Press, 1997. 98–115.

Kingsley, Charles. *Glaucus; or, The Wonders of the Shore.* Cambridge: Macmillan, 1855.

———. *Madame How and Lady Why; or, First Lessons in Earth Lore for Children.* London: Macmillan & Co., 1869.

Lee, Sarah Bowdich. *Excursions in Madeira and Porto Santo.* London: George B. Whittaker, 1825.

———. *Freshwater Fishes of Great Britain Drawn and Described by Mrs. T. Edward Bowdich.* London: printed for the authoress, 1828.

———. *Taxidermy; or The Art of Collecting, Preparing, and Mounting Objects of Natural History for the Use of Museums and Travellers.* London: Longman, Brown, Green, and Longmans, 1843.

Lees, Edwin. "Observations on the Popularity of Natural History." *Naturalist* 3 (1838): 291–301.

Lewes, George Henry. *Sea-side Studies at Ilfracombe, Tenby, the Scilly, and Jersey.* 2d ed. Edinburgh: Blackwood, 1860.

Loudon, Jane. *British Wild Flowers.* London: William S. Orr & Co., 1846.

———. *The Young Naturalist; or the Travels of Agnes Merton and Her Mama.* 1840. London: Routledge, Warne, and Routledge, 1863.

———. *The Young Naturalist's Journey.* London: William Smith, 1840.

Lowry, Delvalle. *Conversations in Mineralogy.* London: Longman, Hurst, Rees, Orme and Brown, 1822.

Marcet, Jane. *Conversations on Chemistry: in which the elements of that science are familiarly explained and illustrated by experiments.* London: Longman, Hurst, Rees and Orme, 1806.

———. *Conversations on Natural Philosophy.* London: Hurst, Rees, Orme and Brown, 1819.

Meredith, Louisa. *My Home in Tasmania During a Residence of Nine Years.* London: John Murray, 1852.

———. *Notes and Sketches of New South Wales during a Residence in that Colony from 1839–1844.* London: John Murray, 1844.

———. *Our Island Home.* London: Marcus Wood, 1879.

———. *Our Wildflowers Familiarly Described and Illustrated.* London: John Murray, 1844.

———. *The Romance of Nature; or The Flower Seasons Illustrated.* London: Tilt, 1836.

———. *Tasmanian Friends and Foes: Feathered, Furred, and Finned.* London: Marcus Ward, 1880.

Merrill, Lynn L. *The Romance of Victorian Natural History.* Oxford: Oxford University Press, 1989.

Myers, Greg. "Fictions and Facts: The Form and Authority of the Scientific Dialogue." *History of Science* 30 (1992): 221–47.

———. "Science for Women and Children: The Dialogue of Popular Science in the Nineteenth Century." *Nature Transfigured: Science and Literature, 1700–1900.* Ed. John Christie and Sally Shuttleworth. Manchester: Manchester University Press, 1989. 172–200.

———. *Writing Biology: Texts in the Social Construction of Scientific Knowledge.* Madison, Wis.: University of Wisconsin Press, 1990.

Plues, Margaret. *Rambles in Search of Ferns.* London: Houlston and Wright, 1861.

Roberts, Mary. *Voices from the Woodlands, Descriptive of Forest Trees, Ferns, Mosses, and Lichens.* London: Reeve and Bentham, 1850.

Sheets-Pyenson, Susan. "Popular Science Periodicals in Paris and London: the Emergence of a Low Scientific Culture, 1820–1875." *Annals of Science* 42 (1985): 549–72.

Shinn, Terry, and R. Whitley. *Expository Science: Forms and Functions of Popularisation.* Dordrecht: D. Reidel, 1985.

Shteir, Ann B. *Cultivating Women, Cultivating Science: Flora's Daughters and Botany in England 1760–1860.* Baltimore: Johns Hopkins University Press, 1996.

Smith, Charlotte. *Rural Walks in Dialogues Intended for the Use of Young Persons.* London: T. Cadell and W. Davies, 1795.

Somerville, Mary. *On the Connexion of the Physical Sciences.* 3d ed. London: J. Murray, 1836.

———. *Personal Recollections, from Early Life to Old Age, of Mary Somerville.* Boston: Roberts Brothers, 1874.

Trimmer, Sarah. *An Easy Introduction to the Knowledge of Nature, and Reading the Holy Scriptures, Adapted to the Capacities of Children.* London: Longman, Robinson and Johnson, 1789.

———. *Fabulous Histories, Designed for the Instruction of Children, Respecting Their Treatment of Animals.* London: Longman, Robinson and Johnson, 1796.

Wakefield, Priscilla. *Domestic Recreations; or Dialogues Illustrative of Natural and Scientific Subjects.* Philadelphia: Robert Carr, 1805.

Ward, Hon. Mrs. *The Microscope.* London: Groombridge and Sons, 1870.

Whitley, Richard. "Knowledge Producers and Knowledge Acquirers: Popularisation as a Relation between Scientific Fields and Their Publics." *Expository Science: Forms and Functions of Popularizations.* Ed. Terry Shinn and Richard Whitley. Dordrecht: D. Reidel, 1885. 3–28.

Wollstonecraft, Mary. *Original Stories from Real Life; with Conversations Calculated to Regulate the Affections and Form the Mind to Truth and Goodness.* London: J. Johnson, 1783.

Wood, J. G. *The Boy's Own Book of Natural History.* London: George Routledge and Sons, 1883.

Wood, Neville, ed. *The Naturalist.* Vol. 3. London: Whittaker and Co, 1838.

Zornlin, Rosina M. *Outlines of Geology for Families and Schools.* London: John W. Parker and Son, 1852.

———. *Recreations in Geology.* 3d ed. London: John W. Parker and Son, 1852.

———. *Recreations in Physical Geography; or the Earth As It Is.* 5th ed. London: John W. Parker and Son, 1855.

———. *The World of Waters; or Recreations in Hydrology.* 3d ed. London: John W. Parker and Son, 1855.

Amateurs or Professionals? (Including Science Studies)

Abir-Am, Pnina, and Dorinda Outram, eds. *Uneasy Careers and Intimate Lives: Women in Science 1789–1979.* New Brunswick: Rutgers University Press, 1987.

Adams, J. F. A. "Is botany a suitable study for young men?" *Science* 9 (1887): 116–17.

Ainley, Marianne Gosztonyi. "Science in Canada's Backwoods: Catharine Parr Traill." *Natural Eloquence: Women Reinscribe Science.* Ed. Barbara T. Gates and Ann B. Shteir. Madison: University of Wisconsin Press, 1997. 79–97.

Alaya, Flavia. "Victorian Science and the 'Genius' of Woman." *Journal of the History of Ideas* 38 (1977): 261–80.

Alic, Margaret. *Hypatia's Heritage: A History of Women in Science from Antiquity through the Nineteenth Century.* Boston: Beacon Press, 1986.

Atkins, Anna. *British Algae: Cyanotype Impressions.* 3 vols. Halstead: Sevenoaks [privately published], 1843–53.

Basalla, George, William Coleman, and Robert H. Kargon, eds. *Victorian Science: A*

Self-Portrait from the Presidential Addresses of the British Association for the Advancement of Science. Garden City: Doubleday/Anchor, 1970.

Beer, Gillian. *Darwin's Plots.* London: Routledge and Kegan Paul, 1983.

———. "'The Face of Nature': Anthropomorphic Elements in the Language of *The Origin of Species.*" *Languages of Nature: Critical Essays in Science and Literature.* Ed. L. J. Jordanova. London: Free Association, 1986. 207–43.

———. *Open Fields: Science in Cultural Encounter.* Oxford: Oxford University Press, 1996.

Benjamin, Marina, ed. *A Question of Identity: Women, Science, and Literature.* New Brunswick: Rutgers University Press, 1993.

———, ed. *Science and Sensibility: Gender and Scientific Enquiry, 1780–1945.* Oxford: Basil Blackwell, 1991.

Blackburn, Jane [Jemima]. *Birds from Moidart and Elsewhere.* Edinburgh: David Douglas, 1895.

———. *Birds Drawn from Nature.* Edinburgh: Edmonston & Douglas, 1862.

———. *Caw! Caw! or, The Chronicle of Crows: a Tale of the Spring-Time.* Glasgow: James Maclehose, 1870.

———. *The Pipits.* Glasgow: James Maclehose, 1872.

Brody, Judit. "The Pen Is Mightier Than the Test Tube." *New Scientist* 105 (1985): 56–58.

Chishom, Alec H. *The Story of Elizabeth Gould.* Melbourne: Hawthorn Press, 1944.

Creese Mary R. S. *Ladies in the Laboratory? America and British Women in Science, 1800–1900: A Survey of Their Contributions to Research.* London: Scarecrow Press, 1998.

Cronin, Helena. *The Ant and the Peacock: Altruism and Sexual Selection from Darwin to Today.* Cambridge: Cambridge University Press, 1991.

Dale, Peter Allen. *In Pursuit of a Scientific Culture: Science, Art, and Society in the Victorian Age.* Madison: University of Wisconsin Press, 1989.

Darwin, Charles. *The Descent of Man and Selection in Relation to Sex.* 2 vols. London: John Murray, 1871.

Daston, Lorraine, and Peter Galison. "The Image of Objectivity." *Representations* 40 (1992): 81–128.

Desmond, Adrian. "Redefining the X Axis: 'Professionals, 'Amateurs,' and the Making of Mid-Victorian Biology—A Progress Report." *Journal of the History of Biology* 34 (2001): 1–47.

Fairley, Robert. *Jemima: The Paintings and Memoirs of a Victorian Lady.* Edinburgh: Canongate, 1988.

———. *Jemima Blackburn's Birds.* Edinburgh: Canongate, 1993.

Gage, Andrew Thomas, and William Thomas Stearn. *A Bicentenary History of The Linnean Society of London.* London: Academic Press, 1988.

Galton, Francis. *Hereditary Genius: An Inquiry into Its Laws and Consequences.* London: Macmillan, 1869.

———. *Essays in Eugenics.* London: Eugenic Education Society, 1909.

Ginzberg, Ruth. "Uncovering Gynocentric Science." *Feminism and Science.* Ed. Nancy Tuana. Bloomington: Indiana University Press, 1989. 69–84.

Gould, John. *The Birds of Australia.* 7 vols. London: J. Gould, 1840–48. Rev. *Naturalist* 2 (1837).

———. *The Birds of Great Britain.* 5 vols. London: J. Gould, 1862–73.

Greville, Robert Kaye. *Algaes Britannicae.* Edinburgh: MacLachlan & Stewart, 1830.

Haraway, Donna J. "A Game of Cat's Cradle: Science Studies, Feminist Theory, Cultural Studies." *Configurations* 1 (1994): 59–71.

———. *Primate Visions: Gender, Race, and Nature in the World of Modern Science.* New York: Routledge, 1989.

Harding, Sandra. *The Science Question in Feminism.* Ithaca: Cornell University Press, 1986.

Harvey, William H. *A Manual of British Algae: Containing Generic and Specific Descriptions of all the Known British Species of Sea-weeds.* London: J. Van Voorst, 1841.

Huxley, Thomas Henry. *Evolution and Ethics.* New York: D. Appleton, 1894.

———. *Man's Place in Nature and Other Anthropological Essays.* 1863. New York: Appleton, 1902.

———. "On the Physical Basis of Life." *Lay Sermons.* London: Macmillan, 1871. 120–46.

Jardine, N., J. A. Secord, and E. C. Spray, eds. *Cultures of Natural History.* Cambridge: Cambridge University Press, 1996.

Jay, Eileen, Mary Noble, and Anne Stevenson Hobbs, eds. *A Victorian Naturalist: Beatrix Potter's Drawings from the Armitt Collection.* London: Frederick Warne, 1992.

Jones, Caroline A., and Peter Galison, eds. *Picturing Science Producing Art.* New York and London: Routledge, 1998.

Jordanova, Ludmilla J. "Gender and the Historiography of Science." *British Journal for the History of Science* 26 (1993): 469–83.

———. "Natural Facts: A Historical Perspective on Science and Sexuality." *Nature, Culture, and Gender.* Ed. Carol MacCormick and Marilyn Strathern. Cambridge: Cambridge University Press, 1980. 42–69.

———. *Sexual Visions: Images of Gender in Science and Medicine.* Madison: University of Wisconsin Press, 1989.

Knoepflmacher, U. C., and G. B. Tennyson, eds. *Nature and the Victorian Imagination.* Berkeley: University of California Press, 1977.

Krasner, James. *The Entangled Eye: Visual Perception and the Representation of Nature in Post-Darwinian Narrative.* New York: Oxford University Press, 1992.

Knight, David. *Science in the Romantic Era.* Aldershot: Ashgate Press, 1998.

Kropotkin, Peter. *Mutual Aid: A Factor in Evolution.* London: William Heinemann, 1902.

Kuklick, Henrika, and Robert E. Kohler, eds. *Science in the Field. Osiris* 11 (1996).

Lang, W. D. "Mary Anning and the Pioneer Geologists of Lyme." *Presidential Address to London Geological Society* 21 (February 1939). 142–64.

Levine, George. *Darwin and the Novelists: Patterns of Science in Victorian Fiction.* Cambridge: Harvard University Press, 1988.

———. "Objectivity and Death: Victorian Scientific Autobiography." *Victorian Literature and Culture* 20 (1992): 273–91.

———. *One Culture: Essays in Science and Literature.* Madison: University of Wisconsin Press, 1987.

———, ed. *Realism and Representation: Essays on the Problem of Realism in Relation to Science, Literature, and Culture.* Madison: University of Wisconsin Press, 1993.

Lightman, Bernard, ed. *Victorian Science in Context.* Chicago: University of Chicago Press, 1997.

Lyell, Charles. *Elements of Geology.* London: J. Murray, 1838.

———. *Principles of Geology.* 11th ed. New York: Appleton, 1890.

Lines, William J. *An All Consuming Passion: Origins, Modernity, and the Australian Life of Georgiana Molloy.* Berkeley: University of California Press, 1994.

MacLeod, Roy. *Public Science and Public Policy in Victorian England.* Aldershot: Variorum Press, 1996.

"Mary Anning, the Fossil Finder." *All the Year Round* 13 (1865): 60–63.

Morrell, Jack. *Science, Culture, and Politics in Britain, 1750–1870.* Aldershot: Ashgate Press, 1997.

Noble, Mary. "Beatrix Potter and Charles McIntosh, Naturalists." *A Victorian Naturalist: Beatrix Potter's Drawings from the Armitt Collection.* Ed. Eileen Jay, Mary Noble, and Anne Stevenson Hobbs. London: Frederick Warne, 1992. 55–135

Outram, Dorinda. "New Spaces in Natural History." *Cultures of Natural History.* Ed. N. Jardine, J. A. Secord, and E. C. Spary. Cambridge: Cambridge University Press, 1996. 249–65.

Paley, William. *Natural Theology, or, Evidences of the Existence and Attributes of the Deity, Collected from the Appearances of Nature.* London: R. Faulder, 1802.

Phillips, Patricia. *The Scientific Lady: A Social History of Woman's Scientific Interests, 1520–1918.* London: Weidenfeld and Nicholson, 1990.

Potter, Beatrix. *Beatrix Potter's Letters.* Ed. Judy Taylor. London: Frederick Warne, 1989.

———. *Complete Tales of Beatrix Potter.* London: Frederick Warne, 1989.

———. *The Journal of Beatrix Potter from 1881–1897.* Transcribed from her code writings by Leslie Linder. London: Frederick Warne, 1966.

Pratt, Anne. *Chapters on the Common Things of the Sea-side.* London: Society for Promoting Christian Knowledge, 1850.

Richards, Eveleen. "Huxley and Woman's Place in Science: The 'Woman Question' and the Control of Victorian Anthropology." *History, Humanity, and Evolution: Essays for John C. Greene.* Ed. James R. Moore. Cambridge: Cambridge University Press, 1989. 253–84.

Ritchie, David. *Darwinism and Politics.* 1890. New York: Charles Scribner's Sons, 1909.

Ritvo, Harriet. *The Platypus and the Mermaid and Other Figments of the Classifying Imagination.* Cambridge: Harvard University Press, 1997.

Romanes, George. *Animal Intelligence.* New York: D. Appleton, 1884.

Schaaf, Larry. *Sun Gardens: Victorian Photograms.* New York: Hans Kraus, 1985.

Taylor, Judy, Joyce Irene Whalley, Anne Stevenson Hobbs, and Elizabeth M. Battrick, eds. *Beatrix Potter, 1866–1943: The Artist and Her World.* London: Frederick Warne, 1987.

Tuchman, Gaye. *Edging Women Out: Victorian Novelists, Publishers, and Social Change.* New Haven: Yale University Press, 1989.

Twining, Elizabeth. *Illustrations of the Natural Orders of Plants with Groups and Descriptions.* London: Sampson Low, Son, and Marston, 1868.

Tyndall, John. *Fragments of Science: Being a Series of Detached Essays, Addresses, and Reviews.* 6th ed. New York: A. L. Burt, 1925.

Wallace, Alfred. "Human Selection." *Fortnightly Review* 54 (1890): 325–37.

Wallace, Robert, ed. *Eleanor Ormerod, LL.D. Economic Entomologist: Autobiography and Correspondence.* New York: E. P. Dutton, 1904.

Whewell, William. Rev. of *On the Connexion of the Physical Sciences,* by Mary Somerville. *Quarterly Review* 51 (1834): 54–68.

Women in Professions, Being the Professional Section of the International Congress of Women, July 1899. London: T. Fisher Unwin, 1900.